Ne

people may look at you funny if you bring your computer to
THE BALL GAME.

Get Nextel and you'll have access to the wireless Web wherever you are. You'll be able to get flight information, stock quotes, the weather, even Edmunds.com. And with Nextel Online℠ Plus, you'll get unlimited Web browsing. Just one more way Nextel gives you more ways than anyone to communicate with everyone.℠

1-800-NEXTEL 9   nextel.com   How business gets done.℠

Nextel phones are manufactured by Motorola, Inc.

Check for Nextel Online availability in your area. To sign up for Nextel Online services, you must also have Nextel digital cellular service. Some restrictions may apply. ©2001 Nextel Communications, Inc. All rights reserved. Nextel, the Nextel logo, Nextel Direct Connect, Nextel Online, More ways than anyone to communicate with everyone, and How business gets done are trademarks and/or service marks of Nextel Communications, Inc. MOTOROLA, The Stylized M Logo and all other trademarks indicated as such herein are trademarks of Motorola, Inc. Reg. U.S. Pat. & Tm. Off. All other product names and services are the property of their respective owners.

Perfect Partners

USED CARS & TRUCKS:
PRICES & RATINGS

For 35 years, Edmunds® has guided smart consumers through the complex used car marketplace. By providing you with the latest trade-in and market value, you are able to determine a fair price for your car before negotiations begin.

Whether buying, selling, or trading, Edmunds® *Used Cars & Trucks: Prices & Ratings* gives all the information you need to get your very best deal.

- Prices Most American and Imported Used Cars, Pickup Trucks, Vans, and Sport Utilities

- Shows Summary Ratings for Most Used Vehicles

- Listings Cover Models Over Last 10 Years

- Price any Vehicle Quickly and Accurately

- Adjust Value for Optional Engines, Equipment and Mileage

For information on all Edmunds® Buyer's Guides, call 914-962-6297

2001

NEW CARS

PRICES & REVIEWS

"WHERE SMART CAR BUYERS START"

Cover photo:
2001 Mercedes-Benz C320

ISBN: 0-87759-667-0
ISSN: 1086-5470

Library of Congress Catalog
Card No: 71-80100

NEW CARS

TABLE OF CONTENTS
SPRING 2001   **VOL N3501-0006**

Introduction 6
Abbreviations 9
Cover Story:
   Mercedes-Benz C320 10
How to Buy Your Next
   New Automobile 18
Specifications 405
Crash Test Data 443
Review:
   Chrysler Sebring 458
Warranties and
   Roadside Assistance 463
Dealer Holdbacks 465
Leasing Tips 468

ACURA
'01 CL-Series 22
'01 Integra 24
'01 RL-Series 26
'01 TL-Series 28

AUDI
'01 A4 30
'01 A6 33
'01 Allroad quattro 37
'01 S4 39
'01 TT 41

BMW
'01 3 Series 45
'01 5 Series 49
'01 Z3 53

BUICK
'01 Century 57
'01 LeSabre 60
'01 Park Avenue 63
'01 Regal 66

CADILLAC
'01 Catera 71
'01 DeVille 73
'01 Eldorado 75
'01 Seville 78

CHEVROLET
'01 Camaro 82
'01 Cavalier 86
'01 Corvette 90
'01 Impala 93
'01 Malibu 97
'01 Monte Carlo 100
'01 Prizm 104

CHRYSLER
'01 300M 107
'01 Concorde 109
'01 LHS 112
'01 Sebring 114

DAEWOO
'01 Lanos 120
'01 Leganza 122
'01 Nubira 124

DODGE
'01 Intrepid 127
'01 Neon 130
'01 Stratus 135

FORD
'01 Crown Victoria 140
'01 Escort ZX2 143
'01 Focus 145
'01 Mustang 147
'01 Taurus 150

HONDA
'01 Accord 154
'01 Civic 157
'01 Insight 159
'01 Prelude 161
'01 S2000 163

HYUNDAI
'01 Accent 165
'01 Elantra 167
'01 Sonata 169
'01 Tiburon 172
'01 XG300 174

INFINITI
'01 G20 177
'01 I30 179
'01 Q45 181

JAGUAR
'01 S-Type 185

KIA
'01 Rio 188
'01 Sephia 189
'01 Spectra 191

LEXUS
'01 ES 300 194
'01 GS-Series 196
'01 IS 300 200
'01 LS 430 202

LINCOLN
'01 Continental 206
'01 LS 208
'01 Town Car 211

MAZDA
'01 626 214
'01 Miata 216
'01 Millenia 218
'00 Protegé 221

MERCEDES-BENZ
'01 C-Class 224
'01 CLK-Class 227
'01 E-Class 230
'01 SLK 233

MERCURY
- '01 Cougar 237
- '01 Grand Marquis 239
- '01 Sable 243

MITSUBISHI
- '01 Diamante 246
- '01 Eclipse 247
- '01 Eclipse Spyder 250
- '01 Galant 252
- '01 Mirage 254

NISSAN
- '01 Altima 257
- '01 Maxima 260
- '01 Sentra 263

OLDSMOBILE
- '01 Alero 266
- '01 Aurora 268
- '01 Intrigue 271

PLYMOUTH
- '01 Neon 275
- '01 Prowler 278

PONTIAC
- '01 Bonneville 280
- '01 Firebird 283
- '01 Grand Am 287
- '01 Grand Prix 290
- '01 Sunfire 295

PORSCHE
- '01 Boxster 300

SAAB
- '01 9-3 307
- '01 9-5 309

SATURN
- '01 L-Series 313
- '01 S-Series 316

SUBARU
- '01 Impreza 320
- '01 Impreza Outback 325
- '01 Legacy 329
- '01 Legacy Outback 336

SUZUKI
- '01 Esteem 342
- '01 Swift 344

TOYOTA
- '01 Avalon 346
- '01 Camry 349
- '01 Camry Solara 355
- '01 Celica 358
- '01 Corolla 361
- '01 Echo 365
- '01 MR2 Spyder 368

VOLKSWAGEN
- '01 Cabrio 373
- '01 Golf 375
- '01 Jetta 378
- '01 New Beetle 381
- '01 Passat 384

VOLVO
- '01 S40/V40 387
- '01 S60 390
- '01 C70 394
- '01 V70 397
- '01 S80 402

© 2001 by Edmunds.com, Inc. All rights reserved. No reproduction in whole or in part may be made without explicit written permission from the publisher. Some images copyright www.arttoday.com and PhotoDisc Inc.

Publisher: Peter Steinlauf
Editor-in-Chief: Christian Wardlaw
Production Manager: Lynette Archbold
Executive Editor: Karl Brauer
Managing Editor: Deborah Gordon
Detroit Editor: John Clor
Senior Features Editor: Brent Romans

Features Editor: Miles Cook
Technical Editor: Scott Memmer
News Editor: Carmen Tellez
Road Test Editor: Neil Chirico
Photography Editor: Scott Jacobs
Associate Editors: Liz Kim, Ed Hellwig, Erin Mahoney

Senior Layout & Design Artist: Robert Archbold
Car Buying Consultant: Phil Reed
Researcher: Erin Riches
Director, Data Coordination: Alison Cooper
Director, New Car Data: Garth Nalleweg
Sr. New Car Data Editor: Charlie Schiavone

New Vehicle Data Editors: Richard Milenkovich, KJ Jones, Roxane Ishimaru
Used Vehicle Editor: John DiPietro
Used Vehicle Data Editor: Wandile Kunene
Maintenance Data Editor: Jose Luis Munoz
Acquisition Specialist: Steven Petrecca
Photo Archivist: Letitia Poteet

Printed in U.S.A.

INTRODUCTION

What's with the dot-com name?

"Where Smart Car Buyers Start" is our motto. It accompanies our logo and serves as an advertising tagline. Call us Edmunds.com, your faithful servant since 1966, bringing you the scoop on car and truck pricing for 35 years.

If you've been living without cable TV in an Airstream trailer on the outskirts of Quartzsite, Ariz., for the past couple of years, you might wonder what all this "dot-com" stuff is about. In a word, the Internet. It's the future of publishing, of retailing, of banking, of investing, of education, and likely a number of things car hacks like us haven't dreamed of.

We publish a free Web site at www.edmunds.com, hence the name of our company. At this Web site, you can gather more facts and figures on mainstream cars and trucks sold in the U.S. than you can by using this book. At the site, there's more than just invoice and retail pricing, reviews, specifications, and how-to-buy articles. The photos are in color. We print the results of full road tests on a weekly basis, and conduct regular comparison tests to determine what the best vehicle is in a given class. Feature content is added regularly. Plus, we can direct you to companies that can help you buy or finance a car, obtain an extended warranty, or provide you with aftermarket accessories.

Our free Web site is updated daily. This book you're holding is updated quarterly. That means our Web site can be more accurate if pricing on a vehicle has recently changed. So if you're looking for pricing on a 2001 model and can't find it here, we've got it on the Web site. Also, you can find out what a given vehicle's True Market Value^{sm} (TMV^{sm}) currently is. TMV^{sm} is the price at which dealers are selling the car, and it's updated weekly to reflect what's currently happening in the market.

We also publish timely incentive and rebate data on the Web site, required information for anyone looking to buy a new car. Finally, because this book is constrained by size and printing costs and the Web site is not, you get more detail on the vehicle you're considering when you visit the Internet than when you visit the local bookstore.

Why do we give all of the information in this book, and more, away for free on our Web site? Because Edmunds is where smart car buyers start. What's smarter than free?

But I don't have a computer. What does this book provide me?

Not everyone owns a computer or has a desire to surf the Web. Others like to have all the available data gathered in one easy-to-read volume that's small enough to be carried around but large enough to offer thorough coverage. Some even like to collect and archive our printed compendiums of automotive facts and figures. If you fit this description, this edition of our traditional print buyer's guide is for you.

Within these pages, we provide you with pricing and specifications for models currently sold in the U.S. that cost less than $55,000. You'll also find editorial about the vehicles, crash-test data, a list of frequently asked questions about the car-buying process and tutorials that should help you if you decide to haggle with the dealer.

There's also a list of our editorial staff's favorite vehicles in a variety of size and type classes, a full road test of the vehicle on the cover, and customer-

INTRODUCTION

assistance phone numbers for the major automakers so you can obtain more information on the models contained in this book.

How do I use this guide?

If you're new to Edmunds.com, or are new to the car-buying experience, here is how to use this guide. Your first step should be to visit car dealerships and test-drive every make and model you're interested in. When you find the car you want to buy, write down all the pertinent information from the window sticker onto a pad of paper. Then, go home and snuggle up with this buyer's guide to start figuring out how to get the best deal on the car of your dreams.

Read the articles about **dealer holdbacks**, **buying your next new automobile**, and **leasing tips**. Then study the make and model that you're interested in. You'll find a representative photo of the vehicle, followed by a synopsis of "What's New?" for the model year. Then, a short review provides facts and opinion about the car. An extensive listing of standard equipment for each trim level comes next, telling you what items are included in the base price of the vehicle. The first paragraph pertains to the base model, and if more than one trim level is available, successive paragraphs will explain what additional features the other trim levels include over the base model.

Next is the meat of this guide: the pricing data. Each vehicle has base invoice price and base MSRP listed for each trim level, and the destination charge, which is the cost of shipping the vehicle from the factory to the dealer. Don't forget to add the destination charge, which is non-negotiable, when pricing a vehicle. Following the base prices and destination charge is a listing of all the optional equipment available on the vehicle from the factory. Along the left margin you'll find a factory code for each option. The dealer invoice price and the MSRP are listed near the right margin. Some option listings have short descriptions that tell you, for example, what might be included in a particular option package, or what trim level the option is available on, or if there are restrictions and requirements regarding availability.

You'll notice that some models do not have options listings. This is because the automaker includes the most popular accessories as standard equipment on a particular trim level, and any additional items that you might like to add to the vehicle will have to be purchased from and installed by the dealer, or are installed at the port of entry. Generally, you can haggle about 25 percent off dealer-installed accessories with little effort.

Looking for the exact specifications of your dream car? Check the back of this book, where you'll find charts displaying the length of the vehicle, the curb weight of the vehicle, and how much power the base engine makes, among others. This format allows you to easily locate and compare specifications between different models and trim levels.

I've followed your advice. Why won't the dealer sell me the car?

Keep in mind that the laws of supply and demand apply to automobiles as much as they apply to any other material commodity. If a vehicle is in great demand and short supply, don't expect to get much of a discount. On the other hand, inflated inventories and tough competition mean that deals are readily available on models that aren't selling well. If a rebate is available on the car or truck you're shopping for, that's an indicator that the dealer will slash the price to the bone to get the car off the lot.

If you have access to our Web site, www.edmunds.com, visit and check out our TMV[sm]

INTRODUCTION

pricing. The published TMV^{sm} is based on a number of factors that determine vehicle price, including supply and demand. We check TMV^{sm} values against actual dealership pricing practices through a nationwide network of dealer personnel, to ensure that we're giving the consumer the best possible information. TMV^{sm} does not, however, take incentives and rebates into account.

If you've got to be the first on your block with a hot new model, you'll pay for the privilege. In fact, dealers sometimes demand profit above the MSRP on ultra-hot models, and they expect to get it. Meanwhile, it is not uncommon for older, stale models to sell below invoice, thanks to hefty incentive programs and rebates, particularly at year-end clearance time. But hot cars will cost more. Sometimes much more.

Contact us.

We strive to give you precise, accurate information so that you can make your very best deal, and we invite your comments. Your best bet for a response is to send e-mail to: manager@edmunds.com. Otherwise, try snail mail to the attention of the Automotive Editors at Edmunds.com; 2401 Colorado Ave.; Suite 250; Santa Monica, CA; 90404.

> NOTE: All information and prices published herein are gathered from sources which, in the editor's opinion, are considered reliable, but under no circumstances is the reader to assume that this information is official or final. All prices are represented as approximations only, in US dollars, and are rounded to the highest whole dollar amount over 50 cents. Unless otherwise noted, all prices are effective as of 1/1/01, but are subject to change without notice. The publisher does not assume responsibility for errors of omission or interpretation. The computerized consumer pricing services advertised herein are not operated by nor are they the responsibility of the publisher. The publisher assumes no responsibility for claims made by advertisers regarding their products or services.

2001 Mercedes-Benz C320

Abbreviations

8V	8-valve		M&S	mud and snow
12V	12-valve		mpg	miles per gallon
16V	16-valve		mph	miles per hour
24V	24-valve		MPI	multi-port injection
2WD	two-wheel drive		MSRP	manufacturer's suggested retail price
4WD	four-wheel drive		N/A	not available OR not applicable
ABS	antilock braking system		NC	no charge
A/C	air conditioning		NHTSA	National Highway and Traffic Safety Administration
ALR	automatic locking retractor			
Amp	ampere		NVH	noise, vibration and harshness
A/S	all-season		OD	overdrive
ASR	automatic slip regulation		OHC	overhead cam
AT	automatic		OHV	overhead valve
Auto	automatic		Opt.	option OR optional
AWD	all-wheel drive		OSRV	outside reverse mirror
BSW	black sidewall		OWL	outline white-letter
Cass.	cassette		Pass.	passenger
CD	compact disc		Pkg.	package
CFC	chloroflourocarbon		PRNDL	Park, Reverse, Neutral, Drive, Low
Conv.	convertible		RBL	raised black-letter
Cpe	coupe		Reg.	regular
Cu. Ft.	cubic foot (feet)		RH	right hand
Cyl.	cylinder		r/l	right and left
DOHC	dual overhead cam		rpm	revolutions per minute
DRL	daytime running light(s)		RWD	rear-wheel drive
DRW	dual rear wheels		SB	shortbed
DSC	dynamic stability control		SBR	steel-belted radial
EDL	electronic differential lock		Sdn	sedan
EFI	electronic fuel injection		SFI	sequential fuel injection
ELR	emergency locking retractor		SLA	short/long arm
EQ	equalizer		SMPI	sequential multi-port injection
ETR	electronically-tuned radio		SOHC	single overhead cam
Ext.	extended		SPI	sequential port injection
ft-lbs.	foot-pounds (measurement of torque)		SRW	single rear wheels
FWD	front-wheel drive		Std.	standard
Gal.	gallon(s)		SUV	sport utility vehicle
GAWR	gross axle weight rating		SWB	short wheelbase
GVW	gross vehicle weight		TDI	turbocharged direct injection
GVWR	gross vehicle weight rating		TMV[sm]	Edmunds.com's True Market Value[sm]
GPS	global positioning satellite		TOD	torque on demand
Hbk.	hatchback		V6	V-type six
HD	heavy duty		V8	V-type eight
Hp	horsepower		V10	V-type ten
HUD	heads-up display		V12	V-type twelve
HVAC	heating, ventilation and air conditioning		VR	v-rated
I-4	inline four		VSC	vehicle skid contrl
I-5	inline five		VTEC	variable valve timing and lift electronic control
I-6	inline six			
L	liter		VVT-i	variable valve timing, intelligence
LB	longbed		Wgn.	wagon
lb(s).	pound(s)		WOL	white outline-letter
LCD	liquid crystal display		WS	work series
LED	light emitting diode		WSW	white sidewall
LEV	low emission vehicle		W/T	work truck
LH	left hand		X-cab	extended cab
LWB	long wheelbase			

EDMUNDS® NEW CARS

REVIEW

2001 Mercedes C320

The Baby Benz Grows Up

BY BRENT ROMANS

So if you had $1.3 billion, what would you do with it? Invest it? Spend it frivolously by buying everything from the Macy's online catalog for each of your 500 closest friends? Donate it to charity? Get Ted Koppel some new hair? (Buying Ted hair would actually be considered a tax-deductible donation.)

Mercedes-Benz has $1.3 billion. Or, rather, it did have it. It blew through that wad of cash for a car—the new C-Class, specifically. That's a pretty stunning amount of money to spend on the development of a car. But Mercedes believes that every penny of its investment was worth it. The C-Class is the company's entry-level luxury car in the United States, competing in a segment that has grown from 623,000 vehicles sold in 1991 to 875,000 sold in 1999. Those vehicles represent the largest portion of the total luxury segment, at over 70 percent. For a luxury-focused company like Mercedes to sell an uncompetitive car in this segment would be almost unthinkable.

The previous C-Class was available from 1994 to 2000. Prestigious and luxurious, the final year was perhaps the car's best, with a lineup including the supercharged C230, a V6-powered C280 and the high-performance C43. The 2000 cars also had additional content in the form of Tele Aid and Touch Shift transmissions. But even with these upgrades, proverbial gray hairs were starting to appear. More recent products from BMW and Lexus were fresher, cheaper and offered a more stimulating drive. Dynamically and stylistically, the C-Class was becoming old.

When a car is redesigned, it is common to see a growth in size, as that keeps the marketing guys happy. But place a 2001 C-Class next to a 2000 model, and you will be hard pressed to notice any dimensional changes. The new car rides on a 106.9-inch wheelbase versus the old car's 105.9-inch measurement. Overall length, height and width are virtually identical, as is cabin volume (88.6 cubic feet vs. 88.0). Trunk space is slightly less with the new car (12.0 vs. 12.9), but passenger accommodations such as legroom and headroom are either identical or slightly more. It would seem that Mercedes considered the previous C-Class "right-sized" and saw little reason to change it.

It is in the other areas of car design — structural engineering, features, safety equipment, and driving dynamics — that Mercedes decided to improve upon. In a way, you could think of the new C-Class as the result of a genetic experiment where C-Class, E-Class and S-Class DNA has been chopped up and placed into the automotive version of a Human Genome Project sequencing machine.

This process is most apparent by looking at the car's exterior styling. The basic profile and shape of the car is remotely similar to the previous C-Class, but it is more modern and draws heavily from the styling applied to the new-for-2000 S-Class. The car is youthful looking now, with swooping C-pillars, a sculpted hood, a trimmer waistline and stronger shoulders. Aerodynamic drag is a super-low 0.27 Cd. The headlights and taillights are styled to fit more closely into the Mercedes-Benz family lineage, with triangle-shaped taillights seemingly straight off an S-Class, LED turn signals fitted in the side mirrors and guitar-shaped headlights that look like the E-Class' quad lamps melted and stuck together. Overall, our staff wasn't drooling over the new C-Class' styling (the headlight design was the most maligned), but certainly nobody hated the styling and we compliment Mercedes for updating the car's looks without being too timid or radical.

Underneath that new sheetmetal is an all-new body structure. Mercedes says it is 26 percent stiffer in static torsional resistance, while bending resistance is 50 percent improved. The front strut-type suspension design has been updated by utilizing two lower links, along with coil springs, twin-tube gas shocks and an antiroll bar. By using two lower links instead of one large link (or control arm), Mercedes says front-impact crash absorption is enhanced. The rear multi-link suspension has also been updated to improve vehicle stability and wheel control at high cornering speeds. Complementing the improved stability are larger and thicker brake rotors, new brake calipers and a more powerful brake booster. There is also a new rack-and-pinion steering system, a change from the previous C-Class' recirculating-ball steering design.

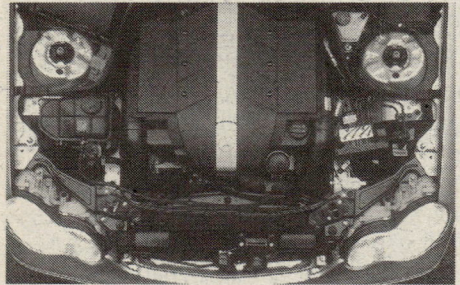

Another C-Class change is the lineup of engines. In fact, all of the engines found in the 2000 C-Class are gone, replaced by two new V6s. The C240 Sedan has a 2.6-liter engine and the C320 has a 3.2-liter V6 (Yes, "240" makes little sense, thereby keeping Mercedes' reputation for cryptic badging intact.). The smaller engine produces 168 horsepower at 5,500 rpm and 177 foot-pounds of torque at 4,500 rpm. The larger engine profits from its extra 0.6 liter of displacement by making 215 horsepower at 5,700 rpm and 221 foot-pounds of torque at 3,000 rpm. As a rather interesting aside, the C320, BMW 330i, Acura TL and Lexus IS 300 make nearly identical amounts of horsepower and torque, so no car has a clear advantage in power output.

Both C-Class engines feature modern Mercedes architecture, with aluminum construction, a double plenum intake manifold, a single overhead camshaft per cylinder bank and twin-spark/three-valve-per-cylinder technology. Mercedes says it uses two spark plugs and three valves per cylinder to reduce emissions without any corresponding loss in horsepower. There's also a computer that takes readings from a variety of sensors to determine optimal service intervals, thereby eliminating scheduled oil changes in the conventional sense.

Two transmissions are offered for the 2001 C-Class. The C240 can be ordered with a six-speed manual transmission, the first time a manual has been offered in a Mercedes sedan in a very long time. The other choice is a five-speed automatic, and that is the only transmission offered in the C320. The automatic features Touch Shift, a feature that first appeared on the C-Class in 2000. Touch Shift allows manual gear selection of the automatic by pushing the shift lever to the left slightly to downshift and to the right slightly to upshift. When in normal drive mode, the electronically controlled automatic can also adapt to both road conditions and driver style.

Another carryover from the previous car is Electronic Stability Program, or ESP. Found on every Mercedes product and tailored to each specific model, ESP uses a steering angle sensor, speed sensors at each wheel, sensors for lateral acceleration and vehicle yaw to calculate the path being asked by the driver (through the steering) versus the vehicle's actual path. If there is a discernable difference, ESP activates to reduce the chances of understeer and oversteer, thereby improving the safety of the vehicle. Traction control and ABS with brake assist are also standard equipment.

If the C-Class does get into an accident, there are plenty of other new measures to keep occupants safe. The body structure itself features new reinforcements in the body floor, doors and roof pillars to improve impact absorption. Tele Aid, Mercedes' cellular-based emergency call system, is standard in both models. Inside the cabin, all five seating positions in the new C-Class are fitted with three-point belts with electronically controlled pre-tensioners. Front passengers get dual-stage front airbags and door-mounted side airbags. Rear outboard passengers also get side airbags, and curtain airbags deploy from the headliner to offer head protection to all outboard passengers. Like before, the C-Class has BabySmart, a system that uses transponders to detect the presence of a BabySmart-compatible child seat to automatically deactivate the front passenger-side airbag. As of this writing, the 2001 C-Class hasn't been tested yet by the NHTSA or IIHS, so we can't comment on how effective the safety systems will be. There should be room for improvement, though; in NCAP tests, the

previous C-Class never achieved five stars in either frontal- or side-impact ratings.

Fortunately, we never had to test the crashworthiness of the C-Class ourselves, but we were able to evaluate nearly every other aspect of the car. Our test vehicle was a C320 equipped with the C6 Sport Package. First impressions? It is obvious that Mercedes has upped the sporting content of the C-Class, a move that certainly has a few BMW execs popping more antacid tablets than usual. The new rack-and-pinion steering system is a big improvement, offering better feel and response. Some people might think it is too heavy for parking lot maneuvers, and it still does not connect the driver to the road in the way that a BMW steering system can. But it weights up nicely while cornering and exhibits little play on center, so you can't ask for too much more.

Equipped with the sport package, our test car's handling abilities seemed better than the old C280 and certainly closer to the high-perfor-

mance C43. Like most Mercedes cars, the car conveys a sense of solid stability. But driven back to back against a 330i, we would say that the C320's suspension engineers still have some more work to do before they can claim superiority. On twisty canyon roads, the C320 doesn't inspire the confidence or generate the level of enthusiasm that the BMW can. There's more body roll (it's 123 pounds heavier than the 2000 C280), and the theoretical payoff in terms of better ride quality doesn't seem to be there.

Still, the fact that the new car begs to be compared to a 3 Series shows just how far it has come. When it comes down to performance handling numbers in the slalom, the Mercedes is about equal to the BMW, and the C320 is certainly more of a pleasure to pilot aggressively than a front-drive Lexus ES 300 or Acura TL.

Another enthusiast bonus is the new 3.2-liter V6 engine. It is very smooth and quiet—as expected—but it also puts out about 10 percent more torque and horsepower than the C280's 2.8-liter V6. At the track, our test car ran from zero to 60 in 7.5 seconds and posted a quarter-mile time of 15.75 seconds at 91 mph. Power is available throughout the rev band, and acceleration seems best from around 3,000 rpm to redline. Braking is simply outstanding. Our car stopped from 60 mph to zero in 111 feet, one of the best figures we have ever recorded.

The enthusiast leanings stop at the transmission, however. Since the manual can't be ordered with the C320, drivers are stuck with the auto. This certainly won't be a problem for the majority of current Mercedes owners, but it won't attract any buyers who insist on having a manual. Like NutraSweet or reading about sex, the Touch Shift function is a poor substitute for the real thing. There is a noticeable time delay between when the driver asks for a shift and the transmission actually acts upon the request. If we lower our expectations to more real-world usage, the transmission's fortunes improve, as it works great around town and on the freeway, always picking the right gear and just generally being transparent.

It's also during those mundane times of urban transit that the C-Class shows how it is still one of the best entry-level cars in terms of luxury and feature content. Wind and road noise are minimal, and the interior design, like the exterior, has gained many family traits found in more expensive Mercedes-Benz cars. Interior material quality has been improved, with every interior plastic panel touchable from the driver's seat being of the soft-touch variety. Leather quality on the seats was high on our sport package-equipped test car, though only one of our editors liked the sport package's engraved aluminum trim; the rest said it looked cheap and unfinished.

An all-new S-Class-inspired gauge cluster features a large analog speedometer along with a smaller fuel gauge and tachometer. The tach is too small in our opinion, but we were very impressed with the menu-driven LCD screen. Operated by large and convenient buttons on the thick steering wheel, the screen can display parameters like running time, language (no Swedish, sorry), outside temperature, service intervals and audio settings. It can also be used to adjust settings of the door locks and exterior lights.

Control ergonomics irked some members of our staff, though it seemed to trouble the newer staffers unfamiliar with the "Mercedes-Benz School of Wonky Control Layout." Window switches? Those would be on the door near the floor. Seat controls? Oh, those are on the door, too. The large allotment of buttons on the dash and for the audio and climate systems can be intimidating. Our more seasoned staffers note, however, that there is logic to the madness, and that after spending time in the car, things do make more sense. Interior storage is better than before, with large door bins and a dual-level center bin. The glove box is also roomy, but the optional CD changer in our test car took up a decent percentage of it. Nobody, but nobody, liked the elegant but nearly useless cupholder.

Best then to use the optional COMAND navigation system to get yourself to a sit-down coffee house. COMAND also integrates the telephone and audio system. Other options include heated seats, high-intensity discharge headlights and an integrated digital cellular phone system. The C2 Package includes a sunroof, rain-sensing windshield wipers and a one-touch power rear-window sunshade. Standard equipment highlights include automatic headlights, an auto-dimming mirror, remote fold-down rear headrests, a power-operated steering wheel (optional on the C240), dual-zone automatic climate control with an active charcoal filter, and a Bose premium audio system (also optional on the C240).

Of course, all of these features don't come free of charge. Pricing is similar to the previous C-Class, but to say that our test car's price is "entry-level" would be a big stretch. Compared to our car, a Lexus IS 300 costs approximately $10,000 less, and an Acura TL with the GPS navigation system (the only feature not standard) is about $12,000 less. Ouch.

But then those cars don't have the three-pointed star on the hood, do they? For consumers who want a solid and prestigious entry-level luxury car with an unparalleled list of options, the C320 is about as good as it gets for 2001. It is also more of a sedan that would appeal to the sporting enthusiast, but for the time being, that crown is still on the head of the 3 Series.

Vehicle Tested:
2001 Mercedes-Benz C320

Base Price: $36,695 (including destination charge)

Options on Test Vehicle: Brilliant Silver Metallic Paint ($625); C2 Package ($1,340 - includes sunroof, rain-sensing windshield wipers, power rear-window sunshade); C3 Package ($425 - includes 60/40 split-fold rear seat and ski sack); C6 Sport Package ($2,950 - includes sport-tuned suspension, 16-inch alloy wheels, sculpted lower body trim, premium leather, engraved aluminum interior trim, sport seats); Compact Disc Changer ($682).

Price of Test Vehicle: $43,617 (including destination charge)

Automobile Manufacturers
Customer Assistance Numbers

Acura	1-800-382-2238
AM General	1-800-348-6833
Audi	1-800-822-2834
BMW	1-800-831-1117
Buick	1-800-521-7300
Cadillac	1-800-458-8006
Chevrolet	1-800-222-1020
Chrysler	1-800-992-1997
Daewoo	1-888-643-2396
Dodge	1-800-992-1997
Ford	1-800-392-3673
GMC	1-800-462-8782
Honda	1-800-999-1009
Hyundai	1-800-633-5151
Infiniti	1-800-662-6200
Isuzu	1-800-255-6727
Jaguar	1-800-452-4827
Jeep	1-800-992-1997
Kia	1-800-333-4542
Land Rover	1-800-637-6837
Lexus	1-800-255-3987
Lincoln	1-800-392-3673
Mazda	1-800-222-5500
Mercedes-Benz	1-800-222-0100
Mercury	1-800-392-3673
Mitsubishi	1-800-222-0037
Nissan	1-800-647-7261
Oldsmobile	1-800-442-6537
Plymouth	1-800-992-1997
Pontiac	1-800-762-2737
Porsche	1-800-545-8039
Saab	1-800-955-9007
Saturn	1-800-553-6000
Subaru	1-800-782-2783
Suzuki	1-800-934-0934
Toyota	1-800-331-4331
Volkswagen	1-800-822-8987
Volvo	1-800-458-1552

HOW TO BUY...

Every automobile buyer has but one thought in mind—to save money by getting a good deal. Your goal should be to pay a minimal amount over the dealer's true cost, not the 10-15 percent the dealer wants you to pay. Use the following guide to help you plan your purchase:

Step 1 Know what type of vehicle you need, and study the different models available.

Step 2 Test-drive, as extensively as possible, each model you're interested in. Pay special attention to safety features, design, comfort, braking, handling, acceleration, ride quality, ease of entry and exit, etc. If possible, rent your final selection for a day or two and take a road trip so you can really "live" with the vehicle.

Step 3 Check insurance rates on the models you're interested in to make sure the premiums fall within your budget.

Step 4 Contact several financial institutions to obtain loan rate information. Later on, you can compare their rates with the dealer's financing plan.

Step 5 Find the exact vehicle you want, and copy the options and prices listed on the window sticker onto a pad of paper. Then, use our pricing information to determine actual dealer cost (if ordering the vehicle from the factory, just use our data to determine what the order will cost when you place it):

a) Total the dealer invoice column for the model and equipment you want.

b) If ordering the vehicle, determine the value of the holdback and subtract this amount. If the dealer orders the vehicle, he won't pay floorplanning (the charge to stock the vehicle), or advertising (an expected cost of business), which the holdback is designed to subsidize.

c) Add a fair profit of about 2-4 percent. Keep in mind that hot-selling models in high demand and short supply will command additional profit, sometimes in excess of MSRP in extreme situations. You can visit our Web site at www.edmunds.com to get the latest True Market Value^{sm} (TMV^{sm}) price for any new car or truck.

d) Add the destination charge, which is non-negotiable. You might be charged advertising fees by the auto manufacturer to help pay for those MTV-style TV commercials that got you thinking about a new car in the first place. Advertising fees should be no more than 1.5 percent of the vehicle's MSRP.

...A NEW CAR

e) Some dealers charge a delivery and handling (D&H) fee. Negotiate this fee. It's just added profit.

f) Deduct any dealer incentives. Incentives get deducted *before* tax is calculated.

g) Add sales taxes.

h) Deduct any customer rebates. Rebates get deducted *after* tax is calculated.

Step 6 Shop this price around to several different dealership sales managers, either over the Internet, in person, or via fax and phone. The dealer who meets or comes closest to your target price should get your business. Be sure that the dealer's price quote will be your final cost (make sure it includes tax and related fees so they don't tack those on later). Get it in writing!

Step 7 If your present vehicle will be used as a trade-in, negotiate the highest possible value for it. Try not to accept a value that is less than Edmunds trade-in value for your car. When trading in your vehicle, you should deduct the trade value from the cost of the new vehicle. If you owe the bank more money than the trade-in is worth to the dealer, you are upside-down on your trade and must add the difference between what you owe and the trade value to the cost of the new vehicle. If you're making a cash down payment, either with or without a trade-in, be sure to deduct this amount from the cost of the new vehicle as well.

Step 8 To the final vehicle cost, add documentation fees and, in some areas, license plate charges.

Step 9 When talking to the finance manager as you close the deal, he or she will try to sell you protection packages, anti-theft systems, dealer-added options, and an extended warranty or service contract. Forget about this stuff, unless the dealer is selling the product for less than you can find elsewhere. Dealers charge a substantial markup on these often useless items to fatten the profit margin on your deal. Some people might want to consider buying an extended warranty or service contract. But remember, this is negotiable, and your new car might already have a strong warranty.

Step 10 Enjoy your new vehicle, knowing that you did everything possible to get the best deal.

Most people have three things in common when they buy a car.

They pay too much,
They waste time,
and
They hate the experience.

Which is exactly why you should call carclub.om. We offer the the quickest and most convenient way to save time and money when you buy a new car or truck. Simple as that.

Just tell us the vehicle and options you want (any make or model-foreign or domestic) and we'll get you a lower price than you can get on your own. Guaranteed in writing. We can factory order any domestic vehicle and usually save you even more.

No haggling. No hassles. No games.

Don't forget to ask about our loans, leases, extended service contracts, gas discounts, deductible reimbursement, and more. It's a terrific way to save even more money on the purchase of your new car

For more information, call carclub.com at 1-800-carclub (1-800-227-2582)

1-800-CARCLUB
or visit us on the web at carclub.com

All new cars arranged for sale are subject to price and availability from the selling franchised new car dealer

You're not alone.℠

ACURA

CL-SERIES

2001 CL-SERIES

What's New?

Acura's CL undergoes a major makeover to gain headway in the luxury coupe market. New from the ground up, the CL receives upgraded 3.2-liter V6 engines making up to 260 horsepower, a five-speed automatic transmission with sequential SportShift, and a full load of standard equipment for a bargain-basement price. A new sport-tuned Type S is worth the extra money if you value performance over ride comfort.

Review

Acura's target market for the 3.2CL is aging baby boomers that are experiencing life without children for the first time in decades. No longer needing that silly SUV or monstrous minivan, these empty nesters are supposed to rediscover the joys of coupe life...preferably in a CL.

Well, there are worse places to go for a midlife crisis. Acura's CL offers spirited performance and competent handling in a package that effectively marries the two with a comfortable, well-appointed cabin. Two models are available: the standard CL or, for those who crave a sportier ride with additional power, the performance-oriented Type S.

Though it will never threaten an NSX in terms of absolute handling nor a Bentley Continental R with regard to lavish trimmings, the stoutly bodied CL may surprise drivers who think that automatic climate control and canyon carving are mutually exclusive.

Highway manners are excellent, with a comfortable ride that provides plenty of feedback. Standard 16-inch wheels and antilock brakes provide sure footing when pushed to the limit, and the variable-assist rack-and-pinion steering is communicative without making low-speed parking maneuvers difficult. A smooth, torquey 3.2-liter, 225-horsepower V6 in standard CLs (or a 260-horsepower version in the Type S model) makes for lively acceleration. The front wheels are driven through a five-speed SportShift automanual transmission.

The extra investment required to purchase the Type S is worth the cost in drivetrain dividends, which include a dual-stage induction system, low-restriction dual exhaust, larger throttle body, increased compression ratio, special cylinder heads, firmer springs, increased shock damping and handsome 17-inch wheels. Type S also gets a Vehicle Stability Assist (VSA) system to keep the car pointed in the direction you want to go. Be warned, however, that the stiffly sprung Type S suffers from a somewhat harsh ride on most urban streets.

Unlike American personal coupes that are often overweight and overtly flashy, or austere German sport coupes, which are often Spartan to the point of monasticism, the CL's interior effectively blends ergonomic simplicity with the look, if not the feel, of rich appointments. Up front, occupants will find comfortable and supportive leather-faced seats, as well as plenty of legroom. Side-impact airbags are standard. Acura calls the CL a 2+2, so it should come as no surprise that backseat passengers will feel a bit pinched if they are over average height.

Standard niceties include an in-dash six-disc CD changer hooked to an Acura/Bose audio system, heated front seats, remote keyless entry, and a power moonroof. The only option on either model is a DVD-based navigation system containing complete mapping of the 48 contiguous states.

As the first Acura designed, engineered, and manufactured almost entirely in the United States, the CL certainly doesn't feel "American." From its high-end accouterments to its sporty road manners, the CL takes personal luxury to a level not commonly found on vehicles in this price range.

CL-SERIES
ACURA

Standard Equipment

3.2 CL (5A): 3.2L V6 SOHC SMPI 24-valve engine with variable valve timing (requires premium unleaded fuel); 5-speed electronic OD automatic transmission with lock-up torque converter; 105-amp alternator; auto-manual transmission; front-wheel drive, traction control, 4.43 axle ratio; stainless steel exhaust with tailpipe finisher; front independent double-wishbone suspension with anti-roll bar, front coil springs, gas-pressurized front shocks, rear independent double-wishbone suspension with anti-roll bar, rear coil springs, gas-pressurized rear shocks; rack-and-pinion power steering with engine-speed-sensing assist; 4-wheel antilock disc brakes; 17.2 gal. capacity fuel tank; side impact bars; front power sliding and tilting glass sunroof with sunshade; front and rear body-colored bumpers; clearcoat monotone paint; aero-composite high intensity headlamps; additional exterior lights include front fog/driving lights; body-colored driver's power remote outside mirror, passenger's power remote with tilt down outside mirror; 16" x 6.5" silver alloy wheels; P205/60VR16 BSW A/S tires; compact steel spare wheel; air conditioning with climate control, air filter; premium AM/FM stereo, seek-scan feature, cassette player, 6-disc CD changer, 6 premium speakers, premium amplifier, theft deterrent, and window grid antenna, radio steering wheel controls; cruise control with steering wheel controls; power door locks with 2 stage unlock, remote keyless entry, power remote trunk release, remote fuel door release; 2 power accessory outlets, driver's foot rest, retained accessory power, garage door opener; instrumentation display includes tachometer, water temperature gauge, in-dash clock, trip odometer; warning indicators include oil pressure, battery, lights on, key in ignition, low fuel, bulb failure, door ajar, trunk ajar, service interval; driver's and passenger's front airbags with occupancy sensor, driver's and front passenger's seat mounted side airbags; ignition disable, panic alarm, security system; tinted windows, power windows with driver's 1-touch down function; variable-speed intermittent front windshield wipers, sun visor strip, rear window defroster; seating capacity of 4, heated-cushion front bucket seats with adjustable headrests, center armrest with storage, driver's seat includes 6-way power adjustment, lumbar support and easy entry, passenger's seat includes 4-way power adjustment and easy entry; rear bucket seat with fixed headrests, center pass-thru armrest; height-adjustable front seatbelts with pretensioners; leather seats, leather door trim insert, full cloth headliner, full carpet floor covering with carpeted floor mats; driver's seat memory includes 2 settings for exterior mirrors; interior lights include dome light, front reading lights, door curb lights, illuminated entry; leather-wrapped steering wheel with tilt adjustment; dual illuminated vanity mirrors; auto-dimming day/night rearview mirror; full floor console, rear console with storage, locking glove box with light, front and rear cupholders, instrument panel covered bin, 2 seatback storage pockets, driver's and passenger's door bins; carpeted cargo floor, cargo net, cargo tray, cargo light; chrome grille, chrome side window moldings, black front windshield molding, black rear window molding and chrome door handles.

3.2 CL TYPE S (5A) (in addition to or instead of 3.2 CL (5A) equipment): 260-HP 3.2L V6 SOHC SMPI 24-valve engine with variable valve timing; 120-amp alternator; sport-ride suspension, electronic stability control; body-colored heated driver's power remote outside mirror; 17" x 7" silver alloy wheels; P215/50VR17 BSW A/S tires.

Base Prices

CODE	DESCRIPTION	INVOICE	MSRP
YA4241FNW	3.2 CL (5A)	25508	27980
YA4261FNW	3.2 CL Type S (5A)	27648	30330
	Destination Charge:	480	480

Interested in seeing what dealers will sell this vehicle for? Check out our True Market Value^{sm} (TMV^{sm}) pricing on our Web site at www.edmunds.com.

Accessories

		INVOICE	MSRP
—	Acura Navigation System	1822	2000
	Includes DVD satellite navigation system and mapping for all 48 contiguous states.		

ACURA

CL-SERIES / INTEGRA

| CODE | DESCRIPTION | | INVOICE | MSRP |

2001 INTEGRA

What's New?

Carpeted floor mats are newly standard, and an emergency trunk release is added to the inside of the sedan's cargo area. Four new colors round out the changes for 2001, Integra's final year before an all-new model debuts for 2002. By the way, this is your last chance for an Integra Sedan — the new car will be offered only as a three-door hatchback.

Review

Yes, yes, we know that the Integra is long in the tooth and that an all-new model will be released in 2002. But don't disrespect the current model.

Since its introduction in 1994, the current Integra has provided many drivers — young, old, male and female — with a sporty, practical, reliable and enjoyable ride. Even 5-year-old Integras still look hot cruising the streets. And the Type R, reintroduced last year after a year's absence, is a bona fide road ripper. There aren't any other cars in the sport compact market with as much longevity, style or popularity.

So, despite being over the hill, the Integra is still a great car. And, just to freshen things up a little bit, this year's model gets standard carpeted floor mats and four new exterior colors. Also, an emergency trunk release has been added to the inside of the sedan's cargo area. Speaking of the sedan, those with a sense of history may want to pick one up in 2001. When the new Integra is released next year it will be available only as a three-door hatchback.

We've always praised the Integra for its thrilling drive. We've even gone so far as to call it one of the top-handling front-drivers in the world. The shifter is one of the best in the industry, with a shape that fits the hand perfectly and a relatively short throw between gears. With a fully independent four-wheel double-wishbone suspension, front and rear stabilizer bars and a thick steering wheel that gives excellent feedback about what's going on down below, the Integra offers nearly the same driving enjoyment you'd get from a BMW 3 Series — if you had twice the money for the dealer, your insurance broker and the service center.

The base (on GS and LS trim levels) 1.8-liter four-cylinder engine produces an adequate, but not ripping 140 horsepower. For mega-thrills, the GS-R boasts a VTEC-enhanced 1.8-liter inline four that cranks out 170 horsepower and 128 foot-pounds of torque. When you run the gutsy Type R to 8,000 rpm, just short of its 8,500-rpm redline, it delivers a street-racer worthy 195 horsepower, mostly due to its hand-polished intake and exhaust ports and a high-flow exhaust system. It's this raw energy that has made the Type R a cult favorite with Japanese road rocket fans.

As part of Honda's larger family, you can also count on the Integra to provide excellent seating, good headroom, straightforward and functional ergonomics and exceptional build quality.

So what if it's an old design; it's one of the best cars ever produced.

Standard Equipment

LS COUPE (5M): 1.8L I4 DOHC SMPI 16-valve engine; 5-speed OD manual transmission; 90 amp alternator; front-wheel drive, 4.27 axle ratio; stainless steel exhaust with tailpipe finisher; front independent double-wishbone suspension with anti-roll bar, front coil springs, gas-pressurized front shocks, rear independent double-wishbone suspension with anti-roll bar, rear coil springs, gas-pressurized rear shocks; rack-and-pinion power steering with engine speed-sensing assist; 4-wheel antilock disc brakes; 13.2 gal. capacity fuel tank; side impact bars; power sliding and

INTEGRA / ACURA

CODE	DESCRIPTION	INVOICE	MSRP

tilting glass sunroof with sunshade; front and rear body-colored bumpers; body-colored bodyside molding; clearcoat monotone paint; projector beam halogen headlamps; driver's and passenger's power remote body-colored folding outside mirrors; 15" x 6" machined alloy wheels; P195/55VR15 BSW A/S tires; trunk mounted compact steel spare wheel; air conditioning; AM/FM stereo radio, seek-scan, single CD player, 6 speakers, theft deterrent, power retractable antenna; cruise control with steering wheel controls; power door locks, power remote hatch release, remote fuel door release; 1 power accessory outlet, front lighter element, driver's foot rest, smokers' package; instrumentation display includes tachometer, water temperature gauge, in-dash clock, trip odometer; warning indicators include oil pressure, battery, lights on, key in ignition, low fuel, door ajar, trunk ajar, service interval; driver's and passenger's front airbags; ignition disable; tinted windows with driver's 1-touch down function; variable-speed intermittent front windshield wipers, rear window wiper, rear window defroster; seating capacity of 4, front bucket seats with adjustable headrests, center armrest with storage, driver's seat includes 8-way adjustment, lumbar support, passenger's seat includes 4-way adjustment, easy entry; 50/50 folding rear bench seat with fixed headrests; cloth seats, cloth door trim insert, full cloth headliner, full carpet floor covering, leather-wrapped gearshift knob; interior lights include dome light, front reading lights; leather-wrapped steering wheel with tilt adjustment; passenger's side vanity mirror; day/night rearview mirror; full floor console, rear console with storage, locking glove box, front cupholder, instrument panel bin, driver's and passenger's door bins; carpeted cargo floor, cargo cover, cargo light; black side window moldings, black front windshield molding, black rear window molding and body-colored door handles.

GS COUPE (5M) (in addition to or instead of LS COUPE (5M) equipment): Rear wing spoiler; leather seats, leatherette door trim insert and locking glove box with light.

GS-R COUPE (5M) (in addition to or instead of GS COUPE (5M) equipment): 1.8L I4 DOHC SMPI 16-valve engine with variable valve timing, (requires premium unleaded fuel) and 4.4 axle ratio.

TYPE-R COUPE (5M) (in addition to or instead of GS-R COUPE (5M) equipment): Engine oil cooler; viscous limited-slip differential; sport ride suspension; rocker panel extensions; P195/55VR15 BSW performance tires; fixed interval front windshield wipers, rear window wiper, front sports seats with adjustable headrests, center armrest with storage, driver's seat includes 4-way adjustment, lumbar support, passenger's seat includes 4-way adjustment, easy entry; cloth seats, cloth door trim insert, carbon fiber dashboard insert, titanium gearshift knob and carbon fiber console insert.

SEDAN (5M) (in addition to or instead of COUPE (5M) equipment): 4.27 axle ratio; P195/55VR15 BSW A/S tires; seating capacity of 5, front bucket seats with adjustable headrests, center armrest with storage, driver's seat includes 8-way adjustment, lumbar support, passenger's seat includes 4-way adjustment and chrome side window moldings.

Base Prices

Code	Description	Invoice	MSRP
DC4351MBW	LS Coupe (5M)	17498	19400
DC4361MBW	GS Coupe (5M)	18983	21050
DC2391MBW	GS-R Coupe (5M)	20109	22300
DC2311EW	Type-R Coupe (5M)	22045	24450
DB7551MBW	LS Sedan (5M)	18218	20200
DB7561MBW	GS Sedan (5M)	19479	21600
DB8591MBW	GS-R Sedan (5M)	20379	22600
	Destination Charge:	480	480

Interested in seeing what dealers will sell this vehicle for? Check out our True Market Value^{sm} (TMV^{sm}) pricing on our Web site at www.edmunds.com.

ACURA — INTEGRA / RL-SERIES

Accessories

CODE	DESCRIPTION	INVOICE	MSRP
—	Transmission: Electronic 4-Speed Automatic with OD (LS/GS Coupe)	720	800

2001 RL-SERIES

What's New?

Acura decides dinging luxury car buyers for floor mats is a bad idea, and so makes them standard for 2001, leaving the DVD-based navigation system alone on the factory option list. Also new is an emergency trunk release located on the inside of the cargo area.

Review

The 3.5 RL, Acura's flagship, is athletic, extremely quiet, luxurious and priced right: All of which makes it a serious contender in the luxury sedan market despite its V6, front-drive layout.

We're most impressed by the efforts taken by Acura engineers to make the RL as quiet, smooth and solid as possible. Mission accomplished. The RL rides like a cloud on greased rails. This welcome feat was accomplished by adding low-friction ball joints in the suspension, Teflon seals on the valves, a liquid-filled rear-trailing arm, foam-filled B- and C-pillars, honeycomb floor panels and vibration-absorbing seats.

Their efforts, however, would have been for naught if the interior designers had slipped even a little. No fear. Switchgear and controls possess the same Acura quality we've counted on for years, the seats are a utopian dream of comfort and the multi-zone climate-control system allows all passengers, including those in the rear, control over their environment.

And don't worry about the sticker being run up when you select a few options — the RL is available in one trim level only and includes everything you'd expect in a luxury sedan, including safety equipment such as high-intensity headlights, side airbags and a new, highly advanced handling control system called Vehicle Stability Assist. And, for 2001, Acura decided it was a bad idea to ding its luxury car buyers for floor mats (well, duh!), so they're now standard. The automaker also added an emergency trunk release located on the inside of the cargo area.

The only thing still optional is the navigation system. We loved it when it was redesigned last year and we still think it's one of the best systems out there. It covers the entire continental United States on a single DVD and supplies verbal instructions that allow drivers to keep their eyes on the road and their hands on the wheel.

Last year we wondered why a V8 engine wasn't included with all the 3.5RL's other advancements, especially considering most of its competitors do offer eight cylinders. We will continue to ask until we are satisfied. It's important to note, though, that we're not complaining about the RL's 210-horsepower V6 - it's an athletic and spirited drive, but we figure a V8, coupled to proper rear-wheel drive, would put the RL over the top.

Standard Equipment

3.5 (4A): 3.5L V6 SOHC SMPI 24-valve engine (requires premium unleaded fuel); 4-speed electronic OD automatic transmission with lock-up torque converter; 110 amp alternator; front-wheel drive, traction control, 3.13 axle ratio; stainless steel exhaust; electronic stability control, front independent double-wishbone suspension with anti-roll bar, front coil springs, gas-pressurized

RL-SERIES

ACURA

CODE	DESCRIPTION	INVOICE	MSRP

front shocks, rear independent double-wishbone suspension with anti-roll bar, rear coil springs, gas-pressurized rear shocks; power-assisted rack-and-pinion steering with speed-sensing assist; 4-wheel antilock disc brakes; 18 gal. capacity fuel tank; side impact bars; front express open sliding and tilting glass sunroof with sunshade; front and rear body-colored bumpers with chrome bumper insert; body-colored bodyside molding with chrome bodyside insert; clearcoat monotone paint; aero-composite high intensity fully auto headlamps; additional exterior lights include front fog/driving lights; driver's and passenger's power remote body-colored heated folding outside mirrors; 16" x 7" machined alloy wheels; P215/60VR16 BSW A/S tires; compact steel spare wheel; air conditioning with climate control, air filter, rear heat ducts; premium AM/FM stereo, seek-scan feature, cassette player, trunk-mounted 6-disc CD changer, 8 premium speakers, theft deterrent, window grid antenna, radio steering wheel controls; cruise control with steering wheel controls; power door locks with 2-stage unlock, remote keyless entry, child-safety rear door locks, power remote trunk release, remote fuel door release; cell phone pre-wiring, 2 power accessory outlets, front lighter element, driver's foot rest, retained accessory power, garage door opener, ashtray; instrumentation display includes tachometer, water temperature gauge, in-dash clock, exterior temp, trip odometer; warning indicators include oil pressure, battery, lights on, key in ignition, low fuel, bulb failure, door ajar, trunk ajar, service interval; driver's and passenger's front airbags, driver's and front passenger's seat-mounted side airbags; ignition disable, panic alarm, security system; tinted windows, power front and rear windows with driver's 1-touch down function; variable-speed intermittent front windshield wipers, sun visor strip, rear window defroster; seating capacity of 5, front bucket seats, heated-cushion driver's and passenger's seats with adjustable tilt headrests, center armrest with storage, driver's seat includes 8-way power adjustment, lumbar support, passenger's seat includes 4-way power adjustment; rear bench seat with tilt headrests, center pass-thru armrest with skibag; height-adjustable front seatbelts with pretensioners; leather seats, leather door trim insert, full cloth headliner, full carpet floor covering, genuine wood dashboard insert, leather-wrapped gearshift knob, genuine wood door panel insert, genuine wood console insert, chrome interior accents; driver's seat memory includes 2 settings for exterior mirrors, steering wheel; interior lights include dome light with fade, front and rear reading lights, door curb lights, illuminated entry; leather-wrapped steering wheel with power tilt and telescopic adjustment; dual illuminated vanity mirrors, dual auxiliary visors; auto-dimming day/night rearview mirror; full floor console, mini overhead console with storage, locking glove box with light, front and rear cupholders, instrument panel covered bin, 2 seatback storage pockets, driver's and passenger's door bins; carpeted cargo floor, carpeted trunk lid, cargo light; chrome grille, chrome side window moldings, black front windshield molding, black rear window molding and body-colored door handles.

Base Prices

KA9651JTW	3.5RL (4A)	37109	42150
Destination Charge:	....	480	480

Interested in seeing what dealers will sell this vehicle for? Check out our True Market Value^{sm} (TMV^{sm}) pricing on our Web site at www.edmunds.com.

Accessories

—	Navigation System	NC	2000
	Includes DVD satellite navigation system and mapping for all 48 contiguous states.		

ACURA

TL-SERIES

2001 TL-SERIES

What's New?

Standard equipment now includes floor mats and an emergency trunk release. No other changes have been made to the hot-selling TL, now in its third model year.

Review

Acura's torchbearer into the burgeoning near-luxury sedan market is the 3.2TL, and it's pitted against some stiff competition in the form of the Audi A4, BMW 3 Series, Infiniti I30, Lexus ES 300, Mercedes C-Class and Volvo S60. Each of these models is well established in the marketplace, which puts the pressure on Acura not only to meet but to exceed what those cars have to offer while simultaneously keeping price in check.

The wildly popular TL, with its promise of luxury, performance and value, has had no problem meeting the challenge, racking up more than 100,000 sales during its first two years on the market. It will likely be front and center for 2001 as well, despite its status as a carryover model.

Based on a Honda global platform shared by the Accord, the TL's wheelbase is 2 inches longer than its pedestrian sibling. Despite this stretch, the rear seat becomes cramped when a tall driver is at the helm, and there's no underseat room for feet. These are not problems in the Accord. We suspect the Acura's more rakish roofline is the culprit, and while some detractors call the TL dull and uninspired in terms of styling, many of our staffers like its angular, chiseled look.

Storage space, unlike rear seat room, is in abundance, including a deep center console and substantial map pockets in the doors. The driver's seat is quite comfortable, although having only the seating surfaces upholstered in leather is disappointing, and the lack of seat height adjustability for the front passenger doesn't win points from our editors.

The only engine is a peppy 3.2-liter V6 that utilizes VTEC technology to produce 225 horsepower and 216 foot-pounds of torque, while still getting 19/29 mpg in city/highway driving. The V6 remains strong in every gear, and it can scoot from zero to 60 in under 8 seconds. This puts the TL ahead of much of its competition in the horsepower race, and we can confirm that it definitely gets out of its own way. The standard SportShift automanual transmission is quite user-friendly, thanks to a shift gate located close to the driver and an intuitive shift pattern.

The TL offers near-luxury equipment without a hefty price, and you get more than just air conditioning and a smattering of leather on the seats. You snag lots of standard equipment, including a power sunroof, a 180-watt sound system with an in-dash CD player, heated front seats, steering-wheel audio controls, rear heat/air vents, micron air-filtration system, traction control, and four-wheel antilock brakes. A super-simple DVD-based navigation system with a smudge-free touch-screen is the only option, and it includes coverage of the entire continental United States on a single disc.

Offering sporty styling and near-luxury features for a price that is well below the class average, the TL continues to deliver both performance and value in an attractive package.

Standard Equipment

3.2 (5A): 3.2L V6 SOHC SMPI 24-valve engine with variable valve timing (requires premium unleaded fuel); 5-speed electronic OD automatic transmission with lock-up torque converter; 105 amp alternator; auto-manual transmission; front-wheel drive, traction control, 4.43 axle ratio; stainless steel exhaust with tailpipe finisher; front independent double-wishbone suspension

TL-SERIES

ACURA

CODE	DESCRIPTION	INVOICE	MSRP

with anti-roll bar, front coil springs, gas-pressurized front shocks, rear independent double-wishbone suspension with anti-roll bar, rear coil springs, gas-pressurized rear shocks; rack-and-pinion power steering with engine speed-sensing assist; 4-wheel antilock disc brakes; 17.2 gal. capacity fuel tank; side impact bars; power sliding and tilting glass sunroof with sunshade; front and rear body-colored bumpers; body-colored bodyside molding; clearcoat monotone paint; aero-composite high intensity auto off headlamps; driver's and passenger's power remote body-colored heated folding outside mirrors; 16" x 6.5" machined alloy wheels; P205/60VR16 BSW A/S tires; compact steel spare wheel; air conditioning with climate control, air filter, rear heat ducts; premium AM/FM stereo, seek-scan feature, cassette player, single-disc CD player, 5 premium speakers, theft deterrent, window grid antenna, radio steering wheel controls; cruise control with steering wheel controls; power door locks with 2-stage unlock, remote keyless entry, child safety rear door locks, power remote trunk release, remote fuel door release; 2 power accessory outlets, driver's foot rest, retained accessory power, garage door opener; instrumentation display includes tachometer, water temperature gauge, in-dash clock, exterior temp, trip odometer; warning indicators include oil pressure, battery, lights on, key in ignition, low fuel, bulb failure, door ajar, trunk ajar, service interval; driver's and passenger's front airbags, driver's and front passenger's seat-mounted side airbags; ignition disable, panic alarm, security system; tinted windows, power front and rear windows with driver's 1-touch down function; variable-speed intermittent front windshield wipers, sun visor strip, rear window defroster; seating capacity of 5, front bucket seats, heated-cushion driver's and passenger's seats with adjustable headrests, center armrest with storage, driver's seat includes 8-way power adjustment, lumbar support, passenger's seat includes 4-way power adjustment; rear bench seat with fixed headrests, center pass-thru armrest; front height-adjustable seatbelts; leather seats, leather door trim insert, full cloth headliner, full carpet floor covering with carpeted floor mats, leather-wrapped gearshift knob, simulated wood door panel insert, simulated wood console insert, chrome interior accents; interior lights include dome light, front reading lights, door curb lights, illuminated entry; leather-wrapped steering wheel with tilt adjustment; dual illuminated vanity mirrors, dual auxiliary visors; auto-dimming day/night rearview mirror; full floor console, mini overhead console with storage, locking glove box with light, front and rear cupholders, 2 seatback storage pockets, driver's and passenger's door bins; carpeted cargo floor, carpeted trunk lid, cargo light; chrome grille, chrome side window moldings, black front windshield molding, black rear window molding and chrome door handles.

Base Prices

UA566YJTW 3.2TL (5A)		25738	28550
Destination Charge:		480	480

Interested in seeing what dealers will sell this vehicle for? Check out our True Market Value^{sm} (TMV^{sm}) pricing on our Web site at www.edmunds.com.

Accessories

—	Navigation System	1799	2000

Includes DVD satellite navigation system and mapping for all 48 contiguous states.

AUDI

A4

| CODE | DESCRIPTION | INVOICE | MSRP |

2001 A4

What's New?

The entire Audi lineup receives a new 4-year/50,000-mile limited warranty and no-charge scheduled maintenance, a 12-year limited warranty against corrosion perforation, and 24-hour Roadside Assistance for 4 years. All A4s are now equipped with head protection airbags, have lengthier oil change intervals, and an optional Electronic Stability Program (ESP). The 1.8T engine gets a horsepower boost from 150 to a racy 170 and meets ULEV standards.

Review

Audi's A4 is sleek, sophisticated, speedy and has won praise from the worldwide automotive media. Small and safe, the A4 has scored well in government crash testing. For U.S. buyers, this translates into a competent alternative to the BMW 3 Series, the Acura TL and the Volvo S40, among others.

For 2001, four versions are available: the A4 1.8T Sedan and 1.8T Avant Wagon, and the A4 2.8 Sedan and 2.8 Avant Wagon. The numerical designations refer to engine size. The 1.8T models get a 1.8-liter turbocharged engine that now produces 170 horsepower and 166 foot-pounds of torque. Vehicles with a 2.8 designation have a 2.8-liter V6 filling their engine bays. The six-cylinder makes 190 horsepower and 207 foot-pounds of torque. Both engines can be ordered with a five-speed manual or a five-speed Tiptronic automanual transmission. Audi's quattro all-wheel-drive system is standard on Avant wagons and optional on the sedans.

Besides engine selection, the 1.8T vehicles differ from the 2.8 models in only minor trim. The 2.8 Sedan and Avant have bigger wheels and tires, 10-way power seats, aluminum trim on the window frames, and wood interior decor. All cars feature goodies like a new Sport 3-spoke steering wheel with Tiptronic control buttons for the auto tranny, automatic climate control, remote keyless entry, heated outside mirrors and windshield-wiper nozzles, an eight-speaker CD audio system, and 60/40 split folding rear seats.

Avant wagons have 31.3 cubic feet of cargo room with the rear seat up and 63.7 cubic feet of cargo room with the seat folded down. They also come with a retractable rear luggage cover, a luggage net, and a three-point center seatbelt. Tether anchors for a child seat are standard as well.

Audi buyers can also personalize their cars by choosing from three different interior themes: Ambition, Ambiente and Advance. The three environments, as Audi calls them, differ by the texture and appearance of the seat upholstery and the color and type of genuine wood or aluminum trim. Main options offered by Audi include a Bose premium sound system, a six-disc CD changer, a navigation system, and sport seats.

With prices starting in the mid-20s, consumers can get a status car that's comfortable and costs less than it does to send your kid to college. Pricing can escalate when heavily equipped, but the A4 is still one of the best entry-luxury sedans on the market.

Standard Equipment

1.8T SEDAN (5M): 1.8L I4 DOHC SMPI 20-valve intercooled turbo, (requires premium unleaded fuel); 5-speed OD manual transmission; engine oil cooler; 90-amp alternator; front-wheel drive, traction control, 3.7 axle ratio; stainless steel exhaust; front independent suspension with anti-roll bar, front coil springs, gas-pressurized front shocks, rear non-independent torsion suspension with anti-roll bar, rear coil springs, gas-pressurized rear shocks; rack-and-pinion power steering

A4

with engine-speed-sensing assist; 4-wheel antilock disc brakes; 15.9 gal. capacity fuel tank; side impact bars; front and rear body-colored bumpers; body-colored bodyside molding; clearcoat monotone paint; projector beam halogen headlamps, headlamp washer; front fog/driving lights; driver's and passenger's power remote body-colored heated folding outside mirrors; 15" x 7" silver alloy wheels; P205/60HR15 BSW A/S tires; full-size alloy spare wheel; air conditioning with climate control, air filter, rear heat ducts; AM/FM stereo, seek-scan, cassette, single-disc CD player, 8 speakers, theft deterrent, and window grid antenna; cruise control; power door locks with 2-stage unlock, remote keyless entry, child-safety rear door locks; cell phone pre-wiring, power accessory outlet, front lighter element, driver's foot rest, smokers' package, first aid kit; instrumentation display includes tachometer, water temperature gauge, volt gauge, in-dash clock, exterior temp, systems monitor, trip computer, trip odometer; warning indicators include oil pressure, battery, low oil level, lights on, key in ignition, low fuel, low washer fluid, door ajar, trunk ajar, service interval; driver's and front passenger's front and seat-mounted side airbags, overhead airbag; security system includes ignition disable and panic alarm; tinted windows, power front and rear windows with 1-touch down function; variable-speed intermittent front windshield wipers with heated washer jets, sun visor strip, rear window defroster; seating capacity of 5, front bucket seats with adjustable tilt headrests, center armrest with storage, driver's and passenger's front seats include 6-way adjustment; 60/40 folding rear bench seat with tilt headrests, rear center armrest with storage; height-adjustable front seatbelts, front and rear seatbelt pretensioners; cloth seats, cloth door trim insert, full cloth headliner, full carpet floor covering with carpeted floor mats, aluminum dashboard insert, leather-wrapped gear shift knob, aluminum door panel insert, chrome interior accents; interior lights include dome light with fade, front and rear reading lights, door curb lights, illuminated entry; leather-wrapped sport steering wheel with tilt and telescopic adjustment; dual illuminated vanity mirrors, driver's side auxiliary visor; day/night rearview mirror; full floor console, locking glove box with light, front cupholder, 2 seatback storage pockets, driver's and passenger's door bins; carpeted cargo floor, cargo net, cargo tie downs, cargo light; chrome grille, black front windshield molding, black side and rear window moldings and body-colored door handles.

1.8T QUATTRO SEDAN (5M) (in addition to or instead of 1.8T SEDAN (5M) equipment): Full-time 4-wheel drive, 3.89 axle ratio; rear independent double-wishbone suspension with anti-roll bar; and a 16.4 gal. capacity fuel tank.

2.8 SEDAN (5M) (in addition to or instead of 1.8T QUATTRO SEDAN (5M) equipment): 2.8L V6 DOHC SMPI 30-valve engine with variable valve timing; electronic OD automatic transmission with lock-up torque converter; 120-amp alternator; front-wheel drive, 3.29 axle ratio; rear non-independent torsion suspension with anti-roll bar, 16" x 7" silver alloy wheels; P205/55HR16 BSW A/S tires; seating capacity of 5, driver's and front passenger's seats include 8-way adjustment, 2-way power lumbar support; genuine wood dashboard insert, genuine wood door panel insert, genuine wood console insert, chrome interior accents and chrome side window moldings.

2.8 QUATTRO SEDAN (5M) (in addition to or instead of 2.8 SEDAN (5A) equipment): 5-speed OD manual transmission; Full-time 4-wheel drive, 3.89 axle ratio; rear independent double-wishbone suspension with anti-roll bar; leather-wrapped sport steering wheel with tilt and telescopic adjustment.

AVANT QUATTRO WAGON (5M) (in addition to or instead of QUATTRO SEDAN (5M) equipment): roof rack; integrated roof antenna; fixed 1/4 vent windows; fixed interval rear wiper; center pass-thru armrest with skibag and a cargo cover.

Base Prices

CODE	DESCRIPTION	INVOICE	MSRP
8D25M4	1.8T Sedan (5M)	21840	24540
8D25M5	1.8T Quattro Sedan (5M)	23590	26290
8D25UK	2.8 Sedan (5A)	27048	30340

AUDI

A4

CODE	DESCRIPTION	INVOICE	MSRP
8D25U5	2.8 Quattro Sedan (5M)	27726	30990
8D55M5	1.8T Avant Quattro Wagon (5M)	24470	27290
8D55U5	2.8 Avant Quattro Wagon (5M)	28606	31990
	Destination Charge:	550	550

Interested in seeing what dealers will sell this vehicle for? Check out our True Market Value^{sm} (TMV^{sm}) pricing on our Web site at www.edmunds.com.

Accessories

		INVOICE	MSRP
—	Jacquard Satin Upholstery	NC	NC
	NOT AVAILABLE with Leatherette or Leather upholstery.		
—	Leather Seat Upholstery (1.8T Quattro Sedan/2.8)	1162	1320
	NOT AVAILABLE with Leatherette or Cloth upholstery.		
—	Perforated Leatherette Upholstery	NC	NC
	NOT AVAILABLE with Leather, Cloth upholstery, or Sport Front Seats.		
—	Transmission: 5-Speed Automatic with Tiptronic	1072	1100
1AT	Electronic Stabilization Program (ESP)	484	550
3X3X	Paint: Melange Metallic	396	450
4Z4Z	Paint: Ebony PL Effect	396	450
5B5B	Paint: Light Silver Metallic	396	450
5H5H	Paint: India Red	396	450
5J5J	Paint: Santorin Blue PL Effect	396	450
7A2	6-Disc CD Changer	484	550
7H7H	Paint: Hibiscus Red PL Effect	396	450
E7E7	Paint: Cactus Green PL Effect	396	450
F2F2	Paint: Brilliant Yellow	396	450
PAW	Cold Weather Package (1.8T Quattro/2.8 Avant)	396	450
	Includes heated front seats and heated driver's door lock.		
PAW	Cold Weather Package (Sedan)	528	600
	Includes ski sack, heated front seats and heated driver's door lock.		
PBS	Bose Premium Sound System	572	650
	Features 150-watt power amplifier and 8 speakers.		
PCX	Premium Package	1056	1200
	Includes power tilt and slide glass sunroof, auto-dimming inside rearview mirror, auto-dimming outside rearview mirrors and Homelink remote transmitter.		
PMT	Integrated Hands-Free Mobile Phone	431	495
PNL	Audi Navigation System (1.8T Quattro Sedan/2.8)	968	1280
	Includes one map CD. Note: Dealer will be invoiced an additional $170.00 for the map CD when it is received.		
PSQ	Sport Package (1.8T)	660	750
	Includes sport suspension, 16" 10-spoke sport wheels and 205/55R16 high performance tires.		
PSQ	Sport Package (1.8T Quattro Sedan/2.8)	440	500
	Includes sport suspension, 16" 10-spoke sport wheels and 205/55R16 high performance tires.		
PX3	Xenon High Intensity Headlights	440	500

A4 / A6 — AUDI

CODE	DESCRIPTION	INVOICE	MSRP
Q1D	Sport Front Seats	440	500
	NOT AVAILABLE with Leatherette upholstery.		
Y4Y4	Paint: Pelican Blue Metallic	396	450

2001 A6

What's New?

All 2001 Audis receive a new 4-year/50,000-mile limited warranty and no-charge scheduled maintenance, a 12-year limited warranty against corrosion perforation, and 24-hour Roadside Assistance for four years. All A6s are now equipped with the high-tech Immobilizer III security system, side-curtain airbags, a 12-millimeter increase in the headrest height adjustment and an optional multifunction steering wheel.

Review

Four flavors of the A6 are available for 2001. The standard 2.8-liter V6, found in the base sedan and the Avant, brews up 200 horsepower and is mated to a standard Tiptronic automatic or an optional five-speed manual transmission. Audi's quattro all-wheel-drive system is optional on the 2.8 and standard on all of the remaining models. This system constantly monitors the grip at all four tires. When one of them starts to lose traction, the quattro system automatically applies power to the tires with the most adhesion to the road surface. Audi's Electronic Stability Program (ESP), standard on the sedans and optional on the 2.8 Avant, applies brakes to the misbehaving wheel and gently points you back on your course.

The A6 2.7T Sedan has a twin-turbo 2.7-liter V6 that produces 250 horsepower and 258 foot-pounds of torque. Audi has used two small turbos rather than one large one to make the engine more responsive. In a nice tip of the hat to enthusiasts, the 2.7T comes with a six-speed manual transmission as standard equipment. A five-speed Tiptronic-controlled automatic transmission is a no-cost option.

The Audi A6 4.2 Sedan features the V8 normally found in the larger A8 Sedan. Obviously this is Audi's challenge to the V8-powered BMW 540i and Mercedes-Benz E430. The 4.2-liter engine produces 300 horsepower and 295 foot-pounds of torque, channeled through a five-speed Tiptronic-controlled automatic transmission. Beyond the engine, the 4.2 also comes with more aggressive styling, bigger wheels and tires, and more standard equipment.

All A6 models feature an interior that is one of the best in its class. Audi greets drivers with a generous amount of supple materials and features. As a bonus, A6 buyers can choose from three different types of interiors. The atmospheres — Ambition, Ambiente and Advance — differ in their use of texture and appearance of the seat upholstery, and the color and type of genuine wood and aluminum trim.

The A6's styling is unmistakably Audi, with a swept greenhouse and muscular fenders. However, the A6 isn't a stunner like the A4. The rounded sheetmetal and sharply creased trim detail don't blend well to our eye, and the taillights on the sedan appear to have been lifted from Chevrolet's lowly S-10 pickup. From some angles, the car looks great. From others, it appears somewhat dumpy and jumbled. Front overhang can appear especially out of balance. Fortunately, the gracefully swept greenhouse on both the sedan and wagon lends a touch of class and elegance to an otherwise characterless profile.

AUDI A6

Despite nitpicks, we believe the A6 is an enticing choice in the hotly contested luxury sedan class. If you're looking for a wagon, the A6 Avant should serve nicely, though it could use a boost in horsepower. Our personal favorite is the A6 2.7T. This version offers better acceleration than the 2.8 and nearly equals the 4.2. It also doesn't cost much more than the 2.8, and certainly costs less than the 4.2.

Standard Equipment

2.8 SEDAN (5A): 2.8L V6 DOHC SMPI 30-valve engine with variable valve timing (requires premium unleaded fuel); 5-speed electronic OD automatic transmission with lock-up torque converter; engine oil cooler; 120 amp alternator; automanual transmission oil cooler; front-wheel drive, traction control, 3.09 axle ratio; dual stainless steel exhaust; front independent suspension with anti-roll bar, front coil springs, gas-pressurized front shocks, rear semi-independent torsion suspension with anti-roll bar, rear coil springs, gas-pressurized rear shocks; rack-and-pinion power steering with vehicle-speed-sensing assist; 4-wheel antilock disc brakes; 18.5 gal. capacity fuel tank; side impact bars; front and rear body-colored bumpers; body-colored bodyside molding rocker panel extensions; metallic monotone paint; projector beam halogen headlamps with washer; additional exterior lights include front fog/driving lights; driver's and passenger's power remote body-colored heated folding outside mirrors; 16" x 7" silver alloy wheels; P205/55HR16 BSW A/S tires; full-size alloy spare wheel; dual-zone front air conditioning with climate control, air filter, rear heat ducts; AM/FM stereo, seek-scan feature, cassette player, single-disc CD player, 8 speakers, amplifier, theft deterrent, window grid antenna; cruise control; power heated door locks with 2-stage unlock, remote keyless entry, child-safety rear door locks, power remote trunk release, power remote fuel door release; cell phone pre-wiring, 2 power accessory outlets, front and rear lighter elements, driver's foot rest, retained accessory power, smokers' package, first aid kit; instrumentation display includes tachometer, water temperature gauge, volt gauge, in-dash clock, exterior temp, systems monitor, trip computer, trip odometer; warning indicators include oil pressure, battery, low oil level, lights on, key in ignition, low fuel, low washer fluid, bulb failure, door ajar, trunk ajar, service interval; driver's and passenger's front airbags, driver's and front passenger's seat-mounted side airbags, overhead airbag; ignition disable, panic alarm, security system; tinted windows, power front and rear windows with front and rear 1-touch down function; variable-speed intermittent front windshield wipers with heated washer fluid jets, sun visor strip, rear window defroster; seating capacity of 5, front bucket seats with adjustable headrests, center armrest with storage, driver's seat includes 8-way power adjustment, power 4-way lumbar support, passenger's seat includes 8-way power adjustment, power 4-way lumbar support; rear bench seat with tilt headrests, center armrest, with storage; height-adjustable front seatbelts with front and rear pretensioners; cloth seats, cloth door trim insert, full cloth headliner, full carpet floor covering with carpeted floor mats, genuine wood dashboard insert, leather-wrapped gearshift knob, genuine wood door panel insert, genuine wood console insert, chrome interior accents; interior lights include dome light with fade, front and rear reading lights, 4 door curb lights, illuminated entry; leather-wrapped steering wheel with tilt and telescopic adjustment; dual illuminated vanity mirrors, driver's side auxiliary visor; day/night rearview mirror; full floor console, locking glove box with light, front and rear cupholders, 2 seatback storage pockets, driver's and passenger's door bins, rear door bins; carpeted cargo floor, cargo net, cargo tie downs, cargo light, concealed cargo storage; chrome grille, chrome side window moldings, black front windshield molding and body-colored door handles.

2.7T QUATTRO SEDAN (6M) (in addition to or instead of BASE SEDAN (5A) equipment): 2.7L V6 DOHC SMPI 30-valve twin turbo engine with variable valve timing (requires premium unleaded fuel); 6-speed OD manual transmission; full-time limited-slip differential, 4.11 axle ratio; electronic stability, front independent suspension with anti-roll bar, front coil springs, gas-pressurized front shocks, rear independent double-wishbone suspension with anti-roll bar, rear coil springs, gas-pressurized rear shocks and P215/55HR16 BSW A/S tires.

4.2 QUATTRO SEDAN (5A) (in addition to or instead of 2.7T QUATTRO SEDAN (6M) equipment): 4.2L V8 DOHC SMPI 40-valve engine with variable valve timing (requires premium unleaded

A6 — AUDI

fuel); 5-speed electronic OD automatic transmission with lock-up torque converter; auto-manual transmission,150 amp alternator, oil cooler; full-time limited-slip differential, 2.73 axle ratio; body colored driver's and passenger's power remote auto-dimming heated folding outside mirrors; auto-dimming rear view mirror;21.7 gal. capacity fuel tank; front express open/close sliding and tilting glass sunroof with sunshade; 16" x 8" silver alloy wheels; P235/50HR16 BSW A/S tires; 8 premium speakers, premium amplifier, radio steering wheel controls; garage door opener; 60/40 folding rear bench seat with tilt headrests, center pass-thru armrest with skibag, with storage; leather seats, leather door trim insert and memory on driver's/passenger's seats with 3 memory setting(s) including settings for exterior mirrors.

AVANT WAGON (5A) (in addition to or instead of BASE SEDAN (5A) equipment): Full-time 4-wheel drive, limited-slip differential, 3.41 axle ratio; roof rack; compact steel spare wheel; AM/FM stereo, seek-scan feature, cassette player, single-disc CD player, 8 speakers, amplifier, automatic equalizer, theft deterrent, and integrated roof antenna; 3 power accessory outlets, rear window wiper; rear blind; center pass-thru armrest with skibag and storage; interior concealed storage, cargo cover and concealed cargo storage.

Base Prices

CODE	DESCRIPTION	INVOICE	MSRP
4B25VK	Base Sedan (5A)	30621	34400
4B257Z	2.7T Quattro Sedan (6M)	35319	39500
4B451Z	4.2 Quattro Sedan (5A)	44031	49400
4B55VZ	Avant Wagon (5A)	33427	37350
Destination Charge:		550	550

Interested in seeing what dealers will sell this vehicle for? Check out our True Market Value^{sm} (TMV^{sm}) pricing on our Web site at www.edmunds.com.

Accessories

CODE	DESCRIPTION	INVOICE	MSRP
—	Transmission: 5-Speed Automatic with Tiptronic (2.7T)	NC	NC
1AT	Electronic Stability Program (ESP) (Avant/Base)	484	550
3Y5	Power Rear and Manual Side Shades (2.7T)	396	450
4X4	Rear Side Airbags	308	350
7A2	6-Disc CD Changer	484	550
	Trunk mounted. NOT AVAILABLE with 6DISC.		
C4H	Wheels: 17" Polished Cast Alloy (4.2)	660	750
	Includes 255/40 performance tires. NOT AVAILABLE with PPS.		
CLOTH	Jacquard Satin Cloth Upholstery (Avant/Base/2.7T)	NC	NC
	NOT AVAILABLE with LTHR or LEATHE.		
LEATHE	Leatherette Seat Upholstery (Avant/Base/2.7T)	NC	NC
	NOT AVAILABLE with CLOTH, LTHR, or PSK.		
LEATHE	Perforated Leatherette Upholstery (Avant)	NC	NC
	NOT AVAILABLE with CLOTH or LTHR.		
LTHR	Leather Seat Upholstery (Avant/Base)	1364	1550
	NOT AVAILABLE with LEATHE or CLOTH.		
PAW	Cold Weather Package (Avant)	418	475
	Includes heated front and rear seats.		
PAW	Cold Weather Package (Base/2.7T)	550	625
	Includes ski sack, heated front and rear seats.		
PBS	Bose Premium Sound System (Avant/Base/2.7T)	660	750

AUDI

A6

CODE	DESCRIPTION	INVOICE	MSRP
PFX	Premium Package (2.7T)	704	800

Includes Xenon high intensity headlights, auto-dimming inside rearview mirror, auto-dimming outside rearview mirrors, multi-function steering wheel, audio controls and telephone controls. REQUIRES PPL. NOT AVAILABLE with PPX.

PHS	Sunroof Package (Avant/Base)	1056	1200

Includes power glass sunroof and Homelink remote transmitter.

PKS	Rear-Facing Children's Bench Seat (Avant)	660	750

Removable.

PMT	Integrated Hands-Free Mobile Phone	431	495
PPL	Celebration Luxury Package (Avant/Base)	1738	1975

Includes leather seat upholstery, sunroof package, power glass sunroof, and Homelink remote transmitter. NOT AVAILABLE with CLOTH, LEATH, PPX, PPY, 7A2, or PMT.

PPL	Preferred Luxury Package (2.7T)	2574	2925

Includes power glass sunroof, outside mirrors and driver's seat memory, leather seat upholstery and Homelink remote transmitter. NOT AVAILABLE with PPX, CLOTH, LEATH.

PPS	Sport Package (4.2)	1540	1750

Includes sport suspension, front sport seats, 17" 5-spoke forged alloy wheels and 255/40 performance tires. NOT AVAILABLE with C4H.

PPX	Premium Package (2.7T)	704	800

Includes Xenon high intensity headlights, auto-dimming inside rearview mirror, auto-dimming outside rearview mirrors, multi-function steering wheel, audio controls and telephone controls. NOT AVAILABLE with PFX.

PPX	Premium Package (4.2)	1298	1475

Includes heated front and rear seats, heated steering wheel, Xenon high intensity headlights, power rear and manual side shades.

PPX	Premium Package (Avant/Base)	902	1025

Includes outside mirrors and memory driver's seat, auto-dimming inside rearview mirror, auto-dimming outside rearview mirrors, Xenon high intensity headlights, multi-function steering wheel, audio controls and telephone controls.

PPY	Guidance Package	1276	1630

Includes Audi navigation system and rear acoustic parking system.

PQP	Wheels: 17" Cross-Spoke Cast Alloy	660	750

Includes 17" performance tires. NOT AVAILABLE with PSK.

PSK	Sport Package (2.7T)	880	1000

Includes sport suspension, front sport seats, 16" twin-spoke alloy wheels and 215/55 performance tires. NOT AVAILABLE with LEATH.

PST	Sport Package with 17" Wheels	1320	1500

Includes sport suspension, front sport seats, 17" cast alloy wheels and performance tires. NOT AVAILABLE with LEATHE, PSK.

QTRO	Quattro IV All-Wheel-Drive System (Base)	1750	1750

Includes front and rear electronic differential locks.

2001 ALLROAD QUATTRO

What's New?

Based on the A6 platform, the height-adjustable allroad debuts this year to fill a slot left in Audi's lineup by the lack of an SUV. This luxury station wagon turned SUV is powered by the A6's 250-horsepower, 2.7-liter V6 engine and features Audi's legendary quattro all-wheel-drive system. Audi blends these features in a distinctive vehicle that can handle a wide range of transportation needs.

Review

A luxury wagon that stands tall when it has to.

That's one way to describe the height-adjustable allroad quattro from Audi. It has a gracefully appointed interior, plenty of guts under the hood and an all-wheel-drive system for occasional off-road adventures. And when you take into consideration the commodious rear cargo area and a variety of convenience packages, you can make this car whatever you want it to be.

The allroad's 250-horsepower, 2.7-liter V6 engine is a proven winner in Audi's A6 2.7T. The engine has five valves per cylinder and uses a twin-turbocharger to generate 258 ft-lbs. of torque over a broad rpm band. The powerplant is mated to a six-speed manual transmission or an optional five-speed Tiptronic automatic, which allows the driver to either leave it in automatic mode or change gears manually. Power is distributed to all wheels using traction-seeking sensors that detect slippage and automatically adjust to give sure-footed handling.

What really distinguishes the allroad (besides the fact that Audi refuses to use a capital letter for its name) is the four-position variable-height pneumatic suspension varying ground clearance up to 2.6 inches. This feature also provides load-leveling capabilities due to the number of passengers or cargo weight. A switch on the dash manually sets the road clearance or you can choose automatic and the height is adjusted according to the demands of the driving situation. For example, the car parks itself in the second-highest setting for slide-in seating. At speeds over 50 mph the car lowers an inch; at 75 mph it lowers another inch. Off-roading can be done with an impressive ground clearance of 8.2 inches. This means the allroad is aerodynamic at high speeds and can still journey over rutted roads without fear of being disemboweled like many wallowy station wagons.

Safety features in the allroad include ABS and a variety of airbags. Besides front airbags, Audi has included drop-down curtain airbags called Sideguard. These airbags protect the head and neck area of passengers, particularly from striking the roof pillars. Additionally, the Sideguard airbags stay inflated for five seconds to offer protection against secondary impact and rollover. Furthermore, if any airbag is deployed, the fuel system is cut off, the doors unlock and the interior lights illuminate. When the rear-facing third-row bench seat is installed, it has its own three-point safety belt and head restraints.

The Audi allroad is offered with a choice of packages. The premium package provides memory positions for the front seats, electronically folding exterior mirrors and auto-dimming rearview and outside mirrors. The convenience package includes heated front and rear seats, a HomeLink transmitter and heated multifunction steering wheel. A warm weather package uses a solar sunroof to power interior cooling fans in hot weather and sunshades to screen the rear windows. The guidance package includes a GPS navigation system and a back-up warning system.

With the allroad, Audi has filled a void left by its lack of an SUV. And it has created a versatile, luxurious car in the process.

AUDI

ALLROAD QUATTRO

CODE	DESCRIPTION	INVOICE	MSRP

Standard Equipment

2.7 (6M): 2.7L V6 DOHC SMPI 30-valve, twin-turbo engine with variable valve timing (requires premium unleaded fuel); 6-speed OD manual transmission; engine oil cooler; 150 amp alternator; full-time limited-slip differential, 4.38 axle ratio; dual stainless steel exhaust with tailpipe finisher; auto ride control, auto-leveling suspension, front independent suspension with anti-roll bar, front air springs, gas-pressurized front shocks, rear independent double-wishbone suspension with anti-roll bar, rear air springs, gas-pressurized rear shocks; rack-and-pinion power steering with vehicle-speed-sensing assist; 4-wheel antilock disc brakes; 18.5 gal. capacity fuel tank; side impact bars; roof rack; front and rear colored bumpers; colored bodyside molding and colored fender flares; metallic monotone paint; projector beam halogen headlamps with washer; additional exterior lights include front fog/driving lights; driver's and passenger's power remote body-colored heated folding outside mirrors; 17" x 7.5" silver alloy wheels; P225/55HR17 BSW AT tires; full-size steel spare wheel; dual-zone front air conditioning with climate control, air filter, rear heat ducts; AM/FM stereo radio, seek-scan feature, cassette player, single-disc CD player, 8 speakers, amplifier, theft deterrent, integrated roof antenna; cruise control; power door locks with 2-stage unlock, remote keyless entry, child-safety rear door locks, power remote hatch release, power remote fuel door release; cell phone pre-wiring, 3 power accessory outlets, front/rear lighter elements, driver's foot rest, retained accessory power, smokers' package, first aid kit; instrumentation display includes tachometer, water temperature gauge, volt gauge, in-dash clock, exterior temp, systems monitor, trip computer, trip odometer; warning indicators include oil pressure, battery, low oil level, lights on, key in ignition, low fuel, low washer fluid, bulb failure, door ajar, trunk ajar, service interval; driver's and passenger's front airbags, driver's and front passenger's seat-mounted side airbags, overhead airbag; ignition disable, panic alarm, security system; tinted windows, power front and rear windows with front and rear 1-touch down function; variable-speed intermittent front windshield wipers with heated washer fluid jets, sun visor strip, rear window wiper, rear window defroster, rear blind; seating capacity of 5, front sports seats with adjustable headrests, center armrest with storage, driver's and passenger's seat includes 8-way power adjustment, power 4-way lumbar support; rear bench seat with tilt headrests, center pass-thru armrest with storage and skibag; height-adjustable front seatbelts with pretensioners; leather seats, leatherette door trim insert, full cloth headliner, full carpet floor covering with carpeted floor mats, genuine wood dashboard insert, wood gearshift knob, genuine wood door panel insert, genuine wood console insert, chrome interior accents; interior lights include dome light with fade, front and rear reading lights, door curb lights, illuminated entry; leather-wrapped steering wheel with tilt and telescopic adjustment; dual illuminated vanity mirrors, driver's side auxiliary visor; day/night rearview mirror; full floor console, locking glove box with light, front and rear cupholders, interior concealed storage, 2 seatback storage pockets, driver's and passenger's door bins, rear door bins; carpeted cargo floor, carpeted cargo mats, cargo cover, cargo net, cargo tie downs, cargo light, concealed cargo storage; chrome grille, chrome side window moldings, black front windshield molding, black rear window molding and body-colored door handles.

Base Prices

4BH579	allroad quattro (6M)	37327	41900
Destination Charge:		550	550

Interested in seeing what dealers will sell this vehicle for? Check out our True Market Value^{sm} (TMV^{sm}) pricing on our Web site at www.edmunds.com.

Accessories

—	Transmission: 5-Speed Automatic with Tiptronic and DSP	972	1000
	Selects from over 200 shift programs to match driver needs and hill detection capability.		

ALLROAD QUATTRO / S4 — AUDI

CODE	DESCRIPTION	INVOICE	MSRP
3FE	Power Tilt and Slide Glass Sunroof	880	1000
	Includes pre-select closing system with pinch protection. NOT AVAILABLE with PWX.		
4X4	Rear Seat-Mounted Side Airbags	308	350
7A2	6-Disc CD Changer	484	550
CF6	Wheels: 17" Dual-Spoke Alloy	836	950
	Includes twin-spoke dimensional effect.		
PBS	Bose Premium Sound System	660	750
	Includes 200-watt amplifier with subwoofer.		
PKS	Rear-Facing Removable Child Bench Seat	660	750
PMT	Integrated Motorola Hands-Free Mobile Phone	431	495
PPD	Convenience Package	704	800
	Includes heated multi-function steering wheel, heated front and rear seats and Homelink remote transmitter.		
PPM	Premium Package	792	900
	Includes Xenon high intensity discharge headlights, auto-dimming inside rearview mirror, auto-dimming outside rearview mirrors, electric folding mirrors, and driver/passenger seat and mirror memory.		
PPY	Guidance Package	1276	1630
	Includes Audi navigation system and rear parktronic acoustic parking system.		
PWX	Warm Weather Package	1540	1750
	Includes solar sunroof and rear side window sun shades. NOT AVAILABLE with 3FE.		

2001 S4

What's New?

The Electronic Stabilization Program is made standard on the S4 Sedan. The S4 Avant debuts for 2001, allowing for more cargo space and family-hauling capabilities. Casablanca White is made available as an exterior color, as are aluminum mirror housings in combination with the Pearl Nappa/Alcantara sets and aluminum trim. A new 4-year/150,000-mile warranty concept is introduced this year.

Review

Although not cheap by any means, the S4 does offer a mouth-watering array of features and improvements over the regular A4 Sedan after which it is modeled.

Starting things out is a 2.7-liter, twin-turbo V6 engine. Sporting twin intercoolers, dual-overhead cams, five valves per cylinder, variable valve timing for the intake camshaft, and optimized combustion chambers, the engine generates 250 horsepower and 258 foot-pounds of torque. Audi has designed the engine to provide much of its power low in the revband. Consequently, the S4 makes quick work of freeway on-ramps and passing maneuvers. Audi gives buyers of the S4 a choice of transmissions; there's a six-speed manual transmission or a five-speed Tiptronic automatic transmission.

All S4s come with Audi's quattro all-wheel-drive system, which constantly monitors the grip of the tires. When one of them starts to lose traction, the quattro system automatically applies

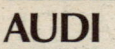

AUDI S4

power to the tires with the most adhesion. Audi says this latest edition of the quattro all-wheel-drive system is capable enough to allow the car to get underway even when only one wheel has reasonable traction.

An S4 Avant is made available for 2001, replete with the 2.7-liter, 250 horsepower, V6 Bi-turbo engine, and such niceties as a retractable luggage cover, retractable dividing cargo net and aluminum-finish roof rails. It's perfect for anyone who needs utility but refuses to give up stellar sport-sedan performance.

The suspension and braking components of the S4 are well tuned. Major items of note are performance-tuned shocks and springs, and unique 17-inch wheels with 225/45R17 tires. This year, the S4 Sedan gains the Electronic Stabilization Program as standard equipment.

The interior retains the same architecture found in the A4, which means an attractive design and an adequate number of features. Special leather upholstery covers standard power seats, and contrasting color suede inserts can be had when ordering the sport interior package. Other options to consider include a sunroof, heated front seats, a six-disc CD changer, and a Bose premium audio system. For safety, there are standard front and head-mounted airbags.

Outside, the S4 differs from regular A4s (not that the A4 is exactly regular, of course) by having the aforementioned 17-inch wheels, larger front air-intake openings, and S4 badging.

The S4 driving experience is a pleasure. The S4 is softer than a BMW M3, but its forgiving nature comes at the expense of pure handling excellence. Taken as a whole, however, we think the 2001 Audi S4 is quite the contender in the sport-sedan market.

Standard Equipment

2.7T (5A): 2.7L V6 DOHC SMPI twin turbo 30-valve engine with variable valve timing (requires premium unleaded fuel); 5-speed electronic OD automatic transmission with lock-up torque converter; engine oil cooler; 120 amp alternator; auto-manual transmission; full-time 4-wheel drive, 3.51 axle ratio; stainless steel exhaust with tailpipe finisher; sport-ride suspension, electronic stability control, front independent suspension with anti-roll bar, front coil springs, gas-pressurized front shocks, rear independent double-wishbone suspension with anti-roll bar, rear coil springs, gas-pressurized rear shocks; rack-and-pinion power steering with engine-speed-sensing assist; 4-wheel antilock disc brakes; 16.4 gal. capacity fuel tank; side impact bars; front and rear body-colored bumpers; body-colored bodyside molding rocker panel extensions; metallic monotone paint; projector beam high intensity headlamps with washer; additional exterior lights include front fog driving lights; driver's and passenger's power remote body-colored heated folding outside mirrors; 17" x 7.5" silver alloy wheels; P225/45YR17 BSW performance tires; full-size alloy spare wheel; air conditioning with climate control, air filter, rear heat ducts; AM/FM stereo radio, seek-scan feature, cassette player, single-disc CD player, 8 speakers, theft deterrent, window grid antenna; cruise control; power heated door locks with 2-stage unlock, remote keyless entry, child-safety rear door locks; cell phone pre-wiring, 1 power accessory outlet, front lighter element, driver's foot rest, retained accessory power, smokers' package, first aid kit; instrumentation display includes tachometer, water temperature gauge, volt gauge, clock, exterior temp, trip computer, trip odometer; warning indicators include oil pressure, battery, low oil level, lights on, key in ignition, low fuel, low washer fluid, door ajar, trunk ajar, service interval; driver's and passenger's front airbags, driver's and front passenger's seat-mounted side airbags, overhead airbag; ignition disable, panic alarm, security system; tinted windows, power front and rear windows with front and rear 1-touch down function; variable-speed intermittent front windshield wipers with heated washer fluid jets, sun visor strip, rear window defroster; seating capacity of 5, front sports seats with adjustable tilt headrests, center armrest with storage, driver's and passenger's seat includes 8-way power adjustment with power 2-way lumbar support; 60/40 folding rear bench seat with tilt headrests, center armrest with storage; height-adjustable front seatbelts with front and rear pretensioners; leather seats, cloth door trim insert, full cloth headliner, full carpet floor covering with carpeted floor mats, genuine wood dashboard insert, leather-wrapped gearshift knob, genuine wood door panel insert, genuine wood console insert, chrome interior accents; interior lights include dome light with fade, front and rear reading lights, door curb lights, illuminated entry; leather-wrapped sport steering wheel with tilt and telescopic adjustment; dual illuminated vanity mirrors, driver's side auxiliary visor; day/night rearview mirror; full floor console, mini overhead console locking glove

S4 / TT   AUDI

box with light, front cupholder, 2 seatback storage pockets, driver's and passenger's door bins; carpeted cargo floor, cargo net, cargo tie downs, cargo light; chrome grille, chrome side window moldings, black front windshield molding, black rear window molding and body-colored door handles.

AVANT (5A) (in addition to or instead of 2.7T (5A) equipment): roof rack; 9 speakers, cargo cover.

Base Prices

CODE	DESCRIPTION	INVOICE	MSRP
8D257Z	S4 2.7T (5A)	34791	38900
8D557Z	S4 Avant (5A)	36199	40500
	Destination Charge:	550	550

Interested in seeing what dealers will sell this vehicle for? Check out our True Market Value^{sm} (TMV^{sm}) pricing on our Web site at www.edmunds.com.

Accessories

CODE	DESCRIPTION	INVOICE	MSRP
—	Transmission: 6-Speed Manual	NC	NC
	Includes 4.111 axle ratio.		
7A2	6-Disc CD Changer	484	550
PAW	Cold Weather Package	528	600
	Includes heated front seats and ski sack.		
PAW	Heated Front Seats	396	450
	Includes individual temperature control.		
PBS	Bose Premium Sound System	572	650
PCX	Premium Package	1056	1200
	Includes power tilt and slide glass sunroof, auto-dimming inside rearview mirror, auto-dimming outside mirrors and Homelink remote transmitter.		
PMT	Integrated Hands-Free Mobile Phone	431	495
PNL	Audi Navigation System	968	1280
	Includes 1 map CD. Dealer will be invoiced an additional $170 for the map CD when it is received.		
WMM	Enhanced Sport Package	352	400
	Includes pearl or silk nappa leather seats with alcantara inserts, silver aluminum belt line trim and silver aluminum outside rear view mirrors.		

2001 TT

What's New?

For 2001 Audi introduces the TT Roadster, which retains the same interior and chassis as the coupe. Makes sense, as the coupe was designed with the roadster version in mind. There's also a 225-horsepower quattro version for both the coupe and convertible.

Review

The Audi TT concept car was introduced in 1995, and we hated it. Subsequently, we've had numerous visual encounters and chances to get behind the wheel. You could say we've developed an acquired taste.

AUDI   TT

| CODE | DESCRIPTION | INVOICE | MSRP |

In person, the car just looks right, appearing aggressive and graceful at the same time. The rear boasts rounded flanks and a cleanly arced roofline. Purposeful styling details are executed with ice-cold precision; it is an instant classic - a shape that will be a topic of discussion for years. The ride ain't too shabby, either.

Audi's entry-level TT comes with a front-engine, front-drive powertrain layout. Its turbocharged, 1.8-liter, four-cylinder engine makes 180 horsepower and is connected to a five-speed manual transmission, achieving zero to 60 in 7.4 seconds. Also available is a massaged 225-horsepower engine that shaves nearly a second off of that time. With standard all-wheel drive, it can reach a top speed of 143 mph. The torque is increased as well, from 173 to 207 foot-pounds, but we still feel that both are lacking in low-range take off. Once you overcome that, though, hang on to your toupees!

The TT Coupe has a sparse interior and a nearly useless rear seat. Inside, Audi has created a visual and tactile feast of aluminum, leather and stainless steel. The effect is successful, appearing to be expensively outfitted, but not luxurious in the traditional sense. And, thanks to the hatchback design for the coupe, the TT offers owners some utility, carrying 13.8 cubic feet of cargo with the rear seat up and 24.2 cubic feet if the rear seat is folded down. The numbers go down for the quattro and convertible versions; but hey, this isn't a minivan.

Standard equipment includes leather sport seats, cruise control, a tachometer, alloy wheels, a split-folding rear seat, and an AM/FM stereo with cassette and speed-sensitive volume control. A CD player is optional. Power seats, a sunroof and a full-size spare tire are not available on this car. The front-wheel drive convertible comes with a manually operated top, while the Quattro comes with a power top, both with glass rear window with defrost.

To keep passengers safe, Audi installed ABS, traction control and a first-aid kit in the TT. Head and thorax side airbags are also standard. Pre-tensioners and force limiters make seatbelts even more effective than conventional systems and next-generation front airbags deploy at lower speeds. Audi contends that through marvelous feats of engineering and dual roll-bar hoops, the protection level for the convertible in a rollover is equal to that of the coupe.

The TT's styling will make it popular with people who like to impress. Whether in coupe or roadster form, the car makes a bold statement you won't soon forget.

Standard Equipment

180 HP FWD COUPE (5M): 1.8L I4 DOHC SMPI 20-valve intercooled turbo engine (requires premium unleaded fuel); 5-speed OD manual transmission; engine oil cooler; 120 amp alternator; front-wheel drive, traction control, 3.94 axle ratio; stainless steel exhaust with tailpipe finisher; electronic stability control, front independent strut suspension with anti-roll bar, front coil springs, gas-pressurized front shocks, rear semi-independent torsion suspension with anti-roll bar, rear coil springs, gas-pressurized rear shocks; rack-and-pinion power steering; 4-wheel antilock disc brakes; 14.5 gal. capacity fuel tank; side impact bars; front and rear body-colored bumpers, rear lip spoiler; clearcoat monotone paint; projector beam halogen headlamps with washer; additional exterior lights include front fog/driving lights; driver's and passenger's power remote body-colored heated folding outside mirrors; 16" x 7" silver alloy wheels; P205/55WR16 BSW performance tires; compact steel spare wheel; air conditioning with climate control, air filter, rear heat ducts; AM/FM stereo radio, seek-scan feature, cassette player, CD changer pre-wiring, in-dash CD pre-wiring, 6 speakers, and window grid diversity antenna; cruise control; central-locking power door locks with 2-stage unlock, remote keyless entry, power remote trunk release, power remote fuel door release; cell phone pre-wiring, 1 power accessory outlet, front lighter element, driver's foot rest, retained accessory power, smokers' package, first aid kit; instrumentation display includes tachometer, water temperature gauge, in-dash clock, exterior temp, systems monitor, trip computer, trip odometer; warning indicators include oil pressure, water temp,

AUDI TT

battery, low coolant, lights on, key in ignition, low fuel, low washer fluid, bulb failure, door ajar, trunk ajar, service interval; driver's front airbag, passenger's cancelable front airbag, driver's and front passenger's seat-mounted side airbags; ignition disable, panic alarm, security system; tinted windows, power windows with driver's and passenger's 1-touch down function; variable-speed intermittent front windshield wipers with heated washer fluid jets, sun visor strip, driver's and passenger's illuminated vanity mirrors, rear window defroster; seating capacity of 4, front sports seats with adjustable tilt headrests, driver's and front passenger's seats include 6-way adjustment; seatbelts with pretensioners; leather seats, leather door trim insert, full cloth headliner, full carpet floor covering with floor mats, aluminum wood trim on instrument panel, aluminum console insert, leather/aluminum gearshift knob; interior lights include dome light with fade, front reading lights, illuminated entry; leather-wrapped sport steering wheel with tilt and telescopic adjustment; dual illuminated vanity mirrors, driver's side auxiliary visor; day/night rearview mirror; full floor console, locking glove box with light, front cupholder, locking interior concealed storage, driver's and passenger's door bins; carpeted cargo floor, cargo cover, cargo light; black grille, black side window moldings and body-colored door handles.

180 HP QUATTRO COUPE (5M) (in addition to or instead 180 HP FWD COUPE (5M) equipment): Full-time 4-wheel drive; 3.32 axle ratio; rear independent multi-link suspension with anti-roll bar, rear coil springs, gas-pressurized rear shocks and 16.3 gal. capacity fuel tank.

180 HP FWD ROADSTER (5M) (in addition to or instead of 180 HP FWD COUPE (5M) equipment): Rear lip spoiler; manual convertible roof with lining, glass rear window, roll-over protection; fixed antenna; seating capacity of 2, front sports seats with fixed headrests and plastic seatback.

225 HP (6M) (in addition to or instead of 180 HP (5M) equipment): 6-speed OD manual transmission; dual stainless steel exhaust with tailpipe finisher; power convertible roof with lining (Roadster); 17" x 7.5" silver alloy wheels and P225/45YR17 BSW performance tires.

Base Prices

CODE	DESCRIPTION	INVOICE	MSRP
8N3E54	180 HP FWD Coupe (5M)	27701	31200
8N9554	180 HP w/o ESP FWD Roadster (5M)	29153	32850
8N3E5N	180 HP Quattro Coupe (5M)	29451	32950
8N9E54	180 HP w/ESP FWD Roadster (5M)	29461	33200
8N3569	225 HP w/o ESP Quattro Coupe (6M)	31915	35750
8N3E69	225 HP w/ESP Quattro Coupe (6M)	32223	36100
8N9569	225 HP w/o ESP Quattro Roadster (6M)	34379	38550
8N9E69	225 HP w/ESP Quattro Roadster (6M)	34687	38900
	Destination Charge:	550	550

Interested in seeing what dealers will sell this vehicle for? Check out our True Market Value[sm] (TMV[sm]) pricing on our Web site at www.edmunds.com.

Accessories

CODE	DESCRIPTION	INVOICE	MSRP
—	Heated Seats (w/o ESP)	396	450
	Includes individual temperature control.		
—	Wheels: 17" 5-Spoke Forged Alloy (225 HP w/o ESP)	440	500
—	Xenon Headlamps (w/o ESP)	440	500
	Includes high intensity discharge with automatic self-leveling.		
0LM	California Emission Requirements	NC	NC
3FN	Power Folding Top (180 HP Roadster)	704	800

AUDI   *TT*

CODE	DESCRIPTION	INVOICE	MSRP
PAS	Audio Package	1056	1200
	Includes Bose premium sound system and 6-disc CD changer.		
PLG	Baseball Optic Leather (Roadster)	880	1000
	NOT AVAILABLE with PLH.		
PLH	Nubbed TT Cloth Seat Insert	NC	NC
	Includes leather bolsters. NOT AVAILABLE with PLG.		
PMT	Integrated Hands-Free Mobile Phone	431	495
PNK	Audi Navigation System	968	1280
PPF	Performance Package (180 HP FWD w/o ESP Roadster)	880	1000
	Includes Xenon headlamps, 17" 6-spoke cast alloy wheels and P225/45YR17 performance tires. NOT AVAILABLE with PPX.		
PPX	Premium Package	1276	1450
	Includes heated seats, Xenon headlamps, 17" 6-spoke forged alloy wheels and P225/45YR17 performance tires. NOT AVAILABLE with PPF.		

A two-minute quote could save you big bucks!

eCoverage's online quote-to-claim insurance services deliver all the benefits savvy Internet buyers like you have come to expect. And eCoverage is backed by some of the world's biggest financial institutions.

VISIT edmunds.com/insurance

3 SERIES — BMW

2001 3 SERIES

What's New?

A boost in engine displacement and technology, plus an available all-wheel-drive system keeps BMW's venerable 3 Series at the top of its game in the competitive entry-level luxury market. Larger wheels and brakes are part of the engine upgrade. Two-stage front airbags, reduced steering effort, a Cold Weather package and Dynamic Brake Control round out the major changes for 2001.

Review

In typical BMW fashion, the 3 Series lineup is being introduced in stages. The first models to change were the sedans, followed by the coupes, the convertible, and the wagon. This allows BMW to maintain customer interest in their best-selling platform over the course of several years.

Sedan buyers can choose from an upgraded 2.5-liter inline six (models with this powerplant will now use the numerical designation of 325) that now makes 184 horsepower, or a new-for-2001 3.0-liter inline six (330 models). The latter engine, which debuted in the X5 3.0i, replaces the 2.8-liter engine across BMW's entire product line. Bumping horsepower and torque from the former engine's 193 and 206, respectively, to 225 and 214 in the 3.0-liter adds some noticeable punch to the 3 Series and helps keep it ahead of rivals like the Audi A4 and new Lexus IS 300.

Riding on the same platform, the 3 Series sedans, coupes and convertible receive a standard five-speed manual transmission, a sport-tuned suspension, and ventilated front and rear disc brakes. Two versions of the coupe are available: the 325Ci, with the aforementioned 2.5-liter inline six, and the 330Ci with the more powerful 3.0-liter engine, larger brakes and standard 17-inch wheels. The more powerful 330 coupe reaches 60 from zero in just 6.4 seconds and features a broad torque band. Both engines meet low-emission vehicle (LEV) standards. A five-speed Steptronic automanual transmission is available for those who don't want to shift their own gears.

Another new option for 2001 is all-wheel drive. It's been 10 years since BMW last offered all-wheel drive on the 3 Series and, not surprisingly, this one is lifted straight from the company's other all-wheel-drive vehicle, the X5. BMW will use "xi" nomenclature to denote models equipped with this system, which includes a 0.7-inch increase in ride height and is available on both 325 and 330 sedans as well as the 325 wagon.

If you opt for the 325Ci convertible, you'll have to lower the top manually unless you pop the extra cash for the power top, but 330Ci consumers get this perk standard. All convertibles come with a glass rear window and rollover protection. Wagon buyers will appreciate the touring models standard roof rack and rear window wiper, but, as with the sedan, don't expect to carry full-sized adults in the backseat for long periods of time.

Safety equipment on all 3 Series models includes All-Season Traction (AST) and Dynamic Stability Control (DSC), along with dual front airbags, door-mounted side airbags and BMW's patented Head Protection System (HPS). New for 2001 is Dynamic Brake Control, which reinforces the driver's effort during emergency braking. Rear side airbags and xenon headlights remain optional.

With the arrival of all-wheel drive and more powerful inline six cylinders, only one 3 Series model still offers superior performance; the all-new M3.

BMW

3 SERIES

| CODE | DESCRIPTION | INVOICE | MSRP |

Standard Equipment

325Ci COUPE (5M): 2.5L I6 DOHC SMPI 24-valve engine with variable valve timing (requires premium unleaded fuel); 5-speed manual transmission; 80 amp alternator; rear-wheel drive, traction control, 3.07 axle ratio; stainless steel exhaust; sport-ride suspension, electronic stability control, front independent strut suspension with anti-roll bar, front coil springs, gas-pressurized front shocks, rear independent multi-link suspension with anti-roll bar, rear coil springs, gas-pressurized rear shocks; rack-and-pinion power steering with engine-speed-sensing assist; 4-wheel antilock disc brakes; 16.6 gal. capacity fuel tank; side impact bars; front and rear body-colored bumpers; body-colored bodyside molding rocker panel extensions; clearcoat monotone paint; aero-composite halogen headlamps with daytime running lights, delay-off feature; additional exterior lights include front fog/driving lights; driver's and passenger's power remote body-colored heated folding outside mirrors; 17" x 7" silver alloy wheels; P205/50HR17 BSW A/S tires; full-size alloy spare wheel; air conditioning with climate control, air filter, rear heat ducts; AM/FM stereo radio, seek-scan feature, cassette player, CD changer pre-wiring, 10 speakers, theft deterrent, window grid diversity antenna, steering-wheel-mounted radio and cruise control controls; heated power door locks with 2-stage unlock, remote keyless entry, power remote trunk release; cell phone pre-wiring, 1 power accessory outlet, front lighter element(s), driver's foot rest, retained accessory power, smokers' package; instrumentation display includes tachometer, water temperature gauge, in-dash clock, exterior temp, systems monitor, check control, trip computer, trip odometer; warning indicators include oil pressure, water temp, battery, low oil level, low coolant, lights on, key in ignition, low fuel, low washer fluid, bulb failure, door ajar, trunk ajar, service interval, brake fluid; driver's and passenger's front airbags, driver's and front passenger's door mounted side airbags, overhead airbag; ignition disable, security system; tinted windows with front and rear 1-touch down function, power 1/4 vent windows; variable-speed intermittent front windshield wipers with heated washer fluid jets, sun visor strip, rear window defroster; seating capacity of 5, front bucket seats with adjustable headrests, center armrest with storage, driver's and front passenger's seats include 6-way adjustment, easy entry; 60/40 folding rear bench seat with adjustable headrests, center armrest; height-adjustable front seatbelts with pretensioners; leatherette seats, leatherette door trim insert, full cloth headliner, full carpet floor covering, aluminum dashboard insert, aluminum door panel insert, aluminum console insert, chrome interior accents; interior lights include dome light with fade, front and rear reading lights, illuminated entry; leather-wrapped steering wheel with tilt and telescopic adjustment; dual illuminated vanity mirrors; day/night rearview mirror; full floor console, mini overhead console locking glove box with light, front cupholder, instrument panel covered bin, 2 seatback storage pockets, driver's and passenger's door bins; carpeted cargo floor, carpeted trunk lid, reversible cargo mats, cargo tie downs, cargo light; chrome grille, chrome side window moldings, black front windshield molding, black rear window molding and body-colored door handles.

325Ci CONVERTIBLE (5M) (in addition to or instead of 325Ci COUPE (5M) equipment): 3.46 axle ratio; manual convertible roof with lining, glass rear window, roll-over protection; 16" x 7" silver alloy wheels; compact steel spare wheel; seating capacity of 4, power adjustable headrests, driver's and passenger's seat includes 14-way adjustment (6-way power), easy entry; driver's seat memory includes settings for exterior mirrors.

325i SEDAN (5M) (in addition to or instead of 325Ci COUPE (5M) equipment): front and rear body-colored bumpers with black rubber strip; black bodyside molding rocker panel extensions; P205/55HR16 BSW A/S tires; child-safety rear door locks; black side window moldings.

325i SPORT WAGON (5M) (in addition to or instead of 325i SEDAN (5M) equipment): Roof rack; rear step bumper; compact steel spare wheel; fixed 1/4 vent windows; flip-up rear window, fixed-interval rear wiper, cargo cover, cargo net and cargo tie downs.

325xi SEDAN/SPORT WAGON (5M) (in addition to or instead of 325i SEDAN/SPORT WAGON (5M) equipment): Full-time all-wheel drive, 3.07 axle ratio with traction control.

3 SERIES — BMW

CODE	DESCRIPTION	INVOICE	MSRP

330Ci COUPE (5M) (in addition to or instead of 325Ci COUPE (5M) equipment): 3L I6 DOHC SMPI 24-valve engine with variable valve timing; 2.93 axle ratio; 17" x 8" silver alloy wheels; P205/50R17 BSW performance tires; driver's and passenger's seat includes 8-way power adjustment, 10-way adjustment, easy entry, center pass-thru armrest and memory on driver's seat with 3 memory settings.

330Ci CONVERTIBLE (5M) (in addition to or instead of 330Ci COUPE (5M) equipment): Power convertible roof with lining, glass rear window, roll-over protection; seating capacity of 4, driver's and passenger's seats include 6-way adjustment; leather seats, and leather door trim insert.

330i SEDAN (5M) (in addition to or instead of 330Ci COUPE (5M) equipment): Front and rear body-colored bumpers with black rubber strip; black bodyside molding rocker panel extensions; P225/45HR17 BSW A/S tires; full size steel spare wheel; child-safety rear door locks; adjustable headrests, center armrest with storage, driver's seat includes 6-way adjustment, leather-wrapped gearshift knob; carpeted cargo mats.

330xi SEDAN (5M) (in addition to or instead of 330i SEDAN (5M) equipment): Full-time all-wheel drive, 2.93 axle ratio; P225/45HR17 BSW A/S tires.

Base Prices

Code	Description	Invoice	MSRP
0133	330Ci Coupe (5M)	31650	34990
0134	325Ci Coupe (5M)	26250	28990
0146	330Ci Convertible (5M)	38320	42400
0141	325Ci Convertible (5M)	32550	35990
0142	330i Sedan (5M)	30750	33990
0144	325i Sedan (5M)	24450	26990
0142	330xi Sedan (5M)	32240	35740
0144-AWD	325xi Sedan (5M)	25940	28740
0135	325i Sport Wagon (5M)	26620	29400
0135-AWD	325xi Sport Wagon (5M)	28110	31150
Destination Charge:		570	570

Interested in seeing what dealers will sell this vehicle for? Check out our True Market Value^{sm} (TMV^{sm}) pricing on our Web site at www.edmunds.com.

Accessories

Code	Description	Invoice	MSRP
—	Leather Upholstery (All except 330Ci Conv)	1235	1450
205	Transmission: Steptronic 5-Speed Automatic (All 325i/330i)	1210	1275
	Includes adaptive transmission control and selectable sport mode.		
249	Cruise Control (325i/325xi /325i Wagon/325xi Wagon)	405	475
261	Rear Side Airbags (Sedan/Wagon)	325	385
	Includes rear side airbag deactivation.		
270	Sport Package (325Ci Convertible)	1020	1200
	Includes sport suspension, 17" alloy wheels, 225/45WR17 performance tires and sport seats. REQUIRES Leather Upholstery.		
270	Sport Package (325Ci Coupe)	850	1000
	Includes 17" alloy wheels, 225/45WR17 performance tires and sport seats.		
270	Sport Package (325i Sedan/325i Wagon)	1275	1500
	Includes sport suspension, 3-spoke leather-wrapped steering wheel, 17" alloy wheels, 225/45WR17 performance tires and sport seats.		

BMW

3 SERIES

CODE	DESCRIPTION	INVOICE	MSRP
270	Sport Package (330Ci Convertible/330xi)	680	800
	Includes sport suspension, sport seats and 17" alloy wheels.		
270	Sport Package (330Ci Coupe)	510	600
	Includes sport seats and 17" alloy wheels.		
270	Sport Package (330i)	1020	1200
	Includes sport suspension, leather-wrapped steering wheel, sport seats, M aerodynamic package and 17" alloy wheels.		
356	Cold Weather Package (Sedan)	850	1000
	Includes fold-down rear seats, ski sack, heated front seats and headlight cleaning system.		
356	Cold Weather Package (Convertible/Coupe)	595	700
	Includes ski bag, heated front seats and headlight washer system.		
3--	Black/Blue/Green Soft Top (Convertible)	NC	NC
	NOT AVAILABLE with 391 or 392.		
403	Power Glass Moonroof (All except Convertible)	895	1050
438	Myrtle Wood Trim	425	500
454	Sport Package (325xi)	1020	1200
	Includes 3-spoke leather-wrapped steering wheel, 17" alloy wheels, 225/45WR17 performance tires and sport seats.		
454	Sport Package (330xi)	765	900
	Includes leather-wrapped steering wheel, sport seats and M aerodynamic package.		
459	Power Front Seats with Driver Memory (325Ci Coupe/325i/330i/330xi)	805	945
465	Fold Down Rear Seats (Sedan)	405	475
	Includes ski sack.		
468	Premium Package (325Ci Convertible)	1615	1900
	Includes fully automatic soft top, auto-dimming mirror, universal garage door opener, myrtle wood trim and automatic air conditioning.		
468	Premium Package (325Ci Coupe)	1785	2100
	Includes power glass moonroof, auto-dimming mirror, myrtle wood trim, electric seats with driver's side memory and automatic air conditioning.		
468	Premium Package (325i/325xi/325i Wagon/325xi Wagon)	2975	3500
	Includes cruise control, power glass moonroof, auto-dimming mirror, myrtle wood trim, electric seats with driver's side memory, front armrest, automatic air conditioning and an on-board computer.		
468	Premium Package (330Ci Conv)	680	800
	Includes auto-dimming mirror, universal garage door opener, myrtle wood trim, lumbar support and rain sensor wipers.		
468	Premium Package (330Ci Coupe)	2465	2900
	Includes power glass moonroof, auto-dimming mirror, myrtle wood trim, lumbar support, rain sensor wipers and leather upholstery.		
468	Premium Package (330i/330xi)	3275	3850
	Includes power glass moonroof, auto-dimming mirror, myrtle wood trim, power front seats with driver memory, lumbar support, rain sensor wipers and leather upholstery.		
494	Heated Front Seats	425	500
508	Park Distance Control (325i Wagon/325xi Wagon/all 330i)	300	350
520	Fog Lights (325i/325xi)	220	260
	Includes heated mirrors and heated washer fluid jets.		

3 SERIES / 5 SERIES — BMW

CODE	DESCRIPTION	INVOICE	MSRP
522	Xenon Lights (All 325i) .... *REQUIRES 520.*	425	500
522	Xenon Lights (All 330i)	425	500
550	On-Board Computer (325i/325xi/325i Wagon/325xi Wagon)	255	300
609	Navigation System (All 325i) .... *REQUIRES 468. NOT AVAILABLE with 662.*	1530	1800
609	Navigation System (All 330i) .... *NOT AVAILABLE with 662.*	1530	1800
662	Radio: AM/FM, CD Player-In Dash (All 330i) .... *NOT AVAILABLE with 609.*	170	200
662	Radio: BMW Business CD (All 325i) .... *Replaces standard cassette. NOT AVAILABLE with 609.*	170	200
674	Harman Kardon Sound System (All 325i)	575	675
674	Harman Kardon Sound System (All 330i) .... *Deletes standard hi-fi audio system.*	575	675
926	Tire: Full-Size Spare (325i Wagon/325xi Wagon)	215	250
982	Hard Top (Convertible)	1950	2295
MP	Paint: Metallic Paint	405	475

2001 5 SERIES

What's New?

The former base 2.8-liter engine gets bumped up to 3.0 liters, with an expected horsepower and torque increase to go along with the larger displacement. A new 2.5-liter engine premieres this year, as do rear seat head airbags, upgraded optional equipment and a slightly freshened exterior.

Review

The 5 Series follows BMW's fine tradition of embodying a "true driver's car" and is offered in three flavors for 2001 - the base 525i, the mid-level 530i, or the top-end 540i. In addition to the sedan body style, a wagon (or estate, as they say in Deutschland) is also available in 525i and 540i versions.

A new 2.5-liter inline six-cylinder engine that makes 185 horsepower moves the 525i models. This base model comes with a standard five-speed manual transmission, or it can be optioned with a five-speed Steptronic automanual transmission.

Step up to the 530i and you get a new 3.0-liter inline six that makes a healthy 225 horsepower at 5,900 rpm and 214 foot-pounds of torque at 3,500 rpm. This engine creates a broad torque band and offers commendable acceleration while meeting low-emission vehicle standards.

Under the hood of the 540i sits a 4.4-liter, 32-valve V8 that manages zero-to-60 times in the low sixes. With 282 horsepower at its command, these Bavarian barnstormers are a blast on the open road. This powerplant comes mated to either a six-speed manual or a five-speed Steptronic automanual (the 540i Sport Wagon comes only with the auto) for those who find the BMW stick shifts a bit too demanding in stop-and-go traffic. The suspension is pleasantly firm on this lively model, making even the most docile of drivers feel like Michael Schumacher. Of course, if you

BMW

5 SERIES

| CODE | DESCRIPTION | INVOICE | MSRP |

really want to experience the pinnacle of BMW performance in a luxury sedan, skip the 540i and step up to the wonderful (and wonderfully expensive) M5 sedan.

As one would expect in a top-end, luxury/sport vehicle, equipment levels are first rate. Standard fare includes a10-speaker premium sound system, car and key programmable memory, dual-zone air conditioning, eight-way power adjustments with memory settings, and cruise control with steering wheel controls. All-Season Traction (AST), Dynamic Stability Control (DSC) and Dynamic Brake Control are standard on all 5 Series cars.

Standard safety equipment includes 9-mph bumpers, dual airbags, door-mounted side-impact airbags, and a head-protection system for front passengers. Three-point seatbelts at all seating positions, impact sensors that unlock the doors and activate the hazard lights in the event of a serious accident, remote keyless entry, two-step unlocking, coded drive-away protection, and a vehicle security system are also standard. Rear-passenger side-impact and head protection airbags are optional for the truly safety conscious.

To list all of the 5 Series' luxury options would take more space than we have. A few of the more noticeable ones include a cold- weather package with heated front seats, Park Distance Control, a navigation system and 17-inch wheels with performance tires.

Yes indeed, the 5 Series is a wonderful car. If you can afford to buy one, we recommend that you do. Sure, there are other great cars out there in this price range; we just think this is one of the best.

Standard Equipment

525i SEDAN (5M): 2.5L I6 DOHC SMPI 24-valve engine with variable valve timing (requires premium unleaded fuel); 5-speed manual transmission; 120 amp alternator; rear-wheel drive, traction control, 2.93 axle ratio; stainless steel exhaust; electronic stability control, front independent strut suspension with anti-roll bar, front coil springs, gas-pressurized front shocks, rear independent multi-link suspension with anti-roll bar, rear coil springs, gas-pressurized rear shocks; rack-and-pinion power steering with engine-speed-sensing assist; 4-wheel antilock disc brakes; 18.5 gal. capacity fuel tank; side impact bars; front and rear body-colored bumpers with black rubber strip, chrome bumper insert; black bodyside molding with chrome bodyside insert; metallic monotone paint; aero-composite halogen headlamps with delay-off feature; additional exterior lights include front fog/driving lights; driver's and passenger's body-colored heated folding outside mirrors, driver's power remote outside mirror, passenger's power remote tilt down outside mirror; 16" x 7" silver alloy wheels; P225/55HR16 BSW A/S tires; full-size alloy spare wheel; dual-zone front air conditioning, air filter, rear heat ducts, residual heat recirculation; premium AM/FM stereo radio, seek-scan feature, cassette player, CD changer pre-wiring, 10 speakers, theft deterrent, window grid diversity antenna, steering wheel radio controls; cruise control; power heated door locks with 2-stage unlock, remote keyless entry, child-safety rear door locks, power remote trunk release; cell phone pre-wiring, 1 power accessory outlet, front lighter elements, driver's foot rest, retained accessory power, smokers' package; instrumentation display includes tachometer, water temperature gauge, in-dash clock, exterior temp, systems monitor, check control, trip computer, trip odometer; warning indicators include oil pressure, water temp, battery, low oil level, low coolant, lights on, key in ignition, low fuel, low washer fluid, bulb failure, door ajar, trunk ajar, service interval, brake fluid; driver's and passenger's front airbags, driver's and front passenger's door-mounted side airbags, overhead airbag; ignition disable and panic alarm security system; tinted windows, power front and rear windows with front and rear 1-touch down function; variable-speed intermittent front windshield wipers with heated washer fluid jets, sun visor strip, rear window defroster; seating capacity of 5, front bucket seats, power adjustable tilt headrests, center armrest with storage, driver's seat includes 8-way power adjustment, passenger's seat includes 4-way adjustment; rear bench seat with adjustable headrests, center armrest; height-adjustable front seatbelts with pretensioners; leatherette seats, leatherette door trim insert, full cloth headliner, full carpet floor covering, chrome interior accents; driver's seat memory includes settings for exterior mirrors, steering wheel, and headrests; interior lights include dome light with fade, front and rear reading lights, illuminated entry; steering wheel with power tilt and telescopic adjustment; dual illuminated vanity mirrors; day/night rearview mirror; full floor console, locking glove box with light, front and

5 SERIES — BMW

rear cupholders, 2 seatback storage pockets, driver's and passenger's door bins, rear door bins; carpeted cargo floor, cargo light; chrome grille, chrome side window moldings, black front windshield molding, black rear window molding and body-colored door handles.

525iA SEDAN (5A) (in addition to or instead of 525i SEDAN (5M) equipment): 5-speed electronic OD automatic transmission with lock-up torque converter; driver's selectable multi-mode auto-manual transmission; 4.1 axle ratio.

525i SPORT WAGON (5M) (in addition to or instead of 525i SEDAN (5M) equipment): roof rack; rear step bumper; trunk pull-down, fixed 1/4 vent windows; flip-up rear window, rear window wiper, 60/40 folding rear bench seat with adjustable headrests, cargo cover, cargo net, cargo light, and locking concealed cargo storage.

525iA SPORT WAGON (5A) (in addition to or instead of 525i SPORT WAGON (5M) equipment): 5-speed electronic OD automatic transmission with lock-up torque converter; and driver's selectable multi-mode auto-manual transmission.

530i SEDAN (5M) (in addition to or instead of 525i SEDAN (5M) equipment): 3.0L I6 DOHC SMPI 24-valve engine with variable valve timing; dual-zone front air conditioning with climate control.

530iA (5A) (in addition to or instead of 530i (5M) equipment): 5-speed electronic OD automatic transmission with lock-up and driver's selectable multi-mode auto-manual transmission; 4.1 axle ratio.

540iA SEDAN (5A) (in addition to or instead of 530iA (5A) equipment): 4.4L V8 DOHC SMPI 32-valve engine with variable valve timing, 2.81 axle ratio; dual stainless steel exhaust; recirculating-ball power steering with engine speed-sensing assist; front express open/close sliding and tilting glass sunroof with sunshade; clearcoat monotone paint; projector beam high intensity headlamps with delay-off feature; garage door opener, rain-detecting wipers, driver's and passenger's seat includes 8-way power adjustment; leather seats, leather door trim insert, genuine wood dashboard insert, leather/wood gearshift knob, genuine wood door panel insert, genuine wood console insert; leather-wrapped steering wheel with power tilt and telescopic adjustment; and auto-dimming day/night rearview mirror.

540i SEDAN (6M) (in addition to or instead of 540iA SEDAN (5A) equipment): 6-speed OD manual transmission; sport-ride suspension, black bumper insert; body-colored bodyside molding with chrome bodyside insert; front 17" x 8" silver alloy wheels, rear 17" x 9" silver alloy wheels; P235/45WR17 BSW performance front tires; 255/40 WR17 BSW performance rear tires; front sports seats, driver's and passenger's seat includes 10-way power adjustment, aluminum dashboard insert, aluminum door panel insert, aluminum console insert, leather-wrapped sport steering wheel with power tilt and telescopic adjustment; black side window moldings.

540iA SPORT WAGON (5A) (in addition to or instead of 540iA SEDAN (5A) equipment): 150 amp alternator; 3.15 axle ratio; auto-leveling suspension, rear air shocks; roof rack; rear step bumper; trunk pull-down, fixed 1/4 vent windows; flip-up rear window, rear window wiper, 60/40 folding rear bench seat with adjustable headrests, cargo cover, cargo net, and locking concealed cargo storage.

Base Prices

CODE	DESCRIPTION	INVOICE	MSRP
0156	525i Sedan (5M)	32020	35400
0150	530i Sedan (5M)	35620	39400
0158	540iA Sedan (5A)	46150	51100
0157	525iA Sedan (5A)	33230	36675

BMW

5 SERIES

CODE	DESCRIPTION	INVOICE	MSRP
0153	540i Sedan (6M)	48670	53900
0155	530iA Sedan (5A)	36830	40675
0154	525i Sport Wagon (5M)	33640	37200
0169	540iA Sport Wagon (5A)	48290	53480
0159	525iA Sport Wagon (5A)	34850	38475
	Destination Charge:	570	570

Interested in seeing what dealers will sell this vehicle for? Check out our True Market Value^{sm} (TMV^{sm}) pricing on our Web site at www.edmunds.com.

Accessories

Code	Description	Invoice	MSRP
—	Montana Leather Upholstery (All 525i and 530i)	1235	1450
220	Self-Leveling Suspension (525i Wagon/525iA Wagon)	645	760
248	Heated Steering Wheel (All 525i/530i/530iA/540iA) *REQUIRES 356.*	130	150
261	Rear Side Airbags *Includes rear side airbag deactivation.*	470	550
269	Sport Premium Package (525i Sedan/525iA Sedan) *Includes 17" cross-spoke composite wheels, 235/45R17 93W performance tires, power glass moonroof, sport suspension, Vavona wood high-gloss trim and MO leather upholstery. NOT AVAILABLE with 270 or 468.*	3315	3900
269	Sport Premium Package (525i Wagon/525iA Wagon) *Includes sport suspension, self-leveling suspension, 17" cross-spoke composite wheels, 235/45R17 93W performance tires, power glass moonroof, Vavona wood high-gloss trim and MO leather upholstery. NOT AVAILABLE with 270 or 468.*	3870	4550
269	Sport Premium Package (530i/530iA) *Includes 17" cross-spoke composite wheels, 235/45R17 93W performance tires, shadowline trim, power glass moonroof, auto-dimming inside rearview mirror, rain sensor wipers, sport suspension, M Sport steering wheel, vavona wood high gloss trim and MO leather upholstery. NOT AVAILABLE with 248, 270, or 468.*	3655	4300
270	Sport Package (525i Sedan/525iA Sedan) *Includes 17" cross-spoke composite wheels, 235/45R17 93W performance tires and sport suspension. NOT AVAILABLE with 269 or 468.*	1275	1500
270	Sport Package (525i Wagon/525iA Wagon) *Includes sport suspension, self-leveling suspension, 17" cross-spoke composite wheels, 235/45R17 93W performance tires. NOT AVAILABLE with 269 or 468.*	1680	1975
270	Sport Package (530i/530iA) *Includes 17" cross-spoke composite wheels, 235/45R17 93W performance tires, shadowline trim, sport suspension and M Sport steering wheel. NOT AVAILABLE with 248, 269, or 468.*	1675	1970
270	Sport Package (540iA) *Includes multi-function M Sport steering wheel and high-gloss satin chrome trim. NOT AVAILABLE with 488 or 248.*	2380	2800
356	Cold Weather Package *Includes heated front seats.*	510	600
403	Power Glass Moonroof (All 525i/530i/530iA)	895	1050
416	Electric Rear Sunshade (Sedan)	490	575
417	Rear Door Window Sun Blinds (Wagon)	155	180

5 SERIES / Z3 — BMW

CODE	DESCRIPTION	INVOICE	MSRP
456	Comfort Seats	1020	1200
465	Fold Down Rear Seats with Ski Bag (All except Wagon)	405	475
	REQUIRES Montana Leather Upholstery (On 525/530 Sedans).		
466	Convenience Package (530i/530iA)	510	600
	Includes universal garage door opener and electric passenger seat. REQUIRES 269, 403, or 468. NOT AVAILABLE with 467.		
466	Convenience Package (All 525i)	1105	1300
	Includes universal garage door opener, electric passenger seat and automatic recirculation. REQUIRES 269, 403 or 468.		
467	Comfort Seats and Convenience Package (530i/530iA)	1530	1800
	Includes universal garage door opener, comfort seats, lumbar support. REQUIRES Montana Leather Upholstery (269, 403, or 468). NOT AVAILABLE with 466 or 481.		
468	Premium Package (530i/530iA)	2635	3100
	Includes power glass moonroof, auto-dimming inside rearview mirror, rain sensor wipers, vavona wood high-gloss trim and MO leather upholstery. NOT AVAILABLE with 269, 270, or 481.		
468	Premium Package (All 525i)	2510	2950
	Includes power glass moonroof, vavona wood high-gloss trim and MO leather upholstery. NOT AVAILABLE with 269 or 270.		
481	Sport Seats (530i/530iA)	405	475
	REQUIRES Montana Leather Upholstery, 466 (270 or 269). NOT AVAILABLE with 467, 468, or 488.		
488	Lumbar Support (530i/530iA)	340	400
	REQUIRES 466. NOT AVAILABLE with 481.		
488	Lumbar Support (540iA)	340	400
	NOT AVAILABLE with 270.		
508	Park Distance Control	595	700
522	Xenon Lights (All 525i/530i/530iA)	425	500
609	Navigation System (All except 540)	1690	1990
	Includes 1 geographic disc plus one 6 month update, premium on-board computer and walnut wood trim. NOT AVAILABLE with 650.		
609	Navigation System (All 540i)	1530	1800
	Includes 1 geographic disc plus one 6 month update. NOT AVAILABLE with 650.		
650	Radio: BMW Business CD	170	200
	NOT AVAILABLE with 609.		
677	Premium Hi-Fi	1020	1200
	Includes AM/FM cassette stereo and digital signal processor.		
788	Wheels: 17" Mixed Parallel Spoke (540i Sedan/540iA Sedan)	255	300
	Styling 66. REQUIRES 270.		

2001 Z3

What's New?

Engine displacement in the 2.8 Roadster and Coupe is bumped from 2.8 liters to 3.0 liters. An associated horsepower and torque increase, along with bigger brakes and larger 17-inch

BMW Z3

wheels and tires, accompanies the new engine. The base 2.5-liter engine also sees a 14 horsepower increase. An optional five-speed Steptronic transmission with manual shifting capability is now available.

Review

The Z3, introduced in 1996, has seen unfaltering popularity with young and old alike even as the line has grown to include more models. It seems that wherever we take these cars, a crowd quickly forms to ask questions about performance and to drool over their lovely shapes.

The Z3 lineup consists of three sportsters: the base Z3 Roadster 2.5i, Z3 Coupe 3.0i and Z3 Roadster 3.0i. The Z3 Roadster has an upgraded 2.5-liter, six-cylinder engine that now makes 184 horsepower while meeting low emission vehicle (LEV) standards. Z3s outfitted with larger, 3.0-liter, 225-horsepower six-cylinder engines are available as coupes or roadsters.

Z3 Roadsters feature L-shaped taillights with clear turn signal lenses, fully lined tops, and sculpted rear flanks. The capable sound system is actually audible at speed and clear instrument gauges, plus an analog clock, give the interior a classic look. Some carefully chosen upgrades in interior plastics would go a long way toward improving the Z3's value equation. And what's with the plastic rear window on roadster models when a $12,000 cheaper MR2 provides glass and a defroster?

The 2.5i gets four-wheel disc brakes, a limited-slip differential and 16-inch V-rated performance tires as standard equipment, while the 3.0i cars have larger brakes and new 17-inch wheels this year. A smooth-shifting five-speed manual transmission is standard on all Z cars, and this year a five-speed Steptronic automatic, capable of being manually shifted, is optional.

All Z3s have a leather-wrapped M-Technic sport steering wheel and standard Dynamic Stability Control, which senses when the car is veering from its intended path and selectively modulates engine torque and the antilock brakes to bring the car under control.

Driving BMW's Z3 cars is a phenomenal experience. Even the most basic Z3 Roadster, with its powerful inline six and ventilated front-disc brakes, is a blast. Only at high speeds does the 2.5 feel winded, but opting for the larger displacement 3.0-liter six in the 3.0i Roadster solves that problem. And for those who must have a rigid structure and protection from the elements, the 3.0i Coupe is a hoot.

With superb steering and excellent brakes, any Z3 is fun to drive and own. Despite their prowess, however, pure performance freaks will want to step up to the M Coupe and M Roadster, which offer increased power and superior handling.

Slotted comfortably between the bargain Mazda Miata/Toyota MR2 and more expensive machines from Mercedes-Benz and Porsche, there is a Z3 to suit anybody's needs. Certainly the thrill of open-air motoring in a European two-seater is appealing to any baby boomer who owned a sporty little convertible while in college, but those seeking a scalpel sharp roadster this price range will want to check out Honda's ultra-capable S2000. The Z3 Coupe 3.0i makes sense for Snowbelt dwellers who have greater storage needs and like a bit of "funk" with their "sport."

Thirty-somethings are attracted to Z3s because of their undeniable sex appeal and attainable price. But let's face it: Everybody who loves to drive loves the Z3.

Standard Equipment

2.5i ROADSTER (5M): 2.5L I6 DOHC SMPI 24-valve engine with variable valve timing, (requires premium unleaded fuel); 5-speed manual transmission; 90 amp alternator; rear-wheel drive, limited-slip differential, traction control, 3.46 axle ratio; stainless steel exhaust; electronic stability

Z3 — BMW

control, front independent strut suspension with anti-roll bar, front coil springs, gas-pressurized front shocks, rear independent trailing arm suspension with anti-roll bar, rear coil springs, gas-pressurized rear shocks; rack-and-pinion power steering, engine-speed-sensing assist; 4-wheel antilock disc brakes; 13.5 gal. capacity fuel tank; side impact bars; manual convertible roof with lining, roll-over protection; front and rear body-colored bumpers; rocker panel extensions; clearcoat monotone paint; aero-composite halogen headlamps with daytime running lights; driver's and passenger's power remote body-colored folding outside mirrors; 16" x 7" silver alloy wheels; P225/50VR16 BSW performance tires; compact steel spare wheel; air conditioning; premium AM/FM stereo radio, seek-scan feature, cassette player, CD changer pre-wiring, 10 speakers, amplifier, theft deterrent, fixed antenna; power door locks with 2-stage unlock; cell phone pre-wiring, 1 power accessory outlet, front lighter elements, driver's foot rest, smokers' package; instrumentation display includes tachometer, water temperature gauge, clock, trip odometer; warning indicators include oil pressure, water temp, battery, lights on, key in ignition, low fuel, service interval, low brake fluid; driver's and passenger's front airbags, driver's and front passenger's door-mounted side airbags; ignition disable, security system; tinted windows with driver's and passenger's 1-touch down function; variable-speed intermittent front windshield wipers, sun visor strip; seating capacity of 2, front bucket seats with fixed headrests, driver's seat includes 10-way adjustment (6-way power), passenger's seat includes 6-way adjustment (2-way power); seatbelts with front pretensioners; leatherette seats, leatherette door trim insert, full cloth headliner, full carpet floor covering, leather-wrapped gearshift knob; interior lights include dome light with fade, illuminated entry; leather-wrapped sport steering wheel; vanity mirrors; day/night rearview mirror; full floor console, locking glove box, front cupholder, driver's and passenger's door bins; carpeted cargo floor, cargo light; chrome grille, black side window moldings, black front windshield molding, black rear window molding and black door handles.

3.0i ROADSTER (5M) (in addition to or instead of 2.5i ROADSTER (5M) equipment): 3L I6 DOHC SMPI 24-valve engine with variable valve timing; front 17" x 7.5" silver alloy wheels, rear 17" x 8.5" silver alloy wheels; P225/45ZR17 BSW front performance tires, 245/40 rear tires; premium AM/FM stereo radio, seek-scan feature, cassette player, CD changer pre-wiring, 10 performance speakers, premium amplifier; cruise control; driver's and passenger's front seats include 10-way adjustment (4-way power); leather seats and leather door trim insert.

3.0i COUPE (5M) (in addition to or instead of 3.0i ROADSTER (5M) equipment): 3.07 axle ratio; additional exterior lights include front fog/driving lights; 9 performance speakers, premium amplifier.

Base Prices

CODE	DESCRIPTION	INVOICE	MSRP
0129	3.0i Coupe (5M)	34090	37700
0125	2.5i Roadster (5M)	28330	31300
0128	3.0i Roadster (5M)	34720	37900
	Destination Charge:	570	570

Interested in seeing what dealers will sell this vehicle for? Check out our True Market Value℠ (TMV℠) pricing on our Web site at www.edmunds.com.

Accessories

CODE	DESCRIPTION	INVOICE	MSRP
—	Classic Leather Upholstery (2.5i)	980	1150
	NOT AVAILABLE with LEATH.		
—	Classic Leather Upholstery (2.5i)	NC	NC
	REQUIRES 468. NOT AVAILABLE with LEATH.		
—	Leather Upholstery (2.5i)	980	1150
	NOT AVAILABLE with CLASSI.		

BMW   Z3

CODE	DESCRIPTION	INVOICE	MSRP
205	Transmission: 5-Speed Automatic with Steptronic	1210	1275
263	Wheels: 17" Alloy (Coupe)	255	300
270	Sport Package (Roadster)	510	600
	Includes 16" alloy wheels and sport seats.		
306	Paint: Atlanta Blue Metallic (2.5i,)	405	475
343	Aluminum-Look Interior Trim	255	300
	NOT AVAILABLE with 435 or 468.		
345	Chrome Line Interior (2.5i)	130	150
354	Paint: Titanium Silver Metallic (2.5i)	405	475
362	Paint: Siena Red Metallic (Roadster)	405	475
364	Paitn: Topaz Blue Metallic	405	475
3--	Black/Beige Top (Roadster)	NC	NC
	NOT AVAILABLE with 394.		
398	Electric Top (Roadster)	640	750
400	Paint: Steel Grey Metallic (Roadster)	405	475
403	Glass Moonroof (Coupe)	255	300
405	Heated Seats and Mirrors	425	500
	Includes heated driver's door lock and heated front seats. REQUIRES 270.		
413	Luggage Net (Coupe)	155	180
418	Paint: Impala Brown Metallic (2.5i)	405	475
430	Paint: Oxford Green Metallic	405	475
435	Wood Trim (Roadster)	340	400
	Includes wood console. NOT AVAILABLE with 343.		
468	Premium Package (2.5i)	1360	1600
	Includes leather upholstery, electric top, wood trim and leather upholstery. NOT AVAILABLE with 343.		
468	Premium Package (3.0i Roadster)	810	950
	Includes electric top, leather upholstery and wood trim. NOT AVAILABLE with 343.		
475	Paint: Black Saphire Metallic (2.5i)	405	475
550	On Board Computer	255	300
658	BMW CD Radio	170	200
674	Harman-Kardon Sound System (2.5i)	575	675
982	Hard Top (Roadster)	1615	1900
Q4	Extended Leather Upholstery (3.0i)	1020	1200
	NOT AVAILABLE with R5, R7, or R8.		
R5	Leather Upholstery (3.0i Roadster)	NC	NC
	NOT AVAILABLE with R7, R8, or Q4.		
R7	Classic Leather Upholstery (3.0i Roadster)	NC	NC
	NOT AVAILABLE with R5, R8, or Q4.		
R8	Classic Extended Leather Upholstery (3.0i Roadster)	1020	1200
	NOT AVAILABLE with R5, R7, or Q4.		

BUICK
CENTURY

2001 CENTURY

What's New?

Buick's midsize Century remains relatively unchanged for 2001. New rear-wheel house liners promise a quieter ride on wet roads, a special appearance package is offered and OnStar in-vehicle safety, security and information service is now standard on Limited models.

Review

Back in 1997, a revamped Century hit the showrooms with a bigger, more ergonomic interior and roomier trunk, all wrapped in smooth, flowing sheetmetal that Buick stylists hoped would have a long shelf life. It appears they got their wish. Now five model-years old, today's Century has been growing in popularity each year, proving we shouldn't underestimate the market power of America's senior citizens, rental car companies or business-class road travelers. Not much has changed for the 2001 model year. New rear-wheel house liners are supposed to minimize road noise and a special appearance package is now offered that includes monochrome exterior paint, blacked-out trim and 15-inch chrome alloy wheels. An inside emergency trunk release has been added to all Centurys, just in case a child decides to play hide-and-seek. Other features include cruise control, a six-way power driver's seat, and an AM/FM cassette player with steering wheel controls. Opt for leather and you'll also get uplevel mirrors, seating and audio.

All Centurys receive the stalwart 3100 V6 that makes 175 horsepower and 195 foot-pounds of torque. The Century's smooth-shifting, electronically controlled, four-speed automatic transmission puts the power to the pavement. Inside, dual-zone climate controls are standard on all models. Electronic dual-zone climate control, which replaces slide-and-knob controls with push buttons and LED and digital indicators, is standard in the upper-level Special Edition and optional on the Limited.

Century comes standard with such features as remote keyless entry, automatic power door locks, daytime running lamps with Twilight Sentinel (which automatically controls the headlamps based on lighting conditions), door courtesy lights, battery rundown protection, antilock brakes, traction control, a tire inflation monitor and GM's PASS-Key II theft-deterrent system. OnStar in-vehicle safety, security and information service is now standard on Limited models.

Century stacks up well in the high-volume midsize sedan market, where it shows continued sales strength against its domestic rivals. A decent safety record and solid build quality make it an enduring favorite, while earning it "top buy" acclaim from more than a few consumer publications and rating organizations along the way. With the highest customer-loyalty rating in the segment, Century buyers seem prepared to stick with this Buick well into the new century.

Standard Equipment

CUSTOM (4A): 3.1L V6 OHV SMPI 12-valve engine; 4-speed electronic OD automatic transmission with lock-up torque converter; 600 amp battery with run down protection; front-wheel drive, traction control, 3.05 axle ratio; stainless steel exhaust; front independent strut suspension with anti-roll bar, front coil springs, rear independent strut suspension with anti-roll bar, rear coil springs; rack-and-pinion power steering; front disc/rear drum brakes with 4-wheel antilock brakes; 17.5 gal. capacity fuel tank; side impact bars; class I trailering; front and rear body-colored bumpers with chrome bumper insert; body-colored bodyside molding with chrome bodyside insert; clearcoat monotone paint; aero-composite halogen fully auto headlamps with daytime running lights, delay-off feature; additional exterior lights include cornering lights,

BUICK

CENTURY

CODE	DESCRIPTION	INVOICE	MSRP

underhood light; driver's and passenger's power remote black folding outside mirrors; 15" x 6" steel wheels; P205/70SR15 BSW A/S tires; compact steel spare wheel; dual zone front air conditioning, air filter, rear heat/AC ducts; AM/FM stereo radio, clock, seek-scan, 6 performance speakers, fixed antenna; power door locks with 2-stage unlock, remote keyless entry, child safety rear door locks, power remote trunk release; 1 power accessory outlet, front lighter element(s), driver's foot rest, smoker's package; instrumentation display includes water temperature gauge, trip odometer; warning indicators include oil pressure, water temp, battery, low oil level, low coolant, lights on, key in ignition, low fuel, low washer fluid, door ajar, trunk ajar, service interval, turn signal on, low tire pressure; driver's and passenger's front airbags; ignition disable, panic alarm; tinted windows, power front and rear windows with driver's 1-touch down function; variable intermittent front windshield wipers, sun visor strip, rear window defroster; seating capacity of 6, 55/45 split-bench front seat with adjustable headrests, center armrest with storage, driver's and passenger's seat includes 4-way adjustment; rear bench seat with fixed headrests; front height adjustable seatbelts; cloth seats, cloth door trim insert, full cloth headliner, full carpet floor covering; interior lights include dome light with fade, front reading lights, illuminated entry; steering wheel with tilt adjustment; vanity mirrors, dual auxiliary visors; day/night rearview mirror; locking glove box with light, front cupholder, driver's and passenger's door bins, rear door bins; carpeted cargo floor, cargo light; chrome grille, chrome side window moldings, black front windshield molding, black rear window molding and body-colored door handles.

LIMITED (4A) (in addition to or instead of CUSTOM (4A) equipment): Vehicle speed-sensing assisted rack-and-pinion power steering; driver's and passenger's power remote body-colored heated folding outside mirrors; AM/FM stereo radio, clock, seek-scan, cassette player, 6 performance speakers, auto equalizer, theft deterrent, window grid antenna; cruise control; retained accessory power, emergency S.O.S. (OnStar); seat mounted driver's side airbag; tracker system; driver's seat includes 6-way power adjustment, 8-way adjustment; rear center armrest; leather seats, leatherette door trim insert; leather-wrapped steering wheel with tilt adjustment; dual illuminated vanity mirrors and 2 seatback storage pockets.

Base Prices

Code	Description	Invoice	MSRP
4WS69	Custom (4A)	18154	19840
4WY69	Limited (4A)	20927	22871
	Destination Charge:	610	610

Interested in seeing what dealers will sell this vehicle for? Check out our True Market Value^{sm} (TMV^{sm}) pricing on our Web site at www.edmunds.com.

Accessories

Code	Description	Invoice	MSRP
1SA	Custom Base Package 1SA (Custom)	NC	NC
	Includes vehicle with standard equipment. NOT AVAILABLE with AG1, UPO, AM9.		
1SB	Custom Premium Package 1SB (Custom)	520	605
	Includes AM/FM stereo radio with seek/scan, cassette player, dual electric remote heated mirrors, cruise control with resume speed, front carpet savers, rear carpet savers, trunk convenience net and rear window antenna.		
1SC	Custom Special Edition Package 1SC (Custom)	1708	1986
	Manufacturer Discount	(430)	(500)
	Net Price	1278	1486
	Includes dual electric remote heated mirrors, cruise control with resume speed, front carpet savers, rear carpet savers, trunk convenience net, rear window antenna, 15" wheels deluxe bolt-on covers, AM/FM stereo radio with seek/scan, cassette player, 6-way power driver seat, dual illuminated visor vanity mirrors, OnStar global positioning system, special appearance package, body-colored bodyside molding,		

CENTURY — BUICK

CODE	DESCRIPTION	INVOICE	MSRP
	black door header trim, Century 2001 badging and steering wheel remote radio controls. NOT AVAILABLE with UN6, UPO, QGZ.		
1SD	Custom Special Edition Package 1SD (Custom)	1966	2286
	Manufacturer Discount	(430)	(500)
	Net Price	1536	1786
	Includes dual electric remote heated mirrors, cruise control with resume speed, front carpet savers, rear carpet savers, trunk convenience net, rear window antenna, AM/FM stereo radio with seek/scan, cassette player, 6-way power driver seat, dual illuminated visor vanity mirrors, OnStar global positioning system, special appearance package, body-colored bodyside molding, black door header trim, Century 2001 badging, steering wheel remote radio controls and 15" alloy wheels. NOT AVAILABLE with UN6, UPO, QGZ.		
1SE	Limited Base Package 1SE (Limited)	NC	NC
	Includes cruise control with resume speed and 6-way power driver seat. NOT AVAILABLE with U85, CF5.		
1SF	Limited Luxury Package 1SF (Limited)	555	645
	Includes cruise control with resume speed, 6-way power driver seat, dual electrochromic outside mirror, 6-way power passenger seat, air conditioning and electrochromic interior rearview mirror.		
1SG	Limited Special Edition Package 1SG (Limited)	1875	2180
	Manufacturer Discount	(430)	(500)
	Net Price	1445	1680
	Includes cruise control with resume speed, 6-way power driver seat, special appearance package, body-colored bodyside molding, black door header trim, Century 2001 badging, steering wheel remote radio controls, 15" alloy wheels, dual electrochromic outside mirror, 6-way power passenger seat, air conditioning, electrochromic interior rearview mirror, Concert Sound III speakers, split folding rear seat, storage armrest and cupholders. NOT AVAILABLE with PH6, QGZ.		
AG1	6-Way Power Driver Seat (Custom)	284	330
	NOT AVAILABLE with 1SA. INCLUDED in 1SE, 1SF, 1SC, 1SG, 1SD.		
AM9	Split Folding Rear Seat	236	275
	Includes storage armrest and cupholders. NOT AVAILABLE with 1SA. INCLUDED in 1SG.		
CF5	Electric Sliding Sunroof (Limited)	598	695
	NOT AVAILABLE with 1SE.		
K05	Engine Block Heater	30	35
K34	Cruise Control (Custom)	202	235
	INCLUDED in 1SE, 1SB, 1SF, 1SC, 1SG, 1SD.		
PH6	Wheels: 15" Aluminum (Limited)	322	375
	NOT AVAILABLE with 1SG.		
QGZ	Tires: P205/70R15 AS WSW	129	150
	NOT AVAILABLE with 1SC, 1SD, 1SG.		
U85	Concert Sound III Speakers (Limited)	181	210
	Includes diversity antenna. NOT AVAILABLE with 1SE. INCLUDED in 1SG.		
UK3	Steering Wheel Remote Radio Controls (Limited)	108	125
	NOT AVAILABLE with 1SE. INCLUDED in 1SC, 1SG, 1SD.		

BUICK   CENTURY / LESABRE

CODE	DESCRIPTION	INVOICE	MSRP
UN6	**Radio: AM/FM Stereo with Cassette (Custom)**	168	195
	Includes power-loading cassette, seek-and-scan, clock, digital display, electronic tuning, preset scan, auto CrO2, Dolby B, clean-tape-head indicator and radio monitor. Radio monitor allows radio to play while cassette player is fast-forwarding/reversing. NOT AVAILABLE with 1SC, 1SD, UP0. INCLUDED in 1SB.		
UP0	**Radio: AM/FM Stereo with CD and Cassette (Custom)**	194	225
	Includes power-loading CD player with next/last CD track selector, seek-scan, auto tone control and clock. NOT AVAILABLE with 1SA, UN6, 1SC, 1SD. INCLUDED in 1SG.		
UP0	**Radio: AM/FM Stereo with CD and Cassette**	172	200
	Includes power-loading CD player with next/last CD track selector, seek-scan, auto tone control and clock. NOT AVAILABLE with 1SA, UN6, 1SB. INCLUDED in 1SG.		

2001 LESABRE

What's New?

The best-selling U.S. full-size car for eight straight years, Buick's LeSabre has been mildly updated after being totally redesigned last year. Changes include dual-stage airbags, standard OnStar in-vehicle safety, security and information service and the engine oil change interval has been increased to 10,000 miles.

Review

Evolutionary in style outside, and revolutionary in style inside, the Buick LeSabre, redesigned last year, appears to have met its designers' goals — keep the good stuff and improve the rest. Give Buick credit for acting on customer input and coming up with a surprisingly competent overall package.

Though this big, front-drive sedan is about an inch narrower than its predecessor, much of its shape and many of its dimensions are little-changed from the previous generation. Buick's signature "waterfall" chrome grille is still there, and the clean-looking front and rear fascias set off the clear-lens headlamps and large tail lamps. Flush, body-colored door handles add a clean look to the LeSabre, and even the bodyside moldings have an integrated look.

Interior storage and safety has also been a Buick hallmark and the 2001 LeSabre doesn't disappoint. In addition to incorporating side airbags, the comfortable and supportive front seats have built-in "self-aligning" head restraints, reducing the risk of whiplash. Front seatbelts are now integrated into the seat frames, and all five seating positions come equipped with shoulder and lap belts. The LeSabre's interior meets the government's new head-impact requirements ahead of the federal deadline. The big news for 2001 is standard dual-stage front airbags.

Rear headroom is as good as in the Ford Crown Victoria or Mercury Grand Marquis, and though legroom back there isn't best-in-class, it is still comfortable. Large rear-door glass lowers nearly all the way down into the doors for better ventilation. Trunk room is a decent 18 cubic feet, bettering the 17 cubic feet found in the Chrysler Concorde.

The LeSabre's platform makes for a stiffer, quieter body than its predecessor. While the front suspension features MacPherson struts with coil springs, the rear's semi-trailing arm / coil-spring

LESABRE — BUICK

setup makes for a more-controlled ride. We'd opt for the LeSabre Limited with the Gran Touring Package, despite the fact that the top-of-the-line P225/60R-16 touring radials are not super handlers. Antilock brakes are standard, with the rear drums being upgraded to discs for better stopping power.

The only available powertrain in both the Custom and Limited models remains the trusty 3.8-liter Series II V6, mated to a smooth four-speed automatic transmission. This motor makes a healthy 205 horsepower at 5,200 rpm, with 230 foot-pounds of torque peaking at a useable 3,700 rpm. What's more, GM's V6 meets federal 2001 low-emission vehicle (LEV) standards.

LeSabres have consistently ranked better than average in owner trouble complaints over the years, and the 2001 model should improve that score further. While the median age of most LeSabre buyers has long been in the 60s, more family-oriented buyers are finding themselves in Buick showrooms. That will not only do much to help the brand shake some of its fuddy-duddy image, but also keep LeSabre among the best sellers.

Standard Equipment

CUSTOM (4A): 3.8L V6 OHV SMPI 12-valve engine; 4-speed electronic OD automatic transmission with lock-up torque converter; battery with run down protection; front-wheel drive, 2.86 axle ratio; stainless steel exhaust; comfort ride suspension, auto-leveling suspension, front independent strut suspension with anti-roll bar, front coil springs, rear independent trailing arm suspension with rear coil springs; rack-and-pinion power steering; 4-wheel antilock disc brakes; 18.5 gal. capacity fuel tank; side impact bars; class I trailering; front and rear body-colored bumpers; body-colored bodyside molding; clearcoat monotone paint; aero-composite halogen fully auto headlamps with daytime running lights, delay-off feature; additional exterior lights include underhood light; driver's and passenger's power remote body-colored folding outside mirrors; 15" x 6" steel wheels; P215/70SR15 BSW A/S tires; compact steel spare wheel; air conditioning; AM/FM stereo radio, clock, seek-scan, cassette player, 4 speakers, window grid diversity antenna; cruise control with steering wheel controls; power door locks with 2-stage unlock, remote keyless entry, child safety rear door locks, power remote hatch/trunk release; 1 power accessory outlet, front lighter element(s), driver's foot rest, retained accessory power, smoker's package; instrumentation display includes water temperature gauge, trip odometer; warning indicators include oil pressure, battery, lights on, key in ignition, turn signal on; driver's and passenger's front airbags, driver's and front passenger's seat-mounted side airbags; ignition disable, panic alarm; tinted windows, power front and rear windows with driver's and passenger's 1-touch down function; variable intermittent front windshield wipers, sun visor strip, rear window defroster; seating capacity of 6, 55/45 split-bench front seat with adjustable headrests, center armrest with storage, driver's seat includes 6-way power adjustment, 8-way adjustment, lumbar support, passenger's seat includes 4-way adjustment, lumbar support; rear bench seat; cloth seats, door trim with carpet lower, full cloth headliner, full carpet floor covering with carpeted floor mats, simulated wood dashboard insert, simulated wood door panel insert; interior lights include dome light with fade, front reading lights, illuminated entry; steering wheel with tilt adjustment; vanity mirrors, dual auxiliary visors; day/night rearview mirror; mini overhead console, locking glove box with light, front cupholder, instrument panel covered bin, driver's and passenger's door bins; carpeted cargo floor, cargo tie downs, cargo light; chrome grille, chrome side window moldings, black front windshield molding, black rear window molding and body-colored door handles.

LIMITED (4A) (in addition to or instead of CUSTOM (4A) equipment): Traction control; bodyside accent stripe; additional exterior lights include cornering lights; driver's and passenger's power remote body-colored heated folding outside mirrors, driver's auto dimming outside mirror; dual zone front air conditioning with climate control, air filter, rear heat ducts; single CD player, 6 performance speakers, auto equalizer, theft deterrent; garage door opener, emergency S.O.S. (OnStar); instrumentation display includes tachometer, compass, exterior temp, trip computer; warning indicators include water temp, low oil level, low coolant, low washer fluid, door ajar, trunk ajar, service interval, low tire pressure; tracker system, security system; rain detecting wipers; heated-cushion driver's and passenger's seats, driver's seat includes 8-way power adjustment, lumbar support, passenger's seat includes 8-way power adjustment, lumbar support; rear

BUICK
LESABRE

| CODE | DESCRIPTION | INVOICE | MSRP |

center pass-thru armrest with storage; premium cloth seats; interior lights include 4 door curb lights; dual illuminated vanity mirrors; auto-dimming day/night rearview mirror; mini overhead console with storage and rear cupholder.

Base Prices

Code	Description	Invoice	MSRP
4HP69	Custom (4A)	22058	24107
4HR69	Limited (4A)	26348	28796
	Destination Charge:	655	655

Interested in seeing what dealers will sell this vehicle for? Check out our True Market Value^{sm} (TMV^{sm}) pricing on our Web site at www.edmunds.com.

Accessories

Code	Description	Invoice	MSRP
—	Nuance Leather Seat Trim (Custom)	671	780
	NOT AVAILABLE with 1SA.		
—	Nuance Leather Seat Trim (Limited)	671	780
1SA	Custom Premium Package (Custom)	NC	NC
	Includes AM/FM stereo radio with seek/scan, cassette player and power driver seat. NOT AVAILABLE with AG2, Nuance Leather Seat Trim, W02, KA1, Y56, N66, PF7.		
1SD	Custom Luxury Package (Custom)	950	1105
	Includes power driver seat, AM/FM stereo radio with cassette player, steering wheel radio controls, electrochromic inside rearview mirror, 15" 5-spoke alloy wheels, 6 speaker Concert Sound II system, dual lighted visor vanity mirrors, air filtration system, group package, tachometer, trunk convenience net and accent paint stripes.		
1SE	Custom Prestige Package (Custom)	1990	2314
	Includes power driver seat, 15" 5-spoke alloy wheels, 6 speaker Concert Sound II system, dual lighted visor vanity mirrors, air filtration system, group package, tachometer, trunk convenience net, accent paint stripes, AM/FM stereo radio with CD and cassette players, steering wheel radio controls, pass-key III theft-deterrent system, power passenger seat, OnStar global positioning system, electrochromic inside rearview mirror, integral compass, rain sensing windshield wipers and universal transmitter.		
1SE	Limited Prestige Package (Limited)	NC	NC
	Includes power driver seat, AM/FM stereo radio with CD and cassette players, power passenger seat, electrochromic inside rearview mirror, integral compass, rain sensing windshield wipers, traction control, driver and passenger heated seats.		
A45	Memory Driver's Seat (Limited)	163	190
	Includes memory for outside mirrors, climate control and radio presets and parallel park assist.		
AG2	Power Passenger Seat (Custom)	284	330
	NOT AVAILABLE with 1SA. INCLUDED in 1SE.		
CF5	Electric Sliding Sunroof (Limited)	899	1045
K05	Engine Block Heater	30	35
KA1	Driver and Passenger Heated Seats (Custom)	224	260
	Includes dual electrochromic power heated mirrors. REQUIRES Nuance Leather Seat Trim and (AG2 or 1SE). NOT AVAILABLE with 1SA.		
N66	Wheels: 16" Cross Lace Aluminum	142	165
	Includes P225/60R16 RADIAL A/S BW tires. NOT AVAILABLE with Y56, PF7, 1SA.		

LESABRE / PARK AVENUE — BUICK

CODE	DESCRIPTION	INVOICE	MSRP
NW9	Traction Control (Custom)	150	175
	NOT AVAILABLE with 1SA. INCLUDED in 1SE.		
PF7	Wheels: 15" Multi-Spoke Aluminum	NC	NC
	NOT AVAILABLE with N66, Y56, 1SA, T1U.		
R6M	New Jersey Cost Surcharge	46	NC
T1U	Driver Confidence Package (Limited)	628	730
	Includes EyeCue head up display and StabiliTrak. NOT AVAILABLE with PF7.		
T1U	Driver Confidence Package (Limited)	757	880
	Includes EyeCue head up display, Self-Sealing Radial tires and StabiliTrak. REQUIRES N66. NOT AVAILABLE with Y56, PF7.		
U1S	Trunk Mounted 12 Disc CD Changer (Limited)	512	595
	Includes remote.		
UP0	Radio: AM/FM Stereo with CD and Cassette (Custom)	172	200
	Includes auto tone control, seek/scan, clock, digital display, preset of 12 FM/6 AM stations, motorized volume control, auto CrO2 and Dolby B, preset scan, clean-tape-head indicator, radio monitor (allows radio to play while cassette player is fast forwarding/rewinding) and Theftlock and steering wheel radio controls. NOT AVAILABLE with 1SA. INCLUDED in 1SE.		
W02	Convenience Console	60	70
	Includes writing surface and cupholders, provisions for phone/fax and auxiliary 12V outlets (2). REQUIRES Nuance Leather Seat Trim. NOT AVAILABLE with 1SA.		
Y56	Gran Touring Package	202	235
	Includes 3.05 axle ratio, 16" alloy wheels, P225/60R16 SBR PLY touring BW tires, leather-wrapped steering wheel, rear stabilizer bar and magnetic variable effort steering. NOT AVAILABLE with N66, PF7, 1SA, T1U (Custom only).		
YF5	California Requirements	NC	NC

2001 PARK AVENUE

What's New?

Enjoying mild sales success since its 1997 redesign, Buick's full-size Park Avenue gets only minor refinements in the areas of safety, convenience and colors for 2001. The biggest news is the addition of the Ultrasonic Rear Park Assist system, improving safety while backing up.

Review

While the coupe segment is seeing a rebirth of sorts, nobody can argue with the viability of a well-executed, fully equipped large sedan in today's market. Clean design is the first thing you notice about the Park Avenue. Classy and dignified, there are no tacky add-ons or exaggerated styling themes here. Sure, a coupe this big would look downright silly (did somebody say Riviera?), but a sedan body looks right at home on this massive platform.

Powertrains for 2001 remain unchanged, and that's not a bad thing. GM's award-winning 3800 Series II V6 provides V8-like

BUICK

PARK AVENUE

power. The 240-horsepower supercharged version is a joy. Luckily, it comes standard on the Ultra, which, when fully loaded, tips the scales at a hefty two tons.

There are two trim levels, the well-equipped base Park Avenue, and the upscale Ultra model. A variety of goodies are standard or optional on either, such as rain-sensing wipers and a heads-up display that projects speed, turn signals, high beams and idiot lights onto the bottom of the windshield. There are also the "prestige" and "convenience plus" option packages, as well as a "gran touring" package, which adds programmable-effort steering, a beefier suspension, larger brake rotors, 16-inch alloy wheels riding on 225/60R16 blackwall tires and a leather-wrapped steering wheel.

Topping the list of improvements for 2001 is Ultrasonic Rear Park Assist, an advanced integrated vehicle parking distance system, which is optional on Ultra and prestige package-equipped vehicles. The system helps the driver to judge the distance between the rear of the vehicle and objects behind the car. Safety is further enhanced with standard seat-mounted side airbags for the driver and right-front passenger, and rear child seat-tether anchors. As on most premium GM models, the OnStar mobile communications system is standard on the Ultra and available on the base model.

Standard Equipment

BASE (4A): 3.8L V6 OHV SMPI 12-valve engine; 4-speed electronic OD automatic transmission with lock-up torque converter; 690 amp battery with run down protection; front-wheel drive, 3.05 axle ratio; stainless steel exhaust; comfort ride suspension, auto-leveling suspension, front independent strut suspension with anti-roll bar, front coil springs, rear independent strut suspension with anti-roll bar, rear coil springs; rack-and-pinion power steering; 4-wheel antilock disc brakes; 18.5 gal. capacity fuel tank; side impact bars; class I trailering; front and rear body-colored bumpers with chrome bumper insert, with body-colored rub strip; body-colored bodyside molding with chrome bodyside insert, rocker panel extensions; clearcoat monotone paint with bodyside accent stripe; aero-composite halogen fully auto headlamps with daytime running lights, delay-off feature; additional exterior lights include cornering lights, underhood light; driver's and passenger's power remote body-colored folding outside mirrors; 16" x 6.5" silver alloy wheels; P225/60SR16 BSW A/S tires; compact steel spare wheel; dual zone front air conditioning with climate control, steering wheel temperature controls, air filter, rear heat ducts; AM/FM stereo radio, clock, seek-scan, cassette player, 6 performance speakers, auto equalizer, theft deterrent, window grid antenna, radio steering wheel controls; cruise control; power door locks with 2-stage unlock, remote keyless entry, child safety rear door locks, power remote trunk release, power remote fuel door release; 2 power accessory outlets, front lighter element(s), driver's foot rest, retained accessory power, smoker's package; instrumentation display includes tachometer, water temperature gauge, exterior temp, trip odometer; warning indicators include oil pressure, water temp, battery, lights on, key in ignition, low fuel, brake fluid, turn signal on; driver's and passenger's front airbags, driver's and front passenger's seat-mounted side airbags; ignition disable, panic alarm, security system; tinted windows, power front and rear windows with driver's 1-touch down function; variable intermittent front windshield wipers, sun visor strip, rear window defroster; seating capacity of 6, 45/45 split-bench front seat with power adjustable headrests, center armrest with storage, driver's and passenger's seats include 8-way power adjustment; rear bench seat with fixed headrests, center pass-thru armrest with storage; front height adjustable seatbelts; leather seats, leatherette door trim insert with carpet lower, full cloth headliner, full carpet floor covering with carpeted floor mats, simulated wood dashboard insert, simulated wood door panel insert; interior lights include dome light with fade, front and rear reading lights, 4 door curb lights, illuminated entry; leather-wrapped steering wheel with tilt adjustment; dual illuminated vanity mirrors, dual auxiliary visors; day/night rearview mirror; mini overhead console with storage, locking glove box with light, front and rear cupholders, 2 seatback storage pockets, driver's and passenger's door bins; carpeted cargo floor, cargo net, cargo light; chrome grille, chrome side window moldings, black front windshield molding, black rear window molding and body-colored door handles.

ULTRA (4A) (in addition to or instead of BASE (4A) equipment): 3.8L V6 OHV SMPI supercharger 12-valve engine (requires premium unleaded fuel); traction control, 2.93 axle ratio; electronic

PARK AVENUE — BUICK

CODE	DESCRIPTION	INVOICE	MSRP

stability; rack-and-pinion power steering with vehicle speed-sensing assist; driver's and passenger's body-colored heated folding outside mirrors, driver's power remote auto dimming outside mirror, passenger's power remote outside mirror with tilt down; cassette player, single CD player, 9 performance speakers, amplifier; cell phone pre-wiring, garage door opener, emergency S.O.S. (OnStar); instrumentation display includes compass, systems monitor, trip computer; warning indicators include low oil level, low coolant, low washer fluid, bulb failure, door ajar, trunk ajar, service interval, low tire pressure; tracker system; rain detecting wipers; heated-cushion driver's and passenger's seats with power adjustable tilt headrests, driver's and passenger's power 4-way lumbar support; rear bench seat with tilt headrests; driver's seat memory includes 2 settings for exterior mirrors and headrests; auto-dimming day/night rearview mirror; rear illuminated vanity mirror and carpeted trunk lid.

Base Prices

Code	Description	Invoice	MSRP
4CW69	Base (4A)	29847	32980
4CU69	Ultra (4A)	33928	37490
	Destination Charge:	720	720

Interested in seeing what dealers will sell this vehicle for? Check out our True Market Value^{sm} (TMV^{sm}) pricing on our Web site at www.edmunds.com.

Accessories

Code	Description	Invoice	MSRP
1SA	Base Option Package 1SA (Base)	NC	NC
	Includes AM/FM stereo radio, cassette player, auto tone control, rear seat storage armrest and leather seat trim. NOT AVAILABLE with Y56, CF5, U1S, UV6, UD7.		
1SE	Prestige Option Package 1SE (Base)	1455	1692
	Includes driver information center, electrochromic outside driver mirror, electrochromic interior rearview mirror, power driver's seat with memory, universal transmitter, driver and passenger 4-way power lumbar, moisture-sensing delay wipers, AM/FM stereo radio, CD player, cassette player, auto tone control, three note horn, rear seat storage armrest, On-Star system and leather seat trim.		
1SE	Ultra Prestige Option Package 1SE (Ultra)	NC	NC
	Includes driver information center, AM/FM stereo radio, CD player, cassette player, auto tone control, three note horn, traction control system, stabilitrak, heated front seats, rear seat storage armrest, Concert Sound III and leather seat trim.		
93U	Paint: White Diamond	387	450
	NOT AVAILABLE with 1SA.		
CF5	Electric Sliding & Tilting Sunroof	942	1095
	NOT AVAILABLE with 1SA.		
JL4	StabiliTrak (Base)	426	495
	Includes auto yaw rate correction system. NOT AVAILABLE with 1SA.		
K05	Electric Engine Block Heater	30	35
KA1	Heated Front Seats (Base)	194	225
NW9	Full Range Traction Control (Base)	150	175
	NOT AVAILABLE with 1SA.		
P05	Wheels: 16" Chrome Plated	632	735
	NOT AVAILABLE with Y56.		
U1S	12-Disc Trunk-Mounted Remote CD Changer	512	595
	REQUIRES 1SE. NOT AVAILABLE with 1SA.		

BUICK   PARK AVENUE / REGAL

CODE	DESCRIPTION	INVOICE	MSRP
U99	Concert Sound III (Base)	241	280
	NOT AVAILABLE with 1SA.		
UD7	Ultrasonic Rear Park Assist	254	295
	Includes sensor indicator. REQUIRES UV6. NOT AVAILABLE with 1SA.		
UP0	Radio: AM/FM Stereo with CD, Cass, Automatic Tone Control (Base)	172	200
	Includes power-loading CD and cassette player with next/last CD track selector, seek/scan, auto tone control, clock and steering wheel radio controls. INCLUDED in 1SE.		
UV6	EyeCue Head-Up Display	236	275
	REQUIRES UD7. NOT AVAILABLE with 1SA.		
W02	5 Person Seating Package (Ultra)	159	185
	Includes 45/45 10-way power split-frame seats convenience console with writing surface, dual cup holder, dual auxiliary power outlets and bi-level rear-seat Comfort Temp, convenience console package and dual auxiliary power outlets.		
Y56	Gran Touring Suspension Package (Base)	245	285
	Includes 16" alloy wheels and P225/60R16 touring BW tires. REQUIRES 1SE. NOT AVAILABLE with 1SA, P05.		
Y56	Gran Touring Suspension Package (Ultra)	172	200
	Includes 16" alloy wheels, leather-wrapped steering wheel and P225/60R16 touring BW tires. NOT AVAILABLE with P05.		

2001 REGAL

What's New?

For the 2001 model year, the "Car for the Supercharged Family" gets new rear-wheel house liners for a quieter ride, a standard trunk entrapment release and two new colors, Graphite Metallic and "White". An Olympic appearance package is now available and OnStar in-vehicle safety, security and information service is standard on GS models.

Review

Back in 1997, Buick released a new Regal Sedan. The slow-selling coupe was dropped, leaving LS and GS versions of the four-door. This new Regal was larger in nearly every dimension, and was designed to reduce squeaks and rattles by increasing structural rigidity with one-piece side-panel stampings and cross bracing behind the instrument panel. A full load of standard equipment and reasonable prices have made this front-drive Regal competitive, and it continues to entice buyers who might normally limit themselves to Toyota or Nissan showrooms to at least visit a Buick store.

Think of the Regal as "Park Avenue Light," or "Century Deluxe." LS models are powered by GM's award-winning 3800 Series II V6, which boasts an even 200 horses. Move up to the GS, and you're getting an honest-to-goodness sport sedan equipped with a supercharged 3.8-liter V6 putting 240 horsepower through a heavy-duty version of Regal's four-speed automatic transmission. With a starting price of around $25,000, the suave, speedy Regal GS makes an excellent argument against purchasing any other sporty midsize V6 sedan.

REGAL — BUICK

Basic design is shared with the lower-rung Century. Regal has a unique front fascia, but barely different rear styling. LS versions are distinguished by a chrome-accented grille, while GS models have a body-colored grille and P225/60R16 radials mounted on 16-inch alloy wheels (chrome is an option).

Inside, a comfortable interior beckons, which features a split-folding rear seat to make hauling long items such as skis and fishing rods easier and more convenient. A 220-watt Monsoon audio system with eight speakers is also optional on GS models. Heated leather seats are again available, and with leather comes the option of a side airbag for the driver.

One thing this Buick offers that few in its class can is the availability of OnStar, an optional mobile communications system formerly available only on Cadillac models. The system is standard on the GS model and optional on the LS. OnStar provides a hands-free link to real-time, person-to-person in-vehicle safety, security and information services from GM's 24-hour, seven-day-a-week OnStar Center. The three-button system eliminates the need for a customer to buy separate cellular phone service to access OnStar services.

The Regal GS comes equipped with full-range traction control, which uses the ABS and engine controls to reduce traction loss on slippery surfaces. Engine modulation provides traction-control assistance on LS versions. Four-wheel antilock disc brakes are standard on both models. An exceptional array of standard features and option packages make the LS a smart choice among premium midsize sedans.

Despite recent efforts to establish strong GM brand identities for each division, sharing platforms between multiple divisions is likely to continue to be a problem. Pontiac's Grand Prix and Oldsmobile's Intrigue share Regal's underpinnings and basic structure. Grand Prix is obviously the driver's car with a youthful image and the "We Build Excitement" marketing theme. Intrigue is gracefully styled and import-oriented. So where does that leave the conservative Buick Regal? Buick officials say the Regal is targeted at 40- to 49-year-olds with families who want a blend of performance, dependability and safety. Basically, Buick is going after the kinds of buyers who snap up thousands of Camrys every year.

The Camry is plainly styled, like the Regal. The Camry is a roomy, safe car, like the Regal. The Camry also has an outstanding reputation for reliability and resale value. Can the Regal compete in this arena as well? Given Buick's penchant for award-winning quality and continued refinement, we wouldn't be too surprised. For now, rest assured that the Regal is an excellent value, and with 240 supercharged horses under the hood, the GS model easily gets our nod.

Standard Equipment

LS (4A): 3.8L V6 OHV SMPI 12-valve engine; 4-speed electronic OD automatic transmission with lock-up torque converter; battery with run down protection; 690 amp battery, 102 amp alternator; front-wheel drive, traction control, 3.05 axle ratio; stainless steel exhaust with tailpipe finisher; front independent strut suspension with anti-roll bar, front coil springs, rear independent strut suspension with anti-roll bar, rear coil springs; rack-and-pinion power steering with vehicle speed-sensing assist; 4-wheel antilock disc brakes; 17.5 gal. capacity fuel tank; side impact bars; class I trailering; front and rear body-colored bumpers with body-colored rub strip, black bumper insert; body-colored bodyside molding with black bodyside insert, body-colored bodyside cladding; clearcoat monotone paint; aero-composite halogen fully auto headlamps with daytime running lights, delay-off feature; additional exterior lights include cornering lights, front fog/driving lights, underhood light; driver's and passenger's power remote body-colored heated folding outside mirrors; 15" x 6" steel wheels; P215/70SR15 BSW A/S tires; compact steel spare wheel; dual zone front air conditioning, air filter, rear heat ducts; AM/FM stereo radio, clock, seek-scan, cassette player, 6 performance speakers, auto equalizer, theft deterrent, window grid antenna; cruise control; power door locks with 2-stage unlock, remote keyless entry, child safety rear door locks, power remote hatch/trunk release; 2 power accessory outlets, front lighter element(s), driver's foot rest, retained accessory power, smoker's package; instrumentation display includes tachometer, water temperature gauge, trip odometer; warning indicators include oil pressure, water temp, battery, low oil level, low coolant, lights on, key in ignition, low fuel, low washer fluid, door ajar, trunk ajar, service interval, turn signal on, low tire pressure; driver's and passenger's front airbags; ignition disable, panic alarm; tinted windows, power front and rear windows with driver's 1-touch down function; variable intermittent front

BUICK

REGAL

CODE	DESCRIPTION	INVOICE	MSRP

windshield wipers, sun visor strip, rear window defroster; seating capacity of 5, front bucket seats with adjustable headrests, center armrest with storage, driver's seat includes 6-way power adjustment, 8-way adjustment, passenger's seat includes 4-way adjustment; 60/40 folding rear bench seat with fixed headrests, center armrest with storage; front height adjustable seatbelts; cloth seats, vinyl door trim insert, full cloth headliner, full carpet floor covering, leather-wrapped gearshift knob, simulated wood door panel insert, simulated wood console insert; interior lights include dome light with fade, front reading lights, 2 door curb lights, illuminated entry; leather-wrapped steering wheel with tilt adjustment; vanity mirrors, dual auxiliary visors; day/night rearview mirror; full floor console, locking glove box with light, front and rear cupholders, 2 seatback storage pockets, driver's and passenger's door bins, rear door bins; carpeted cargo floor, cargo light; body-colored grille, chrome side window moldings, black front windshield molding, black rear window molding and body-colored door handles.

GS (4A) (in addition to or instead of LS (4A) equipment): 3.8L V6 OHV SMPI supercharger 12-valve engine (requires premium unleaded fuel); 770 amp battery; 2.93 axle ratio; touring ride suspension; clearcoat lower accent two-tone paint; 16" x 6.5" silver alloy wheels; P225/60SR16 BSW touring A/S tires; climate control air conditioning; single CD; emergency S.O.S. (OnStar); instrumentation display includes trip computer; seat mounted driver's side airbag; tracker system; leather seats, leatherette door trim insert, carpeted floor mats; rear reading lights; dual illuminated vanity mirrors; cargo net and black side window moldings.

Base Prices

4WB69	LS (4A)	....	20903	22845
4WF69	GS (4A)	....	23877	26095
Destination Charge:		....	610	610

Interested in seeing what dealers will sell this vehicle for? Check out our True Market Value^{sm} (TMV^{sm}) pricing on our Web site at www.edmunds.com.

Accessories

—	Leather Seat Trim (LS)	....	684	795
	Includes side airbag for driver. NOT AVAILABLE with 1SA. INCLUDED in 1SC, 1SD, 1SE, 1SF.			
1SA	Standard Package (LS)	....	NC	NC
	Includes vehicle with standard equipment. NOT AVAILABLE with PW8, Y56, PYO, CF5, KA1.			
1SB	Premium Package (LS)	....	354	412
	Includes front carpet savers, rear carpet savers, trunk convenience net, dual illuminated visor mirrors, AM/FM stereo radio, CD player, cassette player. NOT AVAILABLE with Y56, PYO, CF5, KA1.			
1SC	Luxury Package (LS)	....	1717	1997
	Includes front carpet savers, rear carpet savers, trunk convenience net, dual illuminated visor mirrors, AM/FM stereo radio, CD player, cassette player, 15" alloy wheels, Sierra-Grain leather seat trim, driver side air bag, electronic dual zone climate control, electrochromic inside rearview mirror, electrochromic outside rearview mirrors and steering wheel mounted radio controls. NOT AVAILABLE with PYO.			
1SD	Touring Package (LS)	....	2186	2542
	Includes front carpet savers, rear carpet savers, trunk convenience net, dual illuminated visor mirrors, AM/FM stereo radio, CD player, cassette player, Sierra-Grain leather seat trim, side air bag for driver, electronic dual zone climate control,			

REGAL — BUICK

CODE	DESCRIPTION	INVOICE	MSRP

electrochromic inside rearview mirror, electrochromic outside rearview mirrors, steering wheel mounted radio controls, Gran Touring package, Gran Touring suspension, P225/60R16 tires, 16" alloy wheels (4), monsoon 8-speaker system and diversity antenna. NOT AVAILABLE with PW8, PYO.

1SE * **Prestige Package (LS)** 2826 3286
Includes front carpet savers, rear carpet savers, trunk convenience net, dual illuminated visor mirrors, AM/FM stereo radio, CD player, cassette player, Sierra-Grain leather seat trim, side air bag for driver, electronic dual zone climate control, electrochromic inside rearview mirror, electrochromic outside rearview mirrors, steering wheel mounted radio controls, Gran Touring package, Gran Touring suspension, P225/60R16 tires, 16" alloy wheels (4), monsoon 8-speaker system, diversity antenna, On-Star, 6-way power passenger seat and driver information center. NOT AVAILABLE with PW8.

1SG **Standard Package (GS)** .... NC NC
Includes vehicle with standard equipment. NOT AVAILABLE with PYO, CF5.

1SH **Luxury Package (GS)** 464 540
Includes steering wheel mounted radio controls, electrochromic inside rearview mirror, electrochromic outside rearview mirrors, Monsoon 8-speaker system and diversity antenna. NOT AVAILABLE with PYO, CF5.

1SJ **Prestige Package (GS)** 748 870
Includes steering wheel mounted radio controls, electrochromic inside rearview mirror, electrochromic outside rearview mirrors, Monsoon 8-speaker system, diversity antenna and 6-way power passenger seat.

1SN **LSE Package (LS)** 2576 2995
     Manufacturer Discount .... (430) (500)
     Net Price 2146 2495
Includes front carpet savers, rear carpet savers, dual illuminated visor vanity mirrors, AAM/FM stereo radio, CD player, cassette player, trunk convenience net, electronic dual zone climate control, steering wheel mounted radio controls, electrochromic inside rearview mirror, electrochromic outside rearview mirrors, sierra-grain leather seat trim, driver side impact air bag, Gran Touring package, Gran Touring suspension, P225/60R16 A/S TOURING BW tires, 16" aluminum wheels and LSE appearance package.

1SP **LSE Package (LS)** 2614 3040
     Manufacturer Discount .... (430) (500)
     Net Price 2184 2540
Includes front carpet savers, rear carpet savers, dual illuminated visor vanity mirrors, AM/FM stereo radio, CD player, cassette player, trunk convenience net, electronic dual zone climate control, steering wheel mounted radio controls, electrochromic inside rearview mirror, electrochromic outside rearview mirrors, sierra-grain leather seat trim, driver side impact air bag, Gran Touring package, Gran Touring suspension, P225/60R16 A/S TOURING BW tires, 16" aluminum wheels, LSE appearance package and electric sliding/tilting sunroof with sunshade. NOT AVAILABLE with PYO.

BUICK
REGAL

CODE	DESCRIPTION	INVOICE	MSRP
1SQ	LSE Package (LS)	3173	3690
	Manufacturer Discount	(430)	(500)
	Net Price	2743	3190

Includes front carpet savers, rear carpet savers, dual illuminated visor vanity mirrors, AM/FM stereo radio, CD player, cassette player, trunk convenience net, electronic dual zone climate control, steering wheel mounted radio controls, electrochromic inside rearview mirror, electrochromic outside rearview mirrors, sierra-grain leather seat trim, driver side impact air bag, Gran Touring package, Gran Touring suspension, P225/60R16 A/S TOURING BW tires, 16" aluminum wheels, LSE appearance package and electric sliding/tilting sunroof with sunshade.

1SR	GSE Package (GS)	2331	2710
	Manufacturer Discount	(430)	(500)
	Net Price	1901	2210

Includes front carpet savers, rear carpet savers, AM/FM stereo radio, CD player, cassette player, steering wheel mounted radio controls, electrochromic inside rearview mirror, electrochromic outside rearview mirrors, Sierra-grain leather seat trim, monsoon 8-speaker system, diversity antenna, 6-way power passenger seat, electric sliding/tilting sunroof with sunshade, rearview mirror with reading lights, 16" chrome-plated aluminum wheels and GSE appearance package.

CF5	Electric Sliding/Tilting Sunroof w/Sunshade	598	695

Includes sunshade. NOT AVAILABLE with 1SA, 1SB, 1SG, 1SH. INCLUDED in 1SK, 1SF.

K05	Engine Block Heater	30	35
KA1	Driver and Passenger Heated Seats	194	225

NOT AVAILABLE with 1SA, 1SB.

PW8	Wheels: 15" Aluminum (LS)	301	350

REQUIRES 1SB or 1SC. NOT AVAILABLE with PY0, Y56, 1SA, 1SD, 1SE, 1SF. INCLUDED in 1SC.

PY0	Wheels: 16" Chrome Aluminum	559	650

REQUIRES Y56 and (1SE or 1SJ). NOT AVAILABLE with PW8, 1SA, 1SB, 1SC, 1SD, 1SF, 1SG, 1SH, 1SK.

Y56	Gran Touring Package (LS)	516	600

Includes Gran Touring suspension, P225/60R16 AS Touring SBR BW tires and 16" alloy wheels (4). REQUIRES 1SC. NOT AVAILABLE with PW8, 1SA, 1SB. INCLUDED in 1SD, 1SE, 1SF.

CATERA
CADILLAC

| CODE | DESCRIPTION | INVOICE | MSRP |

2001 CATERA

What's New?

After mildly successful front and rear styling enhancements and a revised interior last year, the 2001 model year brings forth few changes for the Catera. OnStar 2.6 in-vehicle safety, security and information service, vented rear disc brakes and the Solar Protect windshield are now standard on all models. The Catera Sport receives new seats and projector beam headlamps are now standard on the base Catera.

Review

Cadillac was the first domestic luxury automaker to attack the entry-level market head-on with the introduction of the Catera. After its first full year on the market, Catera rolled up sales of 25,411 units, making it the most successful launch of an entry-luxury model in U.S. history to date. Based on the European-market Opel Omega MV6, the Catera features a 200-horsepower, 3.0-liter DOHC V6 engine mated to a four-speed automatic transmission and rear-wheel drive. Built in Russelsheim, Germany, the Catera is touted by Cadillac as a blend of the best of German and American engineering.

Alas, Cadillac encountered a number of stumbling blocks after the Catera's launch. First-year cars suffered serious electrical problems. An attempt to install standard side airbags in 1998 was a complete failure: thousands of Cateras sat in the dockyard for months waiting to have the flawed systems removed before finding their way to dealerships. In 1999, imports didn't begin until six months into the new model year when a redesigned fuel tank was deemed problematic. And last year wasn't any better when problems at the factory forced the delay of the 2000 version. Furthermore, despite rear-wheel drive and a powerful engine, Catera didn't appeal to enthusiast drivers who wanted a manual transmission.

After tidying up the design and fine-tuning the suspension last year, Cadillac continues attempts to remove the tarnish from the Catera nameplate by adding vented rear disc brakes, OnStar's new version 2.6 and a Solar Protect windshield to the Catera and Catera Sport.

Outside, the Catera's sheetmetal remains unchanged; The Catera Sport's cabin has been tweaked this year, downgrading the 10-way power driver's seat to an eight-way power seat that mirrors that of the passenger.

Standard Equipment

CATERA (4A): 3L V6 DOHC SMPI 24-valve engine (requires premium unleaded fuel); driver's selectable multi-mode 4-speed electronic OD automatic transmission with lock-up torque converter; 310 amp battery with run down protection; engine oil cooler; 120 amp alternator; rear-wheel drive, traction control, 3.90 axle ratio; dual stainless steel exhaust with tailpipe finisher; auto-leveling suspension, front independent strut suspension with anti-roll bar, front coil springs, rear independent multi-link suspension with anti-roll bar, rear coil springs; power recirculating ball steering with vehicle-speed-sensing assist; 4-wheel antilock disc brakes; 18 gal. capacity fuel tank; side impact bars; front and rear body-colored bumpers; body-colored bodyside molding; clearcoat monotone paint; projector beam halogen fully auto headlamps with daytime running lights, delay-off feature; additional exterior lights include cornering lights, front fog/driving lights; driver's and passenger's power remote body-colored heated folding outside mirrors; 16" x 7" silver alloy wheels; P225/55HR16 BSW A/S tires; full-size steel spare wheel; dual-zone front air conditioning with climate control, air filter, rear heat ducts; AM stereo/ FM stereo radio, clock, seek-scan feature, cassette player, 8 speakers, theft deterrent, window

CADILLAC — CATERA

grid diversity antenna, radio steering wheel controls; cruise control; power door locks with 2-stage unlock, remote keyless entry, child-safety rear door locks, power remote hatch/trunk release, power remote fuel door release; cell phone pre-wiring, 3 power accessory outlets, front and rear lighter element(s), driver's foot rest, retained accessory power, emergency S.O.S. (OnStar); instrumentation display includes tachometer, oil pressure gauge, water temperature gauge, volt gauge, exterior temp, trip odometer; warning indicators include oil pressure, battery, low oil level, low coolant, lights on, key in ignition, low fuel, low washer fluid, door ajar, trunk ajar, service interval, turn signal on; driver's and passenger's front airbags, driver's and front passenger's seat-mounted side airbags; ignition disable, tracker system; tinted windows, power front and rear windows with front and rear 1-touch down function; heated washer fluid jets variable intermittent front windshield wipers, sun visor strip, rear window defroster; seating capacity of 5, front bucket seats with adjustable headrests, center armrest with storage, driver's seat includes 8-way power adjustment, lumbar support, passenger's seat includes 2-way power adjustment, 6-way adjustment, lumbar support; 40/20/40 folding rear bench seat with adjustable headrests, center pass-thru armrest; front and rear height adjustable front seatbelts with pretensioners; leather seats, leatherette door trim insert with carpet lower, full cloth headliner, full carpet floor covering with carpeted floor mats, simulated wood door panel insert, simulated wood console insert, chrome interior accents; interior lights include dome light with delay front and rear reading lights, 4 door curb lights, illuminated entry; leather-wrapped steering wheel with tilt adjustment; dual illuminated vanity mirrors, dual auxiliary visors; auto-dimming day/night rearview mirror; full floor console, locking glove box with light, front and rear cupholders, 2 seatback storage pockets, refrigerated/cooled box, driver's and passenger's door bins, rear door bins; carpeted cargo floor, carpeted trunk lid, cargo net, cargo tie downs, cargo light, concealed cargo storage; chrome grille, black side window moldings, black front windshield molding, black rear window molding and body-colored door handles.

Base Prices

Code	Description	Invoice	MSRP
6VR69	Catera (4A)	29112	31305
	Destination Charge:	640	640

Interested in seeing what dealers will sell this vehicle for? Check out our True Market Value^{sm} (TMV^{sm}) pricing on our Web site at www.edmunds.com.

Accessories

Code	Description	Invoice	MSRP
CF5	Sunroof with Express Open	846	995
	Slightly reduces headroom.		
DE1	Power Rear Sunshade	251	295
KA1	Heated Front Seats	361	425
P05	Wheels: 16" Chrome	509	795
	NOT AVAILABLE with T24.		
T24	Sport Package	2134	2510
	Includes 8-way power passenger seat adjuster, 8-way power driver seat adjuster, memory package, audible theft-deterrent system, 3 channel garage door opener, rear spoiler, heated front seats, 17" alloy wheels, P235/45R17 A/S S BW tires, Xenon high intensity discharge headlamps and sport suspension. NOT AVAILABLE with P05, TW1.		
TW1	Equipment Group TW1	846	995
	Includes 8-way power passenger seat adjuster, 8-way power driver seat adjuster, memory package, audible theft-deterrent system and 3 channel garage door opener. NOT AVAILABLE with T24.		

CATERA / DEVILLE

CADILLAC

CODE	DESCRIPTION	INVOICE	MSRP
UM5	Radio: Bose AM/FM Stereo with CD, Cassette	827	973
	Includes single-slot CD, weatherband, Radio Data System, digital signal processing, auto volume control, Theftlock and 8 speakers.		

2001 DEVILLE

What's New?

After a complete redesign last year, changes for 2001 are minimal at best. A tire pressure monitoring system is available, Graphite replaces Parisian Blue and Polo Green paint schemes, Dark Gray is added as an interior color and all Devilles are now certified throughout the U.S. as low-emissions vehicles.

Review

Cadillac's DeVille celebrated its 50th anniversary in the marketplace last year with a completely revamped car and the introduction of groundbreaking high-tech features.

This latest generation DeVille is evolutionary in design, yet is more than 2 inches shorter and narrower than its predecessor, giving it a slightly trimmer, cleaner look. The DeVille is available in three models: the base DeVille, a ritzy DeVille High Luxury Sedan (DHS) and a sporty, five-passenger DeVille Touring Sedan (DTS).

This year's car benefits from an optional tire pressure monitoring system. What's more, Cadillac's Northstar V8 has been certified as a low-emission vehicle (LEV) nationwide.

Night Vision is the first automotive application of thermal-imaging technology that helps drivers avoid collisions by enhancing their ability to detect objects well beyond the normal range of their headlights. Another DeVille "first" is the use of Ultrasonic Rear Parking Assist, which uses an array of four sensors to help the driver in parking maneuvers. Then there's StabiliTrak 2.0, the latest version of GM's highly acclaimed stability-control system. Enhanced last year with the addition of active steering effort compensation, which slightly increases turning effort during sudden maneuvers, and side-slip-rate control, the system responds to traction loss at all four wheels by gently applying both front brakes to help the driver regain control. In addition, the DeVille DTS features the second generation of Cadillac's continuously variable road-sensing suspension, called the CVRSS 2.0.

All DeVilles include leading-edge passive restraints, a CD-based navigation system and the OnStar communications system, as well as the industry's first light-emitting diode (LED) taillight and center high-mounted stoplight combination. Building on its reputation for comfort and convenience, the 2001 DeVille also offers such luxury touches as three-zone climate control, adaptive seating, massaging lumbar seats and a new center seat/storage system. Rear-seat passengers enjoy a theater seating layout (for optimum forward visibility), heated seats and power lumbar adjustments.

As Cadillac's flagship sedan, the DeVille is a sophisticated American luxury car that remains true to Cadillac's heritage, yet hints at the division's high-tech future. We think that mix will appeal to both the Town Car set and Cadillac purists alike.

CADILLAC — DEVILLE

| CODE | DESCRIPTION | INVOICE | MSRP |

Standard Equipment

BASE (4A): 4.6L V8 DQHC SMPI 32-valve engine requires premium unleaded fuel; 4-speed electronic OD automatic transmission with lock-up torque converter; battery with run down protection; 140 amp alternator; front-wheel drive, traction control, 3.11 axle ratio; stainless steel exhaust; comfort ride suspension, auto-leveling suspension, front independent strut suspension with anti-roll bar, front coil springs, rear independent multi-link suspension with anti-roll bar, rear coil springs; rack-and-pinion power steering with vehicle-speed-sensing assist; 4-wheel antilock disc brakes; 18.5 gal. capacity fuel tank; front license plate bracket, side impact bars; front and rear body-colored bumpers; body-colored bodyside moldings; clearcoat monotone paint; aero-composite halogen fully auto headlamps with daytime running lights, delay-off feature; additional exterior lights include cornering lights, underhood light; driver's and passenger's power remote body-colored heated folding outside mirrors, driver's auto-dimming outside mirror; 16" x 7" cast aluminum wheels; P225/60SR16 BSW A/S tires; compact steel spare wheel; dual-zone front air conditioning with climate control, rear air conditioning with separate controls, air filter, rear heat ducts; AM stereo/FM stereo radio, clock, seek-scan feature, cassette player, single-disc CD player, 8 speakers, theft deterrent, window grid diversity antenna, radio steering wheel controls; cruise control with steering wheel controls; power door locks with 2-stage unlock, remote keyless entry, child-safety rear door locks, power remote hatch/trunk release, power remote fuel door release; cell phone pre-wiring, front and rear lighter elements, 3 power accessory outlets, smokers' package, retained accessory power, driver's foot rest; emergency S.O.S. (OnStar); digital instrumentation display includes compass, exterior temp, systems monitor, trip computer, trip odometer; warning indicators include oil pressure, water temp, battery, lights on, key in ignition, low fuel, low washer fluid, door ajar, service interval; driver's and passenger's front airbags, driver's and front passenger's seat-mounted side airbags; ignition disable, panic alarm, tracker system, security system; tinted windows, power front and rear windows with front and rear 1-touch down function; variable intermittent front windshield wipers, sun visor strip, rear window defroster; seating capacity of 6, 40/20/40 split-bench front seat, adjustable tilt headrests, center armrest with storage, driver's seat and passenger's seat includes 8-way power adjustment; rear bench seat with fixed headrests, center pass-thru armrest with storage; front height adjustable seatbelts with pretensioners; cloth seats, cloth door trim insert, full cloth headliner, full color-keyed carpet floor covering with carpeted floor mats, simulated wood dashboard insert, simulated wood door panel insert, chrome interior accents; interior lights include dome light with fade, front and rear reading lights, 4 door curb lights, illuminated entry; leather-wrapped steering wheel with tilt adjustment; dual illuminated vanity mirrors, dual auxiliary visors; auto-dimming day/night rearview mirror; mini overhead console, locking glove box with light, front and rear cupholders, 2 seatback storage pockets, driver's and passenger's front/rear door bins; carpeted cargo floor, carpeted trunk lid, cargo net, cargo light; chrome grille, chrome side window moldings, black front windshield molding, black rear window molding and body-colored door handles.

DHS (4A) (in addition to or instead of BASE (4A) equipment): Passenger's power remote outside mirror with tilt down; 16" x 7" chrome cast aluminum wheels; premium AM stereo/FM stereo radio, 8 premium speakers; instrumentation display includes tachometer, water temperature gauge; sun blinds; rain detecting wipers, rear power blind; heated-cushion driver's and passenger's seats, massaging lumbar support; heated rear bench seat with fixed headrests; leather seats, leatherette door trim insert with carpet lower, genuine wood dashboard insert, wood gearshift knob, genuine wood door panel insert; driver's seat memory includes 2 settings for exterior mirrors, steering wheel; leather-wrapped/genuine wood steering wheel with power tilt and telescopic adjustment; rear illuminated vanity mirror and carpeted cargo mats.

DTS (4A) (in addition to or instead of DHS (4A) equipment): 4.6L V8 DOHC SMPI 32-valve engine (requires premium unleaded fuel); 3.71 axle ratio; auto ride control, adaptive auto-leveling suspension, electronic stability; additional exterior lights include front fog/driving lights; 17" x 7.5" cast aluminum wheels; P235/55HR17 BSW performance A/S tires; seating capacity of 5, front 40/40 bucket seats; genuine wood console insert; leather-wrapped steering wheel with tilt adjustment; full floor console and mini overhead console with storage.

DEVILLE / ELDORADO — CADILLAC

CODE	DESCRIPTION	INVOICE	MSRP

Base Prices

6KD69	Base (4A)	37208	40495
6KE69	DHS (4A)	42489	46267
6KF69	DTS (4A)	42489	46267
Destination Charge:		720	720

Interested in seeing what dealers will sell this vehicle for? Check out our True Market Value^{sm} (TMV^{sm}) pricing on our Web site at www.edmunds.com.

Accessories

CODE	DESCRIPTION	INVOICE	MSRP
—	Nuance Leather Seat Trim (Base)	667	785
86U	Paint: Crimson Pearl	552	650
93U	Paint: White Diamond	552	650
AC9	Front Adaptive Seats (DHS/DTS)	846	995
	Eliminates massaging lumbar. REQUIRES WA9.		
AW9	Rear Seat Side Airbags	251	295
CF5	Sunroof with Express Open	1318	1550
	Slightly reduces headroom.		
N30	Wood Trim Package (DTS)	506	595
	Includes wood steering wheel and wood shifter.		
N94	Wheels: 17" Chrome (DTS)	509	795
QC6	Wheels: 16" Chrome (Base)	509	795
U1Z	6 Disc CD Changer	506	595
UV2	Night Vision (DHS/DTS)	1912	2250
	REQUIRES WA8.		
UV8	Fully Integrated Hands-Free Portable Phone	574	675
UY4	On-Board CD-ROM Based Navigation System (DHS/DTS)	1696	1995
	Includes Bose premium audio system. REQUIRES U1Z.		
WA7	Comfort/Convenience Package (Base)	931	1095
	Includes 4-way power lumbar support, memory package, trunk mat, heated front and rear seats.		
WA8	Safety/Security Package (Base, DHS)	888	1045
	Includes StabiliTrak 2.0, ultrasonic rear parking assist, 3 channel garage door opener and low tire pressure indicator.		
WA8	Safety/Security Package (DTS)	468	550
	Includes ultrasonic rear parking assist, 3 channel garage door opener and low tire pressure indicator.		
WA9	Comfort/Convenience Package (DTS)	591	695
	Includes memory package, trunk mat, power tilt and telescopic steering wheel.		

2001 ELDORADO

What's New?

Only three minor changes grace the Eldorado for 2001: Sequoia is added for an exterior color, Dark Gray is added for the interior and the Bose sound system with mini disc player goes away.

CADILLAC — *ELDORADO*

Review

One of the models that lured Cadillac back from the brink of becoming hopelessly behind the times was the current edition of the Eldorado. Introduced in 1992 to critical acclaim, and then substantially improved with the introduction of the Northstar V8 in 1993, the Eldorado (along with its sister car, the Seville) has helped bolster Cadillac's future.

While Eldorado lays claim to being the best-selling prestige luxury coupe in the United States, that's not saying a whole lot. In the wake of the deaths of the Lincoln Mark VIII and Buick Riviera, the Eldorado is currently the only luxury coupe built in North America. Consequently, some auto analysts have been crowing about the demise of the Eldo, but Cadillac insiders insist an all-new Eldorado with rear-wheel-drive and a smaller body will appear in the near future.

Meanwhile, traditional luxo-coupe buyers can contemplate the big, front-drive 2001 models, which gain revamped engines and minor exterior tweaks. Both of Cadillac's 4.6-liter Northstar V8s (the 275-horsepower version in Eldorado and the 300-horse motor in the ETC) were redesigned last year from the inside out to achieve better mileage with regular fuel, smoother and quieter operation, and certification as a low-emission vehicle (LEV) in some states.

MagnaSteer variable-effort steering gear is standard. Optional on the base car and standard on the Touring Coupe is StabiliTrak, which includes stability enhancement and road texture detection. Stability enhancement is designed to correct skids automatically, allowing the Eldorado to better respond to driver inputs. Road texture detection reads the road surface, leading to better antilock brake performance.

The Eldorado's interior is rich with leather and wood. ETC models have memory systems that recall rearview mirror positions, climate-control settings, or even what CD and song the driver was listening to last. Standard is GM's new, three-button OnStar system that is now integrated into the Eldo's rearview mirror, eliminating the need for a separate cellular phone. With OnStar, a driver can alert emergency personnel to an exact location or simply get travel directions. The system can even track your Eldo if it's stolen, or locate the nearest ATM.

While today's Eldorado is on the bulky side and as gizmo-laden as they come, it still has a distinctive look and a wonderful engine, especially in ETC guise. Sure, the luxury SUV craze is killing off cars of this ilk, but we wouldn't be surprised to see an SUV backlash in the coming years, and comfy coupes like this Caddy may likely lead a truck-weary market charge back to cars.

Standard Equipment

ESC (4A): 4.6L V8 DOHC SMPI 32-valve engine (requires premium unleaded fuel); 4-speed electronic OD automatic transmission with lock-up torque converter; 770 amp battery with run down protection; 140 amp alternator; front-wheel drive, traction control, 3.11 axle ratio; stainless steel exhaust with tailpipe finisher; comfort ride suspension, auto-leveling suspension, front independent strut suspension with anti-roll bar, front coil springs, rear independent long & short control arm suspension with anti-roll bar, rear coil springs; rack-and-pinion power steering with vehicle-speed-sensing assist; 4-wheel antilock disc brakes; 19 gal. capacity fuel tank; front license plate bracket, side impact bars; front and rear body-colored bumpers with chrome bumper insert; body-colored bodyside molding with chrome bodyside insert; clearcoat monotone paint; aero-composite halogen fully auto headlamps with daytime running lights, delay-off feature; additional exterior lights include cornering lights, front fog/driving lights, underhood light; driver's and passenger's power remote body-colored heated folding outside mirrors, driver's auto-dimming outside mirror; 16" x 7" cast aluminum wheels; P225/60SR16 BSW A/S tires; compact steel spare wheel; dual-zone front air conditioning with climate control, rear heat

ELDORADO
CADILLAC

CODE	DESCRIPTION	INVOICE	MSRP

ducts; premium AM/FM stereo radio, seek-scan feature, cassette player, CD changer pre-wiring, 6 speakers, theft deterrent, power retractable antenna, radio steering wheel controls; cruise control; power door locks with 2-stage unlock, remote keyless entry, power remote hatch/trunk release, power remote fuel door release; cell phone pre-wiring, 2 power accessory outlets, front and rear lighter element(s), retained accessory power, smoker's' package, emergency S.O.S. (OnStar); instrumentation display includes tachometer, water temperature gauge, in-dash clock, compass, exterior temp, systems monitor, trip computer, trip odometer; warning indicators include oil pressure, water temp, battery, lights on, key in ignition, low fuel, low washer fluid, door ajar, trunk ajar, service interval, turn signal on; driver's and passenger's front airbags; ignition disable, tracker system, security system; tinted windows with driver's 1-touch down function; variable intermittent speed front windshield wipers, sun visor strip, rear window defroster; seating capacity of 5, front bucket seats with adjustable tilt headrests, center armrest with storage, driver and passenger seats include 8-way power adjustment; rear bench seat with 2 fixed headrests, center armrest with storage; front seatbelts with pretensioners; leather seats, leatherette door trim insert, full cloth headliner, full carpet floor covering with carpeted floor mats, genuine wood dashboard insert, leather-wrapped gearshift knob, genuine wood door panel insert, chrome interior accents; interior lights include dome light with delay front and rear reading lights, 2 door curb lights, illuminated entry; leather-wrapped steering wheel with tilt adjustment; dual illuminated vanity mirrors, dual auxiliary visors; auto-dimming day/night rearview mirror; full floor console, mini overhead console with storage, locking glove box with light, front and rear cupholders, 2 seatback storage pockets, driver's and passenger's door bins; carpeted cargo floor, carpeted trunk lid, carpeted cargo mats, cargo net, cargo light; chrome grille, chrome side window moldings, black front windshield molding, black rear window molding and body-colored door handles.

ETC (4A) (in addition to or instead of ESC (4A) equipment): 3.71 axle ratio; touring-ride suspension, auto ride control, stability control (StabiliTrak); passenger's power remote outside mirror with tilt down; P235/60HR16 BSW A/S tires; premium AM stereo/FM stereo radio, cassette player, single-disc CD player, 4 premium speakers; rain detecting wipers, driver and passenger seats include 8-way power adjustment with power 4-way lumbar support, heated cushion; genuine wood console insert; driver's seat memory includes 2 settings for exterior mirrors and body-colored grille.

Base Prices

6EL57	ESC (4A)	36788	40036
6ET57	ETC (4A)	40059	43611
Destination Charge:		720	720

Interested in seeing what dealers will sell this vehicle for? Check out our True Market Value^{sm} (TMV^{sm}) pricing on our Web site at www.edmunds.com.

Accessories

86U	Paint: Crimson Pearl	552	650
93U	Paint: White Diamond	552	650
CF5	Sunroof with Express Open	1318	1550
	Deletes sunglass storage compartment and slightly reduces headroom.		
JL4	StabiliTrak (ESC)	421	495
N26	Wheels: 16" Chrome (ETC)	509	795
N30	Wood Steering Wheel	336	395
QC8	Wheels: 16" Chrome (ESC)	509	795
QDC	Tires: P235/60ZR16 Goodyear LS (ETC)	212	250
	Tires are Z-rated blackwall.		

CADILLAC — ELDORADO / SEVILLE

CODE	DESCRIPTION	INVOICE	MSRP
U1S	12 Disc Trunk-Mounted CD Changer	506	595
UG1	Programmable 3-Channel Garage Door Opener	91	107
UM5	Radio: Bose Sound System with CD, Cassette (ESC)	1036	1219
	Includes AM/FM stereo, single slot CD, weather band, digital signal processing, radio data system, Theftlock and 4-speaker Bose acoustic system.		
WA7	ESC Comfort/Convenience Package (ESC)	808	950
	Includes driver and passenger 4-way power lumbar, memory package and heated front seats.		

2001 SEVILLE

What's New?

Tire pressure monitoring is now available on the STS, as well as an e-mail-capable Infotainment radio, a hands-free integrated cellular phone, 17-inch chrome wheels and high-intensity discharge headlamps. OnStar in-vehicle safety, security and information service is now standard fare on the STS and available on the SLS. Two new SLS and three STS packages round out the changes.

Review

The world premiere of the 1998 Seville was held in September of '97 at the Frankfurt International Auto Show to emphasize the car's global focus. The first Cadillac ever to debut outside the United States, the Seville embodies not only the best America has to offer, but in many respects the best of what the world has to offer, too.

For 2001, Cadillac has extended the gadget and package lists that include options to fit nearly any Seville buyer's desire. The SLS Luxury package includes heated front and rear seats, a tilt/telescoping power steering wheel and the memory package. The Premium SLS luxury package adds a Bose stereo, 16-inch chrome wheels and Ultrasonic rear park assist. Moving to the STS and checking the Luxury package adds all items above, plus a six-disc CD changer and the wood trim package. The STS Premium Luxury Package adds high-intensity discharge headlamps, tire pressure monitoring and trades the 16-inch wheels for larger 17-inch chrome numbers. You can also go for the gusto with the STS Premium Performance Package, which adds an express-open sunroof, an e-mail-capable Infotainment radio and an integrated, hands-free cellular phone.

Both the Seville STS and SLS come standard with the latest version of StabiliTrak, which adds side slip-rate control and active steering effort compensation to an already impressive computer-controlled traction system. Also standard is the next generation of Cadillac's Continuously Variable Road-Sensing Suspension (CVRSS), which GM engineers say now includes inputs for transient roll control, lateral support and stability control interaction from StabiliTrak 2.0.

Inside, there's luxurious leather appointments (Zebrano wood trim is available) and an ergonomically functional control panel highlighted by electro-luminescent analog gauges as well as a driver information system. A heated seat is part of an adaptive seating package available on both models that uses a network of inflatable air cells installed in the seat cushion, seatback and side bolsters to adjust comfort and support. You can even opt for massaging

SEVILLE — CADILLAC

lumbar seats on the STS. Interior storage is outstanding, with a roomy glovebox, clamshell-design center armrest console, and a rear-seat pass-through.

Other notable features include a new airbag suppression system that uses sensors to determine if the front-passenger airbag should be disabled because the seat is either vacant or being occupied by a small child. Also new this year is an ultrasonic rear parking assist feature and GM's three-button OnStar communications service as standard equipment, and an optional advanced navigation system.

We could go on and on about other technology, such as the transmission's Performance Algorithm Shifting feature, or the Magnasteer variable-assist, speed-sensitive power rack-and pinion unit, or the road-texture detection system, or the advanced radio data system stereo and any number of other Seville goodies, but space is limited. What we have here is an outstanding example of American design and engineering excellence.

Standard Equipment

SLS (4A): 4.6L V8 DOHC SMPI 32-valve engine (requires premium unleaded fuel); 4-speed electronic OD automatic transmission with lock-up torque converter; 770 amp battery with run down protection; 138 amp alternator; front-wheel drive, traction control, 3.11 axle ratio; stainless steel exhaust with tailpipe finisher; comfort ride suspension, auto-leveling suspension, electronic stability control, front independent strut suspension with anti-roll bar, front coil springs, rear independent multi-link suspension with anti-roll bar, rear coil springs; rack-and-pinion power steering with vehicle-speed-sensing assist; 4-wheel antilock disc brakes; 18.5 gal. capacity fuel tank; front license plate bracket, rear lip spoiler, side impact bars; front and rear body-colored bumpers; body-colored bodyside molding; clearcoat monotone paint; projector beam halogen fully auto headlamps with daytime running lights, delay-off feature; additional exterior lights include cornering lights, underhood light; driver's and passenger's power remote body-colored heated folding outside mirrors, driver's auto-dimming outside mirror; 16" x 7" silver cast aluminum wheels; P235/60SR16 BSW A/S tires; compact steel spare wheel; dual-zone front air conditioning with climate control, air filter, rear heat ducts; premium AM stereo/FM stereo radio, clock, seek-scan feature, cassette player, single-disc CD player, 8 speakers, amplifier, theft deterrent, window grid diversity antenna, radio steering wheel controls; cruise control with steering wheel controls; power door locks with 2-stage unlock, remote keyless entry, child-safety rear door locks, power remote hatch/trunk release, power remote fuel door release; cell phone pre-wiring, 2 power accessory outlets, driver's foot rest, retained accessory power, garage door opener, emergency S.O.S. (OnStar); instrumentation display includes tachometer, water temperature gauge, compass, exterior temp, systems monitor, trip computer, trip odometer; warning indicators include oil pressure, water temp, battery, lights on, key in ignition, low fuel, low washer fluid, door ajar, service interval, turn signal on; driver's and passenger's front airbags, driver's and front passenger's seat-mounted side airbags; ignition disable, panic alarm, tracker system, security system; tinted windows, power front and rear windows with front and rear 1-touch down function; variable intermittent front windshield wipers, rain detecting wipers, sun visor strip, rear window defroster; seating capacity of 5, front bucket seats with power adjustable tilt headrests, center armrest with storage, driver's seat and passenger's seat includes 8-way power adjustments, power 4-way lumbar support; rear bench seat with tilt headrests, center pass-thru armrest with storage; front height adjustable seatbelts with pretensioners; leather seats, leather door trim insert, full cloth headliner, full carpet floor covering with carpeted floor mats, genuine wood dashboard insert, leather-wrapped gearshift knob, genuine wood door panel insert, genuine wood console insert; interior lights include dome light with delay, front and rear reading lights, 4 door curb lights, illuminated entry; leather-wrapped steering wheel with tilt adjustment; dual illuminated vanity mirrors, dual auxiliary visors; auto-dimming day/night rearview mirror; full floor console, mini overhead console, locking glove box with light, front and rear cupholders, 2 seatback storage pockets, driver's and passenger's door bins; carpeted cargo floor, carpeted trunk lid, carpeted cargo mats, cargo net, cargo tie downs, cargo light, concealed cargo storage; chrome grille, chrome side window moldings, black front windshield molding, black rear window molding and body-colored door handles.

CADILLAC — SEVILLE

CODE	DESCRIPTION	INVOICE	MSRP

STS (4A) (in addition to or instead of SLS (4A) equipment): Requires premium unleaded fuel; 3.71 axle ratio; firm-ride suspension, auto ride control, adaptive auto-leveling suspension; additional exterior lights include front fog/driving lights; driver's power remote auto-dimming outside mirror, passenger's power remote outside mirror with tilt down; P235/60HR16 BSW performance A/S tires; premium amplifier, auto equalizer; heated-cushion driver's and passenger's seats; heated rear bench seat with power tilt headrests; driver's seat memory includes 2 settings for exterior mirrors, steering wheel, headrests and leather-wrapped steering wheel with power tilt and telescopic adjustment.

Base Prices

Code	Description	Invoice	MSRP
6KS69	SLS (4A)	38526	41935
6KY69	STS (4A)	44116	48045
	Destination Charge:	720	720

Interested in seeing what dealers will sell this vehicle for? Check out our True Market Value^{sm} (TMV^{sm}) pricing on our Web site at www.edmunds.com.

Accessories

Code	Description	Invoice	MSRP
1SB	SLS Luxury Package (SLS)	935	1100
	Includes memory package, heated front and rear seats, power tilt and telescopic steering wheel. NOT AVAILABLE with 1SC.		
1SC	SLS Premium Luxury Package (SLS)	2669	3140
	Includes memory package, heated front and rear seats, power tilt and telescopic steering wheel, Bose 4.0 AM/FM stereo radio with CD and cassette players, 16" chrome wheels and ultrasonic rear parking assist. NOT AVAILABLE with 1SB.		
1SD	STS Luxury Package (STS)	1687	1985
	Includes Bose 4.0 AM/FM stereo radio with CD and cassette players, 16" chrome wheels, wood trim package, wood steering wheel, and wood shift knob. NOT AVAILABLE with 1SE, 1SF.		
1SE	STS Premium Luxury Package (STS)	2490	2930
	Includes Bose 4.0 AM/FM stereo radio with CD and cassette players, ultrasonic rear parking assist, wood trim package, wood steering wheel, wood shift knob, 17" chrome wheels, P235/55R17 GOODYEAR EAGLE LS tires, high intensity discharge headlamps and tire pressure monitoring. NOT AVAILABLE with 1SD, 1SF.		
1SF	STS Premium Performance Package (STS)	5440	6400
	Includes Bose infotainment 4.0 AM/FM stereo radio with CD and cassette players, ultrasonic rear parking assist, wood trim package, wood steering wheel, wood shift knob, 17" chrome wheels, P235/55R17 GOODYEAR EAGLE LS tires, high intensity discharge headlamps, tire pressure monitoring and portable integrated hands-free cellular phone. NOT AVAILABLE with 1SD, 1SE.		
86U	Crimson Pearl	552	650
93U	White Diamond	552	650
AC9	Driver's Side Adaptive Seat	846	995
	REQUIRES 1SB or 1SC.		
CF5	Sunroof with Express Open	1318	1550
	REQUIRES 1SB or 1SC or 1SD or 1SE or 1SF.		
K05	Engine Block Heater	30	35

SEVILLE — CADILLAC

CODE	DESCRIPTION	INVOICE	MSRP
N30	Wood Trim Package	506	595
	Includes wood steering wheel and wood shift knob. REQUIRES 1SB or 1SC.		
PX2	Wheels: 16" Chrome (SLS)	509	795
QWM	Tires: P235/55WR17 Goodyear (STS)	212	250
	REQUIRES 1SE or 1SF.		
U1Z	6-Disc CD Changer	506	595
	Located in center console. REQUIRES 1SB or 1SC or UY4 or 1SD or 1SE or 1SF.		
U45	Radio: BOSE 4.0 with Infotainment Radio (STS)	1696	1995
	Includes AM/FM stereo cassette, weather band, digital signal processing, Radio Data System, personal digital assistant (e-mail), text messaging, remote vehicle control, TheftLock and 8 speakers. REQUIRES UV8 or 1SF.		
UD7	Ultrasonic Rear Parking Assist (STS)	251	295
UM5	Radio: BOSE 4.0 AM/FM Stereo with CD, Cassette (SLS)	808	950
	Includes single slot CD player, weather band, digital signal processing, Radio Data System, TheftLock and 8 speakers.		
UV8	Portable Integrated Hands-Free Cellular Phone	574	675
UY4	On-Board CD-ROM Based Navigation System (SLS) ...	2503	2945
	Includes Bose 4.0 premium audio system radio. REQUIRES U1Z.		
UY4	On-Board CD-ROM Based Navigation System (STS) ...	1696	1995
	Includes Bose 4.0 premium audio system radio. REQUIRES U1Z.		

TOWN HALL

Get answers from our editors, discover smart shopping strategies and share your perspectives in this interactive forum of both experts and consumers. Just enter the following address into your Web browser:

townhall.edmunds.com

Where smart shoppers talk about cars, trucks, and related consumer topics.

CHEVROLET — *CAMARO*

2001 CAMARO

What's New?
More horsepower is on tap for the Z28, newly-styled chrome 16" wheels are a new option for base and Z28 models and Sunset Orange Metallic is added to the list of colors.

Review

"From the country that invented rock 'n' roll" claimed the advertisements for this Quebec, Canada-built sport coupe when it was redesigned in 1993. A small technicality, we suppose, but there are no technicalities when it comes to the Camaro's performance abilities, particularly in Z28 or SS guise. These Camaros are blazingly quick, hold the road tenaciously, cost less than the average price of a new car in this country and get decent gas mileage when they're not being hammered along a twisty, two-lane road.

Two trim levels are available for 2001 in either coupe or convertible bodystyles. Base Camaros are powered by a 3800 Series II V6 that makes 200 horsepower. Mated to a four-speed automatic or five-speed manual transmission, this sufficiently stout motor makes a strong argument for avoiding the higher insurance rates and prices of the Z28. An optional performance-handling package puts dual exhaust, tighter steering and a limited-slip differential on the V6 Camaro.

The Z28 is the go-faster Camaro. Equipped with a detuned Corvette 5.7-liter V8, the Z28 makes 310 horsepower, 50 more horses than the Mustang GT. Opt for the SS performance package and you get 320 real horsepower (same as the 1999 Mustang Cobra), thanks to forced air induction through an aggressive-looking hood scoop. The SS gets to 60 mph from rest in a little over five seconds. SLP Engineering—known for working magic with GM's F-Bodies since the late '80s—supplies the parts to turn a Z28 into an SS.

For 2001, revisions are few. Revalved shocks, newly restyled 16" chrome wheels, an additional five horsepower for the LS1-powered Z28 and one new exterior color are available.

The interior of the Camaro is functional, but cheap in appearance. Visibility is nothing to brag about either. The Camaro holds a respectable amount of gear in the cargo hold (more than 33 cubic feet of space with the generally useless rear seats folded down), and airbags and antilock brakes are standard.

Rumors are still flying that GM is set to kill the Camaro, and since no product is scheduled for the Canadian Camaro plant after 2002, those rumors are likely true. Steadily declining sales are to blame, and the company is eager to slice non-performing models from the lineup. If the Camaro dies, it would be a real shame because—from a bang-for-the-buck standpoint—the Z28 is unbeatable. More mature drivers can order traction control, but that option defeats some of the fun of Chevy's pony car: smoky, adolescent burnouts that leave the drivers behind choking on charred Goodyears.

Standard Equipment

BASE COUPE (5M): 3.8L V6 OHV SMPI 12-valve engine; 5-speed OD manual transmission; 690 amp battery with run down protection; 105 amp alternator; rear-wheel drive, 3.23 axle ratio; stainless steel exhaust; firm-ride suspension, front independent suspension with anti-roll bar, front coil springs, gas-pressurized front shocks, rigid rear axle trailing arm suspension with anti-roll bar, rear coil springs, gas-pressurized rear shocks; rack-and-pinion power steering; 4-wheel antilock disc brakes; 16.8 gal. capacity fuel tank; rear wing spoiler, side impact bars; class I trailering; front and rear body-colored bumpers; clearcoat monotone paint; aero-composite

CAMARO — CHEVROLET

CODE	DESCRIPTION	INVOICE	MSRP

halogen fully auto headlamps with daytime running lights; driver's and passenger's body-colored outside mirrors, driver's manual remote outside mirror, passenger's manual outside mirror; 16" x 7.5" steel wheels; P215/60SR16 BSW touring A/S tires; compact steel spare wheel; air conditioning; AM/FM stereo radio, clock, seek-scan feature, cassette player, 4 speakers, fixed antenna; 2 power accessory outlets, front lighter element(s), driver's foot rest, retained accessory power, smoker's package; instrumentation display includes tachometer, oil pressure gauge, water temperature gauge, volt gauge, trip odometer; warning indicators include low oil level, lights on, key in ignition, low fuel, trunk ajar, service interval; driver's and passenger's front airbags; ignition disable; tinted windows; variable intermittent front windshield wipers, sun visor strip; seating capacity of 4, front bucket seats with fixed headrests, center armrest with storage, driver's and passenger's seats include 4-way adjustment; full folding rear bench seat; cloth seats, cloth door trim insert with carpet lower, full cloth headliner, full carpet floor covering with floor mats; interior lights include dome light, front reading lights; steering wheel with tilt adjustment; vanity mirrors; day/night rearview mirror; full floor console, locking glove box with light, front and rear cupholders, driver's and passenger's door bins; carpeted cargo floor, cargo cover, cargo light; black side window moldings, black front windshield molding, black rear window molding and body-colored door handles.

Z28 COUPE (4A) (in addition to or instead of BASE COUPE (5M) equipment): 5.7L V8 OHV SMPI 16-valve engine; 4-speed electronic OD automatic transmission with lock-up torque converter; 525 amp battery with run down protection; viscous limited-slip differential, 2.73 axle ratio; stainless steel exhaust with tailpipe finisher; sport-ride suspension; 16" x 8" cast aluminum wheels; P235/55SR16 BSW touring A/S tires; premium AM/FM stereo radio, 8 premium speakers, premium amplifier, auto equalizer and theft deterrent.

BASE CONVERTIBLE (5M) (in addition to or instead of BASE COUPE (5M) equipment): power convertible roof with lining, glass rear window; body-colored bodyside molding; additional exterior lights include front fog/driving lights; driver's and passenger's power remote body-colored outside mirrors; premium AM/FM stereo radio, 8 premium speakers, premium amplifier, auto equalizer, theft deterrent, radio steering wheel controls; cruise control; power door locks with 2-stage unlock, remote keyless entry, power remote hatch/trunk release; panic alarm, security system; tinted windows with driver's 1-touch down function; rear window defroster; leather-wrapped gearshift knob; interior lights include front reading lights, illuminated entry; leather-wrapped steering wheel.

Z28 CONVERTIBLE (4A) (in addition to or instead of Z28 COUPE (4A) equipment): Power convertible roof with lining, glass rear window; additional exterior lights include front fog/driving lights; radio steering wheel controls; cruise control; power remote hatch/trunk release; panic alarm, security system; power windows with driver's 1-touch down function; driver's and passenger's power remote body-colored outside mirrors; driver's seat includes 4-way power adjustment, 8-way adjustment and leather-wrapped gearshift knob.

Base Prices

1FP87	Base Coupe (5M)	15624	17075
1FP87-Z28	Z28 Coupe (4A)	19805	21645
1FP67	Base Convertible (5M)	22299	24370
1FP67-Z28	Z28 Convertible (4A)	26306	28750
	Destination Charge:	575	575

Interested in seeing what dealers will sell this vehicle for? Check out our True Market Value^{sm} (TMV^{sm}) pricing on our Web site at www.edmunds.com.

CHEVROLET — CAMARO

CODE	DESCRIPTION	INVOICE	MSRP

Accessories

Code	Description	Invoice	MSRP
—	Super Soft Sierra Leather Seat Trim	445	500
1SA	Preferred Equipment Group 1SA (Base)	NC	NC
	Includes vehicle with standard equipment. REQUIRES C49 or R9W. NOT AVAILABLE with Y87.		
1SB	Preferred Equipment Group 1SB (Base Coupe)	1041	1170
	Includes remote keyless entry, electronic cruise control with resume speed, theft deterrent alarm system, fog lamps, dual sport electric remote mirrors, power door locks, power windows with driver's express down and remote hatch release. REQUIRES C49 or R9W.		
1SB	Preferred Equipment Group 1SB (Z28 Convertible)	NC	NC
	Includes remote keyless entry, electronic cruise control with resume speed, theft deterrent alarm system, fog lamps, dual sport electric remote mirrors, power door locks, power windows with driver's express down, remote hatch release, 6-way power driver seat, carpeted rear floor mats and color-keyed body side moldings.		
1SC	Preferred Equipment Group 1SC (Z28 Coupe)	NC	NC
	Includes vehicle with standard equipment. REQUIRES C49 or R9W. NOT AVAILABLE with B84.		
1SD	Preferred Equipment Group 1SD (Z28 Coupe)	1526	1715
	Includes remote keyless entry, electronic cruise control with resume speed, theft deterrent alarm system, fog lamps, dual sport electric remote mirrors, power door locks, power windows with driver's express down, remote hatch release, 6-way power driver seat, leather-wrapped steering wheel, carpeted rear floor mats and color-keyed body side moldings. REQUIRES C49 or R9W.		
AG1	6-Way Power Driver Seat (Base)	240	270
	INCLUDED in 1SB, 1SD.		
B35	Carpeted Rear Floor Mats (Base Coupe)	13	15
	INCLUDED in 1SD.		
B84	Color-Keyed Body Side Moldings (Base Coupe)	53	60
	INCLUDED in 1SB, 1SD.		
BBS	Hurst Performance Shift Linkage (Z28)	289	325
	Short throw. REQUIRES MN6.		
C49	Electric Rear Window Defogger (Coupe)	151	170
	NOT AVAILABLE with R9W.		
CC1	Transparent Removable Hatch Roof Panels (Coupe)	886	995
	Includes locks, lockable stowage provisions and sunshades.		
GU5	3.23 Performance Axle Ratio (Z28)	267	300
	REQUIRES QFZ or QLC. NOT AVAILABLE with MN6.		
MN6	Transmission: 6-Speed Manual (Z28)	NC	NC
	Includes skip shift feature and 3.42 performance axle ratio. NOT AVAILABLE with GU5.		
MX0	Transmission: 4-Speed Automatic with OD (Base)	725	815
	Includes 2nd gear start feature and 3.08 axle ratio.		
N96	Wheels: 16" Silver Cast Aluminum (Base)	245	275
	NOT AVAILABLE with PW7.		
NW9	Acceleration Traction Control (Base)	222	250

CAMARO — CHEVROLET

CODE	DESCRIPTION	INVOICE	MSRP
NW9	Acceleration Traction Control (Z28)	400	450
	QFZ tires recommended for optimum traction.		
PW7	Wheels: 16" Chrome Cast Aluminum (Base)	868	975
	NOT AVAILABLE with N96, Y87, Y3F.		
PW7	Wheels: 16" Chrome Cast Aluminum (Z28)	645	725
	NOT AVAILABLE with WU8.		
QCB	Tires: P235/55R16 BW (Base)	120	135
	Tire chains should not be used as they may cause damage. See owner's manual. REQUIRES N96 or PW7.		
QFZ	Tires: P245/50ZR16 AS Performance (Z28)	200	225
	NOT AVAILABLE with QLC, WU8.		
QLC	Tires: P245/50ZR16 Performance (Z28)	200	225
	Tire chains should not be used as they may cause damage. See owner's manual. NOT AVAILABLE with QFZ, WU8.		
R9W	Rear Window Defogger Not Desired (Coupe)	NC	NC
	NOT AVAILABLE with C49.		
U1S	Trunk Mounted 12 Disc CD Changer	530	595
	REQUIRES UNO or ULO.		
UK3	Leather Wrapped Steering Wheel (Base Coupe)	151	170
	Includes leather parking brake release handle, redundant radio controls and leather-wrapped shift knob. REQUIRES ULO or UNO. NOT AVAILABLE with 1SA. INCLUDED in 1SB, 1SD.		
ULO	Radio: AM/FM Stereo with Cassette, Automatic Tone Control (Base Coupe)	312	350
	Includes Monsoon 500 watt premium sound system with seek/scan, automatic tone control, digital clock, TheftLock, speed compensated volume with 8 speakers and auxiliary amplifier. NOT AVAILABLE with UNO.		
UNO	Radio: AM/FM Stereo with CD, Automatic Tone Control (Base Convertible, Z28)	89	100
	Includes Monsoon 500 watt premium sound system with seek/scan, digital clock, TheftLock, speed compensated volume with 8 speakers and auxiliary amplifier.		
UNO	Radio: AM/FM Stereo with CD, Automatic Tone Control (Base Coupe)	400	450
	Includes Monsoon 500 watt premium sound system with seek/scan, digital clock, TheftLock, speed compensated volume with 8 speakers and auxiliary amplifier. NOT AVAILABLE with ULO.		
V12	Power Steering Cooler (Z28)	89	100
	Intended for Gymkhana and Autocross-type applications.		
WU8	SS Performance and Appearance Package (Z28)	3516	3950
	Includes composite hood with functional air scoop, SS specific rear Deck spoiler, forced-air induction system, dual outlet exhaust system, upgraded suspension components for improved handling, Camaro SS exterior graphics, Zexel-Torsen limited slip differential, 17" x 9" painted alloy wheels, 275/40ZR17 GOODYEAR EAGLE F1 tires and power steering cooler. REQUIRES Y2Y and LS1. NOT AVAILABLE with Y3F, QFZ, QLC, PW7.		
Y2Y	SLP 2nd Sticker Content (Z28)	NC	NC
	This option must be ordered when additional SLP second sticker content is desired. Consult with dealer for additional ordering information.		

CHEVROLET   *CAMARO / CAVALIER*

CODE	DESCRIPTION	INVOICE	MSRP
Y3B	RS Package (Base)	746	849
	Includes grille with Chevrolet bowtie logo, dual heritage stripes, Z28-type exhaust system with dual outlets, RS interior and exterior badging. NOT AVAILABLE with Y3F, Y87, N96, PW7, QCB.		
Y3F	Sport Appearance Package (Base)	1562	1755
	Includes spoiler extension, rocker moldings, 16" silver alloy wheels and P235/55R16 BW tires. NOT AVAILABLE with Y3B, PW7.		
Y3F	Sport Appearance Package (Z28)	1200	1348
	Includes spoiler extension and rocker moldings. NOT AVAILABLE with WU8.		
Y87	Performance Handling Package (Base)	245	275
	Includes sport steering ratio, Zexel-Torsen limited slip differential and dual outlet exhaust. NOT AVAILABLE with 1SA, PW7, Y3B.		

2001 CAVALIER

What's New?

Indigo Blue is added to the exterior palette. A CD player is made standard on the LS Sedan and Z24 Coupe. The Z24 Convertible has vanished from the lineup.

Review

For nearly two decades the Cavalier has been a staple sales leader for Chevy dealers. Understandably so, because the Cavalier offers reasonable value and is priced low enough to compete favorably in the compact market, often undercutting smaller models from other manufacturers. The Cavalier makes for solid transportation, offering adequate room for four adults, decent performance and acceptable interior accommodations. Styling is attractive and contemporary, and there is a model to suit almost everyone's needs.

This year, Cavalier is offered in Base Coupe and Sedan, LS Sedan and Z24 Coupe. The Z24 Convertible has been scratched for 2001.

Inside, Cavalier is reasonably comfortable and well laid-out. An ergonomically friendly instrument panel boasts clear gauges, digital odometer and tripmeter, and stereo controls located above the climate controls for easier access. The center-console shift indicator is illuminated, and air conditioning is standard on all Cavaliers. Uplevel stereos include a six-speaker Premium Amplified Audio System with rear-woofer speakers.

GM's venerable 2.2-liter four-cylinder (whose droning exhaust note you are probably familiar with) is standard in the Cavalier. Equipped with this powerplant, Cavalier lags behind its primary domestic competition in power and acceleration. Optional in the LS Sedan is a 2.4-liter twin-cam engine hooked to a four-speed automatic transmission, a setup that features traction control. The Cavalier is a much more livable car with this engine, and we wish that Chevrolet offered this powertrain in base models as well. The twin-cam engine is standard in the sporty Z24 Coupe. Manually shifted Z24 Coupes are quick from rest to 60 mph. Antilock brakes are standard equipment and provide smooth operation and confident response. A rear defogger is standard.

Though the Cavalier exhibits no glaring deficiencies in terms of driving characteristics, the overly compliant suspension does allow for a fair amount of body roll and wallow through

CAVALIER — CHEVROLET

corners, and steering feedback could be improved. As far as braking is concerned, the standard ABS is a nice feature, but the system is relatively unrefined in application.

With the 2.4-liter twin-cam engine, the Cavalier LS Sedan is a virile alternative to some more lethargic economy sedans, and all trim levels pack in a decent amount of standard equipment. But the Cavalier is aging quickly, and there are no plans to replace this model until 2003 at the earliest. Still, it represents good value. The price is dead-on, low enough to make the Chevrolet Metro sedan an exercise in redundancy. We recommend that you check out the Cavalier if a compact car fits your needs.

Standard Equipment

BASE COUPE (5M): 2.2L I4 OHV SMPI 8-valve engine; 5-speed OD manual transmission; 525 amp battery with run down protection; 105 amp alternator; front-wheel drive, 3.58 axle ratio; stainless steel exhaust; front independent strut suspension with anti-roll bar, front coil springs, rear semi-independent torsion suspension with rear coil springs; rack-and-pinion power steering; front disc/rear drum brakes with 4-wheel antilock brakes; 14.3 gal. capacity fuel tank; side impact bars; front and rear body-colored bumpers; clearcoat monotone paint; aero-composite halogen headlamps with daytime running lights; driver's and passenger's black folding outside mirrors, driver's manual remote outside mirror, passenger's manual outside mirror; 14" x 6" steel wheels; P195/70SR14 BSW A/S tires; compact steel spare wheel; air conditioning, rear heat ducts; AM/FM stereo radio, clock, seek-scan feature, 4 speakers, fixed antenna; 1 power accessory outlet, driver's foot rest, retained accessory power; instrumentation display includes tachometer, water temperature gauge, trip odometer; warning indicators include water temp, battery, low coolant, lights on, key in ignition, low fuel; driver's and passenger's front airbags; ignition disable; tinted windows; fixed interval front windshield wipers, rear window defroster; seating capacity of 5, front bucket seats with adjustable headrests, center armrest with storage, driver's and passenger's seat includes 4-way adjustment; full folding rear bench seat; cloth seats, cloth door trim insert, full cloth headliner, full carpet floor covering; interior lights include dome light with fade; day/night rearview mirror; full floor console, glove box, front and rear cupholders, driver's and passenger's door bins; carpeted cargo floor, cargo light; black side window moldings, black front windshield molding, black rear window molding and black door handles.

Z24 COUPE (5M) (in addition to or instead of BASE COUPE (5M) equipment): 2.4L I4 DOHC SMPI 16-valve engine; 600 amp battery with run down protection; 3.94 axle ratio; sport-ride suspension; front mud flaps, rear lip spoiler; body-colored bodyside molding rocker panel extensions; additional exterior lights include front fog/driving lights; driver's and passenger's power remote black folding outside mirrors; 16" x 6" silver alloy wheels; P205/55SR16 BSW performance A/S tires; single-disc CD player, 4 performance speakers; cruise control; power door locks with 2-stage unlock, remote keyless entry, power remote hatch/trunk release; panic alarm, security system; power tinted windows with driver's 1-touch down function; variable intermittent front windshield wipers; easy entry; carpeted floor mats; interior lights include front reading lights, illuminated entry; steering wheel with tilt adjustment; vanity mirrors and cargo net.

BASE SEDAN (5M) (in addition to or instead of BASE COUPE (5M) equipment): Black bodyside molding; child-safety rear door locks; manual front and rear windows and front height adjustable seatbelts.

LS SEDAN (4A) (in addition to or instead of BASE SEDAN (5M) equipment): 4-speed electronic OD automatic transmission with lock-up torque converter; traction control, 3.63 axle ratio; touring-ride suspension; body-colored bodyside molding; 15" x 6" steel wheels; P195/65SR15 BSW touring A/S tires; single-disc CD player, 4 performance speakers; cruise control; remote hatch/trunk release; carpeted floor mats; interior lights include front reading lights; steering wheel with tilt adjustment; vanity mirrors and cargo net.

CHEVROLET

CAVALIER

CODE	DESCRIPTION	INVOICE	MSRP

Base Prices

1JC37	Base Coupe (5M)	12305	13160
1JF37	Z24 Coupe (5M)	15301	16365
1JC69	Base Sedan (5M)	12398	13260
1JF69	LS Sedan (4A)	13889	14855
	Destination Charge:	540	540

Interested in seeing what dealers will sell this vehicle for? Check out our True Market Value^{sm} (TMV^{sm}) pricing on our Web site at www.edmunds.com.

Accessories

—	**Cloth Seat Trim (Z24 Coupe)**	NC	NC
	NOT AVAILABLE with Sport Cloth Seat Trim.		
—	**Sport Cloth Seat Trim (Z24 Coupe)**	NC	NC
	NOT AVAILABLE with Cloth Seat Trim.		
1SA	**Base Equipment Group (Base Coupe/Base Sedan)**	NC	NC
	Includes vehicle with standard equipment. NOT AVAILABLE with CF5, V11, UP0, PF7, UQ3.		
1SA	**LS Base Equipment Group (LS)**	NC	NC
	Includes AM/FM stereo radio with CD with seek and scan. NOT AVAILABLE with PF7, UP0, UQ3.		
1SA	**Z24 Base Equipment Group (Z24 Coupe)**	NC	NC
	Includes AM/FM stereo radio with CD with seek, scan and remote keyless entry.		
1SB	**LS Preferred Equipment Group 1 (LS)**	747	830
	Includes AM/FM stereo radio with CD with seek, scan, dual power outside mirrors, power windows with driver's express down, remote keyless entry, power door locks and content theft security system.		
1SB	**Preferred Equipment Group 1 (Base Coupe)**	387	430
	Includes cargo area convenience net, front and rear carpeted floor mats, dual covered visor mirrors, color-keyed body side moldings, front mud guards, easy entry passenger seat, mechanical trunk release, variable intermittent windshield wipers, AM/FM stereo radio with CD with seek and scan. NOT AVAILABLE with MX1, V11.		
1SB	**Preferred Equipment Group 1 (Base Sedan)**	372	413
	Includes cargo area convenience net, front and rear carpeted floor mats, dual covered visor mirrors, color-keyed body side moldings, front mud guards, mechanical trunk release, variable intermittent windshield wipers, AM/FM stereo radio with CD with seek and scan. NOT AVAILABLE with MX1.		
1SC	**Preferred Equipment Group 2 (Base Coupe)**	945	1050
	Includes cargo area convenience net, front and rear carpeted floor mats, dual covered visor mirrors, color-keyed body side moldings, front mud guards, easy entry passenger seat, mechanical trunk release, variable intermittent windshield wipers, AM/FM stereo radio with CD with seek, scan, 15" wheels with bolt-on covers, P195/65R15 BW touring tires, electronic cruise control with resume speed and tilt steering wheel. NOT AVAILABLE with MX1, UP0.		
1SD	**Preferred Equipment Group 3 (Base Coupe)**	1588	1764
	Includes cargo area convenience net, front and rear carpeted floor mats, dual covered visor mirrors, color-keyed body side moldings, front mud guards, easy entry passenger		

CAVALIER — CHEVROLET

CODE	DESCRIPTION	INVOICE	MSRP
	seat, variable intermittent windshield wipers, AM/FM stereo radio with CD with seek, scan, electronic cruise control with resume speed, tilt steering wheel, 15" wheels with bolt-on covers, P195/65R15 BW touring tires, dual power outside mirrors, power windows with driver's express down, remote keyless entry, power door locks, and contents theft security system. NOT AVAILABLE with MX1, UP0.		
AU0	**Remote Keyless Entry (Base Coupe)**	333	370
	Replaces mechanical trunk opener, power door locks and content theft security system. INCLUDED in 1SA, 1SB, 1SD.		
AU0	**Remote Keyless Entry (Base Sedan/LS)**	369	410
	Replaces mechanical trunk opener, power door locks and content theft security system. INCLUDED in 1SA, 1SB, 1SD.		
CF5	**Electric Sunroof (Base Coupe)**	536	595
	Includes mirror map light. NOT AVAILABLE with 1SA.		
CF5	**Electric Sunroof with Mirror Map Light (Z24 Coupe)**	536	595
DC4	**Dual Reading Lamps Mounted In Mirror (Base Coupe/Z24 Coupe)**	NC	NC
	REQUIRES CF5.		
K05	**Engine Block Heater**	27	30
KL6	**Natural Gas Provisions (Base Sedan)**	5342	5935
	Includes 15" wheels with bolt-on covers and P195/65R15 BW touring tires. NOT AVAILABLE with MX1.		
LD9	**Engine: 2.4L SFI L4 Twin Cam (LS)**	405	450
	Includes 3.91 axle ratio.		
MX0	**Transmission: 4-Speed Auto with OD (Base Sedan)**	702	780
	Includes traction control and 3.63 axle ratio.		
MX0	**Transmission: 4-Speed Automatic (Base Coupe/Z24 Coupe)**	702	780
	Includes traction control.		
MX1	**Transmission: 3-Speed Automatic (Base Coupe/Base Sedan)**	630	700
	Includes 3.18 axle ratio. REQUIRES 1SA. NOT AVAILABLE with 1SB, 1SC, 1SD, KL6.		
PF7	**Wheels: 15" Aluminum (Base Coupe/LS)**	266	295
	NOT AVAILABLE with 1SA.		
T43	**Rear Deck Spoiler (LS)**	135	150
U1C	**Radio: AM/FM Stereo with CD (Base Coupe/Base Sedan)**	148	165
	Includes digital clock and premium front coaxial speakers. NOT AVAILABLE with UP0. INCLUDED in 1SA, 1SB, 1SC, 1SD.		
UP0	**Radio: AM/FM Stereo with CD, Cassette Player (Base Coupe)**	117	130
	Includes seek-and-scan, digital clock, auto-tone control, speed compensated volume, Theftlock and radio data system controls and premium amplified audio system. NOT AVAILABLE with V11, 1SA, 1SB.		
UP0	**Radio: AM/FM Stereo with CD, Cassette Player (Base Coupe/Z24 Coupe/LS)**	207	230
	Includes seek-and-scan, digital clock, auto-tone control, speed compensated volume, Theftlock and radio data system controls and premium amplified audio system. REQUIRES 1SB. NOT AVAILABLE with V11, 1SA, 1SC, 1SD.		
UQ3	**Premium Amplified Audio System**	90	100
	Includes 6 premium speakers with rear woofer speakers. REQUIRES 1SB. NOT AVAILABLE with 1SA.		

CHEVROLET — CAVALIER / CORVETTE

CODE	DESCRIPTION	INVOICE	MSRP
V11	Sport Package (Base Coupe).. Includes spoiler, premium amplified audio system and tachometer. NOT AVAILABLE with 1SA, UPO, 1SB.	122	135
V11	Sport Package (Base Coupe).. Includes spoiler, premium amplified audio system and tachometer. REQUIRES 1SB. NOT AVAILABLE with 1SA, UPO, 1SC, 1SD.	212	235

2001 CORVETTE

What's New?

The entire Corvette lineup receives a dose of additional horsepower and torque. Z06 model joins the lineup, Active Handling now standard on all Corvettes.

Review

Nearly 45 years after the 1953 Corvette debuted, Chevrolet introduced the fifth-generation Corvette for 1997. With the addition of a hardtop model to the lineup in 1999, Chevrolet brings forth an ace in 2001 with the race-ready Z06 hard top.

Pushrod power — in the form of a 5.7-liter LS1 LEV-compliant V8 — motivates the Corvette. Horsepower is rated 350 at 5,600 rpm, while torque measures 360 foot-pounds at 4,000 rpm. On models with a manual transmission, the torque rating increases to 375 foot-pounds at 4,400 rpm. Equipped with the standard four-speed automatic transmission, the Corvette will hit 60 mph in a shade over five seconds. Opt for the six-speed manual transmission and you'll cut less than half a second off the trap time. To help reign the power in on slippery surfaces, acceleration slip regulation (a.k.a., traction control) is standard equipment.

Placing a check mark next to the Z06 box and you'll be treated to the fastest, lightest and stiffest Corvette to leave the factory. Backed by a new 5.7-liter LS6 V8 producing a pavement-melting 385-horsepower at 6,000 rpm and a standard issue M12 six-speed manual transmission (with aggressive gearing to increase torque multiplication), the Z06 rips from zero-to-60 in four seconds flat and corners at one full G.

Manhole cover-sized four-wheel-disc antilock brakes keep stopping distances short, while massive 17-inch front and 18-inch rear tires contribute to prodigious amounts of road grip. The rubber stays planted well, too, thanks to a fully independent four-wheel SLA height-adjustable suspension. Standard for 2001 on all Corvettes is a second generation Active Handling System (AHS), which keeps the Corvette in line even if the driver isn't.

Body panels are still composed of a material other than metal, though no longer fiberglass. Sheet-molded compound wraps around an ultra-stiff structure that features a full-length perimeter frame with tubular steel side rails. A sandwich composite floor with a lightweight balsa wood core damps noise and vibration while making the floor exceptionally stiff.

Inside, a dash with analog gauges and intuitive radio and climate controls greets passengers. Luggage space beneath the coupe's rear hatch glass is an incredible 25 cubic feet. Even the hardtop and convertible can tote more cargo than any Corvette in history.

Yes, the Corvette is an outstanding effort and competes favorably with the best in the class. Long, low, and lean, the Corvette is certainly attractive. We take issue, however, with the thick truncated tail and the odd-looking air scoops for the front brakes. Still, the Corvette's new shape will wear well into the new century.

CORVETTE

CHEVROLET

Don't let the fact that the C5 will swallow two golf bags sway you into thinking this a gentrified sporting coupe. The 2001 Corvette is among the best true sports cars your money can buy. Ladies and Gentlemen, start your engines.

Standard Equipment

COUPE (4A): 5.7L V8 OHV SMPI 16-valve engine (requires premium unleaded fuel); 4-speed electronic OD automatic transmission with lock-up torque converter; 525 amp battery with run down protection; engine block heater; 110 amp alternator; rear-wheel drive, limited-slip differential, traction control, 2.73 axle ratio; dual stainless steel exhaust with tailpipe finisher; electronic stability control, front independent suspension with anti-roll bar, front springs, rear independent short & long arm suspension with anti-roll bar, rear springs; rack-and-pinion power steering with vehicle-speed-sensing assist, power steering cooler; 4-wheel antilock disc brakes; 18.5 gal. capacity fuel tank; side impact bars; front manual targa steel sunroof; front and rear body-colored bumpers; clearcoat monotone paint; aero-composite halogen headlamps with daytime running lights, delay-off feature; additional exterior lights include underhood light; driver's and passenger's power remote body-colored heated folding outside mirrors; 17" x 8.5" front and 18" x 9.5" rear silver alloy wheels; P245/45ZR17 front and P275/40ZR18 rear BSW run flat tires; air conditioning; AM/FM stereo radio, clock, seek-scan feature, cassette player, 6 premium speakers, amplifier, auto equalizer, theft deterrent, window grid antenna; cruise control; power door locks with 2-stage unlock, remote keyless entry, power remote hatch/trunk release, power remote fuel door release; 2 power accessory outlets, front lighter element(s), driver's foot rest, retained accessory power, smoker's package; instrumentation display includes tachometer, oil pressure gauge, water temperature gauge, volt gauge, systems monitor, exterior temperature, trip computer, trip odometer; warning indicators include oil pressure, water temp, battery, low oil level, low coolant, lights on, key in ignition, low fuel, low washer fluid, door ajar, trunk ajar, service interval, brake fluid, turn signal on, low tire pressure; driver's front airbag, passenger's cancelable front airbag; ignition disable, panic alarm, security system; tinted windows with driver's and passenger's 1-touch down function; variable intermittent front windshield wipers, sun visor strip, rear window defroster; seating capacity of 2, front bucket seats with fixed headrests, center armrest with storage, driver's seat includes 6-way power adjustment, 8-way adjustment, passenger's seat includes 4-way adjustment; leather seats, full cloth headliner, full color-keyed carpet floor covering, leather-wrapped gearshift knob; interior lights include dome light with delay reading lights, illuminated entry; leather-wrapped sport steering wheel with tilt adjustment; dual illuminated vanity mirrors; day/night rearview mirror; full floor console, locking glove box with light, front cupholder; carpeted cargo floor, cargo light, concealed cargo storage; black side window moldings, black front windshield molding, black rear window molding and body-colored door handles.

CONVERTIBLE (4A) (in addition to or instead of BASE COUPE (4A) equipment): Manual convertible roof with lining, glass rear window and power retractable antenna.

Z06 HARDTOP (6M) (in addition to or instead of BASE COUPE (4A) equipment): 6-speed OD manual transmission; 3.42 axle ratio; polished tailpipe finisher, sport-ride suspension, HD front and rear anti-roll bar, HD front and rear shocks; 17" x 9.5" front and 18" x 10.5" rear silver alloy wheels; P265/40ZR17 front and P295/35ZR18 rear BSW performance tires; dual-zone front air conditioning with climate control and fixed antenna.

Base Prices

CODE	DESCRIPTION	INVOICE	MSRP
1YY07	Coupe (4A)	35070	40080
1YY67	Convertible (4A)	40779	46605
1YY37	Z06 Hardtop (6M)	41873	47855
Destination Charge:		645	645

CHEVROLET — CORVETTE

CODE	DESCRIPTION	INVOICE	MSRP

Interested in seeing what dealers will sell this vehicle for? Check out our True Market Value^{sm} (TMV^{sm}) pricing on our Web site at www.edmunds.com.

Accessories

CODE	DESCRIPTION	INVOICE	MSRP
1SA	**Preferred Equipment Group 1SA**	NC	NC
	Includes vehicle with standard equipment.		
1SB	**Preferred Equipment Group 1SB (Convertible)**	1548	1800
	Includes dual zone electronic air conditioning, adjustable sport buckets, 6-way power passenger seat, fog lamps, memory package, twilight sentinel lighting, electrochromic interior rear view mirror and electrochromic driver's outside mirror.		
1SB	**Preferred Equipment Group 1SB (Coupe)**	1462	1700
	Includes dual zone electronic air conditioning, adjustable sport buckets, 6-way power passenger seat, fog lamps, luggage shade, parcel net and memory package.		
1SC	**Preferred Equipment Group 1SC (Convertible)**	2236	2600
	Includes dual zone electronic air conditioning, adjustable sport buckets, 6-way power passenger seat, fog lamps, memory package, manual tilt/power telescoping steering, head-up display, twilight sentinel lighting, electrochromic interior rear view mirror and electrochromic driver's outside mirror. NOT AVAILABLE with AAB.		
1SC	**Preferred Equipment Group 1SC (Coupe)**	2322	2700
	Includes dual zone electronic air conditioning, adjustable sport buckets, 6-way power passenger seat, fog lamps, luggage shade, parcel net, memory package, manual tilt/power telescoping steering, head-up display, twilight sentinel lighting, electrochromic interior rear view mirror and electrochromic driver's outside mirror. NOT AVAILABLE with AAB.		
79U	**Millennium Yellow**	516	600
86U	**Magnetic Red II Metallic (Convertible/Coupe)**	516	600
AAB	**Memory Package (Z06)**	129	150
	Remembers pre-sets for outside mirrors, radio, heater, defroster, air conditioning and driver power seat.		
B34	**Front Floor Mats**	22	25
B84	**Body Side Moldings**	64	75
C2L	**Roof Package (Coupe)**	1032	1200
	Includes removable 1 piece body-color solid panel and blue translucent roof panel.		
CC3	**Blue Translucent Roof Panel (Coupe)**	645	750
	1-piece removable roof panel.		
DD0	**Electrochromic Inside Rear View Mirror (Z06)**	103	120
	Includes electrochromic driver's outside mirror.		
F45	**Selective Real Time Damping (Convertible/Coupe)**	1458	1695
	The handling package for ultimate driver comfort and control through the use of a driver adjustable ride control system. Includes standard suspension components and Delphi adjustable ride control system. NOT AVAILABLE with Z51.		
G92	**3.15 Performance Axle Ratio (Convertible/Coupe)**	258	300
	NOT AVAILABLE with MN6		
MN6	**Transmission: 6-Speed Manual (Convertible/Coupe)**	701	815
	Includes 3.42 axle ratio. NOT AVAILABLE with G92.		

CORVETTE / IMPALA — CHEVROLET

CODE	DESCRIPTION	INVOICE	MSRP
N73	Wheels: Magnesium (Convertible/Coupe)	1720	2000
	Tire chains should not be used. They may cause damage. See owners's manual. NOT AVAILABLE with QF5.		
QF5	Wheels: High Polished Aluminum (Convertible/Coupe)	1032	1200
	Tire chains should not be used. They may cause damage. See owners's manual. NOT AVAILABLE with N73.		
R8C	Corvette Museum Delivery	421	490
	Acknowledgment form required.		
U1S	Remote 12 Disc CD Changer (Convertible/Coupe)	516	600
UL0	Radio: AM/FM Stereo with Cassette (Z06)	(86)	(100)
	Includes digital clock. Deletes standard CD player.		
UN0	Radio: Delco AM/FM Stereo with CD Player (Convertible/Coupe)	86	100
	Includes seek/scan, auto tone control, digital clock, TheftLock and speed compensated volume.		
V49	Front License Plate Frame	13	15
Z51	Performance Handling Package (Convertible/Coupe)	301	350
	Performance oriented package for the Gymkhana/Autocross enthusiast, power steering cooler, stiffer stabilizer bars and stiffer springs. REQUIRES G92 or MN6. NOT AVAILABLE with F45.		

2001 IMPALA

What's New?

GM resurrected the Impala nameplate last year (a staple in Chevy's lineup from 1959 to the early '80s and then briefly from 1994 to '96) and put it on an all-new, full-sized sedan body that rides on the Lumina front-drive platform. Although the Lumina itself is still with us for the 2001 model year, Impala will eventually replace it as Chevy's large-car entry to battle the likes of Ford's Crown Victoria, Buick's LeSabre and Chrysler's LH cars.

Review

The Chevy Impala returned last year, this time as a front-wheel-drive, V6-powered spin-off of the Lumina chassis, which left rear-drive Impala purists aching for the previous generation model. Designed to compete in the full-size market, the Impala is more aggressive-looking than its Lumina sister, with smoked headlight lenses, large circular tail lamps, and a shape that creates a "frown" both front and rear. Stylists looked to Impalas of the '60s for inspiration here, but its C-pillar badges mimic the surprisingly successful and often-mourned Impala SS of the '90s.

Available in base and LS trim levels, the 2001 Impala sedan holds six good-sized adults and 17.6 cubic feet of their luggage. Inside, a clean, straightforward layout features large, easy-to-find controls and gauges.

The standard 3.4-liter V6 engine was borrowed from the Venture minivan, making 180 horsepower at 5,200 rpm and 205 foot-pounds of torque at 4,000 rpm. Step up to LS trim and you get a 3.8-liter V6 making 200 horsepower at 5,200 rpm and 225 foot-pounds of torque at

CHEVROLET

IMPALA

CODE	DESCRIPTION	INVOICE	MSRP

4,000 rpm. Weighing just less than 3,400 pounds, Impala should move along with verve with either engine. A four-speed automatic is the only available transmission.

Structural enhancements make for a stiffer body, which allowed the engineers to reduce noise, vibration and harshness. It also allowed a more precisely tuned suspension to maximize both ride comfort and handling prowess. Standard 16-inch wheels and tires do much to help with both ride and grip, while Impala's standard four-wheel-disc brakes are rated for heavy-duty service in a new Impala police package. Antilock brakes, a tire inflation monitor and traction control are optional on base models and standard on LS.

Occupant safety will be a big selling point for the Impala. Head protection standards for 2003 were met three years in advance, a side airbag is available, and rear-seat tethers will handle up to three child safety seats. Daytime running lights are standard.

Other standard equipment includes air conditioning with dual front temperature controls, rear defogger, rear-seat headrests, power windows and locks, and a Radio Data System (RDS) AM/FM stereo. Plus, the clock automatically adjusts when you drive across time zones, and Impala's remote keyless entry fobs can be programmed with the preferences of two different drivers. While OnStar is an option for the base sedan, it's now standard on the LS.

Although it's still too early to tell from last year's model run, Chevrolet promises improved reliability over the last-generation Impala, thanks to a simplified electrical system and fewer parts used in the assembly process. A coolant loss-protection system keeps the Impala moving even if all the coolant has been lost—just make sure to stop before you've traveled 50 miles. And, if you do get stranded, the OnStar mobile communications system can help rescue you.

Standard Equipment

BASE (4A): 3.4L V6 OHV SMPI 12-valve engine; 4-speed electronic OD automatic transmission with lock-up torque converter; 600 amp battery with run down protection; 105 amp alternator; front-wheel drive, 2.86 axle ratio; stainless steel exhaust; touring ride suspension, front independent strut suspension with anti-roll bar, front coil springs, rear independent strut suspension with anti-roll bar, rear coil springs; power rack-and-pinion steering; 4-wheel disc brakes; 17 gal. capacity fuel tank; side impact bars; front and rear body-colored bumpers with black rub strip; black bodyside molding rocker panel extensions; clearcoat monotone paint; aero-composite halogen fully auto headlamps with daytime running lights, delay-off feature; driver's and passenger's power remote body-colored outside mirrors; 16" x 6.5" steel wheels; P225/60SR16 BSW A/S tires; compact steel spare wheel; air conditioning, rear heat ducts; AM/FM stereo radio, clock, seek-scan, 4 speakers, window grid antenna; power door locks with 2 stage unlock, child safety rear door locks, power remote hatch/trunk release; 2 power accessory outlets, front lighter element(s), driver's foot rest, retained accessory power, smoker's package; instrumentation display includes water temperature gauge, trip odometer; warning indicators include oil pressure, water temp, battery, low oil level, low coolant, lights on, key in ignition, low fuel, low washer fluid, door ajar, trunk ajar, service interval, turn signal on; driver's and passenger's front airbags; ignition disable; tinted windows, power front and rear windows with driver's 1-touch down; variable intermittent front windshield wipers, sun visor strip, rear window defroster; seating capacity of 6, 60/40 split-bench front seat with adjustable headrests, center armrest with storage, driver's and passenger's seat include 4-way adjustment; rear bench seat with fixed headrests; front height adjustable seatbelts; cloth seats, full cloth headliner, full carpet floor covering with carpeted floor mats, simulated wood dashboard insert, simulated wood door panel insert; interior lights include dome light with fade, front reading light; steering wheel with tilt adjustment; vanity mirrors, dual auxiliary visors; day/night rearview mirror; locking glove box with light, front cupholder, 1 seat back storage pocket, driver's and passenger's door bins; carpeted cargo floor, cargo light; grille with chrome bar, black side window moldings, black front windshield molding, black rear window molding and body-colored door handles.

LS (4A) (in addition to or instead of BASE (4A) equipment): 3.8L V6 OHV SMPI 12-valve engine; 690 amp battery with run down protection; traction control, 3.05 axle ratio; sport ride suspension; 4-wheel antilock disc brakes; rear wing spoiler; additional exterior styling; include front fog/driving lights; driver's and passenger's power remote body-colored heated outside mirrors; dual zone front air conditioning, air filter; cassette player, 6 speakers, auto equalizer,

IMPALA — CHEVROLET

CODE	DESCRIPTION	INVOICE	MSRP

theft deterrent; cruise control with steering wheel controls; keyless entry; emergency S.O.S. (OnStar); instrumentation display includes tachometer; warning indicators include low tire pressure; seat mounted driver's side airbag; panic alarm, tracker system; seating capacity of 5, front bucket seats with adjustable headrests, driver's seat includes 6-way power adjustment, 8-way adjustment, lumbar support, passenger's seat includes 4-way adjustment; 60/40 folding rear bench seat with fixed headrests, center armrest; premium cloth seats; interior lights include front and rear reading lights, illuminated entry; leather-wrapped steering wheel with tilt adjustment; dual illuminated vanity mirrors; auto-dimming day/night rearview mirror; instrument panel bin, full floor console, mini overhead console with storage, front and rear cupholders and cargo net.

Base Prices

Code	Description	Invoice	MSRP
1WF19	Base (4A)	17521	19149
1WH19	LS (4A)	21251	23225
	Destination Charge:	610	610

Interested in seeing what dealers will sell this vehicle for? Check out our True Market Value^{sm} (TMV^{sm}) pricing on our Web site at www.edmunds.com.

Accessories

Code	Description	Invoice	MSRP
—	**Custom Cloth Trim Package (Base)**	725	815
	Includes 45/45 bucket seats, 6-way power driver seat, driver side impact air bag, driver side manual lumbar, center floor console with cupholders and split folding rear seat. NOT AVAILABLE with 1SA, Leather Seat Trim, W01.		
—	**Custom Cloth Trim Package (Base)**	681	765
	Includes 6-way power driver seat, driver side impact air bag, driver side manual lumbar and split folding rear seat. NOT AVAILABLE with Leather Seat Trim, 1SA, W01.		
—	**Leather Seat Trim (Base)**	1237	1390
	Includes 6-way power driver seat, driver side impact air bag, driver side manual lumbar and split folding rear seat. REQUIRES (1SB and UK3) or 1SC. NOT AVAILABLE with 1SA, AR9, Custom Cloth Seat Trim.		
—	**Leather Seat Trim (LS)**	556	625
1SA	**Base Equipment Group (Base)**	NC	NC
	Includes vehicle with standard equipment. NOT AVAILABLE with UK3, Leather Seat Trim, Custom Cloth Seat Trim, AR9, QD1, W01, 1SZ.		
1SA	**LS Base Equipment Group (LS)**	NC	NC
	Includes AM/FM stereo RDS radio with cassette, remote keyless entry, dual illuminated visor mirrors, luggage area cargo net, electronic speed control with resume speed, overhead console with storage bin, 3 outboard passenger assist grips, driver and passenger temperature control, OnStar safety and security system and electrochromic mirror.		
1SB	**LS Preferred Equipment Group 1 (LS)**	352	396
	Includes AM/FM stereo RDS radio with cassette, remote keyless entry, dual illuminated visor mirrors, luggage area cargo net, electronic speed control with resume speed, overhead console with storage bin, 3 outboard passenger assist grips, driver and passenger temperature control, OnStar safety and security system, electrochromic mirror, steering wheel radio controls, driver info convenience center, trip computer, outside temperature and compass, Homelink programmable garage door opener, anti-theft alarm system and overhead storage bin delete.		

CHEVROLET — IMPALA

CODE	DESCRIPTION	INVOICE	MSRP
1SB	**Preferred Equipment Group 1 (Base)**	776	872
	Includes electronic speed control with resume speed, AM/FM stereo with cassette, RDS radio, 6 speaker system, remote keyless entry, dual illuminated visor mirrors, luggage area cargo net, overhead console with storage bin and 3 outboard passenger assist grips. NOT AVAILABLE with 1SZ.		
1SC	**Preferred Equipment Group 2 (Base)**	1694	1903
	Includes AM/FM stereo RDS radio with cassette, 6 speaker system, remote keyless entry, dual illuminated visor mirrors, luggage area cargo net, electronic speed control with resume speed, overhead console with storage bin, 3 outboard passenger assist grips, driver and passenger temperature control, 16" custom alloy wheels, OnStar safety and security system, electrochromic mirror, steering wheel radio controls and leather-wrapped steering wheel. NOT AVAILABLE with UNO, UPO, 1SZ.		
1SZ	**Preferred Equipment Group Discount (Base)**	(879)	(988)
	NOT AVAILABLE with W01, UK3, UNO, UPO, CF5, 1SA, 1SB, 1SC, K05, WX9.		
AG2	**6-Way Power Passenger Side Seat (Base)**	271	305
	REQUIRES Leather Seat Trim. NOT AVAILABLE with 1SA, AR9.		
AR9	**45/45 Bucket Seats**	NC	NC
	Includes 6-way power driver seat, driver side-impact air bags, driver-side manual lumbar, driver and front passenger manual recline, front seatback storage, and split-folding rear seat with armrest and cupholders. NOT AVAILABLE with Leather Seat Trim, 1SA, W01.		
CF5	**Electric Sliding Sunroof**	623	700
	NOT AVAILABLE with 1SZ.		
CJ3	**Driver and Passenger Temperature Control (Base)**	89	100
	Front passenger controls only. NOT AVAILABLE with 1SZ. INCLUDED in 1SA, 1SB, 1SC.		
D58	**Spoiler Delete (LS)**	(156)	(175)
JL9	**4-Wheel Antilock Disc Brakes (Base)**	534	600
	Includes tire inflation sensor.		
K05	**Engine Block Heater**	31	35
	NOT AVAILABLE with 1SZ.		
K34	**Electronic Speed Control with Resume Speed (Base)**	214	240
	INCLUDED in 1SA, 1SB, 1SC.		
L36	**Engine: 3.8L SFI V6 (Base)**	878	986
	Includes 4-wheel antilock disc brakes, tire inflation sensor, traction control, sport touring suspension and 3.05 axle ratio. REQUIRES QD1. NOT AVAILABLE with 1SA, 1SZ.		
QD1	**Wheels: 16" Custom Aluminum (Base)**	267	300
	NOT AVAILABLE with 1SA. INCLUDED in 1SC.		
QNX	**Tires: P225/60R16N Touring BW (Base)**	40	45
	NOT AVAILABLE with 1SA, 1SZ.		
U68	**Driver Info Convenience Center (Base)**	245	275
	Includes trip computer, outside temperature and compass, Homelink programmable garage door opener, anti-theft alarm system and overhead storage bin delete. REQUIRES JL9. NOT AVAILABLE with 1SA. INCLUDED in 1SB.		
UK3	**Steering Wheel Radio Controls (Base)**	152	171
	Includes leather-wrapped steering wheel. NOT AVAILABLE with 1SA, 1SZ. INCLUDED in 1SB, 1SC.		

IMPALA / MALIBU — CHEVROLET

CODE	DESCRIPTION	INVOICE	MSRP
UL0	Radio: AM/FM Stereo with Cass, RDS (Base)	251	282
	Includes seek-scan, auto tone control, digital clock, TheftLock, auto speed compensated volume control, antenna located in rear glass and 6 speakers in 4 locations. NOT AVAILABLE with UN0, UP0. INCLUDED in 1SA, 1SB, 1SC.		
UN0	Radio: AM/FM Stereo with CD, RDS (Base)	360	405
	Includes seek-scan, digital clock, auto tone control, TheftLock, auto speed compensated volume control, antenna located in rear glass and performance 8 speaker system in 4 locations with auxiliary amplifier. NOT AVAILABLE with UP0, WX9, 1SB, 1SC.		
UN0	Radio: AM/FM Stereo with CD, RDS	109	123
	Includes seek-scan, digital clock, auto tone control, TheftLock, auto speed compensated volume control, antenna located in rear glass and performance 8 speaker system in 4 locations with auxiliary amplifier. REQUIRES 1SB. NOT AVAILABLE with UP0, WX9, 1SA, 1SZ.		
UP0	Radio: AM/FM Stereo with CD, Cass, RDS (Base)	449	505
	Includes seek-scan, digital clock, auto tone control, TheftLock, auto speed compensated volume control, antenna located in rear glass and performance 8 speaker system in 4 locations with auxiliary amplifier. NOT AVAILABLE with UN0, WX9, 1SB, 1SC.		
UP0	Radio: AM/FM Stereo with CD, Cass, RDS	198	223
	Includes seek-scan, digital clock, auto tone control, TheftLock, auto speed compensated volume control, antenna located in rear glass and performance 8 speaker system in 4 locations with auxiliary amplifier. REQUIRES 1SB. NOT AVAILABLE with UL0, UN0, WX9, 1SA, 1SZ.		
W01	Comfort Seating Package	378	425
	Includes driver and passenger front heated seats. REQUIRES Leather Seat Trim. NOT AVAILABLE with 1SA, AR9, Custom Cloth Seat Trim, 1SZ.		
WX9	Remote CD Wiring Harness	71	80
	Includes performance 8 speaker system with auxiliary amplifier. NOT AVAILABLE with UN0, UP0, 1SZ.		

2001 MALIBU

What's New?

Base models receive black rocker moldings, black molded-in-color outside rearview mirrors and a rear window defogger. LS models get front seatback map pockets. Both models receive auto headlamp on/off, new stereos and new cloth interiors.

Review

Chevrolet is trying to claw its way back from mediocrity. Witness the excellent values to be found in the Blazer, Camaro and Cavalier. The Malibu is more of a good thing. In fact, this is one of the best family cars produced by any domestic automaker today.

Consumer clinics determined much of the Malibu's design. What consumers have demanded is a tight, solid, roomy, fun-to-drive midsize sedan. Guess what? Chevrolet delivers, and delivers big with this car. The Malibu is all of these things and more, wrapped in unobtrusive yet attractive sheetmetal and sold at a price that undercuts similarly equipped imports and domestics.

CHEVROLET

MALIBU

Two models are available. Both Malibus feature the torquey 3100, 3.1-liter V6 engine, making 170 horsepower and 190 foot-pounds of torque, while meeting low-emission vehicle (LEV) standards. Gears are shifted automatically, and standard equipment includes four-wheel antilock brakes, four-wheel independent suspension, battery rundown protection, theft deterrent system, tachometer, air-conditioning, rear-seat heat ducts, tilt steering wheel and remote trunk release. Step up to LS trim and you leave the showroom in a fully loaded car. The LS includes aluminum wheels, fog lights, remote keyless entry, power driver's seat, power windows and door locks, cruise control, uplevel stereo, and a trunk cargo net.

This Chevy goes, slows and turns corners well enough to be entertaining, particularly with last year's boost in power. Interior design elements include a handy, left-handed cupholder (which is really too shallow for drinks and should be relegated to use as a change holder), backlighting for major controls and switches throughout the interior, and heating and air conditioning ducts located on the A-pillar to help direct air flow to rear-seat passengers. Also notable is the retro-style, dash-mounted ignition switch, because the driver doesn't have to crane his neck around to find the key slot.

Malibu has safety concerns covered, too. Dual airbags, four-wheel antilock brakes and child-safe rear door locks are standard. According to Chevrolet, side-impact door beams exceed federal standards for protection, though federal side-impact crash tests indicate that occupants may actually be rather vulnerable in this car. Maintaining the Malibu has been made easy with platinum-tipped spark plugs that last up to 100,000 miles, engine coolant designed to last five years or 150,000 miles, and transmission fluid that never has to be changed or checked.

Our list of gripes is short. The fake wood in the LS is unnecessary. We also want to find an integrated child safety seat on the options list in the future. And why can buyers get traction control on the Cavalier but not the Malibu? The list of improvements for 2001 doesn't address our concerns, though automatic on/off headlamps have been added and new cloth seats and door panels grace the interiors.

Still, the Malibu impresses us. It's one of the few domestic models that can go toe-to-toe with the imports on comfort and features, while beating them on price.

Standard Equipment

BASE (4A): 3.1L V6 OHV SMPI 12-valve engine; 4-speed electronic OD automatic transmission with lock-up torque converter; 600 amp battery with run down protection; 105 amp alternator; front-wheel drive, 3.05 axle ratio; stainless steel exhaust; front independent strut suspension with anti-roll bar, front coil springs, rear independent multi-link suspension with anti-roll bar, rear coil springs; rack-and-pinion power steering; front disc/rear drum brakes with 4-wheel antilock brakes; 14.8 gal. capacity fuel tank; side impact bars; front and rear body-colored bumpers; body-colored bodyside molding rocker panel extensions; clearcoat monotone paint; aero-composite halogen fully auto headlamps with daytime running lights; driver's and passenger's black folding outside mirrors, driver's manual remote outside mirror, passenger's manual outside mirror; 15" x 6" steel wheels; P215/60SR15 BSW touring A/S tires; compact steel spare wheel; air conditioning, rear heat ducts; AM/FM stereo radio, clock, seek-scan feature, 4 speakers, fixed antenna; power door locks, child-safety rear door locks, power remote hatch/trunk release; 2 power accessory outlets, front lighter element(s), smoker's package; instrumentation display includes tachometer, water temperature gauge, trip odometer; warning indicators include oil pressure, battery, low coolant, lights on, key in ignition, low fuel, low washer fluid, door ajar; driver's and passenger's front airbags; ignition disable; tinted windows, manual front and rear windows; variable intermittent front windshield wipers, sun visor strip, rear window defroster; seating capacity of 5, front bucket seats with adjustable headrests, center armrest with storage,

MALIBU
CHEVROLET

driver's and passenger's seat include 4-way adjustment; rear bench seat with fixed headrests; front height adjustable seatbelts; cloth seats, cloth door trim insert, full cloth headliner, full carpet floor covering; interior lights include dome light with fade, illuminated entry; steering wheel with tilt adjustment; vanity mirrors; day/night rearview mirror; full floor console, locking glove box with light, front and rear cupholders, instrument panel bin, driver's and passenger's door bins; carpeted cargo floor, cargo light; grille with chrome bar, black side window moldings, black front windshield molding, black rear window molding and body-colored door handles.

LS (4A) (in addition to or instead of BASE (4A) equipment): Body-colored front and rear mud flaps; additional exterior lights include front fog/driving lights; driver's and passenger's power remote body-colored folding outside mirrors; single-disc CD player, auto equalizer, theft deterrent; cruise control with steering wheel controls; power door locks with 2-stage unlock, remote keyless entry; ignition disable, panic alarm; power front and rear windows with driver's 1-touch down function; driver's seat includes 6-way power adjustment, 8-way adjustment; 60/40 folding rear bench seat with fixed headrests; premium cloth seats, carpeted floor mats; interior lights include front reading lights and passenger's side illuminated vanity mirror.

Base Prices

Code	Description	Invoice	MSRP
1ND69	Base (4A)	15573	17020
1NE69	LS (4A)	17660	19300
Destination Charge:		585	585

Interested in seeing what dealers will sell this vehicle for? Check out our True Market Value^{sm} (TMV^{sm}) pricing on our Web site at www.edmunds.com.

Accessories

Code	Description	Invoice	MSRP
—	**Special Leather Seat Trim (LS)**	536	595
	Includes leather-wrapped steering wheel and leather-wrapped shift knob. INCLUDED in 1SB.		
—G	**Spirit Cloth Seat Trim with Split Folding Rear Seat (Base)**	NC	NC
	NOT AVAILABLE with —H, 1SA.		
—H	**Spirit Cloth Seat Trim (Base)**	NC	NC
	NOT AVAILABLE with —G.		
1SA	**LS Preferred Equipment Group 1SA (LS)**	NC	NC
	Includes AM/FM stereo radio with CD and cassette players, color keyed front and rear carpeted floor mats, power outside rearview left and right mirrors, air conditioning, power door locks, cruise control with resume speed, remote keyless entry, split folding rear seat, color keyed mud guards and 15" alloy cast styled wheels.		
1SA	**Preferred Equipment Group 1SA (Base)**	NC	NC
	Includes AM/FM stereo radio, black left and right breakaway outside mirrors, air conditioning, power door locks and 15" steel bolt-on full cover wheels. NOT AVAILABLE with PF7, UPO, —G.		
1SB	**LS Preferred Equipment Group 1SB (LS)**	1188	1320
	Includes AM/FM stereo radio with CD and cassette players, color keyed front and rear carpeted floor mats, power outside rearview left and right mirrors, air conditioning, power door locks, cruise control with resume speed, remote keyless entry, split folding rear seat, color keyed mud guards, 15" alloy cast styled wheels, special leather seat trim, leather-wrapped steering wheel, leather-wrapped shift knob, rear Deck spoiler and electric sliding sunroof.		

CHEVROLET — MALIBU / MONTE CARLO

CODE	DESCRIPTION	INVOICE	MSRP
1SB	**Preferred Equipment Group 1SB (Base)**	896	995
	Includes AM/FM stereo radio with cassette, color keyed front and rear carpeted floor mats, power outside rearview left and right mirrors, rearview mirror with dual reading lamps, air conditioning, power door locks, power windows, cruise control with resume speed and 15" steel bolt-on full cover wheels. NOT AVAILABLE with UN0.		
AM9	**Split-Folding Rear Seat (Base)**	176	195
	Includes luggage area cargo net. REQUIRES — G. NOT AVAILABLE with 1SA, —H. INCLUDED in 1SA, 1SB.		
AU0	**Remote Keyless Entry (Base)**	135	150
	NOT AVAILABLE with 1SA. INCLUDED in 1SA, 1SB.		
B37	**Color-Keyed Front & Rear Carpeted Floormats (Base)**	36	40
	INCLUDED in 1SA, 1SB.		
CF5	**Power Sliding Sunroof (LS)**	585	650
	INCLUDED in 1SB.		
K05	**Engine Block Heater**	27	30
K34	**Electronic Cruise Control with Resume Speed (Base)**	216	240
	INCLUDED in 1SA, 1SB.		
PF7	**Wheels: 15" Cast Aluminum (Base)**	279	310
	NOT AVAILABLE with 1SA. INCLUDED in 1SA, 1SB.		
T43	**Rear Decklid Spoiler (LS)**	158	175
	INCLUDED in 1SB.		
UL0	**Radio: AM/FM Stereo with Cassette (Base)**	198	220
	Includes seek-scan, auto tone, digital clock and Radio Data System (RDS). NOT AVAILABLE with UP0, UN0. INCLUDED in 1SB.		
UN0	**Radio: AM/FM Stereo with CD (Base)**	90	100
	Includes seek-scan, auto tone, digital clock and Radio Data System (RDS). NOT AVAILABLE with UL0, UP0, 1SA.		
UN0	**Radio: AM/FM Stereo with CD (Base)**	288	320
	Includes seek-scan, auto tone, digital clock and Radio Data System (RDS). NOT AVAILABLE with UL0, UP0, 1SB.		
UP0	**Radio: AM/FM Stereo with CD and Cassette (Base)**	180	200
	Includes seek-scan, auto tone, digital clock and Radio Data System (RDS). NOT AVAILABLE with UL0, 1SA, UN0. INCLUDED in 1SA, 1SB.		
VH4	**Black Front & Rear Mud Guards (Base)**	68	75
	INCLUDED in 1SA, 1SB.		
Y11	**Enhanced Gold Package (LS)**	112	125
	Includes gold center grille bar, wheel center cap emblems and interior and exterior gold badging.		

2001 MONTE CARLO

What's New?

Chevy's large personal-luxury coupe receives optional sport appearance packages, a standard driver's side-impact airbag and traction control and OnStar comes with the SS model.

MONTE CARLO — CHEVROLET

| CODE | DESCRIPTION | INVOICE | MSRP |

Review

Heritage design is popular these days, and Chevrolet has employed this styling trend on the Monte Carlo. From the traditional "Knight's Crest" badge, script lettering and distinctive headlight treatment to the sculpted fenders and vertical taillights, the MC strongly recalls the '70s and '80s models that made the nameplate a hit.

Under the skin, the Monte Carlo shares a platform with the Chevrolet Impala, which means this is a big coupe — the full Monte, if you will. Two models are available: the LS comes equipped with a 3.4-liter, V6 engine making 180 horsepower, while the SS benefits from 20 additional ponies and more torque, thanks to the venerable 3.8-liter V6 under the hood. Either model comes well-equipped, but to emphasize performance, the SS gets fog lights, rocker-panel moldings, a rear spoiler, 16-inch alloy wheels, a full complement of gauges and twin exhaust outlets routed from dual mufflers.

A tower-to-tower structural brace under the hood, combined with a magnesium dashboard support beam, contributes to a rigid platform, improves handling and helps reduce squeaks and rattles. Large four-wheel-disc ABS brakes with front cooling ducts provide confidence-inspiring stopping ability. A four-wheel independent MacPherson strut suspension is matched to front and rear stabilizer bars and meaty Goodyear Eagle RS-A performance tires to help make Monte Carlo fun in the curves. But you're going to have to settle for an automatic transmission in this Chevy; a manual is not available. Traction control is now standard on both models.

Inside, buyers looking for healthy doses of comfort will find it in Monte Carlo, whose cavernous innards were designed specifically to maximize harmony between the car and the driver. Special attention was paid to control placement and seat design, and engineers strove to provide top-notch brake pedal and steering feel. Good visibility, thanks to generous expanses of glass, a standard rear-window defogger, and large side-view mirrors, is a new Monte Carlo hallmark, though the wide C-pillars will likely block vision in certain parking and lane-change maneuvers.

All Monte Carlos come with air conditioning, power door locks, power windows, tilt steering wheel, a driver message center with oil life monitor, RDS radio technology, theatre-dimming interior lighting, daytime running lights, a tire-pressure monitor and an inside trunk release designed to prevent a child from becoming locked in the luggage compartment. Step up to the SS model, and you get, in addition to traction control and performance/cosmetic enhancements, a cargo net, cruise control, leather-wrapped steering wheel with redundant audio controls, remote keyless entry, dual-zone temperature controls and a pollen filter. Options include leather seating, premium stereo with CD player, power front seats, heated exterior mirrors, OnStar (standard fare on the SS) and a power sunroof.

Compared to the bland Lumina-based model sold a few years ago, this Monte Carlo is a tremendous improvement.

Standard Equipment

LS (4A): 3.4L V6 OHV SMPI 12-valve engine; 4-speed electronic OD automatic transmission with lock-up torque converter; 600 amp battery; 100 amp alternator; front-wheel drive, traction control, 2.86 axle ratio; stainless steel exhaust; comfort ride suspension, front independent strut suspension with anti-roll bar, front coil springs, rear independent strut suspension with anti-roll bar, rear coil springs; rack-and-pinion power steering; 4-wheel antilock disc brakes; 17 gal. capacity fuel tank; side impact bars; front and rear body-colored bumpers; body-colored bodyside molding rocker panel extensions; clearcoat monotone paint; aero-composite halogen fully auto headlamps with daytime running lights; driver's and passenger's power remote black

CHEVROLET

MONTE CARLO

outside mirrors; 16" x 6.5" steel wheels; P225/60SR16 BSW touring A/S tires; compact steel spare wheel; air conditioning, rear heat ducts; AM/FM stereo radio, clock, seek-scan feature, cassette player, 4 speakers, auto equalizer, theft deterrent, window grid antenna; power door locks, power remote hatch/trunk release; 1 power accessory outlet, front lighter element(s), driver's foot rest, smoker's package; instrumentation display includes tachometer, water temperature gauge, trip odometer; warning indicators include battery, low oil level, low coolant, lights on, key in ignition, service interval, low tire pressure; driver's and passenger's front airbags; ignition disable; tinted windows with driver's 1-touch down function; variable intermittent front windshield wipers, sun visor strip, rear window defroster; seating capacity of 5, front bucket seats with adjustable headrests, center armrest with storage, driver's seat and passenger's seat includes 4-way adjustment; 60/40 folding rear bench seat with fixed headrests, center armrest; cloth seats, cloth door trim insert, full cloth headliner, full carpet floor covering with carpeted floor mats; interior lights include dome light with fade, front reading lights; steering wheel with tilt adjustment; vanity mirrors, dual auxiliary visors; day/night rearview mirror; full floor console, full overhead console with storage, locking glove box with light, front and rear cupholders, 1 seatback storage pocket, driver's and passenger's door bins; carpeted cargo floor, cargo light; body-colored grille, black side window moldings, black front windshield molding, black rear window molding and body-colored door handles.

SS (4A) (in addition to or instead of LS (4A) equipment): 3.8L V6 OHV SMPI 12-valve engine; 3.29 axle ratio; sport-ride suspension; rear lip spoiler; additional exterior lights include front fog/driving lights; 16" x 6.5" sport aluminum wheels; dual-zone front air conditioning, air filter; radio steering wheel controls; cruise control with steering wheel controls; power door locks with 2-stage unlock, remote keyless entry; emergency S.O.S. (OnStar); instrumentation display includes oil pressure gauge, volt gauge; seat mounted driver's side airbag; panic alarm, tracker system; driver's seat includes lumbar support; premium cloth seats; interior lights include illuminated entry; leather-wrapped steering wheel with tilt adjustment; dual illuminated vanity mirrors; auto-dimming day/night rearview mirror and cargo net.

Base Prices

Code	Description	Invoice	MSRP
1WW27	LS (4A)	17907	19570
1WX27	SS (4A)	20496	22400
	Destination Charge:	610	610

Interested in seeing what dealers will sell this vehicle for? Check out our True Market Value^{sm} (TMV^{sm}) pricing on our Web site at www.edmunds.com.

Accessories

Code	Description	Invoice	MSRP
—	Leather Accent Seat Trim (LS)	685	770
	Includes driver side impact air bag. REQUIRES AG1.		
—	Leather Accent Seat Trim (SS)	556	625
	REQUIRES AG1.		
1SA	Base Preferred Equipment Group	NC	NC
	Includes vehicle with standard equipment. NOT AVAILABLE with UK3, CF5, DK5, U68, ZOK.		
1SB	Preferred Equipment Group 1 (LS)	654	735
	Includes electronic cruise control with resume speed, remote keyless entry, illuminated entry, cargo net and styled alloy wheels.		
1SB	Preferred Equipment Group 1 (SS)	547	615
	Includes driver info convenience center, trip computer, outside temperature and compass, Homelink programmable garage door opener, anti-theft alarm system,		

MONTE CARLO — CHEVROLET

CODE	DESCRIPTION	INVOICE	MSRP

...overhead storage bin delete, dual power outside heated mirrors and 6-way power driver seat.

1SC — Preferred Equipment Group 2 (LS) .... 1226 · 1378
Includes electronic speed control with resume speed, remote keyless entry, illuminated entry, cargo net, styled alloy wheels, driver and passenger temperature controls, left and right illuminated visor vanity mirrors, electrochromic inside rearview mirror and OnStar.

AG1 — 6-Way Power Driver Seat .... 271 · 305
INCLUDED in 1SB.

AG2 — 6-Way Power Passenger Seat .... 271 · 305
REQUIRES AG1, Leather Accent Seat Trim and KA1.

AU0 — Remote Keyless Entry (LS) .... 147 · 165
Includes illuminated entry. INCLUDED in 1SB, 1SC.

BYP — High Sport Appearance Package (SS) .... 1869 · 2100
Includes ground effects, race inspired spoiler and instrumentation cluster panel identification, unique 16" alloy wheels and stainless steel exhaust tips. NOT AVAILABLE with D58.

CF5 — Electric Sliding Sunroof .... 623 · 700
Includes overhead storage bin delete. NOT AVAILABLE with 1SA.

CJ3 — Driver and Front Passenger Temperature Controls (LS) .... 89 · 100
INCLUDED in 1SC.

D58 — Spoiler Delete (SS) .... (156) · (175)
NOT AVAILABLE with BYP.

DK5 — Dual Power Outside Heated Mirrors (LS) .... 31 · 35
NOT AVAILABLE with 1SA. INCLUDED in 1SB.

K05 — Engine Block Heater .... 31 · 35

K34 — Electronic Cruise Control with Resume Speed (LS) .... 214 · 240
INCLUDED in 1SB, 1SC.

KA1 — Driver and Front Passenger Heated Seats .... 107 · 120
REQUIRES AG1, AG2 and Leather Accent Seat Trim.

QD1 — Wheels: 16" Styled Aluminum (LS) .... 267 · 300
NOT AVAILABLE with ZOK. INCLUDED in 1SB, 1SC.

U68 — Driver Info Convenience Center (LS) .... 245 · 275
Includes trip computer, outside temperature and compass, Homelink programmable garage door opener, anti-theft alarm system and overhead storage bin delete. NOT AVAILABLE with 1SA. INCLUDED in 1SB.

UK3 — Leather-Wrapped Steering Wheel with Radio Controls (LS) .... 152 · 171
NOT AVAILABLE with 1SA.

UN0 — Radio: AM/FM Stereo with CD .... 109 · 123
Includes seek-scan, digital clock, auto tone control, Theft Lock, speed compensated volume, radio data systems technology and antenna in rear glass and premium 6 speaker system. NOT AVAILABLE with UP0, WX9.

UP0 — Radio: AM/FM Stereo with CD and Cassette .... 198 · 223
Includes seek and scan, digital clock, auto tone control, Theft Lock, auto speed compensated volume control, radio data systems technology and antenna in rear glass and premium 6 speaker system. NOT AVAILABLE with UN0, WX9.

VK4 — Front License Plate Depression Cover .... 9 · 10

CHEVROLET
MONTE CARLO / PRIZM

CODE	DESCRIPTION	INVOICE	MSRP
WX9	Remote CD Wiring Harness	71	80
	Includes performance 6 speaker system. NOT AVAILABLE with UNO, UPO.		
Z0K	Sport Appearance Package (LS)	530	595
	Includes 16" 5-spoke alloy wheels and race inspired spoiler. REQUIRES 1SB or 1SC. NOT AVAILABLE with QD1, 1SA.		

2001 PRIZM

What's New?

The Prizm remains relatively unchanged for 2001. An emergency trunk release becomes standard issue and Medium Red Metallic is added to the color palette.

Review

In short, the Prizm is one solid economy sedan. It does everything capably, and looks good too. Better yet, it is essentially a reskinned Toyota Corolla, which bodes well for reliability, but not necessarily resale value. To top things off, the Prizm has earned very high marks in past initial-quality studies, scoring better than the Infiniti G20 and Honda Accord.

But there is a problem, and that problem is price. Slotted between the Cavalier and Malibu, the small Prizm is no bargain once options are added. A well-equipped Prizm can be more expensive than a similarly loaded Malibu. For 2001, Chevrolet is trying to boost Prizm's value by offering an emergency trunk release and a defroster logic system to the HVAC system in the base price. Bottom-rung models get air conditioning, a four-speaker stereo, floor mats and wheel covers this year, while LSi buyers receive standard power windows, rear defogger, tachometer with outside temperature gauge, tilt steering column, dual reading lights within the rearview mirror and larger tires.

Despite the price of entry, there are compelling reasons to choose the Prizm. Its excellent reliability record, coupled with tasteful styling and outstanding assembly quality, goes a long way toward selling consumers on the Prizm. The car feels substantial, conveying the impression that it will last quite a long time. In contrast, the Cavalier feels somewhat cheap, flimsy and unrefined. The solid Malibu doesn't appeal to buyers looking for a smaller package.

A 1.8-liter four-cylinder engine is standard on all Prizms, which benefits from variable valve timing technology that certainly didn't come from GM. Toyota's VVTi system helps boost power to 125 horsepower and 125 foot-pounds of torque. Interestingly, side airbags are optional on this economy sedan. Front and rear stabilizer bars are standard to improve handling response from the four-wheel independent suspension. All interior fabrics feature Scotchgard stain protection and a power sunroof is available. As on last year's model—and in a break with GM tradition—antilock brakes are optional rather than standard.

Interior accommodations are rather sparse in base Prizms, but LSi's come with uplevel fittings and trim. Either model offers decent ergonomics; all the switches and controls fall readily to hand and the gauges are clear and legible. The seats are rock hard and lacking lumbar and lateral support. The clutch is a joy to work and the five-speed manual snicks fluidly from gear to gear.

Prizm is strictly econo-issue in base trim, but add aluminum wheels and a premium equipment package to an LSi and the Prizm transforms itself into a mini-Camry. Also available are a CD player and extended-range speakers that sound great. Truly, a fully loaded Prizm is a fine package. However, a Prizm LSi with every available option closes quickly on $20,000. For that

PRIZM — CHEVROLET

kind of cash you can buy any number of larger and more substantial sedans. Keep a lid on the options, though, and the Prizm makes much more sense.

Standard Equipment

BASE (5M): 1.8L I4 DOHC SMPI 16-valve engine; 5-speed OD manual transmission; 390 amp battery; 80 amp alternator; front-wheel drive, 3.72 axle ratio; stainless steel exhaust; front independent strut suspension with anti-roll bar, front coil springs, rear independent strut suspension with anti-roll bar, rear coil springs; rack-and-pinion power steering; front disc/rear drum brakes; 13.2 gal. capacity fuel tank; side impact bars; class I trailering; front and rear body-colored bumpers; black bodyside molding; clearcoat monotone paint; aero-composite halogen fully auto headlamps with daytime running lights; driver's and passenger's manual remote black outside mirrors; 14" x 5.5" steel wheels; P175/65SR14 BSW A/S tires; compact steel spare wheel; air conditioning, rear heat ducts; AM/FM stereo radio, clock, seek-scan feature, 4 speakers, fixed antenna; child-safety rear door locks, remote hatch/trunk release, remote fuel door release; 1 power accessory outlet, front lighter element(s), driver's foot rest, smoker's package; instrumentation display includes water temperature gauge, trip odometer; warning indicators include oil pressure, water temp, battery, lights on, key in ignition, low fuel, door ajar, brake fluid; driver's and passenger's front airbags; tinted windows, manual front and rear windows; variable intermittent front windshield wipers, sun visor strip; seating capacity of 5, front bucket seats with adjustable headrests, driver's and passenger's seats include 4-way adjustment; rear bench seat with fixed headrests; front height adjustable seatbelts with pretensioners; cloth seats, cloth door trim insert, full cloth headliner, full color-keyed carpet floor covering with carpeted floor mats; interior lights include dome light with delay; vanity mirrors; day/night rearview mirror; full floor console, glove box with light, front and rear cupholders, instrument panel covered bin, driver's and passenger's door bins; carpeted cargo floor, cargo light; black grille, black side window moldings, black front windshield molding, black rear window molding and black door handles.

LSI (5M) (in addition to or instead of BASE (5M) equipment): Driver's and passenger's power remote black outside mirrors; P185/65SR14 BSW A/S tires; cassette player, 4 performance speakers; cruise control; power door locks with 2-stage unlock, remote keyless entry; instrumentation display includes tachometer, exterior temp; power front and rear windows with driver's 1-touch down function; rear window defroster; center armrest with storage; 60/40 folding rear bench seat with fixed headrests, center pass-thru armrest; premium cloth seats; interior lights include front reading lights, illuminated entry; steering wheel with tilt adjustment and 2 seatback storage pockets.

Base Prices

Code	Description	Invoice	MSRP
1SK19	Base (5M)	13323	13995
1SK19	LSi (5M)	14807	16060
	Destination Charge:	485	485

Interested in seeing what dealers will sell this vehicle for? Check out our True Market Value^{sm} (TMV^{sm}) pricing on our Web site at www.edmunds.com.

Accessories

Code	Description	Invoice	MSRP
1SA	Preferred Equipment Group 1 (Base)	NC	NC
	Includes vehicle with standard equipment. REQUIRES R9W or C49.		
1SB	Preferred Equipment Group 2 (Base)	490	570
	Includes AM/FM stereo radio with cassette, power door locks and electronic cruise control with resume speed. REQUIRES R9W or C49. NOT AVAILABLE with U1C.		

CHEVROLET

PRIZM

CODE	DESCRIPTION	INVOICE	MSRP
1SE	Preferred Equipment Group 1 (LSi)	NC	NC
	Includes AM/FM stereo radio with cassette, power door locks and electronic cruise control with resume speed.		
9J6	Adjustable Tilt Steering Wheel (Base)	69	80
A31	Power Windows with Driver's Express Down (Base)	258	300
	Includes lockout switch.		
AJ7	Driver and Front Passenger Side Airbags	254	295
AN2	Child Safety Seat (LSi)	108	125
AU3	Power Door Locks (Base)	189	220
	Includes driver and passenger side switch. INCLUDED in 1SE, 1SB.		
C49	Rear Window Defogger (Base)	155	180
	NOT AVAILABLE with R9W.		
CF5	Electric Sunroof (Base)	580	675
	Includes mirror map light.		
CF5	Electric Sunroof (LSi)	563	655
	Includes mirror map light. Deletes dual reading lamps built into rearview mirror.		
JM4	4-Wheel Antilock Brake System	555	645
K34	Electronic Cruise Control with Resume Speed (Base)	159	185
	INCLUDED in 1SE, 1SB.		
MS7	Transmission: Electronic 4-Speed Automatic w/OD	688	800
	Includes 2.65 axle ratio. NOT AVAILABLE with MX1.		
MX1	Transmission: 3-Speed Automatic	426	495
	Includes 3.23 axle ratio. NOT AVAILABLE with MS7.		
PG4	Wheels: 14" Alloy	243	283
R9W	Rear Window Defogger Not Desired (Base)	NC	NC
	NOT AVAILABLE with C49.		
U16	Tachometer with Outside Temp Gauge (Base)	60	70
U1C	Radio: AM/FM Stereo with CD (Base)	185	215
	Includes digital clock and 4 premium speakers (front speakers are coaxial). NOT AVAILABLE with 1SB.		
U1C	Radio: AM/FM Stereo with CD	43	50
	Includes digital clock and 4 premium speakers (front speakers are coaxial). NOT AVAILABLE with 1SA.		
UM6	Radio: AM/FM Stereo with Cassette (Base)	142	165
	Includes seek-and-scan, digital clock and 4 premium speakers (front speakers are coaxial). NOT AVAILABLE with U1C. INCLUDED in 1SE, 1SB.		

300M

CHRYSLER

2001 300M

What's New?

DaimlerChrysler ups the feature content for the 300M by including standard steering wheel controls for the stereo, offering the option of side airbags and adding a luxury group package that includes real wood trim and an overhead console-mounted vehicle information center. The rear end gets a makeover in the form of clear lens taillamps and chrome dual exhaust outlets while new 17-inch wheels and anodized aluminum window trim dresses up the 300M's profile. There's now a three-point shoulder/lap belt for the central rear seat passenger and an internal emergency trunk release. Additional luxury package features include an auto dimming rear view mirror and exterior mirrors that tilt down automatically when the vehicle is placed in reverse. Two new exterior colors, Black and Deep Sapphire Blue, plus three new interior colors, Sandstone, Dark Slate Grey, and Taupe, round out the changes for 2001.

Review

The 300M is a 2-year-old iteration of Chrysler's sport sedan. Its styling and letter-series designation pick up where the original '55-'65 muscle cars left off — take one look at its big center grille and fin-like taillights, and you'll be just a notch ahead of your flashback. But the sleek, fluid lines and the streamlined dash remind you that this vehicle does indeed represent the 21st century. This year the 300M gets clear lens taillamps, aluminum side window moldings and chrome dual exhaust outlets to further its performance car image.

For this driver-oriented modernized muscle car, there's a 3.5-liter, aluminum high-output V6 (shared with the Chrysler LHS and the Prowler) that offers respectable power for its size: 253 horsepower at 6,400 rpm and 255 foot-pounds of torque at 3,950 rpm. That's more power than you'll find in such performance sedans as the Nissan Maxima (a 3.0-liter V6 with 222 horses) and the Buick Regal GS (a supercharged 3.8-liter V6 with 240 horsepower). For muscle car fans with a green streak, the 300M's engine is now LEV certified.

The performance theme of the 300M continues underneath. The fully independent suspension has a soft-ride setting as standard, but there's an optional, more aggressive European-tuned performance choice should you want to let the car strut its stuff. We'd opt for the European suspension, just for the promise of an enhanced driving experience. In either soft or taut setting, however, the steering remains first-rate. See, you can bring along the whole canasta club and still have a blast driving them to the Jimmy Buffet Extravaganza in Branson!

The 300M is affectionately known as a 5-meter car (its length is 197.8 inches, or 5.02 meters). Chrysler says that the length was an important consideration from the start, and claims that it can be parked in smaller European garages despite its big-car cabin. The 300M's platform is shared with the Dodge Intrepid and the Chrysler Concorde and LHS, but the 300M is the most fun to drive, thanks in part to its tidy dimensions.

We're disappointed that the 300M's only transmission is an automatic. Chrysler tries to make up for it with AutoStick, which gives manual control of the slushbox, but it's definitely not the same thing as a true manual. In addition to the automatic, other standard features include a leather interior with heated, eight-way power driver's seat, air conditioning, 17-inch wheels, four-wheel ABS, an Infinity 240-watt sound system with new-for-2001 steering wheel controls, heated eight-way power seats, and 17-inch wheels, available painted or with a chromed aluminum finish. Options include side airbags, real wood trim, an overhead console and an in-dash four-disc changer.

CHRYSLER *300M*

CODE	DESCRIPTION	INVOICE	MSRP

Says Chrysler chief engineer Bob Rodger, "The 300 idea is the idea of a powerful, nimble, responsive automotive machine." Of course, Rodger made those comments more than 40 years ago. Amazing how history really does repeat itself.

Standard Equipment

300M (4A): 3.5L V6 SOHC SMPI 24-valve engine; 4-speed electronic OD automatic transmission with lock-up torque converter; 600 amp battery with run down protection; HD radiator; 130 amp alternator; automanual transmission oil cooler; front-wheel drive, traction control, 3.66 axle ratio; stainless steel exhaust with tailpipe finisher; touring ride suspension, front independent strut suspension with anti-roll bar, front coil springs, gas-pressurized front shocks, rear independent multi-link suspension with anti-roll bar, rear coil springs, gas-pressurized rear shocks; power rack-and-pinion steering; 4-wheel antilock disc brakes; 17.3 gal. capacity fuel tank; side impact bars; front and rear body-colored bumpers; body-colored bodyside molding; clearcoat monotone paint; aero-composite halogen fully auto headlamps with delay-off feature; additional exterior lights include front fog/driving lights; driver's and passenger's power remote black heated folding outside mirrors; 17" x 7" silver alloy wheels; P225/55SR17 BSW touring A/S tires; compact steel spare wheel; air conditioning with climate control, rear heat ducts; AM/FM stereo radio, seek-scan, cassette player, single CD player, 9 premium speakers, amplifier, graphic equalizer, window grid antenna, radio steering wheel controls; cruise control with steering wheel controls; power door locks with 2 stage unlock, remote keyless entry, child safety rear door locks, power remote trunk release; 2 power accessory outlets, driver's foot rest, garage door opener; instrumentation display includes tachometer, water temperature gauge, clock, compass, exterior temp, trip computer, trip odometer; warning indicators include oil pressure, water temp, battery, lights on, key in ignition, low fuel, low washer fluid, door ajar, trunk ajar, brake fluid; driver's and passenger's front airbags; ignition disable, panic alarm, security system; tinted windows, power front and rear windows with driver's 1-touch down; variable intermittent front windshield wipers, sun visor strip, rear window defroster; seating capacity of 5, front bucket seats with heated-cushions and adjustable tilt headrests, center armrest with storage, driver's seat includes 8-way power adjustment with lumbar support, passenger's seat includes 8-way power adjustment; 60/40 folding rear bench seat with adjustable headrests and center armrest; front height adjustable seatbelts; leather seats, leatherette door trim insert with carpet lower, full cloth headliner, full carpet floor covering with carpeted floor mats, simulated wood dashboard insert, leather-wrapped gearshift knob, simulated wood door panel insert, chrome interior accents; memory on driver's seat with 2 memory setting(s) includes settings for exterior mirrors; interior lights include dome light with fade, front and rear reading lights, 4 door curb lights, illuminated entry; leather-wrapped steering wheel with tilt adjustment; dual illuminated vanity mirrors, dual auxiliary visors; auto-dimming day/night rearview mirror; full floor console, mini overhead console locking glove box with light, front and rear cupholders, 2 seat back storage pockets, driver's and passenger's door bins; carpeted cargo floor, carpeted trunk lid, cargo net, cargo light; chrome grille, chrome side window moldings, black front windshield molding, black rear window molding and body-colored door handles.

Base Prices

LHYS41	300M (4A)	27451	29640
Destination Charge:		655	655

Interested in seeing what dealers will sell this vehicle for? Check out our True Market Value℠ (TMV℠) pricing on our Web site at www.edmunds.com.

Accessories

26M	Quick Order Package 26M	NC	NC
	Includes vehicle with standard equipment.		

CHRYSLER
300M / CONCORDE

CODE	DESCRIPTION	INVOICE	MSRP
ADE	Cold Weather Group	36	40
	Includes battery heater and engine block heater.		
AFF	Luxury Group	463	520
	Includes exterior driver auto dim mirror, exterior auto adjust in reverse mirrors, wood/leather-wrapped steering wheel, vehicle information center and genuine CA walnut wood trim.		
ARF	Radio: Cassette Player, 4 CD, Amp, 11 Infinity Speakers	458	515
	Includes 360 watt amplifier, 4 disc in-dash CD changer, AM/FM, changer control and 11 Infinity speakers in 9 locations.		
AWS	Smokers' Group	27	30
	Includes front and rear ash receivers and cigar lighter.		
AWT	Performance Handling Group	498	560
	Includes performance 4-wheel disc antilock brakes, high speed engine controller and performance steering, performance suspension and P225/55R17 95V A/S performance tires.		
CGS	Side Supplemental Air Bags	347	390
GWA	Power Sunroof	797	895
PEL	Paint: Inferno Red Tinted Pearlcoat	178	200
TBW	Tire: Full-Size Spare with Matching Wheel	223	250
	NOT AVAILABLE with WF7.		
TBW	Tire: Full-Size Spare with Matching Wheel	343	385
	REQUIRES WF7		
WF7	Wheels: 17" Chrome Aluminum	668	750

2001 CONCORDE

What's New?

Supplemental side airbags are a new option for the year, and an internal trunk release and center shoulder belt for the rear seat are standard. A center console power outlet exists for those models equipped with bucket seats, and all models get steering wheel-mounted audio controls. Two new exterior colors and three new interior colors are available this year, and both engines now meet LEV standards for all 50 states.

Review

The Concorde, along with its sibling Dodge Intrepid, went through a major redesign in 1998, and the folks at Chrysler got it right this time. The Concorde was actually designed and brought to life exclusively through the use of computers, and Chrysler ended up with a modern-day classic. With a front grille reminiscent of certain models from Ferrari, Chrysler brought class and style to full-size sedans.

But looks aren't everything, and sometimes it's what's on the inside that really counts. You can count on 225 horsepower and 225 foot-pounds of torque from the LXi's peppy 3.2-liter V6, which has strong midrange passing power and gets decent mileage. The LX is

CHRYSLER — CONCORDE

| CODE | DESCRIPTION | INVOICE | MSRP |

outfitted with a 2.7-liter V6 worthy of 200 horsepower and 190 foot-pounds of torque. And you say you like 100,000-mile intervals between tune-ups? Your wish has been granted.

Only a four-speed automatic transmission is available, and don't look for an AutoStick anywhere in this lineup. Fret not, you're not missing a whole lot. Our experience with AutoStick showed that it wasn't terribly responsive anyway. Traction control is standard on the LXi and optional for LX seekers, and you can ditto that for ABS. Both the LX and LXi have a touring-tuned four-wheel independent suspension, which is quite compliant. The LXi has speed-sensitive power rack-and-pinion steering, and handling is precise — like a midsize sport sedan, not a car with a 113-inch wheelbase.

Besides V6 power differences between the LX and LXi, there are a few creature comforts made available only on the LXi, including a security system and automatic climate control. But many luxury items are either standard or available to the base model; cruise control, power windows, steering wheel audio controls and an eight-way power driver's seat head up the standard list, while a moonroof, a trip-computer/HomeLink package, power passenger seat, side airbags and leather seats top the optional list.

Packages are also available for the LX that earn the driver a leather-wrapped steering wheel, a 50/50 front bench seat, and eight-way power driver and passenger seats. While we can't be terribly enthusiastic about the quality of the interior materials or the sometimes spotty build quality, we still think that the LX delivers a lot of bang for the buck.

With the last redesign, Chrysler brought class and style to full-size sedans with the Concord. If interior space is your No. 1 priority, this car's hard to beat; with the pool of big ol' American sedans constantly shrinking, there is a case to be made for a car that offers enough trunk space for someone to reside in and actually utilize the internal trunk release that's new for the year. Want a sedan you can lust after? Take a good look at the Concorde. This kind of style will endure for years to come.

Standard Equipment

LX (4A): 2.7L V6 DOHC SMPI 24-valve engine; 4-speed electronic OD automatic transmission with lock-up torque converter; 500 amp battery with run down protection; 120 amp alternator; front-wheel drive, 3.89 axle ratio; stainless steel exhaust; touring ride suspension, front independent strut suspension with anti-roll bar, front coil springs, gas-pressurized front shocks, rear independent multi-link suspension with anti-roll bar, rear coil springs, gas-pressurized rear shocks; power rack-and-pinion steering; 4-wheel disc brakes; 17 gal. capacity fuel tank; side impact bars; front and rear body-colored bumpers; body-colored bodyside molding; clearcoat monotone paint; aero-composite halogen headlamps with delay-off feature; driver's and passenger's power remote black outside mirrors; 16" x 7" steel wheels; P225/60SR16 BSW touring A/S tires; compact steel spare wheel; air conditioning, rear heat ducts; AM/FM stereo radio, clock, seek-scan, cassette player, 4 speakers, window grid antenna; cruise control with steering wheel controls; power door locks with 2 stage unlock, remote keyless entry, child safety rear door locks, power remote trunk release; 2 power accessory outlets, driver's foot rest; instrumentation display includes tachometer, water temperature gauge, trip odometer; warning indicators include oil pressure, water temp, battery, lights on, key in ignition, low fuel, low washer fluid, door ajar, trunk ajar, brake fluid; driver's and passenger's front airbags; panic alarm; tinted windows, power front and rear windows with driver's 1-touch down; variable intermittent front windshield wipers, sun visor strip, rear window defroster; seating capacity of 5, front bucket seats with adjustable headrests, center armrest with storage, driver's seat includes 8-way power adjustment, lumbar support, passenger's seat includes 4-way adjustment; rear bench seat with center pass-thru armrest with storage; front height adjustable seatbelts; premium cloth seats, vinyl door trim insert with carpet, full cloth headliner, full carpet floor covering with carpeted floor mats, simulated wood dashboard insert, simulated wood door panel insert, simulated wood console insert, chrome interior accents; interior lights include dome light with fade, front and rear reading lights, 2 door curb lights, illuminated entry; steering wheel with tilt adjustment; dual illuminated vanity mirrors; day/night rearview mirror; full floor console, locking glove box with light, front and rear cupholders, 1 seat back storage pocket, driver's and passenger's door bins; carpeted cargo floor, carpeted trunk lid, cargo net, cargo light; chrome

CONCORDE — CHRYSLER

grille, black side window moldings, black front windshield molding, black rear window molding and body-colored door handles.

LXi (4A) (in addition to or instead of LX (4A) equipment): 3.2L V6 SOHC SMPI 24-valve engine; 600 amp battery; HD radiator; 130 amp alternator; traction control, 3.66 axle ratio; power rack-and-pinion steering with vehicle speed-sensing assist; 4-wheel antilock brakes; air conditioning with climate control, premium AM/FM stereo radio, clock, seek-scan, cassette player, single CD player, 8 speakers, amplifier, graphic equalizer; garage door opener; compass, exterior temp, trip computer; ignition disable, security system; passenger's seat includes 8-way power adjustment; leather seats, leather-wrapped gearshift knob, leather-wrapped steering wheel with tilt adjustment; auto-dimming day/night rearview mirror; and a mini overhead console.

Base Prices

Code	Description	Invoice	MSRP
LHCH41	LX (4A)	20834	22510
LHCM41	LXi (4A)	24655	26755
	Destination Charge:	625	625

Interested in seeing what dealers will sell this vehicle for? Check out our True Market Value^{sm} (TMV^{sm}) pricing on our Web site at www.edmunds.com.

Accessories

Code	Description	Invoice	MSRP
22C	**Quick Order Package 22C (LX)** — Includes vehicle with standard equipment. NOT AVAILABLE with JPR, AGT, AJD, MP, or ML.	NC	NC
22D	**Quick Order Package 22D (LX)** — Includes universal garage door opener, auto dim rear view mirror, premium cassette player with amplifier and 8 speakers radio, trip computer and 16" alloy wheels. NOT AVAILABLE with AR3.	1010	1135
24F	**Quick Order Package 24F (LXi)** — Includes vehicle with standard equipment.	(285)	(320)
ADE	**Cold Weather Group** — Includes battery heater and engine block heater.	36	40
AGT	**Traction Control/Steering Group (LX)** — Includes premium body controller and speed sensitive steering. REQUIRES BR3. NOT AVAILABLE with 22C.	249	280
AJD	**Leather Interior Group (LX)** — Includes driver's and passenger's 8-way power seats, leather trimmed bucket seats, leather-wrapped shift knob and leather-wrapped steering wheel. NOT AVAILABLE with 22C or QF.	975	1095
AR3	**Radio: Premium Cassette Player, CD, Amp, 8 Speakers (LX)** — Includes 120 Watt amplifier, AM/FM cassette player, equalizer and 8 speakers in 6 locations. NOT AVAILABLE with 22C.	200	225
AR3	**Radio: Premium Cassette Player, CD, Amp, 8 Speakers (LX)** — Includes 120 Watt amplifier, AM/FM cassette playter, equalizer and 8 speakers in 6 locations. NOT AVAILABLE with 22D.	512	575
ARE	**Radio: Cassette Player, 4 CD, Amp, 9 Infinity Speakers (LXi)** — Includes 240 Watt amplifier, steering wheel mounted audio controls, 4 disc in-dash CD changer, AM/FM cassette player, CD changer control and 9 Infinity speakers in 7 locations.	512	575

CHRYSLER

CONCORDE / LHS

CODE	DESCRIPTION	INVOICE	MSRP
AWS	Smokers' Group	27	30
	Includes front and rear ash receivers and cigar lighter.		
BR3	4-Wheel Disc Antilock Brakes (LX)	534	600
CGS	Supplemental Side Air Bags	347	390
GWA	Power Sunroof	797	895
JPR	8-Way Power Driver/Passenger Seats	338	380
	NOT AVAILABLE with 22C.		
ML	Leather Trimmed Bucket Seats	NC	NC
	Includes full length console with cupholders, manual driver lumbar adjust, rear seat with trunk pass-thru and rear armrest with storage/cupholder. REQUIRES 22D and AJD. NOT AVAILABLE with 22C, MP, or QF.		
MP	Leather Trimmed 50/50 Bench Seat	134	150
	Includes front armrest with cupholders, manual driver lumbar adjust, rear seat with trunk pass-thru and rear armrest with storage/cupholder. Deletes floor console and leather-wrapped shift knob. REQUIRES 22D and AJD. NOT AVAILABLE with 22C, QF, or ML.		
QF	Cloth 50/50 Bench Seat (LX)	134	150
	NOT AVAILABLE with ML, MP, and AJD.		
TBB	Tire: Full Size Spare (LX)	142	160
TBW	Full Size Spare with Matching Wheel (LXi)	80	90
	NOT AVAILABLE with WNE.		
TBW	Full Size Spare with Matching Wheel (LXi)	214	240
WNE	Wheels: 16" Chrome Aluminum (LXi)	534	600
	NOT AVAILABLE with TBW.		
WNS	Wheels: 16" Aluminum (LX)	347	390
	INCLUDED in 22D.		

2001 LHS

What's New?

An optional luxury package includes automatic adjusting side mirrors, electrochromic driver's side mirror, walnut wood trim and an overhead console-mounted vehicle information display. There's an additional electrical power outlet in the center console, an overhead console with a driver information display, standard steering wheel-mounted stereo controls, and three new interior colors. The LHS' 17-inch wheels now come in a Sparkle Silver finish while aluminum replaces the chrome window molding trim and two new exterior colors, Black and Deep Sapphire Blue Pearl Coat, further dress up this upscale sedan. For safety's sake, an internal trunk release and a center shoulder belt for the rear seat comes standard while side airbags are now optional for front passengers.

Review

So you call yourself a luxury buyer? Then you've stopped at the right place. The Chrysler LHS, with its fluid lines that echo those of its stablemates, is a full-size sedan that is both affordable and easy on the eyes. It's built on the same platform as the Chrysler 300M, but the LHS is longer and has more luggage space than its sibling. It's got cavernous amounts of space both front and rear, and your in-laws won't find too much to complain about when you tote them for a Sunday jaunt.

If you're torn between the two, keep in mind that the LHS is more of a road pillow - its four-wheel independent suspension is tuned for leisurely driving, whereas the 300M's optional

CHRYSLER

LHS

European-tuned suspension is all about performance.

Unfortunately, the LHS' softer suspension results in some body roll while cornering, and although minor steering correction is required, we have to admit it still boasts agile handling despite a front-wheel-drive setup. It's outfitted with a four-speed overdrive automatic transaxle, and Chrysler does not offer an AutoStick into the equation (it gives you manual control of your automatic tranny). While the AutoStick isn't a substitute for having a real manual transmission, since it shifts itself if it deems you too lax, Chrysler would sure score brownie points for making it available, at least as an option to consumers.

The LHS is powered by the same all-aluminum, 253-horsepower, 3.5-liter, SOHC 24-valve V6 that gives life to both the 300M and the Prowler. Though it makes 39 more horsepower than the last-generation LHS, we'd love to see what a V8 could do to this car. Still, 253 horsepower competes well against the output of luxury cars like the Oldsmobile Aurora and Lincoln Continental, both equipped with eight-cylinder engines. It's both quiet and refined, and gives spirited performance. Additionally, it has been certified as LEV compliant in all 50 states for 2001.

Among the lavish standards are 17-inch wheels, heated and leather-trimmed seats, eight-way power front seats, and Indiglo-style gauges. You can now keep your eyes bolted to the road while tuning out those insipid morning talk show hosts, thanks to the new steering wheel-mounted audio controls. You'll find the seamless dash with its analog clock to be gentrification-cool. Options include side airbags, real wood trim, and an in-dash four-disc changer.

There's an increasing dearth of full-size American sedans for around 30 grand, but there are still a few choices that won't make you feel like you've made a compromise. Though the LHS may be a step down in performance from the 300M, it's tough to beat this luxury car's combination of handsome styling at an affordable price.

Standard Equipment

LHS (4A): 3.5L V6 SOHC SMPI 24-valve engine; 4-speed electronic OD automatic transmission with lock-up torque converter; 600 amp battery with run down protection; HD radiator; 130 amp alternator; transmission oil cooler; front-wheel drive, traction control, 3.66 axle ratio; stainless steel exhaust with tailpipe finisher; touring ride suspension, front independent strut suspension with anti-roll bar, front coil springs, gas-pressurized front shocks, rear independent multi-link suspension with anti-roll bar, rear coil springs, gas-pressurized rear shocks; power rack-and-pinion steering with vehicle speed-sensing assist; 4-wheel antilock disc brakes; 17 gal. capacity fuel tank; side impact bars; front and rear body-colored bumpers; body-colored bodyside molding; clearcoat monotone paint; projector beam halogen fully auto headlamps with delay-off feature; additional exterior lights include front fog/driving lights; driver's and passenger's power remote black heated folding outside mirrors; 17" x 7" silver alloy wheels; P225/55SR17 BSW touring A/S tires; compact steel spare wheel; air conditioning with climate control, rear heat ducts; AM/FM stereo radio, seek-scan, cassette player, single CD player, 9 premium speakers, amplifier, graphic equalizer, window grid antenna, radio steering wheel controls; cruise control with steering wheel controls; power door locks with 2 stage unlock, remote keyless entry, child safety rear door locks, power remote trunk release; 2 power accessory outlets, driver's foot rest, garage door opener; instrumentation display includes tachometer, water temperature gauge, clock, compass, exterior temp, trip computer, trip odometer; warning indicators include oil pressure, water temp, battery, lights on, key in ignition, low fuel, low washer fluid, door ajar, trunk ajar, brake fluid; driver's and passenger's front airbags; ignition disable, panic alarm, security system; tinted windows, power windows with driver's 1-touch down; variable intermittent front windshield wipers, sun visor strip, rear window defroster; seating capacity of 5, front bucket seats with driver's and passenger's heated-cushion and adjustable tilt headrests, center armrest with storage, driver's seat includes 8-way power adjustment,

CHRYSLER

LHS / SEBRING

lumbar support, passenger's seat includes 8-way power adjustment; rear bench seat with fixed headrests and center pass-thru armrest with storage; front height adjustable seatbelts; leather seats, leatherette door trim insert with carpet lower, full cloth headliner, full carpet floor covering with carpeted floor mats, simulated wood dashboard insert, leather-wrapped gearshift knob, simulated wood door panel insert, simulated wood console insert, chrome interior accents; memory on driver's seat with 2 memory setting(s) includes settings for exterior mirrors; interior lights include dome light with fade, front and rear reading lights, 4 door curb lights, illuminated entry; leather-wrapped steering wheel with tilt adjustment; dual illuminated vanity mirrors, dual auxiliary visors; auto-dimming day/night rearview mirror; full floor console, mini overhead console, locking glove box with light, front and rear cupholders, 2 seat back storage pockets, driver's and passenger's door bins; carpeted cargo floor, carpeted trunk lid, cargo net, cargo light; chrome grille, chrome side window moldings, black front windshield molding, black rear window molding and body-colored door handles.

Base Prices

CODE	DESCRIPTION	INVOICE	MSRP
LHCP41	LHS (4A)	26587	28680
	Destination Charge:	680	680

Interested in seeing what dealers will sell this vehicle for? Check out our True Market Value^{sm} (TMV^{sm}) pricing on our Web site at www.edmunds.com.

Accessories

CODE	DESCRIPTION	INVOICE	MSRP
26J	Quick Order Package 26J	NC	NC
	Includes vehicle with standard equipment.		
ADE	Cold Weather Group	36	40
	Includes battery heater and engine block heater.		
AFF	Luxury Group	463	520
	Includes driver auto dim exterior mirror and vehicle information center, exterior auto adjust in reverse mirrors, wood/leather-wrapped steering wheel and genuine California walnut wood trim.		
ARF	Radio: AM/FM Cassette Player with AMP, CD Changer	458	515
	Includes 360 watt amplifier, 4 disc in-dash CD changer with control, and 11 Infinity speakers in 9 locations.		
AWS	Smokers' Group	27	30
	Includes front and rear ash receivers and cigar lighter.		
CGS	Supplemental Side Air Bags	347	390
GWA	Power Sunroof	797	895
TBW	Tire: Full Size Spare with Matching Wheel	343	385
	REQUIRES WFH.		
TBW	Tire: Full Size Spare with Matching Wheel	223	250
WFH	Wheels: 17" Chrome Aluminum	668	750

2001 SEBRING

What's New?

The Sebring Sedan debuts for 2001 along with redesigned versions of the coupe and convertible (the Cirrus Sedan is no more). A new, more powerful V6 joins the enlarged four-cylinder, with a five-speed manual transmission available in the coupe. The Autostick manumatic is still an option for those who can't decide where they stand on the shift issue, but only on

SEBRING — CHRYSLER

upscale LXi models with the V6. An Infinity premium sound system with an in-dash CD changer is also new this year.

Review

Chrysler hopes to continue the success of its Sebring Coupes and Sedans with new designs that closely resemble last year's models, and we don't blame them. The previous Sebring Coupes and Convertibles were good looking, had room for four adults, and provided sporty transportation without the midlife-crisis look. With the addition of the new sedan, practicality invades the Sebring line even further, but don't think boring. The new sedan sports an attractive European inspired design that fits right in with the Sebring mantra of "elegance and engineering."

Apart from the subtle sheetmetal changes, the big news for the Sebring lineup is the new range of powerplants. At the top of the heap sits the Mitsubishi built 3.0-liter V6 cranking out 200 horsepower and 205 ft-lbs. of torque. Available only in the LXi Coupe, it comes standard with a five-speed manual transmission or can be mated to an Autostick manumatic. Standard in convertibles and LXi Sedans is the Chrysler built 2.7-liter V6 rated at 200 hp and 193 ft-lbs of torque coupled to a four-speed automatic with the Autostick shifter. The Autostick is also an option on Limited Convertibles and LXi Sedans.

If you're not in the market for an upscale LXi Coupe or Sedan, a new 2.4-liter four-cylinder powerplant is offered in the base LX trim level. The Chrysler sedan version is rated at 150hp and 167 ft-lbs. of torque while the Mitsubishi-built version in the coupe only claims 142 hp. Both LX Coupes and Sedans offer only a four-speed automatic.

Power may be diminished in the LX models but the standard feature list still continues to impress. Power windows, mirrors and door locks, cruise control, 60/40 split-folding rear seats, and an AM/FM stereo cassette all come standard on both the coupe and the sedan.

Stepping up to the LXi trim level gets you the already mentioned V6 engines along with power adjustable leather seats, premium audio systems, upgraded 16-inch chrome wheels (coupes get 17-inch wheels) and remote keyless entry. The upscale Limited Convertible sports an electroluminescent instrument cluster and a four-disc in-dash CD changer along with chrome interior accents.

The Sebring line still offers extensive safety features including Next Generation multi-stage airbags, improved structural dynamics for frontal- and side-impact protection, and three-point seatbelts for rear seat passengers. The Sebring Sedan also offers side-impact airbags, providing protection for front and rear outboard passengers as an option. Electronic Brake Distribution and advanced "ABS Plus" further improve driver control in the convertible and sedan models.

Regardless of trim level, all Sebring models still remain exceptional values in their class. Even loaded LXi models still sticker in the low 20s with base models coming in well under $20,000. Factor this in with Sebring's generous interior space and classy good looks and it's easy to see why the Sebring, whether coupe, convertible, or sedan, stands out in the crowded midsize market.

Standard Equipment

LX COUPE (4A): 2.4L I4 DOHC SMPI 16-valve engine; 4-speed electronic OD automatic transmission with lock-up torque converter; 510 amp battery with run down protection; 90 amp alternator; front-wheel drive, 3.91 axle ratio; stainless steel exhaust; touring-ride suspension, front independent double-wishbone suspension with anti-roll bar, front coil springs, rear independent double-wishbone suspension with rear coil springs, gas-pressurized front and rear shocks; rack-and-pinion power steering; front disc/rear drum brakes; 16.3 gal. capacity fuel tank; side impact bars; front and rear body-colored bumpers; body-colored bodyside cladding; clearcoat monotone paint; aero-composite halogen headlamps; additional exterior lights include

CHRYSLER — SEBRING

CODE	DESCRIPTION	INVOICE	MSRP

front fog/driving lights; driver's and passenger's power remote black outside mirrors; 16" x 6" steel wheels; P205/55HR16 BSW performance A/S tires; compact steel spare wheel; air conditioning, rear heat ducts; AM/FM stereo radio, clock, seek-scan feature, cassette player, 6 speakers, fixed antenna; cruise control; power auto locking door locks with 2-stage unlock, remote keyless entry, remote trunk release, remote fuel door release; 2 power accessory outlets, front lighter element(s), driver's foot rest, smokers" package; instrumentation display includes tachometer, oil pressure gauge, water temperature gauge, trip odometer; warning indicators include oil pressure, water temp, battery, low coolant, lights on, key in ignition, low fuel, low washer fluid, door ajar, trunk ajar, brake fluid; driver's and passenger's front airbags; ignition disable, panic alarm, security system; tinted windows with driver's 1-touch down function; variable intermittent front windshield wipers, rear window defroster; seating capacity of 5, front bucket seats with adjustable headrests, center armrest with storage, driver's seat includes 6-way adjustment, passenger's seat includes 4-way adjustment, easy entry; 60/40 folding rear bench seat; front height adjustable seatbelts; cloth seats, wood door trim insert, full cloth headliner, full carpet floor covering with carpeted floor mats, simulated wood console insert; interior lights include dome light with fade, front reading lights; sport steering wheel with tilt adjustment; dual illuminated vanity mirrors; auto-dimming day/night rearview mirror; full floor console, locking glove box with light, front and rear cupholders, driver's and passenger's door bins; carpeted cargo floor, cargo net, cargo light; black grille, black side window moldings, black front windshield molding, black rear window molding and body-colored door handles.

LX SEDAN (4A) (in addition to or instead of LX COUPE (4A) equipment): 2.4L I4 SOHC SMPI 16-valve engine; 120 amp alternator; 4-wheel disc brakes; 16 gal. capacity fuel tank; body-colored bodyside molding with chrome bodyside insert; aero-composite halogen headlamps with delay-off feature; 15" x 6" steel wheels; P205/65TR15 BSW A/S tires; CD changer pre-wiring, 4 speakers, child-safety rear door locks, power remote trunk release, 1 power accessory outlet, driver's seat includes 4-way adjustment, lumbar support, cloth door trim insert, and chrome interior accents.

LX CONVERTIBLE (4A): (in addition to or instead of LX COUPE (4A) equipment) 2.7L V6 DOHC SMPI 24-valve engine; engine oil cooler; 120 amp alternator; stainless steel exhaust with tailpipe finisher; power-assisted rack-and-pinion steering with speed-sensing assist; 4-wheel disc brakes; 16 gal. capacity fuel tank; power convertible roof with lining, glass rear window; body-colored bodyside molding with chrome bodyside insert; aero-composite halogen headlamps with delay-off feature; 15" x 6" steel wheels; P205/65TR15 BSW A/S tires; CD changer pre-wiring, 6 speakers, cruise control with steering wheel controls; power door locks with 2-stage unlock, power remote trunk release; 1 power accessory outlet; driver's and passenger's front airbags; power front and rear windows with driver's 1-touch down function; sun visor strip, driver's seat includes 6-way adjustment, passenger's seat includes 4-way adjustment, easy entry; premium cloth seats, cloth door trim insert, chrome interior accents; interior lights include dome light with delay front reading lights, illuminated entry; instrument panel bin, chrome grille, and black door handles.

LXi COUPE (5M) (in addition to or instead of LX COUPE (4A) equipment): 3L V6 SOHC SMPI 24-valve engine; 5-speed OD manual transmission; tailpipe finisher; rear independent double-wishbone suspension with anti-roll bar; 4-wheel disc brakes; driver's and passenger's power remote body-colored outside mirrors; 17" x 6.5" silver alloy wheels; P215/50HR17 BSW performance A/S tires; single-disc CD player, 7 premium speakers, graphic equalizer, compass, exterior temp; driver's seat includes 2-way power adjustment, 6-way adjustment; illuminated entry; and a leather-wrapped steering wheel.

LXi SEDAN (4A) (in addition to or instead of LXi COUPE (4A) equipment): 2.7L V6 DOHC SMPI 24-valve engine; additional exterior lights include front fog/driving lights; 16" x 6.5" silver alloy wheels; P205/60TR16 BSW A/S tires; 4 speakers, child-safety rear door locks; driver's seat includes 6-way power adjustment, 8-way adjustment, lumbar support, leather seats, leatherette door trim insert, leather-wrapped gearshift knob, chrome interior accents and dual illuminated vanity mirrors.

SEBRING CHRYSLER

CODE	DESCRIPTION	INVOICE	MSRP

LXi CONVERTIBLE (4A) (in addition to or instead of LX CONVERTIBLE (4A) equipment): Touring-ride suspension, additional exterior lights include front fog/driving lights; 16" x 6.5" silver alloy wheels; P205/60TR16 BSW A/S tires; single-disc CD player, 6 premium speakers; garage door opener; compass, exterior temp, trip computer, ignition disable, security system; leather seats, leatherette door trim insert with carpet lower, simulated wood dashboard insert, leather-wrapped gearshift knob, simulated wood door panel insert; 2 door curb lights; leather-wrapped steering wheel with tilt adjustment; auto-dimming day/night rearview mirror; 1 seatback storage pocket, black front windshield molding and body-colored door handles.

LIMITED CONVERTIBLE (4A) (in addition to or instead of LXi CONVERTIBLE (4A) equipment): Auto-manual transmission; 4-wheel antilock disc brakes; P205/60TR16 BSW A/S tires; cassette player, and 4-disc CD changer.

Base Prices

Code	Description	Invoice	MSRP
STCS22	LX Coupe (4A)	18449	19910
JRCH27	LX Convertible (4A)	22553	24370
STCP22	LXi Coupe (5M)	19948	21575
JRCP27	LXi Convertible (4A)	24767	26830
JRCH41	LX Sedan (4A)	16668	17975
JRCS27	Limited Convertible (4A)	26644	28915
JRCP41	LXi Sedan (4A)	19264	20860
	Destination Charge:	595	595

Interested in seeing what dealers will sell this vehicle for? Check out our True Market Value℠ (TMV℠) pricing on our Web site at www.edmunds.com.

Accessories

Code	Description	Invoice	MSRP
22H	Quick Order Package 22H (LX Coupe)	NC	NC
	Includes vehicle with standard equipment. REQUIRES and DG1.		
23K	Quick Order Package 23K (LXi Coupe)	NC	NC
	Includes vehicle with standard equipment. NOT AVAILABLE with DHD.		
24H	Quick Order Package 24H (LX)	NC	NC
	Includes vehicle with standard equipment. REQUIRES DG1. NOT AVAILABLE with ATD, AJB, RCC, or GWA.		
24J	Quick Order Package 24J (LX Sedan)	850	955
	Manufacturer Discount	(111)	(125)
	Net Price	739	830
	Includes rear passenger assist handles, front courtesy map lamps, AM/FM CD radio, remote illuminated entry group, illuminated entry, keyless entry, panic alarm, 8-way power driver seat, illuminated vanity mirror sun visors, traveler mini trip computer and low washer fluid warning signal.		
24K	Quick Order Package 24K (LXi Coupe)	NC	NC
	Includes vehicle with standard equipment. REQUIRES and DG1.		
28D	Quick Order Package 28D (LX Conv)	NC	NC
	Includes vehicle with standard equipment.		
28E	Quick Order Package 28E (LXi Conv)	NC	NC
	Includes vehicle with standard equipment.		
28G	Quick Order Package 28G (Limited Conv)	NC	NC
	Includes vehicle with standard equipment.		

CHRYSLER SEBRING

CODE	DESCRIPTION	INVOICE	MSRP
28H	Quick Order Package 28H (LX Sedan)	NC	NC
	Includes vehicle with standard equipment. REQUIRES EES. NOT AVAILABLE with ATD, AJB, RCC, or GWA.		
28J	Quick Order Package 28J (LX Sedan)	850	955
	Manufacturer Discount	(111)	(125)
	Net Price	739	830
	Includes rear passenger assist handles, front courtesy map lamps, AM/FM CD radio, remote illuminated entry group, illuminated entry, keyless entry, panic alarm, 8-way power driver's seat, illuminated vanity mirror sun visors, traveler mini trip computer and low washer fluid warning signal. REQUIRES EES.		
28K	Quick Order Package 28K (LXi Sedan)	NC	NC
	Includes vehicle with standard equipment. REQUIRES EES.		
6R2	Inferno Red Tinted Pearlcoat/Black Vinyl Top (LX Conv/LXi Conv)	178	200
6R4	Inferno Red Tinted Pearlcoat/Sandal Vinyl Top (LX Conv/LXi Conv)	178	200
6R7	Inferno Red Tinted Pearlcoat/Black Convertible Top (LXi Conv)	178	200
6R8	Inferno Red/Sandalwood Convertible Top (LXi Conv)	178	200
ADE	Cold Weather Group (Conv)	27	30
	Includes battery heater and engine block heater.		
ADE	Cold Weather Group (Sedan)	40	36
	Includes battery heater and engine block heater.		
ADT	Touring Group (LX Coupe)	561	630
	Includes compass, temperature gauge, 6-way power driver seat and AM/FM cassette player with CD radio.		
AFF	Luxury Group (LXi Sedan)	1393	1565
	Manufacturer Discount	(178)	(200)
	Net Price	1215	1365
	Includes electroluminescent instrument cluster, Autostick, cargo net, universal garage door opener and 16" x 6.5" chrome alloy wheels.		
AJB	Security Group (LX Conv)	156	175
	Includes security alarm, power auto central locking locks and sentry key theft deterrent system.		
AJB	Security Group (Sedan)	174	195
	Includes power auto central locking locks, security alarm and sentry key theft deterrent system. REQUIRES 24J or 28J. NOT AVAILABLE with 24H or 28H.		
AJD	Leather Interior Group (LXi Coupe)	930	1045
	Includes universal garage door opener, 6-way power driver seat and leather low back bucket seats.		
AJF	Remote/Illuminated Entry Group (LX Sedan)	151	170
	Includes illuminated entry, keyless entry, and panic alarm. INCLUDED in 24J and 28J.		
ATD	Radio: Cassette Player, CD Changer (Sedan)	223	250
	AM/FM Radio with cassette player and CD changer control and 4 disc in-dash CD changer. REQUIRES 24J or 28J. NOT AVAILABLE with 24H, 28H, or RCC.		
ATD	Radio: Cassette, CD Changer (LXi Conv)	223	250
	Includes 4 disc in-dash CD changer and AM/FM cassette player with CD changer control radio.		
AWS	Smokers' Group (Conv)	18	20
	Includes removable front ash tray and cigar lighter.		

CHRYSLER
SEBRING

CODE	DESCRIPTION	INVOICE	MSRP
AWS	Smokers' Group (Sedan)	27	30
	Includes removable ash tray and cigar lighter.		
BL	Leather Low Back Bucket Seats (LXi Coupe)	NC	NC
	REQUIRES AJD.		
BRF	4-Wheel Antilock Disc Brakes (LX Coupe)	503	565
BRF	4-Wheel Antilock Disc Brakes (LXi Coupe)	659	740
	Includes traction control. REQUIRES DG1.		
BRT	4-Wheel Antilock Disc Brakes (Sedan)	503	565
CGS	Side Air Bags (Sedan)	347	390
DG1	Transmission: 4-Speed Automatic (LXi Coupe)	734	825
DHD	Autostick (LXi Coupe)	147	165
	REQUIRES DG1. NOT AVAILABLE with 23K.		
EES	Engine: 2.7L V6 24-Valve with Active Intake (LX Sedan)	757	850
EF7	Engine: 3.0L SOHC 24-Valve V6 (LX Coupe)	757	850
	Includes rear-wheel disc brakes, leather-wrapped steering wheel, leather-wrapped shift knob and bright tip exhaust.		
GWA	Power Sunroof	619	695
	REQUIRES 24J or 28J. NOT AVAILABLE with 24H or 28H.		
H8	Cloth Low-Back Bucket Seats (LXi Sedan)	(111)	(125)
JPV	8-Way Power Driver Seat (LX Sedan)	338	380
	INCLUDED in 24J and 28J.		
RBK	Radio: AM/FM Compact Disc (LX Sedan)	111	125
	INCLUDED in 24J and 28J.		
RBV	Radio: AM/FM, MX with 4 CD In Radio Chgr (LXi Coupe)	NC	NC
RCC	6 Premium Speakers with 120 Watt Amp (Sedan)	312	350
	REQUIRES 24J or 28J. NOT AVAILABLE with 24H, 28H, or ATD.		
RCK	Infinity Speaker System (LX Conv)	423	475
RDW	4 Disc In-Dash CD Changer (LX Conv)	334	375
TBB	Tire: Full Size Spare (LX Conv)	111	125
	NOT AVAILABLE with WNB or TBW.		
TBB	Tire: Full Size Spare (LX Sedan)	142	160
	NOT AVAILABLE with TBW or WNB.		
TBW	Tire: Full Size Spare with Matching Wheel (LX Conv/LXi Conv)	191	215
	REQUIRES WNB. NOT AVAILABLE with TBB.		
TBW	Tire: Full Size Spare with Matching Wheel (LXi Sedan)	343	385
	REQUIRES WN5 or AFF.		
TBW	Tire: Full Size Spare with Matching Wheel (Limited Conv)	325	365
TBW	Tire: Full Size Spare with Matching Wheel (Sedan)	223	250
	REQUIRES WNB. NOT AVAILABLE with TBB.		
WGE	Wheels: 17" Chrome Aluminum (LXi Coupe)	668	750
	REQUIRES AJD.		
WN5	Wheels: 16" X 6.5" Chrome Aluminum (LXi Sedan)	534	600
WNB	Wheels: 16" X 6.5" Aluminum (LX Sedan)	289	325
	Includes P205/60TR16 BSW All Season tires. NOT AVAILABLE with TBB.		
WNS	Wheels: 16" Aluminum (LX Coupe)	325	365

DAEWOO — LANOS

2001 LANOS

What's New?

Daewoo adds the new Sport Hatchback model to the Lanos lineup for 2001, but discontinues the SE Hatchback and SX Sedan. Pacific Blue Mica and Red Rock Mica are added to the palette for the sedan and hatchback, while Super Red and Granada Black Mica are available exclusively on the Sport. The new premium package available on the S models includes power windows, power door locks, power passenger rearview mirror, tilt steering wheel, AM/FM/cassette/CD stereo, digital clock and variable intermittent wipers.

Review

Struggling Korean automaker Daewoo continues to try and convince North American consumers that it's got what it takes to be competitive in the economy car marketplace. Trouble is, few people are buying it, despite the offer of free maintenance for the first year and 12,000 miles. So Daewoo is trying to spark interest in the entry-level Lanos by adding a Sport model, which amounts to little more than cosmetic upgrades.

Available as a three-door hatchback or a four-door sedan, the Lanos is about the size of a Hyundai Accent. That means small. Because the Lanos is such a tiny car, anyone over 6 feet tall should not bother trying find a comfortable seating position. But the price matches the car's size, and for that nominal fee you get suspension tuning from Porsche and styling from ItalDesign. Despite these impressive credentials, creative types in our office refer to this car as the "Lamos."

Lanos comes with a 1.6-liter DOHC 16-valve engine that makes 105 horsepower at 5,800 rpm and 106 foot-pounds of torque at 3,400 rpm. A five-speed manual transmission is also standard, but buyers may choose an optional four-speed automatic. Acceleration, characterized as "spirited" by Daewoo spokespeople, is actually rather leisurely. Zero to 60 takes 11 seconds with the manual and 12.5 seconds with the automatic.

All models are equipped with a MacPherson strut front suspension, which the press kit boasts, "provides resistance to vibration and shock." Also standard for your protection are pre-tensioning seatbelts.

Stiff suspension tuning makes the Lanos fun in corners. Thank you, Porsche. Fit and finish are quite good, and the paint positively shimmers. But the dash is made of what appears to be the least expensive plastic on the planet, and the motor thrashes at higher revs. The lack of a tachometer means you can't tell if you're still within an acceptable operating range or are about to blow the engine.

The new premium package available on the sedan and hatchback includes power windows, power door locks, power passenger-side rearview mirror, tilt steering wheel, CD player, digital clock and variable intermittent wipers. The Sport model includes many of these goodies, plus red leather and brushed aluminum interior trim, alloy wheels, side skirting and a rear spoiler. What's missing is, you guessed it, more power.

Prices for this entry-level car range from just over $9,000 for the bare-bones hatchback to more than $13,000 for a loaded three-door Sport. But with increasingly stiff competition in the inexpensive-car arena from Kia, Hyundai and Toyota, Daewoo will have to come up with more than just new paint colors and a Sport model to prove itself a worthy opponent.

Standard Equipment

S HATCHBACK (5M): 1.6L I4 DOHC MPI 16-valve engine; 5-speed OD manual transmission; 550-amp battery; 85-amp alternator; front-wheel drive, 4.18 axle ratio; partial stainless steel

LANOS
DAEWOO

exhaust; front independent strut suspension with anti-roll bar, front coil springs, rear independent multi-link suspension with anti-roll bar, rear coil springs; rack-and-pinion power steering; front disc/rear drum brakes; 12.7 gal. capacity fuel tank; front and rear mud flaps, side impact bars; front and rear body-colored bumpers; clearcoat monotone paint; aero-composite halogen headlamps; driver's and passenger's manual remote black folding outside mirrors; 14" x 5.5" silver alloy wheels; P185/60SR14 BSW A/S tires; compact steel spare wheel; AM/FM stereo, seek-scan feature, cassette player, CD changer pre-wiring, 4 speakers, theft deterrent, fixed antenna; remote fuel door release; 1 power accessory outlet, front lighter element, driver's foot rest, smokers' package; instrumentation display includes water temperature gauge, trip odometer; warning indicators include oil pressure, water temp, battery, lights on, key in ignition, low fuel, door ajar, brake fluid; driver's and passenger's front airbags; tinted windows; variable-speed intermittent front windshield wipers, sun visor strip, rear window wiper, rear window defroster; seating capacity of 5, front bucket seats with adjustable headrests, driver's seat includes 8-way adjustment and easy entry, passenger's seat includes 4-way adjustment and easy entry; 60/40 folding rear bench seat with fixed headrests; height-adjustable front seatbelts; cloth seats, cloth door trim insert, full cloth headliner, full carpet floor covering; interior lights include dome light; vanity mirrors; day/night rearview mirror; partial floor console, glove box, front cupholder, instrument panel bin, driver's and passenger's door bins; carpeted cargo floor, cargo cover; chrome grille, black side window moldings, black front windshield molding, black rear window molding and black door handles.

SPORT HATCHBACK (5M) (in addition to or instead of S HATCHBACK (5M) equipment): Driver's manual remote, and passenger's power outside mirrors; air conditioning; single-disc CD player; instrumentation display includes in-dash clock; driver's window includes 1-touch down function; leather seats.

S SEDAN (5M) (in addition to or instead of SPORT HATCHBACK (5M) equipment): Driver's and passenger's manual remote outside mirrors; CD changer pre-wiring; child-safety rear door locks, remote trunk release; manual front and rear windows; cloth seats; full floor console, glove box, front cupholder, instrument panel bin, driver's and passenger's door bins; carpeted cargo floor and cargo light.

Base Prices

Code	Description	Invoice	MSRP
D3LS5	S Hatchback (5M)	8003	9199
D3MS5	Sport Hatchback (5M)	11309	12999
D4LS5	S Sedan (5M)	8786	10099
Destination Charge:		430	430

Interested in seeing what dealers will sell this vehicle for? Check out our True Market Value^{sm} (TMV^{sm}) pricing on our Web site at www.edmunds.com.

Accessories

Code	Description	Invoice	MSRP
OFM	Floor Mats	52	60
A/T	Transmission: 4-Speed Automatic with OD	696	800
A/W	Wheels: 14" Alloy (S)	348	400
C60	Air Conditioning (S)	609	700
P02	S Package (S)	783	900

Includes variable-speed intermittent wipers, power windows, power door locks, power passenger side rearview mirror, tilt steering wheel, AM/FM stereo, cassette player, CD player, digital clock, body-colored side skirts and body-colored bodyside molding.

DAEWOO — LEGANZA

2001 LEGANZA

What's New?

Scarlet Mica and Harbor Mist Mica are the new exterior colors. Outside rearview mirrors get a blue tint and a new audio head unit is added for improved sound quality. A new option package for the SE includes front and rear power windows, power door locks, AM/FM/cassette/CD with six speakers, dual body-color heated power rearview mirrors, anti-theft alarm with remote keyless entry, tilt steering wheel and front fog lamps.

Review

Leganza, whose name is derived from a combination of the Italian words "elegante" (elegant) and "forza" (power), is Daewoo's midsize sedan marketed to would-be buyers of pedestrian Honda Accords and Toyota Camrys who want a full load of luxury amenities for a cut-rate bargain price.

Yes, the Leganza is elegant, penned by ItalDesign whiz Giorgetto Giugiaro. But powerful? Hardly. Competing against vehicles commonly equipped with V6 engines, the Leganza is handicapped in the muscle department by its standard and only powerplant; a 2.2-liter, DOHC 16-valve engine making 131 horsepower at 5,200 rpm and 148 foot-pounds of torque at 2,800 rpm is charged with hauling around more than 3,000 pounds of sedan.

Three trim levels are available on the Leganza: SE, SX and CDX. Standard equipment includes a full-size spare tire, power windows and locks, air conditioning, and a tilt steering wheel. A new-for-2001 option package can adorn the base SE with AM/FM/cassette/CD stereo, anti-theft alarm with remote keyless entry, cruise control and fog lamps. Step up to the midlevel SX, and you're rewarded with four-wheel disc antilock brakes, a CD player, leather seats, cruise control, and an automatic transmission, with a moonroof and 15-inch alloy wheels optionally available. The luxurious CDX gets those last two items plus a power driver's seat, automatic temperature control, fake wood trim and traction control.

British suspension-expert Lotus tuned Leganza's four-wheel independent underpinnings, but Daewoo obviously wanted a cushy ride, and the Leganza delivers. Weak tires howl around turns, and the ABS is substandard in refinement and effectiveness. Despite a "Sport" mode for the automatic transmission, it's best to drive the Leganza less enthusiastically than you would, say, anything else on the market.

We've found the Leganza dissatisfying, though plenty of owners report that they enjoy their cars immensely. Our specific complaints include: uncomfortable seats, poor quality interior materials, lousy stereo sound quality, a dearth of engine power, skittish transmission performance, uninspired braking ability, and sloppy steering.

We also know that Daewoo, which has filed for bankruptcy protection, is in big trouble with creditors in Korea, and is desperately searching for another automaker to bail them out of tremendous debt. What's worse is that suitor Ford Motor Company, after reviewing Daewoo's internal records, declined an opportunity to purchase the company. Add to this list of woes substandard crashworthiness as proven by offset crash tests conducted by the Insurance Institute for Highway Safety, and we cannot recommend the Leganza to anyone. Well, anyone we like.

But perhaps the biggest hurdle the Leganza faces is not Daewoo's no-haggle sales strategy, patchy dealer network, financial trouble at home, or poor crash protection, but the extremely fierce competition in the midsize sedan segment. Competing against such entities as the Chevrolet Malibu, Chrysler Sebring, Dodge Stratus, Ford Taurus, Honda Accord, Mazda 626, Mitsubishi Galant, Nissan Altima, Oldsmobile Alero, Saturn LS and Toyota Camry is no small

LEGANZA   DAEWOO

order, especially when the American buying public already knows where to buy and service these models.

Standard Equipment

SE (5M): 2.2L I4 DOHC MPI 16-valve engine; 5-speed OD manual transmission; 610-amp battery; 95-amp alternator; front-wheel drive, 3.72 axle ratio; partial stainless steel exhaust with tailpipe finisher; front independent strut suspension with anti-roll bar, front coil springs, rear independent multi-link suspension with anti-roll bar, rear coil springs; rack-and-pinion power steering; 4-wheel disc brakes; 15.8 gal. capacity fuel tank; front and rear mud flaps, side impact bars; front and rear body-colored bumpers; body-colored bodyside molding; clearcoat monotone paint; projector-beam halogen headlamps; driver's and passenger's power remote body-colored heated folding outside mirrors; 15" x 6" steel wheels; P205/60SR15 BSW A/S tires; full-size steel spare wheel; air conditioning, air filter, rear heat ducts; AM/FM stereo, seek-scan feature, cassette player, 6 speakers, theft deterrent, fixed antenna; power door locks, child-safety rear door locks, remote trunk release, remote fuel door release; 1 power accessory outlet, front lighter element, driver's foot rest, smokers' package; instrumentation display includes tachometer, water temperature gauge, in-dash clock, trip odometer; warning indicators include oil pressure, water temp, battery, lights on, key in ignition, low fuel, door ajar, trunk ajar, brake fluid; driver's and passenger's front airbags; tinted windows, power front and rear windows with driver's 1-touch down function; variable-speed intermittent front windshield wipers, sun visor strip, rear window defroster; seating capacity of 5, front bucket seats with adjustable tilt headrests, center armrest with storage, driver's seat includes 8-way adjustment, passenger's seat includes 4-way adjustment; 60/40 folding rear bench seat with fixed headrests, center armrest; height-adjustable front seatbelts; cloth seats, cloth door trim insert, full cloth headliner, full carpet floor covering, simulated wood dashboard insert, simulated wood door panel insert, simulated wood console insert, chrome interior accents; interior lights include dome light with fade, front reading lights, door curb lights, illuminated entry; steering wheel with tilt adjustment; dual illuminated vanity mirrors; day/night rearview mirror; full floor console, glove box, front cupholder, instrument panel covered bin, driver's and passenger's door bins; carpeted cargo floor, cargo light; chrome grille, black side window moldings, black front windshield molding, black rear window molding and body-colored door handles.

SX (4A) (in addition to or instead of SE (4A) equipment): 4-speed electronic automatic transmission with lock-up converter; 2.65 axle ratio; vehicle-speed-sensing assist; 4-wheel antilock disc brakes; additional exterior lights include front fog/driving lights; single-disc CD player, power retractable antenna; cruise control; remote keyless entry; security system; driver's seat lumbar support; leather seats, leatherette door trim insert, leather-wrapped gearshift knob; leather-wrapped steering wheel.

CDX (4A) (in addition to or instead of SX (4A) equipment): Traction control; front power sliding and tilting glass sunroof with sunshade; full-size alloy spare wheel; climate control; 2 seatback storage pockets.

Base Prices

Code	Description	Invoice	MSRP
F4MR5	SE Sedan (5M)	11899	13999
F4XR4	SX Sedan (4A)	14874	17499
F4CR4	CDX Sedan (4A)	16149	18999
	Destination Charge:	430	430

Interested in seeing what dealers will sell this vehicle for? Check out our True Market Value^{sm} (TMV^{sm}) pricing on our Web site at www.edmunds.com.

DAEWOO

LEGANZA / NUBIRA

CODE	DESCRIPTION	INVOICE	MSRP

Accessories

OFM	Floor Mats	64	75
A/T	Transmission: 4-Speed Automatic with OD (SE)	850	1000
	Includes 2.65 axle ratio.		
A/W	Wheels: 15" Alloy (SX)	425	500
	Includes matching spare.		
CF6	Power Tilt and Slide Glass Moonroof (SX)	430	500
P04	SE Premium Package (SE)	849	999
	Includes AM/FM stereo, cassette player, CD player, anti-theft alarm system with remote keyless entry, cruise control and front fog lamps.		
UP1	CD Changer and DSP Graphic Equalizer (CDX)	383	450

2001 NUBIRA

What's New?

You can now pick up a Daewoo Nubira with Diamond Blue Metallic paint. The sedan gets a new 14-inch standard wheel cover and the wagon has a fresh rear tail lamp design.

Review

Nubira. Sounds like a cloud formation, but it's actually the name of one of the three cars from Daewoo. Nubira means "to go everywhere," and it's Daewoo's best shot at going anywhere in the fickle American marketplace.

The Nubira is available in two trim levels and body styles: SE sedan and CDX trim applied to either sedan or wagon formats. The base SE comes with a height-adjustable driver's seat, six-speaker sound system with cassette player and four-wheel disc brakes. The optional convenience package adds power windows, mirrors and locks, as well as remote keyless entry, tilt steering wheel, a car alarm and fog lights.

Uplevel CDX trim includes a long list of additional standards, in addition to a loaded SE. Air conditioning, CD player, alloy wheels (that resemble a Cuisinart tool), cruise control, heated exterior mirrors and antilock brakes keep CDX buyers happy that they upgraded. Leather seats and a moonroof are optional on CDX. Wagons add a rear wiper and a roof rack. All Nubiras are covered by a scheduled maintenance policy, which takes care of oil changes, tire rotations and the like for the first year and 12,000 miles of ownership.

The sole engine choice for the Nubira is a GM-designed, Australian 2.0-liter four-cylinder engine making 129 horsepower at 5,400 rpm and 136 foot-pounds of torque at 4,400 rpm. This sprightly motor meets LEV standards. Mated to the standard five-speed manual transmission, the Nubira can reach 60 mph in less than 10 seconds, but acceleration is accompanied by plenty of engine racket. The optional automatic requires nearly 2 seconds more to reach expressway velocities.

Overall, the Nubira provides a pleasant ride and decent, if not downright sporty, handling as long as the driver isn't pushing the car for all it's worth. Body roll is kept to a minimum in slower turns, and steering is reasonably responsive if a bit numb. The factory tires, however, could certainly use upgrading, as could the rather weak brakes.

NUBIRA — DAEWOO

Surprisingly, there's plenty of room up front for legs, though rear legroom is severely compromised when the tallest of drivers has the seat moved all the way back in the track. Cabin materials could stand improvement, but at this price, they certainly meet the standard. New exterior colors, taillights (wagon only) and wheelcovers are the only changes for 2001.

The Nubira may be Daewoo's best shot at finding a niche in the crowded economy car market, despite the stiff competition in this segment. It's somewhat attractive, reasonably powerful, and can be loaded to the gills with equipment for a seductively low price. But before Daewoo can find success, it needs to pay some big bills in Korea, or the Nubira will disappear faster than you can say "Yugo."

Standard Equipment

SE SEDAN (5M): 2L I4 DOHC MPI 16-valve engine; 5-speed OD manual transmission; 630-amp battery; 85-amp alternator; front-wheel drive, 3.55 axle ratio; partial stainless steel exhaust; front independent strut suspension with anti-roll bar, front coil springs, rear independent multi-link suspension with anti-roll bar, rear coil springs; rack-and-pinion power steering; 4-wheel disc brakes; 13.7 gal. capacity fuel tank; front and rear mud flaps, side impact bars; front and rear body-colored bumpers; clearcoat monotone paint; aero-composite halogen headlamps; driver's and passenger's manual body-colored folding outside mirrors; 14" x 5.5" steel wheels; P185/65HR14 BSW A/S tires; compact steel spare wheel; rear heat ducts; AM/FM stereo, seek-scan feature, cassette player, 4 speakers, theft deterrent, fixed antenna; cruise control; child-safety rear door locks, remote trunk release, remote fuel door release; 1 power accessory outlet, front lighter element, smokers' package; instrumentation display includes tachometer, water temperature gauge, in-dash clock, trip odometer; warning indicators include oil pressure, water temp, battery, lights on, key in ignition, low fuel, door ajar, trunk ajar, brake fluid; driver's and passenger's front airbags; tinted windows, manual front and rear windows; variable-speed intermittent front windshield wipers, sun visor strip, rear window defroster; seating capacity of 5, front bucket seats with adjustable tilt headrests, center armrest with storage, driver's seat includes 8-way adjustment, passenger's seat includes 4-way adjustment; 60/40 folding rear bench seat with adjustable headrests; height-adjustable front seatbelts with pretensioners; cloth seats, cloth door trim insert, full vinyl headliner, full carpet floor covering, chrome interior accents; interior lights include dome light; vanity mirrors; day/night rearview mirror; full floor console, locking glove box, front cupholder, 2 seatback storage pockets, driver's and passenger's door bins; carpeted cargo floor, cargo light; chrome grille, black side window moldings, black front windshield molding and body-colored door handles.

CDX SEDAN (5M) (in addition to or instead of SE SEDAN (5M) equipment): 4-wheel antilock disc brakes; additional exterior lights include front fog/driving lights; driver's and passenger's power body-colored heated rearview mirrors; air conditioning, air filter, rear heat ducts; single-disc CD player, 6 speakers; power door locks, remote keyless entry; security system; power front and rear windows with driver's 1-touch down function; interior lights include illuminated entry; steering wheel with tilt adjustment.

CDX WAGON (5M) (in addition to or instead of CDX SEDAN (5M) equipment): Exhaust tailpipe finisher; roof rack; integrated roof antenna; variable-speed intermittent front windshield wipers, rear window wiper, rear window defroster; interior lights include front reading lights; carpeted cargo floor, cargo cover and cargo light.

Base Prices

Code	Description	Invoice	MSRP
E4MQ5	SE Sedan (5M)	9803	11399
E4CQ5	CDX Sedan (5M)	12211	14199
EWCQ5	CDX Wagon (5M)	12727	14799

DAEWOO

NUBIRA

CODE	DESCRIPTION	INVOICE	MSRP
	Destination Charge:	430	430

Interested in seeing what dealers will sell this vehicle for? Check out our True Market Value^{sm} (TMV^{sm}) pricing on our Web site at www.edmunds.com.

Accessories

OFM	Floor Mats	56	65
A/T	Transmission: 4-Speed Automatic with OD	696	800
C60	Air Conditioning (SE)	609	700
CF6	Power Tilt and Slide Moonroof (CDX)	430	500
P01	Convenience Package (SE)	654	760
	Includes front and rear power windows, power door locks, body-color heated power rearview mirrors, 6-speaker audio system, anti-theft alarm system, remote keyless entry, tilt steering wheel and front fog lamps.		
W6R	Leather Seating Surfaces (CDX)	559	650

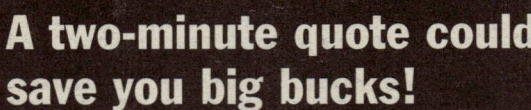

A two-minute quote could save you big bucks!

eCoverage's online quote-to-claim insurance services deliver all the benefits savvy Internet buyers like you have come to expect. And eCoverage is backed by some of the world's biggest financial institutions.

VISIT edmunds.com/insurance

INTREPID
DODGE

2001 INTREPID

What's New?

Changes to this family sedan for the 2001 model year include optional side airbags, a shoulder belt for the central rear passenger, an internal trunk release, three new interior colors, two additional exterior colors, and an additional power outlet in the center console if you get a model with bucket seats. For those cars equipped with the Infinity sound system, you'll receive steering wheel-mounted controls and a four-disc in-dash CD player. SE is now the base Intrepid designation (previously is was the mid-level model) and it includes higher grade fabric this year. All engine choices meet LEV standards and all models receive thicker side glass and upgraded windshield moldings for a quieter ride.

Review

Family-sedan buyers typically want four things in a car: room, style, safety and reliability. Dodge delivers all of this and more in the modern-looking Intrepid. Equipped with a huge interior and gigantic trunk, cutting-edge cab-forward design, and proving itself dependable over the long haul (in our experience, anyway), the Dodge Intrepid represents an excellent argument to avoid cookie-cutter Accords and Camrys for a car with personality. Plus, it scores well in government crash tests.

Three trim levels are available: well-equipped SE or sporty ES, and performance-oriented R/T. SE models include four-wheel disc brakes, air conditioning, rear window defroster, power door locks and windows, cassette player, cruise control, power mirrors, and a tilt steering wheel. ES adds antilock brakes, HomeLink integrated garage door opener, fog lights, premium sound, white-faced gauges, alloy wheels, remote keyless entry, eight-way power driver's seat, leather-wrapped steering wheel and a full-size spare tire. Opt for the R/T and enjoy a higher performance engine, sport-tuned suspension, freer-flowing exhaust, and upgraded brakes, plus a 120-watt AM/FM stereo with cassette/CD player, leather-wrapped shift knob and 17-inch alloy wheels.

SE models, and bottom-rung ES versions, are powered by a twin-cam, 24-valve, 2.7-liter V6. Making 202 horsepower at 5,800 rpm and 190 foot-pounds of torque at 4,850 rpm, this engine moves the 3,400-pound Intrepid along adequately. More impressive is the SOHC, 24-valve, 3.2-liter V6 available in ES models. With 225 horsepower at 6,300 rpm and 225 foot-pounds of torque at 3,800 rpm, this engine's better low-end grunt gets the sportier ES off the line with verve. R/Ts get the Chrysler 300's 3.5-liter V6, but in the Dodge it makes "only" 242 horsepower (11 less than the 300M).

Available only with an automatic transmission, Intrepid at least offers the enthusiast the option of AutoStick, which allows gears to be rowed manually for sporting driving. However, this feature, standard on ES and R/T models, is engineered for the lowest common denominator, and will shift automatically to avoid redlining the engine or fourth-gear starts from a light. Plus, it doesn't improve shift response or acceleration.

If interior space is your No. 1 priority in a sedan, the Intrepid is hard to beat. Rated a large car by the EPA, Intrepid competes with smaller models in price. Room is ample for five adults, and for a family of four, this Dodge seems downright cavernous. It's almost limo-like.

The popular mid-priced sedan segment of the market is saturated with excellent cars, but Dodge is making a strong case for itself. The Intrepid, with its good looks, stable ride and commodious cabin, has carved a niche on this crowded and scarred battleground.

DODGE INTREPID

Standard Equipment

SE (4A): 2.7L V6 DOHC SMPI 24-valve engine; 4-speed electronic OD automatic transmission with lock-up torque converter; 500 amp battery with run down protection; 120 amp alternator; transmission oil cooler; front-wheel drive, 3.89 axle ratio; stainless steel exhaust; touring ride suspension, front independent strut suspension with anti-roll bar, front coil springs, gas-pressurized front shocks, rear independent multi-link suspension with anti-roll bar, rear coil springs, gas-pressurized rear shocks; power rack-and-pinion steering; 4-wheel disc brakes; 17 gal. capacity fuel tank; side impact bars; front and rear body-colored bumpers; body-colored bodyside molding; clearcoat monotone paint; aero-composite halogen headlamps with delay-off feature; driver's and passenger's power remote black outside mirrors; 16" x 7" steel wheels; P225/60SR16 BSW touring A/S tires; compact steel spare wheel; air conditioning, rear heat ducts; AM/FM stereo radio, clock, seek-scan, cassette player, 4 speakers, fixed antenna; cruise control with steering wheel controls; power door locks with 2 stage unlock, child safety rear door locks, power remote trunk release; 1 power accessory outlet, driver's foot rest; instrumentation display includes tachometer, water temperature gauge, trip odometer; warning indicators include oil pressure, water temperature, battery, lights on, key in ignition, low fuel, low washer fluid, door ajar, trunk ajar, brake fluid; driver's and passenger's front airbags; tinted windows, power front and rear windows with driver's 1-touch down; variable intermittent front windshield wipers, sun visor strip, rear window defroster; seating capacity of 5, front bucket seats with adjustable headrests, center armrest with storage, driver's and passenger's seat include 4-way adjustment; rear bench seat; front height adjustable seatbelts; cloth seats, cloth door trim insert with carpet, full cloth headliner, full carpet floor covering with carpeted floor mats; interior lights include dome light with fade, front and rear reading lights; steering wheel with tilt adjustment; vanity mirrors; day/night rearview mirror; full floor console, locking glove box with light, front cupholder, instrument panel bin, driver's and passenger's door bins; carpeted cargo floor, carpeted trunk lid, cargo net, cargo light; body-colored grille, black side window moldings, black front windshield molding, black rear window molding and body-colored door handles.

ES (4A) (in addition to or instead of SE (4A) equipment): HD radiator; 125 amp alternator; automanual transmission, stainless steel exhaust with tailpipe finisher; additional exterior lights include front fog/driving lights; remote keyless entry, panic alarm; driver's seat includes 8-way power adjustment, lumbar support; 60/40 folding rear bench seat with fixed headrests; premium cloth seats, leather-wrapped gearshift knob; 2 door curb lights, illuminated entry; leather-wrapped steering wheel with tilt adjustment; front and rear cupholders, instrument panel bin, and 1 seat back storage pocket.

R/T (4A) (in addition to or instead of ES (4A) equipment): 3.5L V6 SOHC SMPI 24-valve engine; 600 amp battery with run down protection; 130 amp alternator; front-wheel drive, traction control, 3.66 axle ratio; sport ride suspension, 4-wheel antilock disc brakes; 17" x 7" silver alloy wheels; P225/55VR17 BSW performance A/S tires; premium AM/FM stereo radio, clock, seek-scan, cassette player, single CD player, 8 speakers, amplifier, graphic equalizer, fixed antenna; and cloth seats.

Base Prices

CODE	DESCRIPTION	INVOICE	MSRP
LHDH41	SE (4A)	19349	20910
LHDP41	ES (4A)	20875	22605
LHDX41	R/T (4A)	23008	24975
Destination Charge:		625	625

Interested in seeing what dealers will sell this vehicle for? Check out our True Market Valuesm (TMVsm) pricing on our Web site at www.edmunds.com.

INTREPID — DODGE

CODE	DESCRIPTION	INVOICE	MSRP

Accessories

Code	Description	Invoice	MSRP
22C	**Quick Order Package 22C (SE)**	NC	NC
	Includes vehicle with standard equipment.		
23L	**Quick Order Package 23L (ES)**	(107)	(120)
	Includes vehicle with standard equipment. NOT AVAILABLE with BR3, EGW, or TBW.		
24L	**Quick Order Package 24L (ES)**	(107)	(120)
	Includes vehicle with standard equipment. REQUIRES EGW. NOT AVAILABLE with BR3 or TBW.		
24M	**Quick Order Package 24M (ES)**	2844	3195
	Manufacturer Discount	(436)	(490)
	Net Price	2408	2705
	Includes air conditioning with auto temperature control, headliner module, universal garage door opener, auto dim rear view mirror, illuminated vanity mirror sun visors, trip computer, AM/FM cassette player, CD changer radio, steering wheel audio controls, leather trimmed bucket seats, manual driver lumbar adjust, 8-way driver and passenger power seats, security alarm and full size spare tire. REQUIRES EGW. NOT AVAILABLE with BR3, AR3, or TBW.		
25R	**Quick Order Package 25R (RT)**	NC	NC
	Includes vehicle with standard equipment. NOT AVAILABLE with AJF.		
25S	**Quick Order Package 25S (RT)**	1615	1815
	Includes manual driver lumbar adjust, 8-way driver and passenger power seats, 60/40 split folding rear seat, leather trimmed bucket seats, and front door courtesy lamp. NOT AVAILABLE with AJV.		
ADE	**Cold Weather Group**	36	40
	Includes battery heater and engine block heater.		
AJF	**Remote/Illuminated Entry Group (SE/RT)**	200	225
	Includes illuminated entry and keyless entry system. NOT AVAILABLE with 25R.		
AJV	**Driver Convenience Group (RT)**	538	605
	Includes remote/illuminated entry group, illuminated entry, keyless entry system, 8-way power driver seat and 60/40 split folding rear seat. NOT AVAILABLE with 25S.		
AR3	**Radio: Premium AM/FM Stereo with CD and Cassette Player (SE/ES)**	512	575
	Includes 120 watt amplifier, equalizer and 8 speakers in 6 locations. REQUIRES 23L or 24L. NOT AVAILABLE with 24M.		
ARE	**Radio: AM/FM Cassette Player, CD Changer (RT)**	512	575
	Includes 240 watt amplifier, 4 disc in-dash CD changer, 9 Infinity speakers in 7 locations and steering wheel audio controls. INCLUDED in 24M.		
AWS	**Smokers' Group**	27	30
	Includes front and rear ash receiver and cigar lighter.		
BF	**Cloth 50/50 Bench Seat (SE)**	134	150
	Includes front armrest with cup holders, 2-way front head restraints, integral front seat armrest with flip-out cup holders, storage bin and floor console delete.		
BR3	**4-Wheel Disc Antilock Brakes (ES)**	690	775
	Includes traction control. NOT AVAILABLE with 23L or 24L.		
BR3	**4-Wheel Disc Antilock Brakes (SE/ES)**	534	600
	NOT AVAILABLE with 24M.		
CGS	**Supplemental Side Air Bags**	347	390

DODGE

INTREPID / NEON

CODE	DESCRIPTION	INVOICE	MSRP
CSG	60/40 Split Folding Rear Seat (SE)	187	210
	INCLUDED in 25S.		
EGW	Engine: 3.2L V6 SOHC 24V MPI (ES)	445	500
	NOT AVAILABLE with 23L.		
GWA	Power Sunroof	797	895
JPV	8-Way Power Driver Seat (SE)	338	380
TBB	Tire: Full Size Spare (SE)	142	160
TBW	Full Size Spare Tire with Matching Wheel (ES)	80	90
	NOT AVAILABLE with 23L or 24L.		
TBW	Full Size Spare Tire with Matching Wheel (ES/RT)	223	250
	NOT AVAILABLE with 24M.		
WNG	Wheels: 16" Silver Aluminum (SE)	347	390

2001 NEON

What's New?

The Neon R/T and Neon ACR, both models sporting a 2.0-liter 150-horsepower engine, make their much-anticipated return this year. Side-impact airbags and leather seats are now available in Dodge's economy car, as is a new interior color and four new exterior colors. An internal trunk release keeps young and old from being trapped in the Neon's cargo hold, and four new option packages, one of which includes a four-disc in-dash CD player, further widen its appeal to buyers seeking an American-made economy car.

Review

DaimlerChrysler is billing the current-generation Neon as "quiet, sophisticated and still a lot of fun." Fun seems to be the catchword for the Neon. Its maker obviously wants people to know that while the Neon has grown up, it hasn't grown old. It's probably worthwhile for them to stress the fun factor, since the coupe version has been absent since the 2000-model-year redesign, meaning that a four-door sedan will have to suffice for all those economy car thrill-seekers out there. Available trim levels include the base ES, uplevel SE, sporty R/T, and performance-minded ACR.

The standard 132-horsepower 2.0-liter inline four received improvements to the air induction and intake manifold systems last year to provide torque over a broader rpm range, but the powerplant still makes too much noise at high rpms. Thankfully, with a refined suspension that offers plenty of wheel travel, the Neon's ride is smooth. The power rack-and-pinion steering and precisely tuned suspension also contribute to the Neon's cruising quality while making it an absolute blast when canyon carving. Stopping power comes from a front disc/rear drum combo, but buyers may want to opt for four-wheel discs with ABS and traction control.

A 150-horsepower 2.0-liter engine, absent in 2000, makes a celebrated return this year as standard equipment in the reintroduced R/T and ACR models. The feature-laden R/T model also features 16-inch aluminum wheels, four-wheel disc brakes with ABS, a sport suspension, special body cladding, a performance-tuned exhaust, and high ratio steering, along with a unique steering wheel and shift knob, power front windows, power door locks, air conditioning, and remote keyless entry. Options include leather seats with side airbags. Despite its luxury appointments, a five-speed manual is the only transmission offered with the R/T.

NEON
DODGE

ACRs are targeted at the club racing faithful who have used their Neons for track events since the car's introduction in 1994. The 2001 model comes with 15-inch wheels sporting performance tires and all of the performance upgrades found on the R/T, but without the heavy luxury items that might slow Ricky Roadracer down while strafing cones at the local SCCA event. In this arena, the Neon has proven quite capable.

But whether buying a performance-oriented R/T or ACR model, or just the low-dollar base Neon, make sure you stick with the standard equipment five-speed manual transmission. Dodge has the *cojones* to charge $600 for its lame-oid and out-of-date three-speed automatic while the cheaper Hyundai Elantra and Daewoo Nubira offer four-speed autos. Whatever.

Items like a radio/cassette combo and four Big Gulp-sized cupholders are much appreciated, yet overall feature content is still lacking. We also give Dodge credit for creating an attractive and roomy cabin with available white-faced gauges and a swoopy dash that appears very upscale and Intrepid-like.

Unfortunately for Dodge, competitors like the Ford Focus, Mazda Protege and Nissan Sentra offer more bang for the buck in terms of both refinement and content while still providing enthusiasts a fun-to-drive car. If Chrysler wants to continue to compete in this market, the company will have to address the Neon's failings.

Standard Equipment

HIGHLINE (5M): 2L I4 SOHC SMPI 16-valve engine; 5-speed OD manual transmission; 450 amp battery with run down protection; 83 amp alternator; front-wheel drive, 3.55 axle ratio; stainless steel exhaust; front independent strut suspension with anti-roll bar, front coil springs, rear independent multi-link suspension with anti-roll bar, rear coil springs; power rack-and-pinion steering, power steering cooler; front disc/rear drum brakes; 12.5 gal. capacity fuel tank; side impact bars; front and rear body-colored bumpers; body-colored bodyside molding; clearcoat monotone paint; aero-composite halogen headlamps; driver's and passenger's black outside mirrors, driver's manual remote outside mirror, passenger's manual outside mirror; 14" x 5.5" black steel wheels; P185/65TR14 BSW touring A/S tires; compact steel spare wheel; AM/FM stereo radio, clock, seek-scan, cassette player, CD changer pre-wiring, 6 speakers, fixed antenna; child safety rear door locks; 1 power accessory outlet; instrumentation display includes water temperature gauge, trip odometer; warning indicators include oil pressure, battery, lights on, key in ignition, low fuel, door ajar; driver's and passenger's front airbags; tinted windows, manual front and rear windows; variable intermittent front windshield wipers, sun visor strip, rear window defroster; seating capacity of 5, front bucket seats with adjustable headrests, center armrest with storage, driver's and passenger's seat includes 4-way adjustment; 60/40 folding rear bench seat with fixed headrests; front height adjustable seatbelts; cloth seats, cloth door trim insert, full cloth headliner, full carpet floor covering with carpeted floor mats, deluxe sound insulation; interior lights include dome light with fade; steering wheel with tilt adjustment; passenger's side vanity mirror; day/night rearview mirror; full floor console, locking glove box, front and rear cupholders, instrument panel bin, dashboard storage, driver's and passenger's door bins; carpeted cargo floor, carpeted trunk lid, cargo light; black side window moldings, black front windshield molding, black rear window molding and body-colored door handles.

Base Prices

CODE	DESCRIPTION	INVOICE	MSRP
PLDH41	Highline (5M)	11856	12715
	Destination Charge:	490	490

Interested in seeing what dealers will sell this vehicle for? Check out our True Market Valuesm (TMVsm) pricing on our Web site at www.edmunds.com.

Accessories

CODE	DESCRIPTION	INVOICE	MSRP
21D	Quick Order Package 21D	NC	NC
	Includes vehicle with standard equipment. **REQUIRES HAA or 4XA.**		

DODGE NEON

CODE	DESCRIPTION	INVOICE	MSRP
21G	Quick Order Package 21G	2229	2505
	Manufacturer Discount	(592)	(665)
	Net Price	1637	1840

Includes air conditioning, passenger assist handles, ES badge, color keyed instrument cluster bezel, fog lamps, power convenience group, power heated foldaway mirrors, power front windows, sentry key security group, keyless entry system with 2 transmitters, power auto central locking locks, security alarm, sentry key theft deterrent system, tachometer, power trunklid release, leather-wrapped shift knob, leather-wrapped steering wheel, 15" wheel covers, and P185/60R15 BSW A/S touring tires.

22D	Quick Order Package 22D	NC	NC

Includes vehicle with standard equipment. REQUIRES DGC and (HAA or 4XA).

22G	Quick Order Package 22G	2229	2505
	Manufacturer Discount	(592)	(665)
	Net Price	1637	1840

Includes air conditioning, passenger assist handles, ES badge, color keyed instrument cluster bezel, fog lamps, power convenience group, power heated foldaway mirrors, power front windows, sentry key security group, keyless entry system with 2 transmitters, power auto central locking locks, security alarm, sentry key theft deterrent system, tachometer, power trunklid release, leather-wrapped shift knob, leather-wrapped steering wheel, 15" wheel covers, and P185/60R15 BSW A/S touring tires. REQUIRES DGC.

25E	Quick Order Package 25E	1891	2125
	Manufacturer Discount	(218)	(245)
	Net Price	1673	1880

Includes antilock brake group, 4-wheel antilock disc brakes, tachometer, traction control, 2.0 Magnum Decklid badge, ACR competition group, competition suspension, P185/60R15 BSW A/S performance tires, 15" alloy wheels, cloth low-back bucket seats, dual bright tip exhaust, floor mats delete, radio delete, leather-wrapped shift knob, performance steering and leather-wrapped steering wheel. REQUIRES ECH.

25H	Quick Order Package 25H	3943	4430
	Manufacturer Discount	(765)	(860)
	Net Price	3178	3570

Includes air conditioning, 4-wheel antilock disc brakes, traction control, passenger assist handles, 2.0 Magnum Decklid badge, color keyed instrument cluster bezel, dual bright tip exhaust, fog lamps, light group, console flood lamp, glove box lamp, rear view mirror with reading lamps, illuminated vanity mirror sun visors, power convenience group, power heated foldaway mirrors, power front windows, R/T group, front door dodge R/T badge, sill extensions, light group, console flood lamp, glove box lamp, rear view mirror with reading lamps, illuminated vanity mirror sun visors, trunklid spoiler, sport suspension, P195/50R16 BSW P tires, 16" alloy wheels, cloth low back bucket seats, sentry key security group, keyless entry system with 2 transmitters, power auto central locking locks, security alarm, sentry key theft deterrent system, tachometer, power trunklid release, leather-wrapped shift knob, performance steering and leather-wrapped steering wheel. REQUIRES ECH.

4XA	Air Conditioning Bypass	NC	NC

NOT AVAILABLE with HAA, ADV, or AGS.

NEON — DODGE

CODE	DESCRIPTION	INVOICE	MSRP
ADA	Light Group	116	130

Includes console flood lamp, glove box lamp, rear view mirror with reading lamps and illuminated vanity mirror sun visors. REQUIRES HAA, 21G, or 22G. NOT AVAILABLE with 4XA. INCLUDED in 25H.

ADR	Antilock Brake Group	748	840
	Manufacturer Discount	(218)	(245)
	Net Price	530	595

Includes 4-wheel antilock disc brakes, tachometer and traction control. REQUIRES 21D or 22D. INCLUDED in 25E and 25H.

ADR	Antilock Brake Group	659	740
	Manufacturer Discount	(129)	(145)
	Net Price	530	595

Includes tachometer, 4-wheel antilock disc brakes and traction control. REQUIRES ADV, 21G, or 22G. INCLUDED in 25E and 25H.

ADV	Sport Appearance Group	1433	1610
	Manufacturer Discount	(245)	(275)
	Net Price	1188	1335

Includes spare tire cover and performance steering, trunklid spoiler, sport suspension, tachometer, P195/50R16 83V BSW P tires and 16" alloy wheels.

ADV	Sport Appearance Group	1571	1765
	Manufacturer Discount	(294)	(330)
	Net Price	1277	1435

Includes spare tire cover and performance steering, trunklid spoiler, sport suspension, tachometer, P195/50R16 83V BSW P tires and 16" alloy wheels.

ADV	Sport Appearance Group	1522	1710
	Manufacturer Discount	(271)	(305)
	Net Price	1251	1405

Includes spare tire cover and performance steering, trunklid spoiler, sport suspension, tachometer, P195/50R16 83V BSW P tires and 16" alloy wheels. REQUIRES AGS. NOT AVAILABLE with 4XA.

AGS	Sun and Sound Group	1064	1195
	Manufacturer Discount	(356)	(400)
	Net Price	708	795

Includes passenger assist handles and 15" wheel covers, 4 disc in-dash CD changer, light group, console flood lamp, glove box lamp, rear view mirror with reading lamps, illuminated vanity mirror sun visors, and power sunroof. REQUIRES HAA. NOT AVAILABLE with 4XA.

AJP	Power Convenience Group	338	380

Includes power heated foldaway mirrors and power front windows. REQUIRES HAA. NOT AVAILABLE with 4XA. INCLUDED in 21G, 22G and 25H.

AJV	Driver Convenience Group	1922	2160
	Manufacturer Discount	(369)	(415)
	Net Price	1553	1745

Includes air conditioning, front and rear floor mats, light group, console flood lamp, glove box lamp, rear view mirror with reading lamps, illuminated vanity mirror sun visors, AM/FM cassette player with changer control radio, sentry key security group, keyless entry system with 2 transmitters, power auto central locking locks, security

DODGE — NEON

CODE	DESCRIPTION	INVOICE	MSRP
	alarm, sentry key theft deterrent system, tachometer, and power trunklid release. REQUIRES 25E.		
AJX	Sentry Key Security Group	668	750
	Manufacturer Discount	(369)	(415)
	Net Price	299	335
	Includes keyless entry system with 2 transmitters, power auto central locking locks, security alarm, sentry key theft deterrent system, tachometer and power trunklid release. REQUIRES HAA. NOT AVAILABLE with 4XA. INCLUDED in 21G, 22G and 25H. (Option is no longer available).		
ALF	Value Fun Group	645	725
	Manufacturer Discount	(116)	(130)
	Net Price	529	595
	Includes passenger assist handles and power sunroof. REQUIRES 21G or 22G.		
ALF	Value Fun Group	529	595
	Includes passenger assist handles, light group, console flood lamp, glove box lamp, rear view mirror with reading lamps, illuminated vanity mirror sun visors and power sunroof. REQUIRES 25H.		
B7	Premium Cloth Low Back Bucket Seats	NC	NC
	NOT AVAILABLE with XL.		
CGS	Supplemental Side Air Bags	312	350
DGC	Transmission: 3-Speed Automatic	534	600
	REQUIRES 22D or 22G.		
ECH	Engine: 2.0L 4 Cyl. SOHC 16V High Performance	223	250
	REQUIRES 25E.		
HAA	Air Conditioning	890	1000
	NOT AVAILABLE with 4XA. INCLUDED in 21G, 22G and 25H.		
NHK	Engine Block Heater	18	20
	REQUIRES 21D or 22D.		
NHM	Speed Control	209	235
	REQUIRES 21D or 22D.		
RDW	4 Disc In-Dash CD Changer	334	375
	REQUIRES 21D or 22D.		
RL	Leather Low-Back Bucket Seats	899	1010
	Manufacturer Discount	(142)	(160)
	Net Price	757	850
	Includes Decklid liner and full length floor console with premium armrest and side air bags.		
WJA	Wheels: 15" Aluminum	316	355
	REQUIRES AGS. NOT AVAILABLE with 4XA or ADV.		
WJA	Wheels: 15" Aluminum	365	410
	REQUIRES HAA. NOT AVAILABLE with 4XA or ADV.		
XL	Leather Low-Back Bucket Seats	899	1010
	Manufacturer Discount	(142)	(160)
	Net Price	757	850
	Includes Decklid liner and full length floor console with premium armrest and side air bags. NOT AVAILABLE with B7.		

STRATUS — DODGE

2001 STRATUS

What's New?

The Avenger nameplate has been dropped from the Dodge lineup, replaced by the all-new Stratus Coupe. The Stratus Sedan continues with a full redesign but retains much of its predecessor's look and feel. A new engine debuts along with additional safety features that make the Stratus a family sedan in the truest sense. Last year we marveled at the list of standard options on this moderately priced sedan; this year we're rechecking our numbers again as more features debut for 2001.

Review

Chrysler obviously adhered to the "if it ain't broke, don't fix it" philosophy when they redesigned the 2001 Stratus Sedan and new Stratus Coupe, formerly known as the Avenger. The previous generation benefited from a roomy cabin, stylish design, and a long list of standard features that made it the clear value leader in its class. For 2001, the Stratus retains all the features we have come to expect while still managing to up the ante with even more standard options and an exciting new R/T Coupe.

Dodge felt there was a "void in the market" when it came to stylish sport coupes that didn't require a second mortgage to afford. So they took their already striking Avenger Coupe, gave it some new, slicker styling and added a larger, more powerful 3.0-liter V6 cranking out 200 horsepower and 205 ft-lbs. of torque. Mate that to a five-speed manual transmission (a four-speed automatic with AutoStick is also available), specially tuned suspension and 17-inch performance tires and you have yourself the new Stratus R/T, a legitimate performance coupe for under $25,000.

Coupe customers without a performance penchant can opt for the Stratus Coupe in ES trim and still get a potent 2.4-liter engine capable of 147 horsepower and 158 ft-lbs. of torque. The coupe's interior also underwent revision this year with an easier to read instrument panel and more user-friendly controls meant to focus the driver on one thing — driving.

Of course, if your two-door days are behind you, the new Stratus Sedan is sure to appeal to those looking for something a little more family-oriented. Dodge had a value leader on their hands with the previous model, so when it came time for a redesign they simply built on the already-established strengths and incorporated even more bang for the buck and safety along with a more refined exterior look. The interior received the same treatment as the coupe, getting white-faced gauges and new materials designed to not only look better but feel better as well.

Under the hood the base Stratus SE retains the same 2.4-liter four-cylinder offered in last year's model, putting out 150 horsepower and 167 ft-lbs. of torque. This powerplant can be mated to either a five-speed manual or four-speed automatic and incorporates refinements meant to reduce noise at all engine speeds. SE models still offer an extensive list of standard features including A/C, power windows, power mirrors, cruise control, and an AM/FM stereo cassette while adding new 15-inch wheels and tires, larger four-wheel disc brakes and a front and rear independent suspension.

The upgraded ES Sedan now offers a 2.7-liter V6 that adds 32 more horsepower and 20 more ft-lbs. of torque to last year's numbers, bringing the totals up to 200 and 193, respectively. Power runs through a four-speed Autostick transmission and 16-inch chromed aluminum wheels and tires. Other ES specific highlights include fog lamps, eight-way power driver's seat, and leather-wrapped steering wheel and shift knob.

For the first time ever, the Stratus offers an optional side airbag curtain that protects both front and rear occupants in the event of a side impact. Other new safety features include a rear center shoulder belt, multi-stage front airbags to reduce the potential for injury, along with front

DODGE
STRATUS

seatbelt pre-tensioners and load-limiters for improved occupant safety and the LATCH system of child seat-tether anchors.

The long list of standard features coupled with a competitive price makes it hard to overlook Stratus if you're seeking a fully loaded four-door, while the new coupe continues the philosophy of performance and functionality while still retaining an affordable price.

Standard Equipment

SE COUPE (5M): 2.4L I4 DOHC SMPI 16-valve engine; 5-speed OD manual transmission; 510 amp battery with run down protection; 90 amp alternator; front-wheel drive; stainless steel exhaust; touring ride suspension, front independent double wishbone suspension with anti-roll bar, front coil springs, rear independent double wishbone suspension with anti-roll bar, rear coil springs; power rack-and-pinion steering; front disc/rear drum brakes; 16.3 gal. capacity fuel tank; front mud flaps, rear lip spoiler, side impact bars; front and rear body-colored bumpers with body-colored bumper insert; body-colored bodyside molding; clearcoat monotone paint; aero-composite halogen headlamps; driver's and passenger's power remote black outside mirrors; 16" x 6" steel wheels; P205/55HR16 BSW performance A/S tires; compact steel spare wheel; air conditioning, rear heat ducts; AM/FM stereo radio, clock, seek-scan, cassette player, 6 speakers, fixed antenna; cruise control; power door locks, remote trunk release; 2 power accessory outlets, front lighter element(s), driver's foot rest, smokers' package; instrumentation display includes tachometer, water temperature gauge, trip odometer; warning indicators include oil pressure, water temp, battery, lights on, key in ignition, low fuel, door ajar; driver's and passenger's front airbags; ignition disable; tinted windows; variable intermittent front windshield wipers, sun visor strip, rear window defroster; seating capacity of 5, front bucket seats with adjustable headrests, center armrest with storage, driver's seat includes 6-way adjustment, passenger's seat includes 4-way adjustment; full folding rear bench seat; front height adjustable seatbelts; cloth seats, vinyl door trim insert, full cloth headliner, full carpet floor covering with carpeted floor mats; interior lights include dome light; sport steering wheel with tilt adjustment; vanity mirrors; day/night rearview mirror; full floor console, locking glove box with light, front and rear cupholders, instrument panel bin, driver's and passenger's door bins; carpeted cargo floor, cargo net, cargo light; body-colored grille, black side window moldings, black front windshield molding, black rear window molding and body-colored door handles.

SE SEDAN (4A) (in addition to or instead of SE COUPE (5M) equipment): 2.4L I4 SOHC SMPI 16-valve engine; 4-speed electronic OD automatic transmission with lock-up torque converter; 120 amp alternator; front-wheel drive, 3.94 axle ratio; 4-wheel disc brakes; 16 gal. capacity fuel tank; chrome bodyside insert; aero-composite halogen headlamps with delay-off feature; 15" x 6" black steel wheels; P205/65TR15 BSW A/S tires; 4 speakers, child safety rear door locks, power remote trunk release; 1 power accessory outlet, power front and rear windows with driver's 1-touch down; driver's seat includes 4-way adjustment and a 60/40 folding rear bench seat.

R/T COUPE (5M) (in addition to or instead of SE COUPE (5M) equipment): 3L V6 SOHC SMPI 24-valve engine; tailpipe finisher; sport ride suspension; 4-wheel disc brakes; additional exterior lights include front fog/driving lights; 17" x 6.5" silver alloy wheels; P215/50HR17 BSW A/S tires; single CD player, 7 premium speakers, graphic equalizer; power door locks with 2 stage unlock, remote keyless entry, power remote trunk release; instrumentation display includes compass, exterior temp, trip odometer; panic alarm, security system; leather-wrapped gearshift knob; leather-wrapped sport steering wheel with tilt adjustment; dual illuminated vanity mirrors; auto-dimming day/night rearview mirror.

ES SEDAN (4A) (in addition to or instead of R/T Coupe (5M) equipment): 2.7L V6 DOHC SMPI 24-valve engine; automanual transmission; 16" x 6.5" silver alloy wheels; P205/60TR16 BSW A/S tires; 4 speakers, cruise control with steering wheel controls; child safety rear door locks, garage door opener; instrumentation display includes tachometer, driver's seat includes 8-way power adjustment, lumbar support, premium cloth seats, cloth door trim insert, interior lights include, front reading lights, and illuminated entry.

STRATUS — DODGE

CODE	DESCRIPTION	INVOICE	MSRP

Base Prices

CODE	DESCRIPTION	INVOICE	MSRP
STDH22	SE Coupe (5M)	16474	17810
STDS22	R/T Coupe (5M)	19170	20805
JRDH41	SE Sedan (4A)	16507	17830
JRDP41	ES Sedan (4A)	18879	20465
	Destination Charge:	595	595

Interested in seeing what dealers will sell this vehicle for? Check out our True Market Valuesm (TMVsm) pricing on our Web site at www.edmunds.com.

Accessories

CODE	DESCRIPTION	INVOICE	MSRP
21A	Quick Order Package 21A (SE Coupe)	NC	NC
	Includes vehicle with standard equipment. REQUIRES EY7 and DD6. NOT AVAILABLE with EF7, or DG1.		
22A	Quick Order Package 22A (SE Coupe)	NC	NC
	Includes vehicle with standard equipment. REQUIRES EY7 and DG1. NOT AVAILABLE with EF7, or DD6.		
23L	Quick Order Package 23L (R/T Coupe)	NC	NC
	Includes vehicle with standard equipment. REQUIRES EF7 and DD6. NOT AVAILABLE with DG1.		
24A	Quick Order Package 24A (SE Coupe)	NC	NC
	Includes vehicle with standard equipment. REQUIRES EF7 and DG1. NOT AVAILABLE with EY7 or DD6.		
24B	Quick Order Package 24B (SE Sedan)	NC	NC
	Includes vehicle with standard equipment. REQUIRES EDZ and DGL. NOT AVAILABLE with EES, ATD, AJB, RCC, or GWA.		
24C	Quick Order Package 24C (SE Sedan)	850	955
	Manufacturer Discount	(111)	(125)
	Net Price	739	830
	Includes rear passenger assist handles, premium headliner module, front courtesy map lamps, AM/FM with CD and changer control radio, remote illuminated entry group, illuminated entry, keyless entry, 8-way power driver seat, illuminated vanity mirror sun visors, traveler mini trip computer and low washer fluid warning signal. REQUIRES EDZ and DGL. NOT AVAILABLE with EES.		
24L	Quick Order Package 24L (R/T Coupe)	147	165
	Includes vehicle with standard equipment. REQUIRES EF7 and DG1. NOT AVAILABLE with DD6.		
28B	Quick Order Package 28B (SE Sedan)	NC	NC
	Includes vehicle with standard equipment. REQUIRES EES and DGL. NOT AVAILABLE with EDZ, ATD, AJB, RCC, or GWA.		
28C	Quick Order Package 28C (SE Sedan)	850	955
	Manufacturer Discount	(111)	(125)
	Net Price	739	830
	Includes rear passenger assist handles, premium headliner module, front courtesy map lamps, AM/FM with CD and changer control radio, remote illuminated entry group, illuminated entry, keyless entry, 8-way power driver seat, illuminated vanity mirror		

DODGE — STRATUS

CODE	DESCRIPTION	INVOICE	MSRP
	sun visors, traveler mini trip computer and low washer fluid warning signal. REQUIRES EES and DGL. NOT AVAILABLE with EDZ.		
28L	Quick Order Package 28L (ES Sedan)	NC	NC
	Includes vehicle with standard equipment. REQUIRES EES and DGL.		
ADE	Cold Weather Group (Sedan)	36	40
	Includes battery heater and engine block heater.		
ADT	Touring Group (SE Coupe)	614	690
	Includes keyless entry, AM/FM cassette player with CD radio and security alarm.		
AJB	Security Group (Sedan)	174	195
	Includes security alarm and sentry key theft deterrent system. NOT AVAILABLE with 24B or 28B.		
AJD	Leather Interior Group (R/T Coupe)	930	1045
	Includes universal garage door opener, 6-way power driver seat and leather low-back bucket seats.		
AJF	Remote/Illuminated Entry Group (SE Sedan)	151	170
	Includes panic alarm and trunk lid release, illuminated entry and keyless entry. INCLUDED in 24C and 28C.		
AL	Leather Trimmed Bucket Seats (ES Sedan)	534	600
	Includes driver lumbar support and front passenger seat back map pocket and premium door trim panel.		
ATD	Radio: Cassette Player, CD Changer (Sedan)	223	250
	Includes AM/FM cassette player and CD changer control and 4-disc in-dash CD changer. NOT AVAILABLE with 24B, 28B, or RBK.		
AWS	Smokers' Group (Sedan)	27	30
	Includes removeable ash tray and cigar lighter.		
BRF	Antilock 4-Wheel-Disc Brakes (R/T Coupe)	659	740
	Includes traction control. NOT AVAILABLE with DD6.		
BRF	Antilock 4-Wheel-Disc Brakes (R/T Coupe)	503	565
	NOT AVAILABLE with DG1.		
BRT	Antilock 4-Wheel-Disc Brakes (Sedan)	503	565
CGS	Side Air Bags (Sedan)	347	390
DD6	Transmission: 5-Speed Manual (Coupe)	NC	NC
	NOT AVAILABLE with EF7, 22A, 24A, or 24L.		
DG1	Transmission: 4-Speed Automatic (Coupe)	734	825
	NOT AVAILABLE with 21A, 23L, or BRF.		
DGL	Transmission: 4-Spd Automatic (41TE) (Sedan)	NC	NC
EDZ	Engine: 2.4L 4 Cyl. DOHC 16V SMPI (SE Sedan)	NC	NC
	NOT AVAILABLE with 28B or 28C.		
EES	Engine: 2.7L V6 24V with Active Intake (ES Sedan)	NC	NC
EES	Engine: 2.7L V6 24V with Active Intake (SE Sedan)	757	850
	NOT AVAILABLE with 24B or 24C.		
EF7	Engine: 3.0L SOHC 24V V6 (R/T Coupe)	NC	NC
EF7	Engine: 3.0L SOHC 24V V6 (SE Coupe)	846	950
	Includes rear-wheel disc brakes, bright tip exhaust, leather-wrapped steering wheel and leather shift knob. NOT AVAILABLE with DD6, 21A or 22A.		
EY7	Engine: 2.4L 4 CYL SOHC 16V (SE Coupe)	NC	NC
	NOT AVAILABLE with 24A.		

STRATUS — DODGE

CODE	DESCRIPTION	INVOICE	MSRP
GWA	Power Sunroof	619	695
	NOT AVAILABLE with 24B or 28B.		
JPV	8-Way Power Driver Seat (SE Sedan)	338	380
	INCLUDED in 24C and 28C.		
RBK	Radio: AM/FM with CD and Changer Ctrl (SE Sedan)	111	125
	NOT AVAILABLE with ATD. INCLUDED in 24C and 28C.		
RBV	Radio: AM/FM, MX with 4 CD In Radio Chgr (R/T Coupe)	NC	NC
	Includes Infinity 7 speaker system.		
RCC	6 Premium Speakers with 120 Watt Amp (Sedan)	312	350
	NOT AVAILABLE with 24B or 28B.		
TBB	Tire: Full Size Spare (SE Sedan)	142	160
	NOT AVAILABLE with TBW or WNF.		
TBW	Tire: Full Size Spare with Matching Wheel (ES Sedan)	343	385
	REQUIRES WNE.		
TBW	Tire: Full Size Spare with Matching Wheel (Sedan)	223	250
	REQUIRES WNF. NOT AVAILABLE with TBB.		
WNE	Wheels: 16" Chrome Aluminum (ES Sedan)	534	600
WNF	Wheels: 16" X 6.5" Aluminum (SE Sedan)	312	350
	NOT AVAILABLE with TBB.		
WNY	Wheels: 16" X 6" Aluminum (SE Coupe)	325	365

TOWN HALL

Get answers from our editors, discover smart shopping strategies and share your perspectives in this interactive forum of both experts and consumers. Just enter the following address into your Web browser:

townhall.edmunds.com

Where smart shoppers talk about cars, trucks, and related consumer topics.

FORD

CROWN VICTORIA

2001 CROWN VICTORIA

What's New?

Power from the V8 engine is increased. The interior gets minor improvements, including and an optional adjustable pedal assembly. Safety has been improved via a crash severity sensor, safety belt pretensioners, dual-stage airbags and seat-position sensors.

Review

If you've been pinching your pennies to buy a new full-size, rear-drive American sedan, we hope you like Fords. The Blue Oval is the only manufacturer building such cars these days. Decades-old technology allows Ford to keep the prices low, and the car is a favorite among fleet buyers for taxi companies, police departments, or just those who need space and don't want a minivan or sport-ute.

These days the Ford Crown Victoria and its Mercury Grand Marquis stablemate offer much more value than most compact and midsize cars being peddled at your local auto mall. Think about this: the Crown Vic costs less than 30 grand fully loaded with electric everything and a leather interior. In contrast, a similarly equipped Toyota Avalon runs several thousand dollars more.

The five- or six-passenger Crown Vic is available in either base-model trim or upscale LX trim. Both have similar levels of equipment, though optional features like automatic climate control and leather seating are only available on the LX model.

Both versions get mild interior updates for 2001. There are new front-door map pockets, a relocated digital clock, new switches for the power mirrors, traction control and headlights, and a new horn system. The best addition is the optional adjustable gas and brake pedals. The pedals can be moved up to 3 inches towards the driver to improve comfort and to keep shorter drivers from sitting too close to the steering wheel-mounted airbag.

The Crown Victoria was never a slouch in terms of acceleration (as you would hope, seeing as how so many police departments use it), and this year Ford bumped the output of the 4.6-liter V8 engine to 220 horsepower and 265 foot-pounds of torque. The only transmission offered is a four-speed automatic.

In stock trim, the Crown Victoria drives and handles like you would expect a big American sedan to. It's comfortable, but it's all too happy to float around over bumps. The handling and performance package adds a few horsepower (boosting output to 235) and improves the car's stability in the twisties; we recommend it to anyone who enjoys backcountry highways more than mind-numbing interstates for their family vacations.

And if you do plan to haul around a family, you can sleep better at night knowing that the Crown Victoria scores well in National Highway Traffic Safety Administration crash tests. Last year's model did very well, so the 2001 safety improvements (a crash severity sensor, safety belt pretensioners, dual stage airbags and seat position sensors) should make the Crown Vic even better.

If you're one of the few people unwilling to pay for a sport utility's high insurance premiums and abysmal gas mileage and if you just can't stand the idea of a minivan, we hope that you like the Crown Victoria. It's your only choice for an American, full-size, rear-wheel-drive sedan.

Standard Equipment

BASE (4A): 4.6L V8 SOHC SMPI 16-valve engine; 4-speed electronic OD automatic transmission with lock-up converter; battery with rundown protection; 130-amp alternator; rear-wheel drive,

CROWN VICTORIA

FORD

CODE	DESCRIPTION	INVOICE	MSRP

2.73 axle ratio; stainless steel exhaust; front independent suspension with anti-roll bar, front coil springs, gas-pressurized front shocks, rigid rear axle multi-link suspension with anti-roll bar, rear coil springs, gas-pressurized rear shocks; recirculating-ball power steering with vehicle speed-sensing assist; 4-wheel disc brakes; 19 gal. capacity fuel tank; side impact bars; front and rear body-colored bumpers with chrome bumper insert; body-colored bodyside molding; clearcoat monotone paint; aero-composite halogen fully automatic headlamps with delay-off feature; driver's and passenger's power remote body-colored folding outside mirrors; 16" x 7" steel wheels with P225/60SR16 BSW A/S tires; compact steel spare wheel; air conditioning, rear heat ducts; AM/FM stereo w/clock and seek-scan feature, auto-reverse cassette player, 4 speakers, window grid antenna; cruise control with steering wheel controls; power door locks, child-safety rear door locks, power remote hatch/trunk release; 1 power accessory outlet, front lighter element, driver's foot rest, smokers' package; instrumentation display includes oil pressure gauge, water temperature gauge, volt gauge, trip odometer; warning indicators include battery, water temperature, lights on, key in ignition, low fuel, brake fluid; driver's front airbag, passenger's cancelable front airbag; ignition disable; tinted windows, power front and rear windows with driver's 1-touch down function; variable-speed intermittent front windshield wipers, sun visor strip, rear window defroster; seating capacity of 6, 50/50 split-bench front seat with adjustable headrests, driver's and front passenger's armrests, driver's and passenger's front seats include 4-way adjustment; rear bench seat; height-adjustable front seatbelts front pretensioners; cloth seats, vinyl door trim insert, full cloth headliner, full color-keyed carpet floor covering, deluxe sound insulation, simulated-wood dashboard insert, interior lights include dome light with fade, door curb lights, illuminated entry; steering wheel with tilt adjustment; day/night rearview mirror; locking glove box with light, front cupholder, driver's and passenger's door bins; carpeted cargo floor, cargo light; chrome grille, chrome side window moldings, black front windshield molding, black rear window molding and chrome door handles.

LX (4A) (in addition to or instead of BASE (4A) equipment): Power door locks with 2-stage unlock, remote keyless entry, ignition disable, panic alarm; driver's seat includes 8-way power adjustment with 2-way power lumbar support; rear center armrest; premium cloth seats; interior lights include dual illuminated vanity mirrors; 2 seatback storage pockets.

Base Prices

P73	Base (4A)	20793	21965
P74	LX (4A)	22738	24080
	Destination Charge:	680	680

Interested in seeing what dealers will sell this vehicle for? Check out our True Market Value^{sm} (TMV^{sm}) pricing on our Web site at www.edmunds.com.

Accessories

12Y	Front and Rear Floor Mats	49	55
144	Remote Keyless Entry (Base)	213	240
	NOT AVAILABLE with 999.		
175	Universal Garage Door Opener (LX)	102	115
	Can be programmed for 3 different transmitters.		
21A	Power Driver's Seat (Base)	321	360
41G	Handling and Performance Package (Base)	832	935
	Includes revised springs, shocks and stabilizer bar, P225/60TR16 touring BSW tires, 16" cast alloy wheels, rear air suspension, dual exhaust, 4.6L SEFI V8 engine and 3.27 axle ratio. NOT AVAILABLE with 999, T2A, 508.		

FORD

CROWN VICTORIA

CODE	DESCRIPTION	INVOICE	MSRP
41G	**Handling and Performance Package (LX)**	658	740
	Includes revised springs, shocks and stabilizer bar, P225/60R16 touring BSW tires, 16" cast alloy wheels, rear air suspension, dual exhaust, 4.6L SEFI V8 engine and 3.27 axle ratio. NOT AVAILABLE with 999, T2A, 65E, 508.		
41H	**Engine Block Heater**	23	25
508	**Conventional Spare Tire**	93	105
	Includes full-size steel wheel. Replaces standard mini-spare with ground position tire. NOT AVAILABLE with 41G.		
508	**Conventional Spare Tire**	107	120
	Includes steel spare wheel at extra charge. Replaces standard mini-spare with ground position tire. NOT AVAILABLE with 999, T2A.		
552	**Antilock Braking System**	534	600
553	**Antilock Braking System with Traction Control**	690	175
	NOT AVAILABLE with 999.		
585	**Radio: AM/FM Stereo with CD**	124	140
	Replaces cassette. NOT AVAILABLE with 586, 65E, 919.		
586	**Radio: Premium AM/FM Stereo with Cass (LX)**	321	360
	Includes auto-set radio (selects 6 strongest listenable stations and stores them), seek and scan radio feature (seek also available with tape evaluation), distributed audio system, auto-bass/loudness feature, self-diagnostic capability, 80-Watt power, 4 speakers, Dolby sound and radio data system (RDS). NOT AVAILABLE with 999, 585.		
59C	**Power Adjustable Pedals (Base)**	107	120
65C	**LX Comfort Group (LX)**	801	900
	Includes electronic temperature control air conditioning, 12-spoke alloy wheels, power passenger seat with lumbar, electronic auto-dim mirror, compass and leather-wrapped steering wheel. NOT AVAILABLE with 41G, 999, 65E.		
65E	**LX Comfort Plus Group (LX)**	1691	1900
	Includes antilock braking system, electronic temperature control air conditioning, power passenger seat with lumbar, electronic auto-dim mirror, compass, leather-wrapped steering wheel, electronic instrumentation, tripminder computer, electronic digital instrumentation, leather seating surfaces split bench, premium AM/FM stereo with cassette radio and 16" lace spoke cast alloy wheels. NOT AVAILABLE with 41G, 999, 585.		
68D	**Carpet Group (LX)**	120	135
	Includes interior carpet, trunk carpet, front and rear floor mats and carpeted spare tire cover.		
919	**Trunk Mounted 6-Disc CD Changer (LX)**	312	350
	REQUIRES 586. NOT AVAILABLE with 999, 585.		
999	**Engine: 4.6L Natural Gas**	5487	6165
	Includes engine compartment light, automatic headlamp delete and variable assist power steering delete. REQUIRES 13D or 68D. NOT AVAILABLE with 41G, 553, T2A, 144, 508, 65E, L, 586, 919.		
L	**Leather Seating Surfaces Split Bench (LX)**	708	795
	Includes driver/passenger power recliners, power lumbar and vinyl head restraints. NOT AVAILABLE with 999.		
T2A	**Tires: P225/60SR16 WSW**	71	80
	NOT AVAILABLE with 41G, 999, 508.		

ESCORT ZX2 — FORD

2001 ESCORT ZX2

What's New?
Other than a couple of new exterior colors, the Escort ZX2 is unchanged for 2001. The high-performance S/R Package is no longer available.

Review

The Ford Escort ZX2 Coupe must feel like middle management. It has some decent skills to offer, but it's getting old and definitely feeling the heat from younger and more dynamic members of the team.

The younger and more dynamic teammate would be Ford's Focus ZX3 Hatchback. Both the ZX2 Coupe and the Focus ZX3 are aimed at attracting young buyers through a combination of an affordable price, unique styling, versatility and a fun-to-drive nature. But allow us to be frank: The Focus is a much better car.

The ZX2 has been around since 1998 as the coupe version of the Escort Sedan. It shares the same basic front-drive chassis and suspension components with the Escort Sedan (which is no longer available to the public). The ZX2 has its own unique body panels, however, and its styling could be an attribute to some people, especially for those who dislike the sharp-angled Focus.

Escort ZX2 is available as a single model only. There are no trim levels. The main options include the Comfort Group, the Power Group, air conditioning, leather sport bucket seats, a moonroof, antilock brakes, and an upgraded stereo with a six-disc CD changer. Since the base price is so low, adding a host of options won't kill your budget.

The only engine available is Ford's 2.0-liter Zetec four-cylinder. This is the same engine that's used in the Focus ZX3, and it's rated at 130 horsepower and 127 foot-pounds of torque. The Zetec engine is competitive for this class, and its best attribute is a broad and useable powerband. A five-speed manual transmission is standard, and a four-speed automatic is optional. The manual's shifter is rather floppy and has long throws, but it's clearly the better choice for a more sporting drive.

Inside, the ZX2 has a swoopy (some would say overwrought) instrument panel that blends into the door panels. Both front and rear interior room is good for this class, though the Focus has even more. The same goes for trunk space. The ZX2 will hold 11.8 cubic feet of cargo, while the Focus can manage 18.5 cubic feet. As with most small cars, the ZX2's split rear seatbacks can be flipped forward to make extra space for longer items.

The closest competitors to the ZX2 Coupe are the Focus, the Honda Civic Coupe and the Chevrolet Cavalier Z24 Coupe. Both the Civic and Cavalier have their own distinct advantages, the Civic in refinement, the Cavalier in horsepower.

We see little reason to buy a ZX2 Coupe over a Focus. The ZX2's lower price might be attractive, but the difference isn't that great. All the while the Focus has a roomier interior, better suspension and handling, and better crash test scores. If the ZX2 were middle management, it would probably be fired by now.

Standard Equipment

ZX2 (5M): 2L I4 DOHC SMPI 16-valve engine with variable valve timing; 5-speed OD manual transmission; battery with rundown protection; 48-amp HD alternator; front-wheel drive, 4.1 axle ratio; stainless steel exhaust; front independent strut suspension with anti-roll bar, front coil springs, rear independent multi-link suspension with anti-roll bar, rear coil springs; rack-and-

FORD

ESCORT ZX2

pinion power steering; front disc/rear drum brakes; 12.8 gal. capacity fuel tank; rear wing spoiler, side impact bars; front and rear body-colored bumpers; body-colored bodyside molding; clearcoat monotone paint; aero-composite halogen headlamps; driver's and passenger's power remote black outside mirrors; 15" x 5.5" silver alloy wheels, P185/60TR15 BSW A/S tires; compact steel spare wheel; rear heat ducts; AM/FM stereo w/clock, seek-scan feature, cassette player, 4 performance speakers, fixed antenna; power remote trunk release; 2 power accessory outlets, front lighter element, smokers' package; instrumentation display includes tachometer, water temperature gauge, trip odometer; warning indicators include oil pressure, battery, low coolant, lights on, key in ignition, low fuel; driver's and passenger's front airbags; tinted windows; variable-speed intermittent front windshield wipers, rear window defroster; seating capacity of 4, front sports seats with adjustable headrests, driver's and passenger's front seats include 4-way adjustment, driver's seat includes easy entry feature; 60/40 folding rear bench seat; cloth seats, cloth door trim insert, full cloth headliner, full carpet floor covering; interior lights include dome light with delay; vanity mirrors; day/night rearview mirror; full floor console, glove box, front and rear cupholders, instrument panel bin, driver's and passenger's door bins; carpeted cargo floor, cargo light; black side window moldings, black front windshield molding, black rear window molding and body-colored door handles.

Base Prices

Code	Description	Invoice	MSRP
P11	ZX2 (5M)	11432	12050
	Destination Charge:	490	490

Interested in seeing what dealers will sell this vehicle for? Check out our True Market Value℠ (TMV℠) pricing on our Web site at www.edmunds.com.

Accessories

Code	Description	Invoice	MSRP
12Y	Front and Rear Floor Mats	49	55
13B	Power Sliding Moonroof	530	595
41H	Engine Block Heater	NC	NC
44T	Transmission: 4-Speed Automatic	725	815
	Includes 3.74 axle ratio.		
50A	Comfort Group	352	395
	Includes dual map lights, leather-wrapped steering wheel, speed control and tilt steering wheel. REQUIRES 572.		
552	Antilock Braking System	356	400
572	Air Conditioning	708	795
60A	Power Group	352	395
	Includes all door remote keyless entry, anti-theft system, power windows and power locks.		
64A	Wheels: 14" Chrome 5-Spoke	530	595
	Includes P185/65R14 BSW tires.		
919	Radio: Premium AM/FM Cassette with 6-Disc CD Changer	263	295
	80-Watt power. Includes trunk-mounted CD changer. Due to unique design of the ICP and aftermarket audio upgrades are limited. REQUIRES 572.		
A	Unique Leather Sport Buckets	352	395

FORD

2001 FOCUS

What's New?

Raising the bar for compact vehicles, Ford is offering its stability system—called AdvanceTrac—on ZTS Sedans and ZX3 Hatchbacks. Ford has also made previously optional features standard equipment. Highlights include a driver's armrest on every model except LX and power windows on SE Sedans and Wagons. SE Wagons also get the Zetec engine as standard and can be ordered with a manual transmission. A new manual moonroof is offered on the ZX3 and new 16-inch wheels are standard on ZTS Sedans and optional on ZX3 Hatchbacks.

Review

"Smart design and spirited driving" were the guiding forces behind the development of the Focus. Targeted to be the new volume leader in Ford sales worldwide, the Focus is a highly evolved compact car with "New Edge" styling, a roomy interior, and excellent road manners.

Ford offers the Focus in three body styles: a three-door hatchback, a sedan and a wagon. The sedan can be ordered in one of three trim levels, starting with the base LX model and going up to the mid-level SE and highline ZTS trim. Wagons are available in SE trim only.

One of the key design elements for the Focus is its intelligent use of space. Ford boasts that the car's overall design started on the inside to provide additional cabin space and comfort. The goal was to have the Focus comfortably accommodate humans ranging from a 4-foot-10-inch female weighing 95 pounds to a 6-foot-4-inch male weighing 240 pounds.

Besides providing more space and comfort for passengers, the interior also features thoughtful ergonomics. Controls are large and easy to find. Since most people adjust the radio more than the climate system, the radio head unit is placed above the climate controls.

The interior itself is attractive, and contains styling elements from both the Escort ZX2 and Mercury Cougar. All Focus driver seats can be adjusted in height, though some of our editors dislike the seating position, saying it is too "chair-like." A tilt/telescopic steering wheel is optional.

For safety, the Focus utilizes an optimized body structure, standard driver and passenger airbags, seatbelt pretensioners and load-limiting retractors, and optional side airbags. A three-point safety belt for the center rear seat is standard, as are child-safety-seat anchor points. NHTSA crash test scores are very good for this segment.

The base drivetrain for LX models is a 2.0-liter, 110-horsepower engine and five-speed manual transmission. This same drivetrain is standard in SE sedans, but ZTS sedans, along with SE wagons and the ZX3 coupe, get a more powerful 130-horsepower, 2.0-liter Zetec engine as standard equipment. The Zetec makes 130 foot-pounds of torque at an easily accessible 4,250 rpm. Both engines provide adequate power, though the Zetec engine is the clear choice for enthusiasts.

Enthusiasts should also enjoy Focus' ride quality and handling ability. A fully independent multi-link suspension has been adopted for the rear. Body roll is noticeable while cornering, but the Focus stays planted and inspires confidence. The steering system is surprisingly quick, fluid and responsive.

Ford is serious about retaining its share of the worldwide subcompact market. The Focus reflects not only the company's dedication to this goal, but also its ability to make solid, practical transportation for the 21st century.

FORD

FOCUS

Standard Equipment

ZX3 HATCHBACK (5M): 2L I4 DOHC SMPI 16-valve engine with variable valve timing; 5-speed OD manual transmission; battery with rundown protection; 110-amp alternator; front-wheel drive, 3.82 axle ratio; stainless steel exhaust; front independent strut suspension with anti-roll bar, front coil springs, rear independent short & long arm suspension with anti-roll bar, rear coil springs; rack-and-pinion power steering; front disc/rear drum brakes; 13.2 gal. capacity fuel tank; side impact bars; front and rear body-colored bumpers; black bodyside molding rocker panel extensions; clearcoat monotone paint; aero-composite halogen headlamps; additional exterior lights include front fog/driving lights; driver's and passenger's manual remote black outside mirrors, passenger's folding outside mirror; 15" x 5.5" silver alloy wheels, P195/60SR15 BSW A/S tires; compact steel spare wheel; rear heat ducts; AM/FM stereo w/clock, seek-scan feature, single-disc CD player, 4 speakers, integrated roof antenna; remote hatch release; 1 power accessory outlet, front lighter element, retained accessory power, smokers' package; instrumentation display includes tachometer, water temperature gauge, trip odometer; warning indicators include oil pressure, battery, low coolant, lights on, key in ignition, low fuel, door ajar, trunk ajar; driver's and passenger's front airbags; ignition disable; tinted windows; fixed-interval front windshield wipers, rear window wiper, rear window defroster; seating capacity of 5, front sports seats with adjustable headrests, driver's seat includes 6-way adjustment and easy entry feature, passenger's front seat includes 4-way adjustment and easy entry feature; 60/40 folding split-bench rear seat; height-adjustable front seatbelts with pretensioners; cloth seats, cloth door trim insert, full cloth headliner, full carpet floor covering with carpeted floor mats; interior lights include dome light with fade; leather-wrapped steering wheel; vanity mirrors; day/night rearview mirror; full floor console, glove box, front and rear cupholders, instrument panel bin, driver's and passenger's door bins; carpeted cargo floor, cargo cover, cargo light; black grille, black side window moldings, black front windshield molding and black door handles.

LX SEDAN (5M) (in addition to or instead of ZX3 HATCHBACK (5M) equipment): 2L I4 SOHC SMPI 8-valve engine; 3.61 axle ratio; front license plate bracket; 14" x 5.5" steel wheels, P185/65SR14 BSW A/S tires; cassette player; child-safety rear door locks, front bucket seats; vinyl door trim insert; black rear window molding.

SE SEDAN (5M) (in addition to or instead of LX SEDAN (5M) equipment): Body-colored bodyside molding; driver's and passenger's power remote black outside mirrors; air conditioning, rear heat ducts; power door locks with 2-stage unlock, remote keyless entry, panic alarm; power front and rear windows with driver's 1-touch down feature; variable-speed intermittent front windshield wipers, center armrest with storage; illuminated entry.

ZTS SEDAN (5M) (in addition to or instead of SE SEDAN (5M) equipment): 2L I4 DOHC SMPI 16-valve engine with variable valve timing; 3.82 axle ratio; 4-wheel antilock braking system; additional exterior lights include front fog/driving lights; 16" x 6" silver alloy wheels, P205/50SR16 BSW A/S tires; cruise control with steering wheel controls; driver's seat includes lumbar support; simulated wood dashboard insert, simulated wood door panel insert; interior lights include front reading lights, steering wheel with tilt and telescopic adjustment; 2 seatback storage pockets.

SE WAGON (4A) (in addition to or instead of ZTS SEDAN (4A) equipment): 4-speed electronic OD automatic transmission with lock-up converter; front-wheel drive, 3.9 axle ratio; roof rack; front and rear body-colored bumpers with rear step bumper; 15" x 5.5" silver alloy wheels, P195/60SR15 BSW A/S tires; fixed 1/4 vent windows.

Base Prices

CODE	DESCRIPTION	INVOICE	MSRP
P31	ZX3 Hatchback (5M)	11530	12125
P33	LX Sedan (5M)	11770	12385
P34	SE Sedan (5M)	13292	14040

FOCUS / MUSTANG — FORD

CODE	DESCRIPTION	INVOICE	MSRP
P38	ZTS Sedan (5M)	14414	15260
P36	SE Wagon (4A)	15311	16235
Destination Charge:		490	490

Interested in seeing what dealers will sell this vehicle for? Check out our True Market Value^{sm} (TMV^{sm}) pricing on our Web site at www.edmunds.com.

Accessories

CODE	DESCRIPTION	INVOICE	MSRP
13A	Manual Moonroof (ZX3) — REQUIRES 50P.	441	495
41H	Engine Block Heater	NC	NC
434	SE Sport Group (SE) — Includes integrated fog lamps, leather-wrapped steering wheel, rear spoiler and tachometer.	240	270
44A	Transmission: 4-Speed Automatic (ZX3/LX/SE/ZTS) — REQUIRES 50P.	725	815
47D	Advance Trac (ZX3/ZTS) — Includes traction control. REQUIRES 552 and 50P.	1091	1225
50A	SE Comfort Group (SE/SE Wagon) — Includes tilt/telescoping steering wheel, speed control and front map lights.	307	345
50P	Premium Group (ZX3) — Includes air conditioning, front center armrest, speed control, map lights, tilt/telescoping steering wheel, P205/50R16 tires and 16" multi-spoke alloy wheels.	975	1095
552	Anti-Lock Brakes (ZX3/LX/SE/SE Wagon)	356	400
572	Air Conditioning (ZX3/LX)	708	795
59M	Side Impact Air Bags — Includes rear head restraints.	312	350
60A	Power Group (ZX3) — Includes all door remote-entry and power locks, power mirrors and power windows. REQUIRES 50P.	658	740
67A	Street Edition (SE) — Includes 16", 6-spoke aluminum wheels.	690	775
8	Unique Leather Low Back Buckets (ZTS) — Includes map pockets.	619	695

2001 MUSTANG

What's New?

GT models get unique hood and side scoops, so that you can tell 'em apart from V6 models. They also receive standard 17-inch wheels, and V6 Convertibles get 16-inch wheels as standard. All cars have a revised center console and blacked-out headlights and spoilers. The Mach 460 stereo system comes with an in-dash six-disc CD changer. A new "premium" trim line is created for both V6 and V8 models.

Review

Now 37 years old, the Mustang is quickly approaching middle age. But if it's going through a mid-life crisis, nobody is noticing. The Mustang is as popular as ever.

FORD

MUSTANG

CODE	DESCRIPTION	INVOICE	MSRP

Ford's sport coupe has outsold GM's F-bodies—the Chevrolet Camaro and Pontiac Firebird—the last six years in a row. This is in spite of the fact that the Mustang has suffered a performance disadvantage since its redesign in 1994.

There are four models: the V6 Coupe, the V6 Convertible, the GT Coupe and the GT Convertible. All models can be ordered in either deluxe or premium trim. There is also a standard trim available on V6 coupes only. All V6 models have a 3.8-liter pushrod engine that makes 190 horsepower at 5,250 rpm and 225 foot-pounds of torque at 2,800 rpm. Power is acceptable, though V6 Coupes definitely have a rental-car stigma attached to them.

The GT Coupe and Convertible are more in-tune with what pony cars should be. Equipped with a 4.6-liter SOHC V8, GT output is listed at 260 horsepower at 5,250 rpm and 302 foot-pounds of torque at 4,000 rpm. Still, the Camaro Z28 makes 310 horsepower and 335 foot-pounds of torque.

Since it's not due to outright horsepower, we think that part of the Mustang's sales success can be attributed to the car's comfortable interior. Since 1994, the 'Stang has offered drivers and passengers supportive, upright front chairs, well-placed controls, clear views out the front and side windows, and acceptable dashboard and seat materials.

For 2001, Ford upgrades the center console by adding a larger rear cupholder and repositioning the front cupholder, power point, tissue holder and parking brake boot. The standard, deluxe and premium trim groups offer varying levels of standard and optional equipment, with the premium trim group being the most inclusive.

Another advantage of the Mustang is its demeanor on the road. The Mustang's suspension allows the car to be predictable during hard cornering and side-to-side weight transfers are progressive for added stability during high-speed lane changes. The braking and steering have also impressed us. Rough pavement can make the ride uncomfortable, however, as the rear suspension still uses a solid rear axle.

The Mustang has always been crashworthy, offering drivers and front-seat passengers a high level of protection as rated by the National Highway Traffic Safety Administration. All-speed traction control and antilock brakes are standard on most trim levels. Ford thoughtfully provides a traction-control defeat switch for those people who like roasting the rear tires on a regular basis.

As for the rest of us, Mustang is one of the most recognizable nameplates on the road. And if the rumors about the cancellation of the F-body Camaro and Firebird are true, this may be the only pony car left for the new millennium.

Standard Equipment

BASE COUPE (5M): 3.8L V6 OHV SMPI 12-valve engine; 5-speed OD manual transmission; HD battery; 130-amp HD alternator; rear-wheel drive, 3.27 axle ratio; stainless steel exhaust; front independent strut suspension with anti-roll bar, front coil springs, gas-pressurized front shocks, rigid rear axle multi-link suspension with anti-roll bar, rear coil springs, gas-pressurized rear shocks; rack-and-pinion power steering; 4-wheel disc brakes; 15.7 gal. capacity fuel tank; front license plate bracket, side impact bars; front and rear body-colored bumpers; rocker panel extensions; clearcoat monotone paint; aero-composite halogen headlamps; driver's and passenger's power remote black outside mirrors; 15" x 7" painted alloy wheels, P205/65TR15 BSW A/S tires; compact steel spare wheel; air conditioning; premium AM/FM stereo w/clock, seek-scan feature, cassette player, single-disc CD player, 4 performance speakers, amplifier, fixed antenna; power door locks with 2-stage unlock, remote keyless entry, power remote hatch/trunk release; 2 power accessory outlets, driver's foot rest; instrumentation display includes tachometer, oil pressure gauge, water temperature gauge, volt gauge, trip odometer; warning indicators include battery, lights on, key in ignition, low fuel; driver's and passenger's front airbags; ignition disable, panic alarm; tinted windows with driver's 1-touch down function;

MUSTANG FORD

variable-speed intermittent front windshield wipers, sun visor strip, rear window defroster; seating capacity of 4, front bucket seats with adjustable headrests, center armrest with storage, driver's and front passenger's seats include 4-way adjustment and easy entry; 50/50 folding rear bench seat; cloth seats, cloth door trim insert, full cloth headliner, full carpet floor covering; interior lights include dome light, front reading lights, illuminated entry; steering wheel with tilt adjustment; vanity mirrors; day/night rearview mirror; full floor console, locking glove box, front cupholder, instrument panel bin, driver's and passenger's door bins; carpeted cargo floor; black grille, black side window moldings, black front windshield molding, black rear window molding and body-colored door handles.

GT COUPE (5M) (in addition to or instead of BASE/COUPE (5M) equipment): 4.6L V8 SOHC SMPI 16-valve engine; limited-slip differential; dual exhaust with tailpipe finisher; sport-ride suspension; rear wing spoiler; additional exterior lights include front fog/driving lights; 17" x 8" silver alloy wheels, P245/45ZR17 BSW performance tires; compact alloy spare wheel; warning indicators include low coolant; front sports seats; leather-wrapped steering wheel; carpeted cargo floor, cargo light.

BASE/GT CONVERTIBLE (5M) (in addition to or instead of BASE/GT COUPE (5M) equipment): Power convertible roof with lining, glass rear window; 16" x 7.5" painted alloy wheels, P205/55TR16 BSW A/S tires; cruise control with steering wheel controls; driver's seat includes 14-way adjustment (6-way power); dual illuminated vanity mirrors.

Base Prices

Code	Description	Invoice	MSRP
P40	Base Coupe (5M)	15644	16805
P44	Base Convertible (5M)	20518	22220
P42	GT Coupe (5M)	20716	22440
P45	GT Convertible (5M)	24546	26695
	Destination Charge:	600	600

Interested in seeing what dealers will sell this vehicle for? Check out our True Market Value^{sm} (TMV^{sm}) pricing on our Web site at www.edmunds.com.

Accessories

Code	Description	Invoice	MSRP
110A	3.8L V6 Engine and 5-Speed Manual Transmission (Base Coupe)	509	565
	Includes rear spoiler, color-keyed floor mats, power driver's seat and speed control. NOT AVAILABLE with FMATS.		
120A	3.8L V6 Engine and 5-Speed Manual Transmission (Base Coupe)	1616	1795
	Includes antilock braking system, traction control, 16" bright alloy wheels, P225/55R16 BSW A/S tires, rear spoiler, tape stripe, Mach 460 AM/FM stereo, color-keyed floor mats, leather-wrapped steering wheel, power driver's seat and speed control. NOT AVAILABLE with 54V.		
140A	4.6L V8 Engine and 5-Speed Manual Transmission (GT Coupe)	1035	1150
	Includes 17" premium alloy wheels, Mach 460 AM/FM stereo, leather seating surfaces, sport buckets.		
160A	3.8L V6 Engine and 4-Speed Automatic Transmission (Base Convertible)	2309	2565
	Includes 4-speed automatic transmission with OD, rear spoiler, tape stripe, leather-wrapped steering wheel and leather seating surfaces.		
180A	4.6L V8 Engine and 5-Speed Manual Transmission (GT Convertible)	1034	1150
	Includes 17" premium alloy wheels, Mach 460 AM/FM stereo and leather seating surfaces, sport buckets.		

FORD

MUSTANG / TAURUS

CODE	DESCRIPTION	INVOICE	MSRP
41H	Engine Block Heater	NC	NC
44U	Transmission: 4-Speed Automatic with OD	725	815
	INCLUDED in 160A.		
54V	Sport Appearance Group (Base Coupe)	223	250
	Includes leather-wrapped steering wheel, tape stripe, P225/55R16 BSW A/S tires and 16" bright alloy wheels. NOT AVAILABLE in Base Coupe, 120A.		
552	Antilock Braking System (Base)	650	730
	Includes traction control. REQUIRES 44U. NOT AVAILABLE in Base Coupe. INCLUDED in 120A, 160A.		
58M	Radio: Mach 460 AM/FM Stereo	490	550
	Includes 230-Watt RMS (460 Watts peak power), 60-Watt parametrically equalized amplifier, 85-Watt subwoofer amplifiers (2), 5.5 x 7.5 subwoofer speakers (4), 2.5" midrange/tweeters (4), integrated clock, customer interface, rotary on/off volume control, 18 memory presets (6 AM, 12 FM), automatic station set, hall effect (DSP mode) (e.g.- news, jazz, hall, church and stadium) available, radio data system (RDS) available, compact disc, 6-disc in-dash changer, 3-second anti-skip memory buffer on CD, random shuffle (all discs), random shuffle (1 disc) and direct disc access via automatic presets. NOT AVAILABLE in Base Coupe. INCLUDED in 120A, 140A, 160A, 180A.		
T	Leather Seating Surfaces (Base)	445	500
	Front buckets only.		
X	Leather Seating Surfaces Sport Buckets (GT)	445	500
	Front buckets only.		

2001 TAURUS

What's New?

After the 2000 redesign, updates are minor. A Lower Anchor and Tether for Children (LATCH) is now standard on all models. LATCH is an anchoring system for child safety seats. Also new is Spruce Green Clearcoat Metallic, an increase in fuel tank capacity to 18 gallons, a six-disc CD changer standard on SES models, power locks standard on LX and an optional rear spoiler.

Review

For several years now, the Taurus has been the Yankee entry in the best-selling-car-in-America war. It's like the WWF, but for cars. Each year, the Taurus jumps into the ring to duke it out with the Honda Accord and Toyota Camry. The goal? To earn that prestigious title of No. 1, or the "best-selling car in America."

In hopes of putting the Taurus on top, Ford put its main contender through the automotive equivalent of a Tae-Bo class last year, endowing it with better safety, styling, power and suspension.

The current Taurus' main feature is Ford's Personal Safety System. It's a collection of components that allows the car to more fully understand the nature of a crash and factors in whether or not

TAURUS / FORD

| CODE | DESCRIPTION | INVOICE | MSRP |

the seatbelts are in use. With the system, the dual-stage airbags inflate at two different rates, depending on the situation. Additionally, safety belts are equipped with pre-tensioners that are designed to help reduce the risk of force-related injuries in a crash. Taurus also becomes the first car in North America to offer power-adjustable brake and accelerator pedals, allowing drivers of smaller stature to move the pedals toward their feet, rather than moving the seat too close to the steering wheel.

Last year's styling changes were a welcome improvement. All exterior panels on the 2001 Taurus are carried over from last year.

We give the '01 Taurus high marks in the ride and handling department. On the road, the car transmits truly usable feedback to the wheel, letting the driver know what is happening with the tires. The Taurus has a compliant suspension with excellent rebound shock valving for spirited canyon driving, yet without the harshness that can render a cross-country drive unenjoyable. Drive the Taurus into a turn, prod the throttle and the car responds in a predictable manner. Yet on the highway, passengers are treated to a comfortably smooth ride.

The 2001 Taurus powertrains include the 3.0-liter Vulcan and 3.0-liter Duratec V6s. The main difference between the two engines is the cylinder heads. The base Vulcan has two valves per cylinder, while the Duratec has four. The four-valve motor makes 200 horsepower at 5650 rpm and 200 foot-pounds of torque at 4,400 rpm. The base engine makes do with 155 horsepower at 4,900 rpm and 185 foot-pounds at 3950 rpm.

All Tauri get a four-speed automatic. Both the Vulcan and Duratec engines meet low-emission vehicle (LEV) standards in California and the Northeastern states.

The Taurus has always been a good value and now it's better than ever. And with the number of 2000s out there, the car is apparently a popular American-nameplate alternative to an Accord or Camry. Especially when price is factored into the picture.

Standard Equipment

LX SEDAN (4A): 3L V6 OHV SMPI 12-valve engine; 4-speed electronic OD automatic transmission with lock-up converter; battery with rundown protection; 130-amp alternator; transmission, oil cooler; front-wheel drive, 3.77 axle ratio; stainless steel exhaust; front independent strut suspension with anti-roll bar, front coil springs, gas-pressurized front shocks, rear independent multi-link suspension with anti-roll bar, rear coil springs, gas-pressurized rear shocks; rack-and-pinion power steering with vehicle-speed-sensing assist; front disc/rear drum brakes; 18 gal. capacity fuel tank; side impact bars; front and rear body-colored bumpers; body-colored bodyside molding rocker panel extensions; clearcoat monotone paint; aero-composite halogen headlamps; driver's and passenger's power remote black outside mirrors; 16" x 6" steel wheels, P215/60SR16 BSW A/S tires; compact steel spare wheel; air conditioning, rear ac and heat ducts; AM/FM stereo w/clock, seek-scan feature, 4 speakers, amplifier, fixed antenna; power door locks, child-safety rear door locks, power remote trunk release; 2 power accessory outlets, front lighter element, driver's foot rest, retained accessory power, smokers' package; instrumentation display includes tachometer, water temperature gauge, trip odometer; warning indicators include oil pressure, battery, lights on, key in ignition, low fuel, low washer fluid, bulb failure, door ajar, trunk ajar, brake fluid; driver's and passenger's front airbags; ignition disable; tinted windows, power front and rear windows with driver's 1-touch down function; variable-speed intermittent front windshield wipers, sun visor strip, rear window defroster; seating capacity of 5, front bucket seats with adjustable headrests, center armrest with storage, driver's and front passenger's seats include 4-way adjustment; rear bench seat; height-adjustable front seatbelts with pretensioners; cloth seats, door trim with carpet lower, full cloth headliner, full color-keyed carpet floor covering, chrome interior accents; interior lights include dome light with delay; steering wheel with tilt adjustment; vanity mirrors; day/night rearview mirror; partial floor console, glove box with light, front and rear cupholders, instrument panel bin, 2 seatback storage pockets, audio-media storage, driver's and passenger's door bins, rear door bins; carpeted cargo floor, cargo light; black grille, black side window moldings, black front windshield molding and body-colored door handles.

SE SEDAN (4A) (in addition to or instead of LX SEDAN (4A) equipment): Driver's and passenger's power remote body-colored outside mirrors; air filter; cassette player, CD changer pre-wiring;

FORD

TAURUS

cruise control with steering wheel controls; 2-stage unlock feature, remote keyless entry; panic alarm; premium cloth seats; illuminated entry.

SES SEDAN (4A) (in addition to or instead of SE SEDAN (4A) equipment): 4-wheel antilock braking system; single-disc CD player; seating capacity of 6, front bucket seats with adjustable headrests, driver's seat includes 14-way adjustment (6-way power) and lumbar support; 60/40 folding rear bench seat; interior lights include dual illuminated vanity mirrors and dual auxiliary visors.

SEL SEDAN (4A) (in addition to or instead of SES SEDAN (4A) equipment): 3L V6 DOHC SMPI 24-valve engine; 3.98 axle ratio; fully automatic headlamps with delay-off feature; climate control; trunk-mounted 6-disc CD changer, security system; leather-wrapped steering wheel.

SE WAGON (4A) (in addition to or instead of SEL SEDAN (4A) equipment): 3L V6 OHV SMPI 12-valve engine; 3.77 axle ratio; rear independent short & long arm suspension; 4-wheel disc brakes; roof rack; front and rear body-colored bumpers with rear step; body-colored bodyside molding rocker panel extensions; power retractable antenna; fixed 1/4 vent windows; flip-up rear window, fixed-interval rear wiper; cargo tie downs, locking cargo concealed storage; chrome side window moldings.

Base Prices

Code	Description	Invoice	MSRP
P52	LX Sedan (4A)	17092	18260
P53	SE Sedan (4A)	17606	19035
P55	SES Sedan (4A)	18521	20050
P56	SEL Sedan (4A)	19856	21535
P58	SE Wagon (4A)	18646	20190
	Destination Charge:	625	625

Interested in seeing what dealers will sell this vehicle for? Check out our True Market Value^{sm} (TMV^{sm}) pricing on our Web site at www.edmunds.com.

Accessories

Code	Description	Invoice	MSRP
12H	Front Floor Mats	27	30
12Q	Rear Floor Mats	23	25
13B	Power Moonroof (SES/SEL)	792	890
13K	Rear Spoiler (SES/SEL)	205	230
	REQUIRES 186. NOT AVAILABLE with 184.		
186	5-Passenger Seating (SES/SEL)	93	105
	Includes floor console/shift. NOT AVAILABLE with 184.		
21A	Power Driver's Seat w/Manual Lumbar (Regional) (LX/SE)	352	395
	INCLUDES 59C. NOT AVAILABLE with 41H.		
21J	Power Passenger Seat (SEL)	312	350
	REQUIRES J and 61B.		
41H	Engine Block Heater	NC	NC
	NOT AVAILABLE with 53D, 53E, 524, J, 21A, 53F.		
46S	Split-Fold Rear 60/40 Seat (SE Sedan)	124	140
53A	Premium Audio Group (SES/SE Wagon)	472	530
	AM/FM stereo w/cassette player replaces standard single-disc CD player and 6-disc CD changer. REQUIRES 85A and 96W.		

TAURUS — FORD

CODE	DESCRIPTION	INVOICE	MSRP
53C	LX Plus Group w/Power Seat & Adjustable Pedals (LX)	872	980
53D	SES Plus Group (SES)	387	435
	Includes 3.0L 4V V6 engine, 3.98 axle ratio, 4-speed automatic transmission with OD and 5-passenger seating. NOT AVAILABLE with 992, 184, 41H, J.		
53E	SEL Plus Group (SEL)	45	50
	Includes 5-passenger seating and Mach premium sound. NOT AVAILABLE with 184, 41H.		
53F	SES Wagon Plus Group (SE Wagon)	387	435
	Includes 4-speed automatic transmission with OD and adjustable pedals. REQUIRES 85A. NOT AVAILABLE with 992, 41H, J.		
54P	Heated Mirrors (SES/SE Wagon)	31	35
	REQUIRES 85A.		
552	Antilock Braking System (LX/SE Sedan/SE Wagon)	534	600
553	All-Speed Traction Control (All Except LX)	156	175
	REQUIRES 552 or 85A.		
585	Radio: AM/FM Stereo w/Single-Disc CD Player (SE)	124	140
58H	Radio: AM/FM Stereo Cassette (SES)	(124)	(140)
	NOT AVAILABLE with 53A.		
59C	Adjustable Pedals (All Except LX)	107	120
	REQUIRES 21A.		
61B	Side-Impact Airbags	347	390
	Upgrades LX trim to SE cloth buckets.		
85A	SES Wagon Group (SE Wagon)	925	1040
	Includes illuminated visor mirrors, power driver's seat, manual lumbar support and single-disc CD player. REQUIRES 96W.		
916	MACH Premium Sound (SEL)	285	320
96W	Wagon Group (SE Wagon)	267	300
	Includes cargo cover and rear-facing seat.		
99S	Engine: 3.0L 4V V6 (SES/SE Wagon)	619	695
	Includes 3.98 axle ratio.		
J	Leather Seating Surfaces (SEL, SE Wagon)	797	895
	REQUIRES 85A. NOT AVAILABLE with 992.		

A 15-minute phone call could save you 15% or more on car insurance.
1-800-555-2758

The Sensible Alternative

EDMUNDS® NEW CARS · www.edmunds.com

HONDA ACCORD

2001 ACCORD

What's New?

Freshened exterior styling debuts for 2001, with a more aggressive-looking front fascia and hood, and an all-new taillight and rear decklid design. Honda also ups the safety features list, making dual-stage, dual-threshold front airbags standard and side airbags available on all models. All Accords now either meet or exceed California's low-emission vehicle (LEV) standards, and improvements aimed at reducing road and wind noise have been made. EX models get a standard six-disc in-dash CD changer, and all V6 models come with traction control. Mid-year, a DX four-banger equipped with a special value package debuted, adding an automatic transmission, air conditioning, a CD player, floor mats, fake wood interior accents and special exterior trim.

Review

The benchmark. The best-selling car in America. The highest resale value in its class. These are all statements that have been made with regularity concerning the Honda Accord, a vehicle that is always on the short list of the most popular cars in this country. The Accord won a loyal base of customers by offering notable performance, room for four, frugal fuel economy and a virtual guarantee that, if cared for properly, it would not break.

This sixth-generation Accord is available in coupe and sedan bodies, equipped with basic DX (sedan only), mid-grade LX, or loaded EX trim. The standard 2.3-liter four-banger in the DX Sedan is worth 135 horses. LX and EX models come with a VTEC (Variable Valve Timing and Lift Electronic Control) engine, in your choice of 2.3-liter four-cylinder (which generates 150 horsepower) or 3.0-liter V6 (200 horsepower) configurations.

The spunky fours can be mated to a slick-shifting manual or four-speed automatic transmission driving the front wheels. The V6, available only with the automatic, is a model of refinement, revving smoothly and silently.

Now that we've praised the living daylights out of this car, here's some bad news: The low price of the DX is accompanied by a low level of equipment. Also, the Accord is easy to drive, but it doesn't reward the driver much for the efforts. You won't mistake this for a performance car—look to the Nissan Maxima for competent canyon carving. The Accord is suited more to daily driving in the urban jungle, featuring decent acceleration, strong brakes and light, effortless steering.

As with the Toyota Camry, refinement and attention to detail are the Accord's strengths. Almost all interior materials are pleasing to the eye and touch, and are assembled with great care. Gap tolerances are about half what you'd find in competing American products. Storage room abounds; the Accord mimics a minivan with so many places to stash maps, drinks, change, and assorted detritus. Spacious, comfortable and quiet, the Accord will tote many happy campers for miles on end as long as they don't mind the stiff highway ride. The seats are comfortable, both front and rear, and ergonomics are nearly flawless.

While not exactly spicy, the Honda Accord is the definitive family sedan or personal coupe. A low price, a high level of refinement, a cavernous interior, and a well-deserved reputation for reliability put the Accord at the top of the heap. Even a loaded EX V6 model with leather, alloy wheels, power moonroof, automatic climate control, CD player, premium sound, and steering-wheel radio controls struggles to surpass the $25,000 mark. Accord is the benchmark by which all other midsize cars are measured.

ACCORD — HONDA

| CODE | DESCRIPTION | INVOICE | MSRP |

Standard Equipment

2.3 DX SEDAN (5M): 2.3L I4 SOHC SMPI 16-valve engine; 5-speed OD manual transmission; 80 amp alternator; front-wheel drive, 4.06 axle ratio; stainless steel exhaust; front independent double-wishbone suspension with anti-roll bar, front coil springs, gas-pressurized front shocks, rear independent double-wishbone suspension with anti-roll bar, rear coil springs, gas-pressurized rear shocks; rack-and-pinion power steering with engine speed-sensing assist; front disc/rear drum brakes; 17.1 gal. capacity fuel tank; side impact bars; front and rear body-colored bumpers; clearcoat monotone paint; aero-composite halogen headlamps; driver's and passenger's manual remote black folding outside mirrors; 14" x 5.5" steel wheels; P195/70SR14 BSW A/S tires; compact steel spare wheel; rear heat ducts; AM/FM stereo radio, seek-scan feature, cassette player, 2 speakers, window grid antenna; child-safety rear door locks, remote hatch/trunk release, remote fuel door release; 1 power accessory outlet, driver's foot rest; instrumentation display includes tachometer, water temperature gauge, in-dash clock, trip odometer; warning indicators include oil pressure, battery, lights on, key in ignition, low fuel, bulb failure, door ajar, trunk ajar, service interval; tinted windows; manual front and rear windows; fixed interval front windshield wipers, sun visor strip, rear window defroster; seating capacity of 5, front bucket seats with adjustable headrests, center armrest with storage, driver and passenger seats include 4-way adjustment; full folding rear bench seat with fixed headrests; seatbelts with front pretensioners; cloth seats, cloth door trim insert, full cloth headliner, full carpet floor covering; interior lights include dome light with fade; full floor console, locking glove box with light, front cupholder, instrument panel covered bin, driver's and passenger's door bins, rear door bins; body-colored grille, black side window moldings, black front windshield molding, black rear window molding and black door handles.

2.3 VALUE PACKAGE (4A) (in addition to or instead of 2.3 DX SEDAN (5M) equipment): AM/FM stereo radio, seek-scan feature, cassette player, single-disc CD player, 2 speakers, window grid antenna; power door locks with 2-stage unlock, remote keyless entry; driver's and passenger's front airbags; full carpet floor covering with carpeted floor mats, simulated wood door panel insert, simulated wood console insert, chrome interior accents; 1 seatback storage pocket; body-colored grille, chrome side window moldings and body-colored door handles.

2.3 LX COUPE/SEDAN (5M) (in addition to or instead of 2.3 VALUE PACKAGE (4A) equipment): 2.3L I4 SOHC SMPI 16-valve engine with variable valve timing; driver's and passenger's power remote body-colored folding outside mirrors; 15" x 6" steel wheels; P195/65HR15 BSW A/S tires; air conditioning, air filter; AM/FM stereo radio, seek-scan feature, single-disc CD player, 6 speakers; cruise control with steering wheel controls; retained accessory power; power front and rear windows with driver's 1-touch down function; variable-speed intermittent front windshield wipers, driver's seat includes 8-way adjustment, passenger's seat includes 4-way adjustment, center pass-thru armrest; additional interior lights include front reading lights; dual illuminated vanity mirrors; mini overhead console with storage, front and rear cupholders; chrome side window moldings body-colored grille and body-colored door handles.

2.3 EX COUPE/SEDAN (5M) (in addition to or instead of 2.3 LX COUPE/SEDAN (5M) equipment): 4-wheel antilock disc brakes; 15" X 6" silver alloy wheels; front power sliding and tilting glass sunroof with sunshade; aero-composite halogen auto off headlamps; AM/FM stereo radio, seek-scan feature, cassette player, 6-disc CD changer, 6 speakers, theft deterrent; power door locks with 2-stage unlock, remote keyless entry, power remote hatch/trunk release; driver's and passenger's front airbags, driver's and front passenger's seat-mounted side airbags; ignition disable, panic alarm, security system; driver's seat includes 6-way adjustment, 2-way power; lumbar support, passenger's seat includes 4-way adjustment; chrome interior accents; additional interior lights include 4 door curb lights and illuminated entry.

3.0 LX COUPE/SEDAN (4A) (in addition to or instead of 2.3 EX COUPE/SEDAN (5M) equipment): 3L V6 SOHC SMPI 24-valve engine with variable valve timing; 4-speed electronic OD automatic transmission with lock-up torque converter; 100 amp alternator; traction control, 4.2 axle ratio;

HONDA ACCORD

CODE	DESCRIPTION	INVOICE	MSRP

15" x 6.5" steel wheels; P205/65VR15 BSW A/S tires; AM/FM stereo radio, seek-scan feature, single-disc CD player, 6 speakers, driver's seat includes 8-way power adjustment and passenger's seat includes 4-way adjustment.

3.0 EX COUPE/SEDAN (4A) (in addition to or instead of 3.0 LX SEDAN (4A) equipment): Power sliding and tilting glass sunroof with sunshade; aero-composite halogen auto off headlamps; air conditioning with climate control; AM/FM stereo radio, seek-scan feature, cassette player, 6-disc CD changer, 6 speakers, theft deterrent, radio steering wheel controls; remote keyless entry; 1 power accessory outlet, garage door opener; driver's seat includes 8-way power adjustment, lumbar support, passenger's seat includes 4-way power adjustment; leather seats, leather door trim insert, leather-wrapped gearshift knob, simulated wood console insert, chrome interior accents; leather-wrapped steering wheel with tilt adjustment and dual auxiliary visors.

Base Prices

Code	Description	Invoice	MSRP
CG3141PBW	2.3 LX Coupe (5M)	16727	18790
CF8661PW	2.3 Value Package (4A)	0	17200
CG3151JW	2.3 EX Coupe (5M)	19047	21400
CG3241PBW	3.0 LX Coupe (4A)	19935	22400
CG2251JNW	3.0 EX Coupe (4A)	22335	25100
CF8541PW	2.3 DX Sedan (5M)	13715	15400
CG5541PW	2.3 LX Sedan (5M)	16727	18790
CG5561JW	2.3 EX Sedan (5M)	19047	21400
CG1641PBW	3.0 LX Sedan (4A)	19935	22400
CG1651JNW	3.0 EX Sedan (4A)	22335	25100
Destination Charge:		440	440

Interested in seeing what dealers will sell this vehicle for? Check out our True Market Value^{sm} (TMV^{sm}) pricing on our Web site at www.edmunds.com.

Accessories

Code	Description	Invoice	MSRP
—	Anti-Lock Braking System (2.3 LX Sedan)	889	1000
	REQUIRES 4AT.		
—	Leather Seat Trim (EX Sedan/EX Coupe)	1022	1150
	Includes driver's and passenger's airbags, leather-wrapped steering wheel, 8-way power driver's seat and interior wood trim.		
—	Side Airbags (2.3 LX Sedan/2.3 DX Sedan/2.3 LX Coupe)	222	250
—	Super Ultra Low Emission Vehicle (SULEV) (2.3 EX Sedan)	85	100
	Includes 2.3l SULEV engine. REQUIRES 4AT and LTHR.		
—	Ultra Low Emission Vehicle (ULEV) (2.3)	NC	NC
	Includes 2.3l ULEV engine.		
—	Ultra Low Emission Vehicle (ULEV) (2.3 LX Sedan/2.3 EX Sedan)	NC	NC
	Includes 2.3l ULEV engine.		
4AT	Transmission: Electronic 4-Speed Automatic with OD (2.3)	711	800
	Includes and 4.46 axle ratio.		
4AT	Transmission: Electronic 4-Speed Auto w/ OD (DX Sdn/2.3 LX Sdn/2.3 LX Cpe)	711	800
	Includes and 4.46 axle ratio.		

HONDA

2001 CIVIC

What's New?

Honda redesigns its cars and trucks every four to five years, whether they need it or not. For 2001, it's the Civic's turn. Larger inside and out, with more powerful engines but a less sophisticated suspension, coupes and sedans return in familiar DX, LX and EX trims, while HX models come with two doors only. The GX Sedan is powered by natural gas. Unfortunately, the hatchback dies just when Americans are once again figuring out how useful they can be, and the sporty Si goes on hiatus for a year or two.

Review

Who's your Daddy? That should be the 2001 Civic's advertising tagline. Just when the old model began to get a little moldy around the edges in comparison to the Ford Focus, Mazda Protege and Nissan Sentra, Honda drives an all-new Civic off the drawing board and into showrooms, making the job of choosing a competent compact that much more difficult.

Engineers wanted to make the Civic more fun to drive while simultaneously increasing fuel economy with more efficient engines. Improved crashworthiness, a larger cabin, and a bigger trunk were also design goals. Added refinement and standard equipment would increase value in the eyes of the consumer, Honda thought. Finally, they wanted to improve quality 10 times over the old Civic, which sounds damn near impossible to us. Last year's car was already known to be one of the most reliable and tightly assembled vehicles on the planet.

Unfortunately, the hatchback model got the axe and the zippy Si Coupe disappeared in the process, leaving two- and four-door models available in a wide variety of trim levels. Like last year, base models are known as DX, and include a tilt steering wheel and an AM/FM four-speaker stereo, among other items. Mid-level LX comes with air conditioning (includes a micron air filter), power windows and locks, cruise control and a cassette deck. Top-of-the-line EX receives antilock brakes, a moonroof, 15-inch wheels, a CD player and a more powerful VTEC engine. If fuel economy is a priority, get the HX Coupe, available with an optional continuously variable transmission (CVT) and lightweight alloy wheels. Got an Ed Begley Jr. complex? Try the CVT-equipped GX Sedan, which runs on natural gas and meets super low emission vehicle (SULEV) standards. GX can be equipped with lightweight alloy wheels and ABS.

DX, GX and LX are powered by a 115-horsepower, 1.7-liter four-cylinder engine with more torque than last year's 1.6-liter motor. EX continues with a 127-horse VTEC 1.8-liter motor that boasts added twisting force for 2001. Either engine can be mated to a five-speed manual or four-speed automatic transmission except in the GX, which comes with a standard CVT. HX gets a VTEC-E Lean Burn 1.7-liter motor good for 117 horsepower. A five-speed manual is standard on HX, with the aforementioned CVT tranny available optionally. All gasoline motors meet ultra low emission vehicle (ULEV) standards nationwide, while the CNG-fueled GX manages a SULEV rating and a 200-mile range. Oil changes occur every 10,000 miles or 12 months, whichever comes first. Expect a gasoline/electric hybrid Civic to debut for 2002, showcasing technology developed for the Honda Insight.

Coupes and sedans get unique sheetmetal and styling for 2001 to help differentiate between the sporty Civic and the sensible Civic. Engineers targeted a five-star NHTSA crash-test score when designing the Civic's new structure, all while providing more room and greater comfort in a package equivalent in size to the 2000 model. They succeeded—both the coupe and sedan receive the government's highest score in frontal crash tests.

HONDA

CIVIC

CODE	DESCRIPTION	INVOICE	MSRP

Dual seatbelt pre-tensioners, dual-stage airbag inflators, three-point seatbelts for all five occupants, and optional side airbags with a cutoff system that can detect a child or occupant out of position will help Civic provide the anticipated level of passenger protection. Yet, despite this dedication to making Civic safe, ABS is still available only on the most expensive model, the EX, or the GX natural gas model. A real head scratcher, that.

Rounding out the highlights of the redesign, Civic has a larger cabin and trunk, due in part to a shorter nose made possible by the adoption of a relatively mundane MacPherson strut front suspension arrangement. Sophisticated double-wishbone underpinnings continue to support the rear of the car, but last year's trailing arms are gone to make room for a flat rear floor. Spring rates have been reduced all around to produce a softer, more comfortable ride. Finally, noise, vibration and harshness have been quelled in an effort to bring unparalleled refinement to the economy car class.

If you're shopping for a small car and you skip the redesigned 2001 Honda Civic, you're doing yourself a tremendous disservice.

Standard Equipment

DX COUPE (5M): 1.7L I4 SOHC SMPI 16-valve engine; 5-speed OD manual transmission; 70 amp alternator; front-wheel drive, 4.11 axle ratio; stainless steel exhaust; front independent strut suspension with anti-roll bar, front coil springs, rear independent double-wishbone suspension with rear coil springs; rack-and-pinion power steering; front disc/rear drum brakes; 13.2 gal. capacity fuel tank; side impact bars; front and rear body-colored bumpers; clearcoat monotone paint; aero-composite halogen headlamps; driver's and passenger's manual remote black outside mirrors; 14" x 5" steel wheels; P185/70SR14 BSW A/S tires; compact steel spare wheel; AM/FM stereo radio, clock, seek-scan feature, CD changer pre-wiring, 4 speakers, window grid antenna; remote hatch release, remote fuel door release; 1 power accessory outlet, driver's foot rest; instrumentation display includes water temperature gauge, trip odometer; warning indicators include oil pressure, battery, lights on, key in ignition, low fuel, trunk ajar, service interval; driver's and passenger's front airbags; ignition disable; tinted windows; fixed interval front windshield wipers, rear window defroster; seating capacity of 5, front bucket seats with adjustable headrests, driver's and passenger's seats include 4-way adjustment; 60/40 folding rear bench seat with fixed headrests; cloth seats, cloth door trim insert, full cloth headliner, full carpet floor covering; interior lights include dome light; steering wheel with tilt adjustment; vanity mirrors; day/night rearview mirror; partial floor console, glove box, front cupholder, instrument panel covered bin, driver's and passenger's door bins; carpeted cargo floor, cargo light; body-colored grille, black side window moldings, black front windshield molding, black rear window molding and black door handles.

HX COUPE (5M) (in addition to or instead of DX COUPE (5M) equipment): 1.7L I4 SOHC SMPI 16-valve engine with variable valve timing, (requires natural gas fuel); 3.84 axle ratio; driver's and passenger's power remote black outside mirrors; 14" x 5.5" silver alloy wheels; cruise control with steering wheel controls; instrumentation display includes tachometer; tinted windows with driver's 1-touch down function; easy entry; full floor console and 1 seatback storage pocket.

LX COUPE (5M) (in addition to or instead of HX COUPE (5M) equipment): 4.11 axle ratio; air conditioning, air filter; panic alarm; additional interior lights include front reading lights and illuminated entry.

EX COUPE (5M) (in addition to or instead of LX COUPE (5M) equipment): 4.41 axle ratio; power sliding and tilting glass sunroof with sunshade; P185/65SR15 BSW A/S tires; AM/FM stereo radio, clock, seek-scan feature, single-disc CD player, 6 speakers, theft deterrent; power door locks, remote keyless entry, center armrest, driver's seat includes 8-way adjustment, passenger's seat includes 4-way adjustment and body-colored door handles.

DX SEDAN (5M) (in addition to or instead of DX COUPE (5M) equipment): Black bodyside molding; rear heat ducts; child-safety rear door locks and tinted windows.

CIVIC / INSIGHT — HONDA

LX SEDAN (5M) (in addition to or instead of DX SEDAN (5M) equipment): Body-colored bodyside molding; driver's and passenger's power remote black outside mirrors; air conditioning, air filter; cruise control with steering wheel controls; power front and rear windows with driver's 1-touch down function; additional interior lights include front reading lights; full floor console and 1 seatback storage pocket

EX SEDAN (5M) (in addition to or instead of LX SEDAN (5M) equipment): Front disc/rear drum brakes with 4-wheel antilock brakes; power sliding and tilting glass sunroof with sunshade; 15" x 5" steel wheels; AM/FM stereo radio, clock, seek-scan feature, single-disc CD player, 4 speakers, theft deterrent; power door locks, remote keyless entry; panic alarm; driver's seat includes 8-way adjustment, passenger's seat includes 4-way adjustment; additional interior lights include front reading lights, illuminated entry and body-colored door handles.

Base Prices

Code	Description	Invoice	MSRP
EM2121PW	DX Coupe (5M)	11542	12760
EM2171PW	HX Coupe (5M)	12264	13560
EM2151PW	LX Coupe (5M)	13392	14810
EM2191MW	EX Coupe (5M)	14835	16410
ES1521PW	DX Sedan (5M)	11723	12960
ES1551PW	LX Sedan (5M)	13572	15010
ES2571MW	EX Sedan (0M)	15286	16910
Destination Charge:		440	440

Interested in seeing what dealers will sell this vehicle for? Check out our True Market Value^{sm} (TMV^{sm}) pricing on our Web site at www.edmunds.com.

Accessories

	Description	Invoice	MSRP
—	Dual Side Airbags (SRS)	226	250
—	Transmission: Continuously Variable (HX)	902	1000
—	Transmission: Electric 4-Speed Auto with OD (DX/LX)	722	800
—	Transmission: Electric 4-Speed Auto with OD (EX COUPE)	722	800
—	Transmission: Electric 4-Speed Auto with OD (EX SEDAN)	722	800

2001 INSIGHT

What's New?

A continuously variable transmission (CVT) is available for 2001, and Monte Carlo Blue Pearl replaces Citrus Yellow on the color chart.

Review

With its ultra-low drag styling, aluminum body structure and innovative Integrated Motor Assist (IMA) powertrain, the two-passenger Insight can travel as far as 70 miles on a gallon of gas (theoretically, with a 10.6-gallon fuel tank, you can drive from Los Angeles to Salt Lake City and still have a gallon of gas in reserve).

The heart of the system is a 1.0-liter, three-cylinder engine coupled with an electric motor that assists the gasoline engine under acceleration. The package features an idle-stop feature, which shuts off the engine when the driver places the shift lever in neutral and releases the clutch pedal.

HONDA

INSIGHT

| CODE | DESCRIPTION | INVOICE | MSRP |

Unlike GM's all-electric EV-1, the Insight requires no external power supply to recharge the 144-volt nickel-metal hydride batteries. Regenerative braking via the ABS-assisted disc/drum brakes provides juice to the system. With a full charge, and the electric motor providing full assist, the Insight accelerates swiftly, but passing power is lacking.

The five-speed manual transmission has relatively short first, second and third gears for good city driving performance, with tall overdrive gearing in fourth and fifth to maximize fuel economy.

Like the Acura NSX, the Insight's unitized body is made of aluminum (except for the front fenders, which are made from plastic) and boasts a drag coefficient of only 0.25. Thanks to its aerodynamic bodywork, flat underbody, low rolling resistance tires and extensive use of lightweight materials, the Insight requires 30 percent less power to operate at highway speeds than the previous-generation Honda Civic.

But the effort to save weight pays a price in the handling department. The Insight is highly susceptible to cross winds and the narrow tires easily track any groove in the pavement, causing the driver to adjust the steering continually to compensate.

The Insight's interior is just as futuristic as the exterior with a sweeping dash and a high-tech LCD analog/digital instrument display. Divided into three sections, the cluster displays engine rpm, coolant temperature, and the engine's idiot lights on the left bank; a large digital speedometer, odometer, lifetime fuel economy bar graph and instant fuel economy in the middle; and fuel level, battery level indicator, and the electric motor charge and assist indicator on the right bank.

Dual high-back bucket seats feature good lateral and lumbar support. Controls for power windows, mirrors, AM/FM cassette stereo, ventilation and available climate controls are all within easy reach, but two large adults might find themselves knocking elbows in the tight cockpit. Built fully equipped (the only option is an automatic air conditioning system) with power windows, door locks, exterior mirrors, an AM/FM cassette stereo, dual airbags, rear window defroster and a whole lot more, the Insight is an incredible value — for a hybrid vehicle.

Despite the handling shortcomings and quick-to-drain batteries, Honda has brought forth a realistic ultra-low-emission daily driver with electric assist that can be taken anywhere without the worry of having to find an electrical outlet for battery charging. Despite the arrival of the four-passenger Toyota Prius on the market, we bet Honda will sell every Insight they can produce.

Standard Equipment

BASE (5M): 1L I3 SOHC SMPI 12-valve engine with variable valve timing, hybrid battery power; 5-speed OD manual transmission; front-wheel drive, 3.21 axle ratio; stainless steel exhaust; front independent strut suspension with anti-roll bar, front coil springs, rear semi-independent torsion suspension with rear coil springs; power-assisted rack-and-pinion steering with speed-sensing assist; front disc/rear drum brakes with 4-wheel antilock brakes; 10.6 gal. capacity fuel tank; side impact bars; front and rear body-colored bumpers; clearcoat monotone paint; aero-composite halogen headlamps; driver's and passenger's power remote body-colored folding outside mirrors; 14" x 5.5" silver alloy wheels; P165/65SR14 BSW A/S tires; compact alloy spare wheel; AM/FM stereo radio, clock, seek-scan feature, cassette player, 2 speakers, integrated roof antenna; power door locks, remote keyless entry, remote fuel door release; 1 power accessory outlet, driver's foot rest; digital instrumentation display includes tachometer, water temperature gauge, trip computer, trip odometer; warning indicators include oil pressure, battery, lights on, key in ignition, low fuel, door ajar, trunk ajar; driver's and passenger's front airbags; ignition disable, panic alarm; tinted windows with driver's 1-touch down function; fixed interval front windshield wipers, rear window wiper, rear window defroster; seating capacity of 2, front bucket seats with fixed headrests, driver's and passenger's seats include 4-way adjustment; cloth seats, cloth door trim insert, full cloth headliner, full carpet floor

INSIGHT / PRELUDE

HONDA

covering, chrome interior accents; interior lights include dome light, front reading lights, illuminated entry; driver's side vanity mirror; day/night rearview mirror; full floor console, locking glove box, front cupholder, instrument panel covered bin, 1 seatback storage pocket; carpeted cargo floor, cargo tie downs, cargo light, concealed cargo storage; black side window moldings, black front windshield molding, black rear window molding and body-colored door handles.

Base Prices

Code	Description	Invoice	MSRP
ZE1351EW	Base (5M)	N/A	18980
	Destination Charge:	440	440

Interested in seeing what dealers will sell this vehicle for? Check out our True Market Value^{sm} (TMV^{sm}) pricing on our Web site at www.edmunds.com.

Accessories

—	Air Conditioning	NC	1200
	NOT AVAILABLE with AIR2.		

2001 PRELUDE

What's New?

Floor mats, rear child seat-tether anchors and an emergency trunk opener are added to the '01 Prelude. Two new colors, Electron Blue and Satin Silver, are also available.

Review

The aptly named Prelude has always been a symbol for great things to come. Honda has long used the Prelude to showcase its latest technological developments. Remember Honda's four-wheel steering system, designed to give drivers better control in tight corners? It first debuted on the '88 Prelude. In 1993, the Prelude was also one of the first Hondas to receive a VTEC engine, originally introduced in the 1991 Acura NSX. In 1997, Honda continued this tradition by equipping the Prelude SH with the Active Torque Transfer System (ATTS).

ATTS is designed to give the front-wheel-drive Prelude rear-wheel-drive cornering ability while retaining the wet-weather benefits of a traditional front-wheel-drive car. The system works by monitoring the car's speed, steering angle and yaw rate to determine whether the car is following the driver's intended course. In a tight, fast corner the system works by increasing torque to the outboard front wheel, which in turn increases the vehicle's yaw rate, giving the driver better steering response. Basically, it neutralizes understeer for those times when the corners get a little too tight. What will they think of next?

Both trims of Prelude are powered by the VTEC 2.2-liter four-cylinder engine that, when coupled with the manual transmission, cranks out 200 horsepower at 7,000 rpm and 156 foot-pounds of torque at 5,250 rpm. Equipping the Prelude with the automatic transmission reduces horsepower by 5, but the torque remains the same. Base models are available with either a manual or automatic transmission, but if you want the high-tech Type SH, you better like rowing your own gears since it is available only with the five-speed manual gearbox. The four-speed automatic features a sequential SportShift that gives the driver the option of selecting his own

HONDA   *PRELUDE*

gears, similar to Porsche's Tiptronic. Both the base and Type SH models get standard four-wheel ABS, which pulls the car down from speed quickly.

The Prelude comes standard with a six-speaker audio system, power moonroof, adjustable steering column and a height-adjustable driver's seat. Also standard is a state-of-the-art anti-theft system that uses a digitally coded radio signal to ensure that the key you use is the one that came with the vehicle.

After receiving harsh criticism for the fourth-generation's funky interior, Honda took a conservative approach to the dashboard layout of the current Prelude. It is disappointing to note that Honda went so conservative that there's nothing to distinguish the car from a late-'80s Accord.

Despite the interior shortcomings, the Prelude is an outstanding sport coupe that offers the latest technology at a reasonably affordable price. Unfortunately, its sales numbers have been falling in recent years and now the Honda S2000 and an upcoming redesign for the Acura Integra threaten to make the Prelude redundant.

Standard Equipment

BASE (5M): 2.2L I4 DOHC SMPI 16-valve engine with variable valve timing (requires premium unleaded fuel); 5-speed OD manual transmission; 100 amp alternator; front-wheel drive, 4.27 axle ratio; stainless steel exhaust with tailpipe finisher; front independent double-wishbone suspension with anti-roll bar, front coil springs, rear independent double-wishbone suspension with anti-roll bar, rear coil springs; rack-and-pinion power steering with engine speed-sensing assist; 4-wheel antilock disc brakes; 15.9 gal. capacity fuel tank; side impact bars; front power sliding and tilting glass sunroof with sunshade; front and rear body-colored bumpers; rocker panel extensions; clearcoat monotone paint; aero-composite halogen headlamps; driver's and passenger's power remote body-colored folding outside mirrors; 16" x 6.5" silver alloy wheels; P205/50VR16 BSW A/S tires; compact steel spare wheel; air conditioning, air filter; AM/FM stereo radio, seek-scan feature, single-disc CD player, 6 speakers, theft deterrent, window grid antenna; cruise control with steering wheel controls; power door locks with 2-stage unlock, remote keyless entry, remote hatch/trunk release, remote fuel door release; 1 power accessory outlet, driver's foot rest, retained accessory power; instrumentation display includes tachometer, water temperature gauge, in-dash clock, trip odometer; warning indicators include oil pressure, water temp, battery, lights on, key in ignition, low fuel, bulb failure, door ajar, trunk ajar, service interval; driver's and passenger's front airbags; ignition disable, panic alarm; tinted windows with driver's 1-touch down function; fixed interval front windshield wipers, rear window defroster; seating capacity of 4, front bucket seats with adjustable headrests, center armrest with storage, driver's seat includes 6-way adjustment, passenger's seat includes 4-way adjustment, easy entry; full folding rear bench seat; front height adjustable seatbelts; cloth seats, vinyl door trim insert, full cloth headliner, full carpet floor covering with carpeted floor mats, chrome interior accents; interior lights include dome light, front reading lights, 2 door curb lights, illuminated entry; leather-wrapped steering wheel with tilt adjustment; vanity mirrors; day/night rearview mirror; partial floor console, locking glove box, front and rear cupholders, instrument panel bin, 1 seatback storage pocket, driver's and passenger's door bins; carpeted cargo floor, cargo light; black grille, black side window moldings, black front windshield molding, black rear window molding and body-colored door handles.

TYPE SH (5M) (in addition to or instead of BASE (5M) equipment): Front-wheel drive, limited-slip differential; rear wing spoiler; leatherette door trim insert, leather-wrapped gearshift knob and chrome interior accents.

Base Prices

CODE	DESCRIPTION	INVOICE	MSRP
BB6141JW	Base (5M)	21081	23600
BB6151JW	Type SH (5M)	23311	26100
	Destination Charge:	440	440

Interested in seeing what dealers will sell this vehicle for? Check out our True Market Value^{sm} (TMV^{sm}) pricing on our Web site at www.edmunds.com.

PRELUDE / S2000

HONDA

CODE	DESCRIPTION	INVOICE	MSRP

Accessories

— Transmission: 4-Spd Sequential SportShift with OD (Base) 892 1000
Includes 4.79 axle ratio and engine: 2.2L DOHC vtec.

2001 S2000

What's New?

Indy Yellow is a new color for 2001, good for those folks who wish to attract the attention of local gendarmes as they scream to the S2000's ridiculously high redline. Floor mats, a rear wind deflector, a clock and an emergency trunk release are also new standard items. But Honda has failed to add a passenger airbag shut-off switch, much to our chagrin.

Review

It's all about that little red button. Located on the left side of the driver's console and labeled "engine start," the button reflects the racing heritage found on the S2000 roadster.

Honda's two-seat, open-topped roadster is based on the SSM concept car first shown at the 1995 Tokyo Motor Show. Designed to be fun to drive, the S2000 uses a front-engine, rear-wheel-drive configuration. As is often the case with Honda's performance vehicles, the S2000 contains many new technological advances that will surely trickle down to less-expensive models as time rolls by.

The centerpiece is a 2.0-liter, DOHC four-cylinder engine. It is equipped with an updated version of Honda's VTEC system, which can alter both valve timing and valve lift. The VTEC system allows the engine to produce maximum power while still being tractable enough for urban driving. If you need proof of Honda's technological prowess, look no further than the specifications: 240 horsepower at 8,300 rpm and 153 foot-pounds of torque at 7,500 rpm. Twist the key, hit the red start button, and the engine will give you the highest specific output (120 horsepower per liter) of any normally aspirated mass-production engine in the world. It will also spin to speeds that most other engines would choke on — redline is 8,900 rpm. If this still isn't impressive enough, Honda also says that the engine will meet low-emission vehicle status.

Power is routed though a six-speed, close-ratio transmission. The transmission is a compact design and features a direct shift linkage with excellent feel and short throws. A Torsen limited-slip differential is standard equipment.

Honda's expertise is also evident in the S2000's responsive handling. The exceptionally rigid chassis has an ideal 50/50 front-to-rear weight distribution. Both the suspension and power steering systems are unique designs. The suspension is a four-wheel double-wishbone type with a racing-inspired "in-wheel" design. And in place of conventional hydraulic power steering, the S2000 uses an electrically assisted system. This makes the steering feel much more responsive.

Visually, the S2000 is compact and angular. The convertible top is power operated, but the rear window is plastic, not glass. There is only one version of the S2000, so all cars get 16-inch wheels and high-intensity discharge headlights as standard equipment. For occupant safety, Honda says it has designed the car to absorb as much crash energy as possible. It also has installed seatbelts with load limiters and pre-tensioners, driver and passenger airbags, and roll bars. Inside, the S2000 comes with air conditioning, a digital instrument panel, a CD audio system and leather seats.

Honda's new roadster provides an excellent alternative to the Audi TT, BMW Z3, Mercedes-Benz SLK, and Porsche Boxster. Out of that group, the S2000 is the most performance-

HONDA

S2000

oriented. It's not as apt at city use, nor does it have the prestige that comes with owning a car emblazoned with a German marque. But for a visceral (and less-expensive) driving experience, the S2000 is the car to get.

Standard Equipment

BASE (6M): 2.0L I4 DOHC SMPI 16-valve engine with variable valve timing; 6-speed OD manual transmission; rear-wheel drive, limited-slip differential, 4.1 axle ratio; stainless steel exhaust with tailpipe finisher; front independent double-wishbone suspension with anti-roll bar, front coil springs, gas-pressurized front shocks, rear independent double-wishbone suspension with anti-roll bar, rear coil springs, gas-pressurized rear shocks; rack-and-pinion power steering with vehicle-speed-sensing assist; 4-wheel antilock disc brakes; 13.2 gal. capacity fuel tank; side impact bars; power convertible roof with roll-over protection, fixed wind blocker; front and rear body-colored bumpers; clearcoat monotone paint; projector beam high intensity headlamps with; driver's and passenger's power remote body-colored folding outside mirrors; front 16" x 6.5" machined alloy wheels rear 16" x 7.5" machined alloy wheels; P205/55WR16 BSW performance front tires; 225/50 rear tires; compact steel spare wheel; air conditioning, air filter; AM/FM stereo radio, clock, seek-scan feature, single-disc CD player, 4 speakers, fixed antenna; cruise control with steering wheel controls; power door locks with 2-stage unlock, remote keyless entry, power remote hatch release, remote fuel door release; 1 power accessory outlet, driver's foot rest; digital instrumentation display includes tachometer, water temperature gauge, trip odometer; warning indicators include oil pressure, battery, lights on, key in ignition, low fuel, door ajar, trunk ajar, service interval; driver's and passenger's front airbags; ignition disable, panic alarm; tinted windows with driver's 1-touch down function; fixed interval front windshield wipers; seating capacity of 2, front bucket seats with fixed headrests, driver's and passenger's seats include 4-way adjustment; seatbelts with front pretensioners; leather seats, leatherette door trim insert, full carpet floor covering with floor mats, aluminum gearshift knob; interior lights include dome light, front reading lights, illuminated entry; leather-wrapped steering wheel with tilt adjustment; passenger's side vanity mirror; day/night rearview mirror; full floor console, front cupholder, locking interior concealed storage, 2 seatback storage pockets; carpeted cargo floor, cargo light; black side window moldings, black front windshield molding and body-colored door handles.

Base Prices

		INVOICE	MSRP
AP1141ENW	S2000 Convertible (6M)	28733	32300
	Destination Charge:	440	440

Interested in seeing what dealers will sell this vehicle for? Check out our True Market Value^{sm} (TMV^{sm}) pricing on our Web site at www.edmunds.com.

Accessories

CODE	DESCRIPTION	INVOICE	MSRP
—	6 Disc Trunk-Mounted CD Changer	NA	535
—	Aero Screen	NA	279
—	Cargo Net	NA	39
—	Floor Mats	NA	60
	Includes S2000 logo.		
—	Front Under Spoiler	NA	499
	Color-matched.		
—	Security System	NA	448
	Includes 2 remote controls and attachment.		
—	Titanium Shift Knob	NA	159
—	Trunk Spoiler	NA	489
—	Wheel Locks	NA	35

HYUNDAI

2001 ACCENT

What's New?

For 2001, Accent GL and GS get a more powerful and fuel efficient 1.6-liter, DOHC inline four-cylinder engine.

Review

Hyundai is on a mission to reinvent itself in the minds of the American car-buying public. After a rocky period in the early '90s that had people saying, "Hyundais sure are inexpensive...and you get what you pay for," the company has unleashed several winners in a row. The Elantra offers impressive power and sophistication for its price, the Sonata is a roomy and well-built midsize sedan that undercuts competitors by thousands, the Santa Fe is larger than most mini-utes, if not more powerful, and the Tiburon? Uh, well, the Tiburon is a unique piece of work. Additionally, all Hyundais come with an impressive 10-year/100,000-mile drivetrain warranty, helping instill peace in the consumer's mind.

The entry-level Accent is no exception to Hyundai's new rule. Three versions are available. The base L and midlevel GS come in hatchback format while the highline GL model is available only as a sedan. The base engine on L models is a 1.5-liter, SOHC four-cylinder making 92 horsepower. A larger, 105-horsepower 1.6-liter is optional on L and standard on GS and GL. This new DOHC design offers more power and increased fuel economy over the standard engine. An available four-speed automatic performs admirably, but can only be added to the GS or the GL.

Under the Accent's attractively creased bodywork sits a MacPherson strut independent front and a dual-link rear suspension. Stabilizer bars at both ends do a poor job of controlling body lean, and skinny 13-inch wheels and tires do little to inspire confidence in Accent's handling. But the use of hydraulic engine mounting means reduced noise, vibration and harshness. Safety features include depowered airbags and seatbelt pre-tensioners. Unfortunately, ABS for the front disc/rear drum braking system is not even available as an option.

Interiors feature a modern instrument pod and a clean, simple center stack with straightforward climate and radio controls. Rear seat heating and ventilation ducts help keep backseat riders comfortable and the use of noise-reduction material in the A- and B-pillars attempts to quiet the ride. The driver's seat features adjustments for height and rake, as well as fore and aft settings. Oh, and a nifty fold-down armrest is standard.

Standard equipment includes a cassette player, rear defroster, trip odometer, and power steering. Step up to the GS or GL and you'll receive upgraded carpeting, a digital clock, a tachometer, lumbar support for the driver, a 60/40 folding rear seat, a passenger visor vanity mirror and tinted glass. Upgraded trims also open the door to the few factory options that are available, such as power front windows, power exterior mirrors, air conditioning, and a CD player. Port-installed options on any Accent include carpeted floor mats, a rear spoiler, a center armrest, mudguards and a cargo net for the trunk.

Hyundai has made great strides with regard to quality in the last few years and we're gaining respect for its products. In the subcompact world of shoddy Kias, questionable Daewoos and overpriced Toyotas, the Accent has plenty to offer the buyers who must have that new-car smell and new-car warranty. But at a welterweight 2,280 pounds, Accent doesn't offer much crash protection from the hulking SUVs and pickups on the roads. Our advice? Spend the few dollars you have on a larger, slightly used vehicle from one of the major Japanese manufacturers. In the long run, you'll probably be happier.

HYUNDAI ACCENT

| CODE | DESCRIPTION | INVOICE | MSRP |

Standard Equipment

L HATCHBACK (5M): 1.5L I4 SOHC MPI 12-valve engine; 5-speed OD manual transmission; 500-amp battery; engine oil cooler; 75-amp alternator; front-wheel drive, 3.65 axle ratio; partial stainless steel exhaust; front independent strut suspension with anti-roll bar, front coil springs, rear independent multi-link suspension with anti-roll bar, rear coil springs; rack-and-pinion power steering; front disc/rear drum brakes; 11.9 gal. capacity fuel tank; side impact bars; front and rear body-colored bumpers; black bodyside molding; clearcoat monotone paint; aero-composite halogen headlamps; driver's and passenger's manual remote black folding outside mirrors; 13" x 5" steel wheels; P175/70SR13 BSW A/S tires; compact steel spare wheel; rear heat ducts; AM/FM stereo, seek-scan feature, cassette player, 4 speakers, fixed antenna; remote fuel door release; 1 power accessory outlet, front lighter element, driver's foot rest, smokers' package; instrumentation display includes water temperature gauge, trip odometer; warning indicators include oil pressure, battery, lights on, key in ignition, low fuel, door ajar, trunk ajar, brake fluid; driver's and passenger's front airbags; variable-speed intermittent front windshield wipers, rear window defroster; seating capacity of 5, front bucket seats with adjustable headrests, driver's and front passenger's seats include 4-way adjustment and easy entry; full-folding rear bench seat with fixed headrests; height-adjustable front seatbelts with pretensioners; cloth seats, vinyl door trim insert, full vinyl headliner, full carpet floor covering; interior lights include dome light; day/night rearview mirror; full floor console, glove box, front and rear cupholders, driver's and passenger's door bins; carpeted cargo floor, cargo cover, cargo light; body-colored grille, black side window moldings, black front windshield molding, black rear window molding and black door handles.

GS HATCHBACK (5M) (in addition to or instead of L HATCHBACK (5M) equipment): 1.6L I4 SOHC MPI 12-valve engine; body-colored bodyside molding; instrumentation display includes tachometer, dash-mounted clock; tinted windows; sun visor strip, rear window wiper, driver's armrest, driver's seat includes 6-way adjustment and lumbar support; 60/40 folding rear bench seat; cloth door trim insert; passenger's side vanity mirror; 2 seatback storage pockets.

GL SEDAN (5M) (in addition to or instead of GS HATCHBACK (5M) equipment): Child-safety rear door locks, remote trunk release.

Base Prices

13303	L Hatchback (5M)	8610	8999
13333	GS Hatchback (5M)	8797	9399
13423	GL Sedan (5M)	9265	9899
Destination Charge:		435	435

Interested in seeing what dealers will sell this vehicle for? Check out our True Market Value[sm] (TMV[sm]) pricing on our Web site at www.edmunds.com.

Accessories

—	Transmission: 4-Speed Automatic (GS)	562	600
	Includes 3.66 axle ratio.		
1AA	Option Package No.1	NC	NC
	Includes AM/FM stereo with cassette player and power steering.		
2AB	Option Package No.2	686	750
	Includes AM/FM stereo with cassette player, power steering and air conditioning.		
3AC	Option Package No.3 (GS)	1053	1150
	Includes power steering, deluxe interior, deluxe cut pile carpet and door trim, tachometer and digital clock, multi-adjustable driver's seat, tinted glass, air conditioning, AM/FM stereo with CD player, power windows, mirrors and door locks.		

ACCENT / ELANTRA — HYUNDAI

CODE	DESCRIPTION	INVOICE	MSRP
AD	Air Conditioning	686	750
	INCLUDED in 2AB, 3AC.		
CA	California Emissions	70	75
CF	Carpeted Floor Mats	38	60
CN	Trunk Cargo Net	23	38
MG	Mud Guards	35	55
RS	Rear Spoiler	264	395

2001 ELANTRA

What's New?

Bigger inside and out, the redesigned 2001 Elantra boasts stylish sheetmetal, a refined 140-horsepower engine and improved NVH characteristics. Poised to tackle the best in the class, the Elantra comes well equipped for less than $13,000. Though the useful station wagon model has been stricken from the lineup, a five-door hatchback is set to debut later this year.

Review

Already a winner to our editors, the amazingly competent Elantra gets a complete overhaul for 2001, adding interior space and exterior size, along with a full load of standard equipment, without a substantial boost in the price. Stickering for less than $13,000 and sold in a single trim level with a handful of options, the new, more refined Elantra is set to compete head to head with the best in the compact sedan class, beating everyone on price if not overall quality.

Elantra's 140-horsepower, 2.0-liter DOHC engine provides decent acceleration, suffering a bit in terms of performance due to Elantra's weight gain of 300 pounds over last year. A four-speed automatic transmission is optional, and features fuzzy-logic software to optimize shifting and hold a gear on hills, but we'd go with the less expensive manual transmission to extract maximum acceleration.

A four-wheel independent suspension, multi-link with an antiroll bar at the rear, makes for smooth, stable handling, while the speed-sensitive rack-and-pinion steering system communicates improved road feel to the driver for 2001. Four-wheel disc ABS is optional, as is traction control.

Inside the Elantra, consumers will find a roomy cabin with supportive, comfortable seats front and rear. Extensive use of sound-deadening materials helps quiet this formerly buzzy compact car. Equipment levels are impressive, with power windows/locks/mirrors, side airbags, air conditioning, a cassette player and 15-inch wheels standard. Options, aside from the ABS and traction control previously mentioned, are limited to a power moonroof, CD player, cruise control and a smattering of port- and dealer-installed goodies.

Later this year, Hyundai will introduce the Elantra GT. Configured as a five-door hatchback, the GT is designed to appeal to those who may have purchased the discontinued station wagon model, as well as buyers who desire the utility of a hatchback configuration. The GT gets rear disc brakes, a sport-tuned suspension, alloy wheels, and a host of other standard items for a premium of about $1,000 over the sedan.

Elantra also comes with an outstanding warranty. Called the Hyundai Advantage, this buyer-assurance program is a great incentive to buy a Hyundai over one of the many other compact choices on the market. Consumers receive an awesome 10-year/100,000-mile powertrain

HYUNDAI — ELANTRA

| CODE | DESCRIPTION | INVOICE | MSRP |

warranty. If the car is sold within those first 10 years, the new owner will still be entitled to the balance of a five-year/60,000-mile powertrain warranty. Also part of the program is five-year/100,000-mile corrosion coverage and a limited bumper-to-bumper warranty for five years or 60,000 miles. Additionally, the program offers free 24-hour roadside assistance for five years, which includes towing and lockout service.

Attractive, well equipped, and backed up by one of the most extensive warranties in America, Hyundai has a winner in the upgraded and redesigned Elantra. Though it likely won't match the refinement or attention to detail found in segment leaders like the Honda Civic and Ford Focus, the savings to be found up front will certainly sway buyers for whom every penny spent up front counts.

Standard Equipment

GLS SEDAN (5M): 2L I4 DOHC MPI 16-valve engine; 5-speed OD manual transmission; 75-amp alternator; front-wheel drive, 3.84 axle ratio; partial stainless steel exhaust with tailpipe finisher; front independent strut suspension with anti-roll bar, front coil springs, gas-pressurized front shocks, rear independent multi-link suspension with anti-roll bar, rear coil springs, gas-pressurized rear shocks; rack-and-pinion power steering with engine-speed-sensing assist; front disc/rear drum brakes; 14.5 gal. capacity fuel tank; side impact bars; front and rear body-colored bumpers; body-colored bodyside molding; clearcoat monotone paint; aero-composite halogen headlamps; driver's and passenger's power remote body-colored heated folding outside mirrors;15" x 5.5" steel wheels, P195/60HR15 BSW A/S tires; compact steel spare wheel; air conditioning, rear heat ducts; AM/FM stereo, seek-scan feature, cassette player, 4 speakers, fixed antenna; power door locks, child-safety rear door locks, remote trunk release, remote fuel door release; 1 power accessory outlet, front lighter element, smokers' package; instrumentation display includes tachometer, water temperature gauge, in-dash clock, trip odometer; warning indicators include oil pressure, battery, lights on, key in ignition, low fuel, door ajar, trunk ajar, brake fluid; driver's and passenger's front airbags, driver's and front passenger's seat-mounted side airbags; tinted windows, power front and rear windows with driver's 1-touch down function; variable-speed intermittent front windshield wipers, sun visor strip, rear window defroster; seating capacity of 5, front bucket seats with adjustable headrests, center armrest with storage, driver's seat includes 6-way adjustment, lumbar support, front passenger's seat includes 4-way adjustment; 60/40 folding rear bench seat with adjustable headrests; height-adjustable front seatbelts with pretensioners; cloth seats, cloth door trim insert, full cloth headliner, full carpet floor covering; interior lights include dome light, front reading lights, door curb lights; steering wheel with tilt adjustment; passenger side vanity mirror; day/night rearview mirror; full floor console, locking glove box with light, front cupholder, instrument panel bin, driver's and front passenger's door bins; carpeted cargo floor, cargo light; chrome grille, black side window moldings, black front windshield molding, black rear window molding and body-colored door handles.

Base Prices

Code	Description	Invoice	MSRP
42443	GLS Sedan (5M)	11504	12499
	Destination Charge:	435	435

Interested in seeing what dealers will sell this vehicle for? Check out our True Market Value^{sm} (TMV^{sm}) pricing on our Web site at www.edmunds.com.

Accessories

Code	Description	Invoice	MSRP
—	Transmission: 4-Speed Automatic	732	800
	Includes 3.66 axle ratio.		
1AA	Package 1	NC	NC
	Includes air conditioning, AM/FM stereo with cassette player, power windows, power mirrors, power door locks; driver's and front passenger's side airbags. NOT AVAILABLE with WD.		

ELANTRA / SONATA — HYUNDAI

CODE	DESCRIPTION	INVOICE	MSRP
2AB	Package 2	344	400
	Includes air conditioning, AM/FM stereo with cassette player, power windows, power mirrors, power door locks, driver's and front passneger's side airbags, cruise control and keyless-entry system with alarm. NOT AVAILABLE with WD.		
3AC	Package 3	633	750
	Includes air conditioning, power windows, power mirrors, power door locks, driver's and front passneger's side airbags, cruise control, keyless-entry system with alarm and AM/FM stereo with CD player. NOT AVAILABLE with WD.		
4AD	Package 4	1174	1400
	Includes air conditioning, power windows, power mirrors, power door locks, driver's and front passneger's side airbags, cruise control, keyless-entry system with alarm, AM/FM stereo with CD player and power moonroof with sunshade.		
5AE	Package 5	1046	1150
	Includes air conditioning, AM/FM stereo with cassette player, power windows, power mirrors, power door locks, driver's and front passneger's side airbags, cruise control, keyless-entry system with alarm and antilock braking system. NOT AVAILABLE with WD.		
CA	California Emissions	94	100
CF	Carpeted Floor Mats	44	78
CN	Trunk Cargo Net	23	38
MG	Mud Guards	38	60
WD	Sunroof Wind Deflector	35	62
	REQUIRES 4AD. NOT AVAILABLE with 1AA, 2AB, 3AC, 5AE.		

2001 SONATA

What's New?

The Sonata gets only minor trim changes for 2001, such as a new grille design and some tweaks to the rear deck lid. Additional features are ladled onto the standard equipment list.

Review

The Sonata is a thoughtfully designed family sedan that makes for a viable alternative to the more expensive and popular Honda Accord and Toyota Camry.

Under the hood of base models is a standard 2.4-liter four-cylinder engine making 150 horsepower and 156 foot-pounds of torque. Buyers can upgrade to a more powerful V6 or get it standard if they spring for GLS trim. This V6 is an aluminum, 2.5-liter DOHC motor making 170 horsepower at 6,000 rpm and 167 foot-pounds of torque that peak at 4,000, which means power off the line can be a bit lacking. Sonatas can be ordered with automatic or manual transmissions mated to either engine. Higher in the rev range the V6 can get clamorous and the Sonata's automatic transmission can be easily befuddled, causing occasionally hard shifts.

Sonata offers decent steering feedback and body roll is kept to a minimum. Road and wind noise are adequately muffled, and the brakes stop the car with confidence. Riding on a front

HYUNDAI   *SONATA*

| CODE | DESCRIPTION | INVOICE | MSRP |

double-wishbone suspension and a rear five-link setup, the Sonata's ride and handling can be characterized as stable, smooth and responsive.

Inside the monochromatic cabin are plush seats, an adequate driving position and a nice-looking dashboard. Drivers will also find well laid-out radio and HVAC controls, a nifty penholder and a leather shift knob on the GLS model. The trunk is spacious with an extremely low lift-in height for ease of use and rear seats on the GLS fold down conveniently in a 60/40 configuration to expand the cargo area.

Standard safety features such as side airbags, seatbelt pre-tensioners and a passenger-presence airbag detection system all contribute to a safer environment in the Sonata. Optional ABS is offered.

Hyundai has one big advantage over most other manufacturers peddling bread-and-butter sedans these days. Aptly called the Hyundai Advantage, the company's warranty program is a great incentive to buy a Hyundai over one of the many other choices on the market. With the purchase of any Hyundai vehicle, consumers will receive an awesome 10-year/100,000-mile powertrain warranty, five-year/100,000-mile corrosion coverage and a limited bumper-to-bumper warranty for five years or 60,000 miles. Roadside assistance is part of the deal, too, for five years and unlimited mileage.

Incorporating dependability and cutting-edge style in affordable packaging, Hyundai has come a long way lately, and the Sonata is proof of it. Desirable, safe and well equipped, Sonata is perfect for hauling the family around town. If you're still not convinced that the Sonata could lure you away from that bare-bones Camry, Accord or Passat you've been salivating over, go drive one. You'll be surprised by what you discover.

Standard Equipment

BASE (5M): 2.4L I4 DOHC MPI 16-valve engine; 5-speed OD manual transmission; 90-amp alternator; front-wheel drive, 3.88 axle ratio; partial stainless steel exhaust; front independent double-wishbone suspension with anti-roll bar, front coil springs, rear independent multi-link suspension with anti-roll bar, rear coil springs; rack-and-pinion power steering; front disc/rear drum brakes; 17.2 gal. capacity fuel tank; side impact bars; front and rear body-colored bumpers; body-colored bodyside molding; clearcoat monotone paint; aero-composite halogen headlamps; driver's and passenger's power remote body-colored folding outside mirrors; 15" x 6" silver alloy wheels; P205/60HR15 BSW A/S performance tires; compact steel spare wheel; air conditioning, rear heat ducts; AM/FM stereo, seek-scan feature, cassette player, 4 speakers, fixed antenna; cruise control with steering wheel controls; power door locks, child-safety rear door locks, remote trunk release, remote fuel door release; 2 power accessory outlets, front lighter element, driver's foot rest, retained accessory power, smokers' package; instrumentation display includes tachometer, water temperature gauge, dash-mounted clock, trip odometer; warning indicators include oil pressure, battery, lights on, key in ignition, low fuel, bulb failure, door ajar, trunk ajar, brake fluid; driver's and passenger's front airbags, driver's and front passenger's seat-mounted side airbags; tinted windows, power front and rear windows with driver's 1-touch down function; variable-speed intermittent front windshield wipers, sun visor strip, rear window defroster; seating capacity of 5, front bucket seats with adjustable headrests, center armrest with storage, driver's seat includes 6-way adjustment, passenger's seat includes 4-way adjustment; rear bench seat with adjustable headrests; height-adjustable front seatbelts with pretensioners; cloth seats, cloth door trim insert, full cloth headliner, full carpet floor covering; interior lights include dome light with fade; steering wheel with tilt adjustment; passenger's side vanity mirror; day/night rearview mirror; full floor console, locking glove box with light, front cupholder, instrument panel bin, 2 seatback storage pockets, driver's and passenger's door bins; carpeted cargo floor, cargo light; chrome grille, black side window moldings, black front windshield molding, black rear window molding and body-colored door handles.

GLS (5M) (in addition to or instead of BASE (5M) equipment): 2.5L V6 DOHC MPI 24-valve engine; 600-amp battery; engine oil cooler; 95-amp alternator; 4-wheel disc brakes; body-colored bodyside molding with chrome bodyside insert; single-disc CD player, 6 speakers, power retractable antenna; driver's seat includes lumbar support; 60/40 folding rear bench

SONATA — HYUNDAI

CODE	DESCRIPTION	INVOICE	MSRP

seat; premium cloth seats, simulated wood dashboard insert, simulated wood door panel insert, chrome interior accents; interior lights include front reading lights, door curb lights; dual illuminated vanity mirrors.

GLS W/LEATHER (5M) (in addition to or instead of GLS (5M) equipment): Cassette player, 10 speakers, driver's seat includes 8-way adjustment; leather seats, leatherette door trim insert, leather-wrapped gearshift knob; leather-wrapped steering wheel.

Base Prices

Code	Description	Invoice	MSRP
23403	Base (5M)	13805	14999
23453	GLS (5M)	15116	16999
23463	GLS w/Leather (5M)	16294	18324
	Destination Charge:	435	435

Interested in seeing what dealers will sell this vehicle for? Check out our True Market Value℠ (TMV℠) pricing on our Web site at www.edmunds.com.

Accessories

Code	Description	Invoice	MSRP
—	Transmission: 4-Speed Automatic (Base)	499	500
	Includes 3.77 axle ratio.		
—	Transmission: 4-Speed Automatic (GLS/GLS w/Leather)	499	500
	Includes 3.35 axle ratio.		
01AA	Package 1	NC	NC
	Includes air conditioning, power package (power windows, power mirrors, power door locks, side airbags, cruise control,) 15" alloy wheels and Michelin tires.		
02AB	Package 2 (Base)	679	800
	Includes air conditioning, AM/FM stereo w/CD player upgrade, power package (power windows, power mirrors, power door locks, side airbags, cruise control,) 15" alloy wheels and Michelin tires; power tilt/slide moonroof with sunshade.		
10AJ	Package 10 (GLS)	834	975
	Includes air conditioning, AM/FM stereo with CD/cassette player upgrade, power package (power windows, power mirrors, power door locks, side airbags, cruise control,) 15" alloy wheels and Michelin tires; power tilt/slide moonroof with sunshade.		
12AL	Package 12 (GLS w/Leather)	458	550
	Includes air conditioning, AM/FM stereo with CD/cassette player upgrade, power package (power windows, power mirrors, power door locks, side airbags, cruise control,) 15" alloy wheels and Michelin tires, leather package, power driver's seat; power tilt/slide moonroof with sunshade.		
13AM	Package 13 (GLS w/Leather)	1113	1250
	Includes air conditioning, AM/FM stereo with CD/cassette player upgrade, power windows, power mirrors, power door locks, side airbags, cruise control,) 15" alloy wheels and Michelin tires, leather package, power driver's seat, power tilt/slide moonroof with sunshade, antilock braking system, traction control.		
CA	California Emissions	100	100
CF	Carpeted Floor Mats	45	78
CN	Trunk Cargo Net	23	38

HYUNDAI — SONATA / TIBURON

CODE	DESCRIPTION	INVOICE	MSRP
K1	Keyless Remote Entry with Security System	255	385
KR	Keyless Remote Entry System	120	180
MG	Mud Guards	43	75
RS	Rear Spoiler	295	440
WD	Sunroof Wind Deflector	35	62

2001 TIBURON

What's New?

Following last year's freshening, the Tiburon sees only minor trim changes for 2001, such as redesigned wheels and the addition of a rear spoiler as standard equipment.

Review

Several years ago, Hyundai displayed a mouth-watering concept car at national auto shows—the HCD-II. Show-goers could hardly swallow the fact that the same company that produced the dowdy Excel could, or would, dream up something like this futuristic sport coupe. Hyundai execs promised that a production version of the show car was on the drawing board.

The following year, HCD-III arrived and contained an innovative sidesaddle rear seat that a passenger could sit in sideways and stretch out. Excellent concept, Hyundai. Young consumers drooled in anticipation of the forthcoming HCD production car with the cool backseat.

Alas, it was not meant to be. The Tiburon arrived as a compromise between federal regulations and designer fantasy. Still, its swoopy sheetmetal and sporty interior got it noticed. It sports large, bold quad projector-beam headlights, a standard rear spoiler, and distinctive styling that you either love or hate.

A 140-horse, four-cylinder engine propels the Tiburon's front wheels, and can be mated to either a five-speed manual transmission or a four-speed automatic. Acceleration is lively, and thanks to a sport-tuned suspension, cornering is one of the Tiburon's favorite activities. Ride quality, however, is somewhat harsh, and the steering not exactly accurate. Brakes operate with authority.

Thanks to its hatchback body style, Tiburon offers outstanding utility when the rear seats are folded flat. Standard equipment includes 15-inch alloy wheels, power door locks and mirrors, and four-wheel disc brakes. Option packages can get you leather trim, a power sunroof, AM/FM stereo with CD/cassette and antilock brakes.

Hyundai customers will be delighted with the company's buyer-assurance program, called the "Hyundai Advantage." With the purchase of any Hyundai vehicle, consumers will receive an awesome 10-year/100,000-mile powertrain warranty. If the car is sold within those first 10 years, the new owner will still be entitled to the balance of a five-year/60,000-mile powertrain warranty. Also part of the program is five-year/100,000-mile corrosion coverage and a limited bumper-to-bumper warranty of five years or 60,000 miles. Additionally, the program offers free 24-hour roadside assistance for five years, which includes towing and lockout service.

The Tiburon's target market is the same young, style-conscious, financially impaired bunch that buys the Ford Focus ZX3, Honda Civic Coupe and Pontiac Sunfire GT. The stylish Tiburon competes well and, with the Hyundai Advantage warranty backing up the Tib's credentials, many young buyers may look at this coupe with newfound enthusiasm.

TIBURON

HYUNDAI

CODE	DESCRIPTION	INVOICE	MSRP

Standard Equipment

TIBURON (5M): 2L I4 DOHC MPI 16-valve engine; 5-speed OD manual transmission; 90-amp alternator; front-wheel drive, 3.84 axle ratio; partial stainless steel exhaust with tailpipe finisher; sport-ride suspension, front independent strut suspension with anti-roll bar, front coil springs, gas-pressurized front shocks, rear independent multi-link suspension with anti-roll bar, rear coil springs, gas-pressurized rear shocks; rack-and-pinion power steering; 4-wheel disc brakes; 14.5 gal. capacity fuel tank; rear wing spoiler, side impact bars; front and rear body-colored bumpers; clearcoat monotone paint; projector-beam halogen headlamps; driver's and passenger's power remote black folding outside mirrors; 15" x 6" silver alloy wheels, P195/55HR15 BSW A/S performance tires; compact steel spare wheel; air conditioning, rear heat ducts; AM/FM stereo, seek-scan feature, cassette player, 6 speakers, fixed antenna; cruise control; power door locks, remote hatch release, remote fuel door release; 1 power accessory outlet, front lighter element, driver's foot rest, smokers' package; instrumentation display includes tachometer, water temperature gauge, in-dash clock, trip odometer; warning indicators include oil pressure, battery, lights on, key in ignition, low fuel, door ajar, trunk ajar, brake fluid; driver's and passenger's front airbags; tinted windows; variable-speed intermittent front windshield wipers, sun visor strip, rear window defroster; seating capacity of 4, front bucket seats with adjustable headrests, driver's and front passenger's seats include 4-way adjustment, driver's seat features lumbar support; 50/50 folding rear bench seat; height-adjustable front seatbelts with pretensioners; cloth seats, vinyl door trim insert, full vinyl headliner, full carpet floor covering; interior lights include dome light, front reading lights; steering wheel with tilt adjustment; front passenger's vanity mirror; day/night rearview mirror; full floor console, mini overhead console with storage, locking glove box, front cupholder, instrument panel bin, driver's and passenger's door bins; carpeted cargo floor, cargo cover, cargo light; black grille, black side window moldings, black front windshield molding, black rear window molding and body-colored door handles.

Base Prices

| 51323 | Tiburon (5M) .... | 13194 | 14499 |
| | Destination Charge: .... | 435 | 435 |

Interested in seeing what dealers will sell this vehicle for? Check out our True Market Value^{sm} (TMV^{sm}) pricing on our Web site at www.edmunds.com.

Accessories

—	Transmission: 4-Speed Automatic w/OD	732	800
	Includes 3.977 axle ratio.		
1AA	Package 1	NC	NC
	Includes AM/FM stereo w/cassette player, power windows, mirrors and door locks, air conditioning, cruise control, 15" alloy wheels, rear spoiler.		
2AB	Package 2	935	1124
	Includes power windows, mirrors and door locks, air conditioning, cruise control, 15" alloy wheels, rear spoiler, AM/FM stereo w/cassette player, CD player upgrade, power sunroof.		
3AC	Package 3	561	599
	Includes AM/FM stereo w/cassette player, power windows, mirrors and door locks, air conditioning, cruise control, 15" alloy wheels, rear spoiler, leather package (two-tone seat trim, black leather-wrapped steering wheel, black leather-wrapped shift knob).		
4AD	Package 4	956	1074
	Includes power windows, mirrors and door locks, air conditioning, cruise control, 15" alloy wheels, rear spoiler, AM/FM stereo w/cassette, CD player upgrade, leather		

HYUNDAI   TIBURON / XG300

CODE	DESCRIPTION	INVOICE	MSRP
	package (two-tone leather seat trim, black leather-wrapped steering wheel, black leather-wrapped shift knob).		
5AE	Package 5	1496	1723
	Includes power windows, mirrors and door locks, air conditioning, cruise control, 15" alloy wheels, rear spoiler, AM/FM stereo w/cassette, CD player upgrade, leather package (two-tone leather seat trim, black leather-wrapped steering wheel, black leather-wrapped shift knob; power sunroof.		
6AF	Package 6	1963	2222
	Includes power windows, mirrors and door locks, air conditioning, cruise control, 15" alloy wheels, rear spoiler, AM/FM stereo w/cassette, CD player upgrade, leather package (two-tone leather seat trim, black leather-wrapped steering wheel, black leather-wrapped shift knob), power sunroof and antilock braking system.		
AR	Console Armrest	81	130
	REQUIRES 1AA or 2AB.		
CA	California Emissions	117	125
CF	Carpeted Floor Mats	44	75
CN	Trunk Cargo Net	23	38
MG	Mud Guards	38	60

2001 XG300

What's New?

Hyundai goes after the Honda Accord V6 and Toyota Camry V6 by offering more for less. Fully loaded with equipment, the new XG300 undercuts both competitors on price. But, as we all know, there's more to the value equation than an attractive MSRP, especially in the meat of the sedan marketplace.

Review

We're as surprised as anybody. We didn't give Hyundai much of a chance in North America after the atrocious Excel of the 1980s. But the Korean marque has dutifully soldiered on, getting better and better every year.

Now, the manufacturer is aiming high. Following this year's release of its surprisingly good and sharp-looking sport-ute, the Santa Fe, Hyundai has launched the XG300, an all-new six-cylinder sedan aimed at taking on the V6 versions of the Nissan Maxima, Honda Accord and Toyota Camry.

The XG300 was created as Hyundai's flagship model and is meant to lead the automaker's fleet proudly into the new millennium. Hyundai's goal is to use the XG300 to garner serious consideration from consumers. It sure beats Hyundai's previous status as the Oh-God-I-want-a-new-car-but-don't-have-enough-money-for-anything-but-a-Hyundai alternative.

Powered by a 3.0-liter, six-cylinder engine, the XG300 manages a smooth 192 horsepower (at 6,000 rpm) that allows for comfortable highway cruising and merging and passing with elan. A five-speed automatic with a manual shifting provision, called H-matic, is standard. In the next year or so, Hyundai plans to make available a 3.5-liter V6 powerplant that should rocket the flagship past its competitors in terms of power.

XG300 — HYUNDAI

Bigger than the four-door Sonata and about the same size as the Nissan Maxima, the XG300 purportedly seats five comfortably. In an attempt to attract attention, Hyundai loaded the XG300 with many standard features, including four-wheel disc brakes with ABS, 15-inch alloy wheels with Michelin V-rated tires, leather upholstery, power driver and passenger seats, power windows, locks and mirrors, six-speaker stereo with CD player, air conditioning, cruise control, keyless remote entry, trip computer, projector beam headlights and driver and passenger front- and side-impact airbags.

For a sedan priced in the mid-$20,000 range, XG300 offers a whole lot of content, and makes for a compelling alternative to the competition. Hyundai's generous 10-year/100,000-mile warranty and substantial roadside assistance program further sweeten the deal.

In every month of 2000, Hyundai set sales records. But this success hasn't made Hyundai think it can knock Nissan, Toyota and Honda off their pedestals; the company plans to hawk only 15,000 XGs per year. We, learning from our past mistakes, won't discount Hyundai's ability to meet, or exceed, that goal. And, if you're in the market for a new, mid-range sedan, maybe you shouldn't either.

Standard Equipment

BASE (5A): 3L V6 DOHC MPI 24-valve engine; 5-speed electronic OD automatic transmission with lock-up converter; 600-amp battery; engine oil cooler; 120-amp alternator; auto-manual transmission; front-wheel drive, 3.33 axle ratio; partial stainless steel exhaust; front independent double-wishbone suspension with anti-roll bar, front coil springs, gas-pressurized front shocks, rear independent multi-link suspension with anti-roll bar, rear coil springs, gas-pressurized rear shocks; rack-and-pinion power steering; 4-wheel antilock disc brakes; 18.5 gal. capacity fuel tank; side impact bars; front and rear body-colored bumpers with body-colored rub strip, chrome bumper insert; body-colored bodyside molding with chrome bodyside insert; clearcoat monotone paint; projector beam halogen headlamps; driver's and passenger's power remote body-colored heated folding outside mirrors; 15" x 6" silver alloy wheels, P205/65VR15 BSW A/S tires; compact steel spare wheel; air conditioning with climate control, air filter, rear heat ducts; AM/FM stereo, seek-scan feature, single-disc CD player, 6 speakers, automatic equalizer, window grid diversity antenna; cruise control with steering wheel controls; power door locks, child-safety rear door locks, power remote trunk release, power remote fuel door release; 2 power accessory outlets, front and rear lighter elements, driver's foot rest, retained accessory power, smokers' package; instrumentation display includes tachometer, water temperature gauge, in-dash clock, exterior temp, trip computer, trip odometer; warning indicators include oil pressure, battery, lights on, key in ignition, low fuel, bulb failure, door ajar, trunk ajar, brake fluid; driver's and front passenger's airbags, driver's and front passenger's seat-mounted side airbags; ignition disable, security system; tinted windows, power front and rear windows with driver's 1-touch down function; variable-speed intermittent front windshield wipers, sun visor strip, rear window defroster; seating capacity of 5, front bucket seats with adjustable tilt headrests, center armrest with storage, driver's seat includes 8-way power adjustment and lumbar support, front passenger's seat includes 4-way power adjustment and lumbar support; 60/40 folding rear bench seat with tilt headrests, center armrest with storage; height-adjustable front seatbelts with pretensioners; leather seats, leatherette door trim insert, full cloth headliner, full carpet floor covering, simulated wood dashboard insert, leather-wrapped gearshift knob, simulated wood door panel insert, simulated wood console insert, chrome interior accents; interior lights include dome light with fade, front reading lights, door curb lights; leather-wrapped steering wheel with tilt adjustment; dual illuminated vanity mirrors, dual auxiliary visors; day/night rearview mirror; full floor console, locking glove box with light, front and rear cupholders, instrument panel bin, 2 seatback storage pockets, driver's and passenger's door bins; carpeted cargo floor, cargo light; chrome grille, chrome side window moldings, black front windshield molding, black rear window molding and chrome door handles.

L (5A) (in addition to or instead of BASE (5A) equipment): Power sliding/tilting glass sunroof with sunshade; premium AM/FM stereo, cassette player, heated driver's and front passenger's seat cushions; driver's seat memory includes 2 settings; leather/simulated wood steering wheel.

HYUNDAI　　　　　　　　　　　　　　　　　　　　　　XG300

CODE	DESCRIPTION	INVOICE	MSRP

Base Prices

70442	Base (5A)	21018	23499
70452	L (5A)	22359	24999
Destination Charge:		435	435

Interested in seeing what dealers will sell this vehicle for? Check out our True Market Value^{sm} (TMV^{sm}) pricing on our Web site at www.edmunds.com.

Accessories

01AA	Package 1	(447)	(500)

Includes leather seat trim, front-seat side airbags, 15" alloy wheels with Michelin tires, power windows, mirrors and door locks, cruise control, fully automatic air conditioning delete.

02AB	Package 2 (Base)	177	250

Includes leather seat trim, AM/FM stereo with CD player, front-seat side airbags, 15" alloy wheels with Michelin tires, power windows, mirrors and door locks, cruise control, power tilt and slide moonroof with sunshade, fully automatic air conditioning delete.

04AD	Package 4 (L)	NC	NC

Includes leather seat trim, leather and woodgrain-trimmed steering wheel, AM/FM stereo with CD changer and cassette player, power tilt and slide moonroof with sunshade, power windows, mirrors and door locks, electrochromic auto-dimming rear view mirror, front-seat side airbags, cruise control, 15" alloy wheels with Michelin tires, fully automatic air conditioning delete.

05AE	Package 5	NC	NC

Includes fully automatic air conditioning, leather seat trim, front-seat side airbags, 15" alloy wheels with Michelin tires, power windows, mirrors and door locks and cruise control.

06AF	Package 6 (Base)	624	750

Includes fully automatic air conditioning, leather seat trim, AM/FM stereo with CD changer, front-seat side airbags, 15" alloy wheels with Michelin tires, power windows, mirrors and door locks, cruise control, power tilt and slide moonroof with sunshade.

07AG	Package 7 (L)	447	500

Includes fully automatic air conditioning, leather seat trim, leather and woodgrain-trimmed steering wheel, AM/FM stereo with CD changer and cassette player, power tilt and slide moonroof with sunshade, power windows, mirrors and door locks, electrochromic auto-dimming rear view mirror, front-seat side airbags, cruise control, 15" alloy wheels with Michelin tires.

CF	Carpeted Floor Mats	48	78
CN	Trunk Cargo Net	23	38
WD	Moonroof Wind Deflector	35	62

G20

INFINITI

2001 G20

What's New?

G20t comes with standard leather and a power sunroof this year. Luxury models can be equipped with leather and a manual transmission simultaneously. And hold on to your hat — the side marker lights switch from amber lenses to clear.

Review

Infiniti aims its G20 at the young, affluent 25- to 35-year-old demographic that aspires to own an Audi A4, BMW 3 Series or Lexus IS 300 but can't quite squeeze one of those models into the budget. Essentially a Japan-market Nissan with a chrome grille and an Infiniti badge, G20 promises buyers a stimulating and luxurious experience but has difficulty delivering either in a convincing fashion.

Two models are available. Luxury editions provide buyers with goodies like side-impact airbags, fake wood cabin trim, remote keyless entry, Bose audio with 100 watts of power, and the usual battery of power conveniences. Touring models add automatic climate control, a limited-slip differential, fog lights, a rear spoiler, and more aggressive tires. For 2001, G20t, as the Touring model is badged, includes leather seats and a power sunroof. Leather and a sunroof are optional on the G20 Luxury, bundled into a package that also includes automatic climate control. A heated seats package can be added to either model.

One neat option unusual for a car in this price range is the Infiniti Communicator (IC) telematics system. Featuring one-touch calling for help in an emergency or to get roadside assistance, IC also helps retrieve your G20 if it's been stolen, monitors fiddling with the car's standard Vehicle Immobilizer System, and can unlock your doors remotely in the event you lock them in the car or lose them. But the IC costs plenty to install, and we're not sure it's worthwhile, despite the fact that the asking price includes a four-year subscription.

G20's 145-horsepower, 2.0-liter DOHC engine revs freely and smoothly, but can be deemed spirited only when equipped with a manual transmission. The optional four-speed automatic saps power, emasculating the performance part of the car's equation. Curvy roads are where the G20 shines, thanks to a well-tuned suspension and communicative engine-speed sensitive steering. Four-wheel disc brakes with ABS haul the 3,000-pound G20 to a stop assertively.

Cabin space is decent for four adults, though rear seat legroom is rather tight. Sturdy assembly is evident throughout, and the dash sports clearly labeled gauges and properly placed controls.

Despite the fact that the G20 is an attractive set of well-equipped wheels, its downmarket positioning and overall feel dictate that it cannot compete with the Audis, BMWs and Lexuses in which young up-and-comers are interested. We know that the Infiniti dealer body is respectful and courteous to consumers, but think about it this way: a similarly powered Ford Focus ZTS, Nissan Sentra SE or Mazda Protege ES stickers for as much as $10,000 less than the G20. Is 10 grand worth a couple of nice doodads, a better warranty and getting your butt kissed at the dealership?

Furthermore, for the price of a loaded G20t, you can waltz into a Nissan showroom and blast out in a roomier, more powerful Maxima SE. That fact alone is reason enough to forget the G20 even exists.

INFINITI G20

CODE	DESCRIPTION	INVOICE	MSRP

Standard Equipment

LUXURY MODEL (5M): 2L I4 DOHC SMPI 16-valve engine; 5-speed OD manual transmission; battery with run down protection; 90 amp alternator; front-wheel drive, 4.18 axle ratio; stainless steel exhaust; front independent suspension with anti-roll bar, front coil springs, rear non-independent multi-link suspension with anti-roll bar, rear coil springs; rack-and-pinion power steering with engine speed-sensing assist; 4-wheel antilock disc brakes; 15.9 gal. capacity fuel tank; side impact bars; front and rear body-colored bumpers; body-colored bodyside molding, rocker panel extensions; monotone paint; aero-composite halogen auto off headlamps; driver's and passenger's power remote body-colored folding outside mirrors; 15" x 6" silver alloy wheels; P195/65HR15 BSW A/S tires; compact steel spare wheel; air conditioning, rear heat ducts; premium AM/FM stereo radio, clock, seek-scan feature, cassette player, single-disc CD player, 6 premium speakers, power retractable diversity antenna; cruise control with steering wheel controls; power door locks with 2-stage unlock, remote keyless entry, child-safety rear door locks, power remote hatch/trunk release, remote fuel door release; 1 power accessory outlet, driver's foot rest, retained accessory power; instrumentation display includes tachometer, water temperature gauge, trip odometer; warning indicators include oil pressure, battery, lights on, key in ignition, low fuel, low washer fluid, door ajar, brake fluid; driver's and passenger's front airbags, driver's and front passenger's seat-mounted side airbags; ignition disable, panic alarm, security system; tinted windows, power front and rear windows with driver's 1-touch down function; variable-speed intermittent front windshield wipers, sun visor strip, rear window defroster; seating capacity of 5, front bucket seats with adjustable headrests, center armrest with storage, driver's seat includes 8-way adjustment, passenger's seat includes 4-way adjustment; 60/40 folding rear bench seat with adjustable headrests, center armrest; height-adjustable front seatbelts with pretensioners; cloth seats, cloth door trim insert, full cloth headliner, full carpet floor covering with carpeted floor mats, simulated wood console insert; interior lights include dome light with fade, front reading lights, illuminated entry; steering wheel with tilt adjustment; dual illuminated vanity mirrors; day/night rearview mirror; full floor console, locking glove box with light, front and rear cupholders, 2 seatback storage pockets, driver's and passenger's door bins; carpeted cargo floor, carpeted trunk lid, cargo net, cargo light; chrome grille, black side window moldings, black front windshield molding, black rear window molding and body-colored door handles.

TOURING MODEL (5M) (in addition to or instead of LUXURY MODEL (5M) equipment): Viscous limited-slip differential; rear wing spoiler, side impact bars; power sliding and tilting glass sunroof with sunshade; additional exterior lights include front fog/driving lights; P195/60HR15 BSW A/S tires; air conditioning with climate control; garage door opener; driver's seat includes 4-way power adjustment, 8-way adjustment, passenger's seat includes 4-way adjustment; leather seats, leatherette door trim insert and leather-wrapped gearshift knob.

Base Prices

92051	Luxury (5M)	19522	21395
92851	Touring Model (5M)	21738	24095
	Destination Charge:	525	525

Interested in seeing what dealers will sell this vehicle for? Check out our True Market Value^{sm} (TMV^{sm}) pricing on our Web site at www.edmunds.com.

Accessories

4AT	Transmission: 4-Speed Automatic (Luxury)	730	800
4AT	Transmission: 4-Speed Automatic (Touring)	722	800
H02	Infiniti Communicator	1378	1599
	Includes 4 years of Infiniti Response Center Service and cellular service fees. REQUIRES V01.		

G20 / I30

INFINITI

CODE	DESCRIPTION	INVOICE	MSRP
K15	Painted Splash Guards	71	100
R13	6-Disc CD Changer	337	460
V01	Leather and Convenience Package (Luxury)	1132	1500
	Includes leather seating surfaces, leather-wrapped steering wheel, leather-wrapped shift knob, simulated leather door trim, power sliding glass sunroof with sunshade, 4-way power driver's seat, auto temperature control, HVAC microfilter ventilation and Homelink universal transceiver.		
X03	Heated Seats Package	362	420
	Includes heated driver and front passenger seats and heated outside mirrors. REQUIRES V01.		

2001 I30

What's New?

This year two new colors are added along with steering wheel-mounted controls, an anti-glare rearview mirror with integrated compass, and an emergency inside trunk release. The brilliant blue xenon headlights previously available only on Touring models can now be ordered on base Luxury trim cars as well.

Review

Last year brought about big changes for the I30. A new look and a new engine transformed this formerly glorified Nissan Maxima into a true performance luxury sedan. We like the current I30's combination of a buttery-smooth V6 fronting a roomy interior encapsulated in stylish sheetmetal that finally distances it from its cheaper Nissan-badged cousin.

Central to the I30's personality is a 3.0-liter, 24-valve DOHC aluminum V6 engine that makes 227 horsepower; 5 more horses than any Maxima save the 20th Anniversary special edition. Alas, in the Infiniti only a four-speed automatic transmission is available, transferring power to the front wheels.

The I30 boasts computer-assisted, speed-sensitive power steering that automatically adjusts to driving conditions, providing more assist when needed for easy parking, and more effort at high speeds for better feel and feedback. The multi-link beam rear underpinnings contribute to a smooth yet controlled ride, but you'd think a $30,000 entry-luxury sedan might offer a true independent rear suspension. Struts hold up the front end, and stabilizer bars front and rear keep body roll in check. Four-wheel disc ABS is standard, and traction control is optional.

Available in two trim levels, Luxury and Touring, Infiniti I30 comes well equipped in either guise. Luxury models include the usual upscale gewgaws, including leather seats, an express-open sunroof, automatic climate control, 200-watt Bose audio system and the much-ballyhooed (for good reason) power rear sunshade as standard equipment. Step up to the Touring model and Infiniti adds a viscous limited-slip differential, sport-ride suspension, xenon high-intensity headlamps, 17-inch wheels and performance-oriented P225/50VR17 tires.

Inside the I30, consumers will find comfortable seating for five adults and a surprisingly roomy rear seat. The eight-way power-adjustable driver's seat includes lumbar support, two-position memory and an automatic entry/exit system. Side airbags that protect the head and chest deploy from the sides of both front seats. A height-adjustable center armrest with dual-level

INFINITI
I30

storage compartment, signature Infiniti analog clock, and one-touch open and close power windows are also included on all I30s.

Other interesting features on the I30 include active front headrests, which automatically move up and forward during a rear-end collision to protect against whiplash. A HomeLink universal transmitter, which allows you to activate your house lights and garage door from inside the car, is standard on Touring models. Buyers can opt for a Birdview navigation system that pops up from the top of the dashboard, and a trunk-mounted six-CD changer is available, though we wish Infiniti used an in-dash model for optimal convenience. Infiniti Communicator, a telematics system similar to OnStar from General Motors, is also optional on I30, providing one-touch calling for emergency or roadside assistance.

With its classy looks, smooth and powerful V6, and long list of standard and available features, the I30 Luxury delivers a true luxury sedan experience that doesn't entail typical luxury sedan payments. And if you're looking for a reliable, good-looking sport sedan with room for five, the I30 Touring should be on your test drive list.

Standard Equipment

LUXURY (4A): 3L V6 DOHC SMPI 24-valve engine (requires premium unleaded fuel); 4-speed electronic OD automatic transmission with lock-up torque converter; battery with run down protection; 110 amp alternator; front-wheel drive, 3.79 axle ratio; stainless steel exhaust with tailpipe finisher; comfort ride suspension, front independent strut suspension with anti-roll bar, front coil springs, rear non-independent multi-link suspension with anti-roll bar, rear coil springs; rack-and-pinion power steering with engine speed-sensing assist; 4-wheel antilock disc brakes; 18.5 gal. capacity fuel tank; side impact bars; express-open/close sliding and tilting glass sunroof with sunshade; front and rear body-colored bumpers with chrome bumper insert; body-colored bodyside molding; clearcoat monotone paint; aero-composite halogen fully auto headlamps; additional exterior lights include cornering lights, front fog/driving lights; driver's and passenger's power remote body-colored folding outside mirrors; 16" x 6.5" silver alloy wheels; P215/55HR16 BSW A/S tires; compact steel spare wheel; air conditioning with climate control, air filter, rear heat ducts; premium AM/FM stereo radio, seek-scan feature, cassette player, single-disc CD player, 7 premium speakers, amplifier, auto equalizer, window grid diversity antenna, radio steering wheel controls; cruise control with steering wheel controls; power door locks with 2-stage unlock, remote keyless entry, child-safety rear door locks, power remote hatch/trunk release, power remote fuel door release; 2 power accessory outlets, front lighter element(s), driver's foot rest, retained accessory power, garage door opener, smokers' package; instrumentation display includes tachometer, water temperature gauge, clock, compass, exterior temp, trip odometer; warning indicators include oil pressure, battery, lights on, key in ignition, low fuel, bulb failure, door ajar, trunk ajar, brake fluid; driver's and passenger's front airbags, driver's and front passenger's seat-mounted side airbags; ignition disable, panic alarm, security system; tinted windows, power front and rear windows with driver's and passenger's 1-touch down function; variable-speed intermittent front windshield wipers, sun visor strip, rear window defroster, rear power blind; seating capacity of 5, front bucket seats with adjustable headrests, center armrest with storage, driver's seat includes 8-way power adjustment, lumbar support, passenger's seat includes 4-way power adjustment; 60/40 folding rear bench seat with adjustable headrests, center armrest; height-adjustable front seatbelts with pretensioners; leather seats, leatherette door trim insert, full cloth headliner, full carpet floor covering with carpeted floor mats, leather-wrapped gearshift knob, simulated wood door panel insert, simulated wood console insert, chrome interior accents; memory on driver's seat with 2 memory setting(s); interior lights include dome light with fade, front reading lights, 2 door curb lights, illuminated entry; leather-wrapped steering wheel with tilt adjustment; dual illuminated vanity mirrors, dual auxiliary visors; auto-dimming day/night rearview mirror; full floor console, mini overhead console with storage, locking glove box with light, front and rear cupholders, instrument panel covered bin, 2 seatback storage pockets, driver's and passenger's door bins; carpeted cargo floor, carpeted trunk lid, cargo net, cargo light; chrome grille, chrome side window moldings, black front windshield molding, black rear window molding and chrome door handles.

I30 / Q45 — INFINITI

CODE	DESCRIPTION	INVOICE	MSRP

TOURING (4A) (in addition to or instead of LUXURY (4A) equipment): Viscous limited-slip differential, sport-ride suspension; aero-composite high intensity fully auto headlamps; 17" x 7" silver alloy wheels; P225/50VR17 BSW A/S tires.

Base Prices

		Invoice	MSRP
95011	Luxury (4A)	26935	29465
95711	Touring (4A)	28079	31540
	Destination Charge:	525	525

Interested in seeing what dealers will sell this vehicle for? Check out our True Market Value^{sm} (TMV^{sm}) pricing on our Web site at www.edmunds.com.

Accessories

Code	Description	Invoice	MSRP
B03	Touring Sport Package (Touring) *Includes rear spoiler and side sills.*	887	1000
H02	Infiniti Communicator *Includes 4 years of Infiniti Response Center Service and 4 years cellular service fees. NOT AVAILABLE with J10.*	1378	1599
J10	Sunroof and Sunshade Delete (Luxury) *Deletes power sunroof with 1-touch open feature and power rear sunshade. NOT AVAILABLE with H02, T01, N05.*	(868)	(1000)
K60	6-Disc CD Changer *NOT AVAILABLE with U01.*	336	460
N05	Xenon Headlights (Luxury) *NOT AVAILABLE with J10.*	416	500
R02	Side Sills (Touring)	445	500
T01	Traction Control System *REQUIRES X03. NOT AVAILABLE with J10.*	268	300
U01	Infiniti Navigation System and Audio Package *Includes trunk-mounted 6-disc CD autochanger. NOT AVAILABLE with K60.*	2166	2400
W11	Painted Splash Guards	82	110
X03	Heated Seats Package *Includes heated front seats, heated sideview mirrors, heavy duty battery and low windshield washer fluid warning light.*	374	420

2001 Q45

What's New?

Few changes accompany the current Q45 as it gasps a few final breaths before a welcome, and long overdue, redesign debuts in spring of 2001. A new Luxury model replaces last year's Anniversary Edition. All Qs get body-colored door handles and license plate surrounds, revised taillights, real bird's eye maple wood interior trim, and a leather-wrapped steering wheel rim trimmed in ersatz timber. The Touring model has standard bright-finish 17-inch wheels.

Review

As the second-generation Q45 enters its final year of production, Infiniti openly admits that the current car represents less than the sum of its parts. A new Q is due soon, and Nissan's

INFINITI   Q45

luxury division is hyping the redesigned car as a true performance-oriented competitor to the Lexus LS 430, BMW 7 Series and Mercedes-Benz S-Class. Currently, the Q45 more effectively dukes it out with the likes of the mushy Acura RL and the cushy Cadillac DeVille.

Not surprisingly, changes to the Q45 for 2001 are limited. A new Luxury model replaces last year's Anniversary Edition, while the sport-themed Touring model continues to slot in as the top-dog version of Infiniti's flagship. Real bird's eye maple wood trim decorates the cabins of both versions, though the lumber on the steering wheel rim is simulated. Touring models get standard bright-finish 17-inch alloy wheels.

Just as one would expect inside a premium sedan from a luxury marque, all Qs overflow with sumptuous features. Eight-way power leather seats, a 200-watt Bose sound system, driver's seat memory, automatic climate control, power sunroof, power tilt/telescoping steering wheel, power rear sunshade, and keyless entry are standard.

An optional navigation system with an exclusive 3D "Birdview" display is available, but it relies on nine regional CDs to map the entire country, and the car comes standard only with the disc that details the region where you live. Better get a Rand McNally. Heated front seats, a cellular phone, Infiniti Communicator and a six-disc CD changer are other notable options.

Powered by a DOHC, 4.1-liter V8 engine, the rear-wheel-drive Q45 is swift if not quick, despite its 266 horsepower and 278 ft-lbs. of torque. At least the tune-up interval measures 100,000 miles, and fuel economy is decent at 18/23 city/highway.

Overall, the Q45 offers a luxurious ride that is perfect for cross-country cruising but not canyon carving. The Luxury model comes with a four-wheel independent suspension, speed-sensing power-assisted steering, traction control and a viscous limited-slip differential. Sixteen-inch alloy wheels and four-wheel disc brakes, with ABS of course, give this Infiniti a secure and confident feel.

You can opt for the Touring model if your tastes run to the performance end of the luxury-sedan spectrum. While the addition of an electronically controlled suspension (complete with driver-adjustable settings) and 17-inch wheels wearing performance tires give the Touring Q a more commanding feel of the road, don't fool yourself into thinking that you can keep up with the 540i that just blew by you. The smaller Bimmer's got a 16-horsepower advantage and an optional six-speed manual transmission while the Q45 comes only in four-speed automatic form.

Infiniti has built a small but loyal following for the Q45 by offering a solid mix of luxurious appointments and stylish sheetmetal backed by a legendary red carpet service experience. Add to this the relatively low sticker price and the current Q45 has plenty to offer the luxury-sedan buyer.

If you care more about a quiet and comfortable highway ride than you do about quarter-mile times and slalom speeds, the current Q45 makes an excellent choice. But time is running out to acquire Japan's vision of the Buick Park Avenue. The 2002 Q returns the nameplate to its performance roots this March.

Standard Equipment

BASE (4A): 4.1L V8 DOHC SMPI 32-valve engine with variable valve timing (requires premium unleaded fuel); 4-speed electronic OD automatic transmission with lock-up torque converter; 110 amp alternator; rear-wheel drive, viscous limited-slip differential, traction control, 3.69 axle ratio; stainless steel exhaust with tailpipe finisher; front independent strut suspension with anti-roll bar, front coil springs, rear independent multi-link suspension with anti-roll bar, rear coil springs; rack-and-pinion power steering with vehicle-speed-sensing assist; 4-wheel antilock disc brakes; 21.4 gal. capacity fuel tank; side impact bars; express open/close sliding and tilting glass sunroof with sunshade; front and rear body-colored bumpers with chrome bumper insert;

Q45

INFINITI

| CODE | DESCRIPTION | INVOICE | MSRP |

with chrome bodyside insert; clearcoat monotone paint; internally adjustable aero-composite high intensity fully auto headlamps; additional exterior lights include front fog/driving lights, underhood light; driver's and passenger's power remote body-colored heated folding outside mirrors; 16" x 7" silver alloy wheels; P215/60VR16 BSW A/S tires; compact alloy spare wheel; air conditioning with climate control, air filter, rear heat ducts; premium AM/FM stereo radio, seek-scan feature, cassette player, single-disc CD player, 8 premium speakers, power retractable diversity antenna, radio steering wheel controls; cruise control with steering wheel controls; power door locks with 2-stage unlock, remote keyless entry, child-safety rear door locks, power remote hatch/trunk release, power remote fuel door release; cell phone pre-wiring, 4 power accessory outlets, front and rear lighter element(s), trunk pull-down, driver's foot rest, retained accessory power, garage door opener, smokers' package; instrumentation display includes tachometer, water temperature gauge, clock, exterior temp, trip odometer; warning indicators include oil pressure, battery, lights on, key in ignition, low fuel, low washer fluid, bulb failure, door ajar, trunk ajar, brake fluid; driver's and passenger's front airbags, driver's and front passenger's seat-mounted side airbags; ignition disable, panic alarm, tracker system, security system; tinted windows, power front and rear windows with driver's and passenger's 1-touch down function; variable-speed intermittent front windshield wipers, sun visor strip, rear window defroster, rear power blind; seating capacity of 5, front bucket seats with adjustable tilt headrests, center armrest with storage, driver's seat includes 8-way power adjustment and power 2-way lumbar support, passenger's seat includes 8-way power adjustment and power 2-way lumbar support; rear bench seat with adjustable headrests, center armrest with storage; height-adjustable front seatbelts with pretensioners; leather seats, leatherette door trim insert, full cloth headliner, full carpet floor covering with carpeted floor mats, genuine wood dashboard insert, leather-wrapped gearshift knob, genuine wood door panel insert, genuine wood console insert, chrome interior accents; driver's seat memory includes 2 settings for steering wheel; interior lights include dome light with fade, front and rear reading lights, 4 door curb lights, illuminated entry; leather/simulated wood steering wheel with power tilt and telescopic adjustment; dual illuminated vanity mirrors, dual auxiliary visors; auto-dimming day/night rearview mirror; full floor console, locking glove box with light, front and rear cupholders, 2 seatback storage pockets, driver's and passenger's door bins, rear door bins; carpeted cargo floor, carpeted trunk lid, carpeted cargo mats, cargo net, cargo light; chrome grille, chrome side window moldings, chrome front windshield molding, chrome rear window molding and body-colored door handles.

TOURING (4A) (in addition to or instead of BASE (4A) equipment): Sport-ride suspension, driver adjustable ride control, 17" x 7.5" machined alloy wheels; P225/50VR17 BSW performance A/S tires and black grille.

Base Prices

94311	Base (4A)	44014	48895
94811	Touring (4A)	45039	50595
Destination Charge:		525	525

Interested in seeing what dealers will sell this vehicle for? Check out our True Market Value^{sm} (TMV^{sm}) pricing on our Web site at www.edmunds.com.

Accessories

E10	Two-Tone Paint	431	500
G50	Painted Splash Guards	81	110
H02	Infiniti Communicator	1378	1599
	Includes 4 years of Infiniti Response Center service and cellular service fees.		
K02	6-Disc CD Changer	332	460
K60	6-Disc CD Changer	332	460
	Trunk-mounted. NOT AVAILABLE with K02.		

INFINITI   Q45

CODE	DESCRIPTION	INVOICE	MSRP
S92	Rear Spoiler	395	530
U01	Infiniti Navigation System and Audio Package	2166	2400
	Includes 6-disc CD autochanger. NOT AVAILABLE with K02 or K60.		
X03	Heated Front Seats	378	420

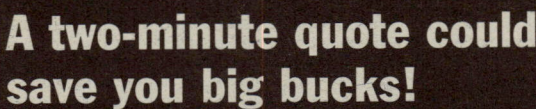

A two-minute quote could save you big bucks!

eCoverage's online quote-to-claim insurance services deliver all the benefits savvy Internet buyers like you have come to expect. And eCoverage is backed by some of the world's biggest financial institutions.

VISIT edmunds.com/insurance

S-TYPE — JAGUAR

2001 S-TYPE

What's New?

The S-Type gets new 10-spoke alloy wheels for 2001, along with exterior color options Onyx White and Roman Bronze. The folks at Jaguar have decided to move the six-disc CD changer from the glove box to the trunk. ISOFIX is added to the rear for securing child seats and Reverse Park Control now comes standard. An electronically controlled, speed-proportional power steering system is new this year and the software for the Voice Activation Control system has been upgraded. A Deluxe Communications Package featuring a Motorola Timeport digital phone system is a new option.

Review

The S-Type's exterior is the first clue that this is no XJ/XK knock-off. The quad headlights and small front grille give the sedan a classic look not seen on Jaguars for 30 years. Subtle character lines run down the otherwise smooth body, but some say the roofline and taillight section bear a resemblance to Ford's Taurus.

Inside, the S-Type is pure Jaguar in appearance, with acres of wood and leather covering every surface. However, much of the interior's componentry and switchgear is identical to that found in the less expensive Lincoln LS, which rides on the same platform. Despite its smaller exterior size, the S-Type boasts a longer wheelbase than Jaguar's XJ models and interior dimensions on par with its larger sedans. A standard split-folding rear seat further adds to this Jag's utility.

But the S-Type's interior has problems that go beyond the preponderance of Ford switchgear. The overall layout is functional but some serious flaws keep it from living up to what we'd expect from a $50,000 automobile. Items like the shallow and dull wood grain trim with ash pattern, the insultingly cheap plastic panel beneath the steering column, and a one-touch down window for no one but the driver leave us unimpressed.

Power for the S-Type comes from either Jaguar's 4.0-liter V8 or Ford's 3.0-liter Duratec V6. While the V8 is a slightly less-powerful version of the engine found in Jaguar's XK8, it still makes 281 horsepower and 287 foot-pounds of torque. The V6 uses a Ford block while Jaguar's variable-valve-timing heads, intake system and drive-by-wire throttle body top the Blue Oval low-end. These changes add 55 horsepower to the Duratec V6, giving it 240 horsepower and 212 foot-pounds of torque. A five-speed automatic is the only transmission available in the S-Type.

As with the LS, suspension components in the S-Type are primarily forged aluminum. Unlike the Lincoln, however, the Jaguar offers a sport package featuring a Computer Active Technology Suspension (CATS) system that constantly adjusts the car's Bilstein shocks. A yaw-control system is also on tap to keep the S-Type from misbehaving even when the driver does.

Additional high-tech toys include a reverse-park control system, a GPS navigation system, and a voice-operated climate control system.

Looks notwithstanding, the S-Type is anything but a classic Jaguar, which, for the purposes of mass-market appeal, is not a bad thing.

Standard Equipment

3.0L V6 (5A): 3L V6 DOHC SMPI with variable valve timing 24-valve engine, (requires premium unleaded fuel); 5-speed electronic OD automatic transmission with lock-up converter; 680-amp battery with rundown protection; driver's selectable multi-mode transmission; rear-wheel drive,

JAGUAR

S-TYPE

| CODE | DESCRIPTION | INVOICE | MSRP |

traction control, 3.31 axle ratio; dual stainless steel exhaust with tailpipe finisher; front independent double-wishbone suspension with anti-roll bar, front coil springs, rear independent double-wishbone suspension with anti-roll bar, rear coil springs; rack-and-pinion power steering with vehicle-speed-sensing assist; 4-wheel disc brakes with 4-wheel antilock braking system; 18.4 gal. capacity fuel tank; side impact bars; front and rear body-colored bumpers with chrome bumper insert; clearcoat monotone paint; aero-composite halogen fully automatic headlamps with delay-off feature; additional exterior lights include front fog/driving lights; driver's and passenger's power remote body-colored heated folding outside mirrors; 16" x 7.5" silver alloy wheels with P225/55HR16 BSW A/S tires; full-size alloy spare wheel; dual-zone front air conditioning with climate control, air filter, rear heat ducts; AM/FM stereo w/clock, seek-scan feature, cassette player, CD changer pre-wiring, 4 speakers, window grid diversity antenna, radio steering wheel controls; cruise control with steering wheel controls; power door locks with 2-stage unlock, remote keyless-entry, child-safety rear door locks, power remote hatch/trunk release, power remote fuel door release; cellphone pre-wiring, 1 power accessory outlet, front lighter element, driver's foot rest, retained accessory power, smokers' package; instrumentation display includes tachometer, water temperature gauge, exterior temp, systems monitor, trip computer, trip odometer; warning indicators include oil pressure, water temp, battery, low coolant, lights on, key in ignition, low fuel, low washer fluid, bulb failure, door ajar, trunk ajar, brake fluid; driver's and passenger's front airbags, driver's and front passenger's seat-mounted side airbags; ignition disable, panic alarm, security system; tinted windows, power front and rear windows with driver's 1-touch down function; heated variable-speed intermittent front windshield wipers, rear window defroster; seating capacity of 5, front bucket seats with adjustable tilt headrests, center armrest with storage, driver's and front passenger's seats include 8-way power seat with lumbar support; 60/40 folding rear bench seat with adjustable headrests, center armrest; height-adjustable front seatbelts with pretensioners; leather seats, leather door trim insert, full cloth headliner, full carpet floor covering with carpeted floor mats, genuine-wood dashboard insert, wood gearshift knob, genuine-wood door panel insert, genuine-wood console insert, chrome interior accents; interior lights include dome light with fade, front and rear reading lights, door curb lights, illuminated entry; leather/genuine-wood steering wheel with power tilt and telescopic adjustment; dual illuminated vanity mirrors; day/night rearview mirror; full floor console, mini overhead console locking glove box with light, front cupholder, instrument panel covered bin, 2 seatback storage pockets, driver's and passenger's door bins, rear door bins; carpeted cargo floor, carpeted trunk lid, cargo tie downs, cargo light; chrome grille, chrome side window moldings, black front windshield molding, black rear window molding and body-colored door handles.

4.0L V8 (5A) (in addition to or instead of 3.0L V6 (5A) equipment): 4L V8 DOHC SMPI with variable valve timing 32-valve engine, front express-open sliding and tilting glass sunroof with sunshade; trunk-mounted 6-disc CD changer, amplifier; garage door opener; instrumentation display includes park distance control; driver's and front passenger's seats include power 2-way lumbar support; driver's seat memory includes 2 settings for exterior mirrors and steering wheel; auto-dimming day/night rearview mirror.

Base Prices

JAG1	3.0L V6 (5A)	39289	43655
JAG2	4.0L V8 (5A)	44419	49355
Destination Charge:		595	595

Interested in seeing what dealers will sell this vehicle for? Check out our True Market Value^{sm} (TMV^{sm}) pricing on our Web site at www.edmunds.com.

S-TYPE JAGUAR

CODE	DESCRIPTION	INVOICE	MSRP

Accessories

Code	Description	Invoice	MSRP
DC	Deluxe Communications Package	3644	4300

Includes 4-year subscription to Jaguar Assist emergency messaging system (VEMS), console-mounted portable cellular phone with voice-activated controls, voice-activated audio controls; navigation system. REQUIRES PM. NOT AVAILABLE with PHONE.

| NS | Navigation System | 1680 | 2000 |

Parts of the continental USA, Alaska, Hawaii and Puerto Rico are not detail-mapped. Please consult your Map Data CD Coverage Guide for a complete listing of these areas. REQUIRES PM.

| PM | Power/Memory Package (V6) | 1680 | 2000 |

Includes power tilt and slide glass moonroof, driver's seat memory includes settings for mirrors and steering wheel, power driver/passenger lumbar, electrochromic rearview mirror with compass, programmable garage door opener and electric steering wheel adjust.

| PS | Premium Sound Package (V6) | 1260 | 1500 |

Includes 175-Watt sound system, AM/FM radio cassette player and compact 6-disc CD autochanger. REQUIRES PM.

| PW | Power/Memory/Weather Package (V6) | 2688 | 3200 |

Includes heated front seats, rain-sensing wipers, Dynamic Stability Control (DSC), power/memory package, power tilt and slide glass moonroof, driver's seat memory includes settings for mirrors and steering wheel, power driver/passenger lumbar, electrochromic rearview mirror with compass, programmable garage door opener, electric steering wheel adjust. NOT AVAILABLE with WR.

| SK | Sport Package (SK) | 924 | 1100 |

Includes 17" sport wheels and P235/50ZR17 tires; Computer Active Technology Suspension (CATS). REQUIRES PM.

| WA | Weather/Sport Package (V8) | 1932 | 2300 |

Includes weather package, heated front seats, rain-sensing wipers, Dynamic Stability Control (DSC).

| WQ | Power/Memory/Weather/Sport Package (V6) | 3612 | 4300 |

Includes heated front seats, rain-sensing wipers, Dynamic Stability Control (DSC), power tilt and slide glass moonroof, driver's seat memory includes settings for mirrors and steering wheel, power driver/passenger lumbar, electrochromic rearview mirror with compass, programmable garage door opener, electric steering wheel adjust; 17" sport wheels with P235/50ZR17 tires, Computer Active Technology Suspension (CATS). NOT AVAILABLE with WR.

| WR | Power/Memory/Sport Package (V6) | 2604 | 3100 |

Includes power tilt and slide glass moonroof, driver's seat memory includes settings for mirrors and steering wheel, power driver/passenger lumbar, electrochromic rearview mirror with compass, programmable garage door opener, electric steering wheel adjust, 17" sport wheels with P235/50ZR17 tires, Computer Active Technology Suspension (CATS). NOT AVAILABLE with WQ, PW.

| WT | Weather Package (V8) | 1008 | 1200 |

Includes heated front seats, rain-sensing wipers and Dynamic Stability Control (DSC).

KIA

RIO

CODE	DESCRIPTION	INVOICE	MSRP

2001 RIO

What's New?

With a base MSRP that makes it the least expensive car in America, the roomy little Rio is a peppy 96-horsepower entry-level sedan. While the design of and materials used on this car are nothing to write home about, build quality is impressively tight. And Kia's new Long Haul Warranty Program offers the added security of a 10-year/100,000-mile limited powertrain warranty, along with impressive levels of bumper-to-bumper and roadside assistance coverage.

Review

Kia's determined to get a tenacious hold on the econo-car market, and with the introduction of the appealingly inexpensive Rio, along with their impressive new Long Haul Warranty Program, they may well be on their way to doing just that.

The 1.5-liter DOHC four-cylinder, the only engine available on the Rio, is surprisingly peppy, making 98 foot-pounds of torque at 4,500 rpm, and providing quick acceleration from a stop as well as adequate passing power on the highways. Over 75 mph, the engine serenades the driver with an incessant whine, but maintains speed quite well. The optional four-speed automatic tranny has an overdrive-off button to avoid gear searching in the hills.

The wedge-shaped exterior design of the Rio is inoffensive, if generic, while the interior is solidly screwed together, although the materials used reflect the bargain-basement price of this subcompact sedan. Hard plastics and cheesy upholstery abound, but rattles and squeaks are still kept to a minimum within the cabin. Outside, the Rio boasts upscale-looking clear lens headlights and, with the $380 upgrade package, wheel covers and bodyside moldings. Alloy wheels are available as an independent option for $275, and you get a nifty spoiler for 85 bones.

Antilock brakes are not standard equipment, but you can get them for $400 with or without the upgrade package. Air conditioning, which works beautifully without hampering engine power too much, will run you another $750, and you can choose either an AM/FM/cassette stereo or an AM/FM/CD stereo, but you can't get both.

The inside of this thrifty sedan is logically and simply laid out. Radio controls are conveniently placed above the HVAC switchgear, although the climate controls are set a little too low in the center stack for optimum ergonomic affability. Buttons and switches are all big enough and easy to find and use, and the front seats are comfy, but lack lumbar support. The rear seat feels like a park bench, but interior room is pretty impressive for a vehicle of this size. One accouterment of which Kia is especially proud is the driver's seat fold-down armrest, but it's pretty much useless with the stick shift, and in fact impedes arm movement somewhat even in the folded-up position.

The Rio behaves well on the road, with a tight suspension that keeps body roll to a minimum, but communicates irregularities in the tarmac directly to the driver. The steering is tight and accurate for a vehicle at this price point, but the lack of refinement is apparent in the vibration through the gas pedal and shifter.

The Rio competes with the Hyundai Accent, the Daewoo Lanos and the Toyota Echo, while being cheaper than all three and still displaying solid build quality. It's definitely worth checking out if you're low on ducats.

RIO / SEPHIA

KIA

| CODE | DESCRIPTION | INVOICE | MSRP |

Standard Equipment

BASE (5M): 1.5L I4 DOHC MPI 16-valve engine; 5-speed OD manual transmission; front-wheel drive; partial stainless steel exhaust; front independent strut suspension with anti-roll bar, front coil springs, rear semi-independent torsion suspension with anti-roll bar, rear coil springs; rack-and-pinion manual steering; front disc/rear drum brakes; 11.9 gal. capacity fuel tank; side impact bars; front and rear body-colored bumpers; clearcoat monotone paint; aero-composite halogen headlamps; driver's and passenger's manual remote black folding outside mirrors; 13" x 5" steel wheels, P175/70HR13 BSW A/S tires; compact steel spare wheel; 4 speakers, manual retractable antenna; child-safety rear door locks, remote trunk release, remote fuel door release; 2 power accessory outlets, front lighter element; driver's foot rest, smokers' package; instrumentation display includes water temperature gauge, trip odometer; warning indicators include oil pressure, battery, lights on, key in ignition, low fuel, door ajar; driver's and passenger's front airbags; tinted windows, manual front and rear windows; fixed-interval front windshield wipers, rear window defroster; seating capacity of 5, front bucket seats with adjustable headrests, center armrest, driver's and front passenger's seat includes 4-way adjustment; rear bench seat; height-adjustable front seatbelts with pretensioners; cloth seats, cloth door trim insert, full cloth headliner, full carpet floor covering; interior lights include dome light; day/night rearview mirror; full floor console, glove box, front cupholder, instrument panel bin, 2 seatback storage pockets, driver's and passenger's door bins; carpeted cargo floor, cargo light; black grille, black side window moldings, black front windshield molding, black rear window molding and black door handles.

Base Prices

31201	Base Sedan (5M)	8466	8895
Destination Charge:	....	450	450

Interested in seeing what dealers will sell this vehicle for? Check out our True Market Value^{sm} (TMV^{sm}) pricing on our Web site at www.edmunds.com.

Accessories

AB	4-Wheel Antilock Brakes	362	400
AC	Air Conditioning	672	750
AT	Transmission: 4-Speed Automatic with OD	826	875
AW	Wheels: 13" Alloy	233	275
CD	Radio: AM/FM CD Stereo	337	395
	NOT AVAILABLE with RM.		
CF	Carpeted Floor Mats	50	69
RM	Radio: AM/FM Cassette Stereo	260	320
	NOT AVAILABLE with CD player.		
SP	Rear Spoiler	68	85
UP	Upgrade Package	326	380
	Includes power steering, tilt steering wheel, full wheel covers, bodyside moldings and dual vanity mirrors.		

2001 SEPHIA

What's New?

The 2001 Sephia features new safety items such as child seat anchors, front seatbelt pretensioners and an emergency internal trunk release. Changes for the 2001 model year also include dual visor vanity mirrors, a coin tray and a gas-cap tether.

KIA SEPHIA

Review

The Kia Sephia is proving itself a contender in the compact sedan market, greatly aided by its extreme affordability. Two trim levels are offered and both come equipped with a 1.8-liter four-cylinder engine that delivers 125 horsepower to the front wheels through a standard five-speed manual transmission. A responsive four-speed automatic is optional.

Base equipment on the Sephia includes power steering, four-wheel independent suspension with front and rear stabilizer bars, wheel covers, dual exterior mirrors, theft-deterrent system, rear defogger, cassette stereo, 60/40 split-folding rear seat and fabric upholstery. The upgraded LS adds air conditioning, power windows and door locks, bodyside moldings, tilt steering wheel and a driver's seat cushion tilt feature. Buyers can add wood grain dash appliqués, a rear spoiler and floor mats to any Sephia, but goodies like cruise control, alloy wheels, power mirrors and ABS are limited to the more expensive LS.

Upscale styling tweaks make Sephia appear more expensive than a car this cheap has a right to look. Even build quality ranks high for a vehicle in this class, based upon our experience. Slam any one of the four doors and you will be rewarded with an impressive "thunk" usually reserved for Hondas and Toyotas. Oddly, however, Kia often scores well below average in terms of initial quality according to J.D. Power & Associates, as reported by owners of the car.

The Sephia is certainly not a performance car, despite its optional rear spoiler, but the motor makes a decent 108 ft-lbs. of torque. This allows the 2,500-pound Sephia to scoot away from stoplights with authority, but the engine doesn't generate much passing thrust at higher rpms where the engine makes more racket than power.

Boasting a capable, Lotus-tuned suspension, Sephia is severely hampered by cheap original equipment tires, which are noisy and make for sloppy handling in the twisties. The front disc/rear drum brakes, available with ABS on LS models, won't help in this regard, proving weak and generally ineffective with lousy pedal feel.

Perhaps the Sephia's greatest strength, aside from a low price and extensive warranty package, lies in its roomy interior, which, according to Kia, is larger than the 2000 Honda Civic and Toyota Corolla, among others. With a truly useable rear seat, four adults can fit with a minimum of contortion.

Sephia offers better up front, out-of-pocket value than many competitors. The new Kia Long Haul Warranty Program helps this value equation. It consists of a 10-year/100,000-mile limited powertrain warranty, a five-year/60,000-mile limited basic warranty, a five-year/100,000-mile anti-perforation warranty (which protects against holes in the body caused by rust) and a five-year, unlimited mileage roadside assistance plan.

But, is that enough to sway buyers? Unimpressive mechanicals and a bad rep for quality will, for some penny-pinching consumers, be offset by the low price and great warranty. The Sephia would never be called a great car, but for some, it might prove to be a good bargain.

Standard Equipment

BASE (5M): 1.8L I4 DOHC MPI 16-valve engine; 5-speed OD manual transmission; 520-amp battery; 70-amp alternator; front-wheel drive, 4.78 axle ratio; partial stainless steel exhaust; front independent strut suspension with anti-roll bar, front coil springs, rear independent multi-link suspension with anti-roll bar, rear coil springs; rack-and-pinion power steering with engine-speed-sensing assist; front disc/rear drum brakes; 13.2 gal. capacity fuel tank; side impact bars; front and rear body-colored bumpers; clearcoat monotone paint; aero-composite halogen headlamps; driver's and passenger's manual remote body-colored folding outside mirrors; 14" x 5.5" steel wheels, P185/65HR14 BSW A/S tires; compact steel spare wheel; AM/FM stereo, seek-scan feature, cassette player, 4 speakers, fixed antenna; child-safety rear door locks,

SEPHIA / SPECTRA — KIA

remote trunk release, remote fuel door release; 1 power accessory outlet, front lighter element, driver's foot rest, smokers' package; instrumentation display includes water temperature gauge, in-dash clock, trip odometer; warning indicators include oil pressure, battery, lights on, key in ignition, low fuel, door ajar, brake fluid; driver's and passenger's front airbags; tinted windows, manual front and rear windows; fixed-interval front windshield wipers, rear window defroster; seating capacity of 5, front bucket seats with adjustable headrests, center armrest with storage, driver's and front passenger's seats include 4-way adjustment; 60/40 folding rear bench seat with fixed headrests; height-adjustable front seatbelts; cloth seats, cloth door trim insert, full cloth headliner, full carpet floor covering; interior lights include dome light; day/night rearview mirror; full floor console, glove box, front cupholder, instrument panel bin, driver's and passenger's door bins; carpeted cargo floor, cargo light; body-colored grille, black side window moldings, black front windshield molding, black rear window molding and body-colored door handles.

LS (5M) (in addition to or instead of BASE (5M) equipment): Body-colored bodyside molding; air conditioning; instrumentation display includes tachometer, power front and rear windows; driver's seat includes 6-way adjustment; steering wheel with tilt adjustment; passenger's side vanity mirror.

Base Prices

Code	Description	Invoice	MSRP
14203	Base Sedan (5M)	9914	10595
14243	LS Sedan (5M)	11325	12195
	Destination Charge:	450	450

Interested in seeing what dealers will sell this vehicle for? Check out our True Market Value^{sm} (TMV^{sm}) pricing on our Web site at www.edmunds.com.

Accessories

Code	Description	Invoice	MSRP
AC	Air Conditioning (Base)	772	900
AT	Transmission: 4-Speed Automatic w/OD	889	975
	Includes 3.83 axle ratio.		
AW	Wheels: Alloy (LS)	284	340
BM	Body-Color Bodyside Molding (Base)	63	85
CC	Cruise Control (LS)	208	250
CD	Radio: AM/FM Stereo w/CD Player (LS)	254	295
CF	Carpeted Floor Mats	53	70
CG	CD Changer (LS)	280	335
	REQUIRES CD.		
CP	Cruise Package (LS)	362	400
	Includes cruise control, tweeters, variable-speed windshield wipers, power mirrors.		
RK	Remote Keyless-Entry (LS)	173	250
SP	Rear Spoiler	137	175
WG	Woodgrain Appearance Package	114	149

2001 SPECTRA

What's New?

2001 sees few changes to Kia's sporty five-door hatchback, which was introduced last year to attract younger customers to the brand. The top-rung GSX trim level gets a gas-cap tether, coin holder and dual visor vanity mirrors. Kia's Long Haul Warranty Program has also been introduced for this model year.

KIA   SPECTRA

Review

Five-door hatchbacks have always been hot sellers in Asian and European markets, but American buyers have shunned the concept — so much so that Ford left the five-door hatchback out of the Focus lineup. The Spectra's duplicitous design does a good job of hiding the fact that it is indeed a five-door hatchback, and therein lays its appeal.

Two trim levels are available: GS and GSX. The sparsely equipped GS includes fabric upholstery, split-folding rear seat, cassette player, rear defroster and two-speed wipers. Optional equipment includes A/C, body-color side moldings, rear wiper/washer, floor mats and an automatic transmission. GSX adds alloy wheels, a rear spoiler, tape stripes and special fabric for a sporty look. It also provides power windows and locks, air conditioning and a tilt steering wheel. ABS, a CD player, cruise control and power windows are available only on GSX.

Powered by a Sephia-derived, 125-horsepower, 1.8-liter DOHC four-cylinder engine and mated to a standard five-speed manual gearbox (a four-speed automatic is optional), the Spectra provides decent fuel economy (23 city and 29 highway) but lacks capable acceleration off idle and during passing maneuvers. Additionally, the raucous motor makes an incessant whine at higher revs, which can grate on the driver's nerves.

Spectra proves to be a competent handler, exhibiting limited body roll and responsive steering. Cheap tires ruin the fun in the twisties. On the highway, the Spectra smoothes out any pavement irregularities, but floats like a boat over highway expansion joints despite the Lotus-tuned suspension. Front disc/rear drum brakes are barely adequate, requiring lots of pedal pressure that results in mediocre stopping performance.

Firm front seats are reasonably comfortable, with a decent amount of lumbar and thigh support, and the simple layout of the dashboard and controls makes the Spectra easy to manipulate. Rear seat riders get minimal legroom, and the canted rear glass impedes valuable headroom. Interior materials are not the Spectra's strong suit with headliner, dash panel, and seat fabric quality well below that of slightly more expensive competitors.

Higher-grade interior materials, along with a more powerful engine and improved brakes, would do wonders for this Kia's overall desirability. Still, you can't deny its substantial price and utility advantages over the competition. Plus, it looks good and sporty, thanks to aggressive styling in front and the fastback-style rear window.

Another incentive to consider the Spectra is Kia's new-for-2001 Long Haul Warranty Program, which consists of a 10-year/100,000-mile limited powertrain warranty, a five-year/60,000-mile limited basic warranty, a five-year/100,000-mile anti-perforation warranty (which protects against holes in the body caused by rust) and a five-year, unlimited mileage roadside assistance plan. This impressive package should add some peace of mind to Spectra ownership.

For first-time buyers and college students trying to survive on Top Ramen, as well as those who desire the utility that only a five-door hatchback can provide, the Spectra is worth a look. Others might want to consider shopping around, especially when Hyundai introduces the well-equipped and more powerful five-door Elantra GT later this year.

Standard Equipment

GS (5M): 1.8L I4 DOHC MPI 16-valve engine; 5-speed OD manual transmission; 520-amp battery; 70-amp alternator; front-wheel drive, 4.11 axle ratio; partial stainless steel exhaust with tailpipe finisher; front independent strut suspension with anti-roll bar, front coil springs, rear independent multi-link suspension with anti-roll bar, rear coil springs; rack-and-pinion power steering, engine-speed-sensing assist; front disc/rear drum brakes; 13.2 gal. capacity fuel tank; side impact bars; front and rear body-colored bumpers; clearcoat monotone paint; aero-composite halogen headlamps; driver's and passenger's manual remote body-colored folding

SPECTRA KIA

outside mirrors; 14" x 5.5" steel wheels, P185/65HR14 BSW A/S tires; compact steel spare wheel; rear heat ducts; AM/FM stereo w/seek-scan feature, cassette player, 4 speakers, fixed antenna; child-safety rear door locks, remote trunk release, remote fuel door release; 1 power accessory outlet, front lighter element, driver's foot rest, smokers' package; instrumentation display includes tachometer, water temperature gauge, in-dash clock, trip odometer; warning indicators include oil pressure, battery, lights on, key in ignition, low fuel, door ajar, brake fluid; driver's and passenger's front airbags; tinted windows, manual front and rear windows; fixed-interval front windshield wipers, rear window defroster; seating capacity of 5, front bucket seats with adjustable headrests, center armrest, driver's and front passenger's seats include 4-way adjustment; 60/40 folding rear bench seat with fixed headrests; height-adjustable front seatbelts; cloth seats, cloth door trim insert, full cloth headliner, full carpet floor covering; interior lights include dome light; day/night rearview mirror; full floor console, glove box, front cupholder, instrument panel bin, driver's and passenger's door bins; carpeted cargo floor, cargo light; body-colored grille, black side window moldings, black front windshield molding, black rear window molding and body-colored door handles.

GSX (5M) (in addition to or instead of GS (5M) equipment): Rear spoiler; rocker panel extensions; bodyside accent stripe; 14" x 6" silver alloy wheels; air conditioning; power front and rear windows with driver's 1-touch down function; leather-wrapped gearshift knob; leather-wrapped steering wheel with tilt adjustment.

Base Prices

Code	Description	Invoice	MSRP
24201	GS Sedan (5M)	10326	10995
24241	GSX Sedan (5M)	12391	13195
	Destination Charge:	450	450

Interested in seeing what dealers will sell this vehicle for? Check out our True Market Value^{sm} (TMV^{sm}) pricing on our Web site at www.edmunds.com.

Accessories

Code	Description	Invoice	MSRP
AB	4-Wheel Antilock Brakes (GSX)	769	800
AC	Air Conditioning (GS)	772	900
AT	Transmission: 4-Speed Automatic w/OD	889	975
	Includes 3.83 axle ratio.		
BM	Body-Color Bodyside Molding	63	85
CC	Cruise Control (GSX)	208	250
CD	Radio: AM/FM Stereo w/CD Player (GSX)	254	295
CF	Carpeted Floor Mats	53	70
CG	CD Changer (GSX)	280	335
	REQUIRES CD.		
CP	Cruise Package (GSX)	362	400
	Includes cruise control, tweeters, variable-speed intermittent wipers, power mirrors.		
RK	Remote Keyless Entry (GSX)	173	250
RW	Rear Wiper	68	95
SP	Rear Spoiler (GS)	161	200

LEXUS

ES 300

2001 ES 300

What's New?

A glow-in-the-dark emergency trunk release handle is now located in the cargo compartment, while child seat-tether anchors have been added inside.

Review

Starting this year, Lexus offers buyers with between $30,000 and $40,000 burning a hole in their pocket two decidedly different choices in the entry-luxury sedan arena. For those who love to drive, but not so much they'd like to shift their own gears, there is the small but stunning IS 300. For those who want what amounts to a high-quality Buick Regal with decent brand cachet, there is this Camry-based ES 300. The IS is hard-edged and muscular, while the ES is soft and pudgy around the middle. We predict that buyers of either car will likely resemble those remarks.

Fortunately, Lexus has done a much better job of masking the ES 300's lineage than Infiniti has done with the Maxima-derived I30. From the outside, you need to look deep beyond the ES 300's stylish duds to see the dowdy Toyota hiding in the structural framework. Inside, it's easier to tell that the Lexus is made of Toyota parts, thanks to shared switchgear between the two models. Is this a bad thing? Not necessarily, as Toyotas are generally solid, reliable, and refined. It just isn't different or better, making it harder to justify the extra premium over a loaded Camry XLE V6.

But then, you take a gander at the specifications sheet. The more powerful ES 300's smooth and silent 3.0-liter V6 produces 210 horsepower and 220 foot-pounds of torque, thanks in part to its Variable Valve Timing with intelligence system (VVT-i). The engine is capable of making 80 percent of peak torque available at 1,600 rpm, resulting in zero-to-60 runs of 8.3 seconds, according to Lexus. A slick-shifting four-speed automatic transmission sends power to the front wheels.

Standard goodies include multi-adjustable power front seats, automatic climate control, real California walnut wood trim, and a first-aid kit. A seven-speaker audio system with 195 watts of amplification is included, and a 230-watt Nakamichi sound system with an in-dash CD changer is optional. Notable available features include leather upholstery, a one-touch-open moonroof, upgraded 16-inch wheels and tires, an adaptive variable suspension system, high-intensity discharge headlights, and heat for the seats and exterior mirrors.

On the safety front, Lexus includes front and side airbags, antilock brakes, traction control, daytime running lights, and ALR/ELR, force-limiting three-point safety belts in all seating locations. Optional on ES 300 is Vehicle Skid Control (VSC), a stability control system that includes Brake Assist (a computerized controller that applies maximum braking force in panic stops quicker than the driver can). For 2001, Lexus has added a glow-in-the-dark release handle inside the trunk, as well as interior tether anchors for child safety seats.

Though the ES 300 is now the duller of the company's entry-luxury offerings in terms of raw performance, it perfectly suits those who want a comfortable, cushy cruiser that goes fast in a straight line, stops quickly, and looks good doing it.

Standard Equipment

ES 300 (4A): 3L V6 DOHC SMPI 24-valve engine with variable valve timing, (requires premium unleaded fuel); 4-speed electronic automatic transmission with lock-up torque converter; 80 amp alternator; driver's selectable multi-mode transmission oil cooler; front-wheel drive, traction

ES 300 — LEXUS

control, 2.64 axle ratio; stainless steel exhaust with tailpipe finisher; front independent strut suspension with anti-roll bar, front coil springs, rear independent strut suspension with anti-roll bar, rear coil springs; rack-and-pinion power steering with engine speed-sensing assist; 4-wheel antilock disc brakes; 18.5 gal. capacity fuel tank; side impact bars; front and rear colored bumpers; colored bodyside cladding; clearcoat lower accent two-tone paint; aero-composite halogen fully auto headlamps with daytime running lights, delay-off feature; additional exterior lights include front fog/driving lights; driver's and passenger's power remote body-colored heated folding outside mirrors, driver's auto-dimming outside mirror; 15" x 6" silver alloy wheels; P205/65VR15 BSW performance tires; full-size steel spare wheel; air conditioning with climate control, rear heat ducts; premium AM/FM stereo radio, seek-scan feature, cassette player, CD changer pre-wiring, 7 performance speakers, amplifier, graphic equalizer, theft deterrent, window grid diversity antenna; cruise control; power door locks with 2-stage unlock, remote keyless entry, child-safety rear door locks, power remote trunk release, power remote fuel door release; cell phone pre-wiring, 2 power accessory outlets, front lighter element(s), driver's foot rest, retained accessory power, smokers' package, first aid kit; instrumentation display includes tachometer, water temperature gauge, in-dash clock, exterior temp, trip odometer; warning indicators include oil pressure, battery, low oil level, lights on, key in ignition, low fuel, low washer fluid, bulb failure, door ajar; driver's and passenger's front airbags, driver's and front passenger's seat-mounted side airbags; ignition disable, panic alarm, security system; tinted windows, power front and rear windows with driver's and passenger's 1-touch down function; variable-speed intermittent front windshield wipers, sun visor strip, rear window defroster; seating capacity of 5, front bucket seats with adjustable tilt headrests, center armrest with storage, driver's seat includes 8-way power adjustment, power 2-way lumbar support, passenger's seat includes 8-way power adjustment; rear bench seat with tilt headrests, center pass-thru armrest; height-adjustable front seatbelts with pretensioners; premium cloth seats, cloth door trim insert, full cloth headliner, full carpet floor covering with carpeted floor mats, genuine wood dashboard insert, leather-wrapped gearshift knob, genuine wood door panel insert, genuine wood console insert; interior lights include dome light with delay front reading lights, 2 door curb lights, illuminated entry; leather-wrapped steering wheel with tilt adjustment; dual illuminated vanity mirrors, dual auxiliary visors; auto-dimming day/night rearview mirror; full floor console, mini overhead console with storage, locking glove box with light, front and rear cupholders, instrument panel bin, 2 seatback storage pockets, driver's and passenger's door bins; carpeted cargo floor, cargo light; chrome grille, chrome side window moldings, black front windshield molding, chrome rear window molding and body-colored door handles.

Base Prices

CODE	DESCRIPTION	INVOICE	MSRP
9000	ES 300 (4A)	27365	31505
	Destination Charge:	545	545

Interested in seeing what dealers will sell this vehicle for? Check out our True Market Value^{sm} (TMV^{sm}) pricing on our Web site at www.edmunds.com.

Accessories

CODE	DESCRIPTION	INVOICE	MSRP
DC	Lexus In-Dash 6 CD Auto-Changer	864	1080
EA	Adaptive Variable Suspension (AVS)	496	620
	REQUIRES LA or VP or VK.		
FT	Tires: All Season	NC	NC
	NOT AVAILABLE with TI, TU.		
GP	Gold Kit	179	279
	Includes all gold plated emblems on the vehicle (except wheels).		
HH	Heated Front Seats	352	440
	REQUIRES LA or VP or VK.		
HL	High Intensity Discharge (HID) Headlamps	412	515

LEXUS — ES 300 / GS-SERIES

CODE	DESCRIPTION	INVOICE	MSRP
LA	Leather Trim Package	1508	1885
	Includes leather seat trim, driver seat with memory, interior air filter and programmable garage door opener.		
LM	Trunk Mat	40	66
NK	Nakamichi Premium Audio System	1277	1630
	Includes Lexus in-dash 6 CD auto-changer. NOT AVAILABLE with VP.		
SR	Power Tilt/Slide Moonroof with Sunshade	800	1000
TI	Tires: 16" with Chrome Wheels	870	1740
	NOT AVAILABLE with TU, FT.		
TU	Tires: 16"	32	40
	NOT AVAILABLE with TI, FT.		
VK	Nakamichi Audio Package	2264	2515
	Includes Nakamichi premium audio system, Lexus in-dash 6 CD auto-changer, leather trim package, leather seat trim, driver seat with memory, interior air filter, programmable garage door opener and; power tilt/slide moonroof with sunshade. NOT AVAILABLE with VP.		
VP	Lexus Value Package	1769	1965
	Includes leather trim package, leather seat trim, driver seat with memory, interior air filter, programmable garage door opener, Lexus in-dash 6 CD auto-changer and power tilt/slide moonroof with sunshade. NOT AVAILABLE with VK, NK.		
VV	Vehicle Skid Control (VSC)	440	550
WL	Wheel Locks	31	52
WU	Wood Steering Wheel	240	300

2001 GS

What's New?

GS 430 gets a new ULEV-certified, 4.3-liter V8 good for 300 horsepower and 325 ft-lbs. of torque, resulting in sub-6-second acceleration times to 60 mph. GS 300 has new E-shift buttons on the steering wheel for manual control of the automatic transmission's shift points. On the safety front, standard side curtain airbags debut on both models, and a new sensor detects if the front passenger seat is unoccupied, deactivating the front passenger airbag if nobody is sitting in that seat. Additionally, a new child seat-tether restraint has been added, along with impact-detecting door locks and an emergency trunk release handle that glows in the dark inside the cargo area. Exterior changes include water-repellent front door glass, a new grille with a bigger "L" badge, revised taillights, larger exhaust pipes with stainless steel tips and new six-spoke alloy wheels. HID headlights are optional on GS 300 but standard on GS 430. Inside, steering wheel controls for the audio system come standard, a compass has been added, and a new DVD-based navigation system is optional. Bummer that it's bundled with trip computer, audio and climate control systems. Mark Levinson audio is newly optional, replacing Nakamichi as the premium sound supplier. GS 300 gets more wood trim inside the cabin, while GS 430 dashboards have new metallic-gray trim. A wood and leather steering wheel is optional on the 430. Four new colors round out this long list of updates for 2001.

GS-SERIES

LEXUS

CODE	DESCRIPTION	INVOICE	MSRP

Review

Looking to create the ultimate sport sedan in both price and performance, Lexus redesigned its GS series in 1998 and came up with a truly exceptional car that has aged extraordinarily well. Available in either GS 300 or new GS 430 format for 2001, this is one model that can hang with the best Europe has to offer.

A distinctive quad-headlight design sweeps back into the hood and fenders in much the same manner as Mercedes' E-Class cars. Short front and rear overhangs give the GS a sporty look, and tidy hindquarters with creative rear taillights keep this car from blending in with the rest of today's high-line sport sedans.

Appearances are supported by powerful drivetrains. The GS 300 uses a 3.0-liter inline six that develops 220 horsepower at 5,800 rpm and 220 foot-pounds of torque at 3,800 rpm. The GS 430 packs a new 4.3-liter V8 that develops 300 horsepower at 5,600 rpm and 325 foot-pounds of torque at 3,400 rpm. Both of these engines use Variable Valve Timing with intelligence (VVT-i) to produce additional power and provide optimal fuel efficiency. A five-speed automatic is the only transmission available. To take advantage of the transmission's five forward gears, the GS 300 features manual upshift and downshift buttons on the steering wheel spokes for 2001, controlled by the thumb and forefinger of either hand.

A roomy cabin provides the driver and front passenger with space to stretch out. An impressive 44 inches of legroom and 58 inches of shoulder room accommodate the long-limbed and broad-shouldered in the front seats. Rear-seat passengers don't fare as well, however, and get only 34.3 inches of legroom. Luxury touches include a standard dual-zone climate control, a power tilt and telescoping steering wheel, and the normal roster of power goodies typically found on luxury cars. Worthwhile options include a Mark Levinson premium sound system and a DVD-based navigation system that employs touch-screen controls to program routes. Unfortunately, Lexus has decided to bundle it with the audio and climate controls, which always work better with traditional buttons and knobs.

Both models come standard with Vehicle Skid Control (VSC), which is a system that employs the sensors, actuators and computer electronics of the antilock braking and traction control systems to help reduce vehicle skids caused by understeer or oversteer conditions. VSC is teamed with Brake Assist ABS; front, side and curtain airbags; and traction control to provide top-notch occupant protection.

As with other vehicles in the Lexus line, road feel and absolute performance take a backseat to pure luxury and refinement. BMW's 5 Series offers a bit more fun, and the Mercedes E-Class has, well, the Mercedes emblem on the hood. But for a reliable daily driver with more than a hint sporting capability, it's tough to beat the Lexus GS.

Standard Equipment

GS 300 (5A): 3L I6 DOHC SMPI 24-valve engine with variable valve timing, (requires premium unleaded fuel); 5-speed electronic OD automatic transmission with lock-up torque converter; 80 amp alternator; driver's selectable multi-mode auto-manual transmission; rear-wheel drive, traction control, 3.92 axle ratio; dual stainless steel exhaust with tailpipe finisher; electronic stability control control, front independent double-wishbone suspension with anti-roll bar, front coil springs, gas-pressurized front shocks, rear independent double-wishbone suspension with anti-roll bar, rear coil springs, gas-pressurized rear shocks; rack-and-pinion power steering with vehicle-speed-sensing assist; 4-wheel antilock disc brakes; 19.8 gal. capacity fuel tank; side impact bars; front and rear body-colored bumpers with chrome insert; chrome bodyside insert, body-colored bodyside cladding; clearcoat monotone paint; aero-composite halogen fully auto headlamps with daytime running lights, delay-off feature; additional exterior lights include front fog/driving lights; driver's and passenger's power remote body-colored heated folding auto-dimming outside mirrors; 16" x 7.5" silver alloy wheels; P215/60VR16 BSW performance tires; full-size alloy spare wheel; dual-zone front air conditioning with climate control, air filter, rear heat ducts; premium AM/FM stereo radio, seek-scan feature, cassette player, CD changer pre-wiring, 7 speakers, amplifier, theft deterrent, window grid diversity antenna, radio steering wheel controls; cruise control; power door locks with 2-stage unlock, remote keyless entry, child-safety

LEXUS

GS-SERIES

rear door locks, power remote hatch release, power remote fuel door release; cell phone pre-wiring, 2 power accessory outlets, front lighter element(s), driver's foot rest, retained accessory power, garage door opener, smokers' package, first aid kit; instrumentation display includes tachometer, water temperature gauge, in-dash clock, compass, exterior temp, trip odometer; warning indicators include oil pressure, battery, low oil level, lights on, key in ignition, low fuel, low washer fluid, door ajar; driver's and passenger's front airbags, driver's and front passenger's seat-mounted side airbags, overhead airbag; ignition disable, panic alarm, security system; tinted windows, power front and rear windows with front and rear 1-touch down function; variable-speed intermittent front windshield wipers, sun visor strip, rear window defroster; seating capacity of 5, front bucket seats with adjustable tilt headrests, center armrest with storage, driver and passenger seats include 8-way power adjustment, power 2-way lumbar support; rear bench seat with tilt headrests, center armrest; height-adjustable front seatbelts with pretensioners; cloth seats, cloth door trim insert, full cloth headliner, full color-keyed carpet floor covering with carpeted floor mats, leather-wrapped gearshift knob, genuine wood door panel insert, genuine wood console insert, chrome interior accents; interior lights include dome light with fade, front and rear reading lights, 4 door curb lights, illuminated entry; leather-wrapped steering wheel with power tilt and telescopic adjustment; dual illuminated vanity mirrors; auto-dimming day/night rearview mirror; full floor console, locking glove box with light, front and rear cupholders, 2 seatback storage pockets, driver's and passenger's door bins; carpeted cargo floor, cargo light; chrome grille, chrome side window moldings, black front windshield molding, black rear window molding and body-colored door handles.

GS430 (5A): 4.3L V8 DOHC SMPI 32-valve engine with variable valve timing; HD battery; 3.27 axle ratio and P225/55VR16 BSW performance tires.

Base Prices

Code	Description	Invoice	MSRP
9300	GS 300 (5A)	33489	38555
9320	GS 430 (5A)	40655	47355
	Destination Charge:	545	545

Interested in seeing what dealers will sell this vehicle for? Check out our True Market Value^{sm} (TMV^{sm}) pricing on our Web site at www.edmunds.com.

Accessories

Code	Description	Invoice	MSRP
CW	Wheels: Chrome	850	1700
	NOT AVAILABLE with FK, TI, TU.		
CW	Wheels: Chrome	850	1700
DC	Lexus In-Dash 6 CD Auto-Changer	864	1080
FK	Chrome Wheels with All-Season Tires	850	1700
FK	Wheels: Chrome with AS Tires	850	1700
	Includes ALL SEASON tires. NOT AVAILABLE with CW, TI, TU.		
FT	Tires: All Season	NC	NC
GP	Gold Kit	174	269
	Includes all gold plated emblems on the vehicle (except wheels).		
HH	Heated Front Seats	352	440
	REQUIRES PM.		
LA	Leather Trim Package with Memory System	1328	1660
	Includes leather seat trim.		

GS-SERIES — LEXUS

CODE	DESCRIPTION	INVOICE	MSRP
LI	Mark Levinson Audio System Package	4710	5965
	Includes Lexus in-dash 6 CD auto-changer, leather trim package with memory system, leather seat trim, power tilt/slide moonroof with sunshade, heated front seats and high intensity discharge headlamps. NOT AVAILABLE with PM.		
LI	Mark Levinson Audio System Package	2970	3790
	Includes ultra-low crossover distortion, state-of-the-art discrete amplifier design, 240 Ws (continuous average power at .01% THD; 20-20,000 Hz) and auto sound levelizer (ASL), Lexus in-dash 6 CD auto-changer, power tilt/slide moonroof with sunshade and heated front seats. NOT AVAILABLE with ND, PM, NL.		
LM	Trunk Mat	40	66
ND	Navigation Package	5472	6715
	Includes compass, leather trim package with memory system, leather seat trim, Lexus in-dash 6 CD auto-changer, power tilt/slide moonroof with sunshade, heated front seats and high intensity discharge headlamps. NOT AVAILABLE with PM, NL.		
ND	Navigation Package	NC	NC
	Includes compass. NOT AVAILABLE with PM.		
ND	Navigation System Package	3732	4540
	Includes navigation system, Lexus in-dash 6 CD auto-changer, power tilt/slide moonroof with sunshade and heated front seats. NOT AVAILABLE with LI, PM, NL.		
NL	Navigation/Mark Levinson Package	6410	7965
	Includes Mark levinson audio system package, Lexus in-dash 6 CD auto-changer, leather trim package with memory system, leather seat trim, power tilt/slide moonroof with sunshade, heated front seats, high intensity discharge headlamps and; navigation package. NOT AVAILABLE with ND, PM.		
NL	Navigation/Mark Levinson Package	4670	5790
	Includes navigation system, Mark levinson audio system package, Lexus in-dash 6 CD auto-changer, power tilt/slide moonroof with sunshade, and heated front seats. NOT AVAILABLE with PM, ND, LI.		
PM	Premium Package	2032	2540
	Includes Lexus in-dash 6 CD auto-changer, power tilt/slide moonroof with sunshade and heated front seats. NOT AVAILABLE with LI, ND, NL.		
PM	Premium Package	3008	3760
	Includes leather trim package with memory system, leather seat trim, Lexus in-dash 6 CD auto-changer and power tilt/slide moonroof with sunshade. NOT AVAILABLE with ND, NL, LI.		
RF	Rear Spoiler	352	440
SR	Power Tilt/Slide Moonroof with Sunshade	816	1020
TI	Upgraded Tire Package with 17" Chrome Wheels	958	1915
	NOT AVAILABLE with TU, CW, FK.		
TU	Upgraded Tire Package with 17" Wheels	172	215
	NOT AVAILABLE with TI, CW, FK.		
WL	Wheel Locks	31	52
WU	Wood and Leather Steering Wheel	240	300
	REQUIRES LI or ND or NL or PM.		

LEXUS

IS 300

| CODE | DESCRIPTION | INVOICE | MSRP |

2001 IS 300

What's New?

Lexus continues to change gears, moving away from single-minded relentless pursuits of perfection to chase performance. The new IS 300, complete with rear-wheel drive and a 215-horse inline six, chases the BMW 3 Series in the entry luxury sport marketplace, and will continue to do so until a proper manual transmission is available.

Review

Lexus, traditional purveyor or highly refined but generally characterless luxury automobiles, is looking to change its staid, reliable, upstanding citizen image. In 1998, the upscale Toyota division lobbed the GS 400 over the net, scoring with consumers who wanted to blend the sporting V8-powered personality of a BMW 5 Series with daring styling and Japanese reliability. But that serve into opposing territory fell somewhat short of the mark in terms of initial quality and outright performance, and a lack of a manual gearbox represented a glaring omission in a vehicle targeting the vaunted 540i.

Has Lexus learned a lesson? The new IS 300, targeting the BMW 3 Series, benefits from the installation of a smooth, 3.0-liter inline six that makes 215 horsepower and 218 foot-pounds of torque at 3,800 rpm. As with the GS 300, whose engine the IS shares, rear-wheel drive is the method of motivation, but for now, we Americans are stuck with a five-speed automatic transmission equipped with E-Shift steering wheel gear-selection buttons, just like in a Formula One car. A manual is on the way, purists, if you can wait a year.

So perhaps the lesson hasn't gone unheeded. We get plenty of power, and a row-'em-yourself transmission is just around the corner. But buyers of these kinds of sedans want performance and style. The IS 300 is mostly successful in this arena, with taut, balanced exterior dimensions stretched over large, available 17-inch wheels optionally finished in smoked chrome. We aren't fans of the circular decklid-mounted taillights, and the clear rear lens covers look too much like the ones you see on the neighbor kid's lowered '94 Accord, but the overall shape is well balanced and attractive.

Inside is where Lexus gets a gold star for imagination, with a chronograph gauge cluster the centerpiece of a highly styled interior. Drilled aluminum pedals announce the IS 300's intentions loud and clear, while fashionable metallic accents litter the cabin.

Double wishbone suspension components front and rear, fine-tuned at Germany's Nurburgring racetrack, keep the standard 16-inch all-season performance tires glued to the ground, while standard four-wheel disc antilock brakes and full-range traction control keep them from sliding and spinning. A limited-slip differential is optional, while standard high-intensity discharge (HID) headlights provide superb nighttime road illumination.

Safety is also addressed, with three-point seatbelts for each of the five seating positions and front seat-mounted side airbags standard. Pre-tensioning and force limiting front harnesses maximize protection in a crash, while an interior trunk lid release handle helps prevent entrapment in the trunk.

With a base price in the low 30s, the IS 300 isn't the bargain the LS 400 was when Lexus debuted a decade ago. With both Audi and BMW offering all-wheel drive technology in their elegant and smooth-riding compact sedans, not to mention superlative interior materials and manual transmissions, Lexus may have its work cut out for it as it learns what it takes to tackle Germany's finest.

IS 300   LEXUS

CODE	DESCRIPTION	INVOICE	MSRP

Standard Equipment

IS 300 (5A): 3.0L I6 DOHC SMPI 24-valve engine with variable valve timing (requires premium unleaded fuel); 5-speed electronic OD automatic transmission with lock-up torque converter; 80 amp alternator; multi-mode auto-manual transmission; rear-wheel drive, traction control, 3.92 axle ratio; stainless steel exhaust with tailpipe finisher; front independent double-wishbone suspension with anti-roll bar, front coil springs, gas-pressurized front shocks, rear independent double-wishbone suspension with anti-roll bar, rear coil springs, gas-pressurized rear shocks; rack-and-pinion power steering with engine speed-sensing assist; 4-wheel antilock disc brakes; 19.8 gal. capacity fuel tank; side impact bars; front and rear body-colored bumpers; body-colored bodyside molding with chrome bodyside insert; clearcoat monotone paint; aero-composite high intensity fully auto headlamps with daytime running lights, delay-off feature; additional exterior lights include front fog/driving lights; driver's and passenger's power remote body-colored heated folding outside mirrors; 17" x 7" silver alloy wheels; P205/45ZR17 performance BSW front tires; 215/45 rear tires; trunk mounted full-size alloy spare wheel; dual-zone front air conditioning with climate control, air filter, rear heat ducts; premium AM/FM stereo radio, seek-scan feature, cassette 6-disc CD changer, 8 performance speakers, amplifier, auto equalizer, theft deterrent, and integrated roof antenna; cruise control; power door locks with 2-stage unlock, remote keyless entry, child-safety rear door locks, power remote hatch/trunk release, power remote fuel door release; cell phone pre-wiring, 2 power accessory outlets, front lighter element(s), driver's foot rest, retained accessory power, smokers' package, first aid kit; instrumentation display includes tachometer, water temperature gauge, volt gauge, in-dash clock, exterior temp, trip odometer; warning indicators include oil pressure, battery, low oil level, lights on, key in ignition, low fuel, low washer fluid, door ajar; driver's and passenger's front airbags, driver's and front passenger's seat-mounted side airbags; ignition disable, panic alarm, security system; tinted windows, power front and rear windows with driver's 1-touch down function; variable-speed intermittent front windshield wipers, sun visor strip, rear window defroster; seating capacity of 5, front bucket seats with adjustable tilt headrests, center armrest with storage, driver and passenger seats include 6-way adjustment and power 2-way lumbar support; rear bench seat with tilt headrests and trunk pass-thru armrest; height-adjustable front seatbelts with pretensioners; cloth seats, cloth door trim insert, full cloth headliner, full color-keyed carpet floor covering with carpeted floor mats, aluminum gearshift knob; interior lights include dome light, front and rear reading lights, 4 door curb lights, illuminated entry; leather-wrapped steering wheel with tilt adjustment; dual illuminated vanity mirrors; auto-dimming day/night rearview mirror; full floor console, locking glove box with light, front and rear cupholders, 2 seatback storage pockets, driver's and passenger's door bins; carpeted cargo floor, carpeted trunk lid, cargo light; chrome grille, black side window moldings, black front windshield molding, black rear window molding and body-colored door handles.

Base Prices

9500	Sport Sedan (5A)	26757	30805
	Destination Charge:	545	545

Interested in seeing what dealers will sell this vehicle for? Check out our True Market Value^{sm} (TMV^{sm}) pricing on our Web site at www.edmunds.com.

Accessories

AL	Wheels: 17" Polished Graphite Alloy	320	400
	NOT AVAILABLE with FT.		
FT	Tires: P205/55R16 AS	NC	NC
	With all season tire pattern. 16" x 6.5" alloy wheels. NOT AVAILABLE with AL.		
GP	Gold Package	298	417
	Includes all gold plated emblems on the vehicle (except wheels).		

LEXUS

IS 300 / LS 430

CODE	DESCRIPTION	INVOICE	MSRP
HH	Heated Front Seats	352	440
	REQUIRES LP or LS.		
LD	Limited Slip Differential	312	390
LM	Carpeted Cargo Mat	40	66
LP	Luxury Leather Package	1444	1805
	Includes ivory/black instrument panel, 8-way power driver/passenger seats, leather/ecsaine trim, wood switchplates and Homelink garage door opener. NOT AVAILABLE with LS.		
LS	Leather Package	1364	1705
	Includes leather/ecsaine trim, 8-way power driver/passenger seats and Homelink garage door opener. NOT AVAILABLE with LP.		
SR	Power Tilt/Slide Moonroof with Sunshade	800	1000
WL	17" Wheel Locks	27	39
	NOT AVAILABLE with FT.		

2001 LS 430

What's New?

The completely redesigned third-generation Lexus flagship features a larger 4.3-liter engine that meets ULEV standards, a freshened aerodynamic shape that allows for a more spacious interior, and a new suspension that offers greater stability and a smoother ride. A richer, more stylish interior with advanced safety and luxury features also debuts.

Review

Japan has perfected the art of refinement in automobiles, as is apparent in the redesign of the 2001 Lexus LS 430, keeping this flagship sedan in step with the rapidly advancing premium luxury segment.

New for 2001, a 4.3-liter engine powers the LS 430, offering the same 290 horsepower as last year, but with 20 foot-pounds more torque for a total of 320. Variable Valve Timing with intelligence (VVT-i) eliminates the compromise between high-rpm horsepower and low-end torque by optimizing valve overlap throughout the rev range. The new engine is matched to a computer-controlled five-speed automatic transmission driving the rear wheels, with Lexus quoting a zero-to-60 time of 6.3 seconds. The industry's first "torque-activated" powertrain control debuts on the 2001 LS 430, so when climbing a hill for example, the controller will increase the throttle opening to provide more power without the driver having to adjust pedal position.

While the new 430 reflects Lexus' established styling theme, the body has a decidedly Teutonic profile, reminding our staff of the Mercedes-Benz S-Class sedan. Tested in the same wind tunnel as Japan's bullet trains, the new, more aerodynamic shape has a coefficient of drag (CD) of .25 when equipped with the available Air Suspension, the lowest of any current passenger sedan. The wheelbase has increased by 3 inches even though overall length remains the same. By comparison, the LS offers more interior cabin volume and a larger trunk than the S-Class.

The more spacious interior features higher grades of wood and leather for 2001. The climate control system uses temperature and sun-sensing air registers to regulate cabin comfort. For

LS 430 — LEXUS

example, if one side of the car is bathed in sunlight the registers deliver more cooling air to that side. The driver's seat includes adjustments for dual lumbar support and an extendable cushion length for thigh support. A new CD changer location for the audio system allows for a larger glove box that complements expanded interior storage compartments. Additional features for 2001 are climate control front seats, parking clearance sonar, power adjustable rear seatbacks with memory, a power rear sunshade and manual door shades, and a rear air conditioner with air purifier. Also optional are a DVD-based navigation system and the first automotive audio application by Mark Levinson, whose components are used in home sound systems costing $100,000 and more.

The LS 430's safety features include four-channel antilock brakes with Brake Assist, Vehicle Skid Control, and new for 2001, advanced variable-force airbags and side curtain front and rear airbags. Sensors determine the force with which to deploy the front airbags in an effort to reduce the chance of airbag-related injuries. Front seats and rear outboard seats are equipped with seatbelt pre-tensioners with force limiters.

Continuing in the stoic tradition of the previous model, but with improvements in terms of performance and pampering, the redesigned Lexus LS 430 will find plenty of favor with buyers looking more for serenity and sanctuary than speed.

Standard Equipment

LS 430 (5A): 4.3L V8 DOHC SMPI 32-valve engine with variable valve timing, (requires premium unleaded fuel); 5-speed electronic OD automatic transmission with lock-up torque converter; 750 amp battery; 100 amp alternator; driver's selectable multi-mode transmission; rear-wheel drive, traction control, 3.27 axle ratio; dual stainless steel exhaust; electronic stability control, front independent double-wishbone suspension with anti-roll bar, front coil springs, gas-pressurized front shocks, rear independent double-wishbone suspension with anti-roll bar, rear coil springs, gas-pressurized rear shocks; rack-and-pinion power steering with vehicle-speed-sensing assist; 4-wheel antilock disc brakes; 22.2 gal. capacity fuel tank; side impact bars; front and rear body-colored bumpers with chrome insert; chrome bodyside insert, body-colored bodyside cladding; clearcoat monotone paint; aero-composite high intensity fully auto headlamps with daytime running lights, delay-off feature; additional exterior lights include cornering lights, front fog/driving lights; driver's and passenger's body-colored heated folding auto-dimming outside mirrors, driver's power remote outside mirror, passenger's power remote with tilt down outside mirror; 16" x 7" machined alloy wheels; P225/60HR16 BSW performance tires; full-size alloy spare wheel; dual-zone front air conditioning with climate control, air filter, rear heat ducts; premium AM/FM stereo radio, seek-scan feature, cassette player, 6-disc CD changer, 7 performance speakers, amplifier, auto equalizer, theft deterrent, window grid diversity antenna, radio steering wheel controls; cruise control with steering wheel controls; power door locks with 2-stage unlock, remote keyless entry, child-safety rear door locks, power remote hatch release, power remote fuel door release; cell phone pre-wiring, 4 power accessory outlets, front and rear lighter element(s), trunk pull-down, driver's foot rest, retained accessory power, garage door opener, smokers' package, first aid kit; instrumentation display includes tachometer, water temperature gauge, in-dash clock, compass, exterior temp, trip computer, trip odometer; warning indicators include oil pressure, battery, low oil level, low coolant, lights on, key in ignition, low fuel, low washer fluid, bulb failure, door ajar, trunk ajar; driver's and passenger's front airbags, driver's and front passenger's seat-mounted side airbags, overhead airbag; ignition disable, panic alarm, security system; tinted windows, power front and rear windows with front and rear 1-touch down function; variable-speed intermittent front windshield wipers, electrically heated window, rain detecting wipers, sun visor strip, rear window defroster; seating capacity of 5, front bucket seats, power adjustable tilt headrests, center armrest with storage, driver's seat includes 10-way power adjustment, power 4-way lumbar support, passenger's seat includes 8-way power adjustment, power 2-way lumbar support; rear bench seat with tilt headrests, center armrest; height-adjustable front seatbelts with pretensioners; leather seats, leather door trim insert, full cloth headliner, full carpet floor covering with carpeted floor mats, genuine wood dashboard insert, leather/wood gearshift knob, genuine wood door panel insert, genuine wood console insert, chrome interior accents; driver's seat memory includes 3 settings for

LEXUS
LS 430

CODE	DESCRIPTION	INVOICE	MSRP

exterior mirrors, steering wheel, headrests; interior lights include dome light with fade, front and rear reading lights, 4 door curb lights, illuminated entry; leather/genuine wood steering wheel with power tilt and telescopic adjustment; dual illuminated vanity mirrors, dual auxiliary visors; auto-dimming day/night rearview mirror; full floor console, locking glove box with light, front and rear cupholders, 2 seatback storage pockets, driver's and passenger's door bins, rear door bins; carpeted cargo floor, cargo light; chrome grille, chrome side window moldings, black front windshield molding, chrome rear window molding and body-colored door handles.

Base Prices

Code	Description	Invoice	MSRP
9100	LS 430 (5A)	46363	54005
	Destination Charge:	545	545

Interested in seeing what dealers will sell this vehicle for? Check out our True Market Value^{sm} (TMV^{sm}) pricing on our Web site at www.edmunds.com.

Accessories

Code	Description	Invoice	MSRP
AT	Ashtray	NC	NC
CW	Wheels: Chrome	850	1700
	Includes chrome plated alloy spare. NOT AVAILABLE with FT, FK, TI, TU.		
FK	Wheels: Chrome	850	1700
	Includes chrome plated alloy spare all season tires. NOT AVAILABLE with CW, TI, TU.		
FT	Tires: All Season	NC	NC
	NOT AVAILABLE with CW, TI, TU.		
GP	Gold Kit	176	261
	Includes all gold plated emblems on the vehicle (except wheels). NOT AVAILABLE with SE, SF, SG."		
HH	Heated Front and Rear Seats	704	880
IN	Black Or Bordeaux Interior Upgrade Package	1684	2105
	Includes semi anilin leather seat trim. REQUIRES UL. NOT AVAILABLE with IR, LH.		
IR	Ecru Interior Upgrade Package	1168	1460
	Includes comfort leather seat trim. REQUIRES UL. NOT AVAILABLE with IN, LG.		
LG	Semi Anilin Leather Seat Trim	NC	NC
	REQUIRES UL and IN. NOT AVAILABLE with LH, IR.		
LH	Comfort Leather Seat Trim	NC	NC
	REQUIRES UL and IR. NOT AVAILABLE with LG, IN.		
LI	Mark Levinson Audio System Package	2530	3240
	Includes Mark Levinson premium audio, power tilt and slide moonroof with sunshade, heated front and rear seats. NOT AVAILABLE with ND, UL.		
LM	Trunk Mat	40	66
MZ	Lexus Link (Mayday)	1015	1215
	Includes 1 year of service.		
ND	Navigation System Package	3300	4000
	Includes navigation system, power tilt and slide moonroof with sunshade, heated front and rear seats. NOT AVAILABLE with LI, NL, UL.		
NL	Navigation/Mark Levinson Package	4230	5240
	Includes navigation system, Mark Levinson audio system package, Mark Levinson premium audio, power tilt and slide moonroof with sunshade, heated front and rear seats and. NOT AVAILABLE with ND, UL.		

LINCOLN

CONTINENTAL

2001 CONTINENTAL

What's New?

The Continental remains relatively unchanged for 2001. A universal garage door opener is standard, and the individual bucket seat option (five-passenger) now requires the Driver's Select System. Two new exterior colors have been added. Like all Lincoln products, the Continental now has complimentary maintenance at no additional charge for the first 3 years/ 36,000 miles in service.

Review

If you are looking for an alternative to Cadillac, then this is your car.

The only front-wheel-drive car in Lincoln's lineup, it's equipped with a 4.6-liter V8 that makes 275 horsepower at 5,750 rpm and 275 foot-pounds of torque at 4,750 rpm. In both size and output, this V8 is very similar to the V8 in Cadillac's big car lineup, though it lacks the marketing push that Cadillac gives its Northstar engine.

A fully independent suspension comes standard on all Continentals. The rear suspension has a load-leveling feature that automatically maintains ride height regardless of passengers or additional cargo. Additionally, Lincoln offers an optional Driver Select System that includes an adjustable shock damping system. It can be set for plush, normal or firm ride control. The Driver Select System also comes with a memory system that allows two separate drivers to adjust seat and exterior mirror settings to their individual tastes.

On the road, the Continental gives a comfortable and stable ride, which is what you should expect out of a large front-drive luxury car. Power from the V8 is more than enough for passing and general highway cruising.

Inside, the Continental's cabin is quiet. Control layout is logical, though the overall ambience is somewhat bland. Storage space is lacking, and the cupholders are not adjustable.

In terms of upgrades, there's an Alpine audio system and Alpine six-disc CD changer for audiophiles, a luxury package with upgraded interior and exterior trim pieces, and a personal security package with a low tire-pressure warning system and run-flat tires. For the ultimate in secure travel, a RESCU package is available with Lincoln's Remote Emergency Satellite Cellular Unit to call for assistance and transmit the vehicle's location via a global positioning satellite (GPS) network.

The Continental's exterior remains unchanged for the 2001 model year. The wide front grille is retained, as are the dual exhaust outlets and the swoopy hood line. This gives the Lincoln a .32 coefficient of drag which, as luxury sedans go, is fairly slippery. If you really want to set yourself apart from other Continentals, the optional six-spoke chrome wheels can add to the car's classic look.

For 2001, all Lincoln models will receive complimentary maintenance. This program covers all routine maintenance — from oil changes to wipers to shocks — for the first three years or 36,000 miles. In addition, the basic Lincoln warranty of four years/50,000 miles remains in place.

Until the LS debuted last year, the Continental used to be Lincoln's smallest offering. It is now mid-pack, sandwiched between the LS and the larger Town Car. Though still a competent and attractive package, the Continental has lost some identity and still faces tough competition from Acura, BMW, Cadillac, Lexus and Mercedes-Benz.

Standard Equipment

CONTINENTAL (4A): 4.6L V8 DOHC SMPI 32-valve engine, (requires premium unleaded fuel); 4-speed electronic OD automatic transmission with lock-up converter; HD battery with rundown protection; 125-amp alternator; front-wheel drive, traction control, 3.56 axle ratio; stainless steel

LS 430 — LEXUS

CODE	DESCRIPTION	INVOICE	MSRP
SP	Euro-Tuned Sport Suspension .... *REQUIRES TU or TI.*	NC	NC
SR	Power Tilt and Slide Moonroof with Sunshade .... *Includes auto open/close feature and pinch protection.*	896	1120
TI	Upgraded Tire Package with 17" Chrome Wheels .... *Includes P225/55R 17 Vrated tires and wheels: 17" chrome. NOT AVAILABLE with TU, CW, FK, FT.*	900	1800
TU	Upgraded Tire Package with 17" Wheels .... *Includes P225/55R 17 Vrated tires and wheels: 17". NOT AVAILABLE with TI, CW, FK, FT.*	80	100
UL	Ultra Luxury Package .... *Includes dynamic laser cruise control, power door closers (all 4 doors), wood/leather steering wheel with voice command button, ecsaine trim located on the sunvisors, headliner, A/B pillars and door trim, additional leather on door armrests/lower dash areas and a rear cooler box. Mark Levinson premium audio, navigation system, Lexus link (Mayday), power tilt and slide moonroof with sunshade, air suspension with avs, laminated side glass, power rear sunshade, intuitive parking assist, power heated rear seats with memory and massage, front climate-controlled seats, rear air conditioner and air filtration, rear seat audio controls and headlamp washers. REQUIRES IN or IR. NOT AVAILABLE with NL, ND, LI.*	9870	12290
WL	Wheel Locks	36	59

One 15-minute call could save you 15% or more on car insurance.

GEICO DIRECT

America's 6th Largest Automobile Insurance Company

1-800-555-2758

CONTINENTAL

LINCOLN

CODE	DESCRIPTION	INVOICE	MSRP

exhaust with tailpipe finisher; auto-leveling suspension, front independent strut suspension with anti-roll bar, front coil springs, gas-pressurized front shocks, rear independent short & long arm suspension with anti-roll bar, rear air springs, gas-pressurized rear shocks; rack-and-pinion power steering with vehicle-speed-sensing assist; 4-wheel disc brakes with 4-wheel antilock braking system; 20 gal. capacity fuel tank; side impact bars; class I towing capability; front and rear body-colored bumpers with chrome bumper insert; body-colored bodyside molding with chrome bodyside insert; clearcoat monotone paint; aero-composite halogen fully automatic headlamps with delay-off feature; additional exterior lights include cornering lights; driver's and passenger's body-colored heated outside mirrors, driver's power remote outside mirror, passenger's power remote outside mirror with tilt-down feature; 16" x 7" silver alloy wheels with P225/60HR16 BSW A/S tires; compact steel spare wheel; air conditioning with climate control, air filter, rear heat ducts; premium AM/FM stereo w/seek-scan feature, cassette player, 4 speakers, amplifier, window grid antenna; cruise control with steering wheel controls; power door locks with 2-stage unlock, remote keyless entry, child safety rear door locks, power remote hatch/trunk release, power remote fuel door release; 2 power accessory outlets, front lighter element, driver's foot rest, retained accessory power, garage door opener, smokers' package; instrumentation display includes tachometer, water temperature gauge, clock, compass, exterior temp, systems monitor, trip computer, trip odometer; warning indicators include oil pressure, water temp, battery, low oil level, low coolant, lights on, key in ignition, low fuel, low washer fluid, bulb failure, door ajar, trunk ajar, service interval, brake fluid, turn signal on; driver's and passenger's front airbags, driver's and front passenger's seat-mounted side airbags; ignition disable, panic alarm, security system; tinted windows, power front and rear windows with driver's 1-touch down function; variable-speed intermittent front windshield wipers, sun visor strip, rear window defroster; seating capacity of 6, 50/50 split-bench front seats with adjustable headrests, center armrest with storage, driver's and front passenger's seats include 6-way power seat, power 2-way lumbar support and easy entry feature; rear bench seat with center armrest; height-adjustable front seatbelts; leather seats, full cloth headliner, full carpet floor covering with carpeted floor mats, genuine wood dashboard insert, leather-wrapped gearshift knob, genuine wood door panel insert, chrome interior accents; driver's seat memory includes 2 memory settings for exterior mirrors; interior lights include dome light with fade, front and rear reading lights, door curb lights, illuminated entry; leather-wrapped steering wheel with tilt adjustment; dual illuminated vanity mirrors, dual auxiliary visors; auto-dimming day/night rearview mirror; partial floor console, mini overhead console with storage, locking glove box with light, front and rear cupholders, 2 seatback storage pockets, driver's and passenger's door bins; carpeted cargo floor, carpeted trunk lid, cargo light; chrome grille, chrome side window moldings, black front windshield molding, black rear window molding and chrome door handles.

Base Prices

M97	Continental (4A)	36412	39380
Destination Charge:		745	745

Interested in seeing what dealers will sell this vehicle for? Check out our True Market Value^{sm} (TMV^{sm}) pricing on our Web site at www.edmunds.com.

Accessories

13B	Power Moonroof	1327	1525
	Includes color-keyed sunshade.		
467	Heated Seats	348	400
	Includes distinct settings for back and bottom heating and 5 temperature settings.		
54A	Luxury Appearance Package	961	1105
	Includes two-tone leather seating surfaces, unique front floor mats and chrome/ argent grille, 6-spoke chrome wheels and steering wheel with real wood trim. REQUIRES 667. NOT AVAILABLE with 675, 64F.		

LINCOLN

CONTINENTAL / LS

CODE	DESCRIPTION	INVOICE	MSRP
6	Individual Bucket Seats	NC	NC
	Includes leather seating surfaces, full-length console and floor shift. REQUIRES 916.		
64F	Wheels: 16" Highly Polished Aluminum	313	360
	NOT AVAILABLE with 64G, 54A.		
64G	Wheels: 6-Spoke Chrome	744	855
	NOT AVAILABLE with 675, 64F, B3D.		
667	Driver Select System	526	605
	Includes driver-selectable ride control (firm, normal and plush) and memory profile system allows 2 drivers to personalize settings for 11 features, semi-active suspension, steering wheel audio controls, auto-dimming outside mirror and individual bucket seats (5-passenger). REQUIRES 916.		
675	Personal Security Package	557	640
	Includes Securi Run-Flat tires with a pressure-alert warning system. REQUIRES 64F. NOT AVAILABLE with 64G, 54A.		
916	Alpine Audio System	501	575
	Includes digital signal processing (DSP), separate subwoofer amplifier, 5-1/2" x 7-1/2" door speakers in rear doors, 5-1/4" round coaxial speakers in front doors and 2- 6 x 9" subwoofers added to rear package tray.		
919	Alpine 6-Disc CD/DJ Changer	526	605
	Located in console. REQUIRES 916.		
B3D	No-Charge 16" Polished Aluminum Wheels	(313)	(360)
	REQUIRES 64F. NOT AVAILABLE with 64G, B3E.		
B3E	No-Charge Power Moonroof	(1327)	(1525)
	REQUIRES 13B. NOT AVAILABLE with B3D.		
HC	Paint: Ivory Parchment Clearcoat Tri-Coat	327	375
WF	Paint: White Pearlescent Clearcoat Metallic Tri-Coat	327	375

2001 LS

What's New?

Now in its second year, the Lincoln LS receives minor changes. V6 models now come with standard traction control and optional AdvanceTrac. All models receive a glow-in-the-dark manual trunk release and child safety-seat anchor points. The sport package has a new 17-inch chrome wheel design and a mini spare tire and wheel instead of the previous 16-inch non-matching aluminum wheel (both late availability). Inside, there is an additional power point, a revised cupholder design, an optional six-disc in-dash CD changer and an optional mirror-mounted compass. In terms of content, Lincoln's RESCU vehicle emergency system couldn't rescue itself from being discontinued for 2001, and the height adjustable rear-seat head restraints have been deleted from V8 automatics. Lastly, Lincoln now offers complimentary maintenance at no additional charge for the first 3 years/36,000 miles in service.

Review

Is it possible to create a car that melds American luxury with European driving dynamics? Sure. Witness the Cadillac Catera. But how about one that's actually good?

Fortunately, the Lincoln LS can answer the call. Now one year old, the LS is one of our favorite entry-level luxury sedans. It is Lincoln's most advanced vehicle in terms of technology, and it is attracting a much younger clientele than Lincoln dealerships are used to seeing.

LS   LINCOLN

| CODE | DESCRIPTION | INVOICE | MSRP |

While many entry-luxury sedans are just warmed-over versions of lower-level cars (like the Infiniti I30 and Nissan Maxima, for instance), the rear-drive LS shares its platform with the more upscale Jaguar S-Type.

From the start, Lincoln aimed the LS squarely at the European and, specifically, BMW market. The LS' front end calls attention to this with its tight quad headlights, swooping central grille and clean hood lines.

Buyers can select from one of two engines that both meet LEV standards. The first is a 3.0-liter V6 that produces 210 horsepower at 6,500 rpm and 205 foot-pounds of torque at 4,750 rpm. It is offered with either a five-speed automatic or a five-speed manual transmission. But with a 3,600-pound curb weight, the V6 LS is somewhat underpowered (given the car's sporting intentions), so Lincoln also offers a V8.

This DOHC, 32-valve, 3.9-liter V8 generates 252 horsepower at 6,100 rpm and 267 foot-pounds of torque at 4,300 rpm. Power delivery is smooth and linear. Zero-to-60 acceleration with the V8 is a quick 7.5 seconds. The engine is hobbled, however, by the five-speed automatic. It is often befuddled, and shifts made using the Sportshift mode (available with the sport package) lag noticeably.

Handling ability is very good, especially when the LS is equipped with the optional sport package. The steering is quick and communicative. Ride quality can sometimes be harsh, but overall, the Lincoln strikes a nice balance between luxury and performance. Traction control is standard and the AdvanceTrac stability control system is optional.

Inside, the LS offers a decent selection of luxury features. The usual suspects are all present, from leather seating surfaces and premium sound to dual-zone climate controls and a driver-preference memory system for seats, mirrors and the steering wheel. Lincoln has also added an optional six-disc in-dash CD changer for this year. GPS navigation, however, is still MIA. Oh, and can we have more interior storage space and better build quality, please?

Minor points aside, the LS is an impressive car. Plunk down $30,000 to $40,000, and you basically get a European sedan with an American nameplate and interior space. If every American carmaker that tried to take on the Europeans succeeded to the extent the LS does, the world would be a far better place.

Standard Equipment

V6 AUTO (5A): 3L V6 DOHC SMPI 24-valve engine; 5-speed electronic OD automatic transmission with lock-up converter; battery with rundown protection; 110-amp alternator; rear-wheel drive, traction control, 3.58 axle ratio; dual stainless steel exhaust; front independent suspension with anti-roll bar, front coil springs, gas-pressurized front shocks, rear independent short & long arm suspension with anti-roll bar, rear coil springs, gas-pressurized rear shocks; rack-and-pinion power steering with vehicle-speed-sensing assist; 4-wheel disc brakes with 4-wheel antilock braking system; 18 gal. capacity fuel tank; side impact bars; class I towing capability; front and rear body-colored bumpers with chrome bumper insert; body-colored bodyside molding; clearcoat monotone paint; aero-composite halogen fully automatic headlamps with delay-off feature; additional exterior lights include front fog/driving lights; driver's and passenger's power remote body-colored heated outside mirrors; 16" x 7" silver alloy with P215/60HR16 BSW A/S tires; compact steel spare wheel; dual-zone front air conditioning with climate control, air filter, rear heat ducts; premium AM/FM stereo w/clock, seek-scan feature, cassette player, 4 speakers, window grid diversity antenna, radio steering wheel controls; cruise control with steering wheel controls; power door locks with 2-stage unlock, remote keyless entry, child safety rear door locks, power remote hatch/trunk release, power remote fuel release; cell phone pre-wiring, 3 power accessory outlets, front lighter element, driver's foot rest, retained accessory power, smokers' package; instrumentation display includes tachometer, water temperature gauge, exterior temp, trip odometer; warning indicators include oil pressure, water temp, battery, low oil level, lights on, key in ignition, low fuel, low washer fluid, bulb failure, door ajar, trunk ajar,

LINCOLN

LS

turn signal on; driver's and passenger's front airbags, driver's and front passenger's seat-mounted side airbags; ignition disable, panic alarm, security system; tinted windows, power front and rear windows with driver's 1-touch down function; heated variable-speed intermittent front windshield wipers, sun visor strip, rear window defroster; seating capacity of 5, front bucket seats with adjustable headrests, center armrest with storage, driver's seat includes 8-way power seat and lumbar support, front passenger's seat includes 6-way power seat, 8-way direction control and lumbar support; 60/40 folding rear bench seat with fixed headrests, rear center armrest; height- adjustable front seatbelts with pretensioners; leather seats, full cloth headliner, full carpet floor covering with carpeted floor mats, simulated wood dashboard insert, wood gearshift knob, simulated wood door panel insert, simulated wood console insert, chrome interior accents; interior lights include dome light with fade, front and rear reading lights, door curb lights, illuminated entry; leather/genuine wood steering wheel with power tilt and telescopic adjustment; dual illuminated vanity mirrors; day/night rearview mirror; full floor console, locking glove box with light, front and rear cupholders, 2 seatback storage pockets, driver's and passenger's door bins, rear door bins; carpeted cargo floor, carpeted trunk lid, cargo light; chrome grille, chrome side window moldings, black front windshield molding, black rear window molding and body-colored door handles.

V6 MANUAL (5M) (in addition to or instead of V6 AUTO (5A) equipment): 5-speed manual transmission; engine oil cooler; 3.07 axle ratio; sport ride suspension, body-colored bumper insert; 17" x 7" silver alloy wheels with P235/50VR17 BSW A/S peformance tires; full-size alloy spare wheel; 6-disc CD changer, 6 premium speakers, amplifier.

V8 AUTO (5A) (in addition to or instead of V6 MANUAL (5M) equipment): 3.9L V8 DOHC SMPI 32-valve engine; 5-speed electronic OD automatic transmission with lock-up converter; 3.31 axle ratio; garage door opener; instrumentation display includes compass, systems monitor, trip computer; warning indicators include service interval, brake fluid; rain-detecting wipers; driver's dual-setting seat-memory feature includes settings for exterior mirrors and steering wheel; auto-dimming day/night rearview mirror.

Base Prices

Code	Description	Invoice	MSRP
M86	V6 Auto (5A)	29383	31665
M86	V6 Manual (5M)	30986	33445
M87	V8 Auto (5A)	33011	35695
	Destination Charge:	610	610

Interested in seeing what dealers will sell this vehicle for? Check out our True Market Value^{sm} (TMV^{sm}) pricing on our Web site at www.edmunds.com.

Accessories

Code	Description	Invoice	MSRP
13B	Power Moonroof	874	1005
	Includes key fob sunroof control.		
556	Advance Trac	640	735
58X	6-Disc In-Dash CD Changer (V6 Auto/V8 Auto)	526	605
	NOT AVAILABLE with 919.		
60L	Convenience Package (V6)	835	960
	Includes electrochromic rearview mirror, compass, universal garage door opener, moisture-sensitive wipers, memory settings, power driver's and front passenger's lumbar.		
60N	Sport Package (V6 Auto/V8 Auto)	1732	1990
	Includes 17" super silver alloy wheels, P235/50VR17 BSW tires, 16" alloy spare wheel, european sport-suspension tuning, Select-Shift automatic transmission, body-		

LS / TOWN CAR — LINCOLN

CODE	DESCRIPTION	INVOICE	MSRP
	colored bumpers, engine oil cooler, leather-wrapped steering wheel, leather-wrapped gearshift knob, Alpine sport audio system, and a 6-disc in-dash CD changer. NOT AVAILABLE with 64X, 919, 916.		
632	Heated Front Seats	348	400
	Heated cushions and seatbacks.		
64C	Wheels: 17" 5-Spoke Chrome Aluminum	735	845
	5-spoke. REQUIRES 60N. NOT AVAILABLE with 64X.		
64X	Wheels: 16" High-Polished Aluminum (V6 Auto/V8 Auto)	352	405
	5-spoke. NOT AVAILABLE with 60N, 64C.		
916	Alpine Audiophile System (V6 Auto/V8 Auto)	501	575
	Includes a 175-Watt, 12-speaker system with 85-Watt subwoofer. NOT AVAILABLE with 60N.		
919	6-Disc Glovebox-Mounted CD Changer (V6 Auto/V8 Auto)	526	605
	NOT AVAILABLE with 58X, 60N.		
HC	Paint: Ivory Parchment Clearcoat Tri-Coat	327	375
WF	Paint: White Pearlescent Clearcoat Metallic Tri-Coat	327	375

2001 TOWN CAR

What's New?

Horsepower has been increased throughout the model lineup. Inside, the Town Car gains adjustable pedals, seat-belt pretensioners, upgraded map pockets and leather grab handles. Signature models have a wood-trimmed steering wheel as standard and the front seats in Executive models have power lumbar adjustment as standard. Lincoln now offers complimentary maintenance at no additional charge for the first 3 years/36,000 miles in service.

Review

It's a special moment in your life when you realize that the car you are driving can also be ordered as a hearse. Or as a limo. You just can't say that about too many cars these days. But it's true for the Lincoln Town Car, the last of the big, rear-drive American luxury sedans.

At over 215 inches in length, its primary mission is to silently and comfortably transport multiple passengers to their destination. For the general consumer, the Town Car is offered in Executive, Signature and Cartier trim. Extended-wheelbase models of the Executive and Cartier are also offered. Made available midway through last year, these vehicles (labeled Executive L and Cartier L) give rear passengers an additional 6 inches of legroom.

Items such as leather seating surfaces, automatic climate control, antilock brakes, traction control, front and side airbags, and memory seating are standard for all models. The new adjustable throttle and brake pedals should help shorter drivers maintain a proper distance from the steering wheel. All 2001 Town Cars also receive complimentary maintenance. This program covers all routine maintenance — from oil changes to wipers to shocks — for the first three years or 36,000 miles.

Stepping up from the Executive to the Signature model adds a few perks such as a powerful Alpine stereo system and steering wheel-mounted controls for the stereo and climate-control

LINCOLN

TOWN CAR

systems. The top-line Cartier gilds the lily with higher-grade leather, heated seats, chrome wheels and, of course, a Cartier clock.

One complaint we had with earlier Town Cars was the lack of horsepower. Lincoln has addressed this in 2001. The Executive and Signature models now have 220 horsepower and 265 foot-pounds of torque. Cartier models get slightly more with 235 horsepower and 276 foot-pounds of torque. All models have a four-speed automatic transmission.

Town Cars work best for highway and urban cruising. The suspension is quite soft, so it's best to order the Signature Touring Sedan option if you think you want a more sporting character. This package adds special trim, the 220-horsepower engine, revised suspension tuning and a shorter axle ratio for better acceleration.

For a large, domestic rear-drive luxury car, the Town Car has no peer. But compared to other vehicles like the BMW 7 Series, Lexus LS 430, and Mercedes S-Class, the Town Car's mediocre level of refinement and material quality quickly stand out. Of course, all of those vehicles cost considerably more. And they can't be ordered direct from the factory as a limo. Advantage: Lincoln.

Standard Equipment

EXECUTIVE (4A): 4.6L V8 SOHC SMPI 16-valve engine; 4-speed electronic OD automatic transmission with lock-up converter; HD battery with rundown protection; 120-amp alternator; rear-wheel drive, traction control, 3.08 axle ratio; stainless steel exhaust; auto-leveling suspension, front independent suspension with anti-roll bar, front coil springs, gas-pressurized front shocks, rigid rear axle multi-link suspension with anti-roll bar, rear air springs, gas-pressurized rear shocks; recirculating-ball power steering with vehicle-speed-sensing assist, steering cooler; 4-wheel disc brakes with 4-wheel antilock braking system; 19 gal. capacity fuel tank; side impact bars; class I towing package; front and rear body-colored bumpers with chrome bumper insert; body-colored bodyside cladding; clearcoat monotone paint; aero-composite halogen fully automatic headlamps with delay-off feature; additional exterior lights include cornering lights, underhood light; driver's and passenger's power remote body-colored heated folding outside mirrors; 16" x 7" silver alloy wheels with P225/60SR16 BSW A/S tires; compact steel spare wheel; air conditioning with climate control, rear heat ducts; premium AM/FM stereo w/clock, seek-scan feature, cassette player, 4 speakers, window grid diversity antenna; cruise control with steering wheel controls; power door locks with 2-stage unlock, remote keyless entry, child-safety rear door locks, power remote hatch/trunk release, power remote fuel door release; 2 power accessory outlets, front lighter element, driver's foot rest, retained accessory power, smokers' package; instrumentation display includes water temperature gauge, exterior temp, systems monitor, trip computer, trip odometer, compass; warning indicators include oil pressure, water temp, battery, low oil level, lights on, key in ignition, low fuel, low washer fluid, bulb failure, door ajar, trunk ajar, brake fluid; driver's and passenger's front airbags, driver's and front passenger's seat-mounted side airbags; ignition disable, panic alarm, security system; tinted windows, power front and rear windows with driver's 1-touch down function; variable-speed intermittent front windshield wipers, sun visor strip, rear window defroster; seating capacity of 6, 40/20/40 split-bench front seat with adjustable headrests, center armrest with storage, driver's and front passenger's seats include 8-way power seat and power 2-way lumbar support; rear bench seat with fixed headrests, center armrest; height-adjustable front seatbelts with pretensioners; leather seats, door trim with carpet, full cloth headliner, full carpet floor covering with carpeted floor mats, plastic/rubber gearshift knob, chrome interior accents; interior lights include dome light with fade, front and rear reading lights, door curb lights, illuminated entry, driver's side mirror; leather-wrapped steering wheel with tilt adjustment; dual illuminated vanity mirrors, dual auxiliary visors; day/night rearview mirror, auto-dimming driver's side mirror; locking glove box with light, front and rear cupholders, interior concealed storage, driver's and passenger's door bins; carpeted cargo floor, carpeted trunk lid, cargo light; chrome grille, chrome side window moldings, black front windshield molding, black rear window molding and chrome door handles.

SIGNATURE (4A) (in addition to or instead of EXECUTIVE (4A) equipment): Driver's auto-dimming outside mirror; premium AM/FM stereo, 9 performance speakers, amplifier, radio

TOWN CAR — LINCOLN

steering wheel controls; garage door opener; additional instrumentation display includes compass; genuine wood dashboard insert, genuine wood door panel insert; driver's seat memory features 2 memory settings for exterior mirrors; leather/genuine wood steering wheel; auto-dimming day/night rearview mirror.

EXECUTIVE L (4A) (in addition to or instead of SIGNATURE (4A) equipment): Dual exhaust; P225/70SR16 WSW A/S tires; rear stereo controls; rear bench seat with tilt headrests, rear illuminated vanity mirror and rear door bins.

CARTIER (4A) (in addition to or instead of EXECUTIVE L (4A) equipment): P225/60SR16 BSW A/S tires; body-side accent gold trim; driver's auto-dimming outside mirror; heated-cushion driver's and front passenger's seats.

CARTIER L (4A) (in addition to or instead of CARTIER (4A) equipment): P225/70SR16 WSW A/S tires; 4 power accessory outlets and heated rear bench seat.

Base Prices

Code	Description	Invoice	MSRP
M81	Executive (4A)	36211	39145
M82	Signature (4A)	38163	41315
M84	Executive L (4A)	39909	43255
M83	Cartier (4A)	40310	43700
M85	Cartier L (4A)	44639	48510
	Destination Charge	745	745

Interested in seeing what dealers will sell this vehicle for? Check out our True Market Value^{sm} (TMV^{sm}) pricing on our Web site at www.edmunds.com.

Accessories

Code	Description	Invoice	MSRP
467	Driver and Passenger Heated Seats (Signature)	348	400
503	Tire: Conventional Spare (All Except Executive L)	114	130
	Includes matching steel wheel.		
60P	Premium Package (Signature/Cartier)	1854	2130
	Manufacturer Discount	(466)	(535)
	Net Price	1388	1595
	Includes trunk-mounted CD changer and power moonroof.		
663	Signature Touring Sedan Package (Signature)	618	710
	Includes argent painted grille with chrome surround, monotone lower bodyside cladding and fascias, birds-eye woodgrain (black) trim on instrument panel and door trim, unique torque converte, revised springs and shocks, 30mm front stabilizer bar and 18mm rear stabilizer bar, 3.55 axle ratio, P235/60SR16 BSW A/S tires, 16" 8-spoke alloy wheels, unique badge, 4.6L EFI V8 engine and dual exhaust. NOT AVAILABLE with 954, T2A.		
919	Trunk Mounted Compact Disc Changer (Signature/Cartier/Cartier L)	526	605
954	Two-Tone Paint (Signature)	226	260
	NOT AVAILABLE with 663.		
T2A	Tires: P225/60SR16 WSW AS (Executive/Signature/Cartier)	91	105
	NOT AVAILABLE with 663.		
WF	Paint: White Pearlescent Clearcoat Metallic Tri-Coat (Executive/Signature)	327	375
X	Leather Perforated 40/20/40 Lounge (Signature)	NC	NC
	REQUIRES 663.		

MAZDA

626

2001 626

What's New?

The 626's interior gains a new modular audio system, a new rear deck with child safety-seat anchors, and an internal emergency trunk release. Mazda has also made EZ-Kool glass standard on all models and side airbags a stand-alone option on models with a V6 and automatic transmissions. All 626s are now 50-state emission compliant, though horsepower has been reduced slightly in the process.

Review

The Mazda 626 has been somewhat of a wallflower these past few years, watching the Ford Taurus, Honda Accord and Toyota Camry receive the most attention from people looking to buy a four-door family sedan. That's a bit unfortunate, as the 626 exhibits some solid attributes.

The Mazda comes in four trim levels: LX, LX-V6, ES and ES-V6. While by no means visually exciting, the 626 still manages to be an attractive sedan. LX and ES models have 15-inch wheels as standard, and the ES-V6 gets 16-inch wheels. The ES-V6 also comes with a sunroof, leather seating, an upgraded audio system, an eight-way driver's seat and heated side mirrors.

Mazda prides itself on building cars that are fun to drive. Aiding the 626's cause is a sporty suspension. Equipped with MacPherson struts up front and Mazda's Twin-Trapezoidal Link (TTL) suspension at the rear, the 626 grips confidently on twisty roads, while out on the highway, the suspension manages to soak up nearly every pothole without jolting passengers into instant kidney failure. The 626's steering and braking are also up to the task of providing a more rewarding experience than your average family sedan.

For power, the LX and ES feature a 2.0-liter four-cylinder engine producing 125 horsepower and 127 foot-pounds of torque. LX and ES cars fitted with the 2.0-liter engine qualify as ultra-low-emission vehicles. The 2.5-liter V6 puts out 165 horsepower and 161 foot-pounds of torque. While both engines are competent, they are a bit down on power when compared to the engines found in the top competitors in this class. Mazda does offer a manual transmission for both engines, making the 626 one of few family sedans available with a V6 and a manual transmission.

Inside, passengers are treated to a clean interior package. It's not exactly luxurious, but most of the controls are positioned for easy reach. HVAC controls are easy enough for a 4-year-old to use, with two large knobs for fan speed and temperature, and two rows of push buttons to control venting, air circulation and air conditioning.

Seating is spacious for its class, but front passengers will be disappointed with the lack of lumbar support and headroom. Rear-seat occupants have a better deal, with good headroom and width for two, a set of cupholders, extra storage in the fold-down center armrest and magazine pockets in the back of the front seats.

Overall, the 626 is a solid alternative in the family sedan market. Its strengths lie in its sporty nature and cult appeal (well, for a family sedan, anyway). If you are in the market to buy a new family sedan, the 626 deserves some of your attention.

Standard Equipment

LX (5M): 2L I4 DOHC SMPI 16-valve engine; 5-speed OD manual transmission; 582-amp battery; 80-amp alternator; front-wheel drive, 4.11 axle ratio; partial stainless steel exhaust; front independent strut suspension with anti-roll bar, front coil springs, rear independent multi-

626 MAZDA

link suspension with anti-roll bar, rear coil springs; rack-and-pinion power steering with engine-speed-sensing assist; front disc/rear drum brakes; 16.9 gal. capacity fuel tank; side impact bars; front and rear body-colored bumpers; body-colored bodyside molding; clearcoat monotone paint; aero-composite halogen auto-off headlamps; driver's and passenger's power remote body-colored outside mirrors; 15" x 6" steel wheels, P205/60SR15 BSW A/S tires; compact steel spare wheel; air conditioning, rear heat ducts; AM/FM stereo w/clock, seek-scan feature, single-disc CD player, 4 speakers, amplifier, window grid antenna; cruise control with steering wheel controls; power door locks with 2-stage unlock, remote keyless entry, child-safety rear door locks, power remote hatch/trunk release, remote fuel door release; 2 power accessory outlets, driver's foot rest; instrumentation display includes tachometer, water temperature gauge, trip odometer; warning indicators include oil pressure, battery, lights on, key in ignition, low fuel, low washer fluid, door ajar, trunk ajar, brake fluid; driver's and passenger's front airbags; tinted windows, power front and rear windows with driver's 1-touch down function; variable-speed intermittent front windshield wipers, sun visor strip, rear window defroster; seating capacity of 5, front bucket seats with adjustable headrests, center armrest with storage, driver's seat includes 6-way adjustment, passenger's seat includes 4-way adjustment; 60/40 folding rear bench seat with fixed headrests, center armrest with storage; height-adjustable front seatbelts; premium cloth seats, cloth door trim insert, full cloth headliner, full carpet floor covering, chrome interior accents; interior lights include dome light with fade, front reading lights, door curb lights, illuminated entry; steering wheel with tilt adjustment; dual illuminated vanity mirrors; day/night rearview mirror; full floor console, mini overhead console with storage, locking glove box with light, front and rear cupholders, instrument panel covered bin, 2 seatback storage pockets, driver's and passenger's door bins; carpeted cargo floor, cargo light; chrome grille, chrome side window moldings, black front windshield molding, black rear window molding and body-colored door handles.

LX V6 (5M) (in addition to or instead of LX (5M) equipment): 2.5L V6 DOHC SMPI 24-valve engine, (requires premium unleaded fuel); 90-amp alternator; 4-wheel disc brakes; P205/60HR15 BSW A/S tires.

ES (4A) (in addition to or instead of LX (5M) equipment): 4-speed electronic OD automatic transmission with lock-up converter, 4.23 axle ratio; leather seats, vinyl door trim insert, simulated wood console insert; leather-wrapped steering wheel.

ES V6 (5M) (in addition to or instead of ES (4A) equipment): 2.5L V6 DOHC SMPI 24-valve engine; 5-speed OD manual transmission; front power sliding and tilting glass sunroof with sunshade; heated outside mirrors; 16" x 6.5" silver alloy wheels, P205/55HR16 BSW A/S tires; cassette player, 4 premium speakers; ignition disable, security system; driver's seat includes 8-way adjustment, leather-wrapped gearshift knob.

Base Prices

Code	Description	Invoice	MSRP
626LX4P	LX (5M)	17088	18735
626LX6P	LX V6 (5M)	18181	19935
626ES4A	ES (4A)	19091	20935
626ES6P	ES V6 (5M)	20911	22935
Destination Charge:		480	480

Interested in seeing what dealers will sell this vehicle for? Check out our True Market Value℠ (TMV℠) pricing on our Web site at www.edmunds.com.

Accessories

Code	Description	Invoice	MSRP
1AB	Antilock Braking System with Traction Control/Airbag (LX-V6/ES-V6) *NOT AVAILABLE with AB4, AB2.*	760	950

MAZDA — 626 / MIATA

CODE	DESCRIPTION	INVOICE	MSRP
1ES	ES Luxury Package (ES)	1040	1300
	Includes power moonroof, anti-theft alarm, 6-way power driver's seat and heated mirrors.		
1LX	LX Luxury Package (LX)	1440	1800
	Includes 15" alloy wheels with locks, power moonroof, anti-theft alarm, 6-way power driver's seat, floor mats and heated mirrors.		
1WP	Wheels: 16" Alloy with Locks (LX-V6)	506	595
	Includes P205/55R16 tires.		
2LX	LX-V6 Premium Package (LX-V6)	1480	1850
	Includes 16" alloy wheels with locks, P205/55R16 tires, power moonroof, 6-way power driver's seat, floor mats, heated mirrors and anti-theft alarm.		
2WP	Wheels: 15" Alloy with Locks (LX)	383	450
3LX	LX-V6 Audio Package (LX-V6)	480	600
	Includes Bose AM/FM with CD/CASSETTE player.		
AB2	Side Airbags (LX-V6/ES-V6)	200	250
	REQUIRES AT1. NOT AVAILABLE with AB4, 1AB.		
AB3	Antilock Braking System (LX/ES)	640	800
	Includes side airbags.		
AB4	Antilock Braking System with Traction Control (LX-V6/ES-V6)	560	700
	REQUIRES AT1. NOT AVAILABLE with 1AB, AB2.		
AT1	Transmission: 4-Speed Automatic (LX/LX-V6/ES-V6)	696	800
CAS	Cassette Deck (LX/LX-V6/ES)	170	200
CD2	6-Disc CD Changer (ES-V6)	180	225
FLM	Floor Mats (LX/LX-V6)	56	80
	NOT AVAILABLE with MATS.		
FOG	Fog Lamps	200	250
GEP	Gold-Tone Emblem Package	120	150
RSP	Rear Spoiler	295	395
	Installed price.		

2001 MIATA

What's New?

For 2001, the Miata receives a host of minor changes. Horsepower has been increased, and a six-speed manual transmission is now optional on Miata LS. Both the exterior and interior have been updated and there are four new exterior colors. Regular Miatas now have 15-inch wheels as standard equipment, while both the Miata LS and cars equipped with the optional suspension package get 16-inch wheels. Safety and security is improved via seatbelt pretensioners, improved ABS, an engine immobilizer, an internal trunk release, and optional keyless remote (standard on Miata LS).

Review

Financially, it certainly pays to buy in bulk. To own a big-and-bad Ford Excursion, you'll have to pay only about $5 per pound (based on MSRP for a base model). To own a lithe 2001 Mazda Miata, you'll have to pay close to $9 per pound. But hey, sometimes you just have to pay more to get the good stuff.

MIATA MAZDA

CODE	DESCRIPTION	INVOICE	MSRP

While it seems strange to pay over $20,000 for a Miata, the price is still considerably less than those asked for roadsters like the BMW Z3, Mercedes-Benz SLK, Porsche Boxster, and Honda S2000. And while the Miata might not be able to match these cars' absolute performance numbers, it certainly equals or exceeds them with regard to the intangibles.

The Miata is about simplicity in design and operation. It's about having fun behind the wheel. It's about feeling free and young on warm summer nights. Not a serious car, the Miata, but that's part of its charm.

For 2001, the Miata receives its most thorough updating since its redesign in 1999. The exterior gains new headlights, a restyled front bumper and fascia, a new five-point air inlet, and an improved boot cover. Mazda has added variable valve timing to the 1.8-liter four-cylinder engine, bumping horsepower to 155 at 7,000 rpm and torque to 125 foot-pounds at 5,000 rpm. The six-speed manual transmission, previously available only on a couple of special limited edition models, is now an option on the Miata LS. Equipped with the six-speed transmission, a 2001 Miata LS should be the fastest Miata ever.

Though the Miata's trunk is miniscule when compared to what can be crammed into the latest SUVs, it can handle daily commuting or weekend getaways. The shifter moves with quick and short precision and all of the switchgear is easy to reach and use. For 2001, the interior features new white-faced gauges with chrome rings, new seats, new interior materials, revised positions for the cupholder and power door-lock switch, and a new modular audio system.

Droning trips on American interstates are not the Miata's forte. But with a lowered top and an open road, the Miata has few equals. The engine is perfectly matched to the suspension and steering, making the car a joy to pilot on curving roads. When equipped with the suspension package (which includes items like a Torsen limited-slip differential and upgraded shock absorbers), the Miata's performance envelope is wider, but some fun is lost in not being able to adjust the tail easily via the throttle.

In our opinion, you can utilize 90 percent of the Miata's abilities under normal driving conditions, while a Porsche Boxster driver is lucky to experience 60 percent of that car's potential most of the time. Toyota will give the '01 Miata some tough competition with its new MR2 Spyder, but that won't change the fact that the Miata continues to be one of the best roadsters available today.

Standard Equipment

BASE (5M): 1.8L I4 DOHC SMPI 16-valve engine; 5-speed OD manual transmission; 70-amp alternator; rear-wheel drive, 4.3 axle ratio; partial stainless steel exhaust with tailpipe finisher; front independent double-wishbone suspension with anti-roll bar, front coil springs, gas-pressurized front shocks, rear independent double-wishbone suspension with anti-roll bar, rear coil springs, gas-pressurized rear shocks; rack-and-pinion power steering with engine-speed-sensing assist; 4-wheel disc brakes; 12.7 gal. capacity fuel tank; side impact bars; manual convertible roof with lining, glass rear window, fixed wind blocker; front and rear body-colored bumpers; clearcoat monotone paint; aero-composite halogen headlamps; additional exterior lights include front fog/driving lights; driver's and passenger's power remote body-colored folding outside mirrors; 15" x 6" silver alloy wheels, P185/60HR15 BSW A/S tires; compact steel spare wheel; air conditioning; AM/FM stereo w/clock, seek-scan feature, single-disc CD player, 2 speakers, theft deterrent, power retractable antenna; remote trunk release, remote fuel door release; 1 power accessory outlet, front lighter element, driver's foot rest, smokers' package; instrumentation display includes tachometer, oil pressure gauge, water temperature gauge, trip odometer; warning indicators include oil pressure, battery, lights on, key in ignition; driver's front airbag, passenger's cancelable front airbag; ignition disable; tinted windows with driver's 1-touch down function; fixed-interval front windshield wipers, rear window defroster; seating capacity of 2, front bucket seats with fixed headrests, center armrest with storage, driver's and front passenger's

MAZDA
MIATA / MILLENIA

seats include 4-way adjustment; cloth seats, full carpet floor covering with floor mats, chrome interior accents; interior lights include dome light; leather-wrapped steering wheel; passenger's side vanity mirror; day/night rearview mirror; full floor console, locking glove box, front cupholder, instrument panel bin, 1 seatback storage pocket, driver's and passenger's door bins; carpeted cargo floor, cargo light; black side window moldings, black front windshield molding, black rear window molding and body-colored door handles.

LS (5M) (in addition to or instead of BASE (5M) equipment): Rear-wheel drive, limited-slip differential, 4.3 axle ratio; rocker panel extensions; 16" x 6" silver alloy wheels, P195/50VR16 BSW A/S performance tires; 4 premium speakers; cruise control; power door locks with 2-stage unlock, remote keyless entry; panic alarm; leather seats; interior lights include illuminated entry.

Base Prices

Code	Description	Invoice	MSRP
MIACP	Base Convertible (5M)	19331	21180
MIALP	LS Convertible (5M)	21836	23930
	Destination Charge:	480	480

Interested in seeing what dealers will sell this vehicle for? Check out our True Market Value^{sm} (TMV^{sm}) pricing on our Web site at www.edmunds.com.

Accessories

Code	Description	Invoice	MSRP
AB1	Antilock Brake System (LS)	468	550
AT1	Transmission: 4-Speed Automatic	782	900
	Includes 4.10 rear axle ratio. REQUIRES AB1. NOT AVAILABLE with SP1, SD1, SP2.		
CAS	Cassette Player	120	150
CV1	Convenience Package (Base)	668	795
	Includes tweeter speakers, power door locks, cruise control and remote keyless-entry system. NOT AVAILABLE with SP1.		
HT1	Detachable Hardtop	1215	1500
MGB	Front and Rear Mud Guards	100	125
MT6	Transmission: 6-Speed Manual with OD (LS)	565	650
RSP	Rear Spoiler	236	295
SD1	Torsen Limited-Slip Differential (Base)	332	395
SP1	Suspension Package (Base)	861	1025
	Includes strut tower brace, Torsen limited-slip differential, 16" alloy wheels with P195/50R16 V-rated Michelin tires, sport suspension, Bilstein shock absorbers. NOT AVAILABLE with CV1.		
SP2	Suspension Package (LS)	332	395
	Includes sport suspension, Bilstein shock absorbers. REQUIRES MT6.		

2001 MILLENIA

What's New?

Mazda has strengthened the Millenia's body structure to improve torsional rigidity 30 percent. Combined with a new rear stabilizer bar and a larger front stabilizer bar, improved handling is the result. Visually, the car should be more appealing thanks to new front and rear styling. The interior has been updated significantly, as well. Hardware changes include larger disc brakes, a revised ABS system and standard side airbags for both models.

MILLENIA — MAZDA

Review

The Mazda Millenia leads a dual-purpose life. It comes in two versions: the Millenia and the Millenia S. In terms of price, the base Millenia competes against cars like the Honda Accord EX V6 and the Nissan Maxima, while the Millenia S goes up against sporty entry-level luxury cars like the Audi A4, Acura TL and Lincoln LS V6.

The Millenia has been around in its current iteration since 1995. To keep the car fresh, Mazda has updated the 2001 car's styling and made minor mechanical changes. Never a standout in terms of styling, the Millenia's new hood, fenders, bumper, grille and headlights should help matters. The rear end also gets new taillights.

Inside, Mazda has ditched the cloth interior on base Millenias and made leather trim standard equipment. It has also given the Millenia a new silhouetted gauge cluster that is similar in design to those found in Lexus vehicles. There's also an upgraded audio system, a new center console with dual-level storage, a leather armrest cover, a 12-volt power point and dual covered cupholders. Materials are better thanks to a new two-tone interior color scheme; a leather-wrapped steering wheel, shift knob and parking brake; and cloth-covered A-pillars. Rounding things out are larger control switch graphics, power lumbar support, rear-seat cupholders and retained accessory power. As was the case last year, traction control and heated front seats are part of the Four-Seasons package.

The main difference between the Millenia and Millenia S is their engines. The base Millenia is powered by a 2.5-liter V6 that makes 170 horsepower at 5,800 rpm and 160 foot-pounds of torque at 4,800 rpm. The supercharged 2.3-liter V6 in the Millenia S makes 210 horsepower at 5,300 rpm and 210 foot-pounds of torque at 3,500 rpm. Both are equipped with four-speed automatic transmissions. Mazda says powertrain improvements have given the Millenia smoother transmission shifts and the Millenia S better acceleration.

The Millenia's 170 horsepower is a bit wanting, so best to step up to the Millenia S if you're looking for power. Acceleration is strong, and because of the Miller-cycle supercharged design, gas mileage remains frugal. On the road, the Millenia's suspension does a good job of soaking up broken pavement. Mazda says it has improved the 2001 car's steering, suspension and body structure for greater stability and response.

Mazda considers the Nissan Maxima, the Infiniti I30, the Toyota Avalon, and the Acura TL to be the Millenia's primary competitors. The Millenia does have some advantages, and this year's improvements should only help matters. However, we still feel that there are simply better choices available. For the price of a base Millenia, we'd take a Honda Accord EX or a Volkswagen Passat GLX. And for the price of a Millenia S, an Acura TL or Lexus IS 300 simply offer more.

Standard Equipment

BASE (4A): 2.5L V6 DOHC MPI 24-valve engine; 4-speed electronic OD automatic transmission with lock-up converter; 90 amp alternator; front-wheel drive, 4.38 axle ratio; partial stainless steel exhaust with tailpipe finisher; front independent suspension with anti-roll bar, front coil springs, gas-pressurized front shocks, rear independent multi-link suspension with rear coil springs, gas-pressurized rear shocks; rack-and-pinion power steering with engine-speed-sensing assist; 4-wheel antilock disc brakes; 18 gal. capacity fuel tank; side impact bars; front and rear body-colored bumpers; body-colored bodyside cladding, rocker panel extensions; clearcoat monotone paint; aero-composite halogen headlamps with auto-off feature; additional exterior lights include front fog/driving lights; driver's and passenger's power remote body-colored heated folding outside mirrors; 16" x 6.5" silver alloy wheels, P215/55VR16 BSW A/S tires; compact steel spare wheel; air conditioning with climate control; AM/FM stereo, seek-scan, cassette player, single-disc CD player, 6 speakers, window grid diversity antenna, radio steering

MAZDA   *MILLENIA*

wheel controls; cruise control with steering wheel controls; power door locks with 2-stage unlock, remote keyless entry, child-safety rear door locks, power remote trunk release, power remote fuel door release; 1 power accessory outlet, front lighter element, driver's foot rest, smokers' package; instrumentation display includes tachometer, water temperature gauge, in-dash clock, exterior temp, trip odometer; warning indicators include oil pressure, battery, lights on, key in ignition, low fuel, door ajar; driver's and passenger's front airbags, driver's and front passenger's seat-mounted side airbags; ignition disable, panic alarm, security system; tinted windows, power front and rear windows with driver's 1-touch down function; variable-speed intermittent front windshield wipers, sun visor strip, rear window defroster; seating capacity of 5, front bucket seats with adjustable tilt headrests, center armrest with storage, driver's seat includes 8-way power adjustment, 2-way power lumbar support, front passenger's seat includes 4-way power adjustment; rear bench seat with fixed headrests, center pass-thru armrest; height-adjustable front seatbelts; cloth seats, cloth door trim insert, full cloth headliner, full carpet floor covering with carpeted floor mats, leather-wrapped gearshift knob, simulated wood door panel insert, simulated wood console insert, chrome interior accents; interior lights include dome light with fade, front and rear reading lights, door curb lights, illuminated entry; leather-wrapped steering wheel with power tilt adjustment; dual illuminated vanity mirrors, driver's side auxiliary visor; day/night rearview mirror; full floor console, locking glove box with light, front and rear cupholders, 2 seatback storage pockets, driver's and passenger's door bins; carpeted cargo floor, cargo light; chrome grille, chrome side window moldings, black front windshield molding, black rear window molding and body-colored door handles.

S (4A) (in addition to or instead of P (4A) equipment): 2.3L V6 DOHC MPI intercooled supercharged 24-valve engine, requires premium unleaded fuel; 110-amp alternator; traction control, 3.81 axle ratio; power sliding and tilting glass sunroof with sunshade; 17" x 7" silver alloy wheels, P215/50VR17 BSW A/S tires; 9 premium speakers, amplifier; front passenger's seat includes 8-way power seat; rear bench seat with adjustable headrests; leather seats and vinyl door trim insert.

Base Prices

MILPA	Base (4A)	25604	28025
MILSA	S (4A)	28340	31025
Destination Charge:	....	480	480

Interested in seeing what dealers will sell this vehicle for? Check out our True Market Value^{sm} (TMV^{sm}) pricing on our Web site at www.edmunds.com.

Accessories

Code	Description	Invoice	MSRP
2CO	4-Seasons Package (Base)	504	600
	Includes heavy-duty windshield wiper motor, heated mirrors and large capacity windshield washer tank, heated front seats, heavy-duty battery, windshield washer fluid indicator light and electronic traction control.		
3CO	4-Seasons Package (S)	252	300
	Includes heavy-duty windshield wiper motor, heated mirrors and large capacity windshield washer tank, heated front seats, heavy-duty battery and windshield washer fluid indicator light.		
3RA	Bose Audio System (Base)	672	800
	Includes AM/FM ETR, cassette player, CD player, power amplifier and Bose 9-speaker sound system.		
5RA	In-Dash 6-Disc CD Changer	420	500
JCP	Two-Tone Paint	319	380
	NOT AVAILABLE with JCR.		

MILLENIA / PROTEGÉ — MAZDA

CODE	DESCRIPTION	INVOICE	MSRP
JCR	White Pearl MC Paint	319	380
	NOT AVAILABLE with JCP.		
PA5	Wheels: 17" Chrome Alloy (S)	420	500

2000 PROTEGÉ

What's New?

Front-seat side airbags and an improved ABS system are new to the LX premium and ES premium packages. The LX and ES also get illuminated power window switches. Chrome plating has been added to the inner door handles, and a Mazda symbol now appears on the steering wheel, the parking brake button, and the automatic transmission shift-lever button. The Twilight Blue Mica exterior color has been discontinued and replaced with Midnight Blue Mica.

Review

Now in its second model year, Mazda's current Protege is a snappy car that competes against vehicles like the Honda Civic, the Toyota Corolla, and the Ford Focus. Sold only as a four-door sedan, the Protege is available in three trim levels: DX, LX and ES. The base-model DX comes with standard features like power steering, tilt steering wheel and a split folding seatback. For options like a driver's height-adjustable seat, power windows and locks, a tachometer, and cruise control, you'll have to step up to either the LX or the ES. The ES also comes with features like standard air conditioning, 15-inch alloy wheels, and optional ABS.

Both the DX and the LX use a 1.6-liter four-cylinder engine that makes 105 horsepower and 107 foot-pounds of torque. Power from the 1.6-liter is tolerable, but buyers looking for more acceleration should go for the ES. This version gets a 1.8-liter engine that puts out 122 horsepower and 120 foot-pounds of torque.

The Protege is one of the best-looking economy sedans on the market. The creased and folded sheetmetal lends the car a more elegant and sophisticated look than you find on a Ford Escort or Nissan Sentra. The attractive brushed-aluminum wheels go a long way toward achieving this upscale appearance. Jewel-like headlight reflectors, angular taillights and chrome accents give the impression of a more expensive car.

The firm seats are comfortable, and the seat height and cushion angle adjustments (on the LX and ES) are greatly appreciated. The driving position is excellent, with a thick steering wheel rim to grip and a properly placed dead pedal for the left foot. There's also a proper Germanic front-passenger door grip, nicely padded upper door panels where elbows often rest, lots of storage nooks and crannies, a large rear seat, a commodious 12.9 cubic foot trunk, and a great stereo. Too bad Mazda decided to go with standard-issue econobox interior plastics, however. While not an unpleasant place to spend time, the Protege's interior is simply an example of form following function. For safety, there's standard dual front airbags and load-limiting front seatbelts with height adjustment.

On the road, the Protege is a bit louder than expected, but it does provide a good drive. The suspension is equal in both performance and ride quality when compared to the other top cars found in this class. Both engines come with either a five-speed manual or four-speed automatic transmission.

MAZDA
PROTEGÉ

CODE	DESCRIPTION	INVOICE	MSRP

The Mazda Protege is a long time favorite of ours. And although the new Ford Focus will be getting a lot of hype this year, the Protege deserves the attention of commuters looking for a comfortably quick commuter with spicy style and a good reliability record.

Standard Equipment

DX (5M): 1.6L I4 DOHC SMPI 16-valve engine; 5-speed OD manual transmission; 70-amp alternator; front-wheel drive, 3.85 axle ratio; partial stainless steel exhaust with chrome tip; front independent strut suspension with anti-roll bar, front coil springs, rear independent strut suspension with anti-roll bar, rear coil springs; power rack-and-pinion steering with engine speed-sensing assist; front disc/rear drum brakes; 13.2 gal. capacity fuel tank; side impact bars; front and rear body-colored bumpers; black bodyside molding; clearcoat monotone paint; aero-composite halogen headlamps; driver's and passenger's manual remote black folding outside mirrors; front and rear 14" x 5.5" styled steel wheels; P185/65SR14 A/S BSW front and rear tires; inside under cargo mounted compact steel spare wheel; rear heat ducts; radio prep, 4 speakers, and manual retractable antenna; child safety rear door locks, remote hatch/trunk release, remote fuel release; 1 power accessory outlet, driver's foot rest, smokers' package; instrumentation display includes water temperature gauge, trip odometer; warning indicators include oil pressure, battery, lights on, low fuel, door ajar; driver's and passenger's front airbags; tinted windows, manual front and rear windows; fixed interval front windshield wipers, rear window defroster; seating capacity of 5, front bucket seats, adjustable headrests, driver's seat includes 4-way direction control, passenger's seat includes 4-way direction control; 60-40 folding rear bench seat; front height adjustable seatbelts; cloth seats, cloth door trim insert, full cloth headliner, full carpet floor covering, plastic/rubber gear shift knob; interior lights include dome light; steering wheel with tilt adjustment; vanity mirrors; day/night rearview mirror; full floor console, glove box, front cupholder, instrument panel covered bin, interior concealed storage, driver's and passenger's door bins; carpeted cargo floor, cargo light; chrome grille, black side window moldings, black front windshield molding, black rear window molding and black door handles.

LX (5M) (in addition to or instead of DX (5M) equipment): Body-colored bodyside molding; driver's and passenger's power remote black folding outside mirrors; AM/FM stereo, clock, seek-scan, single CD, 4 speakers, and manual retractable antenna; cruise control; instrumentation display includes tachometer; power front and rear windows with driver's 1-touch down; center armrest with storage, driver's seat includes 6-way direction control; 60-40 folding rear bench seat with fixed headrests and body-colored door handles.

ES (5M) (in addition to or instead of LX (5M) equipment): 1.8L I4 DOHC SMPI 16-valve engine; 80-amp alternator; 4.11 axle ratio; front and rear 15" x 6" silver alloy wheels; P195/55VR15 A/S BSW front and rear tires; air conditioning, rear heat ducts; power door locks with 2 stage unlock, remote keyless entry; premium cloth seats and interior lights include illuminated entry.

Base Prices

PRODXP	DX (5M)	11679	12215
PROLXP	LX (5M)	12640	13515
PROESP	ES (5M)	14162	15315
Destination Charge:		480	480

Interested in seeing what dealers will sell this vehicle for? Check out our True Market Value^{sm} (TMV^{sm}) pricing on our Web site at www.edmunds.com.

PROTEGÉ
MAZDA

CODE	DESCRIPTION	INVOICE	MSRP

Accessories

Code	Description	Invoice	MSRP
1ES	ES Premium Package (ES)	1296	1580
	Includes side airbags, antilock braking system, power moonroof and carpeted floor mats.		
1LX	LX Premium Package (LX)	1312	1600
	Includes side airbags, antilock braking system, power moonroof, dual front seat map lights, keyless entry and illuminated entry. REQUIRES LXC.		
AT1	Transmission: 4-Speed Automatic with OD	720	800
	Includes 3.90 axle ratio.		
CAS	Cassette Player	213	250
	REQUIRES DXC.		
CE1	NLEV Emissions	84	100
DXF	DX Convenience Package (DX)	1292	1575
	Includes air conditioning, AM/FM stereo with CD and carpeted floor mats.		
FLM	Carpeted Floor Mats	64	80
FOG	Fog Lights	156	195
	Port-installed option.		
KE1	Keyless Entry (LX)	80	100
	Includes illuminated entry.		
LXF	LX Comfort Package (LX)	939	1145
	Includes air conditioning and carpeted floor mats.		
MR1	Power Moonroof (LX/ES)	560	700
	Includes dual front seat map lights. REQUIRES KE1.		
RSP	Rear Spoiler	246	330

A 15-minute phone call could save you 15% or more on car insurance.
1-800-555-2758

The Sensible Alternative

MERCEDES-BENZ
C-CLASS

| CODE | DESCRIPTION | INVOICE | MSRP |

2001 C-CLASS

What's New?

Ever expanding and improving its brood of stately vehicles, Mercedes gives the C-Class a complete overhaul for 2001. A choice of two new engines, increased safety features and sleeker sheetmetal tempt those who seek to gain a foothold into the exalted realms of Mercedes ownership.

Review

Ah, to be a Mercedes owner. More specifically, to be able to tell your friends that you've just bought a Mercedes; that is the stuff of which life is made. Unfortunately, your bank account is not yet plump enough to shell out the bucks for one of the big bad muthas. And, frankly, you kind of wish that a Mercedes had a more sporting attitude.

Enter the all-new 2001 C-Class. Designed to appeal to the sport sedan crowd heretofore untapped by the three-pointed star, Mercedes offers the C-Class as a contender in the entry-level luxury sedan playing field.

Motivating the C-Class is your choice of V6s — the 2.4-liter with 168 horsepower, or a 3.2-liter with 215 horses. And, in an effort to further compete with its venerable statesmen, a six-speed manual tranny will be available for the very first time in a C-Class, but it is reserved for the C240. Those who prefer automatic gear changes will like the tranny on the C320, a five-speeder with TouchShift. It's standard on the 320 and optional on the 240. With an improved five-link rear suspension and a new rack-and-pinion steering system, it should be as pleasurable to go canyon carving in the C-Class as it is to show up at your high school reunion.

Such luxurious features as dual climate control, steering wheel-mounted controls for and wood trim come standard on the C240. Step up to the C320 and receive a Bose stereo system, full power memory front seats and power tilt/telescoping steering wheel. Options include a stand-alone navigation system and Cockpit Management and Data System (COMAND), the center console interface that controls the navigation system, the audio system and the cell phone, xenon headlamps, heated seats, a six-disc CD changer and a sport package that provides higher spring rates, tighter shock valving, a thicker stabilizer bar and larger tires.

The jury's still out on whether or not we like the figure-eight headlamp design that reminds us of an amoeba splitting in two. But the new silhouette of the car, derivative of the S500 but with coupe-like looks, sculpted hood and triangular taillights deserves kudos.

Mercedes went all out to ensure the safety of C-Class buyers. Turn signals in the side mirrors allow others to better spot you. Standard Electronic Stability Program (ESP) that helps bring the car back in line if the system determines that the driver is losing control and four-wheel ABS (with bigger discs than previous versions to help stopping performance) assist drivers in avoiding unseemly situations. Even if you get into a collision, with dual front, four door-mounted side airbags as well as two side curtains ready to deploy, your cabin will be a veritable padded cell. Then you'll hear a concerned, helpful voice through Tele-Aid, which provides emergency services via the cell phone and GPS system.

Yes, the C-Class is the runt of the Mercedes stable. But in its own excellent clique, composed of other Teutonic and Japanese playmates, such as the 3 Series, Audi A4 or the Lexus IS 300, it could very well hold its own.

Standard Equipment

C240 (6M): 2.6L V6 SOHC SMPI 18-valve engine, (requires premium unleaded fuel); 6-speed OD manual transmission; HD battery; 90 amp alternator; rear-wheel drive, traction control, 3.46

C-CLASS — MERCEDES-BENZ

axle ratio; stainless steel exhaust; electronic stability control, front independent double-wishbone suspension with anti-roll bar, front coil springs, gas-pressurized front shocks, rear independent multi-link suspension with anti-roll bar, rear coil springs, gas-pressurized rear shocks; rack-and-pinion power steering with vehicle-speed-sensing assist; 4-wheel antilock disc brakes; 16.2 gal. capacity fuel tank; side impact bars; front and rear body-colored bumpers with body-colored rub strip, chrome bumper insert; body-colored bodyside molding with chrome bodyside insert; clearcoat monotone paint; aero-composite halogen auto on headlamps with daytime running lights, delay-off feature; additional exterior lights include front fog/driving lights; driver's and passenger's power remote body-colored heated folding outside mirrors with turn signal indicators, driver's auto-dimming outside mirror; 16" x 7" silver alloy wheels; P205/55HR16 BSW A/S tires; full-size alloy spare wheel; dual-zone front air conditioning with climate control, air filter, rear heat ducts, residual heat recirculation; AM/FM stereo radio, seek-scan feature, cassette player, CD changer pre-wiring, 7 speakers, theft deterrent, window grid antenna, radio steering wheel controls; cruise control; power door locks with 2-stage unlock, remote keyless entry, child-safety rear door locks, power remote hatch release; cell phone pre-wiring, 1 power accessory outlet, front lighter element(s), driver's foot rest, garage door opener, smokers' package, first aid kit, emergency S.O.S.; instrumentation display includes tachometer, water temperature gauge, in-dash clock, exterior temp, systems monitor, trip odometer; warning indicators include water temp, battery, low oil level, low coolant, lights on, key in ignition, low fuel, low washer fluid, bulb failure, door ajar, trunk ajar, service interval, brake fluid; driver's and passenger's front airbags, driver's and front passenger's door mounted side airbags, overhead airbag; ignition disable, panic alarm, tracker system, security system; tinted windows, power front and rear windows with front and rear 1-touch down function; heated jets variable-speed intermittent front windshield wipers, sun visor strip, rear window defroster; seating capacity of 5, front bucket seats with adjustable tilt headrests, center armrest with storage, driver's seat includes 4-way power adjustment, 8-way adjustment, passenger's seat includes 4-way power adjustment, 8-way adjustment; rear bench seat with power adjustable headrests, center armrest; height-adjustable front seatbelts with pretensioners; leather seats, leatherette door trim insert, full cloth headliner, full carpet floor covering with carpeted floor mats, genuine wood dashboard insert, leather-wrapped gearshift knob, genuine wood door panel insert, genuine wood console insert, chrome interior accents; interior lights include dome light with fade, front reading lights, 2 door curb lights, illuminated entry; leather-wrapped steering wheel with tilt and telescopic adjustment; dual illuminated vanity mirrors; auto-dimming day/night rearview mirror; full floor console, mini overhead console locking glove box with light, front and rear cupholders, instrument panel bin, 2 seatback storage pockets, refrigerated/cooled box, driver's and passenger's door bins; carpeted cargo floor, carpeted trunk lid, cargo light; chrome grille, black side window moldings, black front windshield molding, black rear window molding and chrome door handles.

C320 (5A) (in addition to or instead of C240 (6M) equipment): 3.2L V6 SOHC SMPI 18-valve engine; 5-speed electronic OD automatic transmission with lock-up torque converter; 115 amp alternator; driver's selectable multi-mode auto-manual transmission; 3.27 axle ratio; stainless steel exhaust; driver's power remote auto-dimming outside mirror, passenger's power remote with tilt down outside mirror; premium AM/FM stereo radio, seek-scan feature, cassette player, CD changer pre-wiring, 10 premium speakers; driver's seat includes 8-way power adjustment, passenger's seat includes 8-way power adjustment; memory on driver's and passenger's seats with 3 memory setting(s) includes settings for exterior mirrors, steering wheel and headrests.

Base Prices

C240W	C240 (6M)	27854	29950
C320W	C320 (5A)	34365	36950
Destination Charge:	....	645	645

Interested in seeing what dealers will sell this vehicle for? Check out our True Market Value^{sm} (TMV^{sm}) pricing on our Web site at www.edmunds.com.

MERCEDES-BENZ   C-CLASS

CODE	DESCRIPTION	INVOICE	MSRP

Accessories

CODE	DESCRIPTION	INVOICE	MSRP
—	Personalization Program Paint and Trim (C240/C320)	NC	NC
—	Premium Leather Upholstery (C240/C320)	1279	1375
—	Special Order Personalization Charge (C240/C320)	930	1000
177	Option Package K2 (VPC Installed)	1038	1795
	Includes integrated Motorola digital timeport and 6-disc CD changer. NOT AVAILABLE with 179, CDCHR.		
179	Option Package K2a (VPC Installed)	1355	2190
	Includes integrated motorola digital timeport with voice control and 6-disc CD changer. NOT AVAILABLE with 177, CDCHR.		
189	Paint: Black Opal Met	581	625
197	Paint: Obsidian Black Met	581	625
211	Option Package C1 (C240)	1116	1200
	Includes power front seats with memory, power tilt and telescopic steering wheel and.		
212	Option Package C2	1246	1340
	Includes rain sensing windshield wipers, power tilt/sliding tinted glass sun roof and power rear window sunshade.		
213	Option Package C3	395	425
	Includes ski sack and 60/40 split folding rear seats.		
214	Option Package C4	744	800
	Includes heated headlamp washers and heated seats.		
345	Paint: Orion Blue Met	581	625
352	COMAND Integrated Navigation System	1893	2035
	Includes Global Positioning Satellite navigation assistance and console-mounted screen. Integrates navigation, telephone and audio controls in one control center. Deletes standard cassette player.		
359	Paint: Capri Blue Met	581	625
404	Multi-Contour Driver's Seat	428	460
423	Transmission: 5 Speed Auto with Touch Shift (C240)	1209	1300
	Electronically controlled and driver-adaptive.		
567	Paint: Bordeaux Red Met	581	625
586	Paint: Magma Red Met (C320)	581	625
612	Xenon High Intensity Headlamps	791	850
693	Paint: Desert Silver Met (C320)	581	625
744	Paint: Brilliant Silver Met	581	625
753	Paint: Tectite Gray Met	581	625
772	C6 Sport Package	2744	2950
	Includes unique bumpers, rocker panels and fog lights, sport-tuned suspension, wheels: 16" x 7" 5-spoke sport alloy, tires: P225/50R16 A/S, premium leather upholstery, front sport seats, sculpted lower body trim and engraved aluminum interior trim.		
810	Bose Sound System (C240)	553	595
891	Paint: Aspen Green Met	581	625
904	Paint: Midnight Blue (C240)	581	625
941	Paint: Wedgewood Blue Met	581	625
994	Paint: Amethyst Met	581	625

MERCEDES-BENZ
CLK-CLASS

2001 CLK-CLASS

What's New?

Tele Aid comes standard on every CLK model this year, and the front windows lower slightly when you open the doors and seal (FOOP!) tight when you close them.

Review

Luxury is synonymous with Mercedes, and the CLK lives up to that name. Standard equipment is generous, and the interior is swathed in wood and leather. Based on previous-generation C-Class sedan running gear and available with either a V6 or V8 in coupe or convertible format, the CLK appeals to people who place sports car performance and the availability of manual transmissions secondary to comfort and convenience. But this Benz is no slouch in the driving satisfaction department.

A 3.2-liter V6 engine making 215 horsepower and 229 foot-pounds of torque powers CLK320 models. Mercedes asserts that the 320 Coupe goes from zero to 60 mph in 6.9 seconds. CLK430 models receive a 275-horsepower, 4.3-liter V8 engine, which cranks out 295 ft-lbs. of twist. This shaves nearly a second off the 320's zero-to-60 time. Power is transmitted to the rear wheels through an adaptive logic five-speed automatic transmission that features Touch Shift manual control for drivers wanting to micromanage their automatic's activity. Either car feels well balanced in turns, but a little heavy. The 320 drives more like a sedan than a sports car - surefooted and steady rather than agile and quick. The speedy 430, on the other hand, is tuned for a firm ride and taut handling. In either case, the CLK is an attractive car that turns heads.

Both the CLK320 and the CLK430 can be had in convertible form. The soft-top versions offer open air thrills when the top is down, but inordinately large blind spots when it goes up. Rear seat accommodations are tight in both hard- and soft-top versions, and certain switchgear feels subpar considering the hood badge.

Safety, as well as beauty, is addressed by the CLK. Antilock brakes with Brake Assist and full-range Automatic Slip Control (ASR) traction control come standard. Other standard features include front and side airbags and BabySmart child-detection protection for the front passenger seat. Electronic Stability Programming (ESP), which reduces understeer and oversteer by applying braking force to the wheel that needs it, is standard as well. TeleAid service comes standard with every 2001 CLK, and will notify emergency personnel if your airbags deploy or will put you in touch with a live operator to summon medical or police assistance. Tele Aid also features a roadside assistance function that will allow a Mercedes technician to check on the vehicle's electronic and computer systems via the remote uplink. Finally, Tele Aid incorporates a vehicle tracking system that can be used to locate a car after it has been stolen.

Another high-tech option is the Cockpit Management and Data (COMAND) system that debuted last year on the redesigned S-Class. Integrating radio, navigation, telephone and trip-computer functions into one unit that displays data on a small dash-mounted screen, COMAND is fussy and distracting to operate. Unless you absolutely must have a navigation system on board, skip this option.

The CLK impresses, from the classic and elegant styling, to the smooth and powerful engines, to the comfortable and well-appointed cabin. If you're in the market for a satisfying luxury coupe, it's hard to go wrong with this beautiful Benz.

MERCEDES-BENZ
CLK-CLASS

Standard Equipment

CLK320 (5A): 3.2L V6 SOHC SMPI 18-valve engine, (requires premium unleaded fuel); 5-speed electronic OD automatic transmission with lock-up torque converter; HD battery; 115 amp alternator; driver's selectable multi-mode auto-manual transmission; rear-wheel drive, traction control, 3.07 axle ratio; stainless steel exhaust with tailpipe finisher; electronic stability control, front independent double-wishbone suspension with anti-roll bar, front coil springs, gas-pressurized front shocks, rear independent multi-link suspension with anti-roll bar, rear coil springs, gas-pressurized rear shocks; power recirculating ball steering; 4-wheel antilock disc brakes; 16.4 gal. capacity fuel tank; side impact bars; front and rear body-colored bumpers with body-colored rubber strip; body-colored bodyside molding, rocker panel extensions; clearcoat monotone paint; aero-composite halogen headlamps with delay-off feature; additional exterior lights include front fog/driving lights; driver's and passenger's body-colored heated folding outside mirrors with turn signal indicators, driver's power remote auto-dimming outside mirror, passenger's power remote with tilt down outside mirror; 16" x 7" silver alloy wheels; P205/55HR16 BSW A/S tires; full-size alloy spare wheel; dual-zone front air conditioning with climate control, air filter, rear heat ducts, residual heat recirculation; premium AM/FM stereo radio, seek-scan feature, cassette player, CD changer pre-wiring, 8 premium speakers, theft deterrent, window grid antenna, steering wheel radio controls; cruise control; power door locks with 2-stage unlock, remote keyless entry, power remote hatch release, power remote fuel door release; cell phone pre-wiring, 1 power accessory outlet, front lighter element(s), driver's foot rest, garage door opener, smokers' package, emergency S.O.S.; instrumentation display includes tachometer, water temperature gauge, in-dash clock, exterior temp, systems monitor, trip computer, trip odometer; warning indicators include water temp, battery, low oil level, low coolant, lights on, key in ignition, low fuel, low washer fluid, bulb failure, service interval, low brake fluid; driver's and passenger's front airbags, driver's and front passenger's door mounted side airbags; ignition disable, panic alarm, tracker system, security system; tinted windows with driver's and passenger's 1-touch down function; heated jets with fixed interval front windshield wipers, sun visor strip, rear window defroster; seating capacity of 4, front bucket seats, power adjustable tilt headrests, center armrest with storage, driver and passenger seats include 8-way power adjustment and easy entry; 60/40 folding rear split-bench seat with power adjustable headrests, center armrest; height-adjustable front seatbelts with pretensioners; leather seats, leather door trim insert, full cloth headliner, full carpet floor covering with carpeted floor mats, genuine wood dashboard insert, leather-wrapped gearshift knob, genuine wood door panel insert, genuine wood console insert, chrome interior accents; memory on driver's and passenger's seats with 3 memory setting(s) includes settings for exterior mirrors, headrests; interior lights include dome light with fade, front reading lights, illuminated entry; leather-wrapped steering wheel with telescopic adjustment; dual illuminated vanity mirrors; auto-dimming day/night rearview mirror; full floor console, rear console with storage, locking glove box with light, front and rear cupholders, instrument panel bin, 2 seatback storage pockets, driver's and passenger's door bins; carpeted cargo floor, cargo light; chrome grille, chrome side window moldings, black front windshield molding and chrome door handles.

CLK430 COUPE (5A) (in addition to or instead of CLK320 COUPE (5A) equipment): 4.3L V8 SOHC SMPI 24-valve engine; 2.87 axle ratio; sport-ride suspension; front 17" x 7.5" silver superior alloy wheels rear 17" x 8.5" silver superior alloy wheels; P225/45ZR17 BSW performance front tires; 245/40 rear tires; black side window moldings and body-colored door handles.

CONVERTIBLE (5A) (in addition to or instead of COUPE (5A) equipment): Power convertible roof with lining, glass rear window, roll-over protection, manual wind blocker; premium AM/FM stereo radio, seek-scan feature, cassette player, CD changer pre-wiring, 7 premium speakers, fixed antenna; tinted windows, power front and rear windows with front and rear 1-touch down function; rear bench seat with power adjustable headrests and center armrest.

CLK-CLASS — MERCEDES-BENZ

CODE	DESCRIPTION	INVOICE	MSRP

Base Prices

CLK430C	CLK430 Coupe (5A)	46175	49650
CLK430A	CLK430 Convertible (5A)	52545	56500
CLK320C	CLK320 Coupe (5A)	39014	41950
CLK320 A	CLK320 Convertible (5A)	45477	48900
Destination Charge:		645	645

Interested in seeing what dealers will sell this vehicle for? Check out our True Market Value^{sm} (TMV^{sm}) pricing on our Web site at www.edmunds.com.

Accessories

CODE	DESCRIPTION	INVOICE	MSRP
—	Metallic Paint	581	625
—	Personalization Program Paint and Trim *REQUIRES ORDER.*	NC	NC
—	Special Order Personalization Charge	930	1000
149	Option Package K3 (Coupe) *Includes glass sunroof, auto intermittent rain sensor wipers and electric rear window sunshade.*	1246	1340
150	Option Package K4 (Coupe) *Includes heated front seats, Xenon headlights and headlamp washers.*	1437	1545
159	Option Package K4 (Convertible) *Includes heated front seats, Xenon headlights and headlamp washers.*	1535	1650
177	Option Package K2 *VPC installed, integrated digital timeport phone and integrated 6-disc CD changer. NOT AVAILABLE with 179.*	1038	1795
179	Option Package K2a *VPC installed, integrated digital timeport phone and integrated 6-disc CD changer. NOT AVAILABLE with 177.*	1355	2190
192	Designo Package Espresso Edition *Includes light brown exclusive nappa leather with door inserts, natural maple wood trim, designo light brown/charcoal leather steering wheel/shift knob and charcoal floor mats with light brown leather border and light brown designo script. REQUIRES 873. NOT AVAILABLE with 193.*	5627	6050
193	Designo Package Slate Blue Edition *Includes charcoal/dark blue exclusive nappa leather with door inserts, charcoal natural maple wood trim, charcoal/dark blue nappa leather steering wheel/shift knob and charcoal floor mats with dark blue leather border and dark blue designo script. NOT AVAILABLE with 192.*	6371	6850
352	COMAND System *Command replaces the standard cassette with navigation and CD music capabilities.*	1893	2035
406	Multicontour Front Seat Backs	674	725
731	Burl Walnut Wood Trim (430) *REQUIRES ORDER.*	NC	NC
732	Black Birdseye Maple Wood Trim (320) *REQUIRES ORDER.*	NC	NC
873	Heated Front Seats	577	620

MERCEDES-BENZ

E-CLASS

| CODE | DESCRIPTION | INVOICE | MSRP |

2001 E-CLASS

What's New?

E320 Sedans can now be ordered with the sport package, which includes AMG aerodynamic enhancements, specific fog lights and 17-inch wheels and tires. E-Class sunroofs now feature one-touch opening.

Review

The very popular E-Class has proven to be a solid home run since its last redesign five years ago.

Four different models are available this year. The E320 Sedan and Wagon come equipped with a strong 3.2-liter V6 engine making 221 horsepower and capable of propelling these models from a standstill to 60 mph in 7 to 8 seconds, depending on equipment. The E430 Sedan, available with 4matic all-wheel drive, has a 4.3-liter V8 good for 275 horsepower and runs to 60 mph in the low- to mid-sixes. The ground-tromping E55, discussed in a different review, comes with a massive 349-horsepower 5.5-liter V8. All models have a Touch Shift automanual transmission, which lets the driver select his own gears or leave the slushbox to do the dirty work.

Outside, the E wears a familiar face. The CLK-inspired front end is tapered with a lower hoodline, raked-back dual headlamps and seamlessly integrated bumpers. Along the sides, exterior mirrors have integrated turn signals and trim is body-colored. This year, the base E320 Sedan can now be ordered with a sport package previously reserved for the more expensive E430 models. This package includes AMG aerodynamic enhancements, specific fog lights and 17-inch wheels and tires.

Inside, the multi-function steering wheel, large instrument cluster and central display screen for the optional (but not recommended) Cockpit Management and Data (COMAND) system provide the E-Class driver with a wealth of information. Side airbags are available in each of the four doors, and E320 Wagons come with inflatable side curtains for increased head protection. TeleAid is also a standard service, and can put you in touch with emergency personnel if your airbags deploy or if you suffer a sudden medical problem.

In addition to TeleAid, E-Class comes with a full roster of standard safety equipment. Antilock brakes with Brake Assist, traction control and stability control keep the E-Class going safely and securely in the direction it's been pointed. This year, all E-Class sunroofs feature one-touch opening, giving you even more time to play with COMAND. A BabySmart system automatically deactivates the front passenger airbag when a special dealer-installed child seat is present, but in an E-Class, there's plenty of room in back for the kiddies.

Thanks to a long list of safety and luxury features, the E-Class continues to represent the epitome of luxury, giving its owners a technologically magnificent vehicle in a striking package. The Mercedes E-Class cars make a statement. They say, "I'm rich." Then they add, "But I'm also an intelligent buyer who wants a comfortable and safe car, and that's what I'm paying for." Quite talkative, these cars. But they're correct.

Standard Equipment

E320 RWD SEDAN (5A): 3.2L V6 SOHC SMPI 18-valve engine (requires premium unleaded fuel); 5-speed electronic OD automatic transmission with lock-up torque converter; 100 amp alternator; driver's selectable multi-mode auto-manual transmission; rear-wheel drive, traction control, 3.07 axle ratio; stainless steel exhaust; electronic stability control, front independent double-wishbone suspension with anti-roll bar, front coil springs, gas-pressurized front shocks,

E-CLASS

MERCEDES-BENZ

rear independent multi-link suspension with anti-roll bar, rear coil springs, gas-pressurized rear shocks; rack-and-pinion power steering with vehicle-speed-sensing assist; 4-wheel antilock disc brakes; 21.1 gal. capacity fuel tank; side impact bars; front and rear body-colored bumpers with body-colored rub strip, chrome bumper insert; body-colored bodyside molding with chrome bodyside insert; clearcoat monotone paint; aero-composite halogen headlamps with delay-off feature; additional exterior lights include front fog/driving lights; driver's and passenger's body-colored heated folding outside mirrors with turn signal indicators, driver's power remote auto-dimming outside mirror, passenger's power remote outside mirror with tilt down function; 16" x 7.5" silver alloy wheels; P215/55HR16 BSW A/S tires; full-size alloy spare wheel; dual-zone front air conditioning with climate control, air filter, rear heat ducts, residual heat recirculation; premium AM/FM stereo radio, seek-scan feature, cassette player, CD changer pre-wiring, 8 speakers, theft deterrent, integrated roof antenna, radio steering wheel controls; cruise control; power door locks with 2-stage unlock, remote keyless entry, child-safety rear door locks, power remote trunk release, power remote fuel door release; cell phone pre-wiring, 1 power accessory outlet, front lighter element(s), driver's foot rest, retained accessory power, garage door opener, smokers¿ package, emergency S.O.S.; instrumentation display includes tachometer, water temperature gauge, in-dash clock, exterior temp, systems monitor, trip odometer; warning indicators include oil pressure, water temp, battery, low oil level, low coolant, lights on, key in ignition, low fuel, low washer fluid, bulb failure, service interval, brake fluid; driver's and passenger's front airbags, driver's and front passenger's door mounted side airbags, overhead airbag; ignition disable, panic alarm, tracker system, security system; tinted windows, power front and rear windows with front and rear 1-touch down function; variable-speed intermittent front windshield wipers with heated washer nozzles, sun visor strip, rear window defroster; seating capacity of 5, front bucket seats, power adjustable tilt headrests, center armrest with storage, driver and front passenger seats include 8-way power adjustment; rear bench seat with power adjustable headrests, center armrest; front and rear height adjustable seatbelts with front pretensioners; leather seats, leather door trim insert, full cloth headliner, full carpet floor covering with carpeted floor mats, genuine wood dashboard insert, leather-wrapped gearshift knob, genuine wood door panel insert, genuine wood console insert; memory on driver's and passenger's seats with 3 memory setting(s) includes settings for exterior mirrors, steering wheel, headrests; interior lights include dome light with fade, front reading lights, 4 door curb lights, illuminated entry; leather-wrapped steering wheel with power tilt and telescopic adjustment; dual illuminated vanity mirrors; auto-dimming day/night rearview mirror; full floor console, mini overhead console locking glove box with light, front and rear cupholders, instrument panel covered bin, 2 seatback storage pockets, refrigerated box, driver's and passenger's door bins, rear door bins; carpeted cargo floor, carpeted trunk lid, cargo tie downs, cargo light; chrome grille, black side window moldings, black front windshield molding, black rear window molding and chrome door handles.

E430 RWD SEDAN (5A) (in addition to or instead of E320 RWD SEDAN (5A) equipment): 4.3L V8 SOHC SMPI 24-valve engine; 2.82 axle ratio; 17" x 7.5" silver alloy wheels; P235/45WR17 BSW performance A/S tires; premium AM/FM stereo radio, seek-scan feature, cassette player, CD changer pre-wiring and 8 premium speakers.

E320 RWD WAGON (5A) (in addition to or instead of E320 RWD SEDAN (5A) equipment): Auto-leveling suspension; 18.5 gal. capacity fuel tank; roof rack; 2 power accessory outlets, trunk pull-down; fixed 1/4 vent windows; fixed interval rear wiper with heated jets; seating capacity of 7; 60/40 folding rear split-bench seat 2nd row seat with adjustable headrests, center armrest; full folding 3rd row rear facing bench seat; leatherette door trim insert, genuine wood dashboard insert, cargo cover and cargo net.

4MATIC AWD SEDAN (5A) (in addition to or instead of RWD SEDAN (5A) equipment): Full-time 4-wheel drive.

MERCEDES-BENZ

E-CLASS

CODE	DESCRIPTION	INVOICE	MSRP

Base Prices

Code	Description	Invoice	MSRP
E320 W	E320 RWD Sedan (5A)	44501	47850
E320 W/4	E320 4MATIC AWD Sedan (5A)	47151	50700
E430 W	E430 RWD Sedan (5A)	49476	53200
E430 W/4	E430 4MATIC AWD Sedan (5A)	52127	56050
E320 S	E320 RWD Wagon (5A)	45245	48650
E320 S/4	E320 4MATIC AWD Wagon (5A)	47895	51500
	Destination Charge:	645	645

Interested in seeing what dealers will sell this vehicle for? Check out our True Market Value^{sm} (TMV^{sm}) pricing on our Web site at www.edmunds.com.

Accessories

Code	Description	Invoice	MSRP
—	Metallic Paint	581	625
—	Nappa Leather Seat Trim (Sedan)	674	725
	REQUIRES ORDER. NOT AVAILABLE with 185, 186.		
—	Nappa Leather Seat Trim (Wagon)	1939	2085
	REQUIRES (ORDER) Special Order Personalization Charge. NOT AVAILABLE with 185, 186, (PREM) Premium Leather Seat Trim.		
—	Personalization Program Paint and Trim	NC	NC
	REQUIRES ORDER.		
—	Premium Leather Seat Trim (Wagon)	1279	1375
	NOT AVAILABLE with NAPPA.		
—	Special Order Personalization Charge	930	1000
147	Option Package E1	1023	1100
	Includes Xenon headlamps and headlamp washer system.		
148	Option Package E2 (E320)	1497	1610
	Includes Bose premium sound system, power tilt/sliding tinted glass sun roof and rain sensor wipers.		
148	Option Package E2 (E430)	1139	1225
	Includes power tilt/sliding tinted glass sun roof and rain sensor wipers.		
177	Option Package K2 (VPC Installed)	1038	1795
	Includes integrated digital motorola timeport phone and 6-disc CD changer. NOT AVAILABLE with 179.		
179	Option Package K2a (VPC Installed)	1355	2190
	Includes integrated digital motorola timeport phone and 6-disc CD changer. NOT AVAILABLE with 177.		
185	Designo Package Espresso Edition (E320 RWD Wagon)	6185	6650
	Includes charcoal interior, light brown Nappa leather, natural elm wood trim, and charcoal floor mats with leather trim, natural elm wood and leather steering wheel, natural elm wood and leather shift knob. REQUIRES 873. NOT AVAILABLE with 186, NAPPA.		
185	Designo Package Espresso Edition (RWD Sedan)	5627	6050
	Includes charcoal interior, light brown Nappa leather, natural elm wood trim, and charcoal floor mats with leather trim, natural elm wood and leather steering wheel, natural elm wood and leather shift knob. REQUIRES 873. NOT AVAILABLE with 186, NAPPA.		

E-CLASS / SLK — MERCEDES-BENZ

CODE	DESCRIPTION	INVOICE	MSRP
186	**Designo Package Silver Edition (E320 RWD Wagon)**	6185	6650
	Includes charcoal interior with dark green/charcoal Nappa leather, natural maple wood trim and charcoal floor mats with leather trim, natural maple wood and leather steering wheel, natural maple wood and leather shift knob. REQUIRES 873. NOT AVAILABLE with 185, NAPPA.		
186	**Designo Package Silver Edition (RWD Sedan)**	5627	6050
	Includes charcoal interior with dark green/charcoal Nappa leather, natural maple wood trim and charcoal floor mats with leather trim, natural maple wood and leather steering wheel, natural maple wood and leather shift knob. REQUIRES 873. NOT AVAILABLE with 185, NAPPA.		
217	**Special Order Package ES1**	977	1050
	Includes parktronic and rear reading lamps. REQUIRES ORDER.		
352	**COMAND Integrated Navigation System**	1893	2035
	Includes radio and single-CD player/CD-ROM drive, Includes radio and single-CD player/CD-ROM drive. Deletes standard cassette player and dash pocket.		
401	**Active Ventilated Seats**	1070	1150
	REQUIRES NAPPA or PREM.		
406	**Multi-Contour Driver and Passenger Seats**	674	725
414	**Power Tilt/Sliding Tinted Glass Sun Roof**	1079	1160
	Includes one-touch express-open/close.		
540	**Electric Rear Window Sunshade (Sedan)**	391	420
	Includes one-touch express-up/down.		
772	**E3 Sport Package (RWD Sedan)**	3804	4090
	Includes sculpted front Apron, side sills, rear Apron and round projector-beam front foglamps, wheels: 17" 5-spoke alloy and tires: 235/45R17 94W HIGH performance.		
873	**Front Heated Seats**	577	620

2001 SLK

What's New?

A new, V6-powered SLK320 joins the line-up while the SLK230 gets more power and a $2,100 price reduction. Both versions get a new six-speed manual tranny in addition to the five-speed automatic that's been available since the car's introduction, and all models benefit from a revised interior and exterior.

Review

The SLK's big selling point is its exclusive retractable steel roof that, when raised, makes the car seem as tight and insulated as a Benz sedan. In less than 30 seconds, you can convert the SLK from a closed coupe to a cool convertible without leaving the driver's seat.

The original was available only with an automatic transmission and a 185-horsepower, 2.3-liter four cylinder that had an anemic exhaust note. In 1999, Mercedes equipped the car with a five-speed manual

MERCEDES-BENZ — SLK

transmission as standard equipment, making the slushbox optional. While not appreciably quicker, the manual offered buyers the option of selecting their own gears. When combined with the SLK's precise steering, rev-happy supercharged powerplant, and wonderfully damped suspension, the car was entertaining, though not particularly exhilarating.

This year the company has again raised the SLK's sporting potential by offering a V6-powered model, the SLK320. This version uses a 3.2-liter engine and a new standard six-speed manual transmission to send 215 horsepower to the rear wheels. The four-cylinder engine is also enhanced for 2001 and now makes 190 horsepower. While the six-speed manual is standard on both models, a five-speed automatic is still offered.

An optional sport package for the SLK230 doesn't cure the lame exhaust blat, but does include a muscular-looking body kit and thick 17-inch treads mounted to AMG Monoblock wheels. All SLK320s come standard with new 17-inch, five-spoke wheels, a unique air dam, metal plate door sills, power seats, a telescoping steering column and a wood and leather trimmed interior. Designo editions with special paint and trim are also available and, thankfully, the previous SLK230's carbon fiber inserts are gone. All models get front and side airbags as standard equipment, along with ABS, the ESP Stability Program, and the Tele Aid emergency call system.

The SLK also has a super-reinforced A-pillar, integrated roll bars behind each seat and emergency tensioning seatbelt retractors for enhanced rollover protection. Brake Assist applies full braking force before you can. A BabySmart system allows owners to use a special car seat sold by Benz dealers that keeps the passenger airbag from deploying in an accident. Here's our question: Why no cutoff switch like Mazda and other manufacturers offer? Inside, the 2001 SLK features a new shift lever, a new overhead console, SL-style door panels and a chrome handbrake button. Options like a CD changer, headlight washers, heated seats and, for the first time in SLK history, Xenon headlights can further spruce up this "poor man's" SL.

Standard Equipment

SLK230 (6M): 2.3L I4 DOHC SMPI inter-cooled supercharger 16-valve engine with variable valve timing (requires premium unleaded fuel); 6-speed OD manual transmission; HD battery; 90 amp alternator; rear-wheel drive, traction control, 3.46 axle ratio; stainless steel exhaust with tailpipe finisher; electronic stability control, front independent double-wishbone suspension with anti-roll bar, front coil springs, gas-pressurized front shocks, rear independent multi-link suspension with anti-roll bar, rear coil springs, gas-pressurized rear shocks; power recirculating ball steering; 4-wheel antilock disc brakes; 15.9 gal. capacity fuel tank; side impact bars; power convertible hardtop roof with lining, glass rear window, roll-over protection; front and rear body-colored bumpers with body-colored rubber strip; clearcoat monotone paint; aero-composite halogen headlamps with delay-off feature; additional exterior lights include front fog/driving lights; driver's and passenger's power remote body-colored heated folding outside mirrors; front 16" x 7" silver alloy wheels; rear 16" x 8" silver alloy wheels; P205/55VR16 performance BSW front tires; 225/50 rear tires; trunk mounted compact steel spare wheel; dual-zone front air conditioning, air filter, residual heat recirculation; premium AM/FM stereo radio, seek-scan feature, cassette player, CD changer pre-wiring, in-dash CD pre-wiring, 6 premium speakers, theft deterrent, fixed antenna; cruise control; power door locks with 2-stage unlock, remote keyless entry; cell phone pre-wiring, 1 power accessory outlet, front lighter element(s), driver's foot rest, garage door opener, smokers' package, emergency S.O.S. (OnStar); instrumentation display includes tachometer, water temperature gauge, in-dash clock, exterior temp, systems monitor, trip odometer; warning indicators include water temp, battery, low oil level, low coolant, lights on, key in ignition, low fuel, low washer fluid, bulb failure, service interval; driver's and passenger's front airbags, driver's and front passenger's door mounted side airbags; ignition disable, panic alarm, tracker system, security system; tinted windows with driver's and passenger's 1-touch down function; heated washer bottle; variable-speed intermittent front windshield wipers, rear window defroster; seating capacity of 2, front bucket seats with adjustable headrests, center armrest with storage, driver's and passenger's seats include 6-way adjustment; seatbelts with front pretensioners; leather seats, leather door trim insert, full vinyl headliner, full carpet floor covering with floor mats, aluminum trim on instrument panel; interior lights include dome light with fade, illuminated entry;

SLK — MERCEDES-BENZ

leather-wrapped steering wheel; vanity mirrors; auto-dimming day/night rearview mirror; full floor console, locking glove box with light, front cupholder, instrument panel covered bin, driver's and passenger's door bins; carpeted cargo floor, cargo cover, cargo light; black grille, black side window moldings, black front windshield molding and body-colored door handles.

SLK320 (6M) (in addition to or instead of SLK230): 3.2L V6 SOHC SMPI 18-valve engine; driver's seat includes 6-way power adjustment 8-way adjustment, passenger's seat includes 6-way power adjustment, 8-way adjustment; genuine wood trim on instrument panel, wood gearshift knob; steering wheel with telescopic adjustment.

Base Prices

Description	Invoice	MSRP
SLK230 Komp SLK230 Kompressor (6M)	36177	38900
SLK320 SLK320 Roadster (6M)	40827	43900
Destination Charge:	645	645

Interested in seeing what dealers will sell this vehicle for? Check out our True Market Value^{sm} (TMV^{sm}) pricing on our Web site at www.edmunds.com.

Accessories

Code	Description	Invoice	MSRP
—	Metallic Paint	581	625
169	K1 Package (SLK230)	791	850
	Includes power seats and manual telescoping steering wheel.		
170	K4 Package	1437	1545
	Includes Xenon lights, headlight washers and heated seats.		
177	Option Package K2	1038	1795
	CDMA (Code Division Multiple Access), integrated 6-disc CD changer and integrated portable cellular telephone. NOT AVAILABLE with 178.		
179	Option Package K2a	1355	2190
	CDMA (Code Division Multiple Access), integrated portable telephone and integrated 6-disc CD changer. NOT AVAILABLE with 177, 178, 180.		
194	Designo Package Copper Edition	4743	5100
	Includes two-tone copper/charcoal exclusive nappa leather with door insert, charcoal cinamorra wood trim and steering wheel, nappa leather shift knob and charcoal floor mats with copper leather border and copper designo script. REQUIRES 873 or 170. NOT AVAILABLE with 195.		
195	Designo Package Electric Green Edition	4326	4650
	Includes charcoal exclusive nappa leather with light green stitching with door inserts, charcoal cinamorra wood trim and steering wheel, nappa leather shift knob and charcoal floor mats with charcoal leather border and light green designo script. REQUIRES 873 or 170. NOT AVAILABLE with 194.		
200	Designo Goldenrod Edition	4046	4350
	Includes basic charcoal interior, cinnamora anthracite wood trim, charcoal single colour leather seats, charcoal velour floor mats and charcoal leather steering wheel and shift knob. REQUIRES 873 or 170. NOT AVAILABLE with 194, 195.		
200	Designo Goldenrod Edition	4325	4650
	Includes basic charcoal interior, cinnamora anthracite wood trim, charcoal single colour leather seats, charcoal velour floor mats and cinnamora wood trim/charcoal leather steering wheel and shift knob. REQUIRES 873 or 170. NOT AVAILABLE with 194, 195.		

MERCEDES-BENZ   SLK

CODE	DESCRIPTION	INVOICE	MSRP
423	Transmission: 5 Speed Auto with Touch Shift	884	950
	Includes 3.27 axle ratio.		
772	SP1 Sport Package	3846	4135
	Includes sculpted lower body AMG designed aerodynamic enhancements, projector beam front fog lamps and side sills. silver painted front grill mesh, front 17" x 7.5" Monoblock alloy wheels, rear 17" x 8.5" Monoblock alloy wheels, 225/45ZR17 front tires and 245/40ZR17 rear tires.		
873	Heated Seats	577	620

TOWN HALL

Get answers from our editors, discover smart shopping strategies and share your perspectives in this interactive forum of both experts and consumers. Just enter the following address into your Web browser:

townhall.edmunds.com

Where smart shoppers talk about cars, trucks, and related consumer topics.

2001 COUGAR

What's New?

Exterior and interior changes are extensive for the Cougar. At first glance outside, you'll notice new front and rear fascias, new headlights with a projector and reflector system, a new grille, a new spoiler, new fog lights, and 16-inch painted or 17-inch machined aluminum wheels. New clearcoat metallic colors include Dark Shadow Grey, Tropic Green, French Blue and Sunburst Gold. The Cougar S is finally a go for production (we hope).

Review

The Cougar stands out as one of the more distinctly styled vehicles on the road today. And don't expect Cougar customers to be cross shopping for the 2001 Grand Marquis; this kitty cat is aimed at a much younger crowd.

The Cougar's New Edge look combines sleek, rounded main forms with creased straight-edge detail. The most interesting parts of the Cougar's appearance are the cat-eye headlamps with smoked lenses, large triangular taillights, sculpted doors and hood, and the character line that runs along the lower portion of the greenhouse.

Underneath this eye-catching skin are components that are much more familiar. The Cougar is built on the same European-engineered platform as the old Ford Contour and Mercury Mystique. It also shares roughly 70 percent of its parts with these two entry-level sedans. This is important to Ford, because it keeps the cost of the Cougar down.

The Cougar is blessed with an excellent suspension, neutral handling characteristics and powerful brakes. This translates to plenty of fun on curvy roads. The only thing slowing the Cougar down is an overly heavy steering feel and engines that don't quite measure up to the car's exciting looks. Ford offers either a 125-horsepower, four-cylinder engine or a 2.5-liter V6 that produces 170 horsepower. Compared to the engines found in the Mitsubishi Eclipse or the Volkswagen GTI, the Cougar is a bit shy on power.

Good thing there's the limited-production Cougar S that will be available in early 2001. A high-performance version of the V6-powered car, it comes standard with 200 horsepower. The car's suspension is also performance-tuned to handle the extra power.

For all Cougar interiors, you'll find a conventional control layout with a decidedly unconventional appearance. Accessing the backseat is a breeze, thanks to a front passenger seat that slides forward when the backrest is folded and then returns to its preset position once riders are secured in back. The rear seats are firm and place the rider high in the car; taller adults will find that their heads are squashed into the headliner.

For 2001, the interior has been notably updated with a CD player now standard. Visually, the door inserts have a perforated black material and there's a new steering wheel with revised cruise-control switches and a Cougar head emblem. There's also a new instrument cluster with a satin aluminum face and graphics, new gauge surround rings and pointers, and a new cluster shroud with a technical grain. Many components are also refinished with a new appearance and others will be painted with satin aluminum paint.

The Cougar S should be a welcome sight to performance enthusiasts. And despite the relative lack of power, the regular Cougar still has a lot to offer. It's affordable, functional, fun to drive and neat to look at.

MERCURY — COUGAR

Standard Equipment

I4 (5M): 2L I4 DOHC SMPI 16-valve engine with variable valve timing; 5-speed OD manual transmission; 105-amp alternator; 72-amp battery; front-wheel drive, 3.82 axle ratio; stainless steel exhaust; front independent strut suspension with anti-roll bar, front coil springs, gas-pressurized front shocks, rear independent multi-link suspension with anti-roll bar, rear coil springs, gas-pressurized rear shocks; rack-and-pinion power steering; front disc/rear drum brakes; 16 gal. capacity fuel tank; side impact bars; front and rear body-colored bumpers; clearcoat monotone paint; enclosed projector beam halogen headlamps; driver's and passenger's power remote body-colored heated outside mirrors; 15" x 6" silver alloy wheels, P205/60SR15 BSW A/S tires; compact steel spare wheel; air conditioning, air filter, rear heat ducts; premium AM/FM stereo, seek-scan feature, single-disc CD player, 4 performance speakers, integrated roof antenna; power door locks, power remote hatch release; 1 power accessory outlet, driver's foot rest; instrumentation display includes tachometer, water temperature gauge, in-dash clock, exterior temp, trip computer, trip odometer; warning indicators include oil pressure, battery, low coolant, lights on, key in ignition, low fuel, brake fluid; driver's and passenger's front airbags; ignition disable; tinted windows with driver's 1-touch down function; variable-speed intermittent front windshield wipers, rear window defroster; seating capacity of 4, front bucket seats with fixed headrests, driver's seat includes 8-way adjustment (2-way power), front passenger's seat includes 4-way adjustment with easy entry feature; 50/50 folding rear bucket seat with fixed headrests; height-adjustable front seatbelts; cloth seats, cloth door trim insert, full cloth headliner, full carpet floor covering with floor mats; interior lights include dome light with delay; steering wheel with tilt adjustment; driver's side vanity mirror; day/night rearview mirror; full floor console, glove box, front and rear cupholders, driver's and passenger's door bins; carpeted cargo floor, cargo cover, cargo tie downs, cargo light; black grille, black side window moldings, black front windshield molding, black rear window molding and body-colored door handles.

V6 (5M) (in addition to or instead of I4 (5M) equipment): 2.5L V6 DOHC SMPI 24-valve engine; 130-amp alternator; 4.06 axle ratio; tailpipe finisher; touring-ride suspension.

V6 S (5M) (in addition to or instead of V6 (5M) equipment): Requires premium unleaded fuel; traction control; sport-ride suspension; 4-wheel antilock disc brakes; rear wing spoiler; body-colored bodyside molding; additional exterior lights include front fog/driving lights; 17" x 7" machined alloy wheels, P215/50ZR17 BSW A/S tires; cruise control with steering wheel controls; power door locks with 2-stage unlock, remote keyless entry; warning indicators include low washer fluid, door ajar, service interval; ignition disable, panic alarm; rear window wiper; front sports seats with adjustable tilt headrests, center armrest with storage, driver's seat includes 14-way adjustment (6-way power), 2-way power lumbar support; leather seats, leather-wrapped gearshift knob, aluminum interior accents; interior lights include front reading lights, illuminated entry; leather-wrapped steering wheel; dual illuminated vanity mirrors; glove box with light, 2 seatback storage pockets.

Base Prices

Code	Description	Invoice	MSRP
T60	I4 (5M)	15505	16700
T61	V6 (5M)	15955	17200
T62	S (5M)	20321	22050
Destination Charge:		475	475

Interested in seeing what dealers will sell this vehicle for? Check out our True Market Value^{sm} (TMV^{sm}) pricing on our Web site at www.edmunds.com.

Accessories

Code	Description	Invoice	MSRP
13E	Power Tilt/Slide Sunroof	547	615
13K	Spoiler (I4)	209	235

COUGAR / GRAND MARQUIS — MERCURY

CODE	DESCRIPTION	INVOICE	MSRP
21A	6-Way Power Driver Seat (V6)	209	235
	Includes power lumbar, fore/aft and recline. REQUIRES 97S.		
41H	Engine Block Immersion Heater	18	20
44T	Transmission: 4-Speed Automatic Transmission with OD (V6)	725	815
	Includes 3.77 axle ratio.		
552	Antilock Braking System (I4/V6)	445	500
553	Traction Control (V6)	209	235
	REQUIRES 552.		
586	Radio: AM/FM Stereo with 6-Disc CD Changer (V6)	187	210
	In-dash CD changer. NOT AVAILABLE with 58K, 60L.		
586	Radio: AM/FM Stereo with 6-Disc CD Changer (V6/S)	116	130
	In-dash CD changer. NOT AVAILABLE with 58K.		
58K	Radio: AM/FM Stereo with CD, Cassette (I4/V6)	71	80
	Includes premium sound. NOT AVAILABLE with 586.		
59M	Side Airbags	347	390
60L	V6 Convenience Group (V6)	588	660
	Includes speed control, remote keyless entry, remote trunk release with key fob, panic alarm, illuminated entry, rear window wiper/washer, AM/FM stereo with CD and cassette players.		
63B	Smokers' Package	13	15
646	Wheels: 16" Machined Aluminum (V6)	223	250
	REQUIRES 97S.		
8	Leather Sport Bucket Seats (V6)	797	895
	REQUIRES 21A and 97S.		
94A	I4 Convenience Group (I4)	547	615
	Includes speed control, remote keyless entry, remote trunk release with key fob, panic alarm, illuminated entry and rear window wiper/washer.		
96G	Bodyside Moldings (I4/V6)	45	50
97S	V6 Sport Group (V6)	770	865
	Includes bright doorsill plate, aluminum foot rest, clutch, brake and accelerator pedal pads, leather-wrapped steering wheel, leather shift knob, light group, auxiliary warning system, glove box light, drivers side illuminated visor mirror, map lamps, fog lamps, spoiler, 4-wheel disc brakes, 16" painted aluminum wheels and P215/50X16 BSW tires, and sport cloth bucket seats.		

2001 GRAND MARQUIS

What's New?

Power from the V8 engine is improved. The interior gets minor improvements and an optional adjustable pedal assembly. Safety has been improved via a crash severity sensor, safety belt pretensioners, dual-stage airbags and seat position sensors.

Review

If you've been pinching your pennies to buy a new full-size, rear-drive American sedan, we hereby offer the Mercury Grand Marquis. It's mechanically identical to the Ford Crown Victoria; Ford and Mercury are the only brands building such cars these days.

MERCURY

GRAND MARQUIS

| CODE | DESCRIPTION | | INVOICE | MSRP |

Decades-old technology allows Mercury to keep the prices low, and the car is a favorite among people who need space and don't want a minivan or sport-ute. Think about this: the Grand Marquis costs less than $30 grand fully loaded with electric everything and a leather interior. In contrast, a similarly equipped Toyota Avalon runs several thousand dollars more.

The five- or six-passenger Grand Marquis is available in either GS or LS trim. Both have similar levels of equipment, though optional features like automatic climate control, a power passenger seat and a leather interior are only available on the LS model.

Both versions get mild interior updates for 2001. Storage pouches have been added to the front seat cushion, and there are new traction control, headlight and fuel-door release controls. The best addition is the optional adjustable gas and brake pedal assembly. These pedals can be moved up to 3 inches towards the driver to improve comfort and to keep shorter drivers from sitting too close to the steering wheel-mounted airbag.

The Grand Marquis was never a slouch in terms of acceleration, and this year Mercury has bumped the output of the 4.6-liter V8 engine to 220 horsepower and 265 foot-pounds of torque. The only transmission offered is a four-speed automatic. For even more horsepower, wait until later in 2001 when the special-edition, supercharged Grand Marquis Marauder becomes available as a 2002 model.

In stock trim, this Merc drives and handles like you would expect a big American sedan to. It's comfortable, but it's all too happy to float around over bumps. The handling and performance package adds 20 horsepower and improves the car's stability in the twisties; we recommend it to anyone who enjoys backcountry highways more than mind-numbing interstates for their family vacations.

And if you do plan to haul around a family, you can sleep better at night knowing that the Grand Marquis scores well in National Highway Traffic Safety Administration crash tests. Last year's models did very well, so the 2001 safety improvements (a crash severity sensor, safety belt pretensioners, dual-stage airbags and seat position sensors) should make the Mercury even better.

If you're one of the few people unwilling to pay for a sport utility's high insurance premiums and abysmal gas mileage and if you just can't stand the idea of a minivan, we hope that you like the Grand Marquis. It's your only choice for a premium brand, full-size, rear-wheel-drive sedan.

Standard Equipment

GS (4A): 4.6L V8 SOHC SMPI 16-valve engine; 4-speed electronic OD automatic transmission with lock-up converter; battery with rundown protection; 130-amp alternator; rear-wheel drive, 2.73 axle ratio; stainless steel exhaust; front independent suspension with anti-roll bar, front coil springs, gas-pressurized front shocks, rigid rear axle multi-link suspension with anti-roll bar, rear coil springs, gas-pressurized rear shocks; recirculating-ball power steering with vehicle-speed-sensing assist; 4-wheel disc brakes; 19 gal. capacity fuel tank; side impact bars; front and rear body-colored bumpers with chrome bumper insert; body-colored bodyside molding with chrome bodyside insert; clearcoat monotone paint; aero-composite halogen fully automatic headlamps with delay-off feature; additional exterior lights include cornering lights; driver's and passenger's power remote body-colored folding outside mirrors; 16" x 7" steel wheels, P225/60SR16 BSW A/S tires; compact steel spare wheel; air conditioning, rear heat ducts; AM/FM stereo w/clock, seek-scan feature, cassette player, 4 speakers, window grid antenna; cruise control with steering wheel controls; power door locks, child-safety rear door locks, power remote trunk release, remote fuel door release; 1 power accessory outlet, front lighter element, driver's foot rest, smokers' package; instrumentation display includes oil pressure gauge, water temperature gauge, volt gauge, in-dash clock, trip odometer; warning indicators include battery, lights on,

GRAND MARQUIS — MERCURY

key in ignition, low fuel; driver's and front passenger's airbags; ignition disable; tinted windows, power front and rear windows with driver's 1-touch down function; variable-speed intermittent front windshield wipers, sun visor strip, rear window defroster; seating capacity of 6, 50/50 split-bench front seat with adjustable headrests, driver's and front passenger's armrests, driver's seat includes 8-way power adjustment and power lumbar support, passenger's front seat includes 4-way adjustment; rear bench seat with center armrest; height-adjustable front seatbelts with pretensioners; premium cloth seats, vinyl door trim insert, full cloth headliner, full color-keyed carpet floor covering, deluxe sound insulation, simulated wood dashboard insert, simulated wood door panel insert, chrome interior accents; interior lights include dome light with fade, illuminated entry; steering wheel with tilt adjustment; passenger's side vanity mirror; day/night rearview mirror; locking glove box with light, front cupholder, 2 seatback storage pockets, driver's and passenger's door bins; carpeted cargo floor, cargo light; chrome grille, chrome side window moldings, black front windshield molding, black rear window molding and chrome door handles.

LS (4A) (in addition to or instead of GS (4A) equipment): Bodyside accent stripe; power door locks with 2-stage unlock, remote keyless entry, panic alarm; driver's seat includes 2-way power lumbar support; premium cloth seats; interior lights include front and rear reading lights, dual illuminated vanity mirrors.

Base Prices

			Invoice	MSRP
M74	GS (4A)		21595	22805
M75	LS (4A)		23343	24705
Destination Charge:			680	680

Interested in seeing what dealers will sell this vehicle for? Check out our True Market Value^{sm} (TMV^{sm}) pricing on our Web site at www.edmunds.com.

Accessories

Code	Description	Invoice	MSRP
144	Remote Keyless-Entry System (GS)	213	240
	Includes keypad and 2 remotes.		
155	Electronic Instrumentation (LS)	379	425
	REQUIRES 573.		
175	Homelink Universal Garage Door Opener (LS)	102	115
41G	Handling Package (LS)	476	535
	Includes larger diameter rear stabilizer bar and unique-tuned suspension (shocks, spring rates), 3.27 axle ratio, P225/60R16 BSW tires, rear air suspension with unique springs, 16" lacy-spoke alloy wheels and dual exhaust. REQUIRES (68E or 68F or 60L) and 99W. NOT AVAILABLE with 66B, 64R, 54E.		
41G	Handling Package	761	855
	Includes larger diameter rear stabilizer bar and unique-tuned suspension (shocks, spring rates), 3.27 axle ratio, rear air suspension with unique springs and dual exhaust. REQUIRES 99W. NOT AVAILABLE with 66B, 64R, 54E.		
508	Tires: 16" Conventional Spare	93	105
	Replaces standard mini-spare with full-size steel wheel and ground-position tire.		
508	Tires: 16" Conventional Spare	107	120
	Replaces standard mini-spare with full-size steel wheel and ground-position tire. REQUIRES 41G.		
552	Antilock Brakes	534	600

MERCURY — GRAND MARQUIS

CODE	DESCRIPTION	INVOICE	MSRP
553	Traction Control	690	775
	Includes antilock brakes.		
573	Electronic Automatic Temperature Control (LS)	156	175
	Includes outside temperature display.		
585	Single-Disc CD Player (GS)	124	140
	Replaces cassette player.		
586	Radio: Premium AM/FM with Cassette (LS)	321	360
	Includes radio/tape scan, AM stereo, auto-memory set, unique 4-channel premium amplifier with 80 total Watts RMS, Automatic Dynamic Noise Reduction (DNR) on FM, CrO2 capability on tape, radio play during tape rewind/fast forward, premium dual cone rear speakers and premium front door speakers, CD changer compatible and radio data system (RDS).		
59C	Power Adjustable Pedals (GS)	107	120
60C	GS Standard Equipment Group (GS)	NC	NC
	Includes remote keyless entry system, bodyside paint stripe, luxury light group (dual illuminated visor mirrors, dual beam dome/map light.) REQUIRES B3A.		
60L	LS Standard Equipment Group (LS)	NC	NC
	Includes GS standard equipment group, electronic instrumentation, electronic automatic temperature control, outside temperature display, auto-dimming mirror with compass, premium AM/FM stereo with cassette player, leather twin-comfort seats, 8-way power passenger seat, Homelink universal garage door opener and leather-wrapped steering wheel. REQUIRES B3A and (41G or 54E). NOT AVAILABLE with 68E, 68F, 64R.		
64R	Wheels: 16" Teardrop Aluminum (LS)	285	320
	NOT AVAILABLE with 41G, 54E, 68E, 68F, 60L.		
66B	Rear Air Suspension (LS)	240	270
	Tuned for softer ride. NOT AVAILABLE with 41G.		
68E	Premium Package (LS)	997	1120
	Includes power adjustable pedals, leather-wrapped steering wheel, electronic automatic temperature control, outside temperature display, 8-way power passenger seat and auto-dimming mirror with compass. REQUIRES 41G or 54E. NOT AVAILABLE with 60L, B3A, 64R.		
68F	Ultimate Package (LS)	2243	2520
	Includes premium package, power adjustable pedals, leather-wrapped steering wheel, electronic automatic temperature control, outside temperature display, 8-way power passenger seat, auto-dimming mirror with compass, traction control, antilock brakes, electronic instrumentation and premium AM/FM stereo with cassette player. REQUIRES 41G. NOT AVAILABLE with 60L, B3A, 64R.		
919	Trunk-Mounted 6-Disc CD Changer (LS)	312	350
	REQUIRES 586.		
943	Luxury Light Group (GS)	169	190
	Includes dual illuminated visor mirrors and dual-beam dome/map light.		
972	Bodyside Paint Stripe (GS)	54	60
99W	Engine: 4.6L OHC EFI	NC	NC
	Horsepower on engine increases from 225 to 240 with dual exhaust. REQUIRES 41G.		
B3A	GS California/Hawaii Edition (GS)	443	480

GRAND MARQUIS / SABLE — MERCURY

CODE	DESCRIPTION	INVOICE	MSRP
B3A	LS California/Hawaii Edition (LS) .... *REQUIRES 60L. NOT AVAILABLE with 68E, 68F.*	755	820
J	Leather Twin-Comfort Seats (LS) .... *REQUIRES 68E or 68F.*	708	795

2001 SABLE

What's New?

A new child safety-seat restraint system is in place as well as a larger 18-gallon fuel tank. An AM/FM stereo with a CD player is optional equipment. There's also a clearcoat metallic paint swap, trading Tropic Green for Spruce Green. Otherwise, no changes for the recently freshened Sable.

Review

The Sable has earned a good reputation for safety, thanks to its solid performances in U.S. government crash testing. Mercury builds on that rep with the Sable's new Advanced Restraints System (ARS). This system adapts airbag deployment depending upon impact severity, safety-belt usage and driver-seat position. The ARS includes safety-belt pre-tensioners and retractors. Head-and-chest side airbags are optional for front occupants. Safety goodies include an emergency trunk release (for those times when you accidentally lock yourself in your own trunk), and locking front-seat head restraints.

Inside, the Sable has power-adjustable accelerator and brake pedals. With the touch of a button, the brake and accelerator pedals can, together, be horizontally adjusted up to 3 inches toward the driver from the standard location to provide added driving comfort for a wider range of drivers. Audio and climate controls are grouped in a soft-cornered rectilinear shape. Controls are operated by square buttons, which are arranged in a conventional linear grid fashion for more intuitive use. The flip/fold console in the six-passenger Sable now folds down flat to the floor, allowing easy access to the lower part of the integrated control panel.

We give the '01 Sable high marks in the ride and handling department. On the road, the car transmits truly usable feedback to the wheel, letting the driver know what is happening with the tires. The Sable has a compliant suspension with excellent rebound shock valving for spirited canyon driving, yet without the harshness that can render a cross-country drive unenjoyable. Drive the Sable into a turn, prod the throttle and the car responds in a predictable manner. Yet on the highway, passengers are treated to a comfortably smooth ride.

The 2001 Sable powertrains include the 3.0-liter Vulcan and 3.0-liter Duratec V6s. The main difference between the two engines is the cylinder heads. The base Vulcan has two valves per cylinder, while the Duratec has four. The four-valve motor makes 200 horsepower at 5650 rpm and 200 foot-pounds of torque at 4,400 rpm. The base engine makes do with 155 horsepower at 4,900 rpm and 185 foot-pounds at 3950 rpm. Both engines meet Low-Emissions Vehicle (LEV) standards in California and 13 Northeastern states.

With the optional 24-valve Duratec V6 putting the power down, the Sable is actually quite sporting. The engine features a wide power band with tons of low-end torque. Reaching the upper end of the tachometer, the engine emits a nasty growl and a notable amount of torque steer during upshifts.

We've always liked the Sable and Taurus, but thought they were edged out when compared to the Accord or Camry. The gap is now considerably narrower when comparing the Honda and

MERCURY — SABLE

Toyota benchmarks because the Sable (and Taurus) is now a much better car. Furthermore, you can get a Sable wagon if you desire—no such choice exists with Accord or Camry. Now if they just made the wagon's four-wheel disc brakes available on the sedan.

Standard Equipment

GS SEDAN (4A): 3L V6 OHV SMPI 12-valve engine; 4-speed electronic OD automatic transmission with lock-up converter; battery with rundown protection; 130-amp alternator; transmission, oil cooler; front-wheel drive, 3.77 axle ratio; stainless steel exhaust; front independent strut suspension with anti-roll bar, front coil springs, gas-pressurized front shocks, rear independent multi-link suspension with anti-roll bar, rear coil springs, gas-pressurized rear shocks; rack-and-pinion power steering with vehicle-speed-sensing assist; front disc/rear drum brakes; 16 gal. capacity fuel tank; side impact bars; front and rear body-colored bumpers; body-colored bodyside molding with chrome bodyside insert, rocker panel extensions; clearcoat monotone paint; aero-composite halogen headlamps; driver's and passenger's power remote body-colored heated outside mirrors; 16" x 6" wheels, P215/60TR16 BSW A/S tires; compact steel spare wheel; air conditioning, rear heat ducts; AM/FM stereo w/clock, seek-scan feature, cassette player, CD changer pre-wiring, 4 speakers, fixed antenna; power door locks with 2-stage unlock, remote keyless entry, child-safety rear door locks, power remote trunk release; 2 power accessory outlets, front lighter element, driver's foot rest, retained accessory power, smokers' package; instrumentation display includes tachometer, water temperature gauge, trip odometer; warning indicators include oil pressure, battery, lights on, key in ignition, low fuel, door ajar, trunk ajar, brake fluid; driver's and passenger's front airbags; ignition disable, panic alarm; tinted windows, power front and rear windows with driver's 1-touch down function; variable-speed intermittent front windshield wipers, sun visor strip, rear window defroster; seating capacity of 6, front bucket seats with adjustable headrests, driver's and front passenger's seats include 4-way adjustment; rear bench seat; height-adjustable front seatbelts with pretensioners; cloth seats, full cloth headliner, full color-keyed carpet floor covering with carpeted floor mats, deluxe sound insulation, simulated wood dashboard insert, simulated wood door panel insert, chrome interior accents; interior lights include dome light with delay, front reading lights, illuminated entry; steering wheel with tilt adjustment; vanity mirrors; day/night rearview mirror; partial floor console, locking glove box with light, front and rear cupholders, 2 seatback storage pockets, driver's and passenger's door bins, rear door bins; carpeted cargo floor, cargo tie downs, cargo light; chrome grille, chrome side window moldings, black front windshield and rear window moldings and body-colored door handles.

LS SEDAN (4A) (in addition to or instead of GS SEDAN (4A) equipment): Seating capacity of 5; center armrest with storage; driver's seat includes 14-way adjustment (6-way power), lumbar support.

LS PREMIUM SEDAN (4A) (in addition to or instead of LS SEDAN (4A) equipment): 3L V6 DOHC SMPI 24-valve engine; 3.98 axle ratio; fully automatic headlamps with delay-off feature; additional exterior lights include front fog/driving lights; climate control; security system; dual illuminated vanity mirrors and dual auxiliary visors.

GS WAGON (4A) (in addition to or instead of LS PREMIUM SEDAN (4A) equipment): 3L V6 OHV SMPI 12-valve engine; 3.77 axle ratio; rear independent short & long arm suspension; 4-wheel disc brakes; roof rack; front and rear body-colored bumpers with rear step; power retractable antenna; fixed 1/4 vent windows; flip-up rear window, fixed-interval rear wiper; seating capacity of 8; 3rd-row bench seat facing rear; partial floor console; locking and cargo-concealed storage.

LS PREMIUM WAGON (4A) (in addition to or instead of GS WAGON (4A) equipment): 3L V6 DOHC SMPI 24-valve engine; 3.98 axle ratio; seating capacity of 7, driver's seat includes 14-way adjustment (6-way power), lumbar support.

SABLE — MERCURY

CODE	DESCRIPTION	INVOICE	MSRP

Base Prices

Code	Description	Invoice	MSRP
M50	GS Sedan (4A)	17777	19185
M53	LS Sedan (4A)	18767	20285
M55	LS Premium Sedan (4A)	19937	21585
M58	GS Wagon (4A)	19397	20985
M59	LS Premium Wagon (4A)	20927	22685
	Destination Charge:	625	625

Interested in seeing what dealers will sell this vehicle for? Check out our True Market Value^{sm} (TMV^{sm}) pricing on our Web site at www.edmunds.com.

Accessories

Code	Description	Invoice	MSRP
13B	Power Moonroof (LS/LS Prem Sedan/LS Prem Wagon)	792	890
186	5-Passenger Seating (GS)	93	105
	Includes floor shift and floor console.		
21A	6-Way Power Driver Seat (GS/GS Wagon)	352	395
21J	6-Way Power Passenger Seat (LS Prem Sedan/LS Prem Wagon)	312	350
	REQUIRES 61B and J.		
53A	Audio Group (LS/LS Prem Sedan/LS Prem Wagon)	597	670
	Includes features of AM/FM stereo, cassette player, MACH audio group, 80-Watts, 6 premium speakers, vehicle-specific equalization, external amplifier and 6-disc CD changer. NOT AVAILABLE with 585.		
552	Antilock Braking System	NC	NC
553	All-Speed Traction Control (LS/LS Prem Sedan/LS Prem Wagon)	156	175
	REQUIRES 552.		
585	Radio: AM/FM Stereo, CD Player (GS/LS/GS Wagon)	125	140
	NOT AVAILABLE with 53A.		
59C	Power Adjustable Pedals (GS/GS Wagon)	107	120
	REQUIRES 21A.		
61B	Side-Impact Airbags	347	390
64N	Wheels: 7-Spoke Machined Alloy (GS)	352	395
64W	Wheels: Chrometec (LS/LS Prem Sedan/LS Prem Wagon)	263	295
85B	Secure Group (GS/LS/LS Prem Sedan/GS Wagon)	503	565
	Includes side-impact airbags and antilock braking system.		
99S	Engine: 3.0L Duratec 4V V6 (LS)	619	695
	Includes 3.98 axle ratio.		
J	Leather Seat Trim (LS Prem Sedan/LS Prem Wagon)	NC	NC

MITSUBISHI

DIAMANTE

| CODE | DESCRIPTION | | INVOICE | MSRP |

2001 DIAMANTE

What's New?

This Mitsubishi model doesn't change much from last year, but product planners add tether anchors for child seats, fog lights on the LS, and new seat fabric and wheel cover for the ES. Greenies can rest easy knowing that it meets LEV standards for all states.

Review

Three years ago, Mitsubishi changed the Diamante, stepping up their offering in the near-luxury market and producing another choice for the upper-middle-class shopper. For 2001, both the ES and LS trim designations are equipped with more standard options, but otherwise, no grand changes have occured.

A 3.5-liter V6 drives the front wheels, making 210 horsepower and competing adequately with other sedans in its class. While it makes a strong showing on the skidpad and in 60-to-zero braking, the Diamante goes from zero to 60 in a less-than-spectacular 8.3 seconds. The electronically controlled four-speed automatic transmission will learn if you're a lead foot and adjust itself accordingly. Unfortunately, it will also not shift as well as other transmissions - the "adaptive control management" often manages to do neither, and renders impotent an otherwise competent powertrain.

Exterior styling features a chiseled, BMW-like appearance - emphasis on "like" - and features chrome on the window moldings, grille trim, license plate surround and the alloy wheels. Overall, the interior appears adequate but leaves something to be desired - most specifically, a fold-down rear seat or cargo-area pass-through and better-quality materials. For a car of this price point, we'd expect that engineers would make at least a half-hearted attempt to imitate real wood - but noooo.

Not so important, but possibly an issue, are the pictogram choices on the automatic climate controls. They seem logical to some drivers and ridiculous to others, suggesting that Mitsubishi designers might want to take another look at them. It's indicative of the not-quite-effective execution that seems to plague the car.

The 2001 ES is a cloth-trimmed base model with new wheel covers, an AM/FM stereo with CD player and an anti-theft engine immobilizer. The high-end LS adds a host of features, including leather seats, steering wheel and shift knob, a power-adjustable driver's seat with lumbar support, wood grain accents, power sunroof, a HomeLink transmitter, separate amplifier for the stereo with steering wheel audio controls, fog lights and color-keyed body-side molding. Upgrade the in-dash CD player to a six-disc version in either ES or LS, but the all-weather package - heated mirrors and front seats, and the traction-control system — is available only for LS customers.

While the 2001 Diamante gets points for its roominess and excellent sound system, those features are outweighed by a poorly functioning transmission, build-quality issues and uncomfortable seats. At this price point, competitors like the Acura 3.2 TL, Chrysler 300M, the Lexus IS300 and Infiniti I30 seem to overwhelm the Diamante in terms of getting the most for your hard-earned money. We recommend considering all your options when shopping for your next near-luxury vehicle.

Standard Equipment

ES (4A): 3.5L V6 SOHC SMPI 24-valve engine; 4-speed electronic OD automatic transmission with lock-up torque converter; 110 amp alternator; front-wheel drive, 3.5 axle ratio; stainless steel exhaust; front independent strut suspension with anti-roll bar, front coil springs, rear independent multi-link suspension with anti-roll bar, rear coil springs; rack-and-pinion power steering with engine speed-sensing assist; 4-wheel antilock disc brakes; 19 gal. capacity fuel tank; side impact bars; front and rear body-colored bumpers; black bodyside molding; clearcoat

DIAMANTE / ECLIPSE

MITSUBISHI

CODE	DESCRIPTION	INVOICE	MSRP

monotone paint; aero-composite halogen auto off headlamps; driver's and passenger's power remote body-colored folding outside mirrors; 15" x 6" steel wheels; P205/65HR15 BSW A/S tires; full-size steel spare wheel; air conditioning with climate control, rear heat ducts; AM/FM stereo radio, seek-scan feature, single-disc CD player, 6 speakers, theft deterrent, power retractable diversity antenna; cruise control; power door locks with 2-stage unlock, remote keyless entry, child-safety rear door locks, power remote trunk release, power remote fuel door release; 2 power accessory outlets, front lighter element, driver's foot rest, retained accessory power, smokers' package; instrumentation display includes tachometer, water temperature gauge, in-dash clock, trip odometer; warning indicators include oil pressure, battery, low oil level, low coolant, lights on, key in ignition, low fuel, door ajar; driver's and passenger's front airbags; ignition disable, panic alarm, security system; tinted windows, power front and rear windows with driver's 1-touch down function; variable intermittent speed front windshield wipers, sun visor strip, rear window defroster; seating capacity of 5, front bucket seats with adjustable tilt headrests, center armrest with storage, driver's seat includes 8-way adjustment, passenger's seat includes 4-way adjustment; rear bench seat with adjustable headrests, center armrest; height-adjustable front seatbelts with pretensioners; cloth seats, cloth door trim insert, full cloth headliner, full carpet floor covering with carpeted floor mats; interior lights include dome light with fade, front reading lights, 2 door curb lights, illuminated entry; steering wheel with tilt adjustment; dual illuminated vanity mirrors; day/night rearview mirror; full floor console, locking glove box with light, front and rear cupholders, 2 seatback storage pockets, driver's and passenger's door bins; carpeted cargo floor, carpeted trunk lid, cargo light; chrome grille, chrome side window moldings, black front windshield molding, black rear window molding and chrome door handles.

LS (4A) (in addition to or instead of ES (4A) equipment): Front express open sliding and tilting glass sunroof with sunshade; body-colored bodyside molding; additional exterior lights include front fog/driving lights; 16" x 6" silver alloy wheels; P215/60VR16 BSW A/S tires; premium AM/FM stereo, 8 premium speakers, amplifier, theft deterrent, radio steering wheel controls; garage door opener; driver's seat includes power 2-way lumbar support, passenger's seat includes 8-way power adjustment; leather seats, leatherette door trim insert with carpet; simulated wood dashboard insert, leather-wrapped gearshift knob, simulated wood door panel insert, simulated wood console insert; memory on driver's seat includes 2 settings; leather-wrapped steering wheel with tilt adjustment and mini overhead console.

Base Prices

			Invoice	MSRP
DM42-B	ES (4A)	....	23100	25387
DM42-G	LS (4A)	....	25845	28407
Destination Charge:		....	520	520

Interested in seeing what dealers will sell this vehicle for? Check out our True Market Value^{sm} (TMV^{sm}) pricing on our Web site at www.edmunds.com.

Accessories

P1	All Weather Package (LS)	584	720
	Includes traction control, heated mirrors and heated front seats.		

2001 ECLIPSE

What's New?

The new year for the Eclipse sees a standard spoiler, tether anchors for child seats and engines that meet LEV emissions standards.

MITSUBISHI — ECLIPSE

Review

Since 1990, the Eclipse has delivered edgy styling and quick performance at bargain prices. The 1995 redesign improved on this idea and last year, the Eclipse got another makeover - complete with enhanced four-cylinder engine performance, sophisticated technology and a new image.

Mitsubishi calls the Eclipse's styling "geo-mechanical," with an unbroken roof arch, a swell in the hood that rolls across the upper fenders, a lateral accent line and ribbed contours in its doors and front fascia. The spoiler that reminds us of the St. Louis Gateway Arch is now standard.

Inside, styling is one part futuristic and two parts sporty with a dash of luxury sprinkled in. Featuring a twin-cockpit design, the interior is symmetrical and functional, with some components appearing melded into the dash while others protrude aggressively. Materials include soft-touch appointments with titanium-finish details that look rather cheap.

The Eclipse is offered in three trim levels — RS, GS and GT. The base four-cylinder engine found in the RS and GS models displaces 2.4 liters and produces 155 horsepower. The GT model comes equipped with a 3.0-liter V6 engine making 205 horsepower that offers increased responsiveness to throttle input. The turbo engine has been dropped in favor of the more refined V6. Regardless of engine selection, a five-speed manual transmission is standard fare. For those desiring an automatic tranny, Mitsubishi offers a four-speed automatic with "learned control" that tailors its shifting characteristics to the driver's style, or a Sportronic automanual transmission that allows drivers to change gears without using a clutch.

The Eclipse also incorporates a front suspension with large-diameter front struts and a multi-link rear suspension with tubular steel arms. A stiff sub-frame and a longer wheelbase also add to ride quality. Safety features include front-seat force-limiter seatbelts and front seat-mounted side airbags that are optional on the GT model. Traction control is offered only on GT with an automatic transmission, which leaves us wondering why it isn't available with the manual. And why can't buyers of the RS and GS models get antilock brakes?

With all these features, the value of Eclipse hasn't been lost. Standard equipment on every 2001 model includes power windows and door locks, an engine immobilizer and anti-theft system, microfiltered air conditioning, height-adjustable driver's seat, CD player, auto-off headlights, and alloy wheels. The mid-level GS also gets standard 16-inch wheels, cruise control, power sunroof, remote keyless entry, fog lamps, lumbar support and a split-folding rear seat. Step up to the GT and consumers will receive the V6 engine, 17-inch wheels, improved brakes, upgraded seat fabric and wider tires. The power sunroof is optional on the GT, as well as an audio and premium package with side airbags and a 4-disc CD changer.

Hardcore Eclipse fans will be upset that Mitsubishi no longer offers the turbo and all-weather GSX model in order to focus on attracting middle-market buyers. There's certainly no denying the huge leap that Mitsubishi has taken with the 2001 Eclipse. From styling to drivetrain, the car is totally different from the previous version that wore an "Eclipse" badge.

Standard Equipment

RS (5M): 2.4L I4 SOHC MPI 16-valve engine; 5-speed OD manual transmission; 90 amp alternator; front-wheel drive, 3.72 axle ratio; stainless steel exhaust; front independent strut suspension with anti-roll bar, front coil springs, rear independent multi-link suspension with rear coil springs; rack-and-pinion power steering with engine speed-sensing assist; front disc/rear drum brakes; 16.4 gal. capacity fuel tank; side impact bars; front and rear body-colored bumpers; clearcoat monotone paint; aero-composite halogen auto off headlamps; driver's and passenger's manual black outside mirrors; 15" x 6" silver alloy wheels; P195/65HR15 BSW A/S tires; compact steel spare wheel; air conditioning, air filter; AM/FM stereo radio, seek-scan feature, single-disc CD player, 4 speakers, theft deterrent, fixed antenna; power door locks,

ECLIPSE
MITSUBISHI

remote trunk release; 2 power accessory outlets, front lighter element, driver's foot rest, retained accessory power, smokers' package; instrumentation display includes tachometer, water temperature gauge, in-dash clock, trip odometer; warning indicators include oil pressure, battery, lights on, key in ignition, low fuel, door ajar, trunk ajar, brake fluid; driver's and passenger's front airbags; ignition disable; tinted windows with driver's 1-touch down function; variable - speed intermittent speed front windshield wipers, rear window defroster; seating capacity of 4, front sports seats with adjustable headrests, driver's seat includes 6-way adjustment, passenger's seat includes 4-way adjustment; full-folding rear bench seat; height adjustable front seatbelts; cloth seats, front cloth headliner, full carpet floor covering with carpeted floor mats; interior lights include dome light with fade, front reading lights; steering wheel with tilt adjustment; vanity mirrors; day/night rearview mirror; full floor console, glove box, front cupholder, instrument panel bin, driver's and passenger's door bins; carpeted cargo floor, cargo cover; black side window moldings, black front windshield molding, black rear window molding and body-colored door handles.

GS (5M) (in addition to or instead of RS (5M) equipment): Rear wing spoiler; driver's and passenger's power remote black outside mirrors; 16" x 6" silver alloy wheels; P205/55HR16 BSW A/S tires; 6 speakers, window grid diversity antenna; cruise control; power door locks with 2-stage unlock, remote keyless entry; garage door opener; ignition disable, panic alarm; sun visor strip; 50/50 folding rear bench seat; cloth door trim insert; leather-wrapped gearshift knob; additional interior lights include illuminated entry; leather-wrapped steering wheel with tilt adjustment; cargo net and cargo light.

GT (5M) (in addition to or instead of GS (5M) equipment): 3L V6 SOHC MPI 24-valve engine; engine oil cooler; 85 amp alternator; 3.74 axle ratio; stainless steel exhaust with tailpipe finisher; 4-wheel disc brakes; additional exterior lights include front fog/driving lights; 17" x 6.5" silver alloy wheels; P215/50VR17 BSW A/S tires; additional instrumentation display includes oil pressure gauge and premium cloth seats.

Base Prices

		Invoice	MSRP
EC24-G	RS (5M)	16460	17987
EC24-K	GS (5M)	17196	18797
EC24-P	GT (5M)	19168	20947
Destination Charge:		520	520

Interested in seeing what dealers will sell this vehicle for? Check out our True Market Value^{sm} (TMV^{sm}) pricing on our Web site at www.edmunds.com.

Accessories

Code	Description	Invoice	MSRP
—	Transmission: 4-Speed Automatic with ELC (GS)	915	1000
	Includes 2.4L 16-valve engine.		
—	Transmission: 4-Speed Automatic with ELC (GT)	915	1000
	NOT AVAILABLE with P3.		
—	Transmission: 4-Speed Automatic with ELC (RS)	732	800
	Includes 2.4L 16-valve engine.		
P1	GS Sun and Sound Package (GS)	936	1080
	Includes Infinity AM/FM cassette and CD radio and power sunroof.		
P2	GT Sun and Sound Package (GT)	936	1080
	Includes Infinity AM/FM cassette, CD radio and power sunroof. NOT AVAILABLE with P3 or P4.		
P3	GT Premium Package (GT)	2402	2760
	Includes Infinity AM/FM, cassette player, CD changer radio, leather front seats, power driver's seat, antilock brakes, side airbags, security system, rear wiper and power sunroof. NOT AVAILABLE with P2, P4, or P5.		

MITSUBISHI — *ECLIPSE / ECLIPSE SPYDER*

CODE	DESCRIPTION	INVOICE	MSRP
P4	GT Premium Package (GT)	2652	3050
	Includes Infinity AM/FM, cassette player, CD changer radio, leather front seats, power driver's seat, antilock brakes, side airbags, security system, rear wiper, power sunroof and traction control. NOT AVAILABLE with P2, P3, or P5.		
P5	GT Sun, Sound and Leather Package (GT)	1458	1690
	Includes GT Sun and sound package, Infinity AM/FM cassette player, CD radio, power sunroof and leather seats. NOT AVAILABLE with P3 or P4.		

2001 ECLIPSE SPYDER

What's New?

Mitsubishi's 2001 Eclipse Spyder is all-new inside and out and based on the recently redesigned Eclipse Coupe, embodying a youthful image and providing a sporty drive. But the turbocharged engine is no longer on the menu.

Review

Since 1996, the Eclipse Spyder has delivered edgy, top-down styling and inspiring performance at bargain prices. With a triple-layer power top and designer bodywork, the Spyder was an instant hit - selling at the rate of 1,000 units a month. The second-generation Spyder receives enhanced four-cylinder engine performance, a refined V6, sophisticated technology and a new image.

Mitsubishi calls the new Eclipse's styling "geo-mechanical," with a swell in the hood that rolls across the upper fenders, a lateral accent line and ribbed contours in its doors and front fascia.

Inside, styling is one part futuristic and two parts sporty with a dash of luxury sprinkled in. With a twin-cockpit design, the interior is symmetrical and functional, with some components appearing to be melded into the dash while others protrude aggressively. Materials include soft-touch appointments with titanium-finish details that look rather cheap.

The Spyder is offered in two trim levels—GS and GT. The base 2.4-liter four-cylinder engine found in the GS model produces 147 horsepower. This six-horsepower gain over the 1999 model feels even more substantial because the power peak is 500 rpm lower in the rev range. The GT model comes equipped with a thoroughly responsive 3.0-liter V6 engine making 200 horsepower. The old Spyder's turbo engine has been dropped in favor of the more refined V6. Regardless of engine selection, a five-speed manual transmission is standard fare. For those desiring an automatic tranny, Mitsubishi offers a new four-speed Sportronic automanual transmission that allows drivers to change gears without using a clutch.

The 2001 Spyder also rides on a revised suspension, with large-diameter front struts, a strut tower brace and a multi-link rear suspension incorporating stronger tubular steel arms. A stiffer sub-frame and a longer wheelbase also debut. Safety improvements include front-seat force-limiter seatbelts and front seat-mounted side airbags that are optional on the GT model. Traction control is offered only on the GT with an automatic transmission, which leaves us wondering why it isn't available with the manual. And why can't buyers of the GS models get antilock brakes?

With all these improvements, the Spyder's value hasn't been lost. Standard equipment on every 2001 model includes power windows and door locks, an engine immobilizer and anti-theft system, microfiltered air conditioning, height-adjustable driver's seat, CD player, auto-off headlights, 16-inch wheels, cruise control, remote keyless entry, lumbar support, and dual accessory power outlets. Step up to the GT and receive the V6 engine, 17-inch wheels, improved brakes and wider tires.

ECLIPSE SPYDER — MITSUBISHI

Hardcore Eclipse fans will be upset that Mitsubishi has dropped the turbo this year, focusing instead on attracting middle-market buyers. There's certainly no denying the huge leap that Mitsubishi has taken with the 2001 Eclipse Spyder. From styling to drivetrain, the car is totally different from anything that's previously worn a "Spyder" badge.

Standard Equipment

GS (5M): 2.4L I4 SOHC MPI 16-valve engine; 5-speed OD manual transmission; 90 amp alternator; front-wheel drive, 3.72 axle ratio; stainless steel exhaust; front independent strut suspension with anti-roll bar, front coil springs, rear independent multi-link suspension with anti-roll bar, rear coil springs; rack-and-pinion power steering with engine speed-sensing assist; front disc/rear drum brakes; 16.4 gal. capacity fuel tank; rear wing spoiler, side impact bars; power convertible roof with lining, glass rear window; front and rear body-colored bumpers; clearcoat monotone paint; aero-composite halogen auto off headlamps; additional exterior lights include front fog/driving lights; driver's and passenger's power remote black outside mirrors; 16" x 6" silver alloy wheels; P205/55HR16 A/S BSW tires; compact steel spare wheel; air conditioning, air filter; AM/FM stereo radio, seek-scan feature, single-disc CD player, 7 speakers, theft deterrent, fixed antenna; cruise control; power door locks with 2-stage unlock, remote keyless entry, remote trunk release; 2 power accessory outlets, front lighter element, driver's foot rest, retained accessory power, garage door opener, smokers' package; instrumentation display includes tachometer, water temperature gauge, in-dash clock, trip odometer; warning indicators include oil pressure, battery, lights on, low fuel, door ajar, trunk ajar, brake fluid; driver's and passenger's front airbags; ignition disable, security system; tinted windows, power front and rear windows with driver's 1-touch down function; variable-speed intermittent front windshield wipers, sun visor strip, rear window defroster; seating capacity of 4, front sports seats with adjustable headrests, center armrest with storage, driver's seat includes 6-way adjustment, lumbar support, passenger's seat includes 4-way adjustment; rear bench seat; height-adjustable front seatbelts; cloth seats, cloth door trim insert, front cloth headliner, full carpet floor covering with carpeted floor mats, leather-wrapped gearshift knob; interior lights include dome light with fade, front reading lights; leather-wrapped steering wheel with tilt adjustment; vanity mirrors; day/night rearview mirror; full floor console, glove box, front cupholder, instrument panel bin, driver's and passenger's door bins; carpeted cargo floor, cargo cover, cargo net, cargo light; black side window moldings, black front windshield molding, black rear window molding and body-colored door handles.

GT (5M) (in addition to or instead of GS (5M) equipment): 3.0L V6 SOHC MPI 24-valve engine; engine oil cooler; 85 amp alternator; 3.74 axle ratio; stainless steel exhaust with tailpipe finisher; 4-wheel disc brakes; rocker panel extensions; 17" x 6.5" silver alloy wheels; P215/50VR17 A/S BSW tires; power retractable antenna; instrumentation display includes oil pressure gauge and premium cloth seats.

Base Prices

CODE	DESCRIPTION	INVOICE	MSRP
EC28-K	Spyder GS (5M)	21409	23407
EC28-P	Spyder GT (5M)	23245	25407
	Destination Charge:	520	520

Interested in seeing what dealers will sell this vehicle for? Check out our True Market Value^{sm} (TMV^{sm}) pricing on our Web site at www.edmunds.com.

Accessories

CODE	DESCRIPTION	INVOICE	MSRP
4AT	Transmission: 4-Speed Automatic with Sportronic	910	1000
	NOT AVAILABLE with P5 (GT).		
LS	Leather Front Seats	525	600

MITSUBISHI
ECLIPSE SPYDER / GALANT

CODE	DESCRIPTION	INVOICE	MSRP
P5	GT Premium Package (GT) .... Includes Infinity AM/FM stereo with cassette and CD changer, leather front seats, power driver's seat, antilock brakes and side airbags. NOT AVAILABLE with P6.	2057	2370
P6	GT Premium Package (GT) .... Includes Infinity AM/FM stereo with cassette and CD changer, leather front seats, power driver's seat, antilock brakes, side airbags and traction control. REQUIRES 4AT. NOT AVAILABLE with P5.	2308	2650

2001 GALANT

What's New?

Mitsubishi's fourth-generation Galant features some new standard and optional equipment, like a LATCH system for child seats and traction control and heated mirrors for cold-weather dwellers who purchase the all-weather package. It now meets LEV standards.

Review

The current Galant debuted in 1999, and featured V6 power, BMW knock-off styling, and lots of standard equipment to combat its opponents. It was tailored to appease power-hungry Americans by offering a choice of two engines: a high-torque four-cylinder or a 195-horsepower V6.

Going fast is second nature to the Galant. The vehicle exhibits a smooth powertrain with a Saab-like thrust of forward movement the second your foot hits the gas. Its torquey, 2.4-liter, 16-valve, SOHC four-cylinder engine produces 145 horsepower and 155 foot-pounds of torque, and quells noise and vibration nicely. The 3.0-liter, 24-valve SOHC V6 makes 205 foot-pounds of torque at 4,500 rpm, placing it on par power-wise with the Toyota Camry, Honda Accord and Mazda 626.

The Galant is offered in four trim levels: DE, ES, LS and GTZ. The economical DE is built with the four-cylinder engine, the ES can be purchased with either a four-banger or a V6, and the luxury LS and sport-tuned GTZ both come with V6 power standard. All Galants come standard with an automatic transmission (manual transmissions are not available on Galants), A/C, power package, variable intermittent wipers, AM/FM/CD stereo, auxiliary power outlet, tinted glass and dual trip odometers. Safety features include available front seat-mounted side airbags, automatic headlight shut-off, a new Lower Anchor and Tether for Children (LATCH) system for child seats, and a collapsible steering column.

The ES model comes with a cruise-control memory function, an optional sunroof, and an optional premium package with adjustable driver's lumbar support and an Infinity sound system. If you opt for the LS, you'll automatically receive the premium package, standard V6 engine and traction control. The GTZ model also comes with a V6 engine, color-keyed grille, rear spoiler, leather trim and black-on-white instrument gauges. These refinements, coupled with the sport-tuned suspension, make GTZ the high-end Galant for those seeking crisp handling and the most fun-to-drive ride in the line. It's too bad a manual transmission is not available.

Inside, styling is clean and simple, with appealing interior wood appointments, a thick, leather-wrapped steering wheel, and functional interior controls. The stereo unit is positioned above the automatic climate controls for easier driver access and the console-mounted cupholders don't block any part of the dashboard. Seating in the Galant is comfortable with a good driving position and excellent visibility.

GALANT — MITSUBISHI

| CODE | DESCRIPTION | INVOICE | MSRP |

All 2001 Galants include an anti-theft engine immobilizer, continuous seatbelt warning lamp, rear center three-point safety belt, large 195/65R15 tires and an optional in-dash, six-disc CD changer.

With its balance of styling, performance and standard content, the Galant is an impressive vehicle and one we would recommend to those in the market for a fun family sedan.

Standard Equipment

DE (4A): 2.4L I4 SOHC SMPI 16-valve engine; 4-speed electronic OD automatic transmission with lock-up torque converter; 90 amp alternator; front-wheel drive, 4.04 axle ratio; stainless steel exhaust; front independent strut suspension with anti-roll bar, front coil springs, rear independent multi-link suspension with rear coil springs; rack-and-pinion power steering; front disc/rear drum brakes; 16.3 gal. capacity fuel tank; side impact bars; front and rear body-colored bumpers; black bodyside molding; clearcoat monotone paint; aero-composite halogen auto off headlamps; driver's and passenger's manual remote black outside mirrors; 15" x 6" steel wheels; P195/65HR15 BSW A/S tires; compact steel spare wheel; air conditioning, air filter; AM/FM stereo radio, clock, seek-scan feature, single-disc CD player, 4 speakers, fixed antenna; power door locks with 2-stage unlock, child-safety rear door locks, remote trunk release, remote fuel door release; 2 power accessory outlets, front lighter element, driver's foot rest, retained accessory power, smokers' package; instrumentation display includes tachometer, water temperature gauge, trip odometer; warning indicators include oil pressure, battery, lights on, key in ignition, door ajar; driver's and passenger's front airbags; ignition disable; tinted windows, power front and rear windows with driver's 1-touch down function; variable intermittent speed front windshield wipers, rear window defroster; seating capacity of 5, front bucket seats with adjustable headrests, center armrest with storage, driver's seat includes 6-way adjustment, passenger's seat includes 4-way adjustment; rear bench seat; front height adjustable seatbelts; cloth seats, vinyl door trim insert, full cloth headliner, full carpet floor covering with carpeted floor mats; interior lights include dome light with fade, front reading lights; steering wheel with tilt adjustment; driver's side vanity mirror; day/night rearview mirror; full floor console, locking glove box, front and rear cupholders, instrument panel bin, driver's and passenger's door bins; carpeted cargo floor, cargo light; black grille, black side window moldings, black front windshield molding, black rear window molding and black door handles.

ES (4A) (in addition to or instead of DE (4A) equipment): Body-colored bodyside molding; driver's and passenger's power remote body-colored outside mirrors; theft deterrent, window grid antenna; cruise control; remote keyless entry; sun visor strip; folding rear bench seat with fixed headrests, center pass-thru armrest; premium cloth seats, cloth door trim insert; simulated wood dashboard insert, simulated wood door panel insert, simulated wood console insert; additional interior lights include illuminated entry; dual illuminated vanity mirrors; chrome grille, chrome side window moldings and body-colored door handles.

ES V6 (4A) (in addition to or instead of ES (4A) equipment): 3L V6 SOHC SMPI 24-valve engine; 85 amp alternator; 3.74 axle ratio; 4-wheel antilock disc brakes; 16" x 6" steel wheels; P205/55HR16 BSW A/S tires and rear heat ducts.

LS V6 (4A) (in addition to or instead of ES V6 (4A) equipment): Traction control; front express open sliding and tilting glass sunroof with sunshade; body-colored bodyside cladding; additional exterior lights include front fog/driving lights; driver's and passenger's power remote body-colored heated outside mirrors; 7 premium speakers, amplifier; driver's and front passenger's seat-mounted side airbags; ignition disable, panic alarm, security system; driver's seat includes 8-way power adjustment with lumbar support, passenger's seat includes 4-way adjustment; leather seats, leatherette door trim insert, full cloth headliner, full carpet floor covering with carpeted floor mats, simulated wood dashboard insert, leather-wrapped gearshift knob, leather-wrapped steering wheel with tilt adjustment and 2 seatback storage pockets.

GTZ-V6 (4A) (in addition to or instead of LS V6 (4A) equipment): Sport-ride suspension; rear wing spoiler; garage door opener and body-colored grille.

MITSUBISHI — GALANT / MIRAGE

CODE	DESCRIPTION	INVOICE	MSRP

Base Prices

GA41-B	DE (4A)	16151	17557
GA41-G	ES (4A)	16749	18407
GA41-K	ES V6 (4A)	18481	20307
GA41-X	LS V6 (4A)	21750	23907
GA41-P	GTZ V6 (4A)	21842	24007
	Destination Charge:	520	520

Interested in seeing what dealers will sell this vehicle for? Check out our True Market Value^{sm} (TMV^{sm}) pricing on our Web site at www.edmunds.com.

Accessories

P1	ES Premium Package (ES)	2261	2600

Includes antilock brakes, side airbag system, Mitsubishi/Infinity premium audio system, power glass sunroof with sunshade, leather-wrapped steering wheel, driver's side adjustable lumbar support, 15" alloy wheels and rear seat heater ducts.

P2	ES-V6 Premium Package (ES V6)	2082	2400

Includes side airbag system, Mitsubishi/Infinity premium audio system, leather-wrapped steering wheel, driver's side adjustable lumbar support and 16" bright alloy wheels.

P3	All Weather Package (ES V6)	270	310

Includes heated power mirrors and traction control system.

SR	Power Glass Sunroof with Sunshade (ES, ES V6)	697	850

One-touch with tilt feature.

ULEV	Ultra Low Emission Vehicle (ULEV) (DE,ES)	NC	NC

2001 MIRAGE

What's New?

All 2001 Mirages now have tether anchors for child seats and meet LEV standards. A power sunroof is now available with the coupe's sport package. Sedan buyers can choose from the LS or the new base ES trim model that replaces the DE model. Nothing else has changed but the designation—John Mellencamp? John Cougar? John Cougar Mellencamp?

Review

Available as a coupe in DE and LS trim levels, and as a sedan in ES and LS levels, the Mirage's main competition are sales favorites like the Honda Civic and Toyota Corolla, as well as Korean contenders like the Kia Sephia and Hyundai Elantra.

The entry-level DE Coupe has a 92-horsepower, 1.5-liter engine mated to either a five-speed manual or four-speed automatic transmission. The ES Sedan comes with a larger 1.8-liter, 113-horsepower engine. This same sedan also has a front stabilizer bar that helps the car move nimbly between potholes and slow-moving traffic, and both the DE Coupe and ES Sedan have a four-wheel independent suspension. Several standard features

MIRAGE — MITSUBISHI

are part of the DE Coupe and ES Sedan trim level, including tilt steering, remote outside mirrors and intermittent wipers.

All LS models, which are meant to appeal to the features-conscious crowd, have the larger 1.8-liter engine, a six-way adjustable driver's seat, rear window defroster, a body-colored grille and body-colored door handles. Other upgrades include alloy wheels, a chrome-tipped exhaust, a stereo with integrated CD controls and for the 2001 LS Sedan, a standard sunroof. We found that Mirage's interior appears to be made of higher-quality material than most cars at this price. If you want your Mirage with some "sport" thrown in, the LS Coupe can be ordered with an optional sport package that includes a rear spoiler, chrome tailpipe extension and side air dams. LS Coupes and all sedans come with air conditioning, an AM/FM stereo with CD player, a tachometer and a split folding rear bench seat to access the cargo capacity of 11.5 cubic feet.

Regardless of the specific body style and trim level you order, you can be sure your Mirage won't blend in with the other small cars in the parking lot. Its shape offers more personality than the Toyota Corolla or Honda Civic, although the funky shape of the Ford Focus, or the elegant Protege, may be more suited to your eclectic tastes.

Generally, we like the Mirage. It's got a good look, a quiet interior, stable road characteristics and comfy seats. But the Kia Sephia is still a better value and the 2001 Elantra looks to be a strong contender in terms of refinement, interior space and overall design. And while the Civic and Corolla may not be as sexy, they do come with legendary reliability at a comparable price. Competition in the small-car segment continues to heat up, and we fear this aging Mirage may be fading.

Standard Equipment

DE COUPE (5M): 1.5L I4 SOHC MPI 12-valve engine; 5-speed OD manual transmission; 420 amp battery; 80 amp alternator; front-wheel drive, 3.71 axle ratio; stainless steel exhaust; front independent strut suspension front coil springs, rear independent multi-link suspension with rear coil springs; rack-and-pinion power steering; front disc/rear drum brakes; 12.4 gal. capacity fuel tank; side impact bars; front and rear body-colored bumpers; clearcoat monotone paint; aero-composite halogen headlamps; driver's and passenger's manual remote black folding outside mirrors; 14" x 5.5" steel wheels; P175/65SR14 BSW A/S tires; compact steel spare wheel; prep speakers, manual retractable antenna; remote trunk release, remote fuel door release; 1 power accessory outlet, front lighter element, driver's foot rest, smokers' package; instrumentation display includes water temperature gauge, in-dash clock, trip odometer; warning indicators include oil pressure, battery, lights on, key in ignition, low fuel, door ajar, brake fluid; driver's and passenger's front airbags; tinted windows; fixed interval front windshield wipers, rear window defroster; seating capacity of 5, front bucket seats with fixed headrests, driver's seat includes 6-way adjustment, passenger's seat includes 4-way adjustment; rear bench seat with fixed headrests; front height adjustable seatbelts; cloth seats, cloth door trim insert, full cloth headliner, full carpet floor covering with carpeted floor mats; interior lights include dome light; steering wheel with tilt adjustment; vanity mirrors; day/night rearview mirror; full floor console, glove box, front cupholder, instrument panel bin, driver's and passenger's door bins; carpeted cargo floor, cargo light; black grille, black side window moldings, black front windshield molding, black rear window molding and black door handles.

LS COUPE (5M) (in addition to or instead of DE (5M) equipment): 1.8L I4 SOHC MPI 16-valve engine; 433 amp battery; front-wheel drive, 3.72 axle ratio; front independent strut suspension with anti-roll bar, front coil springs, rear independent multi-link suspension with rear coil springs; rocker panel extensions; driver's and passenger's power remote body-colored folding outside mirrors; P185/65HR14 BSW A/S tires; air conditioning; AM/FM stereo radio, seek-scan feature, single-disc CD player, 4 speakers; cruise control; retained accessory power; instrumentation display also includes tachometer; tinted windows with driver's 1-touch down function; variable-speed intermittent speed front windshield wipers; front bucket seats with adjustable headrests, center armrest with storage; 60/40 folding rear bench seat with fixed headrests; interior lights also include front reading lights; mini overhead console with storage, and body-colored door handles.

ES SEDAN (5M) (in addition to or instead of DE COUPE): 3.72 axle ratio; front independent strut suspension with anti-roll bar; air conditioning; AM/FM stereo radio, seek-scan feature, single-disc

MITSUBISHI — MIRAGE

| CODE | DESCRIPTION | INVOICE | MSRP |

CD player, 4 speakers; child-safety rear door locks; retained accessory power; manual front and rear windows; front bucket seats with adjustable headrests, center armrest with storage; 60/40 folding rear bench seat with fixed headrests, center armrest and body-colored grille.

LS SEDAN (5M) (in addition to or instead of LS COUPE (5M) equipment): 4.04 axle ratio; stainless steel exhaust with tailpipe finisher; express open sliding and tilting glass sunroof with sunshade; additional instrumentation display includes water temperature gauge, in-dash clock, trip odometer; power front and rear windows with driver's 1-touch down function; rear window defroster; body-colored grille, black front windshield molding, black rear window molding and body-colored door handles.

Base Prices

Code	Description	Invoice	MSRP
MG21-B	DE Coupe (5M)	10923	11877
MG41-B	ES Sedan (5M)	12534	13627
MG21-G	LS Coupe (5M)	13541	14717
MG41-G	LS Sedan (5M)	13319	14477
	Destination Charge:	520	520

Interested in seeing what dealers will sell this vehicle for? Check out our True Market Value^{sm} (TMV^{sm}) pricing on our Web site at www.edmunds.com.

Accessories

Code	Description	Invoice	MSRP
—	Transmission: 4-Speed Automatic with ELC (DE)	735	800
	Includes 4.04 axle ratio.		
—	Transmission: 4-Speed Automatic with ELC (ES)	734	800
—	Transmission: 4-Speed Automatic with ELC (LS)	739	810
	Includes 4.04 axle ratio.		
—	Transmission: 4-Speed Automatic with ELC (LS)	729	790
AC	Air Conditioning (DE)	770	880
	REQUIRES P1.		
P1	Convenience Package (DE)	1591	1810
	Includes air conditioning, full cloth seat trim, power door locks, power windows, 60/40 folding rear seat and AM/FM stereo with CD player.		
P1	Premium Package (LS)	1040	1190
	Includes power sunroof, 14" alloy wheels and P185/65R14 tires.		
P2	Sport Package (LS)	901	1030
	Includes side air dam and white face meters, 14" alloy wheels, chrome tailpipe extension, fog lights and rear spoiler.		
PP	Power Package (ES)	425	490
	Includes power door locks and power windows with auto down feature.		
SR	Power Sunroof (LS)	700	800

ALTIMA

NISSAN

2001 ALTIMA

What's New?

GXE is available with a new Limited Edition package, which includes goodies like an eight-way power driver's seat, remote keyless entry, floor mats, special badging and a security system.

Review

When Nissan introduced its Infiniti J30 knockoff, Altima, in 1993, it was an instant hit. The term "affordable luxury" became synonymous with the new sedan, and consumers rushed out in droves to buy this car. Five years later, the Altima was redesigned with the goal of improving on its original style and appeal. Unfortunately, the second-generation edition didn't include the upscale design details and cut-rate luxury cabin that the original car possessed. Sales suffered as a result.

So Nissan made substantial refinements to the current-generation Altima just two years after its debut. Styling was cleaned up, cabin refinements were incorporated, and the powertrain was refined. Noise, vibration and harshness were quelled through the addition of sound-deadening materials, and a trick new automatically adjustable strut suspension improved the ride and handling.

But sales remained stagnant, forcing Nissan to offer hefty customer rebates and dealer incentives to clear inventory. Dear consumer, what this means to you is a good deal on a decent, if not terribly exciting, car. If what you need is a reliable, roomy sedan that offers the ability to have a little fun when the road turns twisty, Nissan's Altima will fill the bill.

Available in base XE, mid-grade GXE, sporty SE and leather-lined GLE trims, Altima is reasonably crashworthy, scoring average or better in government crash testing. Side impact airbags come standard on GLE, and are optional on GXE and SE. Our favorite, not surprisingly, is the SE, since the GLE can't be bought with a manual transmission or four-wheel disc brakes.

When equipped with a stick shift, the standard 155-horsepower, 2.4-liter four-cylinder engine manages to get the 3,000-pound sedan to speed with surprising alacrity, running from rest to 60 mph in a hair over 8 seconds, though without refined noises emanating from beyond the firewall. Handling is an Altima strong point, with sharp steering and a nicely balanced chassis sporting an Acceleration Sensitive Strut Valving (ASSV) four-wheel independent suspension with rear Super Toe Control. Models with 16-inch wheels have a front strut-tower brace for increased rigidity and responsiveness. ABS is optional on all Altimas except XE.

Simple interior design means it's easy to find and use controls and switches. Seating is comfortable front and rear, but beware that the leather used on some models ain't exactly high-quality hide. Wood tone accents dress things up a bit on GXE and GLE Altimas, in an effort to remind you that this Nissan's calling card is "affordable luxury."

Our primary complaint with the Altima, aside from its utter lack of personality and rather gruff truck-based engine, is with the quality of the materials that have gone into its construction. It's too easy to see where corners were cut, and slamming doors and the trunk lid don't impart a sense of solidity.

Nevertheless, the Altima represents a solid value. Want a nice set of wheels for less than $20,000? Drop by your local Nissan store.

Standard Equipment

XE (5M): 2.4L I4 DOHC SMPI 16-valve engine; 5-speed OD manual transmission; 100 amp alternator; front-wheel drive, 3.82 axle ratio; steel exhaust; front independent strut suspension with anti-roll bar, front coil springs, rear independent strut suspension with anti-roll bar, rear coil

NISSAN — ALTIMA

CODE	DESCRIPTION	INVOICE	MSRP

springs; rack-and-pinion power steering with engine speed-sensing assist; front disc/rear drum brakes; 15.9 gal. capacity fuel tank; side impact bars; front and rear body-colored bumpers; body-colored bodyside molding; monotone paint; aero-composite halogen headlamps; additional exterior lights include cornering lights; driver's and passenger's power remote black outside mirrors; 15" x 6" steel wheels; P195/65SR15 BSW A/S tires; compact steel spare wheel; rear heat ducts; window grid antenna; child-safety rear door locks, remote trunk release, remote fuel door release; 1 power accessory outlet, front lighter element, driver's foot rest, smokers' package; instrumentation display includes tachometer, water temperature gauge, trip odometer; warning indicators include oil pressure, battery, lights on, key in ignition, low fuel, door ajar; driver's and passenger's front airbags; ignition disable; tinted windows, power front and rear windows with driver's 1-touch down function; fixed interval front windshield wipers, sun visor strip, rear window defroster; seating capacity of 5, front bucket seats with adjustable headrests, driver's and passenger's seats include 4-way adjustment; rear bench seat with fixed headrests; height-adjustable front seatbelts with pretensioners; cloth seats, vinyl door trim insert, full cloth headliner, full carpet floor covering; interior lights include dome light; steering wheel with tilt adjustment; dual auxiliary visors, passenger's side vanity mirror; day/night rearview mirror; full floor console, glove box, front cupholder, instrument panel bin, driver's and passenger's door bins; carpeted cargo floor, carpeted trunk lid, cargo light; chrome grill, chrome side window moldings, black front windshield molding, black rear window molding and body-colored door handles.

GXE (5M) (in addition to or instead of XE (5M) equipment): Driver's and passenger's power remote body-colored outside mirrors; driver's seat includes 8-way adjustment, passenger's seat includes 4-way adjustment; 60/40 folding rear bench seat with fixed headrests, center armrest; premium cloth seats, simulated wood dashboard insert, simulated wood console insert and 1 seatback storage pocket.

SE (5M) (in addition to or instead of GXE (5M) equipment): Battery with rundown protection; steel exhaust with tailpipe finisher; sport-ride suspension; 4-wheel disc brakes; rear wing spoiler; additional exterior lights include front fog/driving lights; 16" x 6" silver alloy wheels; P205/55HR16 BSW A/S tires; air conditioning, rear heat ducts; premium AM/FM stereo radio, clock, seek-scan feature, 6-disc CD changer, 6 speakers, window grid antenna; cruise control with steering wheel controls; power door locks with 2-stage unlock, remote keyless entry, power remote trunk release, remote fuel door release; garage door opener; ignition disable, panic alarm; variable-speed intermittent front windshield wipers, front sports seats with adjustable headrests, driver's seat includes lumbar support; leather-wrapped gearshift knob; interior lights include dome light with fade, front reading lights, illuminated entry; leather-wrapped steering wheel with tilt adjustment; dual illuminated vanity mirrors, dual auxiliary visors; mini overhead console with storage, locking glove box with light, instrument panel covered bin, cargo net, cargo light and body-colored door handles.

GLE (4A) (in addition to or instead of SE (5M) equipment): 4-speed electronic OD automatic transmission with lock-up torque converter; 4.09 axle ratio; comfort-ride suspension; cassette player, single-disc CD player; 2 power accessory outlets; driver's and passenger's front airbags, driver's and front passenger's seat-mounted side airbags, leather seats and leatherette door trim insert.

Base Prices

05651	XE (5M)	14547	15140
05751	GXE (5M)	15016	16340
05951	SE (5M)	16935	18640
05811	GLE (4A)	18525	20390
Destination Charge:		520	520

Interested in seeing what dealers will sell this vehicle for? Check out our True Market Value^{sm} (TMV^{sm}) pricing on our Web site at www.edmunds.com.

ALTIMA — NISSAN

CODE	DESCRIPTION	INVOICE	MSRP

Accessories

CODE	DESCRIPTION	INVOICE	MSRP
—	Transmission: Electric 4-Speed Automatic with OD (GXE)	735	800
—	Transmission: Electric 4-Speed Automatic with OD (SE)	727	800
—	Transmission: Electric 4-Speed Automatic with OD (XE)	768	800
B07	Anti-Lock Braking System (GXE/GLE/SE)	454	499
	REQUIRES S01 and G02 or J01.		
F02	XE Option Package (XE)	1734	1999
	Includes CFC-free air conditioning, cruise control, 100-Watt AM/FM radio and CD audio system radio.		
F05	Radio: AM/FM, Cassette, CD with 6 Speakers (GXE)	346	399
	REQUIRES G02. NOT AVAILABLE with R94.		
F06	Radio: AM/FM, 6-Disc CD Changer with 6 Speakers (GLE)	346	399
	NOT AVAILABLE with R93.		
G02	GXE Limited Edition Package (GXE)	1263	1375
	Includes gxe vop package, CFC-free air conditioning, 100-Watt AM/FM, CD audio system radio, cruise control, power door locks, 205/60R15 A/S RADIAL tires, variable-speed intermittent wipers, dual illuminated visor vanity mirrors, glove compartment lamp, dual overhead map lamps, sunglass holder, battery saver system, illuminated entry/exit fade out system, storage bin, 8-way cloth power driver's seat, remote keyless entry system, vehicle security system, floor mats and LE badging. REQUIRES 4AT.		
H01	Vehicle Security System (GLE/SE)	172	199
	REQUIRES J01.		
H08	Remote Keyless Entry (GXE)	172	199
	REQUIRES V01.		
J01	Power Glass Sunroof (GXE/GLE/SE)	737	849
	REQUIRES G02.		
K02	Color Keyed Rear Spoiler (GXE/GLE)	293	339
	REQUIRES G02 and B07 or J01.		
L92	Floor Mats	58	79
M02	Splash Guards (GXE/GLE/SE)	69	79
	REQUIRES G02 or V01 or J01.		
N93	Sunroof Wind Deflector (GXE/GLE/SE)	42	59
	REQUIRES J01.		
P01	8-Way Cloth Power Driver's Seat (SE)	346	399
	REQUIRES J01 and M02. NOT AVAILABLE with X03.		
R93	6-Disc CD - 2 DIN (GXE/GLE)	338	459
	REQUIRES F05. NOT AVAILABLE with F06.		
R94	In-Dash 6-Disc CD 1 DIN (GXE)	355	439
	NOT AVAILABLE with F05.		
S01	Front Side Airbags (GXE/SE)	227	249
	REQUIRES G02 or J01.		
T94	In-Cabin Microfilter	36	39
V01	GXE VOP Package (GXE)	918	999
	Includes rear cupholders/rear power point, phone storage compartment and slant-cut tailpipe, CFC-free air conditioning, 100-Watt AM/FM radio, CD audio system, cruise control, power door locks, 205/60R15 A/S RADIAL tires, variable intermittent		

NISSAN
ALTIMA / MAXIMA

CODE	DESCRIPTION	INVOICE	MSRP

wipers, dual illuminated visor vanity mirrors, glove compartment lamp, dual overhead map lamps, sunglass holder, battery saver system, illuminated entry/exit fade out system and storage bin. REQUIRES 4AT.

X03   Leather Seat Trim (GLE) 1126   1299
Includes power driver's seat. REQUIRES J01.

2001 MAXIMA

What's New?

A 20th Anniversary edition includes the 227-horsepower version of the standard 3.0-liter V6 from the Infiniti I30, as well as goodies like bronze-lensed headlight covers, a body kit, ersatz carbon fiber interior trim, drilled metal pedals and a number of features normally optional on the SE. This special model also gets an exclusive color: Majestic Blue. A new Meridian package is optional on all Maximas, bundling side-impact airbags and a low washer fluid indicator with heated front seats and side mirrors, as well as special trunk lid trim. Adding optional traction control to the SE or GLE results in a Z Edition Maxima, for some zany reason.

Review

Sometimes, a car doesn't have to be visually appealing to instill desire. Since 1995, the Nissan Maxima has been such a car. This self-proclaimed "four-door sports car" went from beauty to beast that year, but the mechanicals underneath the bodywork created a symphony no enthusiast could resist. A 1997 reskin helped in the styling department, but the real draw continued to be the stunningly smooth 3.0-liter dual overhead cam V6 engine, which Ward's Auto World dubbed "the best V6 engine available in America." Last year, Nissan released a redesigned Maxima with more of what was good about the car (luxury and performance) and more of what was controversial (odd styling cues ladled over a dull shape).

Let's start with a discussion of the controversial. Wheel arches ripped off from Audi. A gaping, slat-toothed grille that would look right at home on a Buick Regal. Teardrop taillights with smoked lens surrounds (SE only) that appear out of place in a sea of body-color plastic and metal. Love it or hate it, at least Maxima is distinctive.

Besides, from behind the steering wheel, you won't care one whit what the outside looks like. This car is sheer joy to drive. The V6 makes 222 horsepower at 6,400 rpm and 217 foot-pounds of twisting force at 4,000 rpm. Helping to produce that level of motivational force is a specially designed exhaust system that reduces backpressure when the engine is revved hard.

And rev it hard you will, regardless of whether you select the standard five-speed manual transmission or the available four-speed automatic. Handling is also a Maxima strong point, despite the lack of a true rear independent suspension. Four-wheel disc antilock brakes are standard, and traction control is available with the automatic gearbox.

Inside, a sport-oriented theme greets occupants, with the usual luxury enhancements to make the cabin more appealing. Mid-level SE models get titanium-faced gauges, while all models have a 60/40 split-bench seat. A long wheelbase creates a large interior; rear seat riders get plenty of legroom, and trunk space measures 15.1 cubic feet.

Maxima is available in four flavors for 2001: basic GXE, sporty SE, specially-trimmed SE 20th Anniversary Edition and luxurious GLE. Standard equipment on all Maximas includes air conditioning, remote keyless entry, and various power accoutrements. SE adds racy alloy

MAXIMA

NISSAN

wheels, special gauges, a sport suspension, fog lights and a rear decklid spoiler. Anniversary models get a high-output version of the V6 engine, special trim and a unique paint color. GLE models have fake wood accents, leather seats, a 200-Watt Bose audio system, and automatic climate control. A power sunroof, heated seats, and side airbags can be added to any model, while GXE and SE can be equipped with a new Meridian trim package that includes heated seats with integrated side airbags. Select traction control for the SE or GLE and shazzam! You've got yourself a Z Edition.

A treat to drive, the Maxima is an enthusiast's alternative to staid family cars from Honda and Toyota.

Standard Equipment

GXE (5M): 3L V6 DOHC SMPI 24-valve engine (requires premium unleaded fuel); 5-speed OD manual transmission; battery with run down protection; 110 amp alternator; front-wheel drive, 3.82 axle ratio; stainless steel exhaust; front independent strut suspension with anti-roll bar, front coil springs, rear non-independent multi-link suspension with anti-roll bar, rear coil springs; rack-and-pinion power steering with engine speed-sensing assist; 4-wheel antilock disc brakes; 18.5 gal. capacity fuel tank; side impact bars; front and rear body-colored bumpers; body-colored bodyside molding; monotone paint; aero-composite halogen fully automatic headlamps; driver's and passenger's power remote body-colored folding outside mirrors; 15" x 6" steel wheels; P205/65SR15 BSW A/S tires; compact steel spare wheel; air conditioning, rear heat ducts; AM/FM stereo radio, seek-scan feature, cassette player, 4 speakers, window grid diversity antenna; cruise control with steering wheel controls; power door locks with 2-stage unlock, remote keyless entry, child-safety rear door locks, power remote trunk release, power remote fuel door release; cell phone pre-wiring, 2 power accessory outlets, driver's foot rest, retained accessory power; instrumentation display includes tachometer, water temperature gauge, in-dash clock, trip odometer; warning indicators include oil pressure, battery, lights on, key in ignition, low fuel, door ajar, trunk ajar, brake fluid; driver's and passenger's front airbags; ignition disable, panic alarm, security system; tinted windows, power front and rear windows with driver's 1-touch down function; variable-speed intermittent front windshield wipers, sun visor strip, rear window defroster; seating capacity of 5, front bucket seats with adjustable headrests, center armrest with storage, driver's seat includes 8-way adjustment, passenger's seat includes 4-way adjustment; 60/40 folding rear bench seat with fixed headrests, center armrest; height-adjustable front seatbelts with pretensioners; premium cloth seats, cloth door trim insert, full cloth headliner, full carpet floor covering; interior lights include dome light with fade, front reading lights, 2 door curb lights, illuminated entry; steering wheel with tilt adjustment; dual illuminated vanity mirrors, dual auxiliary visors; day/night rearview mirror; full floor console, mini overhead console with storage, locking glove box with light, front and rear cupholders, instrument panel covered bin, driver's and passenger's door bins; carpeted cargo floor, cargo light; chrome grille, chrome side window moldings, black front windshield molding, black rear window molding and chrome door handles.

SE (5M) (in addition to or instead of GXE (5M) equipment): Stainless steel exhaust with tailpipe finisher; sport-ride suspension; rear wing spoiler; additional exterior lights include front fog/driving lights; 16" x 6.5" silver alloy wheels; P215/55HR16 BSW A/S tires; premium AM/FM stereo radio, seek-scan feature, cassette player, single-disc CD player, 6 speakers, radio steering wheel controls; driver's seat includes 8-way adjustment, lumbar support, passenger's seat includes 4-way adjustment; premium cloth seats, leather-wrapped gearshift knob; leather-wrapped steering wheel with tilt adjustment; black grille and body-colored door handles.

SE 20TH ANNIVERSARY EDITION (5M) (in addition to or instead of SE (5M) equipment): Viscous limited-slip differential, 3.82 axle ratio; express open/close sliding and tilting glass sunroof with sunshade; rocker panel extensions; monotone paint with badging; 17" x 6.5" silver alloy wheels; P225/50VR17 BSW A/S tires; carbon fiber gearshift knob, carbon fiber door panel insert and carbon fiber console insert.

NISSAN — MAXIMA

CODE	DESCRIPTION	INVOICE	MSRP

GLE (4A) (in addition to or instead of SE (5M) equipment): 4-speed electronic OD automatic transmission with lock-up torque converter; 3.79 axle ratio; air conditioning with climate control; 7 premium speakers, amplifier, automatic equalizer; garage door opener; additional instrumentation display includes exterior temp; leather seats, leatherette door trim insert, simulated wood console insert, chrome interior accents; 1 seatback storage pocket and cargo net.

Base Prices

Code	Description	Invoice	MSRP
08451	GXE (5M)	19430	21249
08251	SE (5M)	21433	23849
08611	GLE (4A)	23769	26449
08351	SE 20th Anniversary Edition Sedan (5M)	24342	27149
	Destination Charge:	520	520

Interested in seeing what dealers will sell this vehicle for? Check out our True Market Value^{sm} (TMV^{sm}) pricing on our Web site at www.edmunds.com.

Accessories

Code	Description	Invoice	MSRP
—	Transmission: 4-Speed Automatic with OD (Anniversary Edition)	449	500
—	Transmission: 4-Speed Automatic with OD (GXE)	1315	1700
—	Transmission: 4-Speed Automatic with OD (SE)	449	500
G94	In-Cabin Microfilter	42	59
H07	Bose Audio System (SE)	798	899
	Includes acoustically tuned AM/FM/CD/cassette audio system - 200 Ws with Active Equalization, steering-wheel-mounted audio controls, CD changer compatibility, 7 active Bose speakers including 2 tweeters, subwoofer and amplifiers. REQUIRES V03.		
K93	Sunroof Wind Deflector	42	59
	REQUIRES J01 or V03.		
L92	Floor Mats (All Except Anniversary Edition)	58	79
M92	Splash Guards (All Except Anniversary Edition)	63	89
N94	Body-Colored Splash Guards (Anniversary Edition)	82	109
R92	6-Disc CD Changer	338	459
	REQUIRES V01.		
S92	Rear Spoiler (GXE/GLE)	360	479
T01	Z Edition Traction Control System (All Except GXE)	259	299
	REQUIRES 4AT.		
V01	GXE Comfort and Convenience Package (GXE)	950	1069
	Includes height-adjustable center armrest, 16" alloy wheels, P215/55HR16 A/S SBR tires, 8-way power driver's seat, premium AM/FM, CD, cassette player, cargo net, Homelink universal transceiver and auto-dimming rear view mirror. REQUIRES 4AT.		
V03	SE Comfort and Convenience Package (SE)	1598	1799
	Includes power sliding glass sunroof, 17" performance alloy wheels, P225/50VR17 A/S tires, 8-way power driver's seat, Homelink universal transceiver, cargo net and auto-dimming rear view mirror.		
W08	Meridian Edition	467	539
	Includes heated front seats, heated outside mirrors, low washer fluid warning light, front seat side supplemental airbags and trunk lid trim. REQUIRES 4AT (except on GLE & SE) and V01 or V03.		

MAXIMA / SENTRA

CODE	DESCRIPTION	INVOICE	MSRP
X03	SE Leather Trim Package (SE)	1171	1349

Includes automatic temperature control, 4-way power front passenger's seat, simulated leather upper door trim, passenger-side seatback pocket and digital outside temperature display. REQUIRES V03 and H07.

2001 SENTRA

What's New?

Redesigned and released late in the 2000 model year, the 2001 Sentra is carrying over unchanged in XE, GXE, SE and super low-emission CA trims.

Review

Nissan says the Sentra was created to break the compact, economy-car stereotype of small cabin space, minimal options, ho-hum styling and "rental car-like" driving traits. The message is: This car is not your everyday economy sedan. It's cool. Young people, come right this way.

But the emphasis in advertising for, and published road tests of, the new Sentra is on the sporty, 145-horsepower SE model, which our staff has dubbed "mini-Maxima." With plenty of smooth-revving power, taut handling, sharp steering and responsive brakes, it's hard not to love this rather homely Sentra. Add in an impressive, optional 150-Watt sound system with in-dash CD changer and a relatively low sticker price, and the advertising rings true with regard to the top-of-the-line sport-tuned model. You get lots of bang for the buck with the SE.

How does the message hold up for the other versions of the Sentra, which include the XE, GXE and low-emission CA models? For starters, you don't get available 16-inch wheels and tires, rear disc brakes, a strut-tower brace under the hood, or a sport suspension. You also don't get the powerful engine.

Standard fare for the lower-line Sentra XE and GXE is a 126-horsepower, 1.8-liter motor that makes most of its torque down low for spirited in-town response. The CA (Clean Air) model's engine makes identical power from the same displacement, but emits zero evaporative emissions. So why, you might ask, isn't this motor standard in the XE and GXE? It requires low-sulfur fuel, currently available only in California.

An independent front suspension is married to a sophisticated beam rear axle, as in the Maxima. Front disc, rear drum brakes handle stopping duties on lower-level Sentras, and ABS is reserved only for the GXE and SE models.

All Sentras come with power windows, a rear defroster, tilt steering column and cloth upholstery. Stepping up to the GXE nets the buyer velour seating, air conditioning, cruise control, power exterior mirrors and door locks, and a thumping sound system. CA includes alloy wheels and an automatic transmission. SE adds the previously mentioned go-fast goodies plus titanium-faced gauges, remote keyless entry and the option of a power sunroof. Side airbags can be added to the GXE and SE.

Sentra's primary fault, as has been the case for years, is with rear seat accommodations. There simply isn't enough legroom to keep four tall adults comfortable in this car for more than a few minutes. And the dumpy-looking butt on the Sentra has simply got to go.

Front seats are comfortable, though, and the dash is laid out in a clean fashion, making it easy to find and use the controls. The cabin imparts an upscale feel, like a Maxima, but not.

NISSAN *SENTRA*

So, is the Sentra a breakthrough vehicle? No, it still has a tight cabin and pedestrian styling. But enthusiasts on a budget will love the SE.

Standard Equipment

XE (5M): 1.8L I4 DOHC SMPI 16-valve engine with variable valve timing; 5-speed OD manual transmission; 80 amp alternator; front-wheel-drive, 3.83 axle ratio; stainless steel exhaust; front independent strut suspension with anti-roll bar, front coil springs, rear non-independent multi-link suspension with anti-roll bar, rear coil springs; rack-and-pinion power steering with engine speed-sensing assist; front disc/rear drum brakes; 13.2 gal. capacity fuel tank; side impact bars; front and rear body-colored bumpers; body-colored bodyside molding; clearcoat monotone paint; aero-composite halogen headlamps; driver's and passenger's manual remote black outside mirrors; 14" x 5.5" steel wheels; P185/65SR14 BSW A/S tires; compact steel spare wheel; rear heat ducts; radio prep speakers, fixed antenna; child-safety rear door locks, remote trunk release, remote fuel door release; 1 power accessory outlet, driver's foot rest; instrumentation display includes water temperature gauge, trip odometer; warning indicators include oil pressure, battery, lights on, key in ignition, low fuel, low washer fluid, door ajar, brake fluid; driver's and passenger's front airbags; tinted windows, manual front and rear windows; fixed interval front windshield wipers, sun visor strip, rear window defroster; seating capacity of 5, front bucket seats with adjustable headrests, center armrest with storage, front driver's and passenger's seat include 4-way adjustment; rear bench seat with fixed headrests; height-adjustable front seatbelts with pretensioners; cloth seats, cloth door trim insert, full cloth headliner, full carpet floor covering, chrome interior accents; interior lights include dome light; steering wheel with tilt adjustment; passenger's side vanity mirror; day/night rearview mirror; full floor console, glove box, front cupholder, instrument panel covered bin, driver's and passenger's door bins; carpeted cargo floor; chrome grille, black side window moldings, black front windshield molding, black rear window molding and black door handles.

GXE (5M) (in addition to or instead of XE (5M) equipment): Battery with run down protection; 4.18 axle ratio; driver's and passenger's power remote body-colored outside mirrors; air conditioning; AM/FM stereo radio, clock, seek-scan feature, single-disc CD player, 4 speakers; cruise control with steering wheel controls; additional instrumentation display includes tachometer; power front and rear windows with driver's 1-touch down function; variable-speed intermittent front windshield wipers, driver's seat includes 8-way adjustment; premium cloth seats; vanity mirrors; cargo light and body-colored door handles.

SE (5M) (in addition to or instead of GXE (4A) equipment): 2L I4 DOHC SMPI with variable valve timing; stainless steel exhaust with tailpipe finisher; sport-ride suspension; 4-wheel disc brakes; additional exterior lights include front fog/driving lights; P195/60HR15 BSW A/S tires; 2 power accessory outlets; 60/40 folding-rear bench seat with fixed headrests; leather-wrapped gearshift knob; leather-wrapped steering wheel with tilt adjustment and cargo net.

Base Prices

CODE	DESCRIPTION	INVOICE	MSRP
42151	XE (5M)	10956	11649
42251	GXE (5M)	12343	13499
42451	SE (5M)	13624	14899
	Destination Charge:	520	520

Interested in seeing what dealers will sell this vehicle for? Check out our True Market Value^{sm} (TMV^{sm}) pricing on our Web site at www.edmunds.com.

SENTRA

CODE	DESCRIPTION	INVOICE	MSRP

Accessories

CODE	DESCRIPTION	INVOICE	MSRP
—	Transmission: 4-Speed Automatic with OD (GXE)	732	800
—	Transmission: 4-Speed Automatic with OD (SE)	731	800
—	Transmission: 4-Speed Automatic with OD (XE)	705	750
F05	XE Option Package (XE)	1040	1199
	Includes air conditioning, AM/FM radio and cassette with 4 speakers radio.		
G03	GXE Convenience Package (GXE)	131	150
	Includes 60/40 split fold-down rear seat, remote keyless entry system, rear auxiliary power outlet and valet key.		
H01	Immobilizer/Vehicle Security System (GXE/SE)	259	299
	REQUIRES G03.		
J01	Power Sunroof (SE)	519	599
	REQUIRES P04 or V02.		
K93	Rear Spoiler	259	339
	NOT AVAILABLE with V02.		
L92	Floor Mats	58	79
N94	Splash Guards	50	79
	NOT AVAILABLE with SPLASH, V02.		
P04	Premium 180-Watt CD Audio System (SE)	172	199
	Includes 7 speakers.		
R02	6-Disc In-Dash CD Changer (GXE/SE)	346	399
	REQUIRES V09 or P04 or V02. NOT AVAILABLE with (DISC) 6 Disc Trunk Mounted CD Autochanger.		
S01	Side-Impact Airbags/ABS (GXE/SE)	606	699
	REQUIRES G03.		
T94	In-Cabin Microfilter	31	39
	NOT AVAILABLE with VENT.		
V02	SE Performance Package (SE)	606	699
	Includes overhead sunglasses holder, 16" alloy wheels, 195/55R16 tires, rear spoiler, premium 180-Watt CD audio system, body color side sill extensions, dual illuminated visor vanity mirrors, overhead storage console, map lights and sport cloth seat trim. REQUIRES 4AT. NOT AVAILABLE with K93, N94.		
V02	SE Performance Package (SE)	779	899
	Includes overhead sunglasses holder, 16" alloy wheels, 195/55R16 tires, rear spoiler, viscous limited slip differential, premium 180-Watt CD audio system, body color side sill extensions, dual illuminated visor vanity mirrors, overhead storage console, map lights and sport cloth seat trim. NOT AVAILABLE with K93, N94.		
V09	GXE Luxury Package (GXE)	563	649
	Includes 15" alloy wheels, 195/60HR15 tires, premium 180-Watt CD audio system, dual illuminated visor vanity mirrors, overhead storage console, map lights and immobilizer/vehicle security system. REQUIRES G03.		

OLDSMOBILE

ALERO

2001 ALERO

What's New?

A five-speed manual transmission is now available with the four-cylinder engine, an eight-speaker premium sound system is now standard on the GLS (optional on GL). A refined ABS system and 16-inch wheels are also standard on the GLS.

Review

Introduced to the public at the 1998 North American International Auto Show, the Oldsmobile Alero was an instant hit with the automotive press and consumers alike. Both a sedan and a coupe are available, with your choice of three trim levels and two engines. While the Alero is technically a replacement for the Achieva, this stylish compact is light years ahead of previous attempts by the division to build and market a small car.

Like big-brother Intrigue, the Alero is entertaining to drive. GX and GL models come with a 2.4-liter, dual-overhead-cam, four-cylinder engine that makes 150 horsepower. A four-speed automatic is standard with a five-speed manual optional for those who prefer to row gears. Optional on GL and standard on GLS is a 3.4-liter V6 that makes 170 horsepower mated only to the automatic. Both engines now meet low-emission vehicle (LEV) standards.

While neither engine is particularly quiet during operation, they both deliver spirited performance. Alero employs what Olds engineers call an Active Response System (ARS) to increase driver enjoyment. ARS is simply a combination of 16 desirable attributes, such as a stiff body structure, four-wheel independent suspension, all-speed traction control and four-wheel disc brakes with improved-for-2001 ABS. As part of an optional sport package for the GL or GLS Sedan, the firmer-riding suspension rolls on upsized, V-rated, 16-inch performance rubber.

Inside, the Alero is a four-fifths version of the Intrigue. Well laid-out with seating for five, this car has features such as air conditioning, power locks, rear window defogger and split/folding rear seats all standard. But side airbags, offered by some under-$20,000 competitors from Toyota and Chevrolet, aren't available or planned. On the minus side, the cloth upholstery isn't very attractive, and the leather looks and feels too much like vinyl for our tastes.

Overall, the Alero is a stylish, powerful, sporting car that is willing to play if you are. It can serve family duty when necessary, won't embarrass the owner when pulling up to a swanky restaurant, zooms confidently along when the road turns twisty, and won't break the bank when the payment book arrives in the mail. However appealing, the Alero, like the rest of Oldsmobile's lineup, will eventually join its extinct brothers from Edsel, Studebaker and Plymouth.

Standard Equipment

GX COUPE (4A): 2.4L I4 DOHC SMPI 16-valve engine; 4-speed electronic OD automatic transmission with lock-up torque converter; 600 amp battery with run down protection; 105 amp alternator; front-wheel drive, traction control, 3.42 axle ratio; stainless steel exhaust; touring ride suspension, front independent strut suspension with anti-roll bar, front coil springs, rear independent multi-link suspension with anti-roll bar, rear coil springs; power rack-and-pinion steering; 4-wheel antilock disc brakes; 14.3 gal. capacity fuel tank; front license plate bracket, side impact bars; front and rear body-colored bumpers; body-colored bodyside molding; clearcoat monotone paint; aero-composite halogen fully auto headlamps with daytime running lights, delay-off feature; additional exterior lights include underhood light; driver's and passenger's manual black folding outside mirrors; 15" x 6" steel wheels; P215/60SR15 BSW touring A/S

ALERO — OLDSMOBILE

tires; compact steel spare wheel; air conditioning, rear heat/AC ducts; AM/FM stereo radio with RDS, clock, seek-scan, speed sensitive volume, single CD player, 4 speakers, auto equalizer, theft deterrent, window grid antenna; cruise control with steering wheel controls; power door locks, power remote hatch/trunk release; 2 power accessory outlets, front lighter element(s), smoker's package; instrumentation display includes tachometer, water temperature gauge, trip odometer; warning indicators include oil pressure, battery, low coolant, lights on, key in ignition, low fuel, low tire pressure, low washer fluid, service interval; driver's and passenger's front airbags; ignition disable; tinted windows; variable intermittent front windshield wipers, sun visor strip, rear window defroster; seating capacity of 5, front bucket seats with adjustable headrests, center armrest with storage, driver's and passenger's seat includes 4-way adjustment, easy entry; 70/30 folding rear bench seat with fixed headrests; cloth seats, cloth door trim insert, full cloth headliner, full carpet floor covering with carpeted floor mats; interior lights include dome light with fade, illuminated entry; steering wheel with tilt adjustment; dual vanity mirrors; day/night rearview mirror; full floor console, mini overhead console with storage, locking glove box with light, front and rear cupholders, instrument panel bin, 2 seat back storage pockets; carpeted cargo floor, cargo light; chrome side window moldings, black front windshield molding, black rear window molding and body-colored door handles.

GL1 COUPE (4A) (in addition to or instead of GX COUPE (4A) equipment): Power rack-and-pinion steering with vehicle speed-sensing assist; driver's and passenger's power remote body-colored folding outside mirrors; 6 speakers; remote keyless entry; panic alarm; tinted windows with driver's 1-touch down; driver's seat includes 2-way power adjustment, 6-way adjustment, lumbar support; premium cloth seats; dual auxiliary visors; driver's and passenger's door bins and cargo net.

GL2 COUPE (4A) (in addition to or instead of GL1 COUPE (4A) equipment): Sport ride suspension; rear wing spoiler; additional exterior lights include front fog/driving lights; 16" x 6.5" silver alloy wheels; P225/50SR16 BSW performance A/S tires; leather-wrapped gearshift knob and leather-wrapped steering wheel with tilt adjustment.

GLS COUPE (4A) (in addition to or instead of GL2 COUPE (4A) equipment): 3.4L V6 OHV SMPI 12-valve engine; 3.05 axle ratio; stainless steel exhaust; touring ride suspension; rear wing spoiler (Coupe only); P225/50SR16 BSW touring A/S tires; cassette player, single CD player, amplifier, 8 performance speakers; warning indicators include low oil level, low tire pressure; driver's seat includes 6-way power adjustment, 8-way adjustment, lumbar support; leather seats and leatherette door trim insert.

SEDAN (4A) (in addition to or instead of COUPE (4A) equipment): Child safety rear door locks.

Base Prices

Code	Description	Invoice	MSRP
3NK37	GX Coupe (4A)	16091	17210
3NL37	GL1 Coupe (4A)	17037	18620
3NL37	GL2 Coupe (4A)	17865	19525
3NF37	GLS Coupe (4A)	20082	22190
3NK69	GX Sedan (4A)	16091	17210
3NL69	GL1 Sedan (4A)	17037	18620
3NL69	GL2 Sedan (4A)	17865	19525
3NF69	GLS Sedan (4A)	19878	21965
	Destination Charge:	575	575

Interested in seeing what dealers will sell this vehicle for? Check out our True Market Value^{sm} (TMV^{sm}) pricing on our Web site at www.edmunds.com.

OLDSMOBILE — ALERO / AURORA

CODE	DESCRIPTION	INVOICE	MSRP

Accessories

CODE	DESCRIPTION	INVOICE	MSRP
1SA	GL1 Package (GL1)	NC	NC
	Includes vehicle with standard equipment.		
1SA	GLS Package (GLS)	NC	NC
	Includes vehicle with standard equipment.		
1SA	GX Package (GX)	NC	NC
	Includes vehicle with standard equipment.		
1SB	GL2 Package (GL2)	NC	NC
	Includes vehicle with standard equipment.		
AG1	6-Way Power Driver's Side Seat Adjuster (GL1/GL2)	271	305
	Includes manual lumbar adjuster.		
CF5	Power Sunroof (GLS)	623	700
K05	Engine Block Heater	31	35
LA1	Engine: 3.4L V6 OHV SMPI (GL1/GL2)	583	655
	Includes 3.05 axle ratio. NOT AVAILABLE with MM5.		
MM5	Transmission: 5-Speed Manual with OD (GX/GL2)	(699)	(785)
	Includes transmission delete and 3.94 axle ratio.		
R7T	Feature Package (GL1)	725	815
	Manufacturer Discount	(267)	(300)
	Net Price	458	515
	Includes 15" alloy wheels, fog lamps, leather-wrapped steering wheel and leather shifter.		
R7Y	Sun and Sound Package (GL1/GL2)	979	1100
	Manufacturer Discount	(227)	(255)
	Net Price	752	845
	Includes power sunroof, AM/FM stereo, CD, cassette and radio premium sound system with 8-speakers.		
R9P	Performance Suspension Package (GLS)	222	250
	Includes touring suspension and P225/50R16 performance tires.		
T43	Rear Decklid Spoiler (GL1/GLS Sedan)	200	225
	REQUIRES R7T.		
Y11	Gold Package (GL1/GL2/GLS)	134	150
	Includes gold-tinted front and rear emblems and Alero and Oldsmobile lettering on rear panel.		

2001 AURORA

What's New?

Oldsmobile has redesigned the Aurora, plopping its flagship sedan onto a more rigid but still front-drive platform. Remaining stylish and contemporary, Aurora is more conventional in appearance but overall, remains an enticing package. 3.5 V6 and 4.0 V8 versions are available, each equipped with a full load of luxury accoutrements.

Review

Aurora debuted to the public in 1994, a sensually shaped replacement for the Toronado coupe and a sign of things to come from Oldsmobile. At the time one of the stoutest sedans

AURORA

OLDSMOBILE

CODE	DESCRIPTION	INVOICE	MSRP

in the world, the car's delicious styling, smooth-revving overhead-cam V8, and emphasis on composed performance impressed critics.

Now Oldsmobile introduces a completely redesigned 2001 Aurora flagship, in 3.5 and 4.0 versions. Like its predecessor, the new Aurora is quite rigid, providing a solid sense of quality. Unlike the old version, the new model is rather svelte, shedding weight due to a more compact body and the use of aluminum in key parts of the design.

Improved performance should be the translation, especially since the DOHC 4.0-liter V8 engine makes more power while still delivering 17 mpg in the city and 25 mpg on the highway. It sends 250 horsepower to the front wheels through a four-speed automatic transmission. The 3.5-liter twin-cam V6, which first appeared in the lower-priced Intrigue and gets a few additional miles per gallon, makes 215 horses, but is charged with moving 120 fewer pounds.

Four-wheel disc ABS brakes and speed-sensitive rack-and-pinion steering that provides better feel and feedback are standard, and so are fat tires and attractive spoked aluminum wheels. The 3.5 is shod with 16-inch Goodyears while 4.0 models receive 17-inch Michelins. A precision control system (read: traction and stability control) keeps the 4.0 traveling the straight and narrow when it senses that a loss of control may be imminent.

Since the Aurora is a luxury car, you should know about a few of the goodies. All Auroras are equipped with leather seats and real walnut trim in a two-tone interior. Driver-oriented with a beautifully swept arc of a control panel, the cabin includes a 27-function Driver Information Center. Chrome accents around the gated shifter and gauges lend a touch of class.

Head, shoulder, and hip room have all been increased, but legroom is down slightly. Though the trunk is smaller, it's more accessible thanks to a larger opening and lower liftover height. Side airbags are mounted to the front seats, and two drivers can personalize the remote keyless entry system to their individual tastes.

With a lower price point for the 3.5, Oldsmobile expects to double sales of the Aurora. The car's combination of style, luxury and value could have led to success. However, with Olds now on the General's chopping block, Aurora's long-term outlook is rather dim.

Standard Equipment

3.5 (4A): 3.5L V6 DOHC SMPI 24-valve engine; 4-speed electronic OD automatic transmission with lock-up torque converter; battery with run down protection; 105 amp alternator; front-wheel drive, 3.29 axle ratio; stainless steel exhaust with powdercoated exhaust tip; sport ride suspension, auto-leveling suspension, front independent strut suspension with anti-roll bar, front coil springs, rear independent multi-link suspension with anti-roll bar, rear coil springs; power rack-and-pinion steering with vehicle speed-sensing assist; 4-wheel antilock disc brakes; 18.5 gal. capacity fuel tank; side impact bars; front and rear body-colored bumpers; body-colored bodyside molding; clearcoat monotone paint; projector beam halogen fully auto headlamps with daytime running lights; additional exterior lights include front fog/driving lights; driver's and passenger's power remote body-colored heated folding outside mirrors; 16" x 7" silver alloy wheels; P225/60HR16 touring A/S BSW tires; compact steel spare wheel; air conditioning with climate control, air filter, rear heat ducts; AM/FM stereo radio, clock, seek-scan, cassette player, single CD player, 6 speakers, auto equalizer, and window grid diversity antenna, radio steering wheel controls; cruise control; power door locks with 2 stage unlock, remote keyless entry, child safety rear door locks, power remote hatch/trunk release, power remote fuel release; 2 power accessory outlets, driver's foot rest, retained accessory power; instrumentation display includes tachometer, water temperature gauge, systems monitor, trip computer, trip odometer, exterior temp; warning indicators include oil pressure, water temp, battery, low oil level, low coolant, lights on, key in ignition, low fuel, low washer fluid, door ajar, trunk ajar, service interval, brake fluid; driver's and passenger's front airbags, driver's and front passenger's seat mounted side airbags; ignition disable, panic alarm, security system, valet key, emergency

OLDSMOBILE — AURORA

"S.O.S."(OnStar); tinted windows, power front and rear windows with driver's and passenger's 1-touch down; variable intermittent front windshield wipers, sun visor strip, rear window defroster; seating capacity of 5, front bucket seats with adjustable tilt headrests, center armrest with storage, driver's seat includes 6-way power adjustment, passenger's seat includes 4-way adjustment; rear bench seat with fixed headrests, center pass-thru armrest; leather seats, leatherette door trim insert, full cloth headliner, full carpet floor covering with carpeted floor mats, genuine wood trim on instrument panel, leather-wrapped gearshift knob; interior lights include dome light with fade, front and rear reading lights, 4 door curb lights, illuminated entry, ignition switch; leather-wrapped steering wheel with tilt adjustment; dual illuminated vanity mirrors, dual auxiliary visors; day/night rearview mirror; full floor console, mini overhead console with storage, instrument panel covered bin storage, audio media storage, locking glove box with light, front and rear cupholders, 2 seat back storage pockets, driver's and passenger's door bins; carpeted cargo floor, carpeted trunk lid, cargo net, cargo light; chrome side window moldings, black front windshield molding, black rear window molding and body-colored door handles.

4.0 (4A) (in addition to or instead of 3.5 (4A) equipment): 4.0L V8 DOHC SMPI 32-valve engine (requires premium unleaded fuel); traction control, 3.71 axle ratio; electronic stability; 17.5 gal. capacity fuel tank; body-colored heated folding driver's power remote outside mirror, passenger's power remote with tilt down outside mirror; 17" x 7.5" polished alloy wheels; P235/55HR17 touring A/S BSW tires; dual zone front air conditioning with climate control; garage door opener; instrumentation display includes compass; variable intermittent front rain detecting wipers; passenger's seat includes 6-way power adjustment; rear bench seat with fixed headrests, center pass-thru armrest with storage and memory on driver's seat with 2 memory setting(s) includes settings for exterior mirrors and auto-dimming day/night rearview mirror.

Base Prices

Code	Description	Invoice	MSRP
3GR29	3.5 (4A)	27879	30469
3GS29	4.0 (4A)	31699	34644
	Destination Charge:	670	670

Interested in seeing what dealers will sell this vehicle for? Check out our True Market Value^{sm} (TMV^{sm}) pricing on our Web site at www.edmunds.com.

Accessories

Code	Description	Invoice	MSRP
1SA	Option Package 1SA (3.5)	NC	NC
	Includes vehicle with standard equipment.		
1SB	Option Package 1SB (4.0)	NC	NC
	Includes vehicle with standard equipment.		
93U	Paint: White Diamond	352	395
BA5	Gold Graphics Package	156	175
	Includes gold finish on emblems and rear panel script.		
CF5	Electric Sliding Glass Panel Sunroof	975	1095
	Includes tinted gray glass and universal garage door opener.		
K05	Engine Block Heater	36	40
KA1	Driver's & Passenger's Heated Front Seats	307	345
	REQUIRES T1U or T2C.		
N94	Wheels: 17" Chrome-Plated Aluminum (4.0)	712	800
PH2	Wheels: 16" Chrome-Plated Aluminum (3.5)	712	800
T1U	Passenger Comfort Package (3.5)	392	440
	Includes 8-way power passenger's seat with power lumbar adjustment, rear storage armrest with stowable cupholders and dual zone climate control.		

AURORA / INTRIGUE — OLDSMOBILE

CODE	DESCRIPTION	INVOICE	MSRP
T2C	All Weather Package (3.5)	512	575
	Includes all-speed traction control and precision control system. REQUIRES T1U. INCLUDED in 1SB.		
T2U	Convenience Package (3.5)	503	565
	Includes electrochromic inside day/night mirror, compass, memory controls, universal garage door opener, rain-sensing auto wipers and personalization features.		
U1F	Radio: Bose AM/FM Stereo with CD/Cassette	445	500
	Includes auto-reverse cassette, seek-and-scan, 8-speaker premium sound system, diversity antenna, and reception elements in rear window and windshield. REQUIRES T1U.		
U1S	12-Disc Trunk-Mounted Remote CD Changer	409	460

2001 INTRIGUE

What's New?

The Intrigue receives only minor changes for 2001, including two new exterior colors and a standard air filtration system. The OnStar driver assistance system is now standard on GLS models while Precision Control System equipped models receive exterior "PCS" badging.

Review

Since being introduced in the 1998 model year, the Intrigue has played a key role in helping Oldsmobile redefine its struggling brand identity. Aimed squarely at the imports, Intrigue features a functional sedan design inside and out that delivers a minimum of glitz and a maximum of ergonomic operation. Providing tight space for five adults, the Intrigue offers acceptable interior room without a bulky exterior size or hefty curb weight.

Built off a rigid structural backbone, Olds gave its midsize front-driver four-wheel independent suspension, disc brakes and ABS. The GX is a fully equipped base model, while moving up to the GL nets extras such as a dual-zone air conditioner, fog lamps, keyless entry and upgraded mirrors, seats and sound system. The GLS pops for top-of-the-line items such as a now standard OnStar vehicle assistance system, leather, fake wood trim, and a CD player. Need more pizzazz? The gold exterior badge package and special Sterling (as in silver) Edition model offered in 2000 remain available for 2001. All models receive a standard air filtration system for 2001.

All Intrigues are now powered by GM's 24-valve 3.5-liter V6 (based on the Aurora V8) that sends a torquey 215 horsepower through a four-speed electronically controlled transaxle. Last year the Intrigue debuted the PCS driver control system that uses sensors to measure the speed of each wheel as well as steering and yaw angles. If a panic stop, quick swerve or slick pavement forces the car into a skid, the system hydraulically adjusts the individual ABS unit(s) needed to bring the car back under control.

Driving the Intrigue feels more like driving an import than a typical Oldsmobile. Speed-sensitive steering offers good feedback, and the brake pedal is easy to modulate. Seats are comfy and supportive. While the car is fairly big, it doesn't feel like it from the driver's seat, thanks to responsive handling and good visibility. Hoever, the speed-sensitive steering can be rather schizophrenic when its ratio and weighting change in mid corner. Understated styling provides strong family ties to the flagship Aurora in the headlights, front fascia and rear quarters. And

OLDSMOBILE

INTRIGUE

| CODE | DESCRIPTION | INVOICE | MSRP |

Intrigue's twin-cam V6 not only provides stout acceleration and good fuel economy, but it does so without the need for premium fuel, unlike many other performance-oriented V6 powerplants in this class.

Pricing is in line with the Toyota Camry LE and XLE V6, the Nissan Maxima SE and GLE, and the Mercury Sable LS. Offering style, room and power, the Oldsmobile Intrigue is one sedan priced in the mid-20s that shoppers should at least test drive when searching for their next family sedan—unless they are squeamish about the parent company's impending demise.

Standard Equipment

GX (4A): 3.5L V6 DOHC SMPI 24-valve engine; 4-speed electronic OD automatic transmission with lock-up; 690 amp battery with run down protection; 105 amp alternator; front-wheel drive, 3.05 axle ratio; stainless steel exhaust; touring ride suspension, front independent strut suspension with anti-roll bar, front coil springs, gas-pressurized front shocks, rear independent strut suspension with anti-roll bar, rear coil springs, gas-pressurized rear shocks; power rack-and-pinion steering with vehicle speed-sensing assist; 4-wheel antilock disc brakes; 18 gal. capacity fuel tank; side impact bars; front and rear body-colored bumpers; body-colored bodyside molding rocker panel extensions; clearcoat monotone paint; aero-composite halogen fully auto headlamps with daytime running lights, delay-off feature; additional exterior lights include cornering lights; driver's and passenger's power remote black folding outside mirrors; 16" x 6.5" silver finish aluminum wheels silver finish aluminum; P225/60SR16 BSW touring A/S tires; compact steel spare wheel; air conditioning, air filter, rear heat ducts; AM/FM stereo radio, clock, seek-scan, cassette, 4 speakers, auto equalizer, theft deterrent, window grid antenna; cruise control with steering wheel controls; power door locks, child safety rear door locks, power remote hatch/trunk release, power remote fuel release; 2 power accessory outlets, driver's foot rest, retained accessory power; instrumentation display includes tachometer, water temperature gauge, systems monitor, trip odometer; warning indicators include oil pressure, battery, low oil level, low coolant, lights on, key in ignition, low fuel, low washer fluid, service interval; driver's and passenger's front airbags; ignition disable; tinted windows, power front and rear windows with driver's 1-touch down; variable intermittent front windshield wipers, sun visor strip, rear window defroster; seating capacity of 5, front bucket seats with adjustable headrests, center armrest with storage, driver's and passenger's seat includes 4-way adjustment; rear bench seat with fixed headrests, center armrest; front height adjustable seatbelts; cloth seats, vinyl door trim insert, full cloth headliner, full carpet floor covering with carpeted floor mats, plastic/rubber gearshift knob; interior lights include dome light with fade, front and rear reading lights, illuminated entry; steering wheel with tilt adjustment; vanity mirrors, dual auxiliary visors; day/night rearview mirror; full floor console, locking glove box with light, front and rear cupholders, instrument panel covered bin, 2 seat back storage pockets, driver's and passenger's door bins, rear door bins; carpeted cargo floor, cargo light; chrome side window moldings, black front windshield molding, black rear window molding and body-colored door handles.

GL (4A) (in addition to or instead of GX (4A) equipment): Traction control; additional exterior lights include front fog/driving lights; driver's and passenger's power remote body-colored folding outside mirrors; dual zone front air conditioning with climate control; cassette, single CD, 6 performance speakers, radio steering wheel controls; power door locks with 2 stage unlock, remote keyless entry; instrumentation display includes exterior temp, systems monitor; panic alarm; driver's seat includes 6-way power seat, 8-way adjustment; 60/40 folding rear bench seat with fixed headrests; leather-wrapped gearshift knob; leather-wrapped steering wheel with tilt adjustment; dual illuminated vanity mirrors and cargo net.

GLS (4A) (in addition to or instead of GL (4A) equipment): Emergency S.O.S. (OnStar); instrumentation display includes compass; tracker system; heated-cushion driver's and passenger's seats, passenger's seat includes 6-way power seat, 8-way adjustment; leather seats, leatherette door trim insert, simulated wood door panel insert, simulated wood console insert and auto-dimming day/night rearview mirror.

INTRIGUE — OLDSMOBILE

CODE	DESCRIPTION	INVOICE	MSRP

Base Prices

3WH69	GX (4A)	20491	22395
3WS69	GL (4A)	22097	24150
3WX69	GLS (4A)	24261	26515
	Destination Charge:	610	610

Interested in seeing what dealers will sell this vehicle for? Check out our True Market Value^{sm} (TMV^{sm}) pricing on our Web site at www.edmunds.com.

Accessories

Code	Description	Invoice	MSRP
1SA	GX Equipment Package (GX)	NC	NC
	Includes vehicle with standard equiment.		
1SB	GL Equipment Package (GL)	NC	NC
	Includes vehicle with standard equipment.		
1SC	GLS Equipment Package (GLS)	NC	NC
	Includes vehicle with standard equipment.		
1SL	Premium Leather Package (GL)	1420	1595
	Includes dual zone auto air conditioning, air filtration system, rear window grid antenna, cruise control with steering wheel controls, power door locks, power outside rearview fold-away mirrors, tilt steering column, 16" styled alloy wheels, power windows, trunk cargo net, fog lamps, 60/40 split folding rear seat, sun visors with lighted mirrors, steering wheel mounted radio controls, heated front seats, 6-way power passenger seat and Nuance leather seat trim.		
1SS	Precision Sport Package (GLS)	2016	2265
	Includes dual zone auto air conditioning, air filtration system, rear window grid antenna, cruise control with steering wheel controls, power door locks, power outside rearview fold-away mirrors, tilt steering column, power windows, trunk cargo net, fog lamps, 60/40 split folding rear seat, sun visors with lighted mirrors, steering wheel mounted radio controls, Nuance leather seat trim, faux woodgrain interior accents, electrochromic inside rearview mirror, OnStar communications system, precision control system package, 3.29 axle ratio, P225/60R16 H RATED BW performance tires, rear Decklid spoiler, electric sliding glass panel sunroof and 16" chrome plated alloy wheels.		
1SX	Driver Control Package (GX)	881	990
	Includes air conditioning, air filtration system, rear window grid antenna, cruise control with steering wheel controls, power door locks, power outside rearview fold-away mirrors, tilt steering column, 16" silver finish aluminum wheels, power windows, remote keyless entry, 6 speaker dimensional sound system, 6-way power driver seat, leather-wrapped steering wheel, full function traction control system, AM/FM stereo with CD, cassette and auto tone control radio.		
AM9	60/40 Split Folding Rear Seat (GX)	134	150
	Includes fold forward seatback. REQUIRES 1SA, 1SX.		
CF5	Electric Sliding Glass Panel Sunroof (GX/GL)	668	750
	Includes panel in gray tint (reduces headroom). INCLUDED in 1SS.		
D81	Rear Decklid Spoiler (GX/GL)	200	225
	INCLUDED in 1SS.		

OLDSMOBILE — INTRIGUE

CODE	DESCRIPTION	INVOICE	MSRP
JL4	Precision Control System Package (GX/GL)	530	595
	Includes PCS badge, Precision Control System components and Magnasteer II, 3.29 axle ratio and P225/60R16 H RATED BW performance tires. REQUIRES 1SX. NOT AVAILABLE with 1SA. INCLUDED in 1SS.		
K05	Engine Block Heater	36	40
PY1	Wheels: 16" Chrome Plated Aluminum (GL)	619	695
	INCLUDED in 1SS.		
U1F	Radio: Bose AM/FM Stereo with CD, Cassette (GL/GLS)	445	500
	Includes seek-scan, auto-reverse cassette, digital display clock and 8 speaker sound system powered by a rear shelf amplifier.		
Y11	Gold Package	134	150
	Includes exterior gold lettering, wheel and hood emblems.		

TOWN HALL

Get answers from our editors, discover smart shopping strategies and share your perspectives in this interactive forum of both experts and consumers. Just enter the following address into your Web browser:

townhall.edmunds.com

Where smart shoppers talk about cars, trucks, and related consumer topics.

NEON — PLYMOUTH

2001 NEON

What's New?

Side-impact airbags and leather seats are now available in Plymouth's economy car. A center shoulder belt for the rear seat and an internal emergency trunk release further improve this Plymouth's safety consciousness. Both a Sun and Sound or a Value/Fun option group is available this year, each of which includes a sunroof. New interior and exterior options for the Neon pump some life in this fading brand, but if you've got a hankering for the Plymouth nameplate, act fast; as of 2002 Plymouth will be closing shop and subsuming its identity to the gods of DaimlerChrysler.

Review

DaimlerChrysler is billing the current-generation Neon as "quiet, sophisticated and still a lot of fun." Fun seems to be the catchword for the Neon. It's used repeatedly by the manufacturer including, "fun-to-drive handling and steering" and "fun-to-drive attributes." Its maker obviously wants people to know that while the Neon has grown up, it hasn't grown old.

While a fun factor still exists when piloting the Plymouth Neon, the "quiet, sophisticated" aspects are nowhere to be found. The standard 132-horsepower 2.0-liter inline four received refinements to the air induction and intake manifold systems last year to provide torque over a broader rpm range while simultaneously quelling engine noise, but the powerplant still makes too much racket at high rpms.

A word of advice: make sure you stick with the standard equipment five-speed manual transmission. Plymouth has the cojones to charge $600 for its lame-oid and out-of-date three-speed automatic while the cheaper Hyundai Elantra and Daewoo Nubira utilize four-speed autos. Whatever.

With a refined suspension that offers plenty of wheel travel, the Neon's ride is smooth, and it's further enhanced with premium shock absorbers and rear sway bars. The power rack-and-pinion steering and precisely tuned suspension also contribute to the Neon's cruising quality while making it an absolute blast when canyon carving. Stopping power comes from a front disc/rear drum combo, but buyers may want to opt for four-wheel discs with ABS and traction control.

We genuinely like the Neon's exterior features that include jewel-like headlamps, a sleek roofline, and large tail lamps. Utilizing a long wheelbase and wide track, the Neon also offers exceptional interior room and a stable ride.

Plymouth's version of the Neon comes in two models. Base Neons are simply called "Sedan" while upscale models benefit from "LX" badging. Standard items like a radio/cassette combo and four Big Gulp-sized cupholders are much appreciated, yet overall feature content is still lacking. You don't even get power rear windows, a tachometer, or cruise control as standard equipment on the "upscale" LX model. New options for 2001, including side-impact airbags and leather seats, have somewhat expanded the Neon's feature list. You can also get a sunroof as part of the Sun and Sound or Value/Fun option packages. We give Plymouth credit for creating an attractive cabin that appears very upscale and for offering a standard 132-horsepower engine, even in the base Neon.

Unfortunately, competitors like the Ford Focus, Mazda Protege and Nissan Sentra offer more bang for the buck in terms of both refinement and content while still providing enthusiasts with a fun-to-drive car. We bid a fond adieu to Plymouth.

PLYMOUTH

NEON

Standard Equipment

HIGHLINE (5M): 2L I4 SOHC SMPI 16-valve engine; 5-speed OD manual transmission; 450 amp battery with run-down protection; 83 amp alternator; front-wheel drive, 3.55 axle ratio; stainless steel exhaust; front independent strut suspension with anti-roll bar, front coil springs, rear independent multi-link suspension with anti-roll bar, rear coil springs; rack-and-pinion power steering, power steering cooler; front disc/rear drum brakes; 12.5 gal. capacity fuel tank; side impact bars; front and rear body-colored bumpers; body-colored bodyside molding; clearcoat monotone paint; aero-composite halogen headlamps; driver's and passenger's black outside mirrors, driver's manual remote outside mirror, passenger's manual outside mirror; 14" x 5.5" black steel wheels; P185/65TR14 BSW A/S touring tires; compact steel spare wheel; AM/FM stereo radio, clock, seek-scan, cassette player, CD changer pre-wiring, 6 speakers, fixed antenna; child safety rear door locks; 1 power accessory outlet; instrumentation display includes water temperature gauge, trip odometer; warning indicators include oil pressure, battery, lights on, key in ignition, low fuel, door ajar; driver's and passenger's front airbags; tinted windows, manual front and rear windows; variable speed intermittent front windshield wipers, sun visor strip, rear window defroster; seating capacity of 5, front bucket seats with adjustable headrests, center armrest with storage, driver's and passenger's seat includes 4-way adjustment; 60/40 folding rear bench seat with fixed headrests; height adjustable front seatbelts; cloth seats, cloth door trim insert, full cloth headliner, full carpet floor covering with carpeted floor mats, deluxe sound insulation; interior lights include dome light with fade; steering wheel with tilt adjustment; passenger's side vanity mirror; day/night rearview mirror; full floor console, locking glove box, front and rear cupholders, instrument panel bin, dashboard storage, driver's and passenger's door bins; carpeted cargo floor, cargo light; black side window moldings, black front windshield molding, black rear window molding and body-colored door handles.

Base Prices

CODE	DESCRIPTION	INVOICE	MSRP
PLPH41	Highline (5M)	11856	12715
	Destination Charge:	490	490

Interested in seeing what dealers will sell this vehicle for? Check out our True Market Value^{sm} (TMV^{sm}) pricing on our Web site at www.edmunds.com.

Accessories

CODE	DESCRIPTION	INVOICE	MSRP
—	Side Air Bags	312	350
21G	Quick Order Package 21G	2212	2485
	Manufacturer Discount	(592)	(665)
	Net Price	1620	1820

Includes air conditioning, passenger assist handles, LX badge, color keyed instrument cluster bezel, fog lamps, power convenience group, power heated folding mirrors, power front windows, premium cloth low back bucket seats, sentry key security group, keyless entry system with 2 transmitters, power automatic central locking locks, security alarm, sentry key theft deterrent system, tachometer, power trunklid release, leather-wrapped shift knob, leather-wrapped steering wheel, P185/60R15 BSW A/S touring tires, 15" wheel covers and 15" x 6" black wheels. NOT AVAILABLE with DGC.

22G	Quick Order Package 22G	2212	2485
	Manufacturer Discount	(592)	(665)
	Net Price	1620	1820

Includes air conditioning, passenger assist handles, LX badge, color keyed instrument cluster bezel, fog lamps, power convenience group, power heated folding mirrors,

NEON — PLYMOUTH

CODE	DESCRIPTION	INVOICE	MSRP

power front windows, premium cloth low-back bucket seats, sentry key security group, keyless entry system with 2 transmitters, power automatic central locking locks, security alarm, sentry key theft deterrent system, tachometer, power trunklid release, leather-wrapped shift knob, leather-wrapped steering wheel, P185/60R15 BSW A/S touring tires, 15" wheel covers and 15" x 6" black wheels. REQUIRES DGC.

CODE	DESCRIPTION	INVOICE	MSRP
ADA	Light Group	116	130
	Includes console flood lamp, glove box lamp, rearview mirror with reading lamps and illuminated vanity mirror sun visors. REQUIRES HAA, 21G, or 22G.		
ADR	Antilock Brake Group	748	840
	Manufacturer Discount	(218)	(245)
	Net Price	530	595
	Includes 4-wheel antilock disc brakes, tachometer and traction control.		
ADR	Antilock Brake Group	659	740
	Manufacturer Discount	(129)	(145)
	Net Price	530	595
	Includes 4-wheel antilock disc brakes, tachometer and traction control. REQUIRES AJX, 21G, or 22G.		
AGS	Sun and Sound Group	1064	1195
	Manufacturer Discount	(356)	(400)
	Net Price	708	795
	Includes value fun group, light group, glove box lamp, rearview mirror with reading lamps, illuminated vanity mirror sun visors, power sunroof, 4 disc in-dash CD changer, P185/60R15 BSW A/S touring tires, 15" wheel covers and 15" x 6" black wheels. REQUIRES HAA.		
AJP	Power Convenience Group	338	380
	Includes power heated folding mirrors and power front windows. REQUIRES AJX and HAA. INCLUDED in 21G or 22G.		
AJX	Sentry Key Security Group	668	750
	Manufacturer Discount	(369)	(415)
	Net Price	299	335
	Includes keyless entry system with 2 transmitters, power automatic central locking locks, security alarm, sentry key theft deterrent system, tachometer and power trunklid release. REQUIRES HAA. INCLUDED in 21G or 22G.		
ALF	Value Fun Group	645	725
	Manufacturer Discount	(116)	(130)
	Net Price	529	595
	Includes passenger assist handles and power sunroof. REQUIRES 21G or 22G.		
CGS	Supplemental Side Air Bags	312	350
DGC	Transmission: 3-Speed Automatic	534	600
	Includes 2.98 axle ratio. NOT AVAILABLE with 21G.		
HAA	Air Conditioning	890	1000
	INCLUDED in 21G or 22G.		
NHK	Engine Block Heater	18	20
NHM	Speed Control	209	235
RDW	4-Disc In-Dash CD Changer	334	375

PLYMOUTH
NEON / PROWLER

CODE	DESCRIPTION	INVOICE	MSRP
WJA	Wheels: 15" Aluminum	316	355
	REQUIRES AGS, 21G, or 22G.		
WJA	Wheels: 15" Aluminum	365	410
	REQUIRES HAA.		
XL	Leather Low-Back Bucket Seats	899	1010
	Manufacturer Discount	(142)	(160)
	Net Price	757	850

Includes Decklid liner and full length floor console with premium armrest, side airbags and woodgrain instrument cluster bezel.

2001 PROWLER

What's New?

Get your Plymouth Prowler while you can. After 2001 it goes away…and becomes the Chrysler Prowler. Sure, it will be the identical car, but that powerful Plymouth Prowler alliteration will be gone forever! Oh, yeah, you can get these in copper metallic and a silver/black combination this year. New adjustable damper shocks are offered as standard equipment.

Review

Chrysler has taken the drawing board directly into the manufacturing plant. The Prowler is simply a concept car that has magically seen the light of day, and though it's not the most impressive car performance-wise, it is a most impressive display of Chrysler's commitment to fun.

Modeled after traditional hot rods of the 1950s, the Prowler certainly looks the part, despite the federally mandated but truly dopey-looking gray front bumpers. Painted in a variety of colors, including new copper and a silver/black combination for 2001, Prowler is equipped with massive 20-inch chrome wheels in back (fronts are 17s). With its extremely high beltline, you'll feel like you're treading water in a pool, and with the top up, visibility is a joke. Trunk space is even more amusing if you've got more than a briefcase to haul around.

The retro aluminum bodywork is wrapped around an all-aluminum frame supported by an aluminum four-wheel independent suspension. New this year are adjustable dampers that let you soften the ride; a welcome feature, as this roadster tends to ride harshly. Lousy leather-wrapped seats don't promote comfort over the long haul, and Chrysler parts bin bits combine with questionable ergonomics (center-mounted gauges?) to remind you that form definitely takes precedence over function in this vehicle. And if the styling isn't attracting enough attention, you can crank up the 320-watt Infinity sound system, with speed-compensated volume control, to make sure everyone notices you.

Prowler's powertrain somewhat disappoints. A stout 3.5-liter SOHC V6 engine, capable of producing 253 horsepower and 255 foot-pounds of torque, powers this Plymouth from rest to 60 mph in 6 seconds, but without sufficient exhaust rumble. It's mated to Chrysler's lame AutoStick automanual transmission, which is certainly no substitute for a real manual gearbox. So, no V8 and no stick: if this constitutes the hardware of the modern hot rod, we'll take a pass. The Prowler offers better handling than you might think, but the comparably priced Corvette will wax it while offering superior comfort and amenities.

PROWLER
PLYMOUTH

This car will turn heads, even in exotic car-jaded towns like Los Angeles or Palm Beach. If you're not a celebrity but you want to feel like one, here's the recipe: buy a Plymouth Prowler. Drop the top. Cruise up and down your local strip. Wave at the gawking crowd. Just don't try to drag race any real muscle cars.

Standard Equipment

PROWLER (4A): 3.5L V6 SOHC SMPI 24-valve engine; 4-speed electronic OD automanual transmission with lock-up torque converter; 500 amp battery; 90 amp alternator; rear-wheel drive, 3.89 axle ratio; dual stainless steel exhaust with tailpipe finisher; front independent suspension with anti-roll bar, front coil springs, gas-pressurized front shocks, rear independent multi-link suspension with anti-roll bar, rear coil springs, gas-pressurized rear shocks; power rack-and-pinion steering; 4-wheel disc brakes; 12.2 gal. capacity fuel tank; side impact bars; manual convertible roof with a glass rear window, roll-over protection; front and rear colored bumpers; rocker panel extensions; clearcoat monotone paint; projector beam halogen headlamps; driver's and passenger's power remote body-colored outside mirrors; front 17" x 7.5" and rear 20" x 10" chrome alloy wheels; front P225/45VR17 BSW and rear P295/40VR20 run flat tires; alloy spare wheel; air conditioning; premium AM/FM stereo radio, clock, seek-scan, cassette player, 6-disc CD changer, 7 premium speakers, premium amplifier, graphic equalizer, window grid antenna, radio steering wheel controls; cruise control with steering wheel controls; power door locks with 2 stage unlock, remote keyless entry, remote trunk release; 1 power accessory outlet; instrumentation display includes tachometer, oil pressure gauge, water temperature gauge, volt gauge, compass, exterior temp, trip computer, trip odometer; warning indicators include oil pressure, water temp, battery, lights on, key in ignition, low fuel, low washer fluid, door ajar, trunk ajar, low tire pressure; driver's front airbag, passenger's cancelable front airbag; ignition disable, panic alarm, security system; tinted windows with driver's 1-touch down function; variable speed intermittent front windshield wipers, rear window defroster; seating capacity of 2, front bucket seats with fixed headrests, center armrest with storage, driver's seat includes 6-way adjustment, passenger's seat includes 4-way adjustment; leather seats, leatherette door trim insert, full carpet floor covering with floor mats, leather-wrapped gearshift knob; interior lights include dome light, front reading lights, illuminated entry; leather-wrapped steering wheel with tilt adjustment; vanity mirrors; auto-dimming day/night rearview mirror; full floor console, glove box with light, front cupholder, 2 seat back storage pockets; carpeted cargo floor; body-colored grille, black front windshield molding and body-colored door handles.

Base Prices

Code	Description	Invoice	MSRP
PRPS27	Base (4A)	41270	44225
	Destination Charge:	775	775

Interested in seeing what dealers will sell this vehicle for? Check out our True Market Value^{sm} (TMV^{sm}) pricing on our Web site at www.edmunds.com.

Accessories

Code	Description	Invoice	MSRP
21A	Quick Order Package 21A	NC	NC
	Includes vehicle with standard equipment.		
ACB	Black Tie Edition Group	1820	2000
	Includes black hood, Decklid, center high mounted stop lamp, two-tone doors (black upper and silver lower), upper black hood ornament, silver quarter panels, front fascia, hood side panels, grille, door handles, rear valence/tape, headlamps, fenders, front quarter/side sill panels, fuel door, instrument panel cluster bezel and floor mats, two-tone paint application, black exterior mirrors and silver paint stripe.		

PONTIAC — BONNEVILLE

2001 BONNEVILLE

What's New?

Because Pontiac's flagship sedan, built on the Cadillac Seville's platform with rakish styling and high-tech goodies such as an integrated chassis control system, was all-new last year, 2001 sees little change. Heated seats are available on the SE and SLE, and Ivory White is a new color for the year. OnStar telematics with a 1-year membership is optional on the SE but comes standard with the SLE and SSEi.

Review

Billed as "Luxury With Attitude," the Pontiac Bonneville was completely redesigned on a bigger and better platform with an all-new look for 2000. This updated architecture resulted in a 62 percent improvement in torsional stiffness over the previous iteration, providing a rigid body shell for a solid, quiet ride. Rolling on a 112-inch wheelbase, the Bonny backs up Pontiac's "Wide Track" marketing pitch with a class-leading 62.6-inch front and 62.1-inch rear footprint.

Styling combines a steep hood and windshield rake with an aggressive roofline to impart a decidedly wedge-like profile. But the Bonneville still retains such traditional Pontiac design cues as cat's-eye headlamps with large, round fog lamps, a V-shaped hood, and sculpted bodysides with muscular haunches. Three models are available, SE, SLE and SSEi.

Standard on the SE and SLE is GM's 3800 Series II V6 that not only pumps out 205 horsepower though a four-speed automatic transmission, but also can get an amazing 30 miles per gallon on the highway. Move to the SSEi and you get a healthy, 240-horsepower supercharged variant of the 3.8-liter V6 that makes you almost forget that this full-size luxury sport sedan is not available with V8 power.

The base SE is fully equipped, with standard features such as seat-mounted safety belts, driver and front-passenger side-impact airbags, and four-wheel antilock brakes. Other standard items include 16-inch wheels and tires, power mirrors and illuminated entry. The midlevel SLE adds dual climate controls, a programmable driver information center, four-wheel disc brakes with ABS, and an upgrade to 17-inch wheels.

Of course, the SSEi not only packs supercharged punch, but ups the equipment ante with dual exhaust, high-performance 17-inch wheels and tires, GM's StabiliTrak suspension system, and a Bose eight-speaker premium audio unit. You also get other high-tech goodies, such as EyeCue head-up display, variable-effort steering, and 12-way power leather front buckets with memory.

Speaking of the interior, all controls are canted toward the driver in true Pontiac tradition, with full instrumentation backlit in the brand-signature red lighting. If your needs call for six-passenger capability, a 55/45 bench seat with center storage armrest is available on the SE (in cloth only). A lineup of Delco radios is offered, as is GM's three-button OnStar communications system.

Overall, the Bonneville is a stylish and speedy full-size sedan built off a true, world-class platform that has won critical acclaim beneath Cadillac's Seville. If the Bonneville's racy new looks suit you, the only way to improve the breed would be to borrow the Caddy's Northstar V8.

Standard Equipment

SE (4A): 3.8L V6 OHV SMPI 12-valve engine; 4-speed electronic OD automatic transmission with lock-up torque converter; 690 amp battery with run down protection; 140 amp alternator; front-wheel drive, 2.86 axle ratio; stainless steel exhaust; touring ride suspension, auto-leveling

BONNEVILLE

PONTIAC

CODE	DESCRIPTION	INVOICE	MSRP

suspension, front independent strut suspension with anti-roll bar, front coil springs, rear independent trailing arm suspension with anti-roll bar, rear coil springs; power rack-and-pinion steering; 4-wheel antilock disc brakes; 18.5 gal. capacity fuel tank; rear lip spoiler, side impact bars; front and rear body-colored bumpers with chrome bumper insert; body-colored bodyside molding with chrome bodyside insert; clearcoat monotone paint; aero-composite halogen fully auto headlamps with daytime running lights, delay-off feature; additional exterior lights include front fog/driving lights; driver's and passenger's power remote body-colored outside mirrors; 16" x 7" silver alloy wheels; P225/60SR16 BW touring A/S tires; compact steel spare wheel; air conditioning, rear heat ducts; AM/FM stereo radio, clock, seek-scan, cassette player, 6 speakers, auto equalizer, theft deterrent, window grid diversity antenna; cruise control; power door locks with 2 stage unlock, remote keyless entry, child safety rear door locks, power remote hatch/trunk release; 3 power accessory outlets, front lighter element(s), driver's foot rest, retained accessory power, smoker's package; instrumentation display includes tachometer, oil pressure gauge, water temperature gauge, volt gauge, systems monitor, trip odometer; warning indicators include oil pressure, water temp, battery, low oil level, lights on, key in ignition, low washer fluid, door ajar, trunk ajar, turn signal on, low tire pressure; driver's and passenger's front airbags, driver's and front passenger's seat mounted side airbags; ignition disable, panic alarm, security system; tinted windows, power front and rear windows with driver's and passenger's 1-touch down; variable intermittent front windshield wipers, sun visor strip, rear window defroster; seating capacity of 5, front 45/45 bucket seats with adjustable headrests, center armrest with storage, driver's seat includes 6-way power adjustment, 8-way adjustment, lumbar support, passenger's seat includes 4-way adjustment; rear bench seat with fixed headrests, center pass-thru armrest; cloth seats, cloth door trim insert, full cloth headliner, full carpet floor covering with carpeted floor mats; interior lights include dome light with fade, front and rear reading lights, ignition switch light, 4 door curb lights, illuminated entry; steering wheel with tilt adjustment; dual illuminated vanity mirrors, dual auxiliary visors; day/night rearview mirror; full floor console, full overhead console with storage, locking glove box with light, front and rear cupholders, instrument panel bin, 2 seat back storage pockets, driver's and passenger's door bins; carpeted cargo floor, cargo tie downs, cargo net, cargo light; chrome grille, black side window moldings, black front windshield molding, black rear window molding and body-colored door handles.

SLE (4A) (in addition to or instead of SE (4A) equipment): Traction control, 3.05 axle ratio; stainless steel exhaust with poloished tailpipe finisher; sport ride suspension; body-colored bodyside cladding; driver's and passenger's power remote body-colored heated outside mirrors; 17" x 7.5" 17" multi-lace silver cast aluminum wheels; P235/55HR17 BW performance A/S tires; dual zone front air conditioning with climate control, air filter, rear heat ducts; radio steering wheel controls; emergency S.O.S. (OnStar); instrumentation display includes compass, exterior temp, trip computer; warning indicators include low coolant, lights on, low fuel, low washer fluid, service interval, bulb failure; tracker system; rear center pass-thru armrest with storage; memory on driver's seat with 2 memory setting(s) includes settings for exterior mirrors, AC/heat controls, audio settings; leather-wrapped steering wheel with tilt adjustment and body-colored shift.

SSEI (4A) (in addition to or instead of SLE (4A) equipment): 3.8L V6 OHV SMPI supercharger 12-valve engine (requires premium unleaded fuel); 2.93 axle ratio; electronic stability; power rack-and-pinion steering with vehicle speed-sensing assist; passenger's power remote outside mirror with tilt down; single CD player, 8 premium speakers; garage door opener; instrumentation display includes head-up display; seating capacity of 5, front 45/45 bucket seats with adjustable tilt headrests, center armrest with storage, driver's and passenger's seats include 8-way power adjustment, power 4-way lumbar support; leather seats, leatherette door trim insert, leather-wrapped gearshift knob; auto-dimming day/night rearview mirror; carpeted cargo floor, carpeted trunk lid, cargo net and cargo light.

Base Prices

2HX69	SE (4A)	22944	25075
2HY69	SLE (4A)	25661	28045

PONTIAC — BONNEVILLE

CODE	DESCRIPTION	INVOICE	MSRP
2HZ69	SSEi (4A)	29660	32415
	Destination Charge:	655	655

Interested in seeing what dealers will sell this vehicle for? Check out our True Market Value^{sm} (TMV^{sm}) pricing on our Web site at www.edmunds.com.

Accessories

CODE	DESCRIPTION	INVOICE	MSRP
—	**Connolly Prado Leather Seat Trim (SLE)**	756	850
	Includes non-articulating seats, leather-wrapped steering wheel with radio controls, driver manual lumbar and rear storage armrest. INCLUDED in 1SC.		
1SA	**Option Package 1SA (SLE)**	NC	NC
	Includes Delco AM/FM stereo radio with cassette, 6-way power driver seat, trunk storage net, remote keyless entry system, dual illuminated visor vanity mirrors, full feature theft-deterrent system, rear deck spoiler, leather-wrapped steering wheel and traction control.		
1SB	**Option Package 1SB (SE/SSEi)**	NC	NC
	Includes trunk storage net, remote keyless entry system, dual illuminated visor vanity mirrors, full feature theft-deterrent system and rear Deck spoiler. NOT AVAILABLE with U1S.		
1SC	**Option Package 1SC (SE)**	1638	1840
	Includes Delco AM/FM stereo radio with cassette, 6-way power driver seat, trunk storage net, remote keyless entry system, dual illuminated visor vanity mirrors, full feature theft-deterrent system, rear Deck spoiler, dual zone auto air conditioning, 45/45 bucket seats, leather seat trim, rear armrest with storage, leather-wrapped steering wheel, radio controls, 3.05 performance axle ratio, traction control, OnStar, 6 speaker sound system and 16" 5-spoke silver cast alloy wheels. NOT AVAILABLE with AM6.		
1SZ	**Heat and Seat Discount (SE/SLE)**	(178)	(200)
	REQUIRES AG2.		
AG2	**6-Way Power Passenger Seat (SE/SLE)**	472	530
	Includes driver and passenger heated seats. REQUIRES 1SZ.		
AM6	**55/45 Split Bench Seat (SE)**	134	150
	Includes manual recliners, storage armrest with dual cupholders and non-storage rear armrest, floor console delete and rear air vent delete. NOT AVAILABLE with 1SC.		
CF5	**Power Glass Sunroof**	961	1080
	Includes illuminated visor vanity mirrors and overhead console delete.		
K05	**Engine Block Heater**	31	35
KA1	**Driver and Passenger Heated Seats (SSEi)**	200	225
N94	**Wheels: 17" High-Polished Cast Aluminum (SLE/SSEi)**	530	595
	Includes multi-spoke and bright chrome.		
NP5	**Leather-Wrapped Steering Wheel (SE)**	156	175
	Includes radio controls. INCLUDED in 1SA, 1SC.		
NW9	**Traction Control (SE)**	156	175
	INCLUDED in 1SA, 1SC.		
U1P	**Radio: Delco AM/FM Stereo with CD (SE/SLE)**	89	100
	Includes clock, Theftlock, programmable equalization and radio data system.		

BONNEVILLE / FIREBIRD

PONTIAC

CODE	DESCRIPTION	INVOICE	MSRP
U1Q	Radio: Delco AM/FM Stereo with CD, Cassette (SE/SLE)	178	200
	Includes radio data system, programmable equalizer, clock, touch control, seek-and-scan, search and replay, power antenna, TheftLock and 6-speaker system. NOT AVAILABLE with U1P.		
U1S	Trunk-Mounted 12-Disc CD Player	530	595
	NOT AVAILABLE with 1SB.		

2001 FIREBIRD

What's New?

For 2001, V8-equipped Formula and Trans Am receive five more horsepower and five more ft-lb of torque, new exterior and interior colors join the palette, and the Ram Air Formula is dropped from the lineup.

Review

The Pontiac Firebird is a car meant to convey sex appeal. Its blend of angular greenhouse lines and softly bulging sheetmetal creates the automotive equivalent of a supermodel in a silk nightgown. Unfortunately, the bespoiled Trans Am (with its aero skirting, decklid "batwing" and louvered side scoops) ruins the effect. Not to worry; the midlevel Formula provides all of the T/A's hardware and go-fast goodies in a more restrained-looking, lighter, less costly package.

The Firebird's cockpit is a futuristic blend of style and function, and is better executed than that of its corporate twin, the Chevrolet Camaro. Dual airbags and antilock brakes are standard, and the optional traction-control system can be ordered on all models. Additionally, convertible versions of Firebird and Trans Am are available (but not Formula), for a corresponding boost in price.

Performance from the Corvette-derived LS1 V8 is nothing short of astounding, providing enough grunt to get the Firebird to 60 mph faster than your 10-year-old can get to 40 yards. The pushrod 5.7-liter that comes standard on Formula and Trans Am now makes 310 horsepower (up five from last year), and a more-important 340 foot-pounds (five more than last year) of tire-blistering torque. Want even more? A Ram Air WS6 performance and handling package for the T/A is available (the Formula version has been dropped for 2001), featuring twin hood scoops that force cool air into the engine, resulting in 15 extra ponies. WS6 suspension tuning and 275/40ZR-17 rubber keep the Ram Air Firebird planted to the ground, while a dual-outlet exhaust system is the last thing most poor souls trying to catch you will see.

All V8 models come standard with a four-speed automatic transmission; a six-speed manual is a no-cost option. Base Firebirds are powered by a 3800 Series II V6 that makes a peppy 200 horsepower, and can be optioned with a performance package of their own. This "insurance special" includes bigger tires, a limited-slip differential, dual exhaust and uplevel steering. A slick-shifting, five-speed manual transmission is standard on the V6.

With world-class powertrains and hot-looking sheetmetal at a low base price, the Firebird fries Ford's Mustang, not only at the stoplight but also at the racetrack. Problem is, Ford's beloved pony car is pummeling Pontiac's performance flagship in dealer showrooms, outselling this GM F-body at better than a 3-to-1 clip. While Mustang's packaging and refinement may have earned it a wider audience, Firebird wears its modern-day muscle-car crown well.

PONTIAC — FIREBIRD

If this powerful pony car legend has been on your wish list for a while, the time to act is now. The current F-body's days are numbered, with 2002 as the last model year. If the Camaro/Firebird nameplates live on into the new millennium, look for them to be reborn in a vastly different form on an all-new platform.

Standard Equipment

BASE COUPE (5M): 3.8L V6 OHV SMPI 12-valve engine; 5-speed OD manual transmission; 690 amp battery with run down protection; 105 amp alternator; rear-wheel drive, 3.23 axle ratio; stainless steel exhaust; firm ride suspension, front independent suspension with anti-roll bar, front coil springs, gas-pressurized front shocks, rigid rear axle trailing arm suspension with anti-roll bar, rear coil springs, gas-pressurized rear shocks; power rack-and-pinion steering; 4-wheel antilock disc brakes; 16.8 gal. capacity fuel tank; front license plate bracket, rear lip spoiler, side impact bars; class I trailering; front and rear body-colored bumpers; body-colored bodyside molding; clearcoat monotone paint; sealed beam halogen fully auto headlamps with daytime running lights; additional exterior lights include front fog/driving lights; driver's and passenger's body-colored outside mirrors, driver's manual remote outside mirror, passenger's manual outside mirror; 16" x 8" silver alloy wheels; P215/60SR16 BSW touring A/S tires; compact steel spare wheel; air conditioning; AM/FM stereo radio, clock, seek-scan, single CD player, 4 speakers, graphic equalizer, theft deterrent, fixed antenna; cruise control; power remote hatch/trunk release; 2 power accessory outlets, front lighter element(s), driver's foot rest, retained accessory power, smoker's package; instrumentation display includes tachometer, oil pressure gauge, water temperature gauge, volt gauge, trip odometer; warning indicators include battery, low oil level, lights on, trunk ajar, key in ignition, service interval; driver's and passenger's front airbags; ignition disable; tinted windows; variable intermittent front windshield wipers, sun visor strip, rear window defroster; seating capacity of 4, front bucket seats with adjustable headrests, center armrest with storage, driver's seat includes 6-way adjustment, passenger's seat includes 4-way adjustment; full folding rear bench seat; cloth seats, cloth door trim insert, full cloth headliner, full carpet floor covering with carpeted floor mats, leather-wrapped gearshift knob; interior lights include dome light with fade, front reading lights; steering wheel with tilt adjustment; vanity mirrors; day/night rearview mirror; full floor console, locking glove box with light, front and rear cupholders, driver's and passenger's door bins; carpeted cargo floor, cargo cover, cargo light; black side window moldings, black front windshield molding, black rear window molding and body-colored door handles.

BASE 2DR CONVERTIBLE (5M) (in addition to or instead of BASE COUPE (5M) equipment): Power convertible roof with lining, glass rear window; rocker panel extensions; premium AM/FM stereo radio, 8 premium speakers, premium amplifier, power retractable antenna, radio steering wheel controls; power door locks with 2 stage unlock, remote keyless entry, power remote hatch/trunk release; panic alarm, security system; driver's seat includes 6-way power adjustment, 8-way adjustment and interior lights include illuminated entry.

FORMULA COUPE (4A) (in addition to or instead of BASE COUPE (4A) equipment): 5.7L V8 OHV SMPI 16-valve engine; 4-speed electronic OD automatic transmission with lock-up torque converter; 525 amp battery with run down protection; transmission oil cooler; viscous limited slip differential, 2.73 axle ratio; stainless steel exhaust with tailpipe finisher; sport ride suspension; driver's and passenger's power remote body-colored outside mirrors; P245/50ZR16 BSW performance A/S tires; premium AM/FM stereo radio, 10 premium speakers, premium amplifier, power retractable antenna, radio steering wheel controls; warning indicators include low coolant; tinted windows with driver's 1-touch down and leather-wrapped steering wheel with tilt adjustment.

TRANS AM COUPE (4A) (in addition to or instead of FORMULA 2DR COUPE (4A) equipment): Stainless steel exhaust with tailpipe finisher; front manual t-bar glass sunroof with sunshade; body-colored bodyside molding rocker panel extensions; leather seats, leatherette door trim insert with carpet lower and leather-wrapped gearshift knob.

FIREBIRD — PONTIAC

CODE	DESCRIPTION	INVOICE	MSRP

TRANS AM 2DR CONVERTIBLE (4A) (in addition to or instead of TRANS AM COUPE (4A) equipment): Power convertible roof with lining, glass rear window and 8 premium speakers.

Base Prices

Code	Description	Invoice	MSRP
2FS87	Base Coupe (5M)	17133	18725
2FV87-W66	Formula Coupe (4A)	21873	23905
2FS67	Base Convertible (5M)	23191	25345
2FV87	Trans Am Coupe (4A)	24719	27015
2FV67	Trans Am Convertible (4A)	28443	31085
	Destination Charge:	575	575

Interested in seeing what dealers will sell this vehicle for? Check out our True Market Value^{sm} (TMV^{sm}) pricing on our Web site at www.edmunds.com.

Accessories

Code	Description	Invoice	MSRP
—2	Prado Leather Seat Trim (Trans Am)	165	185
	REQUIRES AQ9. NOT AVAILABLE with —3, 1SH.		
—3	Prado Leather Seat Trim (Base/Formula)	512	575
	Includes perforated inserts on seating surfaces. NOT AVAILABLE with 1SA, 1SB, 1SH.		
1SA	Base Equipment Group 1SA (Base Coupe/Formula)	NC	NC
	Includes vehicle with standard equipment. NOT AVAILABLE with W54, W55, U1S, (—3) Prado Leather Seat Trim, P05, W68, QCB.		
1SA	Equipment Group 1SA (Convertible/Trans Am Coupe)	NC	NC
	Includes power group, protection group and 6-way power driver seat.		
1SB	Mid-Level Equipment Group 1SB (Base Coupe)	1344	1510
	Includes power group and 4-speed automatic transmission. REQUIRES QCB. NOT AVAILABLE with —3, CC1.		
1SB	Up-Level Equipment Group 1SB (Formula)	1339	1505
	Includes removable hatch roof, protection group, theft deterrent system, remote keyless entry, 6-way power driver seat, AM/FM stereo radio with CD, equalizer and 4-speed automatic transmission.		
1SC	Up-Level Equipment Group 1SC (Base Coupe)	2180	2450
	Includes power group, protection group, theft deterrent system, remote keyless entry, 6-way power driver seat, AM/FM stereo radio with CD, equalizer, leather-wrapped rim steering wheel, leather-wrapped shift knob and 4-speed automatic transmission. REQUIRES QCB.		
1SH	NHRA Special 4-Speed Edition Package (Formula/Trans Am Coupe)	1041	1170
	Includes 3.23 performance rear axle ratio, power steering cooler, 16" chrome cast aluminum wheels and NHRA Special Edition specific badging. REQUIRES GU5. NOT AVAILABLE with BBS, Prado Leather Seat Trim, AG1, U1S, MN6, WS6, WU6, W54, AQ9.		
1SH	NHRA Special 6-Speed Edition Package (Formula/Trans Am Coupe)	1064	1195
	Includes 3.23 performance rear axle ratio, power steering cooler, hurst performance shift linkage, 16" chrome cast aluminum wheels and NHRA Special Edition specific badging. NOT AVAILABLE with Prado Leather Seat Trim, AG1, U1S, WS6, WU6, W54, AQ9.		
AG1	6-Way Power Driver Seat (Base Coupe/Formula)	240	270
	NOT AVAILABLE with 1SA, 1SH. INCLUDED in 1SA, 1SB, 1SC.		

PONTIAC — FIREBIRD

CODE	DESCRIPTION	INVOICE	MSRP
AQ9	Custom Bucket Seats (Trans Am)	NC	NC
	Includes adjustable lumbar supports. REQUIRES —2. NOT AVAILABLE with —3, 1SH.		
BBS	Hurst Performance Shift Linkage (Trans Am/Formula)	289	325
	REQUIRES MN6. NOT AVAILABLE with 1SH. INCLUDED in 1SH.		
CC1	Removable Locking Hatch Roof (Base Coupe/Formula)	886	995
	Includes locking package and sunshade. NOT AVAILABLE with 1SB. INCLUDED in 1SB.		
GU5	3.23 Performance Rear Axle Ratio (Trans Am/Formula)	267	300
	NOT AVAILABLE with MN6.		
MM5	Transmission: 5-Speed Manual (Base Coupe)	(725)	(815)
	REQUIRES 1SB. NOT AVAILABLE with W68, 1SA.		
MN6	Transmission: 6-Speed Manual (Trans Am/Formula)	NC	NC
	Includes skip shift feature and 3.42 axle ratio. NOT AVAILABLE with GU5, 1SH.		
MX0	Transmission: 4-Speed Automatic (Base)	725	815
	INCLUDED in 1SB, 1SC.		
NW9	Traction Control (Base)	222	250
	Acceleration slip regulation.		
NW9	Traction Control (Trans Am/Formula)	400	450
	Acceleration slip regulation.		
P05	Wheels: 16" x 8" Chrome Cast Aluminum	530	595
	5-spoke. NOT AVAILABLE with WS6, 1SA. INCLUDED in 1SH.		
QCB	P235/55R16 Touring Tires (Base)	120	135
	Tire chains should not be used as they may cause damage. See owner's manual. NOT AVAILABLE with 1SA.		
QLC	P245/50ZR16 Speed Rated Tires (Trans Am/Formula)	NC	NC
	High performance. NOT AVAILABLE with WS6. INCLUDED in 1SH.		
R7X	Protection Group (Base Coupe/Formula)	214	240
	Includes theft deterrent system and remote keyless entry. NOT AVAILABLE with 1SA. INCLUDED in 1SA, 1SB, 1SC.		
U1S	12-Disc Trunk-Mounted Disc Changer	530	595
	NOT AVAILABLE with 1SA, 1SH.		
V12	Power Steering Cooler (Trans Am/Formula)	89	100
	INCLUDED in 1SH.		
W54	Radio: AM/FM Stereo with Cassette Player and Equalizer (Base Coupe)	294	330
	Includes 7-band graphic equalizer, clock, touch control, seek-and-scan, search and replay, Theftlock and 500 watt peak power Monsoon sound system. Hi-performance 10-speaker system includes 6" HS speakers and tweeters in doors, 6" subwoofers in sail panels, subwoofer amplifier as well as 4" speakers and tweeters in rear quarter panels. Also includes remote CD pre-wiring, leather-wrapped rim steering wheel and leather-wrapped shift knob. REQUIRES 1SB. NOT AVAILABLE with W55, 1SA.		
W54	Radio: AM/FM Stereo with Cassette Player and Equalizer (Convertible)	(89)	(100)
	Includes 7-band graphic equalizer, clock, touch control, seek-and-scan, search and replay, Theftlock and 500 watt peak power Monsoon sound system. Hi-performance 10-speaker system includes 6" HS speakers and tweeters in doors, 6" subwoofers in sail panels, subwoofer amplifier as well as 4" speakers and tweeters in rear quarter panels. Also includes remote CD pre-wiring. REQUIRES 1SC. NOT AVAILABLE with W55, 1SA, 1SH.		

FIREBIRD / GRAND AM — PONTIAC

CODE	DESCRIPTION	INVOICE	MSRP
W55	**Radio: AM/FM Stereo with CD and Equalizer (Base Coupe)**	383	430
	Includes 7-band graphic equalizer, clock, touch control, seek-and-scan, search and replay, Theftlock, and 500 watt peak power Monsoon sound system. Hi-performance 10-speaker system includes 6" HS speakers and tweeters in doors, 6" subwoofers in sail panels, subwoofer amplifier as well as 4" speakers and tweeters in rear quarter panels, leather-wrapped rim steering wheel and leather-wrapped shift knob. NOT AVAILABLE with W54, 1SA. INCLUDED in 1SB, 1SC.		
W68	**Sport Appearance Package (Base)**	926	1040
	Includes specific aero appearance and dual outlet exhaust. NOT AVAILABLE with Y87, 1SA.		
WS6	**Ram Air Performance/Handling Package (Trans Am)**	2804	3150
	Includes RAM AIR induction system and specifically tuned suspension, 17"x 9" polished cast alloy wheels, P275/40ZR17 tires, low restriction dual exhaust system and power steering cooler. REQUIRES MN6 or GU5. NOT AVAILABLE with P05, QLC, 1SH.		
X10	**Radio: AM/FM Stereo with Cassette Player and Equalizer (Convertible)**	(89)	(100)
	Includes 7-band graphic equalizer, clock, touch control, seek-and-scan, search and replay, Theftlock and 500 watt peak power Monsoon sound system. Hi-performance 8-speaker system includes 6" HS speakers and tweeters in doors, 6" subwoofers in sail panels, subwoofer amplifier as well as 4" speakers in rear quarter panels. Includes leather-wrapped rim steering wheel with radio controls and leather-wrapped shift knob and parking brake handle.		
Y3C	**Firebird GT Package (Base Coupe)**	509	599
	Includes 2 Firebird GT exterior decals on B-pillars and Firebird GT stripe package and dual-dual exhaust outlets. NOT AVAILABLE with W68, Y87, P05.		
Y87	**3800 V6 Performance Package (Base)**	436	490
	Includes uplevel steering, Torsen limited slip rear differential, dual outlet exhaust and P235/55R16 touring tires. NOT AVAILABLE with W68.		

2001 GRAND AM

What's New?

For 2001, the Grand Am gets audio improvements, a wheel upgrade and revised paint choices.

Review

Boasting bold styling and a wide stance, the sporty Grand Am bears a strong family resemblance to its big brother, the Grand Prix. One noteworthy design quirk is the use of large, round cornering lamps at the lower edges of the rear fascia, looking much like the fog/driving lamps in the front.

Overall, the design is pleasing to the eye because the car's proportions are well balanced. The Grand Am can be had as a coupe or sedan, in two distinct models (SE and GT) plus four option packages (SE, SE1,

PONTIAC GRAND AM

GT and GT1). Base SE Sedans and Coupes are powered by a 150-horse, twin cam 2.4-liter four-cylinder that was fitted with a redesigned composite intake manifold last year for better fuel economy and lower emissions. The base cars also feature air conditioning, antilock brakes and an AM/FM stereo cassette. An electronically controlled four-speed automatic is standard. The SE1 includes cruise, 15-inch wheels, power seats, windows and mirrors, and can be optioned with 16-inch alloys, a CD player and decklid spoiler.

Once you get to the SE2, you gain a 170-horsepower, 3.4-liter V6 that has been reworked for better durability and lower emissions. You also get all the SE1 options as well as traction control and remote keyless entry. Go for the sporty GT, and you'll benefit from a stiffer suspension, four-wheel disc brakes, a set of 16-inch five-spoke wheels and a unique look, including special front and rear fascias and bodyside cladding. GT1 adds a six-way power driver's seat, high-power audio system and power sunroof. Leather seating and chrome wheels are also available.

Grand Am's interior is cockpit-themed, with all center panel controls angled toward the driver, gathered around a contemporary circular cluster panel housing red backlit gauges. Surfaces are soft-touch and low-gloss while control knobs are easy to see and use, and new audio systems (including a Monsoon variant) are available. By putting money into driver-oriented hardware instead of flashy doodads, Pontiac has bolstered Grand Am's market position. This car packs lots of equipment into a well-screwed-together package. But don't look for real enthusiasts to embrace the Grand Am until a five-speed is available in the V6 GT model.

Standard Equipment

SE COUPE (5M): 2.4L I4 DOHC SMPI 16-valve engine; 5-speed OD manual transmission; 600 amp battery with run down protection; 105 amp alternator; front-wheel drive, traction control, 3.94 axle ratio; stainless steel exhaust; touring ride suspension, front independent strut suspension with anti-roll bar, front coil springs, rear independent multi-link suspension with anti-roll bar, rear coil springs; power rack-and-pinion steering; front disc/rear drum brakes with 4-wheel antilock brakes; 15.2 gal. capacity fuel tank; side impact bars; class I trailering; front and rear body-colored bumpers, body-colored bodyside cladding, rocker panel extensions; clearcoat monotone paint; aero-composite halogen fully auto headlamps with daytime running lights, delay-off feature; additional exterior lights include front fog/driving lights; driver's and passenger's black outside mirrors, driver's manual remote outside mirror, passenger's manual outside mirror; 15" x 6" steel wheels; P215/60SR15 BSW touring tires; compact steel spare wheel; air conditioning, rear heat ducts; AM/FM stereo radio, clock, seek-scan, cassette player, 4 speakers, theft deterrent, fixed antenna; power door locks with 2 stage unlock, power remote hatch/trunk release; 1 power accessory outlet, front lighter element(s), driver's foot rest, smoker's package; instrumentation display includes tachometer, water temperature gauge, trip odometer; warning indicators include oil pressure, battery, low coolant, low fuel, lights on, key in ignition, low washer fluid, service interval; driver's and passenger's front airbags; ignition disable; tinted windows; variable intermittent front windshield wipers, sun visor strip, rear window defroster; seating capacity of 5, front bucket seats with adjustable headrests, center armrest with storage, driver's and passenger's seat includes 4-way adjustment, easy entry; rear bench seat with fixed headrests; front height adjustable seatbelts; cloth seats, cloth door trim insert, full cloth headliner, full carpet floor covering with carpeted floor mats; interior lights include dome light with fade, illuminated entry; steering wheel with tilt adjustment; vanity mirrors, dual auxiliary visors; day/night rearview mirror; full floor console, mini overhead console with storage, locking glove box with light, front cupholder, instrument panel bin, driver's and passenger's door bins; carpeted cargo floor, cargo light; black grille, chrome side window moldings, black front windshield molding, black rear window molding and body-colored door handles.

SE1 COUPE (5M) (in addition to or instead of SE COUPE (5M) equipment): Rear wing spoiler, side impact bars; driver's and passenger's power remote black outside mirrors; P215/60SR15 BSW touring A/S tires; single CD player, 6 performance speakers, graphic equalizer; cruise control with steering wheel controls; remote keyless entry; panic alarm; tinted windows with driver's 1-touch down; driver's seat includes 2-way power adjustment, 6-way adjustment and 60/40 folding rear bench seat with fixed headrests.

GRAND AM — PONTIAC

GT COUPE (4A) (in addition to or instead of SE1 COUPE (4A) equipment): 3.4L V6 OHV SMPI 12-valve engine; 4-speed electronic OD automatic transmission with lock-up torque converter; 3.29 axle ratio; stainless steel exhaust with tailpipe finisher; sport ride suspension; power rack-and-pinion steering with vehicle speed-sensing assist; 4-wheel antilock disc brakes; front and rear body-colored bumpers with black bumper insert; with black bodyside insert, body-colored bodyside cladding, rocker panel extensions; driver's and passenger's power remote body-colored outside mirrors; 16" x 6.5" silver alloy wheels; P225/50VR16 BSW performance tires; 8 premium speakers, amplifier; warning indicators include low oil level; front sports seats, driver's seat includes lumbar support; premium cloth seats, leather-wrapped gearshift knob; interior lights include front and rear reading lights; leather-wrapped steering wheel with tilt adjustment; 2 seat back storage pockets; cargo net; black grille and black side window moldings.

GT1 COUPE (4A) (in addition to or instead of GT COUPE (4A) equipment): Front express open sliding and tilting glass sunroof with sunshade; cassette player, single CD and driver's seat includes 6-way power adjustment, 8-way adjustment.

SEDAN (5M) (in addition to or instead of COUPE (5M) equipment): Child safety rear door locks and manual front and rear windows.

Base Prices

CODE	DESCRIPTION	INVOICE	MSRP
2NE37	SE Coupe (5M)	14768	16140
2NF37	SE1 Coupe (5M)	16351	17870
2NW37	GT Coupe (4A)	18515	20235
2NV37	GT1 Coupe (4A)	19677	21505
2NE69	SE Sedan (5M)	15043	16440
2NF69	SE1 Sedan (5M)	16626	18170
2NW69	GT Sedan (4A)	18790	20535
2NV69	GT1 Sedan (4A)	19952	21805
Destination Charge:		585	585

Interested in seeing what dealers will sell this vehicle for? Check out our True Market Value^{sm} (TMV^{sm}) pricing on our Web site at www.edmunds.com.

Accessories

CODE	DESCRIPTION	INVOICE	MSRP
—	Prado Leather Seat Trim (GT/GT1)	423	475
1SA	Option Package 1SA	NC	NC
	Includes vehicle with standard equipment.		
CF5	Power Glass Sunroof (SE1/GT)	578	650
	INCLUDED in 1SA.		
K05	Engine Block Heater	31	35
K34	Cruise Control with Resume Speed (SE)	209	235
	INCLUDED in 1SA.		
LA1	Engine: 3.4L 3400 SFI V6 (SE1)	583	655
	Includes 3.05 axle ratio and variable effort power steering. REQUIRES MX0. NOT AVAILABLE with R6B.		
MX0	Transmission: Electronic 4-Speed Automatic (SE/SE1)	699	785
	Electronically controlled and 3.42 axle ratio. INCLUDED in 1SA.		
PY0	Wheels: 16" Aluminum Multi Spoke (SE1)	436	490
	Includes P225/50R16 GOODYEAR LS touring BW tires.		
PY1	Wheels: 16" Chrome Tech Aluminum (GT/GT1)	574	645

PONTIAC
GRAND AM / GRAND PRIX

CODE	DESCRIPTION	INVOICE	MSRP
R6B	Solid Value Appearance Package (GT)	1326	1490
	Manufacturer Discount	(556)	(625)
	Net Price	770	865
	Includes 16" chrome tech alloy wheels, power glass sunroof, AM/FM stereo radio with CD and cassette.		
R6B	Solid Value Appearance Package (SE1)	1317	1480
	Manufacturer Discount	(556)	(625)
	Net Price	761	855
	Includes 16" alloy multi-spoke wheels, P225/50R16 GOODYEAR LS touring BW tires, AM/FM stereo radio with CD, cassette, 8-speaker monsoon sound system and power glass sunroof. NOT AVAILABLE with LA1.		
R6S	Solid Value Appearance Package (GT1)	997	1120
	Manufacturer Discount	(285)	(320)
	Net Price	712	800
	Includes 16" chrome tech alloy wheels and Prado leather seat trim.		
T43	Rear Deck Spoiler (SE)	174	195
	INCLUDED in 1SA.		
U1P	Radio: Delco AM/FM Stereo with CD Player and Clock (SE)	156	175
	Includes 7 band equalizer and 6 speaker sound system (Replaces standard radio). INCLUDED in 1SA.		
U1Q	Radio: Delco AM/FM Stereo with CD and Cassette Players (GT)	174	195
	Includes seek-and-scan, auto-reverse cassette, 7 band equalizer and clock. INCLUDED in 1SA.		
U1Q	Radio: Delco AM/FM Stereo with CD and Cassette Players (SE1)	303	340
	Includes seek-and-scan, auto-reverse cassette, 7 band equalizer, clock and 8-speaker monsoon sound system. INCLUDED in 1SA.		

2001 GRAND PRIX

What's New?

The Grand Prix receives only minor changes for 2001 including a Special Edition appearance package on GT and GTP models and optional 16-inch, three-spoke aluminum wheels. The OnStar system is now available on GTP models while SE models receive a slight front-end revision.

Review

Loaded with standard features and available in a potent, supercharged 240-horsepower edition, Pontiac's Grand Prix successfully blends form, function and performance into one appealing and affordable package. Buyers can select from one of three models: SE (in sedan form only), GT (coupe or sedan) and GTP, the latter a stand-alone model as either a coupe or sedan.

The SE is still powered by a 3.1-liter V6 that makes 175 horsepower while managing

GRAND PRIX
PONTIAC

to meet low-emission vehicle (LEV) standards. (The supercharged 3.8 also meets the same standard, and the naturally aspirated 3.8 meets ultra-low emission vehicle (ULEV) standards.) Despite the commendable numbers for the 3.1, we recommend the 200-horsepower 3800 Series II V6 (optional on SE Sedan and standard on GT). The award-winning 3.8 offers more power yet still delivers about 19 mpg in the city and 30 mpg on the highway, figures that nearly match the base motor.

GTP models come equipped with a supercharged version of the 3800 V6 that makes a whopping 240 horsepower. Traction control works in conjunction with four-wheel antilock disc brakes, which include beefy rotors and state-of-the-art calipers for better stopping ability. Power is put through the front wheels via a standard four-speed, electronically controlled automatic transmission. The GTP gets a heavy-duty version that allows drivers to pick "normal" or "performance" shift modes.

All Grand Prix models benefit from hydraulic engine mounts to isolate noise and vibration normally transmitted into the cabin. And all powertrains feature long-life fluids and parts, such as coolant designed to last five years or 150,000 miles, and platinum-tipped spark plugs that last 100,000 miles under optimal conditions. Interiors feature analog instrumentation and large, easy-to-use controls. In the Pontiac tradition, the dashboard is a cockpit-style arrangement with gauges designed to look like those in a jet fighter, all backlit in a soothing red glow at night.

There is still no split-bench front seat available in SE Sedans, putting the Grand Prix out of contention when considering a six-place four-door. But dual airbags, air conditioning, power windows, door locks and mirrors are all standard fare. And if you like high-tech, you can opt for the EyeCue head-up display, which projects driver data onto the windshield for easy viewing. New for 2001 is the availability of the OnStar communications system. Standard on all GTP models and optional on GT versions, the OnStar system provides 24-hour driver assistance through an integrated hands-free microphone. Should sporty performance be part of your car-buying equation, Grand Prix delivers in the grand American tradition. This Pontiac packs plenty of power and a wide array of safety and convenience features in a package that's as easy to drive as it is on the pocketbook.

Standard Equipment

SE SEDAN (4A): 3.1L V6 OHV SMPI 12-valve engine; 4-speed electronic OD automatic transmission with lock-up torque converter; 600 amp battery with run down protection; 105 amp alternator; front-wheel drive, traction control, 2.93 axle ratio; stainless steel exhaust; touring ride suspension, front independent strut suspension with anti-roll bar, front coil springs, rear independent multi-link suspension with anti-roll bar, rear coil springs; power rack-and-pinion steering; 4-wheel antilock disc brakes; 18 gal. capacity fuel tank; rear lip spoiler, side impact bars; front and rear body-colored bumpers; body-colored bodyside molding; clearcoat monotone paint; aero-composite halogen fully auto headlamps with daytime running lights, delay-off feature; additional exterior lights include front fog/driving lights; driver's and passenger's power remote body-colored outside mirrors; 15" x 6" steel wheels; P205/70SR15 BSW touring tires; compact steel spare wheel; dual zone front air conditioning; AM/FM stereo radio, clock, seek-scan, cassette player, 6 speakers, theft deterrent, window grid antenna; central locking power door locks, child safety rear door locks, power remote trunk release; 2 power accessory outlets, front lighter element(s), driver's foot rest, retained accessory power, smoker s package; instrumentation display includes tachometer, water temperature gauge, trip odometer; warning indicators include oil pressure, battery, low oil level, low coolant, lights on, key in ignition, low fuel, low washer fluid, door ajar, trunk ajar, service interval, turn signal on; driver's and passenger's front airbags; ignition disable; tinted windows, power front and rear windows with driver's 1-touch down; variable intermittent front windshield wipers, sun visor strip, rear window defroster; seating capacity of 5, front sports seats with adjustable headrests, center armrest with storage, driver's seat includes 4-way adjustment, passenger's seat includes 4-way adjustment; rear bench seat with fixed headrests; front height adjustable seatbelts; cloth seats, cloth door trim insert, full cloth headliner, full carpet floor covering with carpeted floor mats; interior lights include dome light with fade, front reading lights; steering wheel with tilt adjustment; vanity mirrors; day/night rearview mirror; instrument panel storage bin, full floor console, locking glove box with light, front cupholder, 2 seat back storage pockets, driver's and passenger's door bins; carpeted

PONTIAC — GRAND PRIX

cargo floor, cargo light; body-colored grille, black side window moldings, black front windshield molding, black rear window molding and body-colored door handles.

GT COUPE (4A) (in addition to or instead of SE SEDAN (4A) equipment): 3.8L V6 OHV SMPI 12-valve engine; 690 amp battery with run down protection; stainless steel exhaust with tailpipe finisher; power rack-and-pinion steering with vehicle speed-sensing assist; 17.5 gal. capacity fuel tank; body-colored bodyside molding body-colored bodyside cladding, rocker panel extensions; 16" x 6.5" 3-spoke silver cast aluminum wheels; P225/60SR16 BSW touring tires; cruise control; power remote hatch/trunk release; easy entry; center pass-thru armrest with storage and black side window moldings.

GTP COUPE (4A) (in addition to or instead of GT COUPE (4A) equipment): 3.8L V6 OHV SMPI supercharger 12-valve engine (requires premium unleaded fuel); driver's selectable transmission; 770 amp battery with run down protection; 2.93 axle ratio; single CD player, graphic equalizer, theft deterrent, radio steering wheel controls; power door locks with 2 stage unlock, remote keyless entry; instrumentation display includes head-up display, compass, exterior temp, trip computer; panic alarm, security system; driver's seat includes 6-way power adjustment, 8-way adjustment, power 4-way lumbar support; leather-wrapped gearshift knob; leather-wrapped sport steering wheel with tilt adjustment; dual illuminated vanity mirrors; auto-dimming day/night rearview mirror; interior lights include illuminated entry; full overhead console with storage, front and rear cupholders and cargo net.

GT/GTP SEDAN (4A) (in addition to or instead of GT/GTP COUPE (4A) equipment): 18 gal. capacity fuel tank and child safety rear door locks.

Base Prices

Code	Description	Invoice	MSRP
2WK69	SE Sedan (4A)	18629	20360
2WP37	GT Coupe (4A)	20006	21865
2WP69	GT Sedan (4A)	20144	22015
2WR37	GTP Coupe (4A)	23200	25355
2WR69	GTP Sedan (4A)	23365	25535
	Destination Charge:	610	610

Interested in seeing what dealers will sell this vehicle for? Check out our True Market Value^{sm} (TMV^{sm}) pricing on our Web site at www.edmunds.com.

Accessories

Code	Description	Invoice	MSRP
—	Prado Leather Seat Trim (GT Coupe)	463	520
	NOT AVAILABLE with 1SA, B4U, AL9, 1SD. INCLUDED in 1SB, 1SD.		
—	Prado Leather Seat Trim (GT Coupe/GTP Sedan)	463	520
	Includes heated driver's seat. NOT AVAILABLE with 1SA, B4U. INCLUDED in 1SB, 1SD.		
—	Prado Leather Seat Trim (GT Sedan)	463	520
	NOT AVAILABLE with 1SA, B4U. INCLUDED in 1SB, 1SD.		
—	Prado Leather Seat Trim (GTP Coupe/GT Sedan)	463	520
	NOT AVAILABLE with B4U, 1SA, AL9, 1SD. INCLUDED in 1SB, 1SD.		
1SA	Option Package 1SA	NC	NC
	Includes vehicle with standard equipment.		
1SB	1SB GT Mid-Level Equipment Group (GT Coupe/GT Sedan)	681	765
	Includes front licence plate depression cover, rear window antenna, Delco AM/FM stereo radio with cassette, 6-way power driver seat, remote decklid release, cruise		

GRAND PRIX — PONTIAC

CODE	DESCRIPTION	INVOICE	MSRP
	control with resume speed, rear Decklid spoiler, rear seat pass-through, trunk cargo net, P225/60R16 touring SBR BW tires, variable effort power steering and security package.		
1SB	1SB GTP Up-Level Equipment Group (GTP)	1015	1140
	Includes front license plate depression cover, rear window antenna, 6-way power driver seat, Prado leather seat trim, heated driver's seat, remote decklid release, cruise control with resume speed, rear Decklid spoiler, rear seat pass-through, variable effort power steering, premium lighting package and OnStar, 4-way power driver seat lumbar support, EyeCue heads-up display, Delco AM/FM stereo radio with CD and equalizer.		
1SB	1SB SE Up-Level Equipment Group (SE Sedan)	926	1040
	Manufacturer Discount	(378)	(425)
	Net Price	548	615
	Includes remote decklid release, cruise control with resume speed, rear decklid spoiler, rear seat pass-through, trunk cargo net, 16" 5-spoke alloy wheels and P225/60R16 touring SBR BW tires. NOT AVAILABLE with AL9.		
1SC	1SC GT Mid-Level Equipment Group (GT Coupe)	1399	1572
	Includes front licence plate depression cover, rear window antenna, Delco AM/FM stereo radio with cassette, 6-way power driver seat, remote decklid release, cruise control with resume speed, rear decklid spoiler, rear seat pass-through, trunk cargo net, P225/60R16 touring SBR BW tires, variable effort power steering, full overhead console, leather-wrapped sport steering wheel, security package, trip computer, premium lighting package, illuminated visor mirrors, assist grips, electrochromic rearview mirror, compass and temperature display, and OnStar.		
1SC	1SC GT Mid-Level Equipment Group (GT Sedan)	1426	1602
	Includes front licence plate depression cover, remote decklid release, cruise control with resume speed, rear decklid spoiler, rear seat pass-through, trunk cargo net, variable effort power steering, full overhead console, leather-wrapped sport steering wheel, security package, trip computer, premium lighting package, illuminated visor mirrors, rear reading lamps, assist grip, electrochromic rearview mirror, compass and temperature display, and OnStar.		
1SD	1SD GT Up-Level Equipment Group (GT Coupe)	2676	3007
	Includes front license plate depression cover, 6-way power driver seat, remote decklid release, cruise control with resume speed, rear decklid spoiler, rear seat pass-through, trunk cargo net, leather-wrapped sport steering wheel with radio controls, remote keyless entry, theft deterrent system, trip computer, illuminated visor mirrors, assist grips, electrochromic rearview mirror, compass and temperature display, OnStar, 4-way power driver seat lumbar support, EyeCue heads-up display, Prado leather seat trim, heated driver's seat and power spoiler type glass sunroof.		
1SD	1SD GT Up-Level Equipment Group (GT Sedan)	2703	3037
	Includes front license plate depression cover, 6-way power driver seat, remote decklid release, cruise control with resume speed, rear decklid spoiler, rear seat pass-through, trunk cargo net, leather-wrapped sport steering wheel with radio controls, remote keyless entry, theft deterrent system, trip computer, illuminated visor mirrors, assist grips, electrochromic rearview mirror, compass and temperature display, OnStar, 4-way power driver seat lumbar support, EyeCue heads-up display, Prado leather seat trim, heated driver's seat and power spoiler type glass sunroof.		

PONTIAC — GRAND PRIX

CODE	DESCRIPTION	INVOICE	MSRP
A90	Remote Decklid Release (SE Sedan)	53	60
	INCLUDED in 1SA, 1SB, 1SC, 1SD.		
AG1	6-Way Power Driver Seat (GT Coupe/GT Sedan/SE Sedan)	240	270
	INCLUDED in 1SB, 1SC, 1SD.		
AL9	4-Way Power Driver Lumbar Support (GT Coupe/GT Sedan)	134	150
	INCLUDES KA1. REQUIRES Prado Leather Seat Trim. NOT AVAILABLE with 1SA. INCLUDED in 1SD.		
AL9	4-Way Power Driver Lumbar Support (GT Coupe/GT Sedan)	89	100
	NOT AVAILABLE with 1SA. INCLUDED in 1SD.		
AP9	Trunk Cargo Net (SE Sedan)	27	30
	INCLUDED in 1SA, 1SB, 1SC, 1SD.		
B4U	Special Edition Appearance Package (All except SE Sedan)	2238	2515
	Manufacturer Discount	(463)	(520)
	Net Price	1775	1995
	Includes unique spoiler, exhaust tips, hood heat extractors, NASCAR-style roof fences, painted trim plates and interior door emblems. REQUIRES 1SD. NOT AVAILABLE with 1SA, U85, (—2) Prado Leather Seat Trim, V2C, N66.		
CF5	Power Spoiler Type Glass Sunroof (All except SE Sedan)	507	570
	Includes express open and sunshade. NOT AVAILABLE with 1SA, 1SD, 1SB. INCLUDED in 1SB, 1SD.		
CF5	Power Spoiler Type Glass Sunroof (All except SE Sedan)	NC	NC
	Includes express open and sunshade. REQUIRES 1SB. NOT AVAILABLE with 1SA. INCLUDED in 1SB, 1SD.		
K05	Engine Block Heater	31	35
K34	Cruise Control with Resume Speed (SE Sedan)	209	235
	Includes dead pedal (integrated for driver's left foot comfort). INCLUDED in 1SA, 1SB, 1SC, 1SD.		
KA1	Heated Driver's Seat (All except SE Sedan)	44	50
N66	Wheels: 16" 5-Spoke Cast Aluminum (GT Coupe/GTP Coupe)	NC	NC
	NOT AVAILABLE with V2C, B4U.		
N66	Wheels: 16" 5-Spoke Cast Aluminum (Sedan)	NC	NC
	Torque-star. Silver painted. NOT AVAILABLE with 1SA, V2C, B4U.		
NC7	Federal Override	NC	NC
	REQUIRES YF5 or NG1.		
R7K	Rear Seat Pass-Through (SE Sedan)	44	50
	Includes 3-passenger seats with integrated headrests and folding armrest. INCLUDED in 1SA, 1SB, 1SC, 1SD.		
R7X	Security Package (SE Sedan)	187	210
	Includes LED warning, armed tone and panic button on key fob, remote keyless entry and theft deterrent system. NOT AVAILABLE with 1SA. INCLUDED in 1SA, 1SB, 1SC, 1SD.		
TR9	Premium Lighting Package and Onstar (GT Coupe)	540	607
	Includes illuminated visor mirrors, assist grips, electrochromic rearview mirror, compass and temperature display and OnStar. NOT AVAILABLE with 1SA, 1SC, 1SD. INCLUDED in 1SA, 1SB, 1SC, 1SD.		

GRAND PRIX / SUNFIRE — PONTIAC

CODE	DESCRIPTION	INVOICE	MSRP
TR9	Premium Lighting Package and Onstar (GT Sedan)	567	637
	Includes illuminated visor mirrors, rear reading lamps, assist grip, electrochromic rearview mirror, compass and temperature display and OnStar. NOT AVAILABLE with 1SA, 1SC, 1SD. INCLUDED in 1SA, 1SB, 1SC, 1SD.		
U1C	Radio: Delco AM/FM Stereo with CD (GT Coupe/SE Sedan/GT Sedan)	89	100
	Delco 2001 Series. Includes seek-and-scan, TheftLock, 6 speakers and clock. NOT AVAILABLE with UP3, 1SA.		
U1C	Radio: Delco AM/FM Stereo with CD (GTP)	NC	NC
	Delco 2001 Series (includes seek-and-scan, TheftLock, 6 speakers and clock). REQUIRES U85.		
U85	Bose Hi-Performance Sound System (GT)	352	395
	REQUIRES U1C. NOT AVAILABLE with 1SA, B4U, UP3.		
U85	Bose Hi-Performance Sound System (GTP)	329	370
	REQUIRES U1C. NOT AVAILABLE with B4U.		
UP3	Radio: Delco AM/FM Stereo with CD and EQ (GT)	134	150
	Delco 2001 Series (includes seek-and-scan, theftlock, 6 speakers and clock). NOT AVAILABLE with 1SA, U1C, U85. INCLUDED in 1SA, 1SB.		
UV6	EyeCue Head-Up Display (GT)	245	275
	Includes digital speedometer, indicators for turn signals, highbeam, low fuel, check gauges, radio frequency and CD disc/track display if equipped with CD player. NOT AVAILABLE with 1SA, 1SB. INCLUDED in 1SA, 1SB, 1SD.		
V2C	Wheels: 16" Cast Aluminum (All except SE Sedan)	289	325
	Highpolished. NOT AVAILABLE with 1SA, N66, B4U.		

2001 SUNFIRE

What's New?

A standard rear spoiler and a new exterior color are the only new additions to the Sunfire for 2001. The GT convertible is no longer available, leaving the sedan and coupe versions as the only available body styles.

Review

Pontiac's Sunfire is supposed to take on the Cavalier, Focus ZX3, Neon and assorted import compacts by offering value, sporty styling and capable performance in a well-rounded package. Sunfire is available as a coupe or sedan SE (base) trim, and as a coupe in the GT (uplevel) series; the convertible is no longer available.

Dual airbags, ABS and an anti-theft system are standard equipment. Base models come with a 2.2-liter four-cylinder engine. Power is rated at 115 horsepower, and can be fed through the standard five-speed manual or optional three- and four-speed automatics. GT models get a slightly larger 16-valve four-cylinder, good for 150 horsepower. The GT's 2.4-liter, twin-cam motor is optional on the SE, and we highly recommend it, particularly if mated to this year's new, smoother-shifting Getrag five-speed manual transmission.

PONTIAC — SUNFIRE

| CODE | DESCRIPTION | INVOICE | MSRP |

Equipped with the bigger engine and a stick shift, a Sunfire is downright speedy when compared to other four-banger compacts. The automatic raises acceleration times by about a second in the dash to 60 mph. Options on the Sunfire include sharp alloy wheels, a power sunroof and a variety of uplevel sound systems, including the 200-watt Monsoon unit. Equip an SE Coupe to the gills, watch the price soar to the mid-18s, and suddenly Sunfire isn't such a hot deal. But fiddling with the options sheet should land you a sporty, well-equipped coupe priced at around $16,000.

The move to more aggressive-looking fascias and rocker-panel moldings was intended to boost Sunfire's image with young buyers. That goal also fueled the move to better sound systems, as well as improvements in interior functionality, features and storage space for things like compact discs or cassettes. And Pontiac even makes the racy decklid spoiler standard on all models for 2001.

Our only complaint about driving the Sunfire is that when it is pushed to its limits, it tends to exhibit an excessive amount of body roll. We think the GT model should offer a more sporting suspension to back up the car's sporty looks and powerful engine. On the plus side, all the well-equipped models we've tested so far carried an affordable price tag.

We think the Sunfire has merit in the crowded compact marketplace. Feature for feature, Sunfire makes a strong argument against purchasing its slightly larger stablemate, the Grand Am, or its more pedestrian twin at Chevy dealers, the Cavalier. Although the lack of a convertible detracts from its sporty image, the coupe and sedan are still capable and fast cars that deserve a look.

Standard Equipment

SE COUPE (5M): 2.2L I4 OHV SMPI 8-valve engine; 5-speed OD manual transmission; 525 amp battery with run down protection; 105 amp alternator; front-wheel drive, 3.94 axle ratio; stainless steel exhaust; touring ride suspension, front independent strut suspension with anti-roll bar, front coil springs, rear semi-independent torsion suspension with rear coil springs; power rack-and-pinion steering; front disc/rear drum brakes with 4-wheel antilock brakes; 14.3 gal. capacity fuel tank; rear wing spoiler, side impact bars; front and rear body-colored bumpers; body-colored bodyside molding rocker panel extensions; clearcoat monotone paint; aero-composite halogen headlamps with daytime running lights; driver's and passenger's black folding outside mirrors, driver's manual remote outside mirror, passenger's manual outside mirror; 14" x 6" steel wheels; P195/70SR14 BSW A/S tires; compact steel spare wheel; air conditioning, rear heat ducts; AM/FM stereo radio, clock, seek-scan, cassette player, 4 speakers, fixed antenna; remote trunk release; 1 power accessory outlet, front lighter element(s), driver's foot rest, retained accessory power, smoker's package; instrumentation display includes tachometer, water temperature gauge, trip odometer; warning indicators include oil pressure, battery, water temperature, low coolant, low fuel, lights on, key in ignition; driver's and passenger's front airbags; ignition disable; tinted windows; fixed interval front windshield wipers, rear window defroster; seating capacity of 5, front bucket seats with adjustable headrests, center armrest with storage, driver's and passenger's seat include 4-way adjustment, easy entry; full folding rear bench seat; premium cloth seats, cloth door trim insert with carpet lower, full cloth headliner, full carpet floor covering with carpeted floor mats; interior lights include dome light with fade; vanity mirrors; day/night rearview mirror; full floor console, locking glove box with light, front and rear cupholders, driver's and passenger's door bins; carpeted cargo floor, cargo light; body-colored grille, black side window moldings, black front windshield molding, black rear window molding and black door handles.

SE SEDAN (5M) (in addition to or instead of GT COUPE (5M) equipment): 3.58 axle ratio; rear wing spoiler; child safety rear door locks and front height adjustable seatbelts.

GT COUPE (5M) (in addition to or instead of SE COUPE (5M) equipment): 2.4L I4 DOHC SMPI 16-valve engine; stainless steel exhaust with tailpipe finisher; sport ride suspension; body-colored bodyside cladding, rocker panel extensions; additional exterior lights include front fog/driving lights; 16" x 6" silver alloy wheels; P205/55SR16 BSW A/S tires; speed sensitive volume, single CD player, 6 speakers, auto equalizer, theft deterrent; front sports seats, driver's

SUNFIRE — PONTIAC

seat includes lumbar support, easy entry; leather-wrapped gearshift knob; leather-wrapped sport steering wheel with tilt adjustment and 1 seat back storage pocket.

Base Prices

Code	Description	Invoice	MSRP
2JB37	SE Coupe (5M)	13112	14175
2JD37	GT Coupe (5M)	15073	16295
2JB69	SE Sedan (5M)	13348	14430
	Destination Charge:	540	540

Interested in seeing what dealers will sell this vehicle for? Check out our True Market Value^{sm} (TMV^{sm}) pricing on our Web site at www.edmunds.com.

Accessories

Code	Description	Invoice	MSRP
1SA	Base Equipment Group 1SA	NC	NC
	Includes transmission: 5-speed manual. NOT AVAILABLE with LD9, PB1, PF7, PG1, QPD, R9P, U85, V1B, CF5, MX1.		
1SB	Mid-Level Equipment Group 1SB (GT Coupe)	1317	1480
	Includes 2.4l twin-cam 16v 4-cylinder engine, 4-speed automatic transmission, P205/55R16 performance BW SBR tires, 16" cast aluminum GT-specific wheels, AM/FM stereo radio with CD player, 45/45 reclining front buckets with sport interior, cruise control, controlled-cycle wet-arm windshield wipers, security package, content theft alarm system, remote keyless entry system and power door locks. NOT AVAILABLE with CF5, V1B.		
1SB	Mid-Level Equipment Group 1SB (SE)	992	1115
	Includes 2.2l 2200 OHV 4-cylinder engine, 4-speed automatic transmission, P195/70R14 A/S BW SBR tires, 14" wheels with custom bolt-on covers, AM/FM stereo radio with CD and adjustable tilt-wheel steering column. NOT AVAILABLE with LD9, PF7, V1B, CF5.		
1SC	Up-Level Equipment Group 1SC (GT Coupe)	1900	2135
	Includes 2.4l twin-cam 16v 4-cylinder engine, 4-speed automatic transmission, P205/55R16 performance BW SBR tires, 16" cast aluminum GT-specific wheels, AM/FM stereo radio with CD, 45/45 reclining front buckets with sport interior, cruise control, controlled-cycle wet-arm windshield wipers, content theft alarm system, remote keyless entry system, power door locks, trunk net, reading lamps and overhead storage console. NOT AVAILABLE with V1B.		
1SC	Up-Level Equipment Group 1SC (SE Coupe)	1660	1865
	Includes 2.2l 2200 OHV 4-cylinder engine,: 4-speed automatic transmission, P195/70R14 A/S BW SBR tires:, 14" wheels with custom bolt-on covers, AM/FM stereo radio with CD, adjustable tilt-wheel steering column, cruise control, controlled-cycle wet-arm windshield wipers, security package, content theft alarm system, remote keyless entry system, power door locks, convenience package, trunk net, reading lamps and overhead storage console. NOT AVAILABLE with V1B, MX1.		
1SC	Up-Level Equipment Group 1SC (SE Sedan)	1695	1905
	Includes 2.2l 2200 OHV 4-cylinder engine, 4-speed automatic transmission, P195/70R14 A/S BW SBR tires, 14" wheels with custom bolt-on covers, adjustable tilt-wheel steering column, cruise control, controlled-cycle wet-arm windshield wipers,		

PONTIAC — SUNFIRE

CODE	DESCRIPTION	INVOICE	MSRP
	content theft alarm system, remote keyless entry system, power door locks, trunk net, reading lamps and overhead storage console. NOT AVAILABLE with V1B, MX1.		
CF5	Power Glass Sunroof (Coupe)	494	555
	Includes reading lamps and overhead storage delete. Deletes passenger assist grip handles. NOT AVAILABLE with 1SA, 1SB. INCLUDED in R6B.		
CF5	Power Glass Sunroof (Coupe)	530	595
	Includes reading lamps. NOT AVAILABLE with 1SA, 1SC. INCLUDED in R6B.		
K05	Engine Block Heater	31	35
K34	Cruise Control (SE)	209	235
	NOT AVAILABLE with 1SA. INCLUDED in 1SB, 1SC, R6B, R6S.		
LD9	Engine: 2.4L Twin-Cam 16V 4-Cyl (SE)	400	450
	REQUIRES 1SC and QPD. NOT AVAILABLE with 1SA, 1SB, MM5, MX1, R6S. INCLUDED in 1SB, 1SC, R6B.		
MM5	Transmission: 5-Speed Manual	(721)	(810)
	NOT AVAILABLE with 1SA. INCLUDED in 1SA.		
MX0	Transmission: 4-Speed Automatic (GT Coupe)	721	810
	Includes traction control. INCLUDED in 1SB, R6B, 1SC, R6S.		
MX1	Transmission: 3-Speed Automatic (SE)	(98)	(110)
	NOT AVAILABLE with 1SC, 1SA.		
MX1	Transmission: 3-Speed Automatic (SE)	623	700
	NOT AVAILABLE with 1SC, 1SB.		
PB1	Wheels: 15" Chrome-Plated Bolt-On Covers (SE)	49	55
	REQUIRES QPD. NOT AVAILABLE with PF7, PG1, 1SA.		
PF7	Wheels: 15" Rally Cast Aluminum (SE)	263	295
	REQUIRES QPD. NOT AVAILABLE with PB1, PG1, 1SA, 1SB, R6B, R6S.		
PG1	Wheels: 15" Custom Bolt-On Covers (SE)	NC	NC
	REQUIRES QPD. NOT AVAILABLE with PB1, PF7, 1SA.		
QPD	Tires: P195/65R15 Touring BW (SE)	120	135
	REQUIRES ((1SB or 1SC or R6B) and (PB1 or PG1)) or ((1SC or R6B) and PF7) or R6S. NOT AVAILABLE with 1SA. INCLUDED in R6B, R6S.		
R6B	Sun and Sound Package (SE Coupe)	1642	1845
	Includes contents of package 1SB, power glass sunroof and P195/65R15 TOURING BW SBR tires. REQUIRES V1B and (PB1 or PG1). NOT AVAILABLE with 1SA, PF7.		
R6B	Sun and Sound Package (SE Coupe)	2274	2555
	Includes contents of package 1SC, power glass sunroof, overhead storage delete and P195/65R15 TOURING BW SBR tires. REQUIRES V1B and (PB1 or PG1).		
R6B	Sun and Storm Package (GT Coupe)	2394	2690
	Includes contents of package 1SC, power sunroof and 200 watt Monsoon premium sound system with 8 speakers. REQUIRES V1B.		
R6B	Sun and Storm Package (Incl 1SB) (GT Coupe)	2020	2270
	Includes contents of package 1SB, power sunroof and 200 watt Monsoon premium sound system with 8 speakers. REQUIRES V1B.		
R6S	Special Edition Package (SE Sedan)	1873	2105
	Includes contents of package 1SB, content theft alarm system, remote keyless entry system, power door locks, dual power remote sport breakaway mirrors, power windows with driver's express down and P195/65R15 TOURING BW SBR tires. REQUIRES V1B and (PB1 or PG1). NOT AVAILABLE with PF7.		

SUNFIRE — PONTIAC

CODE	DESCRIPTION	INVOICE	MSRP
R6S	Special Edition Package (SE Sedan)	2212	2485
	Includes contents of package 1SC, content theft alarm system, remote keyless entry system, power door locks, trunk net, reading lamps, overhead storage console, dual power remote sport breakaway mirrors, power windows with driver's express down and P195/65R15 TOURING BW SBR tires. REQUIRES V1B and (PB1 or PG1).		
R7X	Security Package (SE Coupe)	329	370
	Includes remote keyless entry, power locks and content anti-theft system. NOT AVAILABLE with 1SA. INCLUDED in 1SB, 1SC, R6S, R6B.		
R7X	Security Package (SE Sedan)	365	410
	Includes remote keyless entry system, power door locks and content theft alarm system. REQUIRES 1SB. NOT AVAILABLE with 1SA. INCLUDED in 1SC, R6S.		
R9P	Power Package (Coupe)	338	380
	Includes power mirrors and power windows. REQUIRES 1SC. NOT AVAILABLE with 1SA, R6B. INCLUDED in R6S, 1SC, R6B.		
R9P	Power Package (SE Sedan)	396	445
	Includes power mirrors and power windows with driver's express down. INCLUDED in R6S, 1SC, R6B.		
U1P	Radio: AM/FM Stereo w/CD (SE)	138	155
	Includes RDS and 6 speaker sound. INCLUDED in 1SB, R6B, 1SC, R6S.		
U1Q	Radio: AM/FM Stereo w/ CD and Cassette Player (GT Coupe)	89	100
	Includes RDS and 6 speakers.		
U85	Monsoon Premium Sound System (Coupe)	174	195
	REQUIRES R7X and (1SB or 1SC or R6B). NOT AVAILABLE with 1SA. INCLUDED in 1SC, R6B.		
V1B	Special Edition Value Package Savings (SE Sedan)	(516)	(580)
	REQUIRES R6S. NOT AVAILABLE with 1SA, 1SB, 1SC.		
V1B	Sun and Sound Value Package Savings (SE Coupe)	(467)	(525)
	REQUIRES R6B. NOT AVAILABLE with 1SA, 1SB, 1SC.		
V1B	Sun and Storm Value Package Savings (GT Coupe)	(445)	(500)
	REQUIRES R6B. NOT AVAILABLE with 1SA, 1SB, 1SC.		
VK4	Front License Plate Cover (GT Coupe)	9	10
	Included at no charge for states with a front plate requirement.		

A 15-minute phone call could save you 15% or more on car insurance.
1-800-555-2758

The Sensible Alternative

PORSCHE — BOXSTER

2001 BOXSTER

What's New?

Minor interior changes occur for 2001. The Boxster S' thicker roof lining has migrated to the regular Boxster. Both cars now feature a hidden cell phone antenna, a gauge cluster design similar to the 911's, improved interior lighting and better dashboard material quality. Porsche has also added a new button to the ignition key to control the driver's seat and outside memory function. In terms of optional equipment, the sophisticated Porsche Stability Management system is now available for the Boxster and Boxster S.

Review

Entering its fifth year of production, Porsche's captivating Boxster is a purpose-built sports car for people who love a challenge, designed to go fast and provide optimum feedback while demanding the driver's undivided attention. It rewards skilled pilots with an unparalleled thrill ride and an unrivaled exhaust note.

There are two models available: the Boxster and the Boxster S. The regular Boxster is equipped with a 2.7-liter flat six engine that produces 217 horsepower at 6,400 rpm and 192 foot-pounds of torque at 4,750 rpm. While these numbers are adequate, they are shy of the numbers posted by the Audi TT Roadster and the BMW M Coupe.

Pop the extra $9,000 for a Boxster S and you get a half-liter increase in engine displacement and 33 more horsepower, for a total of 250, to adequately fling the car through your favorite set of S-turns. The horizontally opposed 3.2-liter flat six also makes 33 more foot-pounds of torque, bringing that number to 225 and endowing the German roadster with a decidedly forceful personality. The S model also gets a six-speed, short-throw manual transmission (as opposed to the Boxster's five-speed), a larger radiator, a revised suspension, 17-inch (up from 16-inch) wheels and more standard equipment. There is still plenty of optional equipment left to order, though, and doing so can quickly jack up the price to Porsche 911 territory. Certainly worth considering is the Porsche Stability Management system, a stability control system that helps to prevent dangerous skids and spins.

Two adults fit just fine in the Boxster, and the supple leather seats are mighty comfortable for most folks. Substantial bolstering holds occupants in place on tight turns, and nicely sculpted door panels provide a great spot to rest an arm while driving. Wind protection isn't great, so prepare to have your hair tousled even with the windows up and the wind blocker in place. On the plus side, cowl shake is nearly non-existent, with only slight amounts of shimmy evident, and there is an ample 9.1 cubic feet of cargo space available.

As a daily driver, the Porsche isn't well equipped to deal with the realities of ever-changing weather conditions, multi-tasking behind the steering wheel, and low-speed traffic situations. Its delicately balanced chassis, confounding interior ergonomics, lack of a cupholder and stiff steering, brakes and clutch conspire to make it a chore around town. Buy a Mercedes SLK320 or Audi TT Roadster if your primary driving environment resembles the Disneyland parking lot.

Rather, the Porsche Boxster shines as a weekend getaway vehicle, providing comfort and space for two adults and their belongings with driving characteristics improving at speed. Take the long way, running hard on as many twisty two-lane roads as you can find with someone who loves road trips just as much as you do, and you'll immensely enjoy one of the most memorable overnight vacations you've had in years.

BOXSTER

PORSCHE

Standard Equipment

BASE (5M): 2.7L H6 DOHC SMPI 24-valve engine with variable valve timing, (requires premium unleaded fuel); 5-speed OD manual transmission; engine oil cooler; 120 amp alternator; transmission oil cooler; rear-wheel drive, 3.56 axle ratio; dual stainless steel exhaust with tailpipe finisher; front independent strut suspension with anti-roll bar, front coil springs, gas-pressurized front shocks, rear independent strut suspension with anti-roll bar, rear coil springs, gas-pressurized rear shocks; rack-and-pinion power steering with engine speed-sensing assist; 4-wheel antilock disc brakes; 17 gal. capacity fuel tank; power retractable rear spoiler, side impact bars; power convertible roof with roll-over protection; front and rear body-colored bumpers; clearcoat monotone paint; aero-composite halogen headlamps; additional exterior lights include front fog/driving lights; driver's and passenger's body-colored heated folding outside mirrors, driver's power remote outside mirror, passenger's power remote with tilt down outside mirror; front 16" x 6" silver alloy wheels rear 16" x 7" silver alloy wheels; P205/55ZR16 BSW performance A/S performance front tires; 225/50 rear tires; full-size alloy spare wheel; air conditioning with climate control, air filter; AM/FM stereo radio, seek-scan feature, cassette player, 4 speakers, theft deterrent, window grid diversity antenna; power door locks; 1 power accessory outlet, front lighter element(s), driver's foot rest, smokers' package; instrumentation display includes tachometer, water temperature gauge, clock, trip odometer; warning indicators include oil pressure, water temp, battery, low oil level, lights on, key in ignition, low fuel, low washer fluid, brake fluid; driver's and passenger's front airbags, driver's and front passenger's door-mounted side airbags; ignition disable; tinted windows with driver's and passenger's 1-touch down function; heated washer fluid jets, fixed interval front windshield wipers, sun visor strip; seating capacity of 2, front bucket seats with fixed headrests, center armrest with storage, driver's and passenger's seats include 8-way adjustment (2-way power); leather seats, leatherette door trim insert, full carpet floor covering, leather-wrapped gearshift knob; interior lights include dome light with delay, door curb lights; leather-wrapped steering-wheel with telescopic adjustment; dual illuminated vanity mirrors; day/night rearview mirror; full floor console, interior concealed storage, driver's and passenger's door bins; carpeted cargo floor, cargo net; black side window moldings, black front windshield molding and body-colored door handles.

S (6M) (in addition to or instead of BASE (5M) equipment): 3.2L H6 DOHC SMPI 24-valve engine with variable valve timing; 6-speed OD manual transmission; HD radiator; 3.44 axle ratio; sport-ride suspension; power convertible roof with lining, roll-over protection; front 17" x 7" silver alloy wheels rear 17" x 8.5" silver alloy wheels; P205/50ZR17 BSW A/S performance front tires; 255/40 rear tires; remote keyless entry, power remote hatch release; security system; heated washer fluid jets, variable speed intermittent front windshield wipers; full cloth headliner; illuminated entry and colored front windshield molding.

Base Prices

986310	Base (5M)	NA	42100
986320	Boxster S (6M)	NA	50200
Destination Charge:	....	765	765

Interested in seeing what dealers will sell this vehicle for? Check out our True Market Value^{sm} (TMV^{sm}) pricing on our Web site at www.edmunds.com.

Accessories

—	Leather Interior Trim	NA	1990

Includes black leather steering wheel, hand brake grip, door handles, shift lever knob; black leatherette shift lever boot and sunvisors; leather top/bottom dashboard in seat color. NOT AVAILABLE with SPCLTH, X99, P70.

PORSCHE — BOXSTER

CODE	DESCRIPTION	INVOICE	MSRP
—	**Special Leather Interior**	NA	2370
	Includes special leather seats, dashboard, top of instrument cluster, center console, storage shelf, roll bar covering and door panels; black leather steering wheel, hand brake grip, door handles and shift knob; black leatherette shift boot and sunvisors. Carpeting is in the color of the special leather and A pillars are in black plastic. NOT AVAILABLE with (OPLTHR) Leather Interior Trim, X99, P70, 982, E51, E53, E55, E61.		
030	**Sport Chassis**	NA	690
	Includes more rigidly tuned springs/shocks and front/rear spring plates.		
249	**Transmission: 5 Speed Automatic with Tiptronic S**	NA	3210
	Includes 4.17 axle ratio. NOT AVAILABLE with Y05, Y06, Y08, P38, P40.		
288	**Headlight Washers**	NA	225
391	**Wheels: 17" Boxster Design (Base)**	NA	1215
	Includes tires: 205/50ZR17 front and 255/40ZR17 rear. NOT AVAILABLE with 413, XRA, XRB, XRL, 400, 414.		
400	**Wheels: 17" Boxster S Design (Base)**	NA	1215
	Includes tires: 205/50ZR17 front and 255/40ZR17 rear. NOT AVAILABLE with 391, 413, XRA, XRB, XRL, 414.		
413	**Wheels: 18" Light Alloy Turbo Look (Base)**	NA	2735
	Pressure-cast. Includes 7.5 x 18 front wheels, 9 x 18 rear wheels and tires: 225/40ZR18 front and 265/35ZR18 rear and anti-theft device. NOT AVAILABLE with 391, XRA, XRB, XRL, 400, 414.		
413	**Wheels: 18" Light Alloy Turbo Look (S)**	NA	1190
	Pressure-cast. Includes 7.5J x 18 front wheels, 9J x 18 rear wheels and tires: 225/40ZR18 front and 265/35ZR18 rear and anit-theft device. NOT AVAILABLE with XRA, XRB, XRL, 414.		
414	**Wheels: 18" High Gloss Turbo Look (Base)**	NA	3705
	Includes tires: 225/40ZR18 front and 265/35ZR18 rear. NOT AVAILABLE with 391, 413, XRA, XRB, XRL, 400.		
414	**Wheels: 18" High Gloss Turbo Look (S)**	NA	2160
	Includes tires: 225/40ZR18 front and 265/35ZR18 rear. NOT AVAILABLE with XRA, XRB, XRL, 413.		
424	**CD Shelf Center Console**	NA	40
	NOT AVAILABLE with 662.		
446	**Wheel Caps with Colored Porsche Crest (4)**	NA	170
476	**Porsche Stability Management**	NA	1215
498	**Delete Model Designation**	NC	NC
51	**Paint: Wimbledon Green Metallic**	2556	3010
53	**Paint: Forest Green Metallic**	2556	3010
54	**Paint: Viola Metallic**	2556	3010
549	**Roof Transport System**	NA	460
55	**Paint: Dark Blue**	2556	3010
550	**Body-Colored Hard Top**	NA	2295
	Includes heatable rear window.		
56	**Paint: Cobalt Blue Metallic**	2556	3010
58	**Paint: Polar Silver Metallic**	2556	3010
59	**Paint: Slate Gray Metallic**	2556	3010
601	**Litronic Headlights**	NA	1070
	REQUIRES 288.		

BOXSTER — PORSCHE

CODE	DESCRIPTION	INVOICE	MSRP
62	Paint: Midnight Blue Metallic	2556	3010
635	Park Assist System	NA	520
	Activated whenever the reverse gear is engaged. An acoustical signal will be heard in intervals whenever the vehicle backs up and approaches an object that is closer than 150 cm (5 feet). At a distance of 30 cm (1 foot) and the tone is continuous.		
662	PCM Information/Navigation System	NA	3540
	Includes cassette radio, GPS Navigation System with separate CD-Rom drive and climate control indicator. Order disks from Navigation Technologies (NavTech) at 1-888-628-6277 and on-board computer. NOT AVAILABLE with 424, P63, P64, P09, P10.		
982	Soft Look Leather Seats In Interior Color	NA	355
	REQUIRES (OPLTHR) Leather Interior Trim. NOT AVAILABLE with P70, (SPCLTH) Special Leather Interior, X99.		
AD	Paint: Black	NC	NC
	NOT AVAILABLE with X45.		
AJ	Paint: Black	NC	NC
	NOT AVAILABLE with X45.		
E3	Paint: Lapis Blue Metallic	687	805
E51	Leather Interior Package	NA	2920
	Includes lower part of instrument panel, trim moulding (groove), side air vents including directional slats, defrost trim, central air vents frame, heat/air conditioning unit frame, left/right switch trims, ignition lock rosette, door handle cover, storage lid, door tube and cover for mirror attachment with leather in interior color. Front loudspeaker cover and central air vent outlet painted in interior color. Door tube adapter painted in silver. REQUIRES (OPLTHR) Leather Interior Trim. NOT AVAILABLE with E53, E55, E60, E61, (SPCLTH) Special Leather Interior, X99, P70.		
E53	Dark Burr Maple Interior Package	NA	4350
	Includes lower part of instrument panel, trim moulding (groove), central air vents frame, heat/air conditioning unit frame, left/right switch covers, door handle cover and door tube handle covered with dark burr maple. Side air vents including directional slats, defroster trim, ignition rosette, storage lid, lower part of door tube and mirror attachment covered with leather in interior color. Front loudspeaker cover and central air vent outlet painted in interior color. Door tube adapter painted in silver. REQUIRES (OPLTHR) Leather Interior Trim. NOT AVAILABLE with E51, E55, E60, E61, (SPCLTH) Special Leather Interior, X99, P70.		
E55	Carbon Interior Package	NA	4350
	Includes lower part of instrument panel, trim moulding (groove), central air vents frame, heat/air conditioning unit frame, left/right switch covers, door handle cover, storage lid and door tube handle covered with carbon. Side air vents including directional slats, defroster trim, ignition rosette, lower part of door tube and mirror attachment covered with leather in interior color. Front loudspeaker cover and central air vent outlet painted in interior color. Door tube adapter painted in silver. REQUIRES (OPLTHR) Leather Interior Trim. NOT AVAILABLE with E51, E53, E60, E61, (SPCLTH) Special Leather Interior, X99, P70.		
E60	Large Arctic Silver Interior Package	NA	3080
	Includes arctic silver painted trim groove, central air vent mounting, left/right switch trim, instrument surround, side air vent slats and loudspeaker grille cover; black leather climate control or digital sound processor trim and lower switch trim; interior		

PORSCHE — BOXSTER

CODE	DESCRIPTION	INVOICE	MSRP
	color leather trimmed side air vents, defroster trim, ignition lock rosette, loudspeaker door finishers, finishers for mirror attachment points, door storage bin cover and door handle cover and interior color painted loudspeaker dashboard finishers. NOT AVAILABLE with E51, E53, E55, E61.		
E61	Small Arctic Silver Interior Package	NA	725
	Includes arctic silver painted trim groove, central air vent mounting, left/right switch trim and instrument surround; black leather trimmed climate control or digital sound processor trim. REQUIRES (OPLTHR) Leather Interior Trim. NOT AVAILABLE with E51, E53, E55, E60, (SPCLTH) Special Leather Interior, X99, P70.		
J4	Paint: Rain Forest Green Metallic	687	805
L1	Paint: Orient Red Metallic	NA	805
M6A	Black Floor Mat with Porsche Lettering	NA	92
M6F	Metropol Blue Floor Mat	NA	92
M6H	Natural Brown Floor Mats	NA	92
M6J	Nephrite Green Floor Mat with Porsche Lettering	NA	92
M6M	Boxster Red Floor Mat with Porsche Lettering	NA	92
M6P	Graphite Grey Floor Mat with Porsche Lettering	NA	92
M6S	Savanna Beige Floor Mat with Porsche Lettering	NA	92
N1	Zanzibar Red	NA	805
P01	Comfort Package	NA	2090
	Includes electrically adjustable front seats, driver's side memory function, left and right adjustable lumbar support. NOT AVAILABLE with P70.		
P09	Sport Package (Base)	NA	2110
	Includes wind stop, sound system, cruise control, alarm system and CD player. NOT AVAILABLE with P10, 662.		
P10	Sport Touring Package (Base)	NA	3420
	Includes wind stop, digital sound system, cruise control, alarm system, CD changer and on-board computer. NOT AVAILABLE with P09, 662.		
P11	Self-Dimming Inner Rearview Mirror	NA	690
	Includes self-dimming driver side rearview mirror and rain sensor.		
P14	Heated Front Seats Package	NA	400
P15	Electrically Adjustable Front Seats	NA	1520
	Includes height, length and left/right backrest adjustment and driver's side memory function. NOT AVAILABLE with P70.		
P38	Design Package (Base)	NA	2578
	Includes arctic silver painted roll bar, stainless steel door sills, aluminum-look instruments, chrome oval exhaust pipe and leather/aluminum shift/brake handle. NOT AVAILABLE with XMK, XMY, P70, Y05, Y08, X45, X69, 249, P39, Y23, Y61, Y63.		
P39	Design Package (Base)	NA	2578
	Includes arctic silver painted roll bar, stainless steel door sills, aluminum-look instruments, chrome oval exhaust pipe, leather/aluminum Tiptronic shifter and hand brake. REQUIRES 249. NOT AVAILABLE with XMK, XMY, P70, X45, X69, P38, Y61, Y63, Y05, Y06, Y08.		
P40	Design Package (S)	NA	1640
	Includes arctic silver painted roll bar, stainless steel door sills and leather/aluminum shift/brake handle. NOT AVAILABLE with XMK, XMY, P70, Y05, Y08, X69, P41, 249, Y23, Y61, Y63.		

BOXSTER — PORSCHE

CODE	DESCRIPTION	INVOICE	MSRP
P41	Design Package (S)	NA	1640
	Includes arctic silver painted roll bar, stainless steel door sills, leather/aluminum Tiptronic shifter and hand brake. REQUIRES 249. NOT AVAILABLE with XMK, XMY, P70, X69, P40, Y61, Y63, Y05, Y06, Y08.		
P63	Sport Package (S)	NA	1560
	Includes wind stop, sound system, cruise control, AM/FM radio and CD player. NOT AVAILABLE with 662, P64.		
P64	Sport Touring Package (S)	NA	2870
	Includes wind stop, digital sound system, cruise control, CD changer and on-board computer. NOT AVAILABLE with 662, P63.		
P70	Sport Design Package	NA	1365
	Includes black leather hand brake grip, door handles, shift knob, airbag cover, roll bar trim, cover of center console and upper part of instrument cover; textured black leatherette side pads of center console front, dashboard, door panels and side panels of center console; metal grey painted bottom of instrument bridge, instrument rims, switch plates, seat buckets, switch plates on seats, outer seat fittings, center console, hand brake cover/lever, ash tray cover plate/lid, left and right door handle tube, panel in front of door lever, storage compartment lid, roll bar, release knob and black leather 3-spoke steering wheel with airbag and sport seats. NOT AVAILABLE with P15, 982, XMK, Y05, Y06, Y08, E51, E53, E55, E61, P38, XMY, P39, P40, P41, P01, XJB, XME, Y23, Y61, Y63, X45, (OPLTHR) Leather Interior Trim, (SPCLTH) Special Leather Interior, X99.		
X1	Arctic Silver Metallic	687	805
X2	Meridian Metallic	NA	805
X45	Painted Instrument Dials In Interior Color	NA	660
	NOT AVAILABLE with P70, P38, P39.		
X69	Carbon Door Sills with Embossed Insignia	NA	765
	NOT AVAILABLE with P40, P38, P39, P41.		
X99	Natural Leather Option	NA	3950
	Includes black leather steering wheel, hand brake grip, door handles and shift knob; black leatherette shift boot and sun visors. Carpeting is in the color of the special leather and A pillars are in black plastic. Code required for transmittal to PAG (internal use only). NOT AVAILABLE with 982, (OPLTHR) Leather Interior Trim, (SPCLTH) Special Leather Interior, P70, E51, E53, E55, E61.		
XAA	Front and Rear Spoilers Aerokit	NA	6225
	Includes left and right rocker panel covers.		
XAB	Rear Speedster In Matching Exterior Color	NA	1465
XJB	Silver Painted Rear Center Console	NA	715
	NOT AVAILABLE with P70, XME.		
XME	Rear Center Console Painted Exterior Color	NA	715
	NOT AVAILABLE with P70, XJB.		
XMK	Roll Bar Painted In Exterior Color	NA	525
	NOT AVAILABLE with P70, P40, XMY, P38, P39, P41.		
XMY	Silver Painted Roll Bar	NA	525
	NOT AVAILABLE with XMK, P70, P38, P39, P40, P41.		
XRA	Wheels: 17" Sport Classic (Base)	NA	2490
	Includes tires: 205/50ZR17 front and 255/40ZR17 rear. NOT AVAILABLE with 391, 413, XRB, XRL, 400, 414.		

PORSCHE — BOXSTER

CODE	DESCRIPTION	INVOICE	MSRP
XRA	Wheels: 17" Sport Classic (S)	NA	1275
	NOT AVAILABLE with 413, XRB, XRL, 414.		
XRB	Wheels: 18" Sport Classic (Base)	NA	4170
	Includes tires: 225/40ZR18 front and 265/35ZR18 rear. NOT AVAILABLE with 391, 413, XRA, XRL, 400, 414.		
XRB	Wheels: 18" Sport Classic (S)	NA	2660
	Includes tires: 225/40ZR18 front and 265/35ZR18 rear. NOT AVAILABLE with 413, XRA, XRL, 414.		
XRL	Wheels: 18" Sport Design (Base)	NA	4170
	Includes tires: 225/40ZR18 front and 265/35ZR18 rear. NOT AVAILABLE with 391, 413, XRA, XRB, 400, 414.		
XRL	Wheels: 18" Sport Design (S)	NA	2660
	Includes tires: 225/40ZR18 front and 265/35ZR18 rear. NOT AVAILABLE with 413, XRA, XRB, 414.		
XSC	Porsche Crest In Headrest	NA	210
XSX	Guards Red Seat Belts	NA	330
	NOT AVAILABLE with XSY, XSZ.		
XSY	Speed Yellow Seat Belts	NA	330
	NOT AVAILABLE with XSZ, XSX.		
XSZ	Riviera Blue Seat Belts	NA	330
	NOT AVAILABLE with XSY, XSX.		
XX2	Footwell Lighting	NA	715
Y05	Carbon/Aluminum Shift/Brake handle (Base)	NA	780
	NOT AVAILABLE with P38, P70, Y06, Y08, P39, 249, Y23, Y61, Y63.		
Y05	Carbon/Aluminum Shift/Brake handle (S)	NA	865
	NOT AVAILABLE with P40, P70, Y06, Y08, P41, 249, Y23, Y61, Y63.		
Y06	Leather/Aluminum Shift/Brake handle (Base)	NA	780
	NOT AVAILABLE with P70, Y05, Y08, P39, 249, Y23, Y61, Y63.		
Y06	Leather/Aluminum Shift/Brake handle (S)	NA	865
	NOT AVAILABLE with P70, Y05, Y08, P41, 249, Y23, Y61, Y63.		
Y08	Dark Wood/Aluminum Shift/Brake handle (Base)	NA	780
	Dark maple burr wood. NOT AVAILABLE with P38, P70, Y05, Y06, P39, 249, Y23, Y61, Y63.		
Y08	Dark Wood/Aluminum Shift/Brake handle (S)	NA	865
	Dark maple burr wood. NOT AVAILABLE with P40, P70, Y05, Y06, P41, 249, Y23, Y61, Y63.		
Y1	Paint: Seal Grey Metallic	NA	805
Y23	Leather/Aluminum Tiptronic Shifter and Hand brake	NA	720
	In interior color leather. Actuating knob is aluminum in color. REQUIRES 249. NOT AVAILABLE with P70, Y61, Y63, Y05, Y06, Y08, P38, P40.		
Y61	Carbon/Aluminum Tiptronic Shifter and Hand brake	NA	720
	Actuating knob is aluminum in color. REQUIRES 249. NOT AVAILABLE with P70, Y23, Y63, Y05, Y06, Y08, P38, P39, P40, P41.		
Y63	Dark Wood/Aluminum Tiptronic Shifter and Hand brake	NA	720
	Dark maple burr wood. Actuating knob is aluminum in color. REQUIRES 249. NOT AVAILABLE with P70, Y23, Y61, Y05, Y06, Y08, P38, P39, P40, P41.		
Z8	Paint: Black Metallic	687	805

SAAB

2001 9-3

What's New?

The base convertible has been dropped for this year while all other models get two new colors. The OnStar telematics system and traction control are now standard.

Review

Despite some shortcomings, we're fond of Saab's uniquely styled coupes and sedans. The base 9-3 comes in a three-door coupe and a five-door hatchback while the convertible has been dropped for 2001. All come equipped with a powerful 185-horsepower four-cylinder engine. This turbocharged 2.0-liter produces stunning acceleration that can char the front tires into bits if the driver so chooses.

Move up to the even more feature-laden SE five-door or convertible, and you're opting for even more performance. All SEs are powered by a high-output version of the turbo four that spins an amazing 205 horses (that's better than 100 horsepower per liter of displacement!) through either a four-speed automatic or five-speed manual gearbox. Perhaps even more impressive is that in stick-shift models, this motor makes its 209 foot-pounds of torque at an amazingly low 2,200 rpm, and then maintains peak torque all the way up to 4,500 rpm. Talk about a useable power band!

In addition to getting bigger wheels and tires, the uplevel SE also boasts a sportier look with a front chin spoiler, flared rocker panels, a low-slung rear valence, body-colored mirrors, chrome exhaust tip and a sports steering wheel. The SE Convertible models add a rear spoiler, while five-door versions come equipped with a specially tuned sport suspension for more responsive handling. For pure enthusiasts, Saab offers the high-performance 9-3 Viggen. With 230 horsepower and a healthy 258 foot-pounds of torque from its high-output turbo 2.3-liter, the Viggen can be had as a coupe, hatch or ragtop, and either in black, Steel Gray or Laser Red.

All 9-3 models feature Saab's patented pendulum-design B-pillar, which deflects side impacts away from head and chest areas; the world's first head-restraint system to reduce the risk of whiplash-type injuries; and seat-mounted, two-stage inflating head and chest side airbags.

The Saab 9-3 is a fun-to-drive, equipment-laden near-luxury car that competes against entries from Volvo, BMW and Mercedes. While the 9-3 is a good car in its own right, the problem is that there are plenty of good cars in the 9-3's price class. If your tastes run a bit on the eccentric side, however, this car's personality and quirkiness may be a better choice for you than a BMW 3 Series or Mercedes C class. You'll certainly stand out more in the crowd, and have fun doing it.

Standard Equipment

BASE 2-DOOR HATCHBACK (5M): 2L I4 DOHC MPI intercooled turbo 16-valve engine; 5-speed OD manual transmission; 130 amp alternator; front-wheel drive, traction control, 3.82 axle ratio;stainless steel exhaust with tailpipe finisher; front independent strut suspension with anti-roll bar, front coil springs, gas-pressurized front shocks, rear non-independent trailing arm suspension with anti-roll bar, rear coil springs, gas-pressurized rear shock; rack-and-pinion power steering; 4-wheel antilock disc brakes; 16.9 gal. capacity fuel tank; rear lip spoiler, side impact bars; front and rear body-colored bumpers with black rub strip; black bodyside molding; clearcoat monotone paint; aero-composite halogen auto off headlamps with washer and wiper, daytime running lights, delay-off feature; additional exterior lights include cornering lights, front fog/driving lights; driver's and passenger's power remote black heated folding outside

SAAB 9-3

CODE	DESCRIPTION	INVOICE	MSRP

mirrors; 15" x 6.5" silver alloy wheels; P195/60VR15 BSW A/S tires; compact steel spare wheel; air conditioning, air filter, rear heat ducts; AM/FM stereo radio, seek-scan, cassette player, CD changer pre-wiring, 4 speakers, theft deterrent, power retractable antenna, radio steering wheel controls; cruise control; power door locks with 2 stage unlock, remote keyless entry, power remote trunk release; 1 power accessory outlet, front lighter element, driver's foot rest, smokers' package, emergency S.O.S. (OnStar); instrumentation display includes tachometer, water temperature gauge, in-dash clock, exterior temp, systems monitor, trip computer, trip odometer; warning indicators include oil pressure, battery, low oil level, lights on, key in ignition, low fuel, low washer fluid, bulb failure, door ajar, service interval, brake fluid; driver's and passenger's front airbags, driver's and front passenger's seat mounted side airbags; ignition disable, tracker system, security system; tinted windows with driver's and passenger's 1-touch down; variable speed intermittent front windshield wipers, rear window wiper, rear window defroster; seating capacity of 5, front bucket seats with adjustable headrests, driver's seat includes 6-way adjustment, lumbar support, easy entry, passenger's seat includes 4-way adjustment, easy entry; 60/40 folding rear bench seat with adjustable headrests, center pass-thru armrest; front height adjustable seatbelts with pretensioners; premium cloth seats, cloth door trim insert, full cloth headliner, full carpet floor covering with carpeted floor mats; interior lights include dome light with fade, front and rear reading lights, illuminated entry; steering wheel with telescopic adjustment; dual illuminated vanity mirrors; day/night rearview mirror; full floor console, locking glove box with light, front cupholder, instrument panel bin, 2 seat back storage pockets, driver's and passenger's door bins; carpeted cargo floor, vinyl trunk lid, cargo cover, cargo tie downs, cargo light; chrome grille, black side window moldings, black front windshield molding, black rear window molding and black door handle.

BASE 4-DOOR HATCHBACK (5M) (in addition to or instead of BASE 2-DOOR (5M) equipment): Child safety rear door locks.

SE 4-DOOR HATCHBACK (5M) (in addition to or instead of BASE 4-DOOR HATCHBACK (5M) equipment): Sport ride suspension; front power sliding and tilting glass sunroof with sunshade; rocker panel extensions; driver's and passenger's power remote body-colored heated folding outside mirrors; 16" x 6.5" silver alloy wheels; P205/50ZR16 BSW A/S tires; air conditioning with climate control; single CD player, 6 speakers; cell phone pre-wiring; driver armrest, driver's and front passenger's seats include 8-way power adjustment; leather seats, genuine wood dashboard insert, leather-wrapped gearshift knob; driver's seat memory includes 3 setting(s) and leather-wrapped sport steering wheel.

VIGGEN 2-DOOR HATCHBACK (5M) (in addition to or instead of SE 4-DOOR HATCHBACK (5M) equipment): 2.3L I4 DOHC MPI 16-valve intercooled turbo engine; 4.05 axle ratio; rear wing spoiler; 17" x 7.5" silver alloy wheels; P215/45ZR17 BSW performance tires; integrated roof antenna; front sports seats; leather door trim insert and chrome interior accents.

VIGGEN 4-DOOR HATCHBACK (5M) (in addition to or instead of VIGGEN 2-DOOR HATCHBACK (5M) equipment): Child safety rear door locks.

SE CONVERTIBLE (5M) (in addition to or instead of SE 4-DOOR HATCHBACK (5M) equipment): Power convertible roof with lining, glass rear window; power front and rear windows with front and rear 1-touch down function; seating capacity of 4, easy entry and full folding rear bench seat with adjustable headrests.

VIGGEN CONVERTIBLE (5M) (in addition to or instead of SE CONVERTIBLE (5M) equipment): 2.3L I4 DOHC MPI 16-valve intercooled turbo engine; front-wheel drive, 4.05 axle ratio; sport ride suspension; rear wing spoiler; 17" x 7.5" silver alloy wheels; P215/45ZR17 BSW performance tires; air conditioning with climate control; front sports seats, passenger's seat includes 8-way power adjustment; leather door trim insert, chrome interior accents; driver's seat with 3 memory setting(s) and leather-wrapped sport steering wheel.

9-3 / 9-5 — SAAB

CODE	DESCRIPTION	INVOICE	MSRP

Base Prices

323M	Base 2-Door Hatchback (5M)	24905	26495
325M	Base 4-Door Hatchback (5M)	25132	26995
355MSR	SE 4-Door Hatchback (5M)	30411	32595
383MSR	Viggen 2-Door Hatchback (5M)	34575	37995
385MSR	Viggen 4-Door Hatchback (5M)	34575	37995
352MT1	SE Convertible (5M)	36995	39995
382MT1	Viggen Convertible (5M)	40945	44995
Destination Charge:		575	575

Interested in seeing what dealers will sell this vehicle for? Check out our True Market Value^{sm} (TMV^{sm}) pricing on our Web site at www.edmunds.com.

Accessories

—	Front Heated Seats	387	450
—	Premium Package (SE Conv)	1286	1495
	Includes automatic climate control, power passenger seat, driver seat with memory, body colored rear spoiler and leather-wrapped sport steering wheel.		
—	Prep and Handling	105	NC
—	Transmission: 4-Speed Automatic (Base/SE Conv)	1032	1200
	Includes 2.86 axle ratio.		
—	Transmission: 4-Speed Automatic (SE Hatchback)	1032	1200
	Includes 2.0L DOHC intercooled turbo engine and 2.86 axle ratio.		
04	Classic Leather Seat Trim (Base)	1161	1350
257	Paint: Midnight Blue Metallic (Base/SE)	387	450
268	Paint: Silver Metallic (Base/SE)	387	450
273	Paint: Sun Green Metallic (Base/SE)	387	450
279	Paint: Steel Gray Metallic	387	450
AS2	In Dash CD Player (Base)	NC	NC
	Deletes the standard cassette player.		
SR	Power Glass Sunroof (Base)	989	1150
SR	Sunroof Delete (Hatchback - SE/Viggen)	NC	NC
T2	Blue Convertible Top (SE Conv)	NC	NC

2001 9-5

What's New?

Entry-level models get more horsepower from the turbo four-cylinder while all models get the OnStar telematics system, turbo gauges, and two new colors.

Review

Saab's premium 9-5 Sedan is designed to compete with everything from near-luxury models, such as the Lexus ES 300 and Cadillac Catera, to full-blown sport sedans, such as the Mercedes-Benz E430 and BMW 540i. But because the 9-5 is a Saab, this car looks and feels a bit different. The sedan lineup consists of a fully equipped base 9-5 model, an SE version packed with amenities, and a performance-oriented Aero model. The standard 2.3-liter turbo

SAAB 9-5

four-cylinder in the 9-5 base models now produces 185 horsepower, a 15-horsepower increase over last year, and is mated to a five-speed manual or optional four-speed auto gearbox. The 9-5 Aero versions feature a 230-horse, 2.3-liter turbo four, making 258 foot-pounds of torque from 1,900 to 3,000 rpm with the manual transmission. All SEs are powered by a 3.0-liter turbo V6 that requires a driver-selectable four-speed automatic. The V6 makes 200 ponies and 229 foot-pounds of torque from 2,500 rpm through the 4,000-rpm mark.

The 9-5's standard equipment list is long, offering antilock brakes, automatic climate controls, premium stereo, side-impact airbags, an active head-restraint system, traction control and a sunroof. Heated front and rear seats are optional, but Saab's cool ventilated front seats and a 200-watt stereo/CD/cassette come standard on the SE. If you want some of the SE's luxury but can't bear doing without a stick shift, Saab makes the base 9-5 available with a premium package that adds leather, upgraded seats and an audio system.

Saab purists who bemoan the fact that the 9-5 is not available as a hatchback need only to drive the wagon. Offered in turbo four, V6 and Aero versions, the 9-5 Wagon boasts almost 73 cubic feet of cargo space with the rear seat folded. What's more, the same kind of fresh thinking that went into the 9-5's safety technology is evident in the convenience features found in the wagon. Unique ideas such as a refrigerated glove box, an aircraft-inspired "CargoTracks" load-securing system, a removable rigid cargo shelf, and even a sliding load floor to ease loading and unloading, all help to make the 9-5 Wagon handle just about any hauling task with ease.

The 9-5 Wagon Gary Fisher Edition features a roof rack system (Saab Limited Edition Gary Fisher mountain bike included), and various cargo area accoutrements, including heavy-duty cargo nets and a 12-volt power outlet. The modified exterior features side skirts, a front-lip spoiler, body-painted rear bumper valence, white side-indicator lamps, and 17-inch Quad design wheels.

Perhaps the nicest thing about the big Saab is its sporting character, with precise steering and powerful brakes that enhance the driving experience. Even in base form, the 9-5's high level of standard equipment and low-30s sticker price make it a bargain for most people shopping the near-luxury class. The Aero models, on the other hand, will run you closer to $40K.

Standard Equipment

2.3T SEDAN (5M): 2.3L I4 DOHC MPI intercooled turbo 16-valve engine; 5-speed OD manual transmission; battery with run down protection; 130 amp alternator; front-wheel drive, traction control, 4.05 axle ratio; stainless steel exhaust; front independent strut suspension with anti-roll bar, front coil springs, gas-pressurized front shocks, rear independent multi-link suspension with anti-roll bar, rear coil springs, gas-pressurized rear shocks; power rack-and-pinion steering; 4-wheel antilock disc brakes; 18.5 gal. capacity fuel tank; front license plate bracket, side impact bars; front power sliding and tilting glass sunroof with sunshade; front and rear body-colored bumpers with black rub strip; black bodyside molding; clearcoat monotone paint; aero-composite halogen auto off headlamps with washer and wiper, daytime running lights, delay-off feature; additional exterior lights include cornering lights, front fog/driving lights; driver's and passenger's power remote body-colored heated folding outside mirrors; 16" x 6.5" silver alloy wheels; P215/55VR16 BSW A/S tires; compact steel spare wheel; dual zone front air conditioning with climate control, air filter, rear heat ducts; premium AM/FM stereo radio, seek-scan, cassette player, single CD player, 7 performance speakers, amplifier, theft deterrent, window grid diversity antenna, radio steering wheel controls; cruise control; power door locks with 2 stage unlock, remote keyless entry, child safety rear door locks, power remote hatch/trunk release, power remote fuel release; cell phone pre-wiring, 2 power accessory outlets, driver's foot rest, emergency S.O.S. (OnStar); instrumentation display includes tachometer, water temperature gauge, in-dash clock, exterior temp, systems monitor, trip computer, trip odometer; warning indicators

SAAB

9-5

| CODE | DESCRIPTION | INVOICE | MSRP |

include oil pressure, battery, low oil level, low coolant, lights on, key in ignition, low fuel, low washer fluid, bulb failure, door ajar, trunk ajar, brake fluid; driver's and passenger's front airbags, driver's and front passenger's seat mounted side airbags; ignition disable, panic alarm, tracker system, security system; tinted windows, power front and rear windows with driver's and passenger's 1-touch function; variable speed intermittent front windshield wipers, sun visor strip, rear window defroster; seating capacity of 5, front bucket seats with adjustable headrests, center armrest with storage, driver's and front passenger's seat includes 8-way power adjustment, lumbar support; 60/40 folding rear bench seat with adjustable headrests, center pass-thru armrest with skibag with storage; front and rear height adjustable front seatbelts with pretensioners; premium cloth seats, cloth door trim insert, full cloth headliner, full carpet floor covering with carpeted floor mats, genuine wood dashboard insert, leather-wrapped gearshift knob, genuine wood console insert; interior lights include dome light with fade, front and rear reading lights, 4 door curb lights, illuminated entry; leather-wrapped steering wheel with tilt and telescopic adjustment; dual illuminated vanity mirrors, dual auxiliary visors; day/night rearview mirror; full floor console, mini overhead console locking glove box with light, front and rear cupholders, 2 seat back storage pockets, driver's and passenger's door bins; carpeted cargo floor, cargo net, cargo tie downs, cargo light; chrome grille, black side window moldings, black front windshield molding, black rear window molding and black door handles.

SE V6T SEDAN (4A) (in addition to or instead of 2.3T SEDAN (5M) equipment): 3L V6 DOHC MPI 24-valve intercooled turbo engine; 4-speed driver's selectable multi-mode electronic OD automatic transmission with lock-up torque converter;2.56 axle ratio; stainless steel exhaust with tailpipe finisher; black bodyside molding rocker panel extensions; 9 premium speakers, premium amplifier; leather seats, leather door trim insert; memory on driver's seat with 3 memory setting(s) includes settings for exterior mirrors and auto-dimming day/night rearview mirror.

AERO SEDAN (5M) (in addition to or instead of SE V6T SEDAN (4A) equipment): 2.3L I4 DOHC MPI intercooled turbo 16-valve engine; 4.05 axle ratio; sport ride suspension and 17" x 6.5" silver alloy wheels; P225/45YR17 BSW A/S.

WAGON (5M) (in addition to or instead of SEDAN (5M) equipment): Roof rack; 19.8 gal. capacity fuel tank; fixed 1/4 vent windows; rear window wiper and center armrest with storage.

Base Prices

504MSR	Base Sedan (5M)	31615	33995
574ASR	SE V6tSedan (4A)	35751	38650
584MSR	Aero Sedan (5M)	37162	40175
505MSR	Base Wagon (5M)	32266	34695
575ASR	SE V6t Wagon (4A)	36399	39350
585MSR	Aero Wagon (5M)	37809	40875
Destination Charge:		575	575

Interested in seeing what dealers will sell this vehicle for? Check out our True Market Value^{sm} (TMV^{sm}) pricing on our Web site at www.edmunds.com.

Accessories

—	Premium Package (2.3t)	1716	1995
	Includes power seats with memory and Harman-Kardon audio system.		
—	Prep. and Handling	105	NC
—	Sunroof Delete	NC	NC
—	Transmission: 4-Speed Automatic	1032	1200
	Includes 2.56 axle ratio.		

SAAB 9-5

CODE	DESCRIPTION	INVOICE	MSRP
08	Leather Seat Trim with Vented Seats	856	995
	REQUIRES Premium Package.		
257	Paint: Midnight Blue Metallic	387	450
268	Paint: Silver Metallic	387	450
273	Paint: Sun Green Metallic (SE/2.3t)	387	450
279	Paint: Steel Gray Metallic	387	450
FRSEAT	Front and Rear Heated Seats	512	595
W1	BBS 17" 1-Piece Wheels and Tire Pkg (2.3t/SE)	1370	1650
W2	BBS 17" 2-Piece Wheel Upgrade (Aero)	1370	1650

TOWN HALL

Get answers from our editors, discover smart shopping strategies and share your perspectives in this interactive forum of both experts and consumers. Just enter the following address into your Web browser:

townhall.edmunds.com

Where smart shoppers talk about cars, trucks, and related consumer topics.

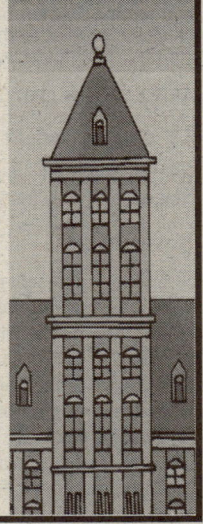

SATURN

L-SERIES

2001 L-SERIES

What's New?

The Saturn L-Series sedans and wagons didn't exactly set the world on fire when they were introduced in 2000, but they return for 2001 virtually unchanged. Saturn has addressed safety concerns by making front and rear head curtain airbags optional on all trim levels. All sedans are now equipped with a three-point seatbelt in the rear center seat, but this feature is still not available in wagons. Later in the model year, sedans will get an emergency trunk release handle. New colors include Cream White, Bright Silver, Silver Blue and Straight Shade Black. Bright White, Silver, Silver Plum and Blackberry have been discontinued.

Review

While Saturn enjoys strong customer loyalty with its line of small cars (almost 50 percent return to buy another Saturn), GM researchers found that when owners move on, they most often move up to a midsize vehicle. So a medium-sized entry makes perfect sense for both Saturn and its loyal customer base. Enter the Saturn L-Series, American-built Opel-based sedans and wagons designed and priced to compete with top imports such as Toyota's Camry and Honda's Accord.

With an overall length of just over 190 inches, the L-Series slots nicely between the segment-leading Camry Sedan and the Ford Taurus. Saturn has changed the L-Series trim level nomenclature slightly for 2001 to avoid confusion with the S-Series model names. Available as base L100, midlevel L200 or top-line L300 Sedans as well as fully equipped LW200 or upmarket LW300 Wagons, all models include air conditioning, four-wheel independent suspension, theft-deterrent system, and front disc/rear drum brakes (disc/disc standard on the 300 models; ABS with traction control is optional).

Inside, the L-Series features a spacious interior with logical, easy-to-use controls. Seats have been designed for all-day comfort. Sedans offer 17.5 cubic feet of trunk space, which is about 3.5 cubic feet more than you'll find in either Camry or Accord. With the rear seats folded, cargo capacity in the wagon is 79 cubic feet—this is 10 more cubic feet than the Subaru Legacy wagon offers and 2 cubic feet less than the Taurus wagon's capacity. Unlike other Saturns, the L-Series has steel quarter panels (remember, this is built off an Opel platform); nevertheless, engineers were able to fit Saturn's signature dent-resistant polymer panels for the doors and fenders. We're hoping that Saturn will take more care in the assembly of its L-Series cars, as 2000 models suffered widely from ill-fitting panels and wavy plastic bodywork.

A pair of DOHC four-valve engines are offered: a Saturn-exclusive 2.2-liter, 137-horsepower four-cylinder with twin balance shafts, and a 3.0-liter, 182-horse V6. The four is standard on L100, L200 and LW200 and comes with a five-speed manual transmission. An electronically controlled four-speed automatic is optional. The V6 is available only in the L300 and LW300 and must be mated to an auto-box. Though the mandatory automatic may not please sport sedan/wagon wannabes, we've found this transmission to be quite savvy—it never picks the wrong gear.

Saturn wanted the L-Series suspension to provide a balance between a smooth ride and European-like handling. This balance holds up until the car is pushed on rough or undulating roads. And while our editors have praised the responsive steering feel in the past, we've also noted that response becomes sluggish during spirited driving on canyon roads.

A head curtain airbag system—for both front and rear passengers—has been added to the option list for all 2001 L-Series cars. When electronic sensors along the sides of the vehicle detect an impact, the bag drops from the roof rail and unfolds as it inflates. Saturn says that the

SATURN — L-SERIES

system will help reduce the severity of head and neck injuries incurred by occupants involved in side-impact crashes. While we approve of this timely safety upgrade (timely indeed, since the 2000 L-Series earned a "poor" rating in the "side impact front" category) we would still like Saturn to add seat-mounted side airbags to protect against torso injuries. We're pleased to see that Saturn has added a three-point seatbelt for the rear center passenger in its L-Series sedan, but we don't understand why the wagons were denied this important safety feature. Saturn claims that its L-Series wagons compete against offerings from Volvo, Subaru, Volkswagen and Audi, but all of these brands offer a standard three-point belt in the center of the rear seat.

Unquestionably, a fully loaded L-Series car offers excellent dollar value (though you will pay the no-haggle MSRP regardless of demand) when compared with similarly equipped Accords, Camrys and Passats—but the Saturn doesn't meet its peers' established standards for build quality and interior materials. Decide whether you're willing to make these concessions before you buy.

Standard Equipment

L100 SEDAN (5M): 2.2L I4 DOHC SMPI 16-valve engine; 5-speed OD manual transmission; 525 amp battery; 96 amp alternator; front-wheel drive, 4.50 axle ratio; stainless steel exhaust; front independent strut suspension with anti-roll bar, front coil springs, gas-pressurized front shocks, rear independent strut suspension with rear coil springs, gas-pressurized rear shocks; power rack-and-pinion steering; front disc/rear drum brakes; 17.9 gal. capacity fuel tank; side impact bars; front and rear body-colored bumpers; clearcoat monotone paint; aero-composite halogen headlamps with daytime running lights; driver's and passenger's manual remote body-colored outside mirrors; 15" x 6" steel wheels; P195/65TR15 BSW touring tires; compact steel spare wheel; air conditioning, air filter, rear heat ducts; AM/FM stereo radio, clock, seek-scan, 8 speakers, fixed antenna; child safety rear door locks, power remote hatch/trunk release; 2 power accessory outlets, front lighter element(s), driver's foot rest, smoker's package; instrumentation display includes tachometer, water temperature gauge, trip odometer; warning indicators include oil pressure, water temp, battery, low coolant, lights on, key in ignition, low fuel, low washer fluid, trunk ajar, service interval, brake fluid; driver's and passenger's front airbags; ignition disable; tinted windows, manual front and rear windows; variable intermittent front windshield wipers, sun visor strip, rear window defroster; seating capacity of 5, front bucket seats with adjustable tilt headrests, driver's and passenger's seat includes 4-way adjustment; 60/40 folding rear bench seat; front height adjustable seatbelts; cloth seats, cloth door trim insert, full cloth headliner, full carpet floor covering, chrome interior accents; interior lights include dome light with delay; steering wheel with tilt adjustment; vanity mirrors; day/night rearview mirror; full floor console, locking glove box, front cupholder, instrument panel bin, driver's and passenger's door bins; carpeted cargo floor, cargo light; grille with chrome bar, black side window moldings, black front windshield molding, black rear window molding and body-colored door handles.

L200 SEDAN (5M) (in addition to or instead of L100 SEDAN (5M) equipment): 525 amp battery with run down protection; driver's and passenger's power remote body-colored heated outside mirrors; single CD player, 8 speakers; cruise control with steering wheel controls; power door locks with 2 stage unlock, remote keyless entry; panic alarm, security system; power front and rear windows with driver's 1-touch down; center armrest with storage, driver's seat includes 6-way adjustment; simulated wood dashboard insert; interior lights include front reading lights, illuminated entry; driver's side illuminated vanity mirror; locking glove box with light and front and rear cupholders.

L300 SEDAN (4A) (in addition to or instead of L200 SEDAN (5M) equipment): 3L V6 DOHC SMPI 24-valve engine; 4-speed electronic OD automatic transmission with lock-up torque converter; 3.29 axle ratio; stainless steel exhaust with tailpipe finisher; sport ride suspension; 4-wheel disc brakes; additional exterior lights include front fog/driving lights; 15" x 6" silver alloy wheels; P205/65HR15 BSW performance tires; cassette player, single CD player, auto equalizer; driver's seat includes lumbar support; 60/40 folding rear bench seat with fixed headrests;

L-SERIES — SATURN

CODE	DESCRIPTION	INVOICE	MSRP

premium cloth seats, full carpet floor covering with carpeted floor mats, simulated wood console insert; interior lights include front and rear reading lights; leather-wrapped steering wheel with tilt adjustment and dual illuminated vanity mirrors.

LW200 WAGON (4A) (in addition to or instead of L200 SEDAN (5M) equipment): 4-speed electronic OD automatic transmission with lock-up torque converter; 3.29 axle ratio; roof rack; integrated roof antenna; fixed 1/4 vent windows; rear window wiper; simulated wood console insert; carpeted trunk lid, cargo cover and cargo net.

LW300 WAGON (4A) (in addition to or instead of L200 WAGON (5M) equipment): 3L V6 DOHC SMPI 24-valve engine; stainless steel exhaust with tailpipe finisher; sport ride suspension; 4-wheel disc brakes; additional exterior lights include front fog/driving lights; 15" x 6" silver alloy wheels; P205/65HR15 BSW performance tires; cassette player, single CD player, auto equalizer; driver's seat includes lumbar support; full carpet floor covering with carpeted floor mats; interior lights include front and rear reading lights; leather-wrapped steering wheel with tilt adjustment and dual illuminated vanity mirrors.

Base Prices

Code	Description	Invoice	MSRP
ZJR19	L100 Sedan (5M)	13335	14495
ZJT19	L200 Sedan (5M)	15410	16750
ZJU35	LW200 Wagon (4A)	17328	18835
ZJW19	L300 Sedan (4A)	17935	19495
ZJW35	LW300 Wagon (4A)	19651	21360
	Destination Charge:	500	500

Interested in seeing what dealers will sell this vehicle for? Check out our True Market Value^{sm} (TMV^{sm}) pricing on our Web site at www.edmunds.com.

Accessories

Code	Description	Invoice	MSRP
—	Transmission: 4-Speed Auto with OD (L100/L200)	791	860
AG1	6-Way Power Driver Seat (All Except L100)	299	325
	Includes lumbar adjustment.		
ASF	Head Curtain Airbags	363	395
	Provides front and rear occupant protection.		
B58	Front and Rear Carpeted Floor Mats (L100/L200/LW200)	64	70
CF5	Power Sunroof (L200/L300)	667	725
D80	Rear Spoiler (L200/L300)	230	250
HAG	Leather Appointments (All Except L100)	1191	1295
	Includes leather-wrapped parking brake grip, 6-way power driver seat, dual heated front seats, leather seat trim and leather-trimmed door panels.		
JL9	Anti-Lock Braking System (L300/LW300)	547	595
	Includes traction control.		
JM4	Anti-Lock Braking System (L100/L200/LW200)	547	595
	Includes traction control.		
QE9	Wheels: 15" Alloy (L200/LW200)	322	350
T96	Fog Lamps (L200/LW200)	207	225
U1C	Radio: AM/FM Stereo with CD, Clock (L100)	267	290
	Includes 8 speaker system. NOT AVAILABLE with UPO.		
U67	Saturn Advanced Audio System (All Except L100)	235	255
	Includes separate amplifier, subwoofer and premium speakers.		

SATURN
L-SERIES / S-SERIES

CODE	DESCRIPTION	INVOICE	MSRP
UP0	Radio: AM/FM CD, Cassette Player and Clock (L100)	469	510
	Includes auto tone control and 8 speaker system. NOT AVAILABLE with U1C.		
UP0	Radio: AM/FM CD, Cassette Player and Clock (L200/LW200)	202	220
	Includes auto tone control and 8 speaker system.		

2001 S-SERIES

What's New?

GM is giving Saturns a major redesign in 2003. As such, the S-Series sees no change from last year, save for optional head-curtain airbags.

Review

Saturn's small cars have enjoyed quite a following over the years, proving both fun to drive and reliable. And Saturn dealers have almost single-handedly sparked a retail revolution that emphasizes the ownership experience over sales commissions. Unfortunately, we want more from Saturn, such as more comfortable seats and better quality switchgear and interior trim.

Last year, Saturn freshened the looks of its SL Sedan and SW Wagon. The ding-, dent- and rust-resistant polymer exterior panels give SL and SW models a contour line that runs the length of the vehicle for an angular appearance. The SC Coupes come with a driver's-side third door, providing better access to the back seat.

Inside, the small sedans and wagons have a one-piece instrument panel cover, ostensibly to eliminate miscolored plastic pieces and ill-fitting seams, but we still find fault with interior fit and finish. Some componentry from the L-Series cars are shared to reduce costs through parts commonality. The seating position is low to the floor, while the seats themselves feel too flimsy for long-haul comfort.

Two engine choices are on the S-Series roster, a 100-horsepower, 1.9-liter four-cylinder or a twin-cam version of the same that generates 124 ponies, with either a five-speed manual or four-speed auto box. Allow us to suggest the twin-cam engine mated to the manual to make for a less-pedestrian sedan or wagon; they're a must if you plan on spirited driving. Rear drum brakes are standard on all models, with no option for disc brakes.

Sedans can be had as a base SL, midrange SL1 or uplevel SL2; wagons are available as the standard SW1 or high-end SW2. Coupes come as the basic SC1 or sportier SC2. Be aware that the standard equipment list is short on all base versions and that features are not packaged well enough to sell you on the midrange models. That means you may be forced into pricey, high-end versions to get the kind of equipment you really want, which puts the price near or beyond such formidable opposition as the Nissan Sentra and the excellent Ford Focus.

Packaging aside, if you're tired of the haggling quagmire, and you're pretty much set on the car and options you want, Saturn's excellent dealer network, money-back guarantee, customer-first philosophy and reputation for reliability are attractive selling points. But we'd recommend that you shop around—many econoboxes of yore have recently been vastly improved so as to not deserve such an ignominious title.

S-SERIES

SATURN

| CODE | DESCRIPTION | INVOICE | MSRP |

Standard Equipment

SL SEDAN (5M): 1.9L I4 SOHC SMPI 8-valve engine; 5-speed OD manual transmission; 525 amp battery; 90 amp alternator; front-wheel drive, 4.06 axle ratio; stainless steel exhaust; front independent strut suspension with anti-roll bar, front coil springs, rear independent strut suspension with rear coil springs; power rack-and-pinion steering; power front disc/rear drum brakes; 12.1 gal. capacity fuel tank; side impact bars; front and rear body-colored bumpers; clearcoat monotone paint; aero-composite halogen headlamps with daytime running lights; driver's and passenger's black outside mirrors, driver's manual remote outside mirror, passenger's manual outside mirror; 14" x 5" steel wheels; P185/65SR14 BSW A/S tires; compact steel spare wheel; rear heat ducts; AM/FM stereo radio, clock, seek-scan, 2 speakers, fixed antenna; child safety rear door locks, remote hatch/trunk release, remote fuel release; 1 power accessory outlet, front lighter element(s), driver's foot rest, smoker's package; instrumentation display includes tachometer, water temperature gauge, trip odometer; warning indicators include oil pressure, battery, low coolant, lights on, key in ignition, low fuel, trunk ajar, service interval; driver's and passenger's front airbags; ignition disable; tinted windows, manual front and rear windows; variable intermittent front windshield wipers, rear window defroster; seating capacity of 5, front bucket seats with fixed headrests, driver's and passenger's seat include 4-way adjustment; 60/40 folding rear bench seat; front height adjustable seatbelts; cloth seats, cloth door trim insert, full cloth headliner, full carpet floor covering; interior lights include dome light with fade; steering wheel with tilt adjustment; passenger's side vanity mirror; day/night rearview mirror; full floor console, glove box, front cupholder, instrument panel bin, driver's and passenger's door bins; carpeted cargo floor, cargo light; black side window moldings, black front windshield molding, black rear window molding and black door handles.

SL1 SEDAN (5M) (in addition to or instead of SL SEDAN (5M) equipment): Power rack-and-pinion steering; 4 speakers.

SL2 SEDAN (5M) (in addition to or instead of SL1 SEDAN (5M) equipment): 1.9L I4 DOHC SMPI 16-valve engine; sport ride suspension, rear independent strut suspension with anti-roll bar; power rack-and-pinion steering with vehicle speed-sensing assist; 15" x 6" steel wheels; P185/65TR15 BSW touring A/S tires; air conditioning, rear heat ducts; seating capacity of 5, adjustable headrests, center armrest with storage, driver's seat includes 6-way adjustment, lumbar support; 1 seat back storage pocket and body-colored door handles.

SC1 COUPE (5M) (in addition to or instead of SL1 SEDAN (5M) equipment): Rear wing spoiler; single CD; seating capacity of 4, easy entry; rear console with storage, front and rear cupholders.

SC2 COUPE (5M) (in addition to or instead of SC1 COUPE (5M) equipment): 1.9L I4 DOHC SMPI 16-valve engine; sport ride suspension, rear independent strut suspension with anti-roll bar; power rack-and-pinion steering with vehicle speed-sensing assist; additional exterior lights include front fog/driving lights; driver's and passenger's power remote body-colored outside mirrors; 15" x 6" steel wheels; P195/60HR15 BSW performance A/S tires; air conditioning; cruise control with steering wheel controls; power door locks with 2 stage unlock, remote keyless entry, power remote hatch/trunk release; panic alarm, security system; tinted windows with driver's 1-touch down; adjustable headrests, driver's seat includes 6-way adjustment, lumbar support; leather-wrapped steering wheel with tilt adjustment; 1 seat back storage pocket and body-colored door handles.

SW2 WAGON (5M) (in addition to or instead of SL2 SEDAN (5M) equipment): Front and rear body-colored bumpers with rear step bumper; P185/65TR15 BSW touring A/S tires; tinted windows, fixed 1/4 vent windows; rear window wiper, cargo cover and cargo net.

SATURN

S-SERIES

CODE	DESCRIPTION	INVOICE	MSRP

Base Prices

ZZR27	SC2 Coupe (5M)	14080	15645
ZZJ35	SW2 Wagon (5M)	12861	14290
ZZN27	SC1 Coupe (5M)	11282	12535
ZZF69	SL Sedan (5M)	9936	10570
ZZJ69	SL2 Sedan (5M)	11606	12895
ZZG69	SL1 Sedan (5M)	10336	11485
	Destination Charge:	465	465

Interested in seeing what dealers will sell this vehicle for? Check out our True Market Value^{sm} (TMV^{sm}) pricing on our Web site at www.edmunds.com.

Accessories

—	Leather Appointments (SW2/SL2/SC2)	630	700
	Includes leather seating surfaces and leather-wrapped parking-brake grip, leather-wrapped steering wheel and leather-wrapped gearshift. REQUIRES HK1 or HN1.		
—	Transmission: Electronic 4-Speed Automatic with OD (All Except SL)	774	860
ASF	Head Curtain Airbags (All Except SL)	292	325
	Provide front occupant protection.		
ASF	Head Curtain Airbags (SL)	306	325
	Provide front occupant protection.		
AU0	Saturn Security System (SW2/SL2/SL1)	333	370
	Includes theft protection, power door locks, and remote keyless entry.		
B58	Front and Rear Floor Mats	63	70
C60	Air Conditioning (SC1/SL/SL1)	864	960
	Includes CFC-free refrigerant.		
CF5	Power Sunroof (SL2/SL1/SC)	652	725
D80	Rear Spoiler (SL2)	202	225
HK1	SW2 Option Package (SW2)	896	995
	Includes cruise control, Saturn security system, power windows and power remote control side mirrors.		
HL1	SC1 Option Package (SC1)	1647	1830
	Includes air conditioning, cruise control, power exterior mirrors, power windows with driver express-down and Saturn security system.		
HM1	SL1 Option Package (SL1)	1760	1955
	Includes air conditioning, cruise control, Saturn security system, power windows and power remote control side mirrors.		
HN1	SL2 Option Package (SL2)	896	995
	Includes cruise control, Saturn security system, power windows and power remote control side mirrors.		
JM4	Anti-Lock Braking System	446	495
	Includes traction control.		
PG5	Wheels: 15" Alloy (SC2)	315	350
PH6	Wheels: 15" Alloy (SC1)	405	450
	Includes P185/65R15 touring A/S SBR BW tires.		
PH6	Wheels: 15" Alloy (SW2/SL2)	315	350
T96	Fog Lamps (SW2/SL2)	153	170

S-SERIES — SATURN

CODE	DESCRIPTION	INVOICE	MSRP
U1C	Radio: AM/FM Stereo with CD (SL)	301	320
	Includes 4 coaxial speakers. NOT AVAILABLE with ULO, UPO.		
U1C	Radio: AM/FM Stereo with CD (SW2/SL2/SL1)	261	290
	Includes 4 coaxial speakers. NOT AVAILABLE with ULO, UPO.		
ULO	Radio: AM/FM Stereo Cassette (SC)	90	100
	Includes theft protection and 4 coaxial speakers. NOT AVAILABLE with UPO.		
ULO	Radio: AM/FM Stereo with Cassette (SL)	395	420
	Includes auto tone control and 4 coaxial speakers. NOT AVAILABLE with U1C, UPO.		
ULO	Radio: AM/FM Stereo with Cassette (SW2/SL2/SL1)	351	390
	Includes auto tone control and 4 coaxial speakers. NOT AVAILABLE with U1C, UPO.		
UPO	Radio: AM/FM Stereo CD and Cassette Player (SC)	198	220
	Includes auto tone control, theft protection and 4 coaxial speakers. NOT AVAILABLE with ULO.		
UPO	Radio: AM/FM Stereo with CD and Cassette Player (SL)	508	540
	Includes auto tone control and 4 coaxial speakers. NOT AVAILABLE with U1C, ULO.		
UPO	Radio: AM/FM Stereo with CD and Cassette Player (SW2/SL2/SL1)	459	510
	Includes auto tone control and 4 coaxial speakers. NOT AVAILABLE with U1C, ULO.		

A 15-minute phone call
could save you 15% or more
on car insurance.

1-800-555-2758

GEICO DIRECT

The Sensible Alternative

SUBARU — IMPREZA

2001 IMPREZA

What's New?
RS models get carbon fiber patterned interior trim, a CD player, and embroidered floor mats.

Review

The Impreza was originally built to battle the Ford Escorts, Toyota Corollas and Chevy Cavaliers that sold so well to young adults, but a zippy advertising campaign touting the underpowered Impreza as "What to Drive" alienated traditional Sube buyers and turned off the young adults it was supposed to attract. Sales of the Impreza were less than successful, and Subaru scrambled to find a solution.

Wonder of wonders, the company decided to reacquaint itself with its legendary all-wheel-drive system. Subaru emphasizes AWD in every ad, article and brochure you can lay your hands on. Ah yes, "The Beauty Of All-Wheel Drive." This AWD model is available in coupe, sedan, wagon, and Outback Sport format. Traditional front-wheel-drive editions have been banished from the roster.

Two trim levels are offered- the base L models and the racy 2.5 RS. Inspired by Subaru's success in the World Rally Championship, the 2.5 RS combines the performance and handling of a race car with the comfort and convenience of a modern Japanese coupe. Additional factory options include short throw shifters, titanium shift knobs, and strut tower braces to reduce body flex in corners. Normally only available in the aftermarket, these trick options show that Subaru knows who its customers are and how they like to drive their cars.

Overall, we find much to like about the Impreza. We've driven 2.5 RS and L Coupe models, and thoroughly enjoyed them. All Imprezas behave like street-legal rally cars, and they're a hoot to toss around. Fling one into a corner, and it clings to the pavement. Imprezas are a blast to drive hard and fast, and the all-wheel-drive system performs brilliantly on a variety of road surfaces. Each Impreza model is available with an $800 automatic transmission. Interiors are comfortable (though the side glass feels a bit too close) and steering and braking are communicative.

There is one thing that bothers us about the Impreza lineup, and that's the lack of an antilock brake option on the L model. To get ABS, you must order the 2.5 RS. This doesn't make much sense coming from a company touting safety in its advertising.

The Impreza's impressive road manners and clean styling make it an interesting alternative for those looking for something distinctly un-Honda Civic-like. Its full-time all-wheel-drive system also makes it a shoe-in for those needing sure-footed winter transportation. Although we love the performance of the current 2.5RS, buyers might want to think twice about getting one now. A fully redesigned version with a turbocharged engine debuts soon and it should be a real screamer.

Standard Equipment

L AWD COUPE (5M): 2.2L H4 SOHC SMPI 16-valve engine; 5-speed OD manual transmission; 75 amp alternator; full-time 3.9 axle ratio; stainless steel exhaust; front independent strut suspension with anti-roll bar, front coil springs, rear independent strut suspension with anti-roll bar, rear coil springs; power rack-and-pinion steering with engine speed-sensing assist; front disc/rear drum brakes; 15.9 gal. capacity fuel tank; rear wing spoiler, side impact bars; front and rear body-colored bumpers; black bodyside molding; clearcoat monotone paint; aero-composite halogen auto off headlamps; driver's and passenger's power remote black folding outside

IMPREZA

SUBARU

| CODE | DESCRIPTION | INVOICE | MSRP |

mirrors; 15" x 6" steel wheels; P195/60HR15 BSW A/S tires; steel spare wheel; air conditioning, rear heat ducts; AM/FM stereo radio, seek-scan, cassette player, 4 speakers, manual retractable antenna; power door locks, remote hatch/trunk release, remote fuel release; 1 power accessory outlet, front lighter element(s), driver's foot rest, smokers' package; instrumentation display includes tachometer, water temperature gauge, in-dash clock, trip odometer; warning indicators include oil pressure, battery, key in ignition, low fuel, door ajar; driver's and passenger's front airbags; tinted windows with driver's 1-touch down; fixed interval front windshield wipers, rear window defroster; seating capacity of 5, front bucket seats with adjustable headrests, center armrest with storage, driver and passenger seats include 4-way adjustment, easy entry; rear bench seat with fixed headrests; front height adjustable seatbelts; cloth seats, cloth door trim insert, full cloth headliner, full color-keyed carpet floor covering; interior lights include dome light; steering wheel with tilt adjustment; passenger's side vanity mirror; day/night rearview mirror; full floor console, locking glove box, front cupholder, instrument panel bin, dashboard storage, driver's and passenger's door bins; carpeted cargo floor; black grille, black side window moldings, black front windshield molding, black rear window molding and black door handles.

2.5 RS AWD COUPE (5M) (in addition to or instead of L AWD COUPE (5M) equipment): 2.5L H4 SOHC SMPI 16-valve engine; full-time viscous limited slip differential, 4.11 axle ratio; stainless steel exhaust with tailpipe finisher; sport ride suspension; 4-wheel antilock disc brakes; front power sliding and tilting glass sunroof; body-colored bodyside molding rocker panel extensions; additional exterior lights include front fog/driving lights; driver's and passenger's power remote body-colored folding outside mirrors; 16" x 7" silver alloy wheels; P205/55VR16 BSW A/S tires; AM/FM stereo radio, seek-scan, cassette player, single CD player, 4 speakers, manual retractable antenna; cruise control; front sports seats with adjustable headrests, center armrest with storage, carbon fiber dashboard insert, leather-wrapped gearshift knob, carbon fiber door panel insert; additional interior lights include front reading lights; leather-wrapped steering wheel with tilt adjustment and body-colored door handles.

SEDAN (5M) (in addition to or instead of COUPE (5M) equipment): Child safety rear door locks.

WAGON (5M) (in addition to or instead of SEDAN (5M) equipment): Front and rear body-colored bumpers with rear step bumper; fixed 1/4 vent windows; rear window wiper; 60/40 folding rear bench seat and cargo cover.

Base Prices

Code	Description	Invoice	MSRP
1MA	L AWD Coupe (5M)	14695	15995
1MC	2.5 RS AWD Coupe (5M)	17868	19495
1JA	L AWD Sedan (5M)	14695	15995
1JC	2.5 RS AWD Sedan (5M)	17868	19495
1LA	L AWD Wagon (5M)	15057	16395
	Destination Charge:	495	495

Interested in seeing what dealers will sell this vehicle for? Check out our True Market Value^{sm} (TMV^{sm}) pricing on our Web site at www.edmunds.com.

Accessories

Code	Description	Invoice	MSRP
—	Air Filter	39	60
	Dealer installed accessory. Includes air filter cover.		
—	Anti-Slip Mat	13	20
	Dealer installed accessory.		
—	Battery Warmer	19	30
	Dealer installed accessory.		

SUBARU — *IMPREZA*

CODE	DESCRIPTION	INVOICE	MSRP
—	Beige Armrest Extension (L)	57	88
	Dealer installed accessory.		
—	Beige Carpet Floor Covers (L)	45	70
	Dealer installed accessory.		
—	Bike Attachment (Wagon)	149	230
	Dealer installed accessory. Includes bike, kayak and cargo basket mounting clamps.		
—	CD Player	251	335
	Dealer installed accessory. NOT AVAILABLE with CD.		
—	Car Cover	58	90
	Dealer installed accessory.		
—	Car Cover Bag	6	10
	Dealer installed accessory.		
—	Cargo Bin (Wagon)	64	99
	Dealer installed accessory.		
—	Cargo Net (Wagon)	17	26
	Dealer installed accessory.		
—	Cargo Tray (PVC) (Wagon)	45	70
	Dealer installed accessory.		
—	Compartment Separator/Dog Guard (Wagon)	91	140
	Dealer installed accessory.		
—	Custom Tail Pipe Cover (L)	15	22
	Dealer installed accessory.		
—	Engine Block Heater	19	30
	Dealer installed accessory.		
—	Fog Lamps (L)	123	190
	Dealer installed accessory.		
—	Full Front End Cover (2.5 RS)	78	120
	Dealer installed accessory.		
—	Full Front End Cover (L)	71	110
	Dealer installed accessory.		
—	Gauge Pack (L)	273	364
	Dealer installed accessory. Includes beige gauge pack housing.		
—	Gauge Pack	273	364
	Dealer installed accessory. Includes gray gauge pack housing.		
—	Gray Armrest Extension (L)	57	88
	Dealer installed accessory.		
—	Gray Carpet Floor Covers (L)	45	70
	Dealer installed accessory.		
—	Hood Deflector	36	55
	Dealer installed accessory.		
—	Hood Front End Cover (L)	29	45
	Dealer installed accessory.		
—	Kayak Carrier (Wagon)	83	127
	Dealer installed accessory. Includes bike, kayak and cargo basket mounting clamps.		
—	Keyless Entry System	135	207
	Dealer installed accessory. Includes illuminated entry.		
—	Lighter Element	3	5
	Dealer installed accessory.		

IMPREZA — SUBARU

CODE	DESCRIPTION	INVOICE	MSRP
—	Moonroof Air Deflector (2.5 RS)	29	45
	Dealer installed accessory.		
—	Rear Bumper Corner Molding (2 Pair)	38	58
	Dealer installed accessory.		
—	Rear Bumper Cover	26	40
	Dealer installed accessory.		
—	Rear Differential Protector	45	70
	Dealer installed accessory.		
—	Rear Spoiler (Primed) (L Coupe/L Sedan)	185	285
	Dealer installed accessory.		
—	Rear Upper Spoiler (Primed) (Wagon)	356	475
	Dealer installed accessory.		
—	Roof Cargo Basket (Wagon)	84	130
	Dealer installed accessory. Includes bike, kayak and cargo basket mounting clamps.		
—	Roof Rack (Wagon)	130	200
	Dealer installed accessory.		
—	Roof Visor (Sedan/Wagon)	68	105
	Dealer installed accessory.		
—	Rubber Floor Mats	32	50
	Dealer installed accessory.		
—	Security System Upgrade Kit	72	110
	Dealer installed accessory.		
—	Ski Attachment (Wagon)	81	125
	Dealer installed accessory. Includes ski attachment mounting clamps.		
—	Splash Guards (L)	39	60
	Dealer installed accessory.		
—	Subwoofer/Amplifier	150	230
	Dealer installed accessory.		
—	Trunk Carpet (All Except Wagon)	10	15
	Dealer installed accessory.		
—	Trunk Net (All Except Wagon)	17	26
	Dealer installed accessory.		
—	Tweeter Kit (Pair)	52	80
	Dealer installed accessory.		
—	Upgraded Speakers (All Except Wagon)	57	88
	Dealer installed accessory.		
—	Upgraded Speakers (Wagon)	116	178
	Dealer installed accessory.		
—	Wheel Locks	16	24
	Dealer installed accessory.		
—	Wheel: 15" Alloy (L)	375	500
	Dealer installed accessory. Includes attachment set.		
4AT	Transmission: Electronic 4-Speed Auto	725	800
BW—	Gray/Beige Carpet Floor Covers (L)	48	74
DEST	Destination Surcharge for Alaska	190	190
DEST	Destination Surcharge for New York/New Jersey	40	40
	New York state and the following New Jersey counties: Bergen, Passaic, Sussex, Warren, Morris, Essex, Hudson, Union, Middlesex, Sommerset and Hunterdon.		

SUBARU — IMPREZA

CODE	DESCRIPTION	INVOICE	MSRP
DWB	Subwoofer/Amplifier	169	260
DWD	Upgraded Speakers (All Except Wagon)	67	103
DWE	Upgraded Speakers (Wagon)	134	206
DXA	Tweeter Kit (Pair)	65	100
EWB	CD Player (L)	267	356
F06	Security Package 1	242	370
	Manufacturer Discount	(13)	NC
	Net Price	229	370

Includes keyless entry system, illuminated entry, panic alarm and security system upgrade kit.

CODE	DESCRIPTION	INVOICE	MSRP
FPD	Roof Rack (Wagon)	162	249
H--	Wheels: 15" Brushed or Painted Aluminum (L)	394	525

Includes attachment set.

CODE	DESCRIPTION	INVOICE	MSRP
I06	Premium Sound Package I (Wagon)	635	922
	Manufacturer Discount	(110)	(227)
	Net Price	525	695

Includes CD player, upgraded speakers, subwoofer/amplifier and tweeter kit (pair).

CODE	DESCRIPTION	INVOICE	MSRP
I07	Premium Sound Package II (L Coupe/L Sedan)	568	819
	Manufacturer Discount	(98)	(194)
	Net Price	470	625

Includes CD player, upgraded speakers, subwoofer/amplifier and tweeter kit (pair).

CODE	DESCRIPTION	INVOICE	MSRP
I09	Premium Sound Package III (RS)	301	463
	Manufacturer Discount	(51)	(128)
	Net Price	250	335

Includes upgraded speakers, subwoofer/amplifier and tweeter kit (pair).

CODE	DESCRIPTION	INVOICE	MSRP
I3A	Popular Equipment Group I (Wagon)	288	443
	Manufacturer Discount	(17)	NC
	Net Price	271	443

Includes custom tail pipe cover, roof rack, splash guards and beige carpet floor covers.

CODE	DESCRIPTION	INVOICE	MSRP
I3B	Popular Equipment Group I (Wagon)	288	443
	Manufacturer Discount	(17)	NC
	Net Price	271	443

Includes custom tail pipe cover, roof rack, splash guards and gray carpet floor covers.

CODE	DESCRIPTION	INVOICE	MSRP
I4A	Popular Equipment Group II (L)	126	194
	Manufacturer Discount	(7)	NC
	Net Price	119	194

Includes custom tail pipe cover, splash guards and beige carpet floor covers.

CODE	DESCRIPTION	INVOICE	MSRP
I4B	Popular Equipment Group II (L)	126	194
	Manufacturer Discount	(7)	NC
	Net Price	119	194

Includes custom tail pipe cover, splash guards and gray carpet floor covers.

CODE	DESCRIPTION	INVOICE	MSRP
JVA	Fog Lamps (L)	154	237
JY--	Leather Seats (PIO) (RS Coupe/Sedan)	860	1295

Port installed option.

CODE	DESCRIPTION	INVOICE	MSRP
KWA	Air Filter	54	82

Includes air filter cover.

CODE	DESCRIPTION	INVOICE	MSRP
KW--	Beige/Gray Armrest Extension (L)	62	94

IMPREZA / IMPREZA OUTBACK — SUBARU

CODE	DESCRIPTION	INVOICE	MSRP
LPA	Splash Guards (L)	58	89
LSE	Custom Tail Pipe Cover (L)	20	31
LTB	Rear Bumper Cover	36	55
LWI	Moonroof Air Deflector (RS)	41	63
MSS	Trunk Net (All Except Wagon)	22	34
MSV	Alloy Wheel Locks	25	38
MVF	Cargo Net (Wagon)	27	42
MVG	Cargo Tray (PVC) (Wagon)	48	74
NWF	Gauge Pack - Beige (L)	281	375
	Includes compass, temperature and altimeter and beige gauge pack housing.		
NWG	Gauge Pack - Gray	281	375
	Includes compass, temperature and altimeter and gray gauge pack housing.		
OVE	Hood Deflector	36	69
PXB	Rear Differential Protector	57	88
RWA	Keyless Entry System	149	228
	Includes illuminated entry and panic alarm.		
RWB	Security System Upgrade Kit	93	142

2001 IMPREZA OUTBACK

What's New?

For 2001, Subaru's Impreza Outback Sport receives no major changes.

Review

All-wheel-drive wagons are making a comeback, and Subaru is leading the charge. While European automakers build a variety of AWD family haulers, none can be had for less than 30 grand. This leaves quite a hole in the low-priced, all-weather wagon market, and Subaru is happy to fill it with the company's expanding Outback line.

The first Subaru to wear an Outback badge was the Impreza Outback Sport Wagon in 1994. The success of this model led to the Legacy-based Outback Wagon in 1995 and the mini-SUV-challenging Forester in 1998.

For 2001, the Subaru Outback Sport continues unchanged with its aggressive bi-level spoilers and body-colored side mirrors, door handles and side molding. We've driven the Outback Sport and thoroughly enjoyed it, especially since it comes with antilock brakes standard. Features unique to this version of the Impreza include a heavy-duty four-wheel independent suspension with 6.5 inches of ground clearance, 205/60 R15 M+S tires, splash guards, a two-tone paint scheme, and a rear bumper step pad. The wagon has a small cargo area when the rear seat is raised, partially due to the steeply raked rear window. Drop the seat, though, and you've got 62 cubic feet to mess around with. Quibbles about the Outback Sport include a cramped rear seat and ugly plastic wheelcovers.

Like most Subarus, the Impreza Outback Sport comes with a long list of standard features. Air conditioning, power windows, a 12-volt power outlet in the cargo area, power side-view mirrors, a tilt steering column and a roof rack are all included in the base price. Those looking to spend

SUBARU
IMPREZA-OUTBACK

more can opt for one of the all-weather packages and get items like a CD player, heated outside mirrors, heated seats, a viscous limited-slip rear differential, side-impact airbags, dual power moonroofs, leather upholstery and a front windshield wiper de-icer.

All Imprezas behave like street-legal rally cars, and they're a hoot to toss around. Fling one into a corner, and it clings to the pavement. They are a blast to drive hard and fast, and the all-wheel-drive system performs brilliantly on a variety of road surfaces. Each model is available with an automatic transmission, but to take full advantage of the 2.2-liter, 142-horsepower boxer engine, we prefer the five-speed manual transmission. Interiors are comfortable (though the side glass feels a bit too close), and steering and braking are communicative.

The Impreza Outback Sport offers a unique combination of utility and fun. If you need a serious people mover or a fully capable off-road vehicle, it likely won't meet your demands. If, however, you want to avoid the mob mentality of buying a mini-SUV while still being able to take the road less traveled occasionally, the Outback Sport could be the ride you've been waiting for.

Standard Equipment

BASE (5M): 2.2L H4 SOHC SMPI 16-valve engine; 5-speed OD manual transmission; 75 amp alternator; full-time 3.9 axle ratio; stainless steel exhaust; HD ride suspension, front independent strut suspension with anti-roll bar, front coil springs, rear independent multi-link suspension with anti-roll bar, rear coil springs; power rack-and-pinion steering with engine speed-sensing assist; front disc/rear drum brakes with 4-wheel antilock brakes; 15.9 gal. capacity fuel tank; front and rear mud flaps, rear wing spoiler, side impact bars; roof rack; front and rear body-colored bumpers with rear step bumper; body-colored bodyside molding; lower accent two-tone paint with badging; aero-composite halogen auto off headlamps; driver's and passenger's power remote body-colored folding outside mirrors; 15" x 6" silver styled steel wheels; P205/60SR15 RWL A/S tires; compact steel spare wheel; air conditioning, rear heat ducts; AM/FM stereo radio, clock, seek-scan, cassette player, 4 speakers, manual retractable antenna; power door locks, child safety rear door locks, remote fuel release; 2 power accessory outlets, driver's foot rest; instrumentation display includes tachometer, water temperature gauge, trip odometer; warning indicators include oil pressure, battery, key in ignition, low fuel, door ajar; driver's and passenger's front airbags; tinted windows, power front and rear windows with driver's 1-touch down, fixed 1/4 vent windows; fixed interval front windshield wipers, rear window wiper, rear window defroster; seating capacity of 5, front bucket seats with adjustable headrests, center armrest with storage, driver's and passenger's seats include 4-way adjustment; 60/40 folding rear bench seat; front height adjustable seatbelts; premium cloth seats, cloth door trim insert, full vinyl headliner, full carpet floor covering; interior lights include dome light; steering wheel with tilt adjustment; passenger's side vanity mirror; day/night rearview mirror; full floor console, locking glove box, front cupholder, instrument panel bin, driver's and passenger's door bins; carpeted cargo floor, vinyl/rubber cargo mats, cargo cover, cargo tie downs, cargo light; black grille, black side window moldings, black front windshield molding, black rear window molding and body-colored door handles.

Base Prices

CODE	DESCRIPTION	INVOICE	MSRP
1LC	Impreza Outback Sport Wagon (5M)	16683	18195
	Destination Charge:	495	495

Interested in seeing what dealers will sell this vehicle for? Check out our True Market Value^{sm} (TMV^{sm}) pricing on our Web site at www.edmunds.com.

Accessories

		INVOICE	MSRP
—	Air Filter	39	60
	Dealer installed accessory. Includes air filter cover.		
—	Anti-Slip Mat	13	20
	Dealer installed accessory.		

SUBARU

IMPREZA OUTBACK

CODE	DESCRIPTION	INVOICE	MSRP
—	**Battery Warmer**	19	30
	Dealer installed accessory.		
—	**Bike Attachment**	149	230
	Dealer installed accessory. Includes bike, kayak and cargo basket mounting clamps.		
—	**CD Player**	251	335
	Dealer installed accessory. NOT AVAILABLE with CD.		
—	**Car Cover**	58	90
	Dealer installed accessory.		
—	**Car Cover Bag**	6	10
	Dealer installed accessory.		
—	**Cargo Bin**	64	99
	Dealer installed accessory.		
—	**Cargo Net**	17	26
	Dealer installed accessory.		
—	**Compartment Separator/Dog Guard**	91	140
	Dealer installed accessory.		
—	**Custom Tail Pipe Cover**	15	22
	Dealer installed accessory.		
—	**Engine Block Heater**	19	30
	Dealer installed accessory.		
—	**Fog Lamps**	123	190
	Dealer installed accessory.		
—	**Full Front End Cover**	71	110
	Dealer installed accessory.		
—	**Gauge Pack**	273	364
	Dealer installed accessory. Includes gray gauge pack housing.		
—	**Gray Armrest Extension**	57	88
	Dealer installed accessory.		
—	**Gray Carpet Floor Covers**	45	70
	Dealer installed accessory.		
—	**Hood Deflector**	36	55
	Dealer installed accessory.		
—	**Hood Front End Cover**	29	45
	Dealer installed accessory.		
—	**Kayak Carrier**	83	127
	Dealer installed accessory. Includes bike, kayak and cargo basket mounting clamps.		
—	**Keyless Entry System**	135	207
	Dealer installed accessory.		
—	**Lighter Element**	3	5
	Dealer installed accessory.		
—	**Rear Bumper Corner Molding (2 Pair)**	38	58
	Dealer installed accessory.		
—	**Rear Differential Protector**	45	70
	Dealer installed accessory.		
—	**Roof Cargo Basket**	84	130
	Dealer installed accessory. Includes bike, kayak and cargo basket mounting clamps.		

SUBARU — IMPREZA OUTBACK

CODE	DESCRIPTION	INVOICE	MSRP
—	Roof Visor	68	105
	Dealer installed accessory.		
—	Rubber Floor Mats	32	50
	Dealer installed accessory.		
—	Security System Upgrade Kit	72	110
	Dealer installed accessory.		
—	Ski Attachment	81	125
	Dealer installed accessory. Includes ski attachment mounting clamps.		
—	Subwoofer/Amplifier	150	230
	Dealer installed accessory.		
—	Tweeter Kit (Pair)	52	80
	Dealer installed accessory.		
—	Upgraded Speakers	116	178
	Dealer installed accessory.		
—	Wheel Locks	16	24
	Dealer installed accessory.		
—	Wheel: 15" Alloy	375	500
	Dealer installed accessory. Includes attachment set.		
4AT	Transmission: Electronic 4-Speed Auto	725	800
BWI	Gray Carpet Floor Covers	48	74
DEST	Destination Surcharge for Alaska	190	190
DEST	Destination Surcharge for New York/New Jersey	40	40
	New York state and the following New Jersey counties: Bergen, Passaic, Sussex, Warren, Morris, Essex, Hudson, Union, Middlesex, Sommerset and Hunterdon.		
DWB	Subwoofer/Amplifier	169	260
DWE	Upgraded Speakers	134	206
DXA	Tweeter Kit (Pair)	65	100
EWB	CD Player	267	356
F06	Security Package 1	242	370
	Manufacturer Discount	(13)	NC
	Net Price	229	370
	Includes keyless entry system, illuminated entry, panic alarm and security system upgrade kit.		
H1A	Wheels: 15" Brushed Aluminum	394	525
	Includes attachment set.		
HWB	Wheels: 15" Painted Aluminum	394	525
	Includes attachment set.		
I06	Premium Sound Package 1	635	922
	Manufacturer Discount	(110)	(227)
	Net Price	525	695
	Includes CD player, upgraded speakers, subwoofer/amplifier and tweeter kit (pair).		
JVA	Fog Lamps	154	237
KWA	Air Filter	54	82
	Includes air filter cover.		
KWD	Gray Armrest Extension	62	94
LSE	Custom Tail Pipe Cover	20	31
MSV	Alloy Wheel Locks	25	38

IMPREZA OUTBACK / LEGACY — SUBARU

CODE	DESCRIPTION	INVOICE	MSRP
MVF	Cargo Net	27	42
NWG	Gauge Pack - Gray	281	375
	Includes compass, temperature and altimeter and gray gauge pack housing.		
OVE	Hood Deflector	36	69
PXB	Rear Differential Protector	57	88
RWA	Keyless Entry System	149	228
	Includes illuminated entry and panic alarm.		
RWB	Security System Upgrade Kit	93	142

2001 LEGACY

What's New?

The Brighton model is stricken from the Legacy lineup. All 2001 Legacys comply with low-emission vehicle (LEV) standards and come with standard 24-hour roadside assistance. Legacy L models now include an ambient temperature gauge, a dual mode digital trip odometer, and a fixed intermittent rear wiper with washer on the wagons. GT models feature a power moonroof, six-way power driver's seat, limited-slip rear differential and multi-reflector halogen fog lights.

Review

Subaru distances itself from mainstream automakers by emphasizing its all-wheel-drive (AWD) lineup, thus carving out a unique niche that other companies are just now beginning to address. Subaru emphasizes that true all-wheel drive is a transmission that "drives all four wheels all the time," thus differentiating their vehicles from other entry-level luxury sedans whose AWD systems turn on the non-powered wheels only when the others lose traction. A wise move, since loyal Subaru buyers stick with the brand partially because of the wide variety of AWD models in the company's stable.

The AWD in the Subaru Legacy GT makes for a more controlled turn, giving the driver more confidence on tight curvy roads by increasing its handling ability. This is enhanced by the fully independent, sport-tuned suspension. The steering, tight and responsive, provides accurate control of the vehicle with no excessive pulling or looseness. Overall, it makes for a well-balanced, powerful ride and allows one to thread through traffic with precision.

All Legacy models have a Phase II 2.5-liter, 16-valve, 165-horsepower boxer engine under the hood. Making 166 foot-pounds of torque at 4,000 rpm, models come with either a five-speed manual or four-speed automatic transmission. Subaru's H-4 design, first developed over 30 years ago for Japanese cars, makes the engine much smoother, as the cylinder vibrations cancel each other out. As a result, this engine growls, instead of roars, when you rev it. While either drivetrain offers substantial low-end torque, a bump in horsepower would greatly enhance the Legacy's fun factor and allow it to challenge more established competitors like Accord, Camry and Maxima.

This year, the Brighton model is no longer available. The Legacy L now includes an ambient temperature gauge, dual mode digital trip odometer, and a fixed intermittent rear wiper with washer on the wagons, while the GT sedans and wagons get a power moonroof (dual on wagons), a six-way power driver's seat, limited-slip rear differential, multi-reflector halogen fog lights and an in-glass antenna.

SUBARU

LEGACY

| CODE | DESCRIPTION | INVOICE | MSRP |

Additionally, all Legacys boast conservative sheetmetal, a hidden tailpipe, standard breakaway mirrors and front and rear cupholders. Safety features for all models include daytime running lights, front seatbelt pre-tensioners and load limiters, and a three-point seatbelt for the rear-seat center position. Side-impact airbags are standard on the Outback Limited and GT Limited, but are not available on lesser trim levels. The Outback has a built-in child seat option.

Subaru has a good thing going with its Legacy, which offers a little something for everyone. Roomy, comfortable and loaded with utility, the Legacy's standard all-wheel drive, along with its many technical and stylistic innovations, should entice you to take a close look.

Standard Equipment

L AWD SEDAN/WAGON (5M): 2.5L H4 SOHC SMPI 16-valve engine; 5-speed OD manual transmission; 430 amp battery; 90 amp alternator; full-time 3.9 axle ratio; stainless steel exhaust; front independent strut suspension with anti-roll bar, front coil springs, rear independent multi-link suspension with anti-roll bar, rear coil springs; power rack-and-pinion steering with engine speed-sensing assist; 4-wheel antilock disc brakes; 16.9 gal. capacity fuel tank; side impact bars; roof rack (wagon), front and rear body-colored bumpers; black bodyside molding; clearcoat monotone paint; aero-composite halogen auto off headlamps with daytime running lights; driver's and passenger's power remote black folding outside mirrors; 15" x 6" steel wheels; P205/60HR15 BSW A/S tires; compact steel spare wheel; air conditioning, rear heat ducts; AM/FM stereo radio, seek-scan, cassette player, 4 speakers, manual retractable antenna; cruise control; power door locks with 2 stage unlock, child safety rear door locks, remote hatch/trunk release, remote fuel release; 1 power accessory outlet, driver's foot rest; instrumentation display includes tachometer, water temperature gauge, in-dash clock, exterior temp, trip odometer; warning indicators include oil pressure, battery, key in ignition, low fuel, door ajar, brake fluid; driver's and passenger's front airbags; tinted windows, power front and rear windows with driver's 1-touch down; fixed interval front windshield wipers, rear window defroster; seating capacity of 5, front bucket seats with adjustable headrests, center armrest with storage, driver's and passenger's seats include 4-way adjustment; rear bench seat with 3 fixed headrests, center pass-thru armrest; front height adjustable seatbelts with front pretensioners; cloth seats, cloth door trim insert, full cloth headliner, full carpet floor covering; interior lights include dome light, front reading lights; steering wheel with tilt adjustment; vanity mirrors; day/night rearview mirror; full floor console, locking glove box with light, front and rear cupholders, instrument panel covered bin, driver's and passenger's door bins; carpeted cargo floor, cargo light, concealed cargo storage; black grille, black side window moldings, black front windshield molding, black rear window molding and black door handles.

GT AWD SEDAN/WAGON (5M) (in addition to or instead of L AWD SEDAN (5M) equipment): Full-time viscous limited slip differential, 4.11 axle ratio; sport ride suspension; rear wing spoiler; front (and rear - wagon only) power sliding and tilting glass sunroof with sunshade; body-colored bodyside molding, rocker panel extensions; additional exterior lights include front fog/driving lights; driver's and passenger's power remote body-colored folding outside mirrors; 16" x 6.5" silver alloy wheels; P205/55HR16 BSW A/S tires; rear A/C ducts; window grid antenna; power door locks with 2 stage unlock, remote keyless entry; panic alarm; variable speed intermittent front windshield wipers, sun visor strip; driver's seat includes 6-way power adjustment, 8-way adjustment, lumbar support, passenger's seat includes 4-way adjustment; premium cloth seats, simulated wood dashboard insert, leather-wrapped gearshift knob, simulated wood console insert; additional interior lights include 2 door curb lights and illuminated entry; leather-wrapped steering wheel with tilt adjustment; dual illuminated vanity mirrors; chrome grille and body-colored door handles.

GT LIMITED AWD SEDAN (5M) (in addition to or instead of GT AWD SEDAN (5M) equipment): 6 speakers; driver's and passenger's front airbags, driver's and front passenger's seat mounted side airbags; leather seats; leatherette door trim insert; front and rear cupholders and instrument panel bin.

LEGACY — SUBARU

CODE	DESCRIPTION	INVOICE	MSRP

Base Prices

Code	Description	Invoice	MSRP
1AA	L AWD Sedan (5M)	17560	19295
1AC	GT AWD Sedan (5M)	20770	22895
1AE	GT Limited AWD Sedan (5M)	22109	24395
1BA	L AWD Wagon (5M)	18187	19995
1BC	GT AWD Wagon (5M)	21577	23795
	Destination Charge:	495	495

Interested in seeing what dealers will sell this vehicle for? Check out our True Market Value^{sm} (TMV^{sm}) pricing on our Web site at www.edmunds.com.

Accessories

Code	Description	Invoice	MSRP
—	6 Disc In-Dash CD Changer (GT)	371	495
	Dealer installed accessory.		
—	6 Pair Ski Attachment (Sedan)	81	125
	Dealer installed accessory. Includes ski mounting clamps (square).		
—	6 Pair Ski Attachment (Cross Bars) (Wagon)	81	125
	Dealer installed accessory. Includes ski mounting clamps.		
—	6 Pair Ski Attachment (Round Cross Bars) (Wagon)	81	125
	Dealer installed accessory. Includes bike, kayak and cargo basket mounting clamps.		
—	Acrylic Hood Deflector	38	58
	Dealer installed accessory.		
—	Air Filtration System	26	40
	Dealer installed accessory.		
—	Anti-Slip Mat	13	20
	Dealer installed accessory.		
—	Auto Dimming Mirror	107	165
	Dealer installed accessory. Includes compass.		
—	Battery Warmer	19	30
	Dealer installed accessory.		
—	Bike Attachment (Sedan)	149	230
	Dealer installed accessory. Includes bike mounting clamps (square).		
—	Bike Attachment (Flat Cross Bars) (Wagon)	149	230
	Dealer installed accessory. Includes bike, kayak and cargo basket mounting clamps.		
—	Bike Attachment (Round Cross Bars) (Wagon)	149	230
	Dealer installed accessory. Includes bike mounting clamps.		
—	CD Player (L, GT Wagon)	251	335
	Dealer installed accessory. NOT AVAILABLE with EYB, EYA.		
—	Car Cover	65	100
	Dealer installed accessory.		
—	Car Cover Bag	6	10
	Dealer installed accessory.		
—	Cargo Bin (Wagon)	84	130
	Dealer installed accessory.		
—	Cargo Net (Wagon)	19	30
	Dealer installed accessory.		

SUBARU

LEGACY

CODE	DESCRIPTION	INVOICE	MSRP
—	Cargo Tray/Mat (Wagon)	45	70
	Dealer installed accessory.		
—	Carpeted Gray Floor Covers	45	70
	Dealer installed accessory.		
—	Compartment Sep/Dog Guard (Wagon)	91	140
	Dealer installed accessory.		
—	Cross Bars (Wagon)	104	160
	Dealer installed accessory.		
—	Engine Block Heater	19	30
	Dealer installed accessory.		
—	Extended Roof Cargo Carrier (AWD Wagon)	319	425
	Dealer installed accessory.		
—	Full Front End Cover	78	120
	Dealer installed accessory.		
—	Hood Front End Cover	32	50
	Dealer installed accessory.		
—	Illuminated Vanity Visor (L)	35	54
	Dealer installed accessory.		
—	Kayak Carrier (Sedan)	83	127
	Dealer installed accessory. Includes kayak and roof basket mounting clamps (square).		
—	Kayak Carrier (Cross Bars) (Wagon)	83	127
	Dealer installed accessory. Includes bike, kayak and cargo basket mounting clamps.		
—	Kayak Carrier (Round Cross Bars) (Wagon)	83	127
	Dealer installed accessory. Includes bike, kayak and cargo basket mounting clamps.		
—	Keyless Entry System (L)	105	162
	Dealer installed accessory.		
—	Leather Shift Knob - A/T (L)	38	59
	Dealer installed accessory. REQUIRES 4AT.		
—	Leather Shift Knob - M/T (L)	32	49
	Dealer installed accessory.		
—	Lighter Element	5	8
	Dealer installed accessory.		
—	Logic Control CD Player (GT)	251	335
	Dealer installed accessory. NOT AVAILABLE with EYA.		
—	Moonroof Air Deflector (GT Sedan)	28	43
	Dealer installed accessory.		
—	Multi Reflector Fog Lights (L)	156	240
	Dealer installed accessory.		
—	Performance Muffler (GT)	281	375
	Dealer installed accessory.		
—	Power Outlet	32	50
	Dealer installed accessory. REQUIRES 4AT.		
—	Rear Bumper Corner Molding (2 Pair)	38	58
	Dealer installed accessory.		
—	Rear Bumper Cover (Wagon)	31	48
	Dealer installed accessory.		

LEGACY — SUBARU

CODE	DESCRIPTION	INVOICE	MSRP
—	Rear Differential Protector	45	70
	Dealer installed accessory.		
—	Rear Gate Bar (Wagon)	29	45
	Dealer installed accessory.		
—	Rear Window Dust Deflector (Wagon)	52	80
	Dealer installed accessory.		
—	Roof Cargo Basket (Sedan)	84	130
	Dealer installed accessory. Includes kayak and roof basket mounting clamps (square).		
—	Roof Cargo Basket (Cross Bars) (Wagon)	84	130
	Dealer installed accessory. Includes bike, kayak and cargo basket mounting clamps.		
—	Roof Cargo Basket (Round Cross Bars) (Wagon)	84	130
	Dealer installed accessory. Includes bike, kayak and cargo basket mounting clamps.		
—	Roof Cargo Carrier (Wagon)	296	395
	Dealer installed accessory.		
—	Round Cross Bar Set (Wagon)	104	160
	Dealer installed accessory.		
—	Rubber Floor Mats	32	50
	Dealer installed accessory.		
—	SD Color-Keyed Spoiler (Sedan)	198	305
	Dealer installed accessory.		
—	SD Primed Spoiler (Sedan)	162	250
	Dealer installed accessory.		
—	SW Primed Spoiler (Wagon)	130	200
	Dealer installed accessory.		
—	SD Color-Keyed Spoiler (Wagon)	198	305
	Dealer installed accessory.		
—	Security System Upgrade	99	152
	Dealer installed accessory.		
—	Splash Guards (GT Wagon, L)	45	70
	Dealer installed accessory.		
—	Square Sedan Cross Bar Set (Sedan)	117	180
	Dealer installed accessory.		
—	Stabilizing Brackets (4) (Wagon)	26	40
	Dealer installed accessory.		
—	Subwoofer/Amplifier	149	228
	Dealer installed accessory. NOT AVAILABLE with DYC.		
—	Trunk Net (Sedan)	17	26
	Dealer installed accessory.		
—	Tweeter Kit (All Except Limited)	60	92
	Dealer installed accessory.		
—	Upgraded Speakers (All Except Limited)	105	162
	Dealer installed accessory. NOT AVAILABLE with DYA.		
—	Wheel Locks	16	24
	Dealer installed accessory.		
—	Wheels: 15" Brushed Aluminum (L)	375	500
	Dealer installed accessory. Includes attachment set. NOT AVAILABLE with HWB, H1A.		

SUBARU   *LEGACY*

CODE	DESCRIPTION	INVOICE	MSRP
—	Wheels: 15" Painted Aluminum (L)	356	474
	Dealer installed accessory. Includes attachment set. NOT AVAILABLE with HWB, H1A.		
—	Woodgrained Patterned Door Switches	55	85
	Dealer installed accessory.		
4AT	Transmission: Electronic 4-Speed Auto (GT)	722	800
	Includes 4.44 axle ratio.		
4AT	Transmission: Electronic 4-Speed Auto (L)	722	800
	Includes 4.11 axle ratio. NOT AVAILABLE with LSB.		
BYA	Gray Carpet Floor Covers	48	74
DEST	Destination Surcharge for Alaska	190	190
DEST	Destination Surcharge for New York/New Jersey	40	40
	New York state and the following New Jersey counties: Bergen, Passaic, Sussex, Warren, Morris, Essex, Hudson, Union, Middlesex, Sommerset and Hunterdon.		
DYA	Upgraded Speakers (All Except Limited)	134	206
DYB	Tweeter Kit (All Except Limited)	65	100
DYC	Subwoofer/Amplifier	174	267
EYA	CD Player (GT Sedan, GT Wagon)	271	361
	Includes logic control.		
EYB	CD Player (L)	271	361
EYC	6-Disc In-Dash CD Changer (GT)	390	520
FYA	Cross Bars (Wagon)	106	172
H1A	Wheels: Brushed Aluminum (L)	394	525
	Includes attachment set.		
HWB	Wheels: 15" Painted Alloy (L)	394	525
	Includes attachment set. NOT AVAILABLE with H1A.		
IYA	Woodgrained Patterned Trim	65	100
	Includes power window switch.		
IYB	A/T Leather Shift Knob (L)	44	67
	REQUIRES 4AT. NOT AVAILABLE with LSB.		
KYA	Air Filtration System	41	62
KYE	Auto Dimming Mirror	119	183
	Includes compass.		
L01	Rough Road Group (Wagon)	161	259
	Manufacturer Discount	(16)	NC
	Net Price	145	259
	Includes acrylic hood deflector, rear differential protector and rear window dust deflector.		
L02	Security Group (L)	238	365
	Manufacturer Discount	(16)	NC
	Net Price	222	365
	Includes keyless entry system and security system upgrade.		
L03	Premium Sound Package 1A (L)	644	934
	Manufacturer Discount	(119)	(239)
	Net Price	525	695
	Includes CD player, upgraded speakers, tweeter kit and subwoofer/amplifier.		

LEGACY — SUBARU

CODE	DESCRIPTION	INVOICE	MSRP
L04	Premium Sound Package 1B (GT Sedan, GT Wagon)	644	934
	Manufacturer Discount	(119)	(239)
	Net Price	525	695
	Includes CD player, upgraded speakers, tweeter kit and subwoofer/amplifier.		
L05	Premium Sound Package 2 (GT Sedan, GT Wagon)	763	1093
	Manufacturer Discount	(163)	(298)
	Net Price	600	795
	Includes 6-disc in-dash CD changer, upgraded speakers, tweeter kit and subwoofer/amplifier.		
L06	Premium Sound Package 3 (GT Limited)	564	787
	Manufacturer Discount	(89)	(152)
	Net Price	475	635
	Includes 6-disc in-dash CD changer and subwoofer/amplifier.		
L1A	Popular Equipment Group 1 (L Wagon)	213	336
	Manufacturer Discount	(20)	NC
	Net Price	193	336
	Includes cross bars, splash guards and gray carpet floor covers.		
L2A	Popular Equipment Group 2 (L Sedan)	107	164
	Manufacturer Discount	(10)	NC
	Net Price	97	164
	Includes splash guards and gray carpet floor covers.		
L3A	Popular Equipment Group 3 (Wagon)	154	246
	Manufacturer Discount	(10)	NC
	Net Price	144	246
	Includes cross bars and gray carpet floor covers.		
L4B	Popular Equipment Group 4 (L)	173	305
	Manufacturer Discount	(13)	NC
	Net Price	160	305
	Includes auto dimming mirror, compass and illuminated visor vanity mirrors.		
L6C	Popular Equipment Group 6 (GT)	243	373
	Manufacturer Discount	(14)	NC
	Net Price	229	373
	Includes auto dimming mirror, compass and security system upgrade.		
LSB	M/T Leather Shift Knob (L)	38	58
LWI	Moonroof Air Deflector (GT Sedan, L Sedan)	41	63
LYA	Rear Gate Bar (Wagon)	45	69
LYC	Rear Window Dust Deflector (Wagon)	69	105
LYD	Multi Reflector Fog Lamps (L)	168	259
LYE	Splash Guards (L Sedan)	59	90
LYF	Splash Guards (L Wagon)	59	90
MSV	Alloy Wheel Locks	25	38
MYC	Trunk Net (Sedan)	21	32
MYD	Cargo Net (Wagon)	31	48
MYG	Cargo Tray/Mat (Wagon)	48	74
MYK	Illuminated Visor Vanity Mirrors (L)	54	122
NYA	Power Outlet	58	89
	REQUIRES 4AT.		

SUBARU — LEGACY / LEGACY OUTBACK

CODE	DESCRIPTION	INVOICE	MSRP
PYA	Rear Differential Protector	54	82
PYC	Acrylic Hood Deflector	38	72
PYD	Rear Bumper Cover (Wagon)	37	57
RYB	Keyless Entry System (L) *Includes illuminated entry and panic alarm.*	114	175
RYC	Security System Upgrade	124	190
S——	SW Color-Keyed Spoiler (L Wagon)	192	295

2001 OUTBACK

What's New?

Two new models, the H6-3.0 L.L.Bean Edition and the H6-3.0 VDC, both featuring a more-powerful 3.0-liter engine, join the happy Outback family.

Review

What recipe does an automotive manufacturer use to boost sagging sales? Ask any Subaru executive and she'll tell you to take one part popular Australian movie star and one part advanced all-wheel-drive system. Stir in an undercurrent of SUV backlash with a dash of resurgence in the station wagon market, and behold: the perfect environment for the Subaru Outback.

Available in either wagon or sedan form, the Outback is Subaru's answer to the question: Why would anyone want to drive an ill-handling, gas-guzzling, difficult-to-park SUV? With 7.3 inches of ground clearance, standard all-wheel drive and a base price in the low 20s, the Outback offers on-road practicality with off-road capability at a bargain price. While no match for the likes of Jeep's Grand Cherokee or Toyota's Land Cruiser in terms of hill climbing, the Outback can hold its own in light to moderate off-road situations without losing an oil pan or cracking a differential.

A Phase II 2.5-liter, 16-valve, 165-horsepower boxer engine, producing 166 foot-pounds of torque at 4,000 rpm, powers the Outback Wagon and Outback Limited Wagon and Sedan models. The all-new-for-2001 Outback H6-3.0 L.L.Bean Edition and Outback H6-3.0 VDC are both powered by an all-new 212-horsepower, DOHC, 24-valve, high-output six-cylinder engine mated to Subaru's four-speed electronic automatic transmission. Both H6-3.0-powered Outback models feature specially designed alloy wheels, a mahogany wood and leather steering wheel, automatic climate control, an eight-way power driver's seat and a nifty rear-seat center armrest.

All 2001-model-year Outback models benefit from a viscous limited-slip rear differential and larger front 11.4-inch ventilated disc brakes with twin piston calipers. Standard interior features include an ambient temperature gauge, dual mode digital trip odometer and front seatback net pockets.

Additionally, all Outbacks receive four-wheel disc brakes, ABS, protective lower body cladding, a heavy-duty four-wheel independent suspension, and 24-hour roadside assistance as standard equipment. Opt for the Outback wagon and you'll also get a 60/40-split folding rear seat, keyless entry, a 12-volt cargo area power outlet, a rear wiper/washer, and breakaway power side-view mirrors.

Safety is another area where Subaru refuses to skimp. The Outback models feature a "Ring-Shaped Reinforcement" body structure for maximum protection against frontal, offset, side and rear impacts. Side beams in both the front and rear doors further enhance side-impact protection.

LEGACY OUTBACK — SUBARU

We like the fact that Subaru offers a viable alternative to the SUV. The Outback proves that safety, style and all-weather traction can be had in a non-truck-based vehicle, and at a reasonable price.

Standard Equipment

BASE WAGON (5M): 2.5L H4 SOHC SMPI 16-valve engine; 5-speed OD manual transmission; 430 amp battery; full-time viscous limited slip differential, 4.11 axle ratio; stainless steel exhaust; HD ride suspension, front independent strut suspension with anti-roll bar, front coil springs, rear independent multi-link suspension with anti-roll bar, rear coil springs; power rack-and-pinion steering with engine speed-sensing assist; 4-wheel antilock disc brakes; 16.9 gal. capacity fuel tank; front and rear mud flaps, side impact bars; front and rear body-colored bumpers with rear step bumper; colored bodyside cladding, rocker panel extensions; clearcoat lower accent two-tone paint; aero-composite halogen auto off headlamps with daytime running lights; additional exterior lights include front fog/driving lights; driver's and passenger's power remote black folding outside mirrors; 16" x 6.5" silver alloy wheels; P225/60HR16 RWL M&S tires; compact steel spare wheel; air conditioning, rear heat ducts; AM/FM stereo radio, seek-scan, cassette player, 4 speakers, manual retractable antenna; cruise control; power door locks with 2 stage unlock, remote keyless entry, child safety rear door locks, remote hatch/trunk release, remote fuel release; 2 power accessory outlets, driver's foot rest; instrumentation display includes tachometer, water temperature gauge, in-dash clock, exterior temp, trip odometer; warning indicators include oil pressure, battery, key in ignition, low fuel, door ajar, trunk ajar, brake fluid; driver's and passenger's front airbags, driver's and front passenger's seat mounted side airbags; tinted windows, power front and rear windows with driver's 1-touch down, fixed 1/4 vent windows; fixed interval front windshield wipers, sun visor strip, fixed interval rear wiper, rear window defroster; seating capacity of 5, front bucket seats with adjustable headrests, center armrest with storage, driver's seat includes 6-way power adjustment, 8-way adjustment, lumbar support, passenger's seat includes 4-way adjustment; 60/40 folding rear bench seat with fixed headrests; front height adjustable seatbelts with front pretensioners; cloth seats, cloth door trim insert, full cloth headliner, full carpet floor covering with carpeted floor mats, simulated wood dashboard insert, simulated wood console insert; interior lights include dome light, front reading lights, illuminated entry; passenger's side vanity mirror; day/night rearview mirror; full floor console, mini overhead console with storage, locking glove box with light, front and rear cupholders, instrument panel bin, 2 seat back storage pockets, driver's and passenger's door bins; carpeted cargo floor, cargo light, concealed cargo storage; chrome grille, black side window moldings, black front windshield molding, black rear window molding and body-colored door handles.

LIMITED WAGON (5M) (in addition to or instead of BASE WAGON (5M) equipment): Engine block heater; front and rear power sliding and tilting glass sunroof with sunshade; clearcoat lower accent two-tone paint with badging; driver's and passenger's power remote body-colored heated folding outside mirrors; AM/FM stereo radio, seek-scan, cassette player, single CD player, 8 speakers, window grid antenna; driver's and passenger's front airbags, driver's and front passenger's seat mounted side airbags; heated variable intermittent front windshield wipers; heated-cushion driver's and passenger's seats; leather seats, leatherette door trim insert, leather-wrapped gearshift knob; leather-wrapped steering wheel with tilt adjustment and dual illuminated vanity mirrors.

LIMITED SEDAN (4A) (in addition to or instead of LIMITED WAGON (5M) equipment): 4-speed electronic OD automatic transmission with lock-up torque converter; 490 amp battery; 90 amp alternator; full-time viscous limited slip differential, 4.44 axle ratio; front and rear colored bumpers; colored bodyside cladding, rocker panel extensions; 16" x 6.5" silver with gold accents alloy wheels; 6 speakers; rear bench seat with fixed headrests and center pass-thru armrest.

H6-3.0 L.L. BEAN EDITION WAGON (4A) (in addition to or instead of LIMITED WAGON (5M) equipment): 3L H6 DOHC SMPI 24-valve engine; 4-speed electronic OD automatic transmission with lock-up torque converter; 490 amp battery; air conditioning with climate control, air filter, rear

SUBARU

LEGACY OUTBACK

| CODE | DESCRIPTION | INVOICE | MSRP |

heat ducts; security system; driver's seat includes 8-way power adjustment; simulated wood door panel insert; leather/genuine wood steering wheel with tilt adjustment and auto-dimming day/night rearview mirror.

H6-3.0 VDC WAGON (4A) (in addition to or instead of H6-3.0 L.L. BEAN EDITION WAGON (4A) equipment): Full-time traction control; HD ride suspension, electronic stability; premium AM/FM stereo radio, seek-scan, cassette player, single CD player, 7 speakers and amplifier.

Base Prices

Code	Description	Invoice	MSRP
1AG	Limited Sedan (4A)	23550	25995
1BO	Base Wagon (5M)	20767	22895
1BW	Limited Wagon (5M)	23815	26295
1BY	L.L. Bean Edition Wagon (4A)	26687	29495
1BZ	VDC Wagon (4A)	28839	31895
	Destination Charge:	495	495

Interested in seeing what dealers will sell this vehicle for? Check out our True Market Value^{sm} (TMV^{sm}) pricing on our Web site at www.edmunds.com.

Accessories

Code	Description	Invoice	MSRP
—	6 Disc In-Dash CD Changer	371	495
	Dealer installed accessory.		
—	6 Pair Ski Attachment (Limited Sedan)	81	125
	Dealer installed accessory. Includes ski mounting clamps.		
—	6 Pair Ski Attachment (Cross Bars) (Wagon)	81	125
	Dealer installed accessory. Includes ski mounting clamps.		
—	6 Pair Ski Attachment (Round Cross Bars) (Wagon)	81	125
	Dealer installed accessory. Includes ski, kayak, and roof basket mounting clamps.		
—	Acrylic Hood Deflector	38	58
	Dealer installed accessory.		
—	Air Filtration System	26	40
	Dealer installed accessory.		
—	All Weather Package (Base Wagon)	452	500
	Dealer installed accessory. Includes heated front seats, heated exterior mirrors and windshield wiper de-icer.		
—	Alloy Wheel Locks	16	24
	Dealer installed accessory.		
—	Anti-Slip Mat	13	20
	Dealer installed accessory.		
—	Auto Dimming Mirror	107	165
	Dealer installed accessory. Includes compass.		
—	Battery Warmer	19	30
	Dealer installed accessory.		
—	Bike Attachment (Limited Sedan)	149	230
	Dealer installed accessory. Includes bike mounting clamps.		
—	Bike Attachment (Flat Cross Bars) (Wagon)	149	230
	Dealer installed accessory. Includes bike, kayak and roof basket mounting clamps.		

LEGACY OUTBACK — SUBARU

CODE	DESCRIPTION	INVOICE	MSRP
—	Bike Attachment (Round Cross Bars) (Wagon)	149	230
	Dealer installed accessory. Includes bike mounting clamps.		
—	Bike Carrier (Trailer Hitch) (Wagon)	130	200
	Dealer installed accessory.		
—	Car Cover	65	100
	Dealer installed accessory.		
—	Car Cover Bag	6	10
	Dealer installed accessory.		
—	Cargo Bin (Wagon)	84	130
	Dealer installed accessory.		
—	Cargo Net (Wagon)	23	35
	Dealer installed accessory.		
—	Compartment Sep/Dog Guard (Wagon)	91	140
	Dealer installed accessory.		
—	Cooler/Warmer (Wagon)	91	103
	Dealer installed accessory.		
—	Engine Block Heater	19	30
	Dealer installed accessory.		
—	Full Front End Cover	78	120
	Dealer installed accessory.		
—	Hood Front End Cover	32	50
	Dealer installed accessory.		
—	Integrated Child Safety Seat (Base Wagon)	180	200
	Dealer installed accessory.		
—	Kayak Carrier (Limited Sedan)	83	127
	Dealer installed accessory. Includes kayak and roof basket mounting clamps.		
—	Kayak Carrier (Flat Cross Bars) (Wagon)	83	127
	Dealer installed accessory. Includes bike, kayak and roof basket mounting clamps.		
—	Kayak Carrier (Round Cross Bars) (Wagon)	83	127
	Dealer installed accessory. Includes ski, kayak and roof basket mounting clamps.		
—	Leather Shift Knob - A/T (Base Wagon)	38	59
	Dealer installed accessory. REQUIRES 4AT.		
—	Leather Shift Knob - M/T (Base Wagon)	32	49
	Dealer installed accessory.		
—	Lighter Element	5	8
	Dealer installed accessory.		
—	Logic Control CD Player (Base Wagon)	251	335
	Dealer installed accessory.		
—	Moonroof Air Deflector (Limited Sedan)	28	43
	Dealer installed accessory.		
—	Power Outlet (Base Wagon)	32	50
	Dealer installed accessory. REQUIRES 4AT.		
—	Rear Bumper Corner Molding (2 Pair)	38	58
	Dealer installed accessory.		
—	Rear Differential Protector	45	70
	Dealer installed accessory.		
—	Rear Gate Bar (Wagon)	29	45
	Dealer installed accessory.		

SUBARU — LEGACY OUTBACK

CODE	DESCRIPTION	INVOICE	MSRP
—	Rear Window Dust Deflector (Wagon)	52	80
	Dealer installed accessory.		
—	Roof Cargo Basket (Limited Sedan)	84	130
	Dealer installed accessory. Includes kayak and roof basket mounting clamps.		
—	Roof Cargo Basket (Cross Bars) (Wagon)	84	130
	Dealer installed accessory. Includes bike, kayak and roof basket mounting clamps.		
—	Roof Cargo Basket (Round Cross Bars) (Wagon)	84	130
	Dealer installed accessory. Includes ski, kayak and roof basket mounting clamps.		
—	Roof Cargo Carrier (Wagon)	296	395
	Dealer installed accessory.		
—	Round Cross Bar Set (Wagon)	104	160
	Dealer installed accessory.		
—	Rubber Floor Mats	32	50
	Dealer installed accessory.		
—	SD Color-Keyed Spoiler (Limited Sedan)	198	305
	Dealer installed accessory.		
—	SD Primed Spoiler (Limited Sedan)	162	250
	Dealer installed accessory.		
—	SW Color-Keyed Spoiler (Wagon)	179	275
	Dealer installed accessory.		
—	SW Primed Spoiler (Wagon - Bass/Limited)	130	200
	Dealer installed accessory.		
—	Security System Upgrade	99	152
	Dealer installed accessory.		
—	Square Sedan Cross Bar Set (Limited Sedan)	117	180
	Dealer installed accessory.		
—	Stabilizing Brackets (4) (Wagon)	26	40
	Dealer installed accessory.		
—	Subwoofer/Amplifier	149	228
	Dealer installed accessory.		
—	Trailer Hitch (Wagon)	172	264
	Dealer installed accessory.		
—	Trunk Net (Limited Sedan)	17	26
	Dealer installed accessory.		
—	Tweeter Kit (Base Wagon)	60	92
	Dealer installed accessory.		
—	Upgraded Speakers (Base Wagon)	105	162
	Dealer installed accessory.		
—	Woodgrained Patterned Door Switches	55	85
	Dealer installed accessory.		
4AT	Transmission: Electronic 4-Speed Auto (Base Wagon)	722	800
	Includes 4.44 axle ratio.		
4AT	Transmission: Electronic 4-Speed Auto (Limited)	722	800
	Includes 4.44 axle ratio.		
DEST	Destination Surcharge for Alaska	190	190
DEST	Destination Surcharge for New York/New Jersey	40	40
	New York state and the following New Jersey counties: Bergen, Passaic, Sussex, Warren, Morris, Essex, Hudson, Union, Middlesex, Sommerset and Hunterdon.		

LEGACY OUTBACK — SUBARU

CODE	DESCRIPTION	INVOICE	MSRP
DYA	Upgraded Speakers (Base Wagon)	134	206
DYB	Tweeter Kit (Base Wagon)	65	100
DYC	Subwoofer/Amplifier (Wagon)	174	267
EYA	CD Player (Base Wagon)	271	361
	Includes logic control.		
EYC	6-Disc In-Dash CD Changer (Wagon)	390	520
IYA	Woodgrained Patterned Trim (Wagon)	65	100
IYB	A/T Leather Shift Knob (Base Wagon)	44	67
	REQUIRES 4AT.		
KYA	Air Filtration System (Wagon)	41	62
KYE	Auto Dimming Mirror (Limited Sedan)	119	183
KYE	Auto-Dimming Mirror (Base/Limited/VDC Wagon)	119	183
L01	Rough Road Group (Wagon)	161	259
	Manufacturer Discount	(16)	NC
	Net Price	145	259
	Includes acrylic hood deflector, rear differential protector and rear window dust deflector.		
L04	Premium Sound Package 1B (Base Wagon)	644	934
	Manufacturer Discount	(119)	(239)
	Net Price	525	695
	Includes CD player, upgraded speakers, tweeter kit and subwoofer/amplifier.		
L05	Premium Sound Package 2 (Base Wagon)	763	1093
	Manufacturer Discount	(163)	(298)
	Net Price	600	795
	Includes 6-disc in-dash CD changer, upgraded speakers, tweeter kit and subwoofer/amplifier.		
L06	Premium Sound Package 3 (Limited)	564	787
	Manufacturer Discount	(89)	(152)
	Net Price	475	635
	Includes 6-disc in-dash CD changer and subwoofer/amplifier.		
L6C	Popular Equipment Group 6 (Wagon)	243	373
	Manufacturer Discount	(14)	NC
	Net Price	229	373
	Includes security system upgrade.		
LSB	M/T Leather Shift Knob (Base Wagon)	38	58
LWI	Moonroof Air Deflector (Limited Sedan)	41	63
LYA	Rear Gate Bar (Wagon)	45	69
LYC	Rear Window Dust Deflector (Wagon)	69	105
LYH	Trailer Hitch (Wagon)	192	295
MSV	Alloy Wheel Locks	25	38
MYC	Trunk Net (Limited Sedan)	21	32
MYD	Cargo Net (Wagon)	31	48
NYA	Power Outlet (Base Wagon)	58	89
	REQUIRES 4AT.		
PYA	Rear Differential Protector	54	82
PYC	Acrylic Hood Deflector	38	72
R1D	Security System Upgrade	124	190
RYC	Security System Upgrade (Wagon)	124	190
S— —	SW White Color-Keyed Spoiler (Wagon)	192	295
S— —	SD Color-Keyed Spoiler (Limited Sedan)	212	325

EDMUNDS® NEW CARS

SUZUKI

ESTEEM

2001 ESTEEM

What's New?

In an effort to ply prospective Esteem buyers, Suzuki has equipped every model with an in-dash CD player. Stereo head units also get larger controls. Elsewhere, you will find gentle cosmetic changes: The front grille has been restyled, the seats are wrapped in a new fabric and floor mats are standard. Sky Blue Metallic is no longer available as an exterior color.

Review

There is nothing really objectionable about the Esteem sedan and wagon, but the economy car segment is not what it used to be - at least not since a Focus and a fresh batch of Sentras, Proteges and Elantras arrived. Now, it seems that customers are looking for value (!), socially acceptable aesthetics and a bit of driving amusement. The Esteem has been around since 1995, and it has never been able to deliver all three, though advertising (that ideally, would get people into the dealerships) has not been especially heavy-handed, either. Slowly, Suzuki has enhanced the Esteem, but we're not sure that the company is moving expediently enough to rescue the car from the cellar of the segment in sales.

One of these improvements came last year when Suzuki made the 1.8-liter DOHC four-cylinder engine standard on all models. This engine makes 122 horsepower at 6,300 rpm and 117 foot-pounds of torque at 3,500 rpm. These numbers are competitive for this class, but we've observed more engine roar in the Esteem from 4,000 to 6,800 rpm than we have in its peers. The noise isn't obnoxious - there is simply more of it.

We've found ride quality acceptable on highways and city streets, at least until the Esteem encounters a pothole or an expansion joint. We suspect that its inability to soak these up has to do with its low-tech suspension setup - MacPherson struts at each corner and a single antiroll bar in the front. Wagons get a second antiroll bar in the rear.

You can buy a sedan or a wagon in one of three trim levels. Base-level GL cars are outfitted with air conditioning, power steering, rear window defogger, fold-down rear seat, breakaway mirrors - and for 2001, floor mats and an in-dash CD player. The addition of this audio essential could help move more Esteems off the lot - among its peers, only the Focus offers this nicety in base models. In comparison, Mazda offers only stereo pre-wiring in the Protege DX. The only option for base models is an automatic transmission. GLX trim offers the most desirable content package: besides the GL bits, you get upgraded upholstery; remote keyless entry; power windows, mirrors and locks; split-folding rear seat and cool alloy wheels. You can option the sedan with a sport package (rear spoiler, fog lights, chrome-tipped exhausts and blue or silver body color).

Now, if only Suzuki would revise its option packages, or allow buyers to purchase certain features a la carte. You see, you have to splurge on top-line GLX+ trim to get "extras" like ABS and cruise control. Or perhaps you want all the goodies of GLX+ trim, except the mandatory automatic transmission. Given this requirement, a bigger engine should be part of the package as well. Despite this rather serious packaging flaw, you can build yourself a rather stunning small wagon if you opt for the two-tone paint (available on GLX+ wagons) - silver under-cladding with a Deep Space Blue or Polar White upper body. GLX+ models also have cassette players along with the in-dash CD.

Esteem interiors are user-friendly and solidly constructed, but they don't make you forget how little you paid. Occupants will find the expected amount of plastic and seats that are reasonably comfortable but lack height adjustment and adequate seatback tilt. Nor does the steering wheel have a tilt or telescope adjustment.

The Esteem's exterior styling might not gouge the sensibilities (in the way that the Focus does), but the mild-mannered may find it pleasant. Suzuki has retouched the grille slightly for

ESTEEM SUZUKI

2001—the additional horizontal slats give the hood a slightly flatter appearance, which we like. GLX and GLX+ models come with trendy 15-inch wheels, which have 195/55VR15 Yokohama tires wrapped around them. The tires are an unexpected treat in the economy car class, because they are large for the size and weight of the vehicle and they are biased toward performance rather than fuel economy. We've observed the payoff in grip when pushing this car around corners.

Our chief concern about the Suzuki Esteem is the lack of value—pricing is high, the trim packaging makes it difficult to tailor a car to your needs and the warranty is weak. Still, the Esteem is an attractive car with no serious faults, so if you negotiate an extra nice deal on one, you might enjoy it. We encourage you to compare it with similarly equipped peers, though, before you buy.

Standard Equipment

GL SEDAN (5M): 1.8L I4 DOHC MPI 16-valve engine; 5-speed OD manual transmission; 390 amp battery; engine oil cooler; 70 amp alternator; front-wheel drive, 3.79 axle ratio; stainless steel exhaust; front independent strut suspension with anti-roll bar, front coil springs, rear independent strut suspension with rear coil springs; power rack-and-pinion steering; front disc/rear drum brakes; 12.7 gal. capacity fuel tank; side impact bars; front and rear body-colored bumpers; black bodyside molding; clearcoat monotone paint; aero-composite halogen headlamps with daytime running lights; driver's and passenger's manual black folding outside mirrors; 14" x 5.5" steel wheels; P185/60SR14 BSW A/S tires; compact steel spare wheel; air conditioning, rear heat ducts; premium AM/FM stereo radio, seek-scan, single CD player, 4 speakers, manual retractable antenna; child safety rear door locks, remote hatch/trunk release, remote fuel release; 1 power accessory outlet, driver's foot rest; instrumentation display includes water temperature gauge, in-dash clock, trip odometer; warning indicators include oil pressure, battery, lights on, key in ignition; driver's and passenger's front airbags; tinted windows, manual front and rear windows; variable intermittent front windshield wipers, rear window defroster; seating capacity of 5, front bucket seats with fixed headrests, center armrest with storage, driver's and passenger's seats include 4-way adjustment; full folding rear bench seat with adjustable headrests; front height adjustable seatbelts; cloth seats, cloth door trim insert, full cloth headliner, full carpet floor covering; interior lights include dome light; day/night rearview mirror; full floor console, glove box, front cupholder, driver's and passenger's door bins; carpeted cargo floor; chrome grille, chrome side window moldings, black front windshield molding, black rear window molding and black door handles.

GL WAGON (5M) (in addition to or instead of GL SEDAN (4A) equipment): 3.72 axle ratio; roof rack; rear window wiper, cargo cover, cargo tie downs and concealed cargo storage.

GLX SEDAN/ WAGON (5M) (in addition to or instead of GL SEDAN/ WAGON (5M) equipment): Front and rear mud flaps, side impact bars; driver's and passenger's power remote black folding outside mirrors; 15" x 5.5" silver alloy wheels; P195/55SR15 BSW A/S tires; power door locks, remote keyless entry; instrumentation display includes tachometer; power front and rear windows with driver's 1-touch down; 60/40 folding rear bench seat with adjustable headrests; interior lights include illuminated entry; passenger's side vanity mirror; 2 seat back storage pockets; carpeted cargo floor and cargo light.

GLX+ SEDAN/ WAGON (4A) (in addition to or instead of GLX SEDAN/ WAGON (5M) equipment): 4-speed electronic OD automatic transmission with lock-up torque converter; 3.85 axle ratio; front disc/rear drum brakes with 4-wheel antilock brakes and cruise control.

Base Prices

CODE	DESCRIPTION	INVOICE	MSRP
SGL77C1	GL 1.8 Sedan (5M)	12671	13199
SGL7751	GLX 1.8 Sedan (5M)	13439	13999
SGL78G1	GLX+ 1.8 Sedan (4A)	15167	15799
WGN77C1	GL 1.8 Wagon (5M)	13151	13699

SUZUKI

ESTEEM / SWIFT

CODE	DESCRIPTION	INVOICE	MSRP
WGN77E1	GLX 1.8 Wagon (5M)	13919	14499
WGM78F1	GLX+ 1.8 Wagon (4A)	15839	16499
Destination Charge:		480	480

Interested in seeing what dealers will sell this vehicle for? Check out our True Market Value^{sm} (TMV^{sm}) pricing on our Web site at www.edmunds.com.

Accessories

—	Cruise Control (GLX)	192	200
—	Protective Floor Carpeting	45	75
—	Sport Package (GLX Sedan)	720	900
	Includes center arm rest, color keyed rear spoiler, fog lights, chrome exhaust tip and cruise control.		
—	Transmission: Electric 4-Speed Auto with OD (GL/GLX)	960	1000
	Includes 3.78 axle ratio.		
—	Two-Tone Paint (GLX+ Wagon)	178	200

2001 SWIFT

What's New?

The 2001 Suzuki Swift remains mechanically unchanged. Suzuki has changed the exterior color options slightly: Bright White and Platinum Silver Metallic replace Polar White and Mercury Silver Metallic.

Review

Last year, we wrote, "This is it. This is the car for those of you who need to buy a new vehicle but don't have much more than the lint in your pockets to spend." But since then, the redesigned Hyundai Accent and the all-new Kia Rio have arrived on the scene, and both offer more powerful engines, more amenities and better dollar value. Even the Daewoo Lanos, the thriftiest product of a troubled manufacturer, has a more appealing package than the Swift.

Calling Suzuki's entry-level hatchback "Swift" borders on false advertising. Its tiny 1.3-liter four-cylinder engine generates just 79 horsepower at 6,000 rpm and 75 foot-pounds of torque at 3,000 rpm. Of course, this engine is used in both Swift models, while the more expensive base Chevrolet Metro (the Swift's twin) makes do with a 55-horsepower, 1.0-liter engine.

Meanwhile, the base Hyundai Accent hatchback comes with a 92-horsepower, 1.3-liter engine, and for little more you can have the hardier 105-horsepower, 1.6-liter engine. The Kia Rio sedan, the cheapest car sold in the United States, offers a 1.5-liter that makes 96 horsepower. The Daewoo Lanos models share a 105-horsepower, 1.6-liter. And all of these cars reach their peak horsepower at lower rpm than the Swift, though the little Suzuki sucks out its maximum torque earlier than all of its peers.

We've said before that, if nothing else, the Swift draws customers with the promise that you can put one in your driveway for less than $10,000. But the Swift isn't alone anymore. The Kia Rio and the base Accent and Lanos models all sticker under $9,000 and offer standard power steering; Accent and Lanos also come with an AM/FM stereo with cassette. You can add air conditioning and ABS to all three models.

SWIFT — SUZUKI

A base Swift GA has an MSRP of just over $9,000, but it doesn't come with power steering. The GA hatchback cannot be optioned with a stereo, air conditioning or ABS, either. Move up to the GL trim level and you'll get a stereo with a mere two speakers and air conditioning but still no power steering or ABS - and you're looking at an MSRP of over $10,000. The only factory-installed option for the Swift is a three-speed automatic transmission.

You'll also find that Suzuki's peers offer far better warranties. Hyundais and Kias come with a best-in-class five-year/60,000-mile basic warranty and a 10-year/100,000-mile powertrain warranty. Daewoos have shorter warranties (three-year/36,000-mile basic and five-year/60,000-mile drivetrain), but customers are treated to free scheduled maintenance for the first year of ownership. And Suzuki is the only manufacturer in the group that does not offer roadside assistance.

So what's left to make the Swift an appealing economy car? Excellent gas mileage - no other gas-powered car in the segment can match its 36 mpg in the city and 42 mpg on the highway. Reliability ratings are encouraging, too. And strangely enough, every Swift is equipped with daytime running lights. Your dealer can also install a CD player to make the car more hospitable.

We agree that the Swift is inexpensive and reliable, and for those who want fabulous fuel economy, it may be a suitable choice. However, buyers should be cautioned that loaded Hyundais and Kias with attractive warranties can be had for about the same price, as can a used Honda.

Standard Equipment

GA (5M): 1.3L I4 SOHC MPI 16-valve engine; 5-speed OD manual transmission; engine oil cooler; front-wheel drive, 3.79 axle ratio; stainless steel exhaust; front independent strut suspension with anti-roll bar, front coil springs, rear independent strut suspension with anti-roll bar, rear coil springs; manual rack-and-pinion steering; front disc/rear drum brakes; 10.3 gal. capacity fuel tank; side impact bars; front and rear black bumpers; black bodyside molding; clearcoat monotone paint; aero-composite halogen headlamps with daytime running lights; driver's and passenger's manual black folding outside mirrors; 13" x 4.5" steel wheels; P155/80SR13 BSW A/S tires; compact steel spare wheel; manual retractable antenna; 1 power accessory outlet, driver's foot rest; instrumentation display includes tachometer, water temperature gauge, trip odometer; warning indicators include oil pressure, battery, lights on, key in ignition; driver's and passenger's front airbags; tinted windows; variable intermittent front windshield wipers, rear window wiper, rear window defroster; seating capacity of 4, front bucket seats with fixed headrests, driver's and passenger's seats include 4-way adjustment; full folding rear bench seat; front height adjustable seatbelts; cloth seats, vinyl door trim insert, full cloth headliner, full carpet floor covering; interior lights include dome light; passenger's side vanity mirror; day/night rearview mirror; full floor console, glove box, front cupholder, instrument panel bin, driver's and passenger's door bins; carpeted cargo floor, cargo cover; black side window moldings, black front windshield molding, black rear window molding and black door handles.

GL (5M) (in addition to or instead of GA (5M) equipment): Air conditioning; AM/FM stereo radio, seek-scan, cassette player, 2 speakers and manual retractable antenna.

Base Prices

		Invoice	MSRP
HES5321	GA (5M)	8741	9299
HES5331	GL (5M)	9681	10299
Destination Charge:		430	430

Interested in seeing what dealers will sell this vehicle for? Check out our True Market Value^{sm} (TMV^{sm}) pricing on our Web site at www.edmunds.com.

Accessories

		Invoice	MSRP
—	Air Conditioning (GA)	681	800
—	Transmission: 3-Speed Automatic	611	650

TOYOTA — AVALON

2001 AVALON

What's New?

Two colors, Cognac Brown and Constellation Blue Pearl, are dumped for 2001, and an emergency trunk release has been added. No other changes have been made to this imitation Buick, which was completely redesigned last year.

Review

It would seem buyers of full-sized sedans generally aren't interested in character. Most big four-doors are dull pieces of machinery to look at and a snooze to drive. The beauty in such a vehicle lies in what it can do for the customer in terms of providing space for people and things without compromising the ride or occupant comfort. It should look upscale, but not gaudy, providing just enough glitz and luxury to let others know you have achieved a degree of success in life. Finally, such a vehicle must also be reliable and able to handle years of daily-driver tasks without so much as a whimper.

Since its introduction in 1995, the Toyota Avalon has fit this description: bland as egg whites, but solid, roomy, and dependable. Last year, the Avalon was redesigned. Substantial changes improved its already attractive qualities, but its mission in the grand scheme of things, ersatz Buick, remained the same.

There are two models to choose from: XL and XLS. The main difference between the two is the level of standard equipment, with XLS representing the more luxurious version with JBL audio, programmable HomeLink remote system, remote keyless entry, and aluminum wheels. Either can be ordered with front bucket or bench seats trimmed in available leather upholstery.

Avalon's 3.0-liter V6 engine features a variable valve timing system (Toyota calls its system VVT-i). It provides additional horsepower, improved fuel economy and torque, lower emissions and smoother shifting. The previous Avalon was no slouch in the power department, so the recent engine improvements are icing on an already refined cake.

Toyota also updated the styling. A side benefit of this is a reduction in noise, vibration and harshness (NVH), not that it was a substantial problem in the first place. There's also increased trunk volume, grocery bag hooks, and a larger storage tray and cargo net.

Vehicle Skid Control (VSC), which includes traction and stability control systems, can be added to Avalon XLS. VSC utilizes the braking system to correct understeer or oversteer conditions in a turn. Traction control reduces tire slippage during acceleration. Avalon also features a brake-assist system that detects emergency braking and applies supplemental line pressure to reduce stopping distances.

Other safety features include a body structure that effectively absorbs and diffuses energy along predictable paths, energy-absorbing material in the roof rails, front pillar and center pillar to help reduce potential head injury, and super-sized rearview mirrors.

With Avalon, Toyota meets and exceeds the full-size sedan buyer's expectations. Sure, the price is higher than offerings from Detroit like the Buick LeSabre, Chrysler Concorde and Mercury Grand Marquis. But unflappable quality doesn't come cheap. Want a Lexus but need six-passenger capacity or huge amounts of rear legroom? The Avalon is your car.

Standard Equipment

XL (4A): 3L V6 DOHC MPI 24-valve engine with variable valve timing (requires premium unleaded fuel); 4-speed electronic OD automatic transmission with lock-up torque converter; HD battery with run down protection; HD starter; HD alternator; front-wheel drive, 3.63 axle ratio; stainless steel exhaust with tailpipe finisher; front independent strut suspension with anti-roll

AVALON — TOYOTA

bar, front coil springs, gas-pressurized front shocks, rear independent strut suspension with anti-roll bar, rear coil springs, gas-pressurized rear shocks; rack-and-pinion power steering with engine speed-sensing assist; 4-wheel antilock disc brakes; 18.5 gal. capacity fuel tank; side impact bars; front and rear body-colored bumpers with chrome bumper insert; body-colored bodyside molding with chrome bodyside insert; clearcoat monotone paint; aero-composite halogen fully auto headlamps with daytime running lights; driver's and passenger's power remote body-colored outside mirrors; 15" x 6" steel wheels; P205/65HR15 BSW A/S tires; full-size steel spare wheel; dual-zone front air conditioning; AM/FM stereo radio, seek-scan feature, cassette player, single-disc CD player, 6 speakers, theft deterrent, window grid antenna cruise control with steering wheel controls; power door locks with 2-stage unlock, child-safety rear door locks, remote hatch/trunk release, remote fuel door release; 2 power accessory outlets, front lighter element(s), driver's foot rest, retained accessory power, smokers' package; instrumentation display includes tachometer, water temperature gauge, in-dash clock, exterior temp, trip odometer; warning indicators include oil pressure, battery, key in ignition, low fuel, bulb failure, door ajar; driver's and passenger's front airbags, driver's and front passenger's seat-mounted side airbags; tinted windows, power front and rear windows with driver's 1-touch down function; variable-speed intermittent front windshield wipers, sun visor strip, rear window defroster; seating capacity of 5, front bucket seats with adjustable headrests, center armrest with storage, driver and passenger seats include 6-way adjustment; rear bench seat with adjustable headrests, center pass-thru armrest; height-adjustable front seatbelts with pretensioners; cloth seats, cloth door trim insert, full cloth headliner, full carpet floor covering, chrome interior accents; interior lights include dome light, front reading lights; steering wheel with tilt adjustment; dual illuminated vanity mirrors, dual auxiliary visors; day/night rearview mirror; full floor console, mini overhead console with storage, locking glove box with light, front and rear cupholders, driver's and passenger's door bins, rear door bins; carpeted cargo floor, carpeted trunk lid, cargo light; chrome grille, chrome side window moldings, black front windshield molding, chrome rear window molding and body-colored door handles.

XLS (4A) (in addition to or instead of XL (4A) equipment): Additional exterior lights include front fog/driving lights; driver's and passenger's power remote body-colored heated outside mirrors; dual-zone front air conditioning with climate control, air filter, rear heat ducts; premium AM/FM stereo radio, seek-scan feature, cassette player, single-disc CD player, 7 premium speakers, remote keyless entry, power remote hatch/trunk release; garage door opener; additional instrumentation display includes compass, trip computer; additional warning indicators include low washer fluid; ignition disable, panic alarm, security system; driver and passenger seats include 8-way power adjustment, power 2-way lumbar support; center pass-thru armrest with storage; premium cloth seats, simulated wood dashboard insert, leather-wrapped gearshift knob, simulated wood door panel insert, simulated wood console insert; interior lights include dome light with fade, front and rear reading lights, 2 door curb lights, illuminated entry; leather-wrapped steering wheel with tilt adjustment; auto-dimming day/night rearview mirror; 2 seatback storage pockets and cargo net.

Base Prices

Code	Description	Invoice	MSRP
3534	Avalon XL (4A)	23000	25845
3544	Avalon XLS (4A)	26756	30405
	Destination Charge:	455	455

Interested in seeing what dealers will sell this vehicle for? Check out our True Market Value^{sm} (TMV^{sm}) pricing on our Web site at www.edmunds.com.

Accessories

Code	Description	Invoice	MSRP
—	Split Bench Seat (XL)	730	820
	Includes floor console delete and increased curb weight. NOT AVAILABLE with GH, GI, GK, LF.		

TOYOTA — *AVALON*

CODE	DESCRIPTION	INVOICE	MSRP
—	Split Bench Seat (XLS)	(88)	(100)
	Includes floor console delete and Decreased curb weight. NOT AVAILABLE with LA.		
B8	5-Spoke Star Alloy Wheel Locks (XL)	31	52
	REQUIRES S5. NOT AVAILABLE with S6, SS.		
B9	15" Mesh Alloy Wheel Locks (XL)	31	52
	REQUIRES S6. NOT AVAILABLE with S5, SS.		
C7	Convenience Package	610	998
	Includes auto-dimming mirror, wood dash and v.i.p. RS 3200 deluxe security system. REQUIRES GH or GI or GJ or GK.		
C7	Convenience Package	195	331
	Includes gold package, alloy wheel locks and glass breakage sensor (GBS).		
CF	Carpet/Cargo Mat Set (5 Piece Set)	97	159
DJ	JBL 3 In 1 Premium Combo (XL)	270	360
	Includes AM/FM cass/CD with 7 speakers. REQUIRES GH or GI or (BENCH) Split Bench Seat. NOT AVAILABLE with LG, FG, GJ.		
DU	Wood Dash (Bucket/Bench) (XL)	299	519
FB	Fabric Seat Trim with Bench Seat (XLS)	NC	NC
	REQUIRES (BENCH) Split Bench Seat. NOT AVAILABLE with LA, LB, GL, GU, GV.		
FG	Fabric Seat Trim with Bench Seat (XL)	NC	NC
	REQUIRES (BENCH) Split Bench Seat. NOT AVAILABLE with LF, LG, GK, DJ, GH, GI.		
GH	Package 1 (XL)	828	1035
	Includes power seat package and keyless entry. NOT AVAILABLE with GI, GJ, GK, LF, LG, FG.		
GI	Package 2 (XL)	1136	1420
	Includes power seat package, keyless entry and 15" x 6" aluminum wheels. NOT AVAILABLE with GH, GJ, GK, LF, LG, FG, S5, S6, SS, WZ, WS.		
GJ	Package 3 (XL)	536	670
	Includes keyless entry and 15" x 6" aluminum wheels. REQUIRES (BENCH) Split Bench Seat. NOT AVAILABLE with GH, GI, GK, LF, DJ, S5, S6, SS, WZ, WS.		
GK	Leather Package 3 (XL)	2072	2590
	Includes leather trim package, leather seat trim with bucket seats, leather shift knob, leather steering wheel, leather power seats, keyless entry and 15" x 6" aluminum wheels. NOT AVAILABLE with GH, GI, GJ, FG, S5, S6, SS, WZ, WS.		
GK	Leather Package 4 (XL)	1456	1820
	Includes leather trim package, leather seat trim with bench seat, leather steering wheel, keyless entry and 15" x 6" aluminum wheels. REQUIRES (BENCH) Split Bench Seat. NOT AVAILABLE with GH, GI, GJ, FG, S5, S6, SS, WZ, WS.		
GL	Package 5 (XLS)	1100	1375
	Includes leather trim package with memory, leather seat trim with bucket seats, 16" x 6" aluminum wheels, P205/60R16 A/S tires. NOT AVAILABLE with GU, GV, GW, FB.		
GN	Cargo Net (XL)	30	45
GP	Gold Package	89	164
GU	Package 6 (XLS)	1288	1625
	Includes leather trim package with memory, leather seat trim with bucket seats, 16" x 6" aluminum wheels, P205/60R16 A/S tires; JBL 3 in 1 premium with in-dash changer. NOT AVAILABLE with GL, GV, GW, FB.		

AVALON / CAMRY — TOYOTA

CODE	DESCRIPTION	INVOICE	MSRP
GV	**Package 7 (XLS)**	1540	1940
	Includes leather trim package with heat and memory, leather seat trim with bucket seats, heated seats, 16" x 6" aluminum wheels, P205/60R16 A/S tires; JBL 3 in 1 premium with in-dash changer. NOT AVAILABLE with GL, GU, GW, FB.		
GW	**Package 8 (XLS)**	252	330
	Includes 16" x 6" aluminum wheels, P205/60R16 A/S tires; JBL 3 in 1 premium with in-dash changer. NOT AVAILABLE with GL, GU, GV, LA, LB.		
LA	**Leather Seat Trim with Bucket Seats (XLS)**	NC	NC
	NOT AVAILABLE with FB, LB, GW.		
LB	**Leather Seat Trim with Bench Seat (XLS)**	NC	NC
	REQUIRES (BENCH) Split Bench Seat. NOT AVAILABLE with FB, LA, GW.		
LF	**Leather Seat Trim with Bucket Seats (XL)**	NC	NC
	NOT AVAILABLE with FG, LG, GJ, GI, GH.		
LG	**Leather Seat Trim with Bench Seat (XL)**	NC	NC
	REQUIRES (BENCH) Split Bench Seat. NOT AVAILABLE with LF, FG, DJ, GH, GI.		
N1	**Auto-Dimming Mirror (XL)**	166	240
PC	**Special Color**	187	220
S5	**Wheels: 15" 5-Spoke Star Style Alloy (XL)**	549	699
	NOT AVAILABLE with S6, SS, B9, GI, GJ, GK, WZ, WS.		
S6	**Wheels: 15" Mesh Style Alloy (XL)**	600	799
	NOT AVAILABLE with S5, SS, B8, GI, GJ, GK, WZ, WS.		
SR	**Power Moonroof with Tilt and Slide**	728	910
SS	**Wheels: 15" 5-Spoke Split Alloy (XL)**	440	592
	NOT AVAILABLE with S5, S6, B8, B9, GI, GJ, GK, WS.		
V2	**Glass Breakage Sensor (GBS) (XLS)**	75	115
V5	**V.I.P. RS3200 Deluxe Security System (XL)**	155	249
	REQUIRES GH or GI or GJ or GK.		
VD	**Vehicle Stability Control (XLS)**	680	850
	Includes traction control.		
WL	**Alloy Wheel Locks**	31	52
WS	**Steel Wheel Locks (XL)**	31	52
	NOT AVAILABLE with S5, S6, SS, GI, GJ, GK.		
WZ	**15" Alloy Wheel Locks (XL)**	31	52
	REQUIRES SS. NOT AVAILABLE with S6, S5, GI, GJ, GK.		

NOTE: Toyotas sold in Alabama, Florida, Georgia, North Carolina and South Carolina may be equipped with option packages not listed in this guide. You can expect to haggle 25% off the window sticker price on these packages.

2001 CAMRY

What's New?

A new special edition Gallery Series model is offered on LE models, including two-tone paint and interior trim, fake carbon fiber trim on the dash, chrome and leather cabin accents, and special alloy wheels. Want air conditioning, power windows/locks/mirrors and variable intermittent wipers on the CE? Buy the Value Package. To get remote keyless entry or a power driver's seat on the LE, you must buy a Value Package. A power moonroof and six-disc in-dash CD changer requires the Leather Value Package on XLE models. CE models have new wheelcovers, LE

TOYOTA   *CAMRY*

V6 models get standard daytime running lights and JBL audio is newly optional on all LEs. The anti-theft system with engine immobilizer is restricted to XLE V6 models.

Review

The Toyota Camry is one of America's most-favored mid-size sedans. The reasons are simple. It boasts room for five adults, can be ordered with a powerful and smooth-revving V6, and comes with the reputation of solid Toyota reliability. But can you believe the recent "I'm Too Sexy" advertising campaign? Featuring the lead singer from one-hit-wonder band Right Said Fred, the TV ads proclaim that the Camry is too sexy for a number of things, including drive-thrus, car washes and dry cleaning pick-up runs. So, uh, what are you supposed to use the innocuously styled sedan for? Picking up hot dates? Running Laguna Seca? Impressing the Joneses?

Camry can be equipped for everything from rugged family life or plush luxury touring, but nothing particularly sexy. Club hopping and canyon carving are not on the menu, though Toyota Racing Development (TRD - how sexy is that acronym? Further evidence supporting our case for truthfulness in advertising.) will sell you a kit that turns this grocery-getter into a competent handler.

There are three different trims: base-level CE, mid-level LE, and the top-level XLE. New for 2001 is the LE Gallery Series model, with special trimmings such as two-tone paint, unique alloy wheels, and fake carbon fiber interior decor. LE and XLE can be equipped with a delicious 3.0-liter V6 engine, which produces 200 horsepower and 214 foot-pounds of torque. Acceleration is impressive, and unlike six-pot Honda Accords and Mitsubishi Galants, the Camry LE V6 can be ordered with a manual transmission. Pop the TRD components on, and you've got a hell of a sleeper. Braking is swift and sure with the antilock system, and Camry hangs on well in corners despite rather meek all-season radials and substantial body roll. This car is tuned for a soft, quiet ride out of the factory.

Inside, controls and gauges are laid-out nicely in a dated but ergonomically correct dashboard. The switches and stalks all exhibit a solid heft, imparting a sense of quality. Abundant storage areas include a deep center console, door bins, and dashboard bins. Front cupholders accommodate 20-ounce bottles of your favorite beverage. The only downside to this cabin is that you might find the seats uncomfortable.

Notable options include side airbags, traction control, a JBL sound system, leather interior trim, and a power moonroof. ABS is standard on LE and XLE models equipped with a V6 engine.

For 2001, Toyota has juggled value package content and stand-alone option availability. Want air conditioning and power windows/locks/mirrors on the CE? How about remote keyless entry or a power driver's seat on the LE? Don't forget a power moonroof and six-disc in-dash CD changer on an XLE. All require the purchase of a Value Package. A JBL audio system is newly optional on all LEs, and an anti-theft system with engine immobilizer is restricted to XLE V6 models.

Overall, Camry works well as a family sedan. Fully optioned, it's considerably more expensive than domestic competitors, but given the Camry's best-seller status, it seems most Americans consider this Toyota to be a worthwhile expenditure.

Standard Equipment

CE (5M): 2.2L I4 DOHC MPI 16-valve engine; 5-speed OD manual transmission; 582 amp HD battery; 80 amp HD alternator; front-wheel drive, 3.94 axle ratio; stainless steel exhaust; front independent strut suspension with anti-roll bar, front coil springs, gas-pressurized front shocks,

CAMRY

rear independent strut suspension with anti-roll bar, rear coil springs, gas-pressurized rear shocks; rack-and-pinion power steering with engine speed-sensing assist; front disc/rear drum brakes; 18.5 gal. capacity fuel tank; side impact bars; front and rear body-colored bumpers; body-colored bodyside molding; monotone paint; aero-composite halogen auto off headlamps; driver's and passenger's manual remote black outside mirrors; 14" x 5.5" steel wheels; P195/70SR14 BSW A/S tires; full-size steel spare wheel; rear heat ducts; AM/FM stereo radio, seek-scan feature, cassette player, single-disc CD player, 4 speakers, window grid antenna; child-safety rear door locks, remote hatch/trunk release, remote fuel door release; 2 power accessory outlets, front lighter element(s), driver's foot rest, smokers' package; instrumentation display includes tachometer, water temperature gauge, in-dash clock, exterior temp, trip odometer; warning indicators include oil pressure, battery, key in ignition, low fuel, bulb failure, door ajar; driver's and passenger's front airbags; tinted windows, manual front and rear windows; fixed interval front windshield wipers, sun visor strip, rear window defroster; seating capacity of 5, front bucket seats with adjustable headrests, center armrest with storage, driver's and passenger's seats include 4-way adjustment; 60/40 folding rear bench seat with adjustable headrests, center armrest; height-adjustable front seatbelts with pretensioners; cloth seats, cloth door trim insert, full cloth headliner, full carpet floor covering; interior lights include dome light; steering wheel with tilt adjustment; vanity mirrors, dual auxiliary visors; day/night rearview mirror; full floor console, mini overhead console with storage, locking glove box with light, front and rear cupholders, instrument panel bin, driver's and passenger's door bins; vinyl cargo floor, cargo light; chrome grille, chrome side window moldings, black front windshield molding, chrome rear window molding and body-colored door handles.

LE (4A) (in addition to or instead of CE (5M) equipment): 4-speed electronic OD automatic transmission with lock-up torque converter; driver's and passenger's power remote body-colored outside mirrors; 15" x 6" steel wheels; P205/65HR15 BSW A/S tires; air conditioning; AM/FM stereo radio, seek-scan feature, cassette player, single-disc CD player, 6 speakers; cruise control; retained accessory power; tinted windows, power front and rear windows with driver's 1-touch down function; variable-speed intermittent front windshield wipers, driver's seat includes 6-way adjustment and passenger's seat includes 4-way adjustment.

LE V6 (5M) (in addition to or instead of LE (4A) equipment): 3L V6 DOHC MPI 24-valve engine (requires premium unleaded fuel); 5-speed OD manual transmission; 3.93 axle ratio; 4-wheel antilock disc brakes and aero-composite halogen fully auto headlamps with daytime running lights.

XLE (4A) (in addition to or instead of LE V6 (5M) equipment): 2.2L I4 DOHC MPI 16-valve engine; 4-speed electronic OD automatic transmission with lock-up torque converter; 3.94 axle ratio; stainless steel exhaust with tailpipe finisher; front disc/rear drum brakes with 4-wheel antilock brakes; body-colored bodyside molding with chrome bodyside insert; driver's and passenger's power remote body-colored heated outside mirrors; air conditioning with climate control; premium AM/FM stereo radio, seek-scan feature, cassette player, single-disc CD player, 8 premium speakers; power door locks with 2-stage unlock, remote keyless entry, ignition disable, panic alarm, security system; driver's seat includes 8-way power adjustment, lumbar support, passenger's seat includes 6-way adjustment; premium cloth seats, simulated wood dashboard insert, simulated wood door panel insert, simulated wood console insert; additional interior lights include illuminated entry; leather-wrapped steering wheel with tilt adjustment; dual illuminated vanity mirrors, 2 seatback storage pockets, carpeted cargo floor, carpeted trunk lid and cargo light.

XLE V6 (4A) (in addition to or instead of XLE (4A) equipment): 3L V6 DOHC MPI 24-valve engine (requires premium unleaded fuel); 3.93 axle ratio; 4-wheel antilock disc brakes; 16" x 6" silver alloy wheels; P205/60HR16 BSW A/S tires.

TOYOTA — CAMRY

CODE	DESCRIPTION	INVOICE	MSRP

Base Prices

2525	CE (5M)	15906	17675
2532	LE (4A)	18169	20415
2533	LE V6 (5M)	19922	22385
2540	XLE (4A)	21442	24095
2544	XLE V6 4A	23339	26225
	Destination Charge:	455	455

Interested in seeing what dealers will sell this vehicle for? Check out our True Market Value^{sm} (TMV^{sm}) pricing on our Web site at www.edmunds.com.

Accessories

CODE	DESCRIPTION	INVOICE	MSRP
—	Transmission: Electronic 4-Speed Automatic w/OD (CE)	720	800
—	Transmission: Electronic 4-Speed Automatic w/OD (LE V6)	710	800
AB	4-Wheel ABS (CE)	521	610
	Includes daytime running lights.		
AL	Wheels: 15" 5-Spoke Aluminum (LE)	308	385
	Includes center ornament. REQUIRES GX or GZ or (4AT). NOT AVAILABLE with AW, FW, S1, S2.		
AW	Wheels: 15" Aluminum (LE)	308	385
	Includes P205/65R15 AS tires and 15" alloy center ornament. NOT AVAILABLE with S5, B8, SS, W2, W4, GX, GZ, W5, S1, S2, AL, FW.		
B8	Alloy Wheel Locks (CE/LE)	31	52
	NOT AVAILABLE with AW, GX, GZ, SS, S5, W4, W5, WZ.		
B8	Star 5-Spoke Alloy Wheel Locks (CE/LE)	31	52
	NOT AVAILABLE with AW, GX, GZ, SS, W2, W4, W5, WZ.		
BE	Driver & Passenger and Side Airbags	215	250
	REQUIRES HU.		
BN	Black Pearl Emblems (CE/V6)	89	164
BN	Black Pearl Emblems (LE/XLE)	79	149
C1	Cargo Mat (CE/LE)	45	74
C7	Camry Convenience Package	871	1371
	Includes rear spoiler, 15" 5-spoke split alloy wheels and auto-dimming mirror. NOT AVAILABLE with AW, AL, S5, W2, FW.		
CF	Carpet/Cargo Mat Set (5 Piece Set) (XLE)	92	151
	NOT AVAILABLE with HZ, HX.		
CF	Carpeted Floor Mats (4 Piece Set) (CE/LE)	56	93
	NOT AVAILABLE with HU, VL.		
CL	Cruise Control (CE)	200	250
CV	Center Armrest	40	67
DJ	JBL 3 In 1 Premium Combo (LE)	218	290
	Includes AM/FM, cassette, CD, 8 JBL speakers and metal speaker grille.		
DU	Burlwood Wood Dash (CE/LE)	255	499
FW	Chrome Full Wheel Cover (LE)	96	120
	REQUIRES GX or GZ or 4AT. NOT AVAILABLE with AW, AL.		
GN	Cargo Net	30	45
GP	Gold Package (CE/V6)	99	179

CAMRY

TOYOTA

CODE	DESCRIPTION	INVOICE	MSRP
GP	Gold Package (LE/XLE)	89	164
GX	Gallery Series with VP (LE)	1073	1192

Includes two-tone exterior paint, carbon fiber trim pieces on center stack and shift plate, chrome accent pieces on inside door lock levers and HVAC vents and Gallery Series front fender badging, value package #3, 4-wheel abs, daytime running lights, keyless entry with optical indicator, cloth power driver's seat, gallery series cloth seat trim, leather-wrapped steering wheel, leather-wrapped shift knob, chrome tipped exhaust and unique floor mats. REQUIRES AL or FW. NOT AVAILABLE with S5, B8, GZ, SS, W2, W4, AW, W5, S1, S2.

| GX | Gallery Series with VP (LE V6) .... | 875 | 972 |

Includes two-tone exterior paint, carbon fiber trim pieces on center stack and shift plate, chrome accent pieces on inside door lock levers and HVAC vents and Gallery Series front fender badging, value package #3, keyless entry with optical indicator, cloth power driver's seat, gallery series cloth seat trim, leather-wrapped steering wheel, leather-wrapped shift knob, chrome tipped exhaust, unique floor mats and JBL 3 in 1 premium combo. REQUIRES 4AT and AL or FW. NOT AVAILABLE with VL, S5, B8, SS, W2, W4, AW, W5, S1, S2.

| GZ | Gallery Series with VQ (LE) .... | 704 | 782 |

Includes two-tone exterior paint, carbon fiber trim pieces on center stack and shift plate, chrome accent pieces on inside door lock levers and HVAC vents and Gallery Series front fender badging, keyless entry with optical indicator, cloth power driver's seat, gallery series cloth seat trim, leather-wrapped steering wheel, leather-wrapped shift knob, chrome tipped exhaust and unique floor mats. REQUIRES AL or FW. NOT AVAILABLE with GX, B8, S5, SS, W2, W4, AW, W5, S1, S2.

| HU | Value Package #1 with AC and PO (CE) .... | 700 | 778 |

Includes air conditioner, power package, power windows, power door locks, dual color-keyed power mirrors, variable intermittent windshield wipers and carpeted floor mats. NOT AVAILABLE with CF.

| HX | Value Package #2 with Leather (XLE) .... | 1220 | 1356 |

Includes AM/FM radio with CD, cassette, 8 JBL speakers, leather power seats, front seat back pocket, leather-wrapped shift knob, power tilt and slide moon roof, map light, carpeted floor mats and cargo mat set. NOT AVAILABLE with HZ, CF.

| HX | Value Package #2 with Leather (XLE V6) .... | 770 | 856 |

Includes AM/FM radio with CD, cassette, 8 JBL speakers, leather power seats, front seat back pocket, leather-wrapped shift knob, power tilt and slide moon roof, map light, carpeted floor mats and cargo mat set. NOT AVAILABLE with HZ, CF.

| HZ | Value Package #2 with Leather (XLE) .... | 1445 | 1606 |

Includes AM/FM radio with CD, cassette, 8 JBL speakers, power driver's seat, leather seat trim, leather door trim, front seat back pocket, leather-wrapped shift knob, power tilt and slide moon roof, map light, carpeted floor mats and cargo mat set. NOT AVAILABLE with CF, HX.

| HZ | Value Package #2 with Leather (XLE V6) .... | 995 | 1106 |

Includes AM/FM radio with CD, cassette, 8 JBL speakers, power driver's seat, leather seat trim, leather door trim, front seat back pocket, leather-wrapped shift knob, power tilt and slide moon roof, map light, carpeted floor mats and cargo mat set. NOT AVAILABLE with CF, HX.

| MG | Front and Rear Black Mudguards .... | 48 | 60 |

TOYOTA *CAMRY*

CODE	DESCRIPTION	INVOICE	MSRP
N1	Auto-Dimming Mirror	166	240
P9	6-Disc CD Changer	381	550
RF	Rear Spoiler	329	539
S5	Wheels: 15" Star 5-Spoke (CE/LE)	549	699
	NOT AVAILABLE with AW, GX, GZ, SS, W2, W4, W5, B8, S1, S2, WZ, A9, B2.		
SD	Sunroof Wind Deflector (All Except CE)	35	59
	REQUIRES SR or HZ.		
SR	Power Tilt and Slide Moon Roof (LE)	800	1000
	Includes map light.		
SS	Wheels: 15" 5-Spoke Split Alloy (CE/LE)	440	592
	NOT AVAILABLE with GX, GZ, AW, S5, B8, W2, W4, W5, A9, B2.		
TN	Traction Control (V6)	240	300
	REQUIRES 4AT.		
V2	Glass Breakage Sensor (GBS) (XLE)	75	115
V3	RS3200 Deluxe Security System (CE/LE)	275	439
	REQUIRES HU. NOT AVAILABLE with V4, V5, VL.		
V4	RS3200 Deluxe Security with Trunk Release (CE/LE)	360	575
	REQUIRES HU. NOT AVAILABLE with V3, VL, V5.		
V5	RS3200 Plus Security System (LE)	155	249
	REQUIRES VL. NOT AVAILABLE with V3, V4.		
VL	Value Package #5 with Leather (LE V6)	1052	1290
	Includes keyless entry with optical indicator, power driver's seat, leather seat trim, leather door trim, front seat back pocket, leather-wrapped shift knob, leather-wrapped steering wheel, JBL 3 in 1 premium combo and carpeted floor mats. NOT AVAILABLE with GX, CF, V3, V4.		
VP	Value Package #3 (LE)	369	410
	Includes 4-wheel abs, daytime running lights, keyless entry with optical indicator, cloth power driver's seat and carpeted floor mats. NOT AVAILABLE with AB, GX, GZ, CF, V3, V4.		
VP	Value Package #3 (LE V6)	172	190
	Includes 4-wheel ABS and daytime running lights, keyless entry with optical indicator, cloth power driver's seat, JBL 3 in 1 premium combo and carpeted floor mats. NOT AVAILABLE with VL, GX, CF, V3, V4.		
W2	Wheels: 15" Wide 5-Spoke Painted (CE/LE)	550	699
	NOT AVAILABLE with AW, S5, SS, GX, GZ, W4, W5, S1, S2, WZ, A9, B2.		
WL	Alloy Wheel Locks (All Except CE)	31	52
	REQUIRES AW.		
WS	Steel Wheel Locks (CE/LE)	31	52
WZ	Alloy Wheel Locks (CE/LE)	31	52
	REQUIRES SS. NOT AVAILABLE with S5, B8, W2, W4, W5, B2, A9.		

NOTE: Toyotas sold in Alabama, Florida, Georgia, North Carolina and South Carolina may be equipped with option packages not listed in this guide. You can expect to haggle 25% off the window sticker price on these packages.

CAMRY SOLARA

TOYOTA

| CODE | DESCRIPTION | INVOICE | MSRP |

2001 CAMRY SOLARA

What's New?

Top-level SLE models can be equipped with a new JBL audio system, so long as you order leather upholstery. Option package fiddling makes it easier to equip a Solara the way you like. The anti-theft and engine immobilizer system is restricted to SLEs, while SEs now come standard with a six-speaker cassette stereo. Twilight Blue Pearl is replaced by Indigo Ink as an exterior color.

Review

With its own sheetmetal and a tighter suspension, the Solara is more than just a two-door Camry. Yes, it's based on the Camry platform and uses the same engine and basic components, but almost every aspect of this sporty-looking car has been, uh, Solara-ized to inject it with personality.

Available in two trim levels, SE or SLE, and in your choice of coupe or convertible formats, Solara looks like a promising package. Under the hood you will find either a 2.2-liter, 135-horsepower four-cylinder engine or a 3.0-liter, 200-horsepower V6. Both motors can be had in the SE model, but the premium-grade SLE comes only with the V6 and an automatic transmission. For buyers looking to get the maximum "sport" out of the Solara, the SE V6 with a five-speed manual is your best bet. Note that the Honda Accord Coupe V6 does not offer a manual transmission, or a convertible top, for that matter. Yessireebob, Toyota does give the consumer a wide variety of choice.

For handling duty, Toyota takes the Camry's basic suspension and makes it stiffer by increasing the damping rates and adding a brace that joins the front strut towers together. It also reinforces the transom between the trunk and the passenger compartment and stiffens the front and rear suspension mounts for improved overall body rigidity. Additionally, the Solara features a steering system that is more sport-oriented than the Camry's. However, the Solara is still geared for comfort. If you're looking for true handling excellence, check out the Celica.

The interior is quiet and full of high-quality switchgear laid out in a logical manner. Cloth upholstery is standard, with leather available on SLE models. The pricey convertible features a power folding top, automatic-down power rear-quarter windows and a glass backlight with defogger.

Safety is high on Toyota's list of priorities when it comes to the Solara, but the stuff that matters is optional. Base SE models don't come with standard ABS. Optional side airbags can be ordered on any model. If you purchase an SLE model, traction control can be checked on the options sheet.

For 2001, Solara is largely unchanged. Top-level SLE models can be equipped with a new JBL audio system, so long as you opt for the leather package. The anti-theft and engine immobilizer system is restricted to SLEs, while SEs now come standard with a six-speaker cassette stereo. Twilight Blue Pearl paint is replaced by a new shade called Indigo Ink.

Ultimately, the Solara is a two-door Camry with more aggressive styling and minor suspension differences. Style takes precedence over utility. This makes it a fine choice for those looking for Camry's spaciousness and reliability but who seek a little something whimsical.

Standard Equipment

SE COUPE (5M): 2.2L I4 DOHC MPI 16-valve engine; 5-speed OD manual transmission; front-wheel drive, 3.94 axle ratio; stainless steel exhaust; front independent strut suspension with

TOYOTA .CAMRY SOLARA

anti-roll bar, front coil springs, gas-pressurized front shocks, rear independent strut suspension with anti-roll bar, rear coil springs, gas-pressurized rear shocks; rack-and-pinion power steering with engine speed-sensing assist; front disc/rear drum brakes; 18.5 gal. capacity fuel tank; side impact bars; front and rear body-colored bumpers; body-colored bodyside molding; clearcoat monotone paint; aero-composite halogen auto off headlamps; additional exterior lights include front fog/driving lights; driver's and passenger's power remote body-colored outside mirrors; 15" x 6" steel wheels; P205/65HR15 BSW A/S tires; full-size steel spare wheel; air conditioning, rear heat/AC ducts; AM/FM stereo radio, seek-scan feature, cassette player, single-disc CD player, 6 speakers, window grid antenna; cruise control; power door locks, remote hatch/trunk release, remote fuel door release; 2 power accessory outlets, front lighter element(s), driver's foot rest, retained accessory power, smokers' package; instrumentation display includes tachometer, water temperature gauge, in-dash clock, trip odometer; warning indicators include oil pressure, battery, key in ignition, low fuel, low washer fluid, bulb failure, door ajar; driver's and passenger's front airbags; tinted windows with driver's 1-touch down function; variable intermittent front windshield wipers, sun visor strip, rear window defroster; seating capacity of 5, front bucket seats with adjustable tilt headrests, center armrest with storage, driver's seat includes 8-way adjustment, lumbar support, passenger's seat includes 4-way adjustment, easy entry; 60/40 folding rear bench seat with fixed headrests, center armrest; height-adjustable front seatbelts with pretensioners; premium cloth seats, door trim with carpet lower, full cloth headliner, full carpet floor covering, simulated wood dashboard insert, simulated wood door panel insert; interior lights include dome light with fade, illuminated entry; steering wheel with tilt adjustment; dual illuminated vanity mirrors, dual auxiliary visors; day/night rearview mirror; full floor console, mini overhead console with storage, locking glove box with light, front and rear cupholders, instrument panel covered bin, driver's and passenger's door bins; carpeted cargo floor, carpeted trunk lid, cargo light; chrome grille, chrome side window moldings, chrome front windshield molding, chrome rear window molding and body-colored door handles.

SE V6 COUPE (5M) (in addition to or instead of SE COUPE (5M) equipment): 3L V6 DOHC MPI 24-valve engine (requires premium unleaded fuel); 3.93 axle ratio; 4-wheel antilock disc brakes; aero-composite halogen fully auto with daytime running lights, easy entry and ignition disable.

SLE V6 COUPE (4A) (in addition to or instead of SE V6 COUPE (4A) equipment): Four-speed electronic OD automatic transmission with lock up; driver's and passenger's power remote body-colored heated outside mirrors; 16" x 6" silver alloy wheels; P205/60HR16 BSW A/S tires; air conditioning with climate control; premium AM/FM stereo radio, seek-scan feature, cassette player, single-disc CD player, 8 premium speakers, amplifier; power door locks with 2-stage unlock, remote keyless entry, garage door opener, exterior temp, panic alarm, security system; additional instrumentation display includes compass; driver's seat includes 8-way power adjustment, lumbar support, passenger's seat includes 4-way adjustment; leather seats, leather-wrapped gearshift knob, leather-wrapped steering wheel with tilt adjustment; auto-dimming day/night rearview mirror; overhead storage console, 2 seatback storage pockets, chrome front windshield molding and chrome rear window molding.

CONVERTIBLE (4A) (in addition to or instead of SLE V6 COUPE (4A) equipment): Power convertible roof with lining, glass rear window; 15" x 6" steel wheels; P205/65HR15 BSW A/S tires; premium cloth seats, simulated wood dashboard insert and simulated wood door panel insert.

Base Prices

2731	SE (5M)	17067	18965
2733	SE V6 (5M)	19506	21675
2752	SE Convertible (4A)	22583	25095
2744	SLE V6 (4A)	22755	25165

CAMRY SOLARA — TOYOTA

CODE	DESCRIPTION	INVOICE	MSRP
2754	SE V6 Convertible (4A)	25230	28035
2764	SLE V6 Convertible (4A)	27463	30515
	Destination Charge:	455	455

Interested in seeing what dealers will sell this vehicle for? Check out our True Market Value^{sm} (TMV^{sm}) pricing on our Web site at www.edmunds.com.

Accessories

Code	Description	Invoice	MSRP
—	Transmission: 4-Speed Automatic (SE Coupe)	720	800
—	Transmission: 4-Speed Automatic (SE V6 Coupe)	722	800
AB	Anti-Lock Brakes (SE Coupe/SE Convertible)	521	610
BE	Side Airbags	215	250
CF	Carpet/Cargo Mat Set (5 Piece Set)	101	167
EJ	Radio: JBL 3-In-1 Premium with Changer (SLE)	150	200
	Includes AM/FM radio, cassette, CD, 6-disc changer in-dash and 8 JBL speakers. REQUIRES LQ.		
GP	Gold Package (All V6)	149	224
GP	Gold Package (SE Coupe/SE Convertible)	115	173
LQ	SLE Package (SLE V6)	NC	NC
	Includes power driver seat with 8 way adjuster, power color keyed heated mirrors, anti-theft, keyless entry, garage opener, auto air conditioning, digital heater control, outside temperature gauge, auto rearview mirror dimmer, P205/60R16 tires, 15"x16" alloy wheels, rear spoiler and mudguards. REQUIRES EJ.		
MG	Color-Keyed Mudguards (SE Coupe)	64	80
PC	Special Color	187	220
PE	Cloth Power Driver's Seat (SE/SE V6 Coupe)	312	390
	NOT AVAILABLE with VL.		
RF	Rear Spoiler (Se Coupe)	348	435
SD	Sunroof Wind Deflector (Coupe)	33	55
	REQUIRES SR.		
SR	Power Tilt and Slide Moon Roof (Coupe)	720	900
	Includes map light. REQUIRES PE or VL.		
SW	Grade Package (SE Coupe)	460	575
	Includes leather shift knob, 15 x 6" alloy wheels, smooth leather steering wheel and color-keyed mudguards. NOT AVAILABLE with VF, VH.		
SW	Grade Package (SE Coupe)	508	635
	Includes leather shift knob, 15 x 6" alloy wheels, smooth leather steering wheel and color-keyed mudguards. REQUIRES 4AT. NOT AVAILABLE with VF, VH.		
TN	Traction Control (SLE)	240	300
V3	Deluxe Security System (SE)	275	439
	Available for vehicles without factory security or remote keyless entry. Includes remote keyless entry system, ignition disable and glass breakage sensor. The alarms can be programmed to flash lights or chirp when armed or disarmed. The horn will sound if the glass is broken or if the door is opened without turning off the alarm.		
VF	Upgrade Package #1 (SE Convertible)	732	935
	Includes 15 x 6" alloy wheels, remote keyless entry, JBL 3-in-1 premium combo radio and carpeted floor mats/cargo mat.		

TOYOTA

CAMRY SOLARA / CELICA

CODE	DESCRIPTION	INVOICE	MSRP
VF	**Upgrade Package #1 (SE Coupe)**	623	692
	Includes 15" x 6" alloy wheels, remote keyless entry, JBL 3-in-1 premium combo radio, color-keyed mudguards and carpeted floor mats/cargo mat. NOT AVAILABLE with VH, SW, VL.		
VH	**Sport Trim Package (SE Coupe)**	834	927
	Includes 16" x 6" alloy wheels, remote keyless entry, JBL 3-in-1 premium combo radio, color-keyed mudguards, rear spoiler and carpeted floor mats/cargo mat. NOT AVAILABLE with VF, SW.		
VH	**Sport Trim Package (SE V6)**	1005	1117
	Includes leather shift knob, 16" x 6" alloy wheels, remote keyless entry, JBL 3-in-1 premium combo radio, color-keyed mudguards, rear spoiler, carpeted floor mats/cargo mat and perforated leather steering wheel. NOT AVAILABLE with VL, VF.		
VH	**Sport Trim Package (SE V6 Coupe)**	1059	1177
	Includes leather shift knob, 16" x 6" alloy wheels, remote keyless entry, JBL 3-in-1 premium combo radio, color-keyed mudguards, rear spoiler, carpeted floor mats/cargo mat and perforated leather steering wheel. REQUIRES 4AT. NOT AVAILABLE with VL, VF.		
VL	**Sport Trim Package with Leather (SE V6 Coupe)**	2137	2532
	Includes leather shift knob, 16" x 6" alloy wheels, remote keyless entry, JBL 3-in-1 premium combo radio, color-keyed mudguards, rear spoiler, leather and power seat package, perforated leather steering wheel, leather seat trim and carpeted floor mats/cargo mat. NOT AVAILABLE with PE, VF, VH.		
VL	**Sport Trim Package with Leather (SE V6 Coupe)**	2191	2592
	Includes leather shift knob, 16" x 6" alloy wheels, remote keyless entry, JBL 3-in-1 premium combo radio, color-keyed mudguards, rear spoiler, leather and power seat package, perforated leather steering wheel, leather seat trim and carpeted floor mats/cargo mat. REQUIRES (4AT) 4-speed automatic transmission. NOT AVAILABLE with PE, VF, VH.		
VQ	**Upgrade Package #2 (SE V6 Convertible)**	936	1190
	Includes leather shift knob, 16" x 6" alloy wheels, P205/60R16 A/S tires, remote keyless entry, cloth power driver's seat, perforated leather steering wheel, JBL 3-in-1 premium combo radio and carpeted floor mats/cargo mat.		
WL	**Alloy Wheel Locks**	31	52

NOTE: Toyotas sold in Alabama, Florida, Georgia, North Carolina and South Carolina may be equipped with option packages not listed in this guide. You can expect to haggle 25% off the window sticker price on these packages.

2001 CELICA

What's New?

Brand new last year, the hot Celica motors into 2001 with no changes.

Review

Considerably leaner and meaner than most Celicas produced between 1985 and 2000, the 2001 edition of Toyota's stalwart sport coupe is attracting buyers in droves. Styled in California by Calty Design Research Inc., the cab-forward shape features a high-fashion look with racecar

CELICA
TOYOTA

design elements. Sharp-edged panels, dramatic plunging curves, a tall tail and a radically lowered front fascia create stark contrasts. The look is polarizing, and plenty of consumers are voting on the success of the styling with cash in hand.

There are two versions on sale: a base-level Celica GT, and a more-powerful GT-S. An all-new 1.8-liter, four-cylinder, DOHC aluminum engine powers the Celica GT-S. Hitting an impressive mark of 100 horsepower per liter of displacement, the engine generates 180 ponies at 7,600 rpm and 133 foot-pounds of torque at 6,800 rpm. The GT-S power plant, co-developed with Yamaha, utilizes Toyota's new VVT-i engine technology. Similar in concept to Honda's VTEC, the system can adjust both valve timing and lift. The GT model's adequate 1.8-liter, four-cylinder engine produces 140 horsepower and 125 foot-pounds of torque at 6,400 rpm.

Celica GT and GT-S are both available with different variations of automatic and manual transmissions. GT comes standard with a five-speed manual gearbox. Optional on both trims is a four-speed automatic transmission, equipped with E-shift steering wheel-mounted buttons in the GT-S. These allow for "manual" shifting of the automatic transmission. As an exclusive feature in this class, the manual transmission in the GT-S features six forward gears, but the gates are tight and it's easy to select the wrong gear.

Suspension and braking systems provide outstanding handling and performance. The front suspension utilizes MacPherson struts with offset springs and a solid anti-roll bar. The rear suspension is a double-wishbone design with a camber-control function and a solid anti-roll bar. ABS is optional on both models. The Celica GT rides on 15x6.5-inch steel wheels with 195/60 R15 tires, while the high-grade GT-S features 15x6.5-inch alloy wheels on 205/55 R15 tires. Both models offer optional aluminum alloy wheels, sized 16 inches for the GT-S.

Celica's interior is stylish, functional and comfortable for two adults and a healthy amount of their gear. A simple, downswept dash layout, big analog gauges, sporty bucket seats, faux-drilled metal pedals and fashionable metallic silver accents add to Celica's cockpit ambience. Both GT and GT-S offer a center console big enough to hold eight CD cases, as well as two oversized cups. The rear seatbacks also can be folded forward, providing additional cargo space. Driver and front-passenger airbags are standard, and side airbags are optional. GT-S models can be equipped with leather.

Until recently, Celicas were generally considered slow, overweight and expensive. Detractors claimed they were "secretary's cars." Not anymore.

Standard Equipment

GT (5M): 1.8L I4 DOHC SMPI 16-valve engine with variable valve timing; 5-speed OD manual transmission; 420 amp battery; engine oil cooler; 70 amp alternator; transmission oil cooler; front-wheel drive, 4.31 axle ratio; stainless steel exhaust with tailpipe finisher; front independent strut suspension with anti-roll bar, front coil springs, rear independent double-wishbone suspension with anti-roll bar, rear coil springs; rack-and-pinion power steering; front disc/rear drum brakes; 14.5 gal. capacity fuel tank; side impact bars; front and rear body-colored bumpers; rocker panel extensions; clearcoat monotone paint; projector beam halogen auto on headlamps with daytime running lights; driver's and passenger's power remote body-colored folding outside mirrors; 15" x 6.5" steel wheels; P195/60HR15 BSW A/S tires; compact steel spare wheel; air conditioning; AM/FM stereo radio, seek-scan feature, cassette player, single-disc CD player, 6 speakers, manual retractable antenna; remote fuel door release; 1 power accessory outlet, front lighter element(s), driver's foot rest, smokers' package; instrumentation display includes tachometer, water temperature gauge, in-dash clock, trip odometer; warning indicators include oil pressure, battery, key in ignition, low fuel, door ajar; driver's and passenger's front airbags; tinted windows; variable-speed intermittent front windshield wipers, rear window defroster; seating capacity of 4, front sports seats with fixed headrests, center armrest with

TOYOTA *CELICA*

storage, driver's seat includes 6-way adjustment, passenger's seat includes 4-way adjustment, easy entry; 50/50 folding rear bench seat; seatbelts with front pretensioners; cloth seats, cloth door trim insert, full cloth headliner, full carpet floor covering; interior lights include dome light with fade; steering wheel with tilt adjustment; vanity mirrors; day/night rearview mirror; full floor console, locking glove box with light, front and rear cupholders, instrument panel covered bin, driver's and passenger's door bins; carpeted cargo floor, vinyl trunk lid, cargo cover, cargo tie downs, cargo light; black grille, black side window moldings, black front windshield molding and body-colored door handles.

GT-S (6M) (in addition to or instead of GT (5M) equipment): 1.8L I4 DOHC SMPI 16-valve engine with variable valve timing (requires premium unleaded fuel); 6-speed OD manual transmission; 420 amp HD battery; HD starter; 4.53 axle ratio; 4-wheel disc brakes; additional exterior lights include front fog/driving lights; P205/55VR15 BSW A/S tires; premium AM/FM stereo radio, seek-scan feature, cassette player, single-disc CD player, 8 speakers, amplifier, manual retractable antenna; cruise control; retained accessory power; tinted windows with driver's 1-touch down function; fixed interval rear wiper; premium cloth seats, leather-wrapped gearshift knob, chrome interior accents; additional interior lights include illuminated entry; leather-wrapped steering wheel with tilt adjustment.

Base Prices

Code	Description	Invoice	MSRP
2123	Celica GT (5M)	15369	16985
2133	Celica GTS (6M)	19308	21455
	Destination Charge:	455	455

Interested in seeing what dealers will sell this vehicle for? Check out our True Market Value^{sm} (TMV^{sm}) pricing on our Web site at www.edmunds.com.

Accessories

Code	Description	Invoice	MSRP
—	Transmission: 4-Speed Auto with Sport Shift (GT-S)	631	700
	Includes 3.12 axle ratio.		
—	Transmission: 4-Speed Automatic (GT)	724	800
	Includes 3.92 axle ratio.		
8A	Acculaser Carbon Fiber Dash	199	369
AB	Anti-Lock Brakes	473	550
AW	Wheels: 15" Alloy (GT)	308	385
	Includes 195/60R15 Bridgestone/Dunlap tires. NOT AVAILABLE with WS.		
AW	Wheels: 16" Alloy (GT-S)	48	60
	Includes 205/50R16 tires. NOT AVAILABLE with WS.		
BE	Side Air Bags	215	250
CF	Carpet Floor Mats (4 Piece Set)	46	76
CK	All Weather Guard Package (GT)	223	270
	Includes cold area package, HD battery, heavy duty rear heater, HD rear window defogger and rear intermittent wiper.		
DC	Premium 3-In-1 Combo (GT)	248	330
	Includes premium AM/FM, cassette, CD, 8 speakers and amplifier. REQUIRES UP.		
GN	Cargo Net	30	45
GP	Gold Package	109	179
LA	Leather Seats (GT-S)	496	620
	REQUIRES SR.		
N1	Auto-Dimming Mirror	190	275

CELICA / COROLLA — TOYOTA

CODE	DESCRIPTION	INVOICE	MSRP
P9	6 Disc Trunk-Mounted CD Changer	381	550
RF	Rear Spoiler (GT)	432	540
	Includes fog lamps.		
RF	Rear Spoiler (GT-S)	348	435
SR	Power Tilt/Slide Sunroof	704	880
	REQUIRES UP (GT only).		
UP	Upgrade Package (GT)	656	820
	Includes power windows and locks and cruise control.		
V3	Deluxe Security System	275	439
	REQUIRES UP.		
WL	Alloy Wheel Locks	31	52
	REQUIRES AW. NOT AVAILABLE with WS.		
WS	Steel Wheel Locks	31	52
	NOT AVAILABLE with AW, WL.		

NOTE: Toyotas sold in Alabama, Florida, Georgia, North Carolina and South Carolina may be equipped with option packages not listed in this guide. You can expect to haggle 25% off the window sticker price on these packages.

2001 COROLLA

What's New?

Mid-grade CE trim replaces entry-level VE, top-line LE replaces mid-grade CE, and a sporty new CE-based S model debuts. Front and rear lighting is restyled, and the fascia up front is tweaked and now includes a chrome-ringed grille. An internal trunk release has been added, along with a push-button fresh/recirculate control for the ventilation system. Two new colors replace an equal number of shades that are fading away.

Review

Toyota's venerable Corolla has gone through many changes since it was first introduced in 1968. Over the course of its long life, the Corolla has appeared as a hatchback, coupe, wagon and sedan. The world has seen enough people fall in love with this car to make it the best-selling nameplate in the history of automobiles.

Now, while that's neat and all, we're sure that what's really important to you and your wallet is whether this modern Corolla still has what it takes to stomp out its competitors. In short, it doesn't.

Dating to 1998, the current Corolla faces stiff competition from the Ford Focus, Honda Civic, Hyundai Elantra, Mazda Protege, and Nissan Sentra, all of which have been substantially redesigned or newly introduced since this particular Toyota was fresh out of the blocks. And they are all more satisfying cars.

To help fend them off until the next redesign, the Corolla comes equipped with a zippy, smooth-revving, 1.8-liter, four-cylinder aluminum engine that cranks out 125 horsepower, thanks to a variable valve timing and lift system that Toyota calls VVT-i. VVT-i employs continuously variable intake valve timing to provide greater engine performance, better fuel economy and

TOYOTA

COROLLA

reduced pollution over a wide rev range. When equipped with a manual transmission, this car pulls strongly. Automatic gearboxes are available too, including a technologically advanced (Not!) three-speed unit on base models.

Three trim levels are available on the slightly restyled 2001 Corolla. Base CE, better-equipped LE, and sporty S. The new S model includes "sporty" trim, fog lights, fake leather-wrapped steering wheel, and a tachometer with outside temperature display, among other things.

This year, Toyota is also freshening the exterior styling in a bid to draw buyers into showrooms. Changes include a revised front end with chrome-ringed grille, new headlights and taillights, and body-colored trim for LE and S models. Impulse Red and Indigo Ink replace Venetian Red Pearl and Twilight Blue Pearl on the color palette. Inside, a button has been added to control fresh/recirculated airflow, and in the trunk, and an internal release handle keeps kids from getting trapped.

Our biggest gripe with the Corolla is minimal legroom for both the driver and passengers, and the horribly uncomfortable seats. Center stack ergonomics also aren't up to standards in the class, and the soft suspension keels over in turns, making the tires howl in pain. But the ride is smooth, the cabin is quiet at speed, side airbags are an unusual option for the class, and the parts used in the car's construction exude quality.

Few competitors can match Toyota's run-forever reputation and high levels of build quality. But with lots of better cars competing for slices of the econo-sedan pie, Toyota has its work cut out for it in 2001. Especially since the Chevrolet Prizm, an identical twin of the Corolla, is sold with big, fat, juicy rebates at the Chevy dealer down the street.

Standard Equipment

CE (5M): 1.8L J4 DOHC MPI 16-valve engine with variable valve timing; 5-speed OD manual transmission; 80 amp alternator; front-wheel drive, 3.72 axle ratio; stainless steel exhaust; front independent strut suspension with anti-roll bar, front coil springs, gas-pressurized front shocks, rear independent strut suspension with anti-roll bar, rear coil springs, gas-pressurized rear shocks; rack-and-pinion power steering with engine speed-sensing assist; front disc/rear drum brakes; 13.2 gal. capacity fuel tank; side impact bars; front and rear body-colored bumpers; clearcoat monotone paint; aero-composite halogen fully auto headlamps with daytime running lights; driver's and passenger's manual black outside mirrors; 14" x 5.5" silver styled steel wheels; P175/65SR14 BSW A/S tires; compact steel spare wheel; AM/FM stereo radio, seek-scan feature, 4 speakers, fixed antenna; child-safety rear door locks, remote hatch/trunk release, remote fuel door release; 1 power accessory outlet, driver's foot rest; instrumentation display includes tachometer, water temperature gauge, in-dash clock, exterior temp, trip odometer; warning indicators include oil pressure, battery, key in ignition, lights on, low fuel, door ajar; driver's and passenger's front airbags; tinted windows, manual front and rear windows; seating capacity of 5, front bucket seats with adjustable headrests, center armrest with storage, driver's and passenger's seats include 4-way adjustment; rear bench seat with adjustable headrests; height-adjustable front seatbelts with pretensioners; cloth seats, cloth door trim insert, full cloth headliner, full carpet floor covering; interior lights include dome light with delay; vanity mirrors; day/night rearview mirror; full floor console, glove box, front and rear cupholders, instrument panel covered bin, driver's and passenger's door bins; carpeted cargo floor; body-colored grille, black side window moldings, black front windshield molding, black rear window molding and black door handles.

S (5M) (in addition to or instead of CE (5M) equipment): Body-colored bodyside molding rocker panel extensions; additional exterior lights include front fog/driving lights; driver's and passenger's manual remote black outside mirrors; P185/65SR14 BSW A/S tires; variable-speed intermittent front windshield wipers and body-colored door handles.

LE (5M) (in addition to or instead of S (5M) equipment): Front license plate bracket, side impact bars; driver's and passenger's power remote black outside mirrors; AM/FM stereo radio, seek-scan feature, cassette player, 4 speakers, fixed antenna; retained accessory power; rear window defroster; 60/40 folding rear bench seat with adjustable headrests; additional interior

COROLLA — TOYOTA

| CODE | DESCRIPTION | INVOICE | MSRP |

lights include front reading lights; steering wheel with tilt adjustment; carpeted cargo floor and cargo light.

Base Prices

		INVOICE	MSRP
1711	CE (5M)	11624	12568
1719	S (M5)	11511	12793
1723	LE (M5)	12042	13383
Destination Charge:		455	455

Interested in seeing what dealers will sell this vehicle for? Check out our True Market Value^{sm} (TMV^{sm}) pricing on our Web site at www.edmunds.com.

Accessories

CODE	DESCRIPTION	INVOICE	MSRP
—	4-Speed Automatic Transmission (LE)	733	815
—	Transmission: 3-Speed Automatic (CE)	383	415
	Includes 3.42 axle ratio and tachometer delete.		
—	Transmission: 4-Speed Automatic (S)	736	815
	Includes 2.66 axle ratio.		
2L	Carpet/Cargo Mat Set (5 Piece Set)	82	132
AB	Anti-Lock Brakes (S,LE)	473	550
AG	Appearance Package (CE)	128	160
	Includes black bodyside molding and full wheel covers. NOT AVAILABLE with WC.		
AW	Wheels: 14"x5.5" J Alluminum Alloy (S,LE)	292	365
	Includes P185/65SR14 A/S standard tires. NOT AVAILABLE with SS.		
BE	Driver & Passenger Side Airbags	215	250
	Includes driver and passenger seat-mounted.		
CI	Cargo Mat	34	56
	NOT AVAILABLE with EL, E6, PT1, PV5.		
C7	Corolla Convenience Package	888	1527
	Includes rear spoiler, VIP RS3000 deluxe security system, remote keyless entry system, illuminated entry and 6-disc in-dash CD changer. REQUIRES PL or VP or VQ.		
CF	Carpet Floor Mats	67	95
CK	All Weather Guard Package	59	70
	Includes heavy duty starter, heavy duty heater/ventilator and rear heat ducts. REQUIRES DF.		
CL	Cruise Control (LE)	200	250
CQ	Convenience Package (S)	354	430
	Includes cruise control and tilt steering wheel.		
DA	Burlwood Wood Dash-7 Piece (CE,S)	165	325
	NOT AVAILABLE with PL, V3, VP, VQ, DU.		
DF	Heavy Duty Defogger with Timer (CE,S)	164	205
DU	Burlwood Wood Dash-11 Piece (S,LE)	235	425
	REQUIRES VP or VQ. NOT AVAILABLE with DA.		
EV	Radio: AM/FM Stereo with CD (LE)	75	100
	Includes 4 speakers. NOT AVAILABLE with VP, P5, P6.		
EV	Radio: AM/FM Stereo with CD (S)	233	310
	Includes 4 speakers. NOT AVAILABLE with P5, P6.		

TOYOTA — COROLLA

CODE	DESCRIPTION	INVOICE	MSRP
EX	Radio: Deluxe AM/FM with Cassette (S)	158	210
	Includes 4 speakers. NOT AVAILABLE with EV, P4, P5.		
GN	Cargo Net	30	45
GP	Gold Package	119	179
MG	Front and Rear Black Mudguards (CE,LE)	48	60
P4	Auto-Reverse Cassette Deck (CE,D)	155	220
	REQUIRES EV. NOT AVAILABLE with P5, VP.		
P5	Compact Disc Deck	235	335
	NOT AVAILABLE with P6, P4, EV, VP, P9.		
P6	6 Disc In-Dash CD Changer	414	589
	NOT AVAILABLE with P5, EV, P9.		
P9	6 Disc Trunk-Mounted CD Changer	381	550
	NOT AVAILABLE with P5, P6.		
PL	Power Door Locks (CE)	216	270
	NOT AVAILABLE with DA.		
RF	Rear Spoiler	299	499
SD	Sunroof Wind Deflector (S,LE)	35	59
	REQUIRES SR.		
SR	Sunroof (LE)	572	715
	Includes day/night inner mirror.		
SR	Sunroof (S)	588	735
	Includes day/night inner mirror.		
SS	14" Curved Star Alloy Wheels	375	499
	NOT AVAILABLE with WE3, AW, WL.		
V3	V.I.P. RS3000 Deluxe Security System	275	439
	Available for vehicles without factory security or remote keyless entry. Includes remote keyless entry system, illuminated entry, ignition disable and glass breakage sensor. The alarms can be programmed to flash lights or chirp when armed or disarmed. The horn will sound if the glass is broken or if the door is opened without turning off the alarm. REQUIRES PL or VP or VQ. NOT AVAILABLE with DA.		
VP	Extra Value Package #1 (CE)	658	730
	Includes air conditioning, deluxe AM/FM radio with cassette and digital clock. NOT AVAILABLE with P4, P5.		
VP	Extra Value Package #1 (LE)	923	1025
	Includes air conditioning, power windows and power door locks. NOT AVAILABLE with VQ, EV, P5.		
VP	Extra Value Package #1 (S)	986	1095
	Includes air conditioning, digital clock, power windows and power door locks. NOT AVAILABLE with VQ, DA, P5.		
VQ	Extra Value Package #2 (LE)	1049	1165
	Includes air conditioning, power windows and power door locks. NOT AVAILABLE with VP.		
VQ	Extra Value Package #2 (S)	1112	1235
	Includes air conditioning, digital clock, power windows and power door locks. NOT AVAILABLE with VP, DA.		
WC	Painted Wheel Covers (CE)	50	85
	NOT AVAILABLE with AG.		

COROLLA / ECHO — TOYOTA

CODE	DESCRIPTION	INVOICE	MSRP
WL	Alloy Wheel Locks (S,LE) .... NOT AVAILABLE with SS, WZ.	31	52
WS	Steel Wheel Locks .... NOT AVAILABLE with WZ.	31	52
WZ	Alloy Wheel Locks .... REQUIRES SS. NOT AVAILABLE with WS, WL.	31	52

NOTE: Toyotas sold in Alabama, Florida, Georgia, North Carolina and South Carolina may be equipped with option packages not listed in this guide. You can expect to haggle 25% off the window sticker price on these packages.

2001 ECHO

What's New?

In an effort to better protect occupants of this lightweight economy car, Toyota makes side airbags optional for 2001. Brilliant Blue Pearl is a new color.

Review

Despite what seems at first to be a pretty good deal, we think you'd be wise to shop around before settling on an Echo. But don't take our word for it; ask Car and Driver magazine. They called it a "big mistake."

Yes, it's a Toyota, so it'll probably run until your first gray hair sprouts (or you wind up in a pine box, if you already have gray hairs.) Yes, it gets great gas mileage, doubly important now that OPEC has figured out that Americans will pay higher gas prices before they give up their SUVs. Yes, it has a roomy interior with lots of cubbies to store your stuff. Yes, acceleration is impressive from the sophisticated 108-horsepower, VVTi motor.

But, when you cut through the marketing hype and peek behind Toyota's veneer of bulletproof reliability, what you find might not be pretty.

Neither is the Echo. Hey, styling is a subjective point, but take a good look at this thing. Do you really want people to think you've borrowed a prop from Disneyland's Toontown when you pull up to the curb? But it's cheap, you say. Advertisements brag about a low sticker price that starts under $10,000, but in reality, when you've got the car optioned in a manner that makes it suitable as a daily driver, the value of the Echo starts to evaporate.

Air conditioning, a rear defogger and a clock are all optional. Heck, even power steering is on the a la carte menu. Add these features and you're paying nearly $12,000 for a two-door. At this price, you're still rowing your own gears through gridlocked traffic. Pop for an automatic transmission and you're spending another $800. Now approaching $13,000, you still don't have antilock brakes or side impact airbags. Loaded up with every possible option, an Echo Sedan runs close to $15,000, and you're still rolling down your own windows and manually setting the sideview mirrors.

Beyond the dubious value equation, there is the issue of crashworthiness. Considering the fact that Echo's base curb weight is a feather-light 2,035 pounds, and the average SUV-driving soccer dad pilots a rig at least twice that mass, basic physics dictates that the Echo driver is putting herself at risk. Toyota maintains that Echo was engineered to provide crash and injury protection that matches the larger Camry, and internal company test data indicates their design goal was met. However, U.S. crash testing has not been conducted on the Echo at this writing,

TOYOTA — *ECHO*

so we cannot determine through third party results if Toyota has been able to successfully refute Sir Issac Newton's second law. Until then, order the side airbags.

Echo does have a few redeeming qualities, but not enough to garner a recommendation from our staff. If you're into storage bins, there are big gaping ones in the dash. And the interior is almost as roomy as the more expensive Corolla, a car that we actually find to be a bit cramped. Finally, the sprightly 1.5-liter, twin-cam four-cylinder engine makes 108 horsepower, resulting in surprising acceleration times of 8.5 seconds in the dash from zero to 60.

But with skinny, low rolling resistance, 14-inch tires, a tall stance and center of gravity, and slab-sided bodywork, handling is not Echo's forte. Plus, crosswinds severely hamper the ability to stay in your own lane, and ABS is a costly $590 add-on that is inexplicably bundled with daytime running lights (evidently, Toyota feels buyers of Echos without ABS aren't interested in increased visibility to other drivers.)

Want to know what else you could buy with your hard-earned money? Let's see. How about a certified-used Honda Civic that's bigger inside, several hundred pounds heavier, and won't embarrass you when you meet potential in-laws? And there's the pre-owned Mazda Protégé, a classy small car that resembles the upscale Audi A4. Heck, even many new economy cars could be better bets, like the award-winning Ford Focus, the refined Nissan Sentra, and the surprisingly entertaining, easily affordable and thoroughly warranteed Hyundai Elantra.

Ssssh! Hear that Echo? That's empty Toyota showrooms.

Standard Equipment

COUPE (5M): 1.5L I4 DOHC MPI 16-valve engine with variable valve timing; 5-speed OD manual transmission; front-wheel drive, 3.53 axle ratio; partial stainless steel exhaust; front independent strut suspension with anti-roll bar, front coil springs, gas-pressurized front shocks, rear semi-independent torsion suspension with rear coil springs; manual rack-and-pinion steering; front disc/rear drum brakes; 11.9 gal. capacity fuel tank; front license plate bracket, side impact bars; front and rear body-colored bumpers; clearcoat monotone paint; aero-composite halogen headlamps; driver's and passenger's manual black folding outside mirrors; 14" x 5.5" steel wheels; P175/65SR14 BSW A/S tires; compact steel spare wheel; AM/FM stereo radio, seek-scan feature, 4 speakers, fixed antenna; remote hatch/trunk release, remote fuel door release; 1 power accessory outlet, front lighter element(s), driver's foot rest, smokers' package; instrumentation display includes water temperature gauge, trip odometer; warning indicators include oil pressure, water temp, battery, lights on, key in ignition, low washer fluid, door ajar; driver's and passenger's front airbags, side impact airbags; tinted windows; seating capacity of 5, front bucket seats with adjustable headrests, driver's and passenger's seats include 4-way adjustment, easy entry; rear bench seat with adjustable headrests; height-adjustable front seatbelts with pretensioners; cloth seats, cloth door trim insert, full cloth headliner, full carpet floor covering; interior lights include dome light; steering wheel with tilt adjustment; driver's side vanity mirror; day/night rearview mirror; partial floor console, glove box, front and rear cupholders, instrument panel bin, interior concealed storage, 2 seatback storage pockets, driver's and passenger's door bins, front underseat tray; carpeted cargo floor, carpeted trunk lid, cargo light; black grille, black side window moldings, black front windshield molding, black rear window molding and body-colored door handles.

SEDAN (5M) (in addition to or instead of COUPE (5M) equipment): Child-safety rear door locks.

Base Prices

Code	Description	Invoice	MSRP
1413	Coupe (5M)	9393	9995
1415	Sedan (5M)	9893	10525
Destination Charge:		455	455

Interested in seeing what dealers will sell this vehicle for? Check out our True Market Value^{sm} (TMV^{sm}) pricing on our Web site at www.edmunds.com.

ECHO — TOYOTA

Accessories

CODE	DESCRIPTION	INVOICE	MSRP
—	Transmission: 4-Speed Automatic (Coupe)	752	800
	Includes 3.85 axle ratio.		
—	Transmission: 4-Speed Automatic (Sedan)	753	800
	Includes 3.85 axle ratio.		
AB	Anti-Lock Brakes	505	590
	Includes daytime running lights. REQUIRES GJ and CK.		
AC	Air Conditioning	740	925
	REQUIRES AQ and RC.		
AQ	Auto Idling Control	NC	NC
	REQUIRES CK or PS or GI or AC or GJ.		
BE	Side Impact Airbags	215	250
CF	Carpet Floor Mats (4 Piece Set)	40	65
CK	All Weather Guard Package	220	275
	Includes cold area package, heavy duty battery, heavy duty rear heater, and heavy duty rear defogger. REQUIRES AQ and RC and (QS or GI or RU). NOT AVAILABLE with DE.		
DE	Light Duty Rear Window Defogger	164	205
	NOT AVAILABLE with CK.		
DQ	Digital Clock	56	70
DZ	Radio: Deluxe 3-In-1 Combo	203	270
	Includes AM/FM stereo radio, cassette, CD, 6 speakers and audio indicator. NOT AVAILABLE with EX.		
EX	Radio: Deluxe with Cassette	128	170
	Includes AM/FM stereo radio, cassette with 6 speakers and audio indicator. NOT AVAILABLE with DZ, GJ.		
GI	Upgrade Package #1	832	1020
	Includes sports package indicator, sports body cladding, power steering, fixed intermittent wipers, dual remote control exterior mirrors, 60/40 Split Folding Rear Seat, and digital clock. REQUIRES AQ. NOT AVAILABLE with QS or SB.		
GJ	Upgrade Package #2 (Coupe)	1123	1420
	Includes air conditioning, deluxe 3-in-1 combo radio and power door locks. REQUIRES AQ and RC and (GI or RU). NOT AVAILABLE with QS, EX.		
GJ	Upgrade Package #2 (Sedan)	1159	1465
	Includes air conditioning, deluxe 3-in-1 combo radio and power door locks. REQUIRES AQ and RC and (GI or RU). NOT AVAILABLE with QS, EX.		
GN	Cargo Net	30	45
	NOT AVAILABLE with PC1.		
P4	Auto-Reverse Cassette Deck	155	220
	NOT AVAILABLE with P5, P6, EX, DZ, GJ, RC2.		
P5	Compact Disc Deck	194	275
	NOT AVAILABLE with P4, P6, DZ, GJ, RD1, RD7.		
P6	6 Disc In-Dash Changer	414	589
	NOT AVAILABLE with P4, P5, DZ, GJ, RD7, RD1.		
PL	Power Door Locks (Coupe)	180	225
PL	Power Door Locks (Sedan)	216	270

TOYOTA — ECHO / MR2 SPYDER

CODE	DESCRIPTION	INVOICE	MSRP
PS	Power Steering	231	270
	REQUIRES AQ.		
QS	Quarter Stone Protector	NC	NC
	REQUIRES AQ and RC and CK. NOT AVAILABLE with GI, GJ, RU.		
RC	Radiator Cover	NC	NC
	REQUIRES CK or AC or GJ.		
RF	Rear Lip Spoiler	80	100
	Limited colors.		
RU	Sports Body Cladding	320	400
	Includes front painted bumper with molding. NOT AVAILABLE with QS.		
SB	60/40 Split Folding Rear Seat (Coupe)	132	165
	NOT AVAILABLE with GI.		
SB	60/40 Split Folding Rear Seat (Sedan)	132	165
	NOT AVAILABLE with GI.		
SS	Alloy Wheels	375	499
V3	V.I.P. RS3200 Deluxe Security System	275	439
	Available for vehicles without factory security or remote keyless entry. Includes remote keyless entry system, ignition disable and glass breakage sensor. The alarms can be programmed to flash lights or chirp when armed or disarmed. The horn will sound if the glass is broken or if the door is opened without turning off the alarm. REQUIRES PL. NOT AVAILABLE with QS9.		
WS	Steel Wheel Locks	31	52
WZ	Alloy Wheel Locks	31	52

NOTE: Toyotas sold in Alabama, Florida, Georgia, North Carolina and South Carolina may be equipped with option packages not listed in this guide. You can expect to haggle 25% off the window sticker price on these packages.

2001 MR2 SPYDER

What's New?

Brand new last year, the spunky but not spacious MR2 Spyder rolls into 2001 without changes.

Review

Given the popularity of two-seat roadsters, it was only a matter of time before Toyota joined the fray. Last year, the company resurrected an old timer of the performance line, the MR2, in a new convertible incarnation called the Spyder. Although it has its work cut out for it with the plethora of roadster competitors on the market these days, its relatively low price is its selling point. The MR2 is one of three new vehicles (the others being the Echo and Celica) recently trotted out by Toyota to appeal to younger, first-time buyers.

The Spyder rides on a low-slung, long-wheelbase platform with MacPherson struts supporting each corner. A five-speed manual transmission drives the rear wheels, and an amazingly sharp

MR2 SPYDER

TOYOTA

and responsive electric hydraulic power steering system makes this little droptop a blast when ripping along canyon roads.

Sharing an engine with the Celica GT, MR2 Spyder's 1.8-liter, twin-cam, 16-valve, four-cylinder engine produces 138 horses at 6,400 rpm and 127 foot-pounds of torque at 4,400 rpm, thanks in part to VVT-i variable valve timing technology. Weighing in at a diminutive 2,200 pounds, it provides plenty of vroom from the get-go, reaching 60 mph in about 7 seconds. Not to worry, however, because a wide track and sticky tires will keep you firmly planted to the asphalt. With the mid-engine design and its speedy recovery ability, acrobatics on curvy roads equal some good times.

The kids will have fun with the exterior sheetmetal, which features steel panels bolted onto a rigid unit-body that allows for aftermarket customization. Considering the no-frills, form-over-function style of the dated-looking interior, this may be the only outlet to express your inner artiste.

The MR2 Spyder comes one way and pretty much includes any features you might want. Air conditioning, ABS, power windows and door locks and a tilt steering wheel are all standard. Plus, it boasts something its higher-priced competitor, the Honda S2000, doesn't have: a glass rear window with defroster. However, the ragtop, though made by the same company that makes lids for the S2000 and the Miata, is a bit more cumbersome than those two models. It is necessary to get out of the car before putting it up or down. Plus, you can't get leather upholstery.

Some might find contention with the chunky styling of the little machine, Danny DeVito-esque being one of the ways to describe the bulging headlights and rotund yet busy lines of the sheetmetal, especially when compared to the sleek and curvaceous Miata. But one sometimes feels more affection for the less comely child...

Besides, once you get the MR2 Spyder revved up and onto the proper racing line at a track, you'll be smitten no matter what your opinion of the styling, inside or out. Thinking of autocrossing a small, inexpensive roadster? This Toyota is your car.

Ah, to be young, beautiful, and racing around town in a convertible. You may not be the first two, but you could have the last for a lot less money than you might expect.

Standard Equipment

BASE (5M): 1.8L I4 DOHC MPI 16-valve engine with variable valve timing; 5-speed OD manual transmission; 80 amp alternator; rear-wheel drive, 4.31 axle ratio; stainless steel exhaust with tailpipe finisher; front independent strut suspension with anti-roll bar, front coil springs, rear independent strut suspension with anti-roll bar, rear coil springs; rack-and-pinion power steering; 4-wheel antilock disc brakes; 12.7 gal. capacity fuel tank; side impact bars; manual convertible roof with lining, glass rear window, manual wind blocker; front and rear body-colored bumpers; monotone paint; aero-composite halogen fully auto headlamps with daytime running-lights; driver's and passenger's power remote body-colored folding outside mirrors; front 15" x 6" silver alloy wheels rear 15" x 6.5" silver alloy wheels; P185/55SR15 BSW A/S front tires; 205/50 rear tires; compact steel spare wheel; air conditioning; AM/FM stereo radio, seek-scan feature, cassette player, single-disc CD player, 4 speakers, fixed antenna; power door locks, remote hatch/trunk release, remote fuel door release; 1 power accessory outlet, driver's foot rest, retained accessory power; instrumentation display includes tachometer, water temperature gauge, in-dash clock, trip odometer; warning indicators include oil pressure, battery, lights on, low fuel, door ajar; driver's front airbag, passenger's cancelable front airbag; ignition disable; tinted windows with driver's 1-touch down function; variable-speed intermittent front windshield wipers, rear window defroster; seating capacity of 2, front sports seats with fixed headrests, driver and passenger seat's include 4-way adjustment; height-adjustable front seatbelts with pretensioners; cloth seats, cloth door trim insert, full cloth headliner, full carpet floor covering, leather-wrapped gearshift knob, aluminum interior accents; interior lights include dome light with delay, front reading lights; leather-wrapped steering wheel with tilt adjustment; day/night rearview mirror; full floor console, glove box, front cupholder, instrument panel covered bin, locking interior concealed storage, driver's and passenger's door bins; carpeted cargo floor, cargo light; black side window moldings, black front windshield molding and body-colored door handles.

TOYOTA

MR2 SPYDER / PRIUS

CODE	DESCRIPTION	INVOICE	MSRP

Base Prices

3233	Base Convertible (5M)	21342	23585
	Destination Charge:	455	455

Interested in seeing what dealers will sell this vehicle for? Check out our True Market Value^{sm} (TMV^{sm}) pricing on our Web site at www.edmunds.com.

Accessories

8A	Acculaser Carbon Fiber Dash Applique	199	369
CF	Carpet Floor Mats (2-Piece Set)	37	62
LA	Leather Package	496	620
	Includes leather door trim ornament and tan color top and leather seats. NOT AVAILABLE with LP.		
WL	Alloy Wheel Locks	31	52

NOTE: Toyotas sold in Alabama, Florida, Georgia, North Carolina and South Carolina may be equipped with option packages not listed in this guide. You can expect to haggle 25% off the window sticker price on these packages.

2001 PRIUS

What's New?

Toyota's Prius, a gas/electric hybrid that follows in the more-expensive Honda Insight's footsteps, offers space for five adults coupled with class-leading fuel economy.

Review

Commend Toyota for taking the gasoline/electric hybrid one step further than Honda did when it released the two-seat Insight last year. The new Prius, though it gives up ultimate fuel economy for increased utility, holds five passengers and a good bit of cargo, meaning it functions as a useable family car.

On sale in Japan since 1997, Toyota is keen on pointing out that Prius, and not Insight, was the first mass-produced gas/electric hybrid vehicle in the world. The company held off on introducing the model to U.S. customers until it could gauge consumer interest and boost power levels.

An all-aluminum 1.5-liter gasoline engine makes 70 horsepower at 4,500 rpm, 12 more than Japan-market models. Torque is less than robust, measuring a meager 82 foot-pounds at a rather high 4,200 rpm. Variable valve timing with intelligence (VVT-i) helps maximize engine efficiency while minimizing emissions, and power is put to the ground via a continuously variable transmission driving the front wheels. With a curb weight of 2,765 pounds, we're thinking Prius is for use primarily in the city and not for blitzkrieg runs to Vegas.

Like the engine, the sealed nickel-metal hydride battery pack powering the supplementary electric motor has been boosted 20 percent to 25 kilowatts (kW), resulting in 34 supplementary horsepower. Lighter than Japan-market batteries, U.S. spec power packs are also smaller, providing increased cargo area in the trunk, amounting to 11.8 cubic feet of space. Regenerative

PRIUS

TOYOTA

antilock brakes recharge the battery pack with each use, and if the electrical power completely depletes, the gas engine will help energize them.

Driven with care, Prius will achieve 52 mpg in the city and 45 on the highway while meeting SULEV emissions standards, according to the EPA. With its 11.9-gallon gas tank, that gives the car a maximum city range of just over 600 miles.

A single model is available, loaded with amenities like air conditioning, remote keyless entry, cassette stereo, power windows/locks/mirrors, height-adjustable front seats, and 14-inch alloy wheels. Options are available, most notably side air bags and a CD player.

Gauges and controls are located in the center of the dashboard, like in Toyota's goofy Echo subcompact, to make Prius easy to configure for multiple world markets. Thanks to a tall stance, seating is upright with plenty of head- and foot room. Toyota likes to refer to Prius as a "real car," intimating that Honda's hybrid Insight is not a real car. If the definition of "real" is capacity for more than two people and 10 cubic feet of stuff, then they're not fibbing.

Whatever the case may be, it is obvious that hybrids are meeting with acceptance in the court of public opinion. Like Insight, Prius offers a viable alternative to gasoline power plants without the limitations posed by electric-only cars like the GM EV1. If your blood runs green and not red, drop by your local Toyota dealer for a test drive.

Standard Equipment

PRIUS: 1.5L I4 DOHC SMPI 16-valve engine with variable valve timing, requires 91-or-greater octane fuel; single-speed electronically controlled Continuously Variable Transmission; front-wheel drive, 3.91 axle ratio; stainless steel exhaust; front independent strut suspension with anti-roll bar, front coil springs, rear independent torsion suspension with anti-roll bar, rear torsion springs; rack-and-pinion power steering; front disc/rear drum brakes with 4-wheel antilock brakes; 11.9 gal. capacity fuel tank; side impact bars; front and rear body-colored bumpers with black rub strip, rear wing spoiler; clearcoat monotone paint; aero-composite halogen headlamps with daytime running lights; driver's and passenger's power remote body-colored outside mirrors; 14" x 5.5" silver alloy wheels; P175/65SR14 BSW A/S tires; compact steel spare wheel; air conditioning with climate control, air filter, rear heat ducts; AM/FM stereo radio, seek-scan feature, cassette player, 4 speakers, integrated roof antenna; power door locks with 2-stage unlock, remote keyless entry, remote fuel door release, remote trunk release, child-safety rear door locks; power accessory outlet, front lighter element, driver's foot rest, smokers' package; digital instrumentation includes exterior temp, systems monitor, display trip odometer; warning indicators include oil pressure, water temp, battery, lights on, door ajar; driver's and passenger's front airbags; security system includes ignition disable and panic alarm; tinted windows, power front and rear windows, driver's 1-touch down function; variable-speed intermittent front windshield wipers, rear window defroster; seating capacity of 5, front bucket seats with adjustable headrests, center armrest with storage, driver's and passenger's seats include 6-way adjustment; 60/40 folding rear bench seat with adjustable headrests; height-adjustable front seatbelts with pretensioners; cloth seats, cloth door trim insert, full cloth headliner, full carpet floor covering; interior lights include front reading light, illuminated entry, dome light with delay; steering wheel with tilt adjustment; vanity mirrors; day/night rearview mirror; partial floor console, glove box, front and rear cupholders, instrument panel bin, driver's and passenger's door bins, seatback storage pockets, front underseat tray; carpeted cargo floor, cargo light; black grille, black front windshield molding, black side and rear window moldings, body-colored door handles.

Base Prices

1222	Base Sedan	18793	19995
Destination Charge:		455	455

Interested in seeing what dealers will sell this vehicle for? Check out our True Market Value^{sm} (TMV^{sm}) pricing on our Web site at www.edmunds.com.

TOYOTA   PRIUS

CODE	DESCRIPTION	INVOICE	MSRP

Accessories

CF	Carpet Floor Mats (4 Piece Set)	43	70
GN	Cargo Net	30	45
P5	Compact Disc Deck	235	335
	NOT AVAILABLE with P6.		
P6	6 Disc In-Dash CD Changer	385	550
	NOT AVAILABLE with P5.		
V2	V.I.P. Glass Breakage Sensor (GBS)	75	115
WL	Alloy Wheel Locks	31	52

NOTE: Toyotas sold in Alabama, Florida, Georgia, North Carolina and South Carolina may be equipped with option packages not listed in this guide. You can expect to haggle 25% off the window sticker price on these packages.

TOWN HALL

Get answers from our editors, discover smart shopping strategies and share your perspectives in this interactive forum of both experts and consumers. Just enter the following address into your Web browser:

townhall.edmunds.com

Where smart shoppers talk about cars, trucks, and related consumer topics.

VOLKSWAGEN

CABRIO

2001 CABRIO

What's New?

A top-of-the-line GLX trim level has been added to the existing lineup for 2001. All models get an anti "trunk entrapment" button to keep people from getting stuck in the cargo hold.

Review

Volkswagen's Cabrio is good fun. A four-seat convertible with simple good looks, spry performance and premium sound, the Golf-based drop top is the perfect summertime cruiser. Road feel is superb, and the thick, four-spoke steering wheel falls readily to hand. At high speeds, the VW feels solid and sure; this is a car that will get you speeding tickets if you're not careful. Handling is excellent, in the Volkswagen tradition. The chassis and suspension communicate clearly with the driver, and Cabrio's multi-adjustable seats are comfortable. All Cabrios come with a fixed, integrated roll bar and a stout top, sporting six layers and latching tightly to the windshield header.

Three trim levels are available for 2001: value-packed GL, mid-level GLS, and high-end GLX. All three come with CFC-free air conditioning, ABS, an AM/FM stereo with CD changer pre-wiring, a glass rear window with defogger, side airbags and an anti-theft system. The GL has a vinyl top and a leather-covered steering wheel while GLS models add power windows, power mirrors, heated seats, cruise control, and a cloth top. Pop for the GLX and you get all of the GLS' features plus a power top, leather seating, newly-designed 14-inch wheels and fog lights. For 2001, all Cabrios receive an anti-entrapment button that allows individuals to escape from the trunk.

All models are powered by the same 115-horsepower, 2.0-liter, four-cylinder engine that motivated previous-generation ragtops. A five-speed manual transmission comes standard and an automatic tranny is optional. Despite its 122 foot-pounds of torque, this inline four is no barnstormer, and will feel downright sluggish underfoot if mated to the automatic. Nonetheless, the latest Cabrio is a solid, refined and comfortable ride, whether cruising at highway speeds or clipping apexes on your favorite mountain road. Capable underpinnings include MacPherson struts and an anti-roll bar that controls front-end movement, while Volkswagen's own "independent track-correcting torsion-beam rear axle" keeps the Cabrio's hindquarters in line. This suspension is complimented by a perfectly weighted, power-assisted rack-and-pinion steering system that offers excellent turn-in and fantastic feedback.

Inside the Cabrio you'll find classy chrome accents and an instrument panel that illuminates with indigo blue and red lighting. Climate and radio controls are within easy reach and have a logical layout. Front seats offer substantial bolstering, firm padding, and a wide range of adjustments to satisfy drivers of all sizes. This is one of the few small cars we've driven recently that had front legroom to spare.

The Cabrio imparts a sense of class and sophistication, and with a conservative price tag, a fantastic two-year/24,000-mile new vehicle warranty, a 10-year/100,000-mile powertrain warranty, two years of free roadside assistance, and free scheduled maintenance during the first two years or 24,000 miles of ownership, we think this Volkswagen will appeal to those who appreciate a capable drop-top.

Standard Equipment

GL (5M): 2.0L I4 SOHC SMPI 8-valve engine; 5-speed OD manual transmission; engine oil cooler; 90 amp alternator; front-wheel drive, 3.67 axle ratio; stainless steel exhaust; front

VOLKSWAGEN *CABRIO*

independent strut suspension with anti-roll bar, front coil springs, rear semi-independent torsion suspension with rear coil springs, gas-pressurized rear shocks; rack-and-pinion power steering; 4-wheel antilock disc brakes; 13.7 gal. capacity fuel tank; side impact bars; manual convertible roof with lining, glass rear window, rollover protection; front and rear body-colored bumpers with body-colored rub strip; body-colored bodyside molding; clearcoat monotone paint; aero-composite halogen headlamps with daytime running lights; driver's and passenger's manual remote body-colored heated folding outside mirrors; 14" x 6" steel wheels; P195/60HR14 A/S BSW tires; compact steel spare wheel; air conditioning, air filter, rear heat ducts; premium AM/FM stereo radio, seek-scan feature, cassette player, CD changer pre-wiring, in-dash CD pre-wiring, 8 speakers, theft deterrent, fixed antenna; 2-stage power door locks, remote keyless entry, power remote trunk release; power accessory outlet, driver's foot rest; instrumentation display includes tachometer, water temperature gauge, in-dash clock, trip odometer; warning indicators include oil pressure, battery, lights on, trunk ajar, key in ignition; driver's and passenger's front airbags, driver's and front passenger's seat-mounted side airbags; security system features ignition disable and panic alarm; tinted windows, manual front and rear windows; fixed-interval front windshield wipers with heated jets, rear window defroster; seating capacity of 4, front bucket seats with adjustable tilt headrests, driver's and front passenger's seats include 6-way adjustment; full-folding rear bench seat with fixed headrests; height-adjustable front seatbelts; cloth seats, cloth door trim insert, full cloth headliner, full carpet floor covering with carpeted floor mats, leather gearshift knob, chrome interior accents; interior lights include dome light, door curb lights, illuminated entry; leather-wrapped steering wheel with tilt adjustment and audio component controls; dual illuminated vanity mirrors; day/night rearview mirror; full floor console, front and rear cupholders, 2 seatback storage pockets, driver's and passenger's door bins; carpeted cargo floor, cargo net, cargo light; body-colored grille, black side window moldings, black front windshield molding, black rear window molding and body-colored door handles.

GLS (5M) (in addition to or instead of GL (5M) equipment): Additional exterior lights include front fog/driving lights; driver's and passenger's power remote body-colored heated folding outside mirrors; cruise control; power front and rear windows with driver's and passenger's 1-touch down function; heated-cushion front bucket seats.

GLX (5M) (in addition to or instead of GLS (5M) equipment): Power convertible roof, heated-cushion front sports seats; leather seats, and leatherette door trim insert.

Base Prices

1V74L4	GL (5M)	17947	19600
1V75L4	GLS (5M)	18856	20600
1V77L4	GLX (5M)	20400	22300
Destination Charge:		525	525

Interested in seeing what dealers will sell this vehicle for? Check out our True Market Value^{sm} (TMV^{sm}) pricing on our Web site at www.edmunds.com.

Accessories

—	Transmission: 4-Speed Automatic (GL/GLS/GLX)	864	875
	Includes adaptive "fuzzy logic" shift points, shift lock and 4.22 Axle Ratio.		
PMC	California and Northeast Emissions (GL/GLS/GLX)	99	100
	Northeast states include NH, NY, MA, CT, RI, PA, NJ, DE, MD, VA, VT and DC.		

GOLF VOLKSWAGEN

2001 GOLF

What's New?

All Golf models get clear side marker lights, trunk entrapment buttons, new cupholders and head protection airbags. Golf GL and GLS get higher-quality interior fabrics and the GTI benefits from a new 16-inch wheel design, optional 17-inch wheels, and multi-function steering wheel controls.

Review

We've always liked the Golf, a fun-to-drive, chunky-but-spunky hatchback that has been a bestseller in Europe for more than two decades. Here in the States, the fourth-generation Golf does battle against a range of compacts, many of them with less sporting credentials.

The Golf is available as a base two-door GL, an uplevel four-door GLS, or a sporty two-door GTI in either GLS or GLX trim. There are three powertrains for the GL and GLS. The standard 2.0-liter, four-cylinder engine is good for 115 horsepower, while an optional, fuel-sipping, 1.9-liter Turbo Direct Injection (TDI) diesel engine is available. You can also opt for the turbocharged 1.8T motor, which increases horsepower to 150, produces lots of low-end torque across a wide rev range, and can now be had with an optional sports suspension.

The GTI comes standard with the 1.8T turbo engine and new sports suspension in GLS trim, or you can get the GLX version which serves up a smooth 2.8-liter narrow-angle V6 with a wide torque band. Horsepower is rated 174 at 5,800 rpm, while torque is 181 foot-pounds at 3,200 revs. This year the GLX gets a new 16-inch wheel design and standard multi-function steering wheel controls for the radio and cruise control system (steering wheel controls are optional on GTI models in GLS trim). New 17-inch alloy wheels are optional on all GTI models.

All Golfs are available with a standard five-speed manual or optional four-speed automatic transmission (except the GTI VR6, which is five-speed only). Silky and playful, both the turbo engine and the VR6 make for high-spirited driving. Ownership piece of mind comes from VW's two-year/24,000-mile limited warranty with free scheduled maintenance for the same period.

The Golf offers a long list of standard features, including side-impact airbags, four-wheel-disc ABS, 15-inch wheels and tires, clear halogen headlamps, tilt/telescoping steering wheel, sliding sun-visor extenders, a brake-wear indicator, an anti-theft alarm, remote keyless entry, a split-folding rear seat with three headrests and an optional, dealer-installed, in-dash CD player. An eight-speaker Monsoon sound system is also available. New standard features for 2001 include an improved cupholder design, a trunk entrapment button and head protection airbags.

Consumers will be impressed by Golf's structural rigidity, which not only provides a solid, quiet body with precise gaps between the doors and body panels, but an overall feel of quality. It all rides on front MacPherson struts and a rear independent torsion-beam axle. Separate shock and coil-spring mounts reduce intrusion into the luggage compartment and cut road noise.

Inside, the instrument panel is stylish yet functional, and the dark wood trim in the GLX model blends well with the high-quality fit and finish of the soft-textured surfaces. Like the New Beetle, gauges are backlit in blue with vibrant red pointers. Volkswagen wanted this combination to be marque-specific, noting that they are the same colors used by international air traffic on airfields at night. Seats are firm and supportive, and the back seat folds down for expanded cargo-carrying capacity.

Behind the wheel of the Golf, whether swayed by value or performance, drivers will be racing to start their engines.

VOLKSWAGEN GOLF

Standard Equipment

GL (5M): 2.0L I4 SOHC SMPI 8-valve engine, requires unleaded fuel; 5-speed OD manual transmission; engine oil cooler; 90 amp alternator; front-wheel drive, 4.24 axle ratio; stainless steel exhaust; front independent strut suspension with anti-roll bar, front coil springs, gas-pressurized front shocks, rear semi-independent torsion suspension with anti-roll bar, rear coil springs, gas-pressurized rear shocks; rack-and-pinion power steering; 4-wheel antilock disc brakes; 14.5 gal. capacity fuel tank; side impact bars; front and rear body-colored bumpers with body-colored rubber strip; body-colored bodyside molding; clearcoat monotone paint; aero-composite halogen headlamps with daytime running lights; driver's and passenger's manual remote body-colored heated folding outside mirrors; 15" x 6" steel wheels; P195/65HR15 BSW A/S tires; full-size steel spare wheel; air conditioning, air filter, rear heat ducts; premium AM/FM stereo radio, seek-scan feature, cassette player, CD changer pre-wiring, in-dash CD pre-wiring, 8 speakers, theft deterrent, and integrated roof antenna; power door locks with 2-stage unlock, remote keyless entry, power remote hatch/trunk release, power remote fuel door release; 2 power accessory outlets, driver's foot rest, retained accessory power; instrumentation display includes tachometer, water temperature gauge, in-dash clock, trip odometer; warning indicators include oil pressure, battery, lights on, key in ignition, low fuel, low washer fluid, trunk ajar; driver's and passenger's front airbags, driver's and front passenger's seat-mounted side airbags, driver's and passenger's overhead airbags; ignition disable, panic alarm, security system; tinted windows; variable intermittent front windshield wipers, sun visor strip, fixed interval rear wiper, rear window defroster; seating capacity of 5, front bucket seats with adjustable tilt headrests, driver's and front passenger's seats include 6-way adjustment, easy entry; 60/40 folding rear bench seat with tilt headrests; height-adjustable front seatbelts with pretensioners; cloth seats, cloth door trim insert, full cloth headliner, full carpet floor covering with carpeted floor mats, chrome interior accents; interior lights include dome light with fade, front and rear reading lights, door curb lights, illuminated entry; steering wheel with tilt and telescopic adjustment; dual illuminated vanity mirrors, driver's side auxiliary visor; day/night rearview mirror; full floor console, locking glove box with light, front and rear cupholders, instrument panel bin, driver's and passenger's door bins; carpeted cargo floor, cargo cover, cargo tie downs, cargo light, concealed cargo storage; body-colored grille, black side window moldings, black front windshield molding and body-colored door handles.

GL TDI (5M) (in addition to or instead of GL (5M) equipment): 1.9L I4 SOHC direct diesel injection intercooled turbo 8-valve engine, requires diesel fuel and 3.39 axle ratio and cruise control.

GLS (5M) (in addition to or instead of GL TDI (5M) equipment): 2.0L I4 SOHC SMPI 8-valve engine; 4.24 axle ratio; driver's and passenger's power remote body-colored heated folding outside mirrors; child-safety rear door locks, power front and rear windows; front bucket seats with adjustable tilt headrests, center armrest with storage; height-adjustable front and rear seatbelts with front pretensioners; premium cloth seats; 2 seatback storage pockets.

GLS TDI (5M) (in addition to or instead of GLS (5M) equipment): 1.9L I4 SOHC direct diesel injection intercooled turbo 8-valve engine, requires diesel fuel and 3.39 axle ratio.

GLS 1.8T (5M) (in addition to or instead of GLS TDI (5M) equipment): 1.8L I4 DOHC SMPI intercooled turbo 20-valve engine (requires premium unleaded fuel); traction control and 3.94 axle ratio.

GTI GLS (5M) (in addition to or instead of GLS 1.8T (5M) equipment): sport-ride suspension, rear semi-independent torsion suspension with anti-roll bar, front express open/close sliding and tilting glass sunroof with sunshade; additional exterior lights include front fog/driving lights; driver's and passenger's power remote body-colored heated folding outside mirrors and driver's and front passenger's head airbags.

GOLF — VOLKSWAGEN

CODE	DESCRIPTION	INVOICE	MSRP

GTI GLX (5M) (in addition to or instead of GLS (5M) equipment): 2.8L V6 SOHC SMPI 12-valve engine; traction control, 3.39 axle ratio; sport suspension; 16" x 6.5" silver alloy wheels; P205/55HR16 BSW A/S tires; air conditioning with climate control, radio steering wheel controls; exterior temp, trip computer, trip odometer; heated jets variable-speed intermittent front windshield wipers, rain-detecting wipers, heated-cushion driver's and passenger's seats, leather seats, leatherette door trim insert, genuine wood dashboard insert, wood gearshift knob, genuine wood door panel insert, genuine wood console insert, leather-wrapped steering wheel with tilt and telescopic adjustment, auto-dimming day/night rearview mirror, and leather-wrapped gearshift knob.

Base Prices

Code	Description	Invoice	MSRP
1J14G4	GL Hatchback (5M)	13904	14900
1J1414	GL TDI Hatchback (5M)	15101	16195
1J15G4	GLS Hatchback (5M)	15244	16350
1J1514	GLS TDI Hatchback (5M)	16214	17400
1J15N4	GLS 1.8L Turbo Hatchback (5M)	16675	17900
1J16N4	GLS Hatchback (5M)	17554	19275
1J16U4	GLX Hatchback (5M)	20829	22900
	Destination Charge:	525	525

Interested in seeing what dealers will sell this vehicle for? Check out our True Market Value^{sm} (TMV^{sm}) pricing on our Web site at www.edmunds.com.

Accessories

Code	Description	Invoice	MSRP
—	Transmission: 4-Speed Automatic (All Except GTI GLX)	864	875
	Includes a 3.20 axle ratio.		
4X3	Side Curtain Protection	133	150
	Added to all models at extra cost.		
PJA	Wheels: 17" Monte Carlo Alloy (GTI GLS)	530	600
PJA	Wheels: 17" Monte Carlo Alloy (GTI GLX)	353	400
PLB	Leather Package	929	1050
	Includes leather seat trim, multifunction leather steering wheel, cold weather package, heatable front seats and heated washer nozzles.		
PLX	Luxury Package (GLS, GLS TDI, GLS 1.8T)	1082	1225
	Includes power sunroof and 15" alloy wheels.		
PMC	California and Northeast Emissions	99	100
	States include CA, NH, NY, MA, CT, RI, PA, NJ, DE, MD, VA, VT and DC.		
PSF	Sport Suspension (GLS 1.8T)	177	200
RMA	Monsoon Sound System (GLS)	287	325
WW1	Cold Weather Package (GLS, GLS TDI, GLS 1.8T)	133	150
	Includes heatable front seats and heated windshield washer nozzles.		
-WW1	Cold Weather Package with 4AT (GLS)	133	150
	Includes heatable front seats and heated windshield washer nozzles. REQUIRES 4AT. NOT AVAILABLE with PLT or WW9.		

VOLKSWAGEN — JETTA

2001 JETTA

What's New?

For 2001, improved cloth and velour interior materials come standard in the GL and GLS trim. Side curtain airbags that offer head protection for front and rear passengers are introduced this year, and steering wheel controls for the audio and cruise systems are available on GLS/GLX trim models. Optional 17-inch wheels and a sport suspension can be had on GLS models with the 1.8T or VR6 engine. The new sport suspension comes standard with GLX trim and all models get redesigned cupholders and a trunk entrapment release button. VW has also brought back the sporty Wolfsburg Edition of the Jetta with many features that appeal to the driving enthusiast. For those seeking more utility in the Jetta line up, a wagon model is promised for the spring of 2001.

Review

The Jetta, Volkswagen's sedan version of the Golf, has always been one of our favorites. Like many cars conceived in Germany, the Jetta possesses an uncanny ability to keep the driver in touch with every undulation and irregularity on the road without sacrificing comfort. For 2001, the fourth-generation of VW's best-selling Jetta will see only minor equipment changes.

Jetta's entry-level GL model comes with a 2.0-liter, four-cylinder engine that produces 115 horsepower and makes 122 foot-pounds of torque at 2,600 rpm for quick off-the-line acceleration. The GL also has standard side airbags, a cassette stereo and ABS. The next step up the Jetta ladder is the GLS trim level, which can be ordered with one of four powertrains and offers more standard goodies like cruise control, power windows and mirrors, and a center armrest.

A turbocharged direct injection (TDI) diesel engine is optional on the GL and GLS models. When mated to a manual transmission, the TDI will achieve approximately 49 mpg. A gas-powered turbo 1.8-liter engine, sourced from Audi and providing 150 horsepower, is also available with GLS trim and imbues Jetta with a spirited ride. Optional on GLS and standard on top-of-the-line Jetta GLX is a buttery-smooth, 174-horsepower VR6 engine. GLX also provides nifty equipment like rain-sensor wipers, automatic climate control, leather seats, self-dimming rearview mirrors and wood trim. The Wolfsberg Edition offers many features including a sports-tuned suspension, bolstered seats, a three-spoke leather steering wheel, 16-inch alloy wheels, a leather shift knob, boot and brake handle and exterior badges. A power sunroof, Monsoon sound system and a cold weather packages are options for the Wolfsberg Edition.

For 2001, all Jettas get a side curtain protection system that provides head airbags for front and rear passengers. GLS and GLX models can now be had with multi-function steering wheel controls and 17-inch wheels. A sport suspension is available on GLS models with the 1.8T or VR6 engine; this suspension comes standard on GLX trim Jettas.

The car's exterior is sleek and curvaceous; built with high-tech bonding agents and laser-welding techniques, the Jetta is structurally rigid, which makes for crisp handling and a solid feel. Jetta has always been a driver's car, providing an enjoyable experience despite a simple MacPherson-strut front suspension and a torsion-beam rear axle. Accented by stabilizer bars and four-wheel disc brakes with ABS, Jetta's underpinnings provide decent handling and braking qualities.

Due to its popularity and subsequent price increases, Jetta is not quite the bargain it used to be. Still, Volkswagen's bread-and-butter sedan offers upscale interior components and the top-level GLX model feels downright luxurious. If cost is not your primary concern in selecting a compact sedan, you should give the Jetta a look.

JETTA   VOLKSWAGEN

| CODE | DESCRIPTION | INVOICE | MSRP |

Standard Equipment

GL (5M): 2.0L I4 SOHC SMPI 8-valve engine; 5-speed OD manual transmission; engine oil cooler; 90 amp alternator; front-wheel drive, 4.24 axle ratio; stainless steel exhaust; front independent strut suspension with anti-roll bar, front coil springs, gas-pressurized front shocks, rear semi-independent torsion suspension with anti-roll bar, rear coil springs, gas-pressurized rear shocks; rack-and-pinion power steering; 4-wheel antilock disc brakes; 14.5 gal. capacity fuel tank; side impact bars; front and rear body-colored bumpers with body-colored rub strip; body-colored bodyside molding; clearcoat monotone paint; aero-composite halogen headlamps with daytime running lights; driver's and passenger's manual remote body-colored heated folding outside mirrors; 15" x 6" steel wheels; P195/65HR15 BSW A/S tires; full-size steel spare wheel; air conditioning, air filter, rear heat ducts; premium AM/FM stereo radio, seek-scan feature, cassette player, CD changer pre-wiring, in-dash CD pre-wiring, 8 speakers, theft deterrent, and integrated roof antenna; power door locks with 2-stage unlock, remote keyless entry, child-safety rear door locks, power remote trunk release, power remote fuel door release; 2 power accessory outlets, driver's foot rest, retained accessory power; instrumentation display includes tachometer, water temperature gauge, in-dash clock, trip odometer; warning indicators include oil pressure, battery, lights on, key in ignition, low fuel, low washer fluid, trunk ajar; driver's and passenger's front airbags, driver's and front passenger's seat-mounted side airbags, driver's and front passenger's head airbags; ignition disable, panic alarm, security system; tinted windows, manual front and rear windows; variable-speed intermittent speed front windshield wipers, sun visor strip, rear window defroster; seating capacity of 5, front bucket seats with adjustable tilt headrests, driver's and front passenger's seats include 6-way adjustment; 60/40 folding rear bench seat with tilt headrests; height-adjustable front seatbelts with pretensioners; cloth seats, cloth door trim insert, full cloth headliner, full carpet floor covering with carpeted floor mats, chrome interior accents; interior lights include dome light with fade, front and rear reading lights, door curb lights, illuminated entry; steering wheel with tilt and telescopic adjustment; dual illuminated vanity mirrors, driver's side auxiliary visor; day/night rearview mirror; covered storage floor console, locking glove box with light, front and rear cupholders, instrument panel bin, 2 seatback storage pockets, driver's and passenger's door bins; carpeted cargo floor, cargo tie downs, cargo light, concealed cargo storage; body-colored grille, black side window moldings, black front windshield molding and body-colored door handles.

GL TDI (5M) (in addition to or instead of GL (5M) equipment): 1.9L I4 SOHC direct diesel injection intercooled turbo 8-valve engine, requires diesel fuel and 3.39 axle ratio.

GLS (5M) (in addition to or instead of GL (5M) equipment): Driver's and passenger's power remote body-colored heated folding outside mirrors; cruise control; power front and rear windows with driver's and passenger's 1-touch down function; center armrest with storage; premium cloth seats.

GLS TDI (5M) (in addition to or instead of GLS (5M) equipment): 1.9L I4 SOHC direct diesel injection intercooled turbo 8-valve engine, requires diesel fuel and 3.39 axle ratio.

GLS 1.8T (5M) (in addition to or instead of GLS (5M) equipment): 1.8L I4 DOHC SMPI 20-valve intercooled turbo engine (requires premium unleaded fuel); traction control, and a 3.94 axle ratio.

GLS VR6 (5M) (in addition to or instead of GLS 1.8T (5M) equipment): 2.8L V6 SOHC SMPI 12-valve engine; 3.39 axle ratio.

GLX (5M) (in addition to or instead of GLS VR6 (5M) equipment): Front express open/close sliding and tilting glass sunroof with sunshade; additional exterior lights include front fog/driving lights; 16" x 6.5" silver alloy wheels; P205/55HR16 BSW A/S tires; climate control, 8 premium speakers, amplifier; cruise control; instrumentation display includes exterior temp, trip computer; variable-speed intermittent front windshield wipers with heated washer fluid jets, rain detecting wipers, rear blind; front bucket seats with heated-cushion driver's and passenger's seats,

VOLKSWAGEN *JETTA*

| CODE | DESCRIPTION | INVOICE | MSRP |

driver's and front passenger's seats include 8-way power adjustment, lumbar support; leather seats, leatherette door trim insert, genuine wood dashboard insert, wood gearshift knob, genuine wood door panel insert, genuine wood console insert; driver's seat memory includes 2 settings; leather-wrapped steering wheel; auto-dimming day/night rearview mirror.

WOLFSBURG EDITION (5M) (in addition to or instead of GLS 1.8T (5M) equipment): Sport-ride suspension; power-assisted rack-and-pinion steering; 16" x 6.5" silver alloy wheels; P205/55HR16 BSW A/S tires; cruise control; front sports seats with adjustable tilt headrests; leather-wrapped gearshift knob; leather-wrapped steering wheel with tilt and telescopic adjustment; full floor console.

Base Prices

9M24L4	GL Sedan (5M)	15228	16700
9M25L4	GLS Sedan (5M)	16087	17650
9M2414	GL TDI Sedan (5M)	16764	17995
9M2514	GLS TDI Sedan (5M)	17414	18700
9M25N4	GLS 1.8L Turbo Sedan (5M)	17486	19200
9M2WN4	Wolfsburg (5M)	17713	19450
9M25U4	GLS VR6 Sedan (5M)	18164	19950
9M27U4	GLX Sedan (5M)	22094	24300
Destination Charge:		525	525

Interested in seeing what dealers will sell this vehicle for? Check out our True Market Value^{sm} (TMV^{sm}) pricing on our Web site at www.edmunds.com.

Accessories

—	Transmission: 4-Speed Automatic (GL TDI)	1149	1185
	Includes 3.20 axle ratio and 15"x6" alloy wheels.		
—	Transmission: 4-Speed Automatic (GL/GLS)	864	875
	Includes 4.88 axle ratio.		
—	Transmission: 4-Speed Automatic (GLS 1.8T)	864	875
	Includes 4.43 axle ratio.		
—	Transmission: 4-Speed Automatic (GLS TDI)	1151	1185
	Includes 3.20 axle ratio and 15" alloy wheels. NOT AVAILABLE with PEA.		
—	Transmission: 4-Speed Automatic (GLS VR6/GLX)	864	875
	Includes 4.27 axle ratio.		
3FE	Power Sunroof (GLS TDI/Wolfsburg)	808	915
	REQUIRES 4AT.		
4X3	Side Curtain Protection	133	150
	Mandatory option added to all models at extra cost.		
CANE	California & Northeast Emissions (GL and GLS)	90	100
	States include CA, NH, NY, MA, CT, RI, PA, NJ, DE, MD, VA, VT and DC.		
PCA	Cold Weather Package (GLS/Wolfsburg)	133	150
	Includes heated front seats and heated washer nozzles.		
PDA	Luxury Package (GLS VR6)	1258	1425
	Includes power sunroof, 16" alloy wheels, and P205/55H16 BSW A/S tires. NOT AVAILABLE with PZA.		
PEA	Luxury Package (GLS/GLS 1.8T/GLS TDI)	1082	1225
	Includes 15" alloy wheels. NOT AVAILABLE with PZA.		

JETTA / NEW BEETLE — VOLKSWAGEN

CODE	DESCRIPTION	INVOICE	MSRP
PL5	Leather Package (GLS/GLS 1.8T/GLS VR6/GLS TDI)	796	900
	Includes leather shift knob/hand brake, cold weather package (heated front seats, heated windshield washer nozzles) and lumbar support. REQUIRES PEA, PZA, PDA, or 3FE. NOT AVAILABLE with PLA.		
PLA	Lthr Pkg w/Multi-Function Steering Wheel (GLS/GLS 1.8T/GLS VR6/GLS TDI)	929	1050
	Includes multi-function leather steering wheel, leather shift knob/hand brake, cold weather package (heated front seats, heated washer nozzles) and lumbar support. REQUIRES PEA, PZA, or PDA.		
PMC	California and Northeast Emissions (all except GL and GLS)	99	100
	States include CA, NH, NY, MA, CT, RI, PA, NJ, DE, MD, VA, VT and DC.		
PSA	Wheels: 17" Alloy (GLX)	530	600
	Includes 225/45R17 tires.		
PVA	Sport Suspension (GLS 1.8T/GLS VR6/GLX)	177	200
PZA	Sport Luxury Package (GLS 1.8T/GLS VR6)	1788	2025
	Includes power sunroof, 17" alloy wheels and sport suspension. NOT AVAILABLE with PEA or PDA.		
RSM	Monsoon Sound System (All GLS/Wolfsburg)	287	325

2001 NEW BEETLE

What's New?

Optional 17-inch alloy wheels can be ordered on GLS 1.8T and GLX models. Exterior mirrors are larger, high intensity discharge headlights and a Monsoon sound system are available, and all New Beetles benefit from redesigned cupholders and a trunk entrapment release button. Rain-sensing wipers and a self-dimming rearview mirror now come on GLX models.

Review

The New Beetle is a bundle of contradictions. It's a blast from the past and a gateway to the 21st century. It's small but it's safe. It's pretty but it can also be pretty powerful.

Volkswagen's New Beetle debuted at the 1998 North American International Auto Show in Detroit to classic '60s tunes and daisies dotting the dashboards. As a Volkswagen executive said, "It's the birth of a legend, a love affair continued, a dream come true."

The trademark Beetle body shape is immediately recognizable, though it shares no parts with the old Beetle. It's both larger, with 96.3 cubic feet inside, and more powerful than its predecessor and the motor is no longer in the back. Three engines are available: a turbocharged 150-horsepower, 1.8-liter four-cylinder engine, a 115-horsepower, 2.0-liter four-banger, or a high-tech Turbo Direct Injection diesel engine that gets 48 mpg on the highway and has a driving range of 700 miles.

Performance is surprisingly good on all New Beetles, but the 1.8T really shines when pushed to the limit. With 156 foot-pounds of torque available between 2,200 and 4,200 rpm, the New Beetle 1.8T never feels underpowered or overworked. Fun comes both from watching people stare and wave at you and from blasting down the highways or up a canyon road. Steering is responsive and the little car takes corners without too much fuss, making it easy to rack up

VOLKSWAGEN

NEW BEETLE

CODE	DESCRIPTION	INVOICE	MSRP

speeding tickets if you're not careful. Like most VWs, the New Beetle is fun-to-drive, but we'd love to see the company add a stiffer suspension option to go along with the peppy 1.8T engine.

The safety system features energy-absorbing crush zones, pre-tensioning safety belts, daytime running lights, dual airbags, optional side airbags for front-seat passengers and excellent bumper crash-test scores. Other standard features include four beverage holders, a remote locking system, anti-theft alarm, a passenger-assist handle above the glove compartment, driver and passenger height adjusters, mesh pockets on the doors, and a bud vase on the dash. Nice touch.

For 2001, the New Beetle gets redesigned cupholders, larger exterior mirrors and a trunk release entrapment button. GLX models now come standard with a Monsoon sound system, rain-sensing wipers and a self-dimming rearview mirror. Optional high-intensity discharge headlights are available on GLS and GLX trimmed New Beetles, as are new 17-inch alloy wheels.

The New Beetle offers a unique combination of safety, fun, practicality and value. There's no denying it: It's Beetle-mania all over again.

Standard Equipment

GL (5M): 2.0L I4 SOHC SMPI 8-valve engine; 5-speed OD manual transmission; engine oil cooler; 90 amp alternator; front-wheel drive, 4.24 axle ratio; stainless steel exhaust; front independent strut suspension with anti-roll bar, front coil springs, gas-pressurized front shocks, rear semi-independent torsion suspension with anti-roll bar, rear coil springs, gas-pressurized rear shocks; rack-and-pinion power steering; 4-wheel antilock disc brakes; 14.5 gal. capacity fuel tank; side impact bars; front and rear body-colored bumpers; rocker panel extensions; clearcoat monotone paint; projector beam halogen enclosed headlamps with daytime running lights; driver's and passenger's power remote body-colored heated folding outside mirrors; 16" x 6.5" steel wheels, P205/55HR16 BSW A/S tires; full-size steel spare wheel; air conditioning, air filter, rear heat ducts; premium AM/FM stereo radio, seek-scan feature, cassette player, CD changer pre-wiring, in-dash CD player pre-wiring, 6 speakers, theft deterrent, and integrated roof antenna; power door locks with 2-stage unlock, remote keyless entry, power remote hatch, and fuel door releases; 3 power accessory outlets, driver's foot rest, retained accessory power; instrumentation display includes tachometer, water temperature gauge, clock (inside overhead console), exterior temp, trip odometer; warning indicators include oil pressure, battery, lights on, key in ignition, low fuel, trunk ajar; driver's and passenger's front airbags and seat-mounted side airbags; security system features ignition disable and panic alarm; tinted windows; variable-speed intermittent front windshield wipers, sun visor strip, rear window defroster; seating capacity of 4, front bucket seats with adjustable tilt headrests, driver's and front passenger's seats include 6-way adjustment and easy entry; full-folding rear bench seat with adjustable headrests; height-adjustable front seatbelts with pretensioners; premium cloth seats, vinyl door trim insert, full cloth headliner, front carpet floor covering with carpeted floor mats, chrome interior accents; interior lights include dome light with fade, front and rear reading lights, door curb lights, illuminated entry; steering wheel with tilt and telescopic adjustment; dual illuminated vanity mirrors; day/night rearview mirror; full floor console, mini overhead console with storage, locking glove box with light, front and rear cupholders, 2 seatback storage pockets, driver's and passenger's door bins; carpeted cargo floor, cargo cover, cargo light; black side window moldings and body-colored door handles.

GLS (5M) (in addition to or instead of GL (5M) equipment): Additional exterior lights include front fog/driving lights; cruise control; driver's and passenger's window features 1-touch down function; center armrest with storage.

GLS TDI (5M) (in addition to or instead of GLS (5M) equipment): 1.9L I4 SOHC 8-valve direct-diesel-injection intercooled turbo engine, (requires diesel fuel); 3.39 axle ratio.

GLS 1.8T (5M) (in addition to or instead of GLS TDI (5M) equipment): 1.8L I4 DOHC SMPI 20-valve intercooled turbo engine, (requires premium unleaded fuel); traction control, 3.94 axle ratio; power retractable rear spoiler.

NEW BEETLE — VOLKSWAGEN

CODE	DESCRIPTION	INVOICE	MSRP

GLX (5M) (in addition to or instead of GLS 1.8T (5M) equipment): Front power sliding and tilting glass sunroof with sunshade; alloy wheels; variable-speed intermittent front windshield wipers with heated fluid jets, heated-cushion front bucket seats; leather seats, leather-wrapped gearshift knob and leather-wrapped steering wheel with tilt and telescopic adjustment.

Base Prices

Code	Description	Invoice	MSRP
1C13L4	GL (5M)	15151	15900
1C18L4	GLS (5M)	15706	16850
1C1814	GLS TDI (5M)	16675	17900
1C18N4	GLS 1.8T (5M)	17691	19000
1C17N4	GLX (5M)	19700	21175
	Destination Charge:	525	525

Interested in seeing what dealers will sell this vehicle for? Check out our True Market Value^{sm} (TMV^{sm}) pricing on our Web site at www.edmunds.com.

Accessories

Code	Description	Invoice	MSRP
—	Leatherette Seat Trim (1.8T) *NOT AVAILABLE with PLA.*	NC	NC
—	Leatherette Seat Trim (GLS/TDI) *NOT AVAILABLE with PLA.*	NC	NC
—	Transmission: Adaptive 4-Speed Automatic (1.8T/GLX) *Includes shift lock and 4.43 axle ratio.*	864	875
—	Transmission: Adaptive 4-Speed Automatic (GL/GLS) *Includes shift lock and 4.88 axle ratio.*	864	875
—	Transmission: Adaptive 4-Speed Automatic (TDI) *Includes shift lock and 3.63 axle ratio.*	864	875
CANE	California and Northeast Emissions (GL) *tates include CA, NH, NY, MA, CT, RI, PA, NJ, DE, MD, VA, VT and DC.*	94	100
CANE	California and Northeast Emissions (GLS) *States include CA, NH, NY, MA, CT, RI, PA, NJ, DE, MD, VA, VT and DC.*	92	100
PCA	Cold Weather Package (GLS/TDI/1.8T) *Includes heated front seats and washer nozzles.*	133	150
PDA	Luxury Package (GLS/TDI/1.8T) *Includes power sunroof, 16" alloy wheels and anti-theft wheel locks. NOT AVAILABLE with PZA.*	1082	1225
PLA	Leather Package (GLS/TDI/1.8T) *Includes leather steering wheel, leather shift knob/hand brake, perforated leather seating surfaces, heated front seats and washer nozzles. REQUIRES PDA or PZA. NOT AVAILABLE with Leatherette.*	796	900
PLS	Lifestyle Package (Limited Edition) (GLS) *Includes power tilt and slide glass sunroof with sunshade, 16" x 6.5" alloy wheels, anti-theft wheel locks, leather package, 3-spoke padded leather steering wheel, leather shift knob, cold weather package, perforated leather seating surfaces, heatable front seats and heated windshield washer nozzles . NOT AVAILABLE with PLA, PZA.*	1878	2125
PMC	California and Northeast Emissions (GLS TDI, GLS 1.8T, GLX) *States include CA, NH, NY, MA, CT, RI, PA, NJ, DE, MD, VA, VT and DC.*	99	100

VOLKSWAGEN
NEW BEETLE / PASSAT

CODE	DESCRIPTION	INVOICE	MSRP
PSA	Wheels: 17" Alloy (GLX)	353	400
	Includes 17" all season tires.		
PZA	Sport Luxury Package (1.8T)	1435	1625
	Includes power sunroof and 17" alloy wheels. NOT AVAILABLE with PDA.		
RSM	Monsoon Sound System Package (GLS/GLX)	287	325
	Includes 8 speakers with amplifier, premium AM/FM stereo radio with cassette player, control capability for optional single CD/CD changer and theft deterrent.		

2001 PASSAT

What's New?

Side curtain airbags that offer head protection for front and rear passengers are introduced this year, and optional steering wheel controls for the audio and cruise systems are available on GLS (standard on GLX models). All models receive a trunk entrapment release button as standard equipment.

Review

Volkswagen has been busy in recent years. In between buying up smaller carmakers, designing 12- and 16-cylinder engines, and creating a new line of luxury vehicles, the company has had time to tweak its already excellent Passat sedan and wagon offerings.

The base Passat engine is a 1.8-liter, turbocharged four-cylinder that makes 150 horsepower and an almost lag-free 155 foot-pounds of torque. While not a race engine, this powerplant offers adequate acceleration and contributes more to the Passat's overall grin factor than one might think, especially when mated to the company's excellent five-speed manual transmission.

Stepping up to the 2.8-liter V6 will net you an additional 40 horsepower and 52 more foot-pounds of torque. The V6 comes standard on Passat GLX models and puts the "fun" back in functional with its broad torque band and responsive acceleration. Volkswagen's responsive, five-speed Tiptronic automatic transmission is also available on the GLX.

Regardless of drivetrain choice, all Passats come with superb steering, handling and braking characteristics. With ABS four-wheel discs standard on all trim levels, an independent front and rear suspension, and perfectly weighted power rack-and-pinion steering, the Passat is one of the most entertaining sedans (or wagons) in the midsize class. Some drivers note a bit too much body roll during canyon runs, but the pay-off comes in its excellent overall ride quality. For those living in cold-weather climates, or drivers who enjoy the added stability of all-wheel drive, the Passat can be had with Volkswagen's 4-Motion system.

In addition to its mechanical pedigree, the Passat offers up an impressive list of standard features. Items like air conditioning, cruise control, one-touch power windows, power locks, remote keyless entry, a remote trunk release, a full-size conventional spare, side airbags and heated exterior mirrors are included on the base GLS models. GLX trim adds the aforementioned V6 engine, sunroof, heated front seats with driver's seat memory, leather seat coverings and door inserts, variable intermittent wipers with heated jets and an auto-dimming day-night mirror.

New this year as standard equipment on Passat GLX (optional on GLS models) are multi-function steering wheel controls for the audio and cruise systems. All Passats get a trunk entrapment release button and side curtain protection airbags to better protect both front and rear passengers from head injuries.

PASSAT — VOLKSWAGEN

CODE	DESCRIPTION	INVOICE	MSRP

Based on a stretched Audi A4 platform and using plenty of Audi parts in its construction, the Passat looks, feels, smells and drives like a more substantial car than its base price tag would lead you to believe. Its contemporary styling will wear well into the new century and its solid construction should keep the car feeling new as the miles add up.

Before rushing out to buy that new Accord, Camry or Taurus, you'd do well to at least test-drive a Passat.

Standard Equipment

GLS SEDAN (5M): 1.8L I4 DOHC SMPI intercooled turbo 20-valve engine (requires premium unleaded fuel); 5-speed OD manual transmission; engine oil cooler; 90 amp alternator; front-wheel drive, traction control, 3.7 axle ratio; stainless steel exhaust; front independent suspension with anti-roll bar, front coil springs, gas-pressurized front shocks, rear semi-independent torsion suspension with anti-roll bar, rear coil springs, gas-pressurized rear shocks; rack-and-pinion power steering; 4-wheel antilock disc brakes; 16.4 gal. capacity fuel tank; side impact bars; front and rear body-colored bumpers with body-colored rub strip; body-colored bodyside molding rocker panel extensions; clearcoat monotone paint; aero-composite halogen headlamps with daytime running lights; additional exterior lights include front fog/driving lights; driver's and passenger's power remote body-colored heated folding outside mirrors; 15" x 6" steel wheels; P195/65HR15 BSW A/S tires; full-size steel spare wheel; air conditioning, air filter, rear heat ducts; premium AM/FM stereo radio, seek-scan feature, cassette player, CD changer pre-wiring, in-dash CD pre-wiring, 8 speakers, theft deterrent, and integrated roof antenna; cruise control; power door locks with 2-stage unlock, remote keyless entry, child-safety rear door locks, power remote hatch/trunk release, power remote fuel door release; 2 power accessory outlets, front lighter element, driver's foot rest, retained accessory power, smokers' package; instrumentation display includes tachometer, water temperature gauge, in-dash clock, exterior temp, trip computer, trip odometer; warning indicators include oil pressure, water temp, battery, lights on, key in ignition, low fuel, low washer fluid, trunk ajar; driver's and passenger's front airbags, driver's and front passenger's seat-mounted side airbags, overhead airbag; ignition disable, panic alarm, security system; tinted windows, power front and rear windows with driver's and passenger's 1-touch down function; variable-speed intermittent front windshield wipers, sun visor strip, rear window defroster; seating capacity of 5, front bucket seats with adjustable tilt headrests, center armrest with storage, driver's and passenger's seats include 6-way adjustment; 60/40 folding rear bench seat with adjustable headrests; height-adjustable front seatbelts with front and rear pretensioners; premium cloth seats, cloth door trim insert, full cloth headliner, full carpet floor covering with carpeted floor mats, chrome interior accents; interior lights include dome light with fade, front and rear reading lights, door curb lights, illuminated entry; steering wheel with tilt and telescopic adjustment; dual illuminated vanity mirrors, driver's side auxiliary visor; day/night rearview mirror; full floor console, locking glove box with light, front and rear cupholders, instrument panel bin, 2 seatback storage pockets, refrigerated/cooled box, driver's and passenger's door bins; carpeted cargo floor, cargo tie downs, cargo light, concealed cargo storage; black grille, black side window moldings, black front windshield molding and body-colored door handles.

GLS V6 SEDAN (5M) (in addition to or instead of GLS SEDAN (5M) equipment): 2.8L V6 DOHC SMPI 30-valve engine; dual stainless steel exhaust; genuine wood dashboard insert, and genuine wood door panel insert.

GLS V6 4MOTION SEDAN (5A) (in addition to or instead of GLS V6 SEDAN (5M) equipment): 5-speed electronic OD automatic transmission with lock-up torque converter; auto-manual transmission; full-time all-wheel drive 3.73 axle ratio and rear independent double-wishbone suspension.

GLX SEDAN (5M) (in addition to or instead of GLS V6 SEDAN (5M) equipment): front express open/close sliding and tilting glass sunroof with sunshade; 16" x 6.5" silver alloy wheels; P205/55HR16 BSW A/S tires; climate control, 8 premium speakers, amplifier, radio steering wheel controls; cruise control with steering wheel controls; variable-speed intermittent front windshield wipers with heated jets, rain detecting wipers, rear blind; heated-cushion driver's and passenger's

VOLKSWAGEN
PASSAT

CODE	DESCRIPTION	INVOICE	MSRP

seats, driver's and front passenger's seats include 8-way power adjustment, lumbar support; leather seats, leatherette door trim insert, wood gearshift knob, genuine wood door panel insert, driver's seat memory includes 3 settings; leather-wrapped steering wheel; auto-dimming day/night rearview mirror.

GLX 4MOTION SEDAN (5A) (in addition to or instead of GLX SEDAN (5M) equipment): 5-speed electronic OD automatic transmission with lock-up torque converter; auto-manual transmission; full-time all-wheel drive 3.73 axle ratio and rear independent double-wishbone suspension.

WAGON (5M/5A) (in addition to or instead of SEDAN (5M/5A) equipment): 3 power accessory outlets, fixed 1/4 vent windows; cargo cover.

Base Prices

Code	Description	Invoice	MSRP
3B24X5	GLS Sedan (5M)	19519	21450
3B54X5	GLS Wagon (5M)	20242	22250
3B24SR	GLS V6 Sedan (5M)	21868	24050
3B54SR	GLS V6 Wagon (5M)	22591	24850
3B24SU	GLS V6 4MOTION Sedan (5A)	24770	26875
3B54SU	GLS V6 4MOTION Wagon (5A)	25493	27675
3B25SR	GLX Sedan (5M)	25626	28210
3B55SR	GLX Wagon (5M)	26348	29010
3B25SU	GLX 4MOTION Sedan (5A)	28528	31035
3B55SU	GLX 4MOTION Wagon (5A)	29250	31835
	Destination Charge:	525	525

Interested in seeing what dealers will sell this vehicle for? Check out our True Market Value^{sm} (TMV^{sm}) pricing on our Web site at www.edmunds.com.

Accessories

Code	Description	Invoice	MSRP
—	Transmission: 5-Spd Auto Tiptronic (GLS Sdn/GLS V6 Sdn/GLX Sdn/GLS Wgn) ... Includes 3.73 axle ratio.	1073	1075
—	Transmission: 5-Speed Automatic Tiptronic (GLS V6 Wagon, GLX Wagon)	1073	1075
PJ6	Luxury Package (GLS Sedan/GLS V6 Sedan/GLS V6 AWD Sedan) .... Includes power sunroof, 15" alloy wheels, anti-theft wheel locks and a rear sunshade.	1369	1550
PJ6	Luxury Package (GLS Wagon, GLS V6 Wagon, GLS V6 AWD Wagon) .... Includes power sunroof, 15" alloy wheels and anti-theft wheel locks.	1267	1435
PJ7	Luxury Package (GLS Sedan) .... Includes power tilt and slide glass sunroof with sunshade and manually operated rear sunshade. NOT AVAILABLE with PJ6.	1104	1250
PJ7	Luxury Package (GLS Wagon) .... Includes power tilt and slide glass sunroof with sunshade. NOT AVAILABLE with PJ6.	1002	1135
PLD	Leather Package (GLS Sedan/GLS V6 Sedan/GLS Wagon/GLS V6) .... Includes leather multi-function steering wheel, cold weather package, heated front seats, heated washer nozzles.	1325	1500
RMA	Monsoon Sound System (GLS Sedan/GLS V6 Sedan/GLS Wagon/GLS V6) ...	287	325
WW1	Cold Weather Package (GLS Sedan/GLS V6 Sedan/GLS Wagon/GLS V6) ..... Includes heated front seats and heated washer nozzles.	287	325

S40 and V40

2001 S40 and V40

What's New?
Only a year after debuting them on U.S. shores, Volvo has updated the S40 and V40 for 2001. Both the sedan and wagon gain additional crash protection in the form of standard head-protection airbags, dual-stage front airbags and a new child seat-safety system. Under the hood, engine improvements have been made to increase power and lower emissions. There's also a new five-speed automatic transmission that takes the place of the previous four-speed. Other changes are found in the cabin, with new material colors, a redesigned center stack for better functionality, more durable front-seat materials and improved switchgear. Rounding out the S40 and V40's 2001 changes are restyled headlights, bumpers and fenders.

Review

Now in their second year, the S40 Sedan and V40 Wagon are Volvo's smallest and most affordable vehicles. Designed to appeal to younger buyers, both offer impressive levels of safety equipment and an upscale image.

For 2001, Volvo has given the S40 and V40 standard Inflatable Curtain (IC) head-protection airbags, a system found on other, more expensive Volvo models. The curtains, one on each side, are woven in one piece and hidden inside the roof lining. When deployed, they cover the upper part of the interior, from the A-pillar to the rear side C-pillar, thereby protecting the occupants in the front and rear seats.

Additional crash protection comes from whiplash-reducing front seats, dual-stage front airbags, side airbags for front passengers and seatbelt pre-tensioners. Another safety addition for 2001 is ISO-FIX, a new child seat-safety system. The ISO-FIX system allows owners to safely and conveniently attach and detach a child or infant seat that is a perfect fit for the car.

All S40/V40s are equipped with a turbocharged, 160-horsepower, 1.9-liter four-cylinder engine. Volvo has made minor improvements to the engine for 2001, resulting in increased torque, better fuel mileage and lower emissions. The only transmission available is a new five-speed automatic transmission.

Inside, you'll find a remarkable combination of luxury and value. Comfortable and supportive front seats have that Swedish feel we've come to expect from Volvo's high-end cars, and the interior materials are of high quality for a sub-$40,000 vehicle. The 2001's center stack is updated to be more comfortable and functional. The stack is now more anatomically and ergonomically designed, bearing a much stronger resemblance to the designs found in the V70 and S80. The climate control unit is easier to use and the radio controls are more stylish. Other changes we're glad to see is the addition of a storage area on the center console and window switches relocated to the driver's door panel.

On the road, Volvo has tuned the S40 and V40 to be fairly taut, though comfort ultimately takes precedence over performance. If you are looking for performance, Audi's A4 or BMW's 3 Series is a better choice. Still, the MacPherson struts up front, the rear multilink rear suspension and the rack-and-pinion steering system bring a distinctly Teutonic flavor to these Swedish sedans and wagons.

VOLVO

S40 and V40

If you are in the market for an upscale compact sedan or wagon, Volvo's offerings should be considered, especially if safety is one of your high priorities. The main thing to watch out for is choosing optional equipment. A full load of options can bloom the price of these cars considerably.

Standard Equipment

S40 A SEDAN (5A): 1.9L I4 DOHC MPI 16-valve intercooled turbo engine with variable valve timing; driver's selectable multi-mode 5-speed electronic OD automatic transmission with lock-up converter; 520-amp battery; 100-amp alternator; front-wheel drive, 2.54 axle ratio; stainless steel exhaust with tailpipe finisher; front independent strut suspension with anti-roll bar, front coil springs, rear semi-independent multi-link suspension with anti-roll bar, rear coil springs; rack-and-pinion power steering; 4-wheel disc brakes with 4-wheel antilock braking system; 15.8 gal. capacity fuel tank; side impact bars; front and rear body-colored bumpers with black rub strip; black bodyside molding rocker panel extensions; clearcoat monotone paint; aero-composite halogen headlamps with daytime running lights and delay-off feature; driver's and passenger's power remote body-colored heated folding outside mirrors; 15" x 6" silver alloy wheels with P195/60VR15 BSW A/S tires; compact steel spare wheel; air conditioning with climate control, air filter, rear heat ducts; AM/FM stereo, seek-scan feature, cassette player, 6 speakers, amplifier, theft deterrent, power retractable antenna; cruise control; power door locks with 2-stage unlock, remote keyless-entry, child-safety rear door locks, power remote hatch/trunk release; 1 power accessory outlet, driver's foot rest; instrumentation display includes tachometer, water temperature gauge, in-dash clock, exterior temp, trip odometer; warning indicators include oil pressure, battery, low coolant, lights on, key in ignition, low fuel, low washer fluid, bulb failure, service interval; driver's and passenger's front airbags, driver's and front passenger's seat-mounted side airbags, overhead airbag; ignition disable, panic alarm, security system; tinted windows, power front and rear windows with driver's 1-touch down function; fixed-interval front windshield wipers, rear window defroster; seating capacity of 5, front bucket seats with fixed headrests, center armrest with storage, driver's seat includes 8-way direction control, lumbar support, passenger's seat includes 4-way direction control; rear bench seat with adjustable headrests, center pass-thru armrest; height-adjustable front seatbelts with pretensioners; cloth seats, cloth door trim insert, full cloth headliner, full color-keyed carpet floor covering with carpeted floor mats, plastic/rubber gearshift knob, chrome interior accents; interior lights include dome light with fade, front and rear reading lights, illuminated entry; steering wheel with tilt adjustment; dual illuminated vanity mirrors; day/night rearview mirror; full floor console, locking glove box with light, front and rear cupholders, instrument panel bin, 2 seatback storage pockets, driver's and passenger's door bins, rear door bins; carpeted cargo floor, carpeted trunk lid, cargo tie downs, cargo light; chrome grille, black side window moldings, black front windshield molding, black rear window molding and black door handles.

V40 A WAGON (5A): 1.9L I4 DOHC MPI 16-valve intercooled turbo engine with variable valve timing; 5-speed electronic OD automatic transmission with lock-up converter; 520-amp battery; 100-amp alternator; driver's selectable multi-mode transmission; front-wheel drive, 2.54 axle ratio; stainless steel exhaust with tailpipe finisher; front independent strut suspension with anti-roll bar, front coil springs, rear semi-independent multi-link suspension with anti-roll bar, rear coil springs; rack-and-pinion power steering; 4-wheel disc brakes with 4-wheel antilock braking system; 15.8 gal. capacity fuel tank; side impact bars; front and rear body-colored bumpers with black rub strip; black bodyside molding rocker panel extensions; clearcoat monotone paint; aero-composite halogen headlamps with daytime running lights, delay-off feature; driver's and passenger's power remote body-colored heated folding outside mirrors; 15" x 6" silver alloy wheels with P195/60VR15 BSW A/S tires; compact steel spare wheel; air conditioning with climate control, air filter, rear heat ducts; AM/FM stereo, seek-scan feature, cassette player, 7 speakers, amplifier, theft deterrent, integrated roof antenna; cruise control; power door locks with 2-stage unlock, remote keyless-entry, child-safety rear door locks; 1 power accessory outlet, driver's foot rest; instrumentation display includes tachometer, water temperature gauge, in-dash clock, exterior temp, trip odometer; warning indicators include oil pressure, battery, low coolant, lights on, key in ignition, low fuel, low washer fluid, bulb failure, service interval; driver's and passenger's front airbags, driver's and front passenger's seat mounted side airbags,

S40 and V40

VOLVO

| CODE | DESCRIPTION | INVOICE | MSRP |

overhead airbag; ignition disable, panic alarm, security system; tinted windows, power front and rear windows with driver's 1-touch down function, fixed 1/4 vent windows; fixed-interval front windshield wipers, fixed-interval rear wiper, rear window defroster; seating capacity of 5, front bucket seats with fixed headrests, center armrest with storage, driver's seat includes 8-way adjustment, lumbar support, passenger's seat includes 4-way adjustment; rear bench seat with adjustable headrests, center armrest; height-adjustable front seatbelts with pretensioners; cloth seats, cloth door trim insert, full cloth headliner, full color-keyed carpet floor covering with carpeted floor mats, chrome interior accents; interior lights include dome light with fade, front and rear reading lights, illuminated entry; steering wheel with tilt adjustment; dual illuminated vanity mirrors; day/night rearview mirror; full floor console, locking glove box with light, front and rear cupholders, instrument panel bin, 2 seatback storage pockets, driver's and passenger's door bins, rear door bins; carpeted cargo floor, cargo cover, cargo tie downs, cargo light, cargo concealed storage; roof rack; chrome grille, black side window moldings, black front windshield molding and black door handles.

Base Prices

Code	Description	Invoice	MSRP
6442902191	S40 Sedan (5A)	22090	23500
6452902191	V40 Wagon (5A)	23030	24500
	Destination Charge:	575	575

Interested in seeing what dealers will sell this vehicle for? Check out our True Market Value^{sm} (TMV^{sm}) pricing on our Web site at www.edmunds.com.

Accessories

Code	Description	Invoice	MSRP
—	CD Changer Pre-Wiring	22	27
	Pre-wiring is available to facilitate the installation of the CD changer as a retailer-installed option.		
—	Integrated Child Booster Seat	255	300
—	Leather Upholstery	1020	1200
—	Power Driver's Seat	382	450
—	Power Glass Sunroof	1020	1200
	Includes 1-touch open function. NOT AVAILABLE with ROOF.		
—	Wood Interior Package	127	150
	Includes simulated wood dash trim and wood gearshift lever.		
329	Paint: Silver Metallic	340	400
332	Paint: Midnight Metallic (2.9)	340	400
339	Paint: Torch Red Metallic	340	400
343	Paint: Atlantic Blue Metallic	340	400
344	Paint: Desert Wind Metallic	340	400
345	Paint: Peacock Green Metallic	340	400
AUDIO	Audio Package (S40)	680	800
	Includes AM/FM radio, cassette, CD player and premium speakers.		
AUDIO	Audio Package (V40)	680	800
	Manufacturer Discount	(72)	(85)
	Net Price	608	715
	Includes AM/FM radio, cassette, CD player and premium speakers.		
COLD	Weather Package (S40)	722	850
	Includes dynamic stability assistance, heated front seats and headlamp washer/wiper.		

VOLVO
S40 and V40 / S60

CODE	DESCRIPTION	INVOICE	MSRP
COLD	Weather Package (V40)	722	850
	Manufacturer Discount	(85)	(100)
	Net Price	637	750
	Includes dynamic stability assistance, heated front seats and headlamp washer/wiper.		
LEATH	Leather/CD Package (S40)	1615	1900
	Includes leather upholstery, audio package, AM/FM radio, cassette player, CD player, premium speakers and trip computer. NOT AVAILABLE with ROOF.		
LEATH	Leather/CD Package (V40)	1615	1900
	Manufacturer Discount	(454)	(535)
	Net Price	1161	1365
	Includes leather upholstery, audio package, AM/FM radio, cassette player, CD player, premium speakers, trip computer and 15" 10-spoke dynamic wheels. NOT AVAILABLE with ROOF.		
ROOF	Sunroof/CD Package (S40)	595	700
	Includes audio package and trip computer. NOT AVAILABLE with LEATH.		
ROOF	Sunroof/CD Package (V40)	595	700
	Manufacturer Discount	(454)	(535)
	Net Price	141	165
	Includes audio package, trip computer and 15" 10-spoke dynamic wheels. NOT AVAILABLE with LEATH.		
SPORT	Sport Package (S40)	467	550
	Includes rear spoiler, front fog lights and leather-wrapped sport steering wheel.		
SPORT	Sport Package (V40)	467	550
	Manufacturer Discount	(169)	(200)
	Net Price	298	350
	Includes rear spoiler, front fog lights and leather-wrapped sport steering wheel.		

2001 S60

What's New?

The S60 is Volvo's new sedan that takes the place of the discontinued S70 Sedan. Smaller than the S80 but bigger than the S40, Volvo has designed the S60 to be sporty as well as safe. Like the Audi A4 or BMW 3 Series, it should appeal to drivers who are looking for a sedan that is fun to drive.

Review

The midsize S60 is Volvo's replacement for the discontinued S70 Sedan. But to just say that the S60 is the S70's replacement wouldn't quite be correct. Volvo has higher aspirations for this car. Without sacrificing any of the usual Volvo trademarks such as safety and upscale features, Volvo wants the S60 to be a sporty car, a car that would appeal to someone who likes to drive.

To go about this, Volvo has built the S60 on the P2 platform. This is the same platform that the company uses for its S80 and 2001 V70. Neither the S80 nor the V70 are known for their Olympian athletic ability, however, so for the S60, Volvo reduced the P2 platform's dimensions to give the car more nimble handling. Compared to the 2000 S70, the S60 is 5.7 inches shorter, has a 2-inch shorter wheelbase, and has wider wheel tracks both front and rear.

Besides being smaller than the old S70, the S60 also has fewer trim levels. Volvo will offer three for 2001: the base 2.4, the mid-level 2.4T, and the range-topping T5. The three vary in

S60   VOLVO

levels of standard equipment and what kind of engine the car has. The S60 2.4 comes with a 2.4-liter five-cylinder engine that produces 168 horsepower. The 2.4T, as you might guess, is turbocharged, and it has 197 horsepower. The most powerful engine is the 247-horsepower 2.3-liter turbocharged engine in the T5. Both the 2.4 and T5 can be equipped with either a manual or automatic transmission, while the 2.4T is available only with an automatic.

Making the car look sporty was another priority for Volvo. To do this, stylists gave the car the lines of a coupe without intruding on interior space. This effect is most noticeable when looking at the sloping roofline and thick C-pillars, as they look similar to the ones found on the C70 Coupe. Up front, the raised "V" hood lines hark back to the Volvo's mid-'60s 122 series.

The S60 has an interior that is similar in design to the S80 and V70. The broad instrument panel has large and easy-to-use knobs and buttons for the sound system and climate control. There is seating for five, with more legroom, headroom and shoulder room for front passengers when compared to the 2000 S70. The S60 doesn't have as much rear legroom or trunk space as the S70, however. Making its usual appearance is Volvo's roll call of safety equipment, including dual-stage front airbags, side airbags, and head-protection airbags.

In terms of equipment and safety, there are only a few entry-level luxury cars that can match up to the S60. But would you want to buy one? That probably depends on what you are looking for. If you have owned Volvo sedans in the past, but you want one that's sportier, the S60 would be an excellent match for you. But if driving enjoyment is a top priority, a BMW 330i or Lexus IS 300 would probably be a better choice.

Standard Equipment

2.4M (5M): 2.4L I5 DOHC MPI with variable valve timing 20-valve engine, requires premium unleaded fuel; 5-speed OD manual transmission; 520-amp battery; 100-amp alternator; front-wheel drive; stainless steel exhaust; front independent strut suspension with anti-roll bar, front coil springs, rear semi-independent multi-link suspension with anti-roll bar, rear coil springs; power rack-and-pinion steering; 4-wheel antilock disc brakes; 18.5 gal. capacity fuel tank; side impact bars; front and rear body-colored bumpers with black rub molding; black bodyside molding; clearcoat monotone paint; aero-composite halogen auto off headlamps with daytime running lights, delay-off feature; driver's and passenger's power remote body-colored heated folding outside mirrors; 15" x 6.5" silver alloy wheels; P195/65HR15 BSW A/S tires; compact steel spare wheel; dual-zone front air conditioning, air filter, rear heat ducts; AM/FM stereo, seek-scan, cassette player, CD changer pre-wiring, 6 speakers, theft deterrent, window grid diversity antenna; cruise control; power door locks with 2 stage unlock, remote keyless entry, child safety rear door locks, power remote trunk release, power remote fuel release; cell phone pre-wiring, 2 power accessory outlets, driver's foot rest; instrumentation display includes tachometer, water temperature gauge, in-dash clock, exterior temp, trip odometer; warning indicators include oil pressure, battery, low coolant, lights on, key in ignition, low fuel, low washer fluid, bulb failure, door ajar, trunk ajar, service interval, brake fluid; driver's and passenger's front airbags, driver's and front passenger's seat mounted side airbags, overhead airbag; ignition disable, panic alarm, security system; tinted windows, power front and rear windows with driver's and passenger's 1-touch down; fixed interval front windshield wipers, sun visor strip, rear window defroster; seating capacity of 5, front bucket seats with fixed headrests, center armrest with storage, driver's seat includes 8-way direction control, lumbar support, passenger's seat includes 8-way direction control; 60/40 folding rear bench seat with adjustable headrests and center pass-thru armrest; front height adjustable seatbelts with front and rear pretensioners; cloth seats, vinyl door trim insert, full cloth headliner, full color-keyed carpet floor covering with carpeted floor mats, plastic/rubber gear shift knob, chrome interior accents; interior lights include dome light with fade, front and rear reading lights, illuminated entry; steering wheel with tilt and telescopic

VOLVO   S60

adjustment; dual illuminated vanity mirrors; day/night rearview mirror; full floor console, locking glove box with light, front and rear cupholders, instrument panel bin, 1 seat back storage pocket, driver's and passenger's door bins; carpeted cargo floor, carpeted trunk lid, cargo tie downs, cargo light; chrome grille, black side window moldings, black front windshield molding, black rear window molding and body-colored door handles.

2.4T (5A) (in addition to or instead of 2.4M (5A) equipment): 2.4L I5 DOHC MPI intercooled turbo with variable valve timing 20-valve engine; 5-speed electronic OD automatic transmission with lock-up; driver's selectable multi-mode transmission; 21.1 gal. capacity fuel tank; 16" x 6.5" silver alloy wheels; P205/55HR16 BSW A/S tires; dual zone front air conditioning with climate control; radio steering wheel controls; leather-wrapped gear shift knob, and memory on driver's seat with 3 memory setting(s).

T5 (5M) (in addition to or instead of 2.4T (5M) equipment): 2.3L I5 DOHC MPI intercooled turbo with variable valve timing 20-valve engine; 5-speed OD manual transmission; traction control; stainless steel exhaust with tailpipe finisher; additional exterior lights include front fog/driving lights; 16" x 7" silver alloy wheels; P215/55HR16 BSW A/S tires; premium AM/FM stereo, seek-scan, cassette player, single CD, 8 speakers, garage door opener; additional instrumentation display includes trip computer; driver's and passenger's seat includes 8-way power seat, lumbar support; simulated wood dashboard insert, simulated wood door panel insert; leather-wrapped steering wheel with tilt and telescopic adjustment; and auto-dimming day/night rearview mirror.

Base Prices

Code	Description	Invoice	MSRP
3846132121	2.4M Sedan (5M)	24910	26500
3845832191	2.4T Sedan (5A)	28012	29800
3845332121	T5 Sedan (5M)	29892	31800
	Destination Charge:	575	575

Interested in seeing what dealers will sell this vehicle for? Check out our True Market Value^{sm} (TMV^{sm}) pricing on our Web site at www.edmunds.com.

Accessories

Code	Description	Invoice	MSRP
—	Integrated Phone and ON-CALL Plus System (2.4M)	NC	NC
	Includes sattelite controls on steering wheel. NOT AVAILABLE with TOUR.		
—	Integrated Phone and ON-CALL Plus System (2.4T/T5)	NC	NC
	NOT AVAILABLE with TOUR.		
—	Nidingen Leather/Cloth/Vinyl Seating Surfaces (T5)	850	1000
	Includes front seat storage pockets. NOT AVAILABLE with 9A~~.		
—	Power Glass Sunroof with Tilt and Slide	1020	1200
	Includes sliding sun shade with auto open/close.		
—	Select Leather Seating Surfaces (2.4M/2.4T)	1020	1200
	Includes front seat storage pockets.		
—	Sport Leather Seating Surfaces (T5)	1105	1300
	Includes front seat storage pockets. NOT AVAILABLE with 93~~.		
—	Transmission: 5-Speed Automatic (2.4M)	1000	1000
	Includes winter mode selector switch.		
—	Transmission: 5-Speed Automatic with Geartronic (T5)	1200	1200
	Includes winter mode selector switch.		
000142	Volvo Navigational System (2.4T/T5)	2125	2500
	Includes one free CD map of the customer's choice and one free update. REQUIRES PREM.		

S60 — VOLVO

CODE	DESCRIPTION	INVOICE	MSRP
000227	Dynamic Stability Control (DTSC) (2.4T)	1360	1600
	Includes traction control. NOT AVAILABLE with CLDWTR STC Package.		
000227	Dynamic Stability Control (DTSC) (T5)	935	1100
000258	Geartronic Feature (2.4T)	200	200
000329	Rear Armrest Mounted Dual Cup Holders (2.4M)	38	45
000377	Wheels: 16" Metis 7-Spoke Alloy (2.4T)	212	250
	Includes P215/55HR16 A/S SBR tires. NOT AVAILABLE with 000389.		
000382	Wheels: 16" Mimas 7 Spoke Alloy (2.4M)	425	500
	Includes P205/55R16 A/S tires.		
000389	Wheels: 17" Tethys 17-Spoke Alloy (2.4T/T5)	425	500
	Includes PIRELLI P6 235/45HR17 A/S SBR tires. NOT AVAILABLE with 000377.		
000390	Electric Foldable Rear Head Restraints	55	65
000446	Audio Max 4 CD High End Level Radio (T5)	1020	1200
	Includes AM/FM digital tuner, Dolby ProLogic surround sound with internal 1 x 25 watt amplifier, 4 x 75 watt amplifier and 13 speakers. REQUIRES TOUR.		
426	Paint: Mystic Silver Metallic	340	400
445	Paint: Venetian Red Metallic	340	400
446	Paint: Ash Gold Metallic	340	400
447	Paint: Cypress Green Metallic	340	400
449	Paint: Platinum Green Metallic	340	400
450	Paint: Cosmos Blue Metallic	340	400
451	Paint: Maya Gold Metallic	340	400
INTRO	Introduction Package (2.4M)	531	625
	Includes select leather seating surfaces. REQUIRES SUNRF. NOT AVAILABLE with PREM.		
PREM	Premium Package (2.4M)	1275	1500
	Includes select leather seating surfaces, leather steering wheel, simulated wood trim, single in-dash CD radio and 8-way power driver seat. REQUIRES SUNRF. NOT AVAILABLE with INTRO.		
PREM2	Premium Package (2.4T)	1275	1500
	Includes power driver's seat, select leather seating surfaces, leather steering wheel, simulated wood trim, single in-dash CD radio, 8-way power passenger seat and rear speakers. REQUIRES SUNRF.		
TOUR	Touring Package (2.4M)	680	800
	Includes security laminated side glass, grocery bag holder, homelink, auto dimming rear view mirror, trip computer and electric foldable rear head restraints.		
TOUR2	Touring Package (2.4T)	765	900
	Includes dash cup holder, security laminated side glass, grocery bag holder, air quality system, memory outside mirrors, homelink, auto dimming rear view mirror, trip computer and electric foldable rear head restraints. NOT AVAILABLE with PHONE, 000227.		
TOUR3	Touring Package (T5)	467	550
	Includes Homelink, auto-dimming mirror and trip computer, dash cup holder, security laminated side glass, grocery bag holder, air quality system, memory outside mirrors and electric foldable rear head restraints. NOT AVAILABLE with PHONE.		
WTHR	Cold Weather STC Package (2.4M/2.4T)	722	850
	Includes traction control (STC), heated front seats and headlight wiper/washer system. NOT AVAILABLE with CLDWTR.		

VOLVO   S60 / C70

CODE	DESCRIPTION	INVOICE	MSRP
WTHR2	Cold Weather Package (2.4T/T5)	382	450
	Includes heated front seats and headlight wiper/washer system. NOT AVAILABLE with WTHR.		

2001 C70

What's New?

Volvo has dropped the C70 Coupe light-pressure turbo (LPT), meaning only the high-pressure turbo coupe (HPT) is offered. A new five-speed automatic transmission is optional equipment. Exterior styling remains the same, but there are new 16-inch wheels for all models, with the 17-inch wheels still being optional. Simulated wood trim replaces the previous car's burled walnut wood trim. The coupe's previously standard equipment of the trip computer, auto-dimming rearview mirror, simulated wood trim, leather upholstery and sunroof are now part of the Grand Touring option package. The premium audio system is optional on the HPT coupe and standard on the HPT convertible.

Review

Forget what you think you know about Volvo. Well, almost everything you know. Volvos are still safe cars, but they aren't necessarily boxy or boring. The C70 Coupe and Convertible are proof of that.

With the mission of going after buyers looking for a little excitement, Volvo's svelte C70 offers impressive performance and room for four bona-fide adults. Volvo groups both the C70 and V70 Wagon under the 70-Series name, but the two cars are different in that the C70 continues to be built on Volvo's old S70/V70 platform, while the 2001 V70 has been redesigned and is now based on the larger and more luxurious S80 platform.

The C70 is available as either a coupe or a convertible. For 2001, the coupe's only engine is a turbocharged, 2.3-liter five-cylinder engine that makes 236 horsepower at 5,400 rpm and 244 foot-pounds of torque at 2,400 rpm. A five-speed manual transmission is standard equipment, with a five-speed automatic being optional. The C70 Convertible is also available with this engine, or a more sedate 2.4-liter five-cylinder turbo that makes 190 horsepower and 199 foot-pounds of torque. This engine is available only with the automatic.

The convertible's top is raised or lowered with the press of a single button. The rear seat is notably wide and spacious for this type of car. If you don't need to transport rear passengers, the accessory mesh-screen wind blocker allows draft-free cruising at even elevated highway speeds. With the top up, the C70 Convertible is slightly noisier than other cars in this class.

One of Volvo's priorities for the C70 was structural rigidity, and the results show when driving it along winding roads. This coupe is rock-solid but the convertible exhibits more cowl shake than we expected. In keeping with Volvo's tradition of providing safe transportation, the C70 has dual two-stage front airbags, side airbags for front passengers and three-point seatbelts at all four positions. Additionally, convertibles provide a rollover protection system (ROPS).

Inside, the C70's gauges are easy to read, and the secondary controls are lined up on either side of the steering column. As with most Volvo products, the seats in the C70 are without peer. Superbly comfortable, they offer a wide array of power adjustment, and up to three different memory settings. Combined with a tilting and telescoping steering column, it is simple to find a comfortable position in the driver's seat. Leather seating is optional on the coupe and standard equipment on the convertible. The price tag for the optional premium audio system (standard

C70 — VOLVO

on the HPT convertible) might seem exorbitant, but allow us to say that its sound quality is truly exceptional.

The C70 competes against cars like the Mercedes-Benz CLK, the BMW 3 Series and the Saab 9-3. It is not as performance-oriented as the Mercedes or BMW, but the C70 does have its own unique advantages. If you are shopping for an attractive coupe or convertible with plenty features and safety, the C70 is a car to look at.

Standard Equipment

HT COUPE (5M): 2.3L I5 DOHC MPI 20-valve intercooled turbo engine, (requires premium unleaded fuel); 5-speed OD manual transmission; 520-amp battery; engine oil cooler; 80-amp alternator; front-wheel drive, 4.0 axle ratio; stainless steel exhaust with tailpipe finisher; sport-ride suspension, front independent strut suspension with anti-roll bar, front coil springs, rear semi-independent multi-link suspension with anti-roll bar, rear coil springs; rack-and-pinion power steering; 4-wheel disc brakes with 4-wheel antilock braking system; 18.5 gal. capacity fuel tank; body-colored front mud flaps, side impact bars; front and rear body-colored bumpers; body-colored bodyside molding; clearcoat monotone paint; aero-composite halogen headlamps with auto-off feature; headlamp washer and wiper, daytime running lights with delay-off feature; additional exterior lights include front fog/driving lights; driver's and passenger's power remote body-colored heated folding outside mirrors; 16" x 7" silver alloy wheels with P225/50SR16 BSW A/S tires; compact steel spare wheel; dual-zone front air conditioning with climate control, air filter, rear heat ducts; premium AM/FM stereo, seek-scan feature, cassette player, single-disc CD player, 10 speakers, amplifier, theft deterrent, power retractable diversity antenna; cruise control; power door locks with 2-stage unlock, remote keyless-entry, power remote hatch/trunk release, power remote fuel door release; cellphone pre-wiring, 2 power accessory outlets, driver's foot rest, garage door opener; instrumentation display includes tachometer, water temperature gauge, in-dash clock, exterior temp, trip odometer; warning indicators include oil pressure, battery, low coolant, key in ignition, low fuel, low washer fluid, bulb failure, trunk ajar, service interval, brake fluid; driver's and passenger's front airbags, driver's and front passenger's seat-mounted side airbags; ignition disable, panic alarm, security system; tinted windows with driver's 1-touch down function; variable-speed intermittent front windshield wipers, sun visor strip, rear window defroster; seating capacity of 4, front bucket seats with fixed headrests, center armrest with storage, driver's and front passenger's seats include 8-way power seat, lumbar support, easy entry; rear bench seat with fixed headrests, center pass-thru armrest; front and rear seatbelts with pretensioners; cloth-leather seats, leatherette door trim insert, full cloth headliner, full carpet floor covering with carpeted floor mats, plastic/rubber gearshift knob, chrome interior accents; driver's 3-setting seat memory; interior lights include dome light with fade, front and rear reading lights, door curb lights, illuminated entry; leather-wrapped steering wheel with tilt and telescopic adjustment; dual illuminated vanity mirrors; day/night rearview mirror; full floor console, locking glove box with light, front cupholder, 2 seatback storage pockets, driver's and passenger's door bins; carpeted cargo floor, carpeted trunk lid, cargo light; chrome grille, black side window moldings, black front windshield molding and body-colored door handles.

LT CONVERTIBLE (4A) (in addition to or instead of HT COUPE (5M) equipment): 2.4L I5 DOHC MPI 20-valve intercooled turbo engine with variable valve timing; 5-speed electronic OD automatic transmission with lock-up converter; driver's selectable multi-mode transmission; 2.54 axle ratio; comfort-ride suspension; power convertible roof with lining, glass rear window, rollover protection; P205/55SR16 BSW A/S tires; power front and rear windows; leather seats.

HT CONVERTIBLE (5M) (in addition to or instead of LT CONVERTIBLE (4A) equipment): 5-speed OD manual transmission; 4.0 axle ratio; touring-ride suspension, rear semi-independent multi-link suspensions; P225/50SR16 BSW A/S tires; premium AM/FM stereo, 3-disc CD changer; instrumentation display includes trip computer; simulated wood dashboard insert, wood gearshift knob, simulated-wood console insert; auto-dimming day/night rearview mirror.

VOLVO C70

CODE	DESCRIPTION	INVOICE	MSRP

Base Prices

8725380121	HT Coupe (5M)	32430	34500
8735680091	LT Convertible (4A)	40890	43500
8735380021	HT Convertible (5M)	42770	45500
	Destination Charge:	575	575

Interested in seeing what dealers will sell this vehicle for? Check out our True Market Value^{sm} (TMV^{sm}) pricing on our Web site at www.edmunds.com.

Accessories

Code	Description	Invoice	MSRP
—	**Cold Weather Package (HT/LT Convertible)**	552	650
	Includes heated front seats and stability traction control system (STC).		
—	**Grand Touring Package (HT Coupe)**	1870	2200
	Includes power sliding and tilting sunroof, leather seating surfaces, trip/information center, simulated wood trim/dash/console, wood gearshift knob and auto-dimming rearview mirror. NOT AVAILABLE with SHIFT.		
—	**Leather Seating Surfaces (HT Coupe)**	1020	1200
—	**Power Sliding and Tilting Sunroof (HT Coupe)**	1020	1200
	Includes automatic sliding shade.		
—	**Touring Package (LT Convertible)**	340	400
	Includes trip/information center, simulated wood trim/dash/console, wood gearshift knob and auto-dimming rearview mirror. NOT AVAILABLE with SHIFT.		
—	**Transmission: 5-Speed Automatic (HT)**	1000	1000
	Includes winter mode.		
000011	**Heated Front Seats (HT/LT Convertible)**	212	250
000049	**Trip/Information Center (HT Coupe/LT Convertible)**	212	250
	Includes digital clock, ambient temperature gauge and mileage information.		
000156	**Wheels: 17" Hollow 5-Spoke Alloy (HT/LT Convertible)**	340	400
	Includes P225/45ZR17 tires. NOT AVAILABLE with 000411.		
000164	**Radio: Dolby ProLogic Surround Sound System (HT Convertible)**	510	600
	Includes 12 Dynaudio speakers.		
000164	**Radio: SC 901 Premium Audio System (HT Coupe/LT Convertible)**	1020	1200
	Includes 3-disc in-dash CD player, full-logic cassette player, AM/FM stereo with RDS, Dolby ProLogic surround sound, 400-Watt amplifier and 12 Dynaudio speakers.		
000168	**Auto-Dimming Rearview Mirror (HT Coupe/LT Convertible)**	85	100
000178	**Stability Traction Control System (STC) (HT/LT Convertible)**	467	550
000396	**Simulated Wood Trim/Dash/Console (HT Coupe/LT Convertible)**	170	200
000411	**Wheels: 17" BBS 2-Piece Alloy (HT/LT Convertible)**	1275	1500
	Includes P225/45ZR17 tires. NOT AVAILABLE with 000156.		
000453	**Wood Gearshift Knob (HT Coupe/LT Convertible)**	29	35
	NOT AVAILABLE with SHIFT.		

2001 V70

What's New?

The Volvo V70 has been redesigned for 2001. Major changes include a new body structure, fresh styling, a revised interior and upgraded feature content. Safety figures prominently with the new V70 (as usual), but it is also more sporting than before, especially in T5 trim.

Review

Ask your neighbor to name a family-oriented wagon with a reputation for safety, and most likely he or she will name Volvo. For 2001, however, Volvo is looking to go beyond that confining image with its redesigned V70 Wagon.

For the new V70, Volvo set out to improve interior space, versatility, comfort and performance. The new V70 shares its platform with the S80, Volvo's top-of-the-line sedan. As a result, the new V70 is slightly shorter than the 2000 model, but it has a longer wheelbase, wider front and rear tracks, and about 2 more inches of width and height. The change in dimensions gives passengers plenty of interior space, and four adults will have no problem getting comfortable. Fold the rear seats down, and there is 71.4 cubic feet of cargo space at your disposal.

The new V70 has plenty to offer in terms of performance. The base 2.4T and all-wheel-drive Cross Country models comes with a 197-horsepower, 2.4-liter, turbocharged five-cylinder engine. The up-level T5 also has a turbocharged five-cylinder engine, but output on this model reaches 247 horsepower and 243 foot-pounds of torque.

Both V70s have a MacPherson-strut front suspension and multi-link rear suspension to give the wagon a level of performance and confidence not normally associated with, well, a wagon. On the twisty roads, the V70 feels planted and predictable on fast sweepers and quick transitions. Steering feel is on the heavy side with no discernible on-center dead spot and a quick ratio that makes navigating tight switchbacks a pleasure.

The V70 boasts a long list of safety and convenience features perfect for hauling the brood and associated gear. The front seats offer the kind of comfort and support we've come to expect from Swedish automobiles, while also providing Volvo's anti-whiplash protection technology. All five seating positions have three-point inertia-reel safety belts. Additional safety features include dual-stage front airbags, front side airbags, front-and-rear head airbags, and child-seat ISOFIX attachment points.

Highlights from the optional equipment list include stability control, a third-row seat, a foldable rear table, heated seats, a shopping-bag holder for the cargo area, 17-inch alloy wheels, Dolby surround sound and a GPS navigation system. The navigation system's screen is normally hidden inside the dashboard, and rises upwards when a button on the back of the steering wheel is pushed. This feature makes it easier to look at the screen without taking your eyes off the road.

The new V70 is an impressive vehicle, and it offers an excellent combination of utility, performance and safety. The Cross Country, in particular, would make an excellent vehicle for cold climates. V70 pricing starts in the low 30s, which should help Volvo maintains its lead in the luxury wagon segment. A fully loaded T5 or Cross Country can get expensive, however, so it's best to limit the optional equipment if you are on a budget.

VOLVO
V70

Standard Equipment

2.4M (5M): 2.4L I5 DOHC MPI 20-valve engine with variable valve timing, (requires premium unleaded fuel); 5-speed OD manual transmission; 520-amp battery; engine oil cooler; 100-amp alternator; driver's selectable multi-mode transmission; front-wheel drive, 2.8 axle ratio; stainless steel exhaust; front independent strut suspension with anti-roll bar, front coil springs, rear independent multi-link suspension with anti-roll bar, rear coil springs; rack-and-pinion power steering; 4-wheel antilock disc brakes; 21.1 gal. capacity fuel tank; front mud flaps, side impact bars; front and rear body-colored bumpers with black anti-scuff strip, rear step bumper; black bodyside molding; clearcoat monotone paint; aero-composite halogen auto-off headlamps with daytime running lights, delay-off feature; driver's and passenger's power remote body-colored heated folding outside mirrors; 15" x 6.5" silver alloy wheels; P205/55HR16 BSW A/S tires; compact steel spare wheel; dual-zone front air conditioning, air filter, rear heat ducts; premium AM/FM stereo w/clock, seek-scan feature, cassette player, 6 speakers, amplifier, theft deterrent, window grid diversity antenna; cruise control; power door locks with 2-stage unlock, remote keyless entry, child-safety rear door locks, power remote hatch release; 2 power accessory outlets, driver's foot rest; instrumentation display includes tachometer, water temperature gauge, exterior temp, trip odometer; warning indicators include oil pressure, battery, low coolant, key in ignition, low fuel, low washer fluid, bulb failure, door ajar, trunk ajar, service interval; driver's and passenger's front airbags, driver's and front passenger's seat-mounted side airbags, overhead airbag; ignition disable, panic alarm, security system; tinted windows, power front and rear windows with driver's and passenger's 1-touch down function, fixed 1/4 vent windows; variable-speed intermittent front windshield wipers, sun visor strip, fixed-interval rear wiper, rear window defroster; seating capacity of 5, front bucket seats with fixed headrests, center armrest with storage, driver and passenger seats include 8-way adjustment, lumbar support; 60/40 folding rear split-bench seat with adjustable headrests, center armrest with storage; seatbelts with front and rear pretensioners; cloth seats, cloth door trim insert, full cloth headliner, full color-keyed carpet floor covering with carpeted floor mats, aluminum interior accents; interior lights include dome light with fade, front and rear reading lights, illuminated entry; steering wheel with tilt and telescopic adjustment; dual illuminated vanity mirrors; day/night rearview mirror; full floor console, locking glove box with light, front and rear cupholders, 2 seatback storage pockets, driver's and passenger's door bins; carpeted cargo floor, cargo tie downs, cargo light; chrome grille, black side window moldings, black front windshield molding and body-colored door handles.

2.4T WAGON (5A): 2.4L I5 DOHC MPI 20-valve intercooled turbo engine, 5-speed electronic OD automatic transmission with lock-up converter; touring-ride suspension, body-colored front mud flaps; headlamp washer and wiper; additional exterior lights include front fog/driving lights; 16" x 6.5" silver alloy wheels; dual-zone front air conditioning with climate control; premium AM/FM stereo, seek-scan feature, cassette player, 3-disc CD changer, 6 speakers, amplifier, valet key; central locking; power remote fuel door release; cellphone pre-wiring, garage door opener; additional instrumentation display includes in-dash clock, trip computer; additional warning indicators include low brake fluid; illuminated ignition switch; simulated wood dashboard insert, wood gearshift knob, simulated wood console insert; driver's 3-setting seat memory; additional interior lights include door curb lights; leather-wrapped steering wheel with tilt and telescopic adjustment; auto-dimming day/night rearview mirror; audio media storage and cargo tie downs.

T5 WAGON (5M) (in addition to or instead of 2.4T A (5A) equipment): 2.3L I5 DOHC MPI 20-valve intercooled turbo engine with variable valve timing, 5-speed OD manual transmission; traction control; 16" x 7" silver alloy wheels with P215/55HR16 A/S BSW tires; single-disc CD player, 8 speakers, garage door opener.

XC AWD WAGON (4A) (in addition to or instead of T5 WAGON (5M) equipment): 2.4L I5 DOHC MPI 20-valve intercooled turbo engine with variable valve timing; 5-speed electronic OD automatic transmission with lock-up converter; driver's selectable multi-mode auto-manual transmission; full-time limited-slip differential; skid plates; roof rack; front and rear colored bumpers with black

V70 — VOLVO

anti-scuff strip; colored fender flares; driver's and passenger's power remote colored heated folding outside mirrors; P215/65HR16 BSW A/S tires; passenger's front seat includes 8-way direction control and lumbar support; 40/20/40 folding rear split-bench seat, chrome interior accents; 1 seatback storage pocket, reversible cargo mats.

Base Prices

CODE	DESCRIPTION	INVOICE	MSRP
2856132121	2.4M Wagon (5M)	27636	29400
2855832191	2.4T A Wagon (5A)	30456	32400
2855332121	T5 M Wagon (5M)	32148	34200
2955832171	XC AWD Wagon (4A)	32806	34900
	Destination Charge:	575	575

Interested in seeing what dealers will sell this vehicle for? Check out our True Market Value^{sm} (TMV^{sm}) pricing on our Web site at www.edmunds.com.

Accessories

CODE	DESCRIPTION	INVOICE	MSRP
—	Leather Custom-Cut Seating Surface (XC AWD)	1105	1300
	Includes color-coordinated vinyl door inserts with Cross Country unique stitching.		
—	Leather Seat Trim (2.4M)	1020	1200
—	Transmission: 5 Speed Automatic (2.4M)	1000	1000
	Includes winter mode selector switch.		
—	Transmission: 5-Speed Automatic (T5M)	1200	1200
	Includes winter mode.		
000011	Heated Front Seats (2.4T/T5M)	212	250
000142	Volvo Navigation System (2.4T/T5M)	2125	2500
	Covers the cost of 1 free CD map of the customers choice and 1 free update.		
000142	Volvo Navigation System (XC AWD)	2125	2500
	Includes 1 free CD map of the customer's choice and 1 free update. REQUIRES LTHRPK.		
000163	Radio: HU 803 w/4-Disc CD Changer & Premium Sound (2.4T/T5M/XC AWD)	850	1000
	Includes 9 speakers and 4 x 50-Watt amplifier. Replaces cassette player. REQUIRES TOURPK. NOT AVAILABLE with DOLBY1, DOLBY3.		
000178	Traction Control (STC) (2.4)	467	550
	NOT AVAILABLE with 000227.		
000188	Foldable Rear Table (2.4/T5M)	170	200
000227	Dynamic Stability Control (DTSC) (2.4T)	1360	1600
	Includes trip computer and traction control. NOT AVAILABLE with 000178.		
000227	Dynamic Stability Control (DTSC) (T5M)	935	1100
000262	12" Active Subwoofer System	297	350
	REQUIRES TOURPK. NOT AVAILABLE with VERSP2.		
000322	Integrated Booster Seats (2.4/T5M)	255	300
000376	Wheels: 16" Adrastea Alloy (2.4M)	425	500
	Includes tires: P205/55HR16 A/S.		
000378	Wheels: 17" Amalthea Alloy (2.4T)	425	500
	Includes 235/45HR17 A/S BSW tires.		
377	Wheels: 16" Metis Alloy (2.4T)	212	250
417	Paint: Nautic Blue Metallic (2.4/T5)	340	400
421	Paint: Emerald Green Metallic (2.4)	340	400

VOLVO

V70

CODE	DESCRIPTION	INVOICE	MSRP
426	Paint: Mystic Silver Metallic (2.4/T5)	340	400
443	Paint: Moondust Metallic (2.4/T5)	340	400
444	Paint: Polarartic (T5)	340	400
445	Paint: Venetian Red Metallic (2.4/T5)	340	400
446	Paint: Ash Gold Metallic (2.4)	340	400
447	Paint: Cypress Green Metallic (2.4M/T5)	340	400
449	Paint: Platinum Green Metallic (2.4/T5)	340	400
A9	Leather-Faced Seating (2.4T)	1020	1200
	Includes front seat storage pockets. REQUIRES LTHRPK.		
AA	Leather Seat Trim (T5M)	1105	1300
	Includes front sport bucket seats, front seat storage pockets. REQUIRES LTHRPK.		
INTROPK	Introduction Package (XC AWD)	2052	2415
	Includes leather package, leather custom-cut seating surface, steering wheel and gearshift knob, simulated-wood inlays, versatility package, cargo protection net, cargo security cover, grocery bag holder. NOT AVAILABLE with VERSP2.		
LTHRP2	Leather Package (2.4M)	1020	1200
	Includes leather seat trim, leather steering wheel, leather gear shift knob and simulated red wood trim effect.		
LTHRP3	Leather Package (XC AWD)	1500	1765
	Includes leather custom-cut seating surface, steering wheel, gearshift knob and simulated-wood inlays.		
LTHRP4	Leather Package (T5M)	1500	1765
	Manufacturer Discount	(395)	(465)
	Net Price	1105	1300
	Includes leather sport seats, leather-wrapped steering wheel, leather gearshift knob and wood-effect trim.		
LTHRPK	Leather Package (2.4T)	1415	1665
	Manufacturer Discount	(395)	(465)
	Net Price	1020	1200
	Includes leather-faced seating, leather-wrapped steering wheel, leather gearshift knob and simulated redwood trim effect.		
SECURP2	Security Package (XC AWD)	539	635
	Includes security-laminated door windows, level-movement sensor, interior mass-movement sensor and air quality system (AQS).		
SECURP3	Security Package (2.4M)	340	400
	Includes security laminated door windows, level movement sensor and interior (mass) movement sensor.		
SECURPK	Security Package (2.4T/T5M)	433	510
	Manufacturer Discount	(30)	(35)
	Net Price	403	475
	Includes mass-movement sensor, level sensor and security-laminated window with break sensor.		
SNROOF	Power Glass Sunroof (2.4T/T5M)	1020	1200
	Sliding sunshade with automatic open/close.		
SNROOF2	Power Glass Sunroof (XC AWD)	1032	1200
	Includes slide/tilt function and automatic sliding sunshade.		

V70 — VOLVO

CODE	DESCRIPTION	INVOICE	MSRP
SNROOF3	Power Glass Sunroof (2.4M)	1032	1200
	Includes slide/tilt function and sliding sunshade with auto open/close.		
TOURP2	Touring Package (XC AWD)	1197	1410
	Includes 8-way power passenger seat, trip computer, in-dash CD player, radio, auto-dimming mirror and Homelink remote garage door opener.		
TOURP3	Touring Package (2.4M)	1062	1250
	Includes 8-way power passenger seat, trip computer, with in-dash CD player radio, auto dimming mirror and Homelink remote garage door opener.		
TOURPK	Touring Package (2.4T)	1197	1410
	Manufacturer Discount	(135)	(160)
	Net Price	1062	1250
	Includes Homelink remote garage door opener, in-dash CD player, trip computer, auto-dimming mirror and 8-way adjustable power seats.		
VERSP2	Versatility Package w/Third Seat (2.4T/T5M)	1402	1650
	Manufacturer Discount	(425)	(500)
	Net Price	977	1150
	Includes 3rd-row seat, cargo protection net and security cover, 12-volt power outlet. NOT AVAILABLE with 000262, VERSPK.		
VERSP3	Versatility Package (XC AWD)	573	675
	Includes cargo protection net, cargo security cover and grocery bag holder. NOT AVAILABLE with VERSP2.		
VERSP4	Versatility Package with Auxiliary Seat (XC AWD)	1402	1650
	Includes cargo protection net, cargo security cover and 3rd-row seat. NOT AVAILABLE with VERSPK, INTROPK, OQ0262.		
VERSP5	Versatility Package (2.4M)	297	350
	Includes cargo protection net, cargo security cover, grocery bag holder and 12 volt power outlet. NOT AVAILABLE with VERSP2.		
VERSP6	Versatility Package with Third Seat (2.4M)	977	1150
	Includes cargo protection net, cargo security cover, third row seat and 12 volt power outlet. NOT AVAILABLE with 000262, VERSPK.		
VERSPK	Versatility Package (2.4T/T5M)	573	675
	Manufacturer Discount	(276)	(325)
	Net Price	297	350
	Includes grocery bag holder, cargo protection net and security cover, 12-volt power outlet. NOT AVAILABLE with VERSP2.		
WTHRP2	Cold Weather Package (2.4M)	382	450
	Includes heated front seats and headlamp washer/wiper. NOT AVAILABLE with WTHSTC.		
WTHRP3	Cold Weather/STC Package (2.4M)	722	850
	Includes heated front seats, headlamp washer/wiper, stability and traction control. NOT AVAILABLE with WTHRPK.		
WTHRPK	Cold Weather Package (2.4T/T5M/XC AWD)	382	450
	Includes heated front seats.		
WTHSTC	Cold Weather Package (2.4T)	849	1000
	Includes heated front seats and traction control system (STC).		

VOLVO

S80

2001 S80

What's New?

Volvo has added a new trim level, the S80 T6 Executive. Additional standard content for all trim levels comes in the form of leather seating, a luggage holder, remote retractable rear head restraints, memory position mirrors, and Homelink. The 2.9 gets new 16-inch wheels and an auto-dimming rearview mirror as standard. All S80s get dual-stage airbags. The available Security Package for the S80 2.9 and T6 will now include the Interior Air Quality System, or IAQS, which keeps the passenger cabin free from odors and pollutants.

Review

Are you looking to buy a well-appointed luxury sedan with enough horsepower to humble most of today's sporty coupes? Volvo's flagship sedan, the S80, might just be your car.

Volvo offers the S80 in three trim levels—the S80 2.9, the S80 T6 and the S80 T6 Executive. The S80 2.9 is equipped with a 2.9-liter inline six-cylinder engine. It generates a respectable 197 horsepower at 6,000 rpm and 207 foot-pounds of torque at 4,200 rpm. For the T6 models, Volvo takes the 2.9's engine and bolts on two small turbochargers. Even with slightly less displacement (2.8 liters), the T6's engine belts out 268 horsepower at 5,400 rpm and a tree stump-pulling 280 foot-pounds of torque at 2,000 rpm.

As you might expect, the T6's acceleration is very impressive, but the front-wheel-drive layout often conspires to create a lot of torque steer when the throttle is mashed to the carpet. Both engines are mated to four-speed automatic transmissions. The S80 T6 also provides a Geartronic feature, allowing for manual shifting if the driver desires.

The S80 does handle adequately for a front-drive car. A MacPherson strut suspension handles duties up front, while a fully independent multi-link setup keeps the rear planted. Front and rear antiroll bars help the S80 maintain a flat attitude in corners. The suspension's limits quickly become apparent in the T6, however. A dynamic stability control system is optional.

Comfort is a Volvo hallmark, and the S80 boasts one of the better interiors we've encountered. The rear seat is exceptionally roomy, and there are heating and air conditioning vents in the B-pillar to keep the rear passengers at the perfect temperature. Making their return for 2001 are remote retractable rear head restraints for all S80s.

If that still isn't good enough, order the T6 Executive. New for 2001, this model adds 2 more inches of legroom by pushing the rear seat farther back into the rear deck and by removing the folding seat mechanism. It also features wider rear door openings, heated rear seats, extra padding in the rear seat and bottom cushion, a multi-functional rear center armrest/console, an electric rear window sun shade, a small refrigerator, and a DVD player connected to a video screen mounted in the rear console.

Control layout is decent, though deciphering some of the markings will require the assistance of the owner's manual. An astounding Dolby Pro Logic sound system is offered as optional equipment, as is a CD-based navigation system. As with all Volvo cars, safety is paramount, with whiplash-reducing front seats and extensive side-impact collision protection.

There is little wrong with the S80. This isn't the car to get if you are looking for a driver's car, a styling pacesetter, or a value leader. But as a luxury car with cutting-edge safety and technology, the S80 is unmatched.

S80 VOLVO

Standard Equipment

2.9 (4A): 2.9L I6 DOHC MPI 24-valve engine with variable valve timing, (requires premium unleaded fuel); 4-speed electronic OD automatic transmission with lock-up converter; 600-amp battery; 100-amp alternator; driver's selectable multi-mode transmission; front-wheel drive, traction control, 2.8 axle ratio; stainless steel exhaust; front independent strut suspension with anti-roll bar, front coil springs, rear independent multi-link suspension with anti-roll bar, rear coil springs; rack-and-pinion power steering; 4-wheel disc brakes with 4-wheel antilock braking system; 21.1 gal. capacity fuel tank; front mud flaps, side impact bars; front and rear body-colored bumpers with black rub strip; black bodyside molding with chrome bodyside insert; clearcoat monotone paint; aero-composite halogen headlamps with daytime running lights and delay-off feature; driver's and passenger's power remote body-colored heated folding outside mirrors; 16"x7" silver alloy wheels with P215/55SR16 BSW A/S tires; compact steel spare wheel; dual-zone front air conditioning with climate control, air filter, rear heat ducts; premium AM/FM stereo, seek-scan feature, cassette player, single-disc CD player, 8 speakers, amplifier, window grid diversity antenna, radio steering wheel controls; cruise control with steering wheel controls; power door locks with 2-stage unlock, remote keyless entry, child-safety rear door locks, power remote hatch/trunk release, power remote fuel door release; 2 power accessory outlets, driver's foot rest, retained accessory power, garage door opener; instrumentation display includes tachometer, water temperature gauge, in-dash clock, exterior temp, systems monitor, check control, trip computer, trip odometer; warning indicators include oil pressure, battery, low oil level, low coolant, lights on, key in ignition, low fuel, low washer fluid, bulb failure, door ajar, trunk ajar, service interval, brake fluid; driver's and passenger's front airbags, driver's and front passenger's seat-mounted side airbags, overhead airbag; ignition disable, panic alarm, security system; tinted windows, power front and rear windows with driver's and front passenger's 1-touch down function; variable-speed intermittent front windshield wipers, sun visor strip, rear window defroster; seating capacity of 5, front bucket seats with fixed headrests, center armrest with storage, driver's and front passenger's seats include 8-way power seat and lumbar support; 60/40 folding rear bench seat with power adjustable headrests, center pass-thru armrest with storage; height-adjustable front seatbelts, front and rear seatbelt pretensioners; leather seats, full cloth headliner, full carpet floor covering with carpeted floor mats, simulated wood dashboard insert, simulated wood gearshift knob, simulated wood door panel insert, simulated wood console insert, chrome interior accents; driver's 3-setting seat memory includes settings for exterior mirrors; interior lights include dome light with fade, front and rear reading lights, door curb lights, illuminated entry; leather-wrapped steering wheel with tilt and telescopic adjustment; dual illuminated vanity mirrors; auto-dimming day/night rearview mirror; full floor console, locking glove box with light, front and rear cupholders, instrument panel covered bin, 2 seatback storage pockets, driver's and passenger's door bins, rear door bins; carpeted cargo floor, carpeted trunk lid, cargo net, cargo light; chrome grille, black side window moldings, black front windshield molding, black rear window molding and body-colored door handles.

T-6 (4A) (in addition to or instead of 2.9 (4A) equipment): 2.8L I6 DOHC MPI 24-valve twin-turbo engine with variable valve timing; automanual transmission; vehicle-speed-sensing assist; additional exterior lights include front fog/driving lights; P225/55SR16 BSW A/S tires.

T-6 EXECUTIVE (4A) (in addition to or instead of T-6 (4A) equipment): Rear power blind; seating capacity of 4; heated rear bench seat with power adjustable headrests; refrigerated/cooled box.

Base Prices

Code	Description	Invoice	MSRP
1849452151	2.9 (4A)	34686	36900
1849052151	T-6 (4A)	38446	40900
1849052155	T-6 Executive (4A)	43522	46300

VOLVO S80

CODE	DESCRIPTION	INVOICE	MSRP
	Destination Charge:	575	575

Interested in seeing what dealers will sell this vehicle for? Check out our True Market Value^{sm} (TMV^{sm}) pricing on our Web site at www.edmunds.com.

Accessories

CODE	DESCRIPTION	INVOICE	MSRP
—	Power Glass Sunroof	1020	1200
	Includes auto-open/close and anti-trap.		
—	Security Package	425	500
	Includes interior mass movement sensor, level movement sensor and interior air quality system (IAQS) and security laminated side glass.		
—	Warm Weather Package (2.9/T6)	425	500
	Includes infra-red reflective front windshield, rear window and rear door sun curtains. NOT AVAILABLE with 000142.		
000018	Cold Weather Package	382	450
	Includes heated front seats and headlamp washer/wiper.		
000142	Volvo Navigational System	2125	2500
	Covers the cost of 1 free CD map of the customer's choice and 1 free update. NOT AVAILABLE with NAVI, WARM.		
000163	Radio: 4-Disc In-Dash CD Changer with Surround Sound	850	1000
	Replaces cassette player. Includes Dolby ProLogic, 200-Watt amplifier and 10 premium high-output speakers.		
000227	Dynamic Stability Traction Control	935	1100
	Automatically counteracts a skid by comparing the vehicle's direction of travel to steering wheel movements. Brakes are applied to each wheel as necessary to help the driver retain control.		
000297	Wheels: 17" Canopus Alloy (2.9)	425	500
	Includes Michelin MXM4 225/50R/17 A/S tires and speed-sensitive power steering. NOT AVAILABLE with 000336.		
000336	Wheels: 17" Arrakis Alloy (2.9)	425	500
	Includes Michelin MXM4 225/50R/17 A/S tires and speed-sensitive power steering. NOT AVAILABLE with 000297.		
000336	Wheels: 17" Arrakis Alloy (T6/Executive)	340	400
	Includes Michelin MXM4 225/50R/17 A/S tires.		
417	Paint: Nautic Blue Metallic (2.9)	340	400
426	Paint: Silver Metallic (2.9)	340	400
443	Paint: Moondust Metallic (2.9)	340	400
445	Paint: Venetian Red Metallic (2.9)	340	400
446	Paint: Ash Gold Metallic (2.9)	340	400
447	Paint: Cypress Green Metallic (2.9)	340	400
449	Paint: Platinum Green Metallic (2.9)	340	400
998354	Wireless Fax Machine (Executive)	765	900
	Includes single-page copier that requires mobile phone with fax/data capability and service from your phone service provider. Your phone must also include a mobile office adapter kit to connect with the fax machine.		

New Cars Specifications and EPA Mileage Ratings

Contents

Acura	406	Mazda	424
Audi	407	Mercedes-Benz	425
BMW	409	Mercury	426
Buick	411	Mitsubishi	427
Cadillac	412	Nissan	428
Chevrolet	412	Oldsmobile	429
Chrysler	414	Plymouth	430
Daewoo	415	Pontiac	430
Dodge	416	Porsche	432
Ford	417	Saab	432
Honda	418	Saturn	434
Hyundai	420	Subaru	435
Infiniti	421	Suzuki	436
Jaguar	421	Toyota	436
Kia	422	Volkswagen	438
Lexus	422	Volvo	441
Lincoln	423		

specifications

		CL-Series 3.2 CL	CL-Series 3.2 CL Type S	Integra Coupe - LS - GS	Integra GS-R Coupe	Integra GS-R Sedan	Integra Sedan - LS?GS	Integra Type-R	RL-Series 3.5RL	TL-Series 3.2TL
Length (in.)		192	192	172.4	172.4	178.1	178.1	172.4	196.6	192.9
Width (in.)		70.6	70.6	67.3	67.3	67.3	67.3	67.3	71.4	70.3
Height (in.)		55.5	55.5	52.6	52.6	53.9	53.9	51.9	56.5	55.7
Curb Weight (lbs.)		3470	3510	2639	2672	2764	2725	2600	3858	3483
Wheelbase (in.)		106.9	106.9	101.2	101.2	103.1	103.1	101.2	114.6	108.1
Front Head Room (in.)		37.5	37.5	38.6	38.6	38.9	38.9	37.9	38.8	39.9
Rear Head Room (in.)		36.7	36.7	35	35	36	36	35	36.8	36.8
Front Shoulder Room (in.)		56.4	56.4	51.7	51.7	52	52	51.7	56.9	56.2
Rear Shoulder Room (in.)		54.2	54.2	48.8	48.8	50.3	50.3	48.8	56.9	55.7
Front Hip Room (in.)		52.9	52.9	50.3	50.3	50.7	50.7	50.3	55.7	56
Rear Hip Room (in.)		50.4	50.4	44.1	44.1	49.9	49.9	44.1	56.5	55
Front Leg Room (in.)		42.4	42.4	42.7	42.7	42.2	42.2	42.7	42.1	42.4
Rear Leg Room (in.)		33	33	28.1	28.1	32.7	32.7	28.1	35.4	35
Luggage Capacity (cu ft.)		13.6	13.6	13.3	13.3	11	11	13.3	14	14.3
Number of Cylinders		6	6	4	4	4	4	4	6	6
Displacement (liters)		3.2	3.2	1.8	1.8	1.8	1.8	1.8	3.5	3.2
Horsepower @ RPM		225@5600	260@6100	140@6300	170@7600	170@7600	140@6300	195@8000	210@5200	225@5600
Torque @ RPM		216@4700	232@3500	124@5200	128@6200	128@6200	124@5200	130@7500	224@2800	216@4700
Fuel Capacity		17.2	17.2	13.2	13.2	13.2	13.2	13.2	18	17.2
EPA City (mpg) - Manual		NA	NA	NA	NA	NA	NA	NA	NA	NA
EPA Hwy (mpg) - Manual		NA	NA	NA	NA	NA	NA	NA	NA	NA
EPA City (mpg) - Auto		19	19	25	25	25	25	25	18	19
EPA Hwy (mpg) - Auto		29	29	31	30	30	31	30	24	29
SPECIFICATIONS MILEAGE TABLES	ACURA									

specifications

AUDI

SPECIFICATIONS MILEAGE TABLES	A4 1.8T Avant Wagon	A4 1.8T Quattro Sedan	A4 1.8T Sedan	A4 2.8 Quattro Sedan	A4 2.8 Quattro Wagon	A4 2.8 Sedan	A6 2.7T	A6 4.2	A6 Avant
Length (in.)	176.7	178	178	178	176.7	178	192	193.4	192
Width (in.)	68.2	68.2	68.2	68.2	68.2	68.2	76.1	76.1	76.1
Height (in.)	56.7	55.8	55.8	55.8	56.7	55.8	57.2	57	58.2
Curb Weight (lbs.)	3351	3241	2998	3384	3494	3263	3759	4024	3947
Wheelbase (in.)	102.6	102.6	103	102.6	102.6	103	108.7	108.6	108.6
Front Head Room (in.)	38.2	38.2	38.1	38.2	38.2	38.2	39.3	39.3	39.3
Rear Head Room (in.)	37.8	36.9	36.9	36.9	37.8	36.9	37.9	37.9	38.7
Front Shoulder Room (in.)	54.7	54.7	54.7	54.7	54.7	54.7	56.2	56.2	56.2
Rear Shoulder Room (in.)	53.4	53.4	53.4	53.4	53.4	53.4	55.7	55.7	55.7
Front Hip Room (in.)	NA	NA	NA	NA	NA	NA	NA	NA	NA
Rear Hip Room (in.)	NA	NA	NA	NA	NA	NA	NA	NA	NA
Front Leg Room (in.)	41.3	41.3	41.2	41.2	41.3	41.2	41.3	41.3	41.3
Rear Leg Room (in.)	33.4	33.4	33.4	33.4	33.3	33.4	37.3	37.3	37.3
Luggage Capacity (cu ft.)	31.3	13.7	13.7	13.7	31.3	13.7	15.4	15.4	36.4
Number of Cylinders	4	4	4	6	6	6	6	8	6
Displacement (liters)	1.8	1.8	1.8	2.8	2.8	2.8	2.7	4.2	2.8
Horsepower @ RPM	170@5900	170@5900	170@5900	190@6000	190@6000	190@6000	250@5800	300@6200	200@6000
Torque @ RPM	166@1950	166@1950	166@1950	207@3200	207@3200	207@3200	258@1850	295@3000	207@3200
Fuel Capacity	15.9	16.4	15.9	16.4	15.9	16.4	18.5	21.7	18.5
EPA City (mpg) - Manual	NA	22	23	18	18	NA	17	NA	NA
EPA Hwy (mpg) - Manual	NA	30	32	24	24	NA	24	NA	NA
EPA City (mpg) - Auto	22	20	20	18	NA	18	17	17	17
EPA Hwy (mpg) - Auto	30	27	29	25	NA	26	24	25	24

specifications

	A6 Base	Allroad quattro	S4 2.7T	S4 Avant	TT 180 HP AWD Coupe	TT 180 HP FWD Coupe	TT 180 HP FWD Roadster	TT 225 HP AWD Coupe	TT 225 HP AWD Roadster
Length (in.)	192	189.4	176.7	176.7	159.1	159.1	159.1	159.1	159.1
Width (in.)	76.1	76.1	72.7	72.7	73.1	73.1	73.1	73.1	73.1
Height (in.)	57.2	62	54.9	55.8	53	53	53	53	53
Curb Weight (lbs.)	3560	4167	3704	3814	3208	2921	3131	3274	3473
Wheelbase (in.)	108.7	108.5	102.6	102.6	95.6	95.4	95.4	95.6	95.6
Front Head Room (in.)	39.3	39.3	38.1	38.1	37.8	37.8	38.3	37.8	38.3
Rear Head Room (in.)	37.9	38.7	36.8	36.8	32.6	32.6	NA	32.6	NA
Front Shoulder Room (in.)	56.2	58.6	54.7	54.7	55.6	55.6	55.6	55.6	55.6
Rear Shoulder Room (in.)	55.7	56.9	53.4	53.4	48.1	48.1	NA	48.1	NA
Front Hip Room (in.)	NA	NA	NA	NA	NA	NA	NA	NA	NA
Rear Hip Room (in.)	NA	NA	NA	NA	NA	NA	NA	NA	NA
Front Leg Room (in.)	41.3	41.3	41.3	41.3	41.2	41.2	41.2	41.2	41.2
Rear Leg Room (in.)	37.3	37.3	33.4	33.4	20.2	20.2	NA	20.2	NA
Luggage Capacity (cu ft.)	17.2	36.4	13.7	31.3	10.8	13.8	7.8	10.8	6.4
Number of Cylinders	6	6	6	6	4	4	4	4	4
Displacement (liters)	2.8	2.7	2.7	2.7	1.8	1.8	1.8	1.8	1.8
Horsepower @ RPM	200@6000	250@5800	250@5800	250@5800	180@5500	180@5500	180@5500	225@5900	225@5900
Torque @ RPM	207@3200	258@1850	258@1850	258@1850	173@1950	173@1950	173@1950	207@2200	207@2200
Fuel Capacity	18.5	18.5	16.4	16.4	16.3	14.5	14.5	16.3	16.3
EPA City (mpg) - Manual	NA	16	17	NA	20	22	22	20	20
EPA Hwy (mpg) - Manual	NA	21	24	NA	29	31	30	28	28
EPA City (mpg) - Auto	17	15	17	17	NA	NA	NA	NA	NA
EPA Hwy (mpg) - Auto	24	21	24	24	NA	NA	NA	NA	NA

SPECIFICATIONS MILEAGE TABLES

specifications

	3 Series 325Ci Convertible	3 Series 325Ci Coupe	3 Series 325i Sedan	3 Series 325i Sport Wagon	3 Series 325xi Sedan	3 Series 325xi Wagon	3 Series 330Ci	3 Series 330Ci Convertible	3 Series 330i
Length (in.)	176.7	176.7	176	176.3	176	176.3	177	177	176
Width (in.)	69.2	69.2	68.5	68.5	68.5	68.5	69.2	69.2	68.5
Height (in.)	54.6	54.6	55.7	55.5	55.7	55.5	54.6	54.6	55.7
Curb Weight (lbs.)	3560	3153	3153	3351	3153	3351	NA	NA	NA
Wheelbase (in.)	107.3	107.3	107.3	107.3	107.3	107.3	107.3	107.3	107.3
Front Head Room (in.)	38.3	37.5	38.4	38.4	38.4	38.4	36.3	36.3	38.4
Rear Head Room (in.)	36.9	36.5	37.5	37.6	37.5	37.6	36.2	36.2	37.5
Front Shoulder Room (in.)	54.5	54.5	54.4	54.4	54.4	54.4	54.5	54.6	54.4
Rear Shoulder Room (in.)	45.9	52.7	54.2	54.2	54.2	54.2	52.7	52.7	54.2
Front Hip Room (in.)	NA	NA	NA	NA	NA	NA	NA	53.5	NA
Rear Hip Room (in.)	NA	NA	NA	NA	NA	NA	NA	53.3	NA
Front Leg Room (in.)	41.7	41.7	41.4	41.4	41.4	41.4	41.7	41.7	41.4
Rear Leg Room (in.)	32	33.2	34.6	34.6	34.6	34.6	33.2	33.2	34.6
Luggage Capacity (cu ft.)	7.7	9.5	10.7	NA	10.7	NA	14.5	14.5	10.7
Number of Cylinders	6	6	6	6	6	6	6	6	6
Displacement (liters)	2.5	2.5	2.5	2.5	2.5	2.5	3	3	3
Horsepower @ RPM	184@6000	184@6000	184@6000	184@6000	175@6000	184@6000	225@5900	225@5900	225@5900
Torque @ RPM	175@3500	175@3500	175@3500	175@3500	181@3500	175@3500	214@3500	214@3500	214@3500
Fuel Capacity	16.6	16.6	16.6	16.6	16.6	16.6	16.6	16.6	16.6
EPA City (mpg) - Manual	19	20	20	20	19	19	21	20	21
EPA Hwy (mpg) - Manual	27	29	29	29	27	27	30	28	30
EPA City (mpg) - Auto	19	19	19	19	19	19	19	18	19
EPA Hwy (mpg) - Auto	26	27	27	27	26	26	27	26	27

SPECIFICATIONS MILEAGE TABLES — BMW

specifications

SPECIFICATIONS MILEAGE TABLES	3 Series 330xi	5 Series 525i Sedan	5 Series 525i Sport Wagon	5 Series 525iA Sedan	5 Series 525iA Sport Wagon	5 Series 530i Sedan	5 Series 530iA Sedan	5 Series 540i Sedan	5 Series 540iA Sedan	5 Series 540iA Sport Wagon
Length (in.)	176	188	189.2	188	189.2	188	188	188	188	189.2
Width (in.)	68.5	70.9	70.9	70.9	70.9	70.9	70.9	70.9	70.9	70.9
Height (in.)	55.7	56.7	56.7	56.7	56.7	56.7	56.7	56.5	56.7	56.7
Curb Weight (lbs.)	NA	3495	3726	3495	3726	3495	3495	3748	3803	4056
Wheelbase (in.)	107.3	111.4	111.4	111.4	111.4	111.4	111.4	111.4	111.4	111.4
Front Head Room (in.)	38.4	38.7	38.7	38.7	38.7	38.7	38.7	37.4	37.4	37.4
Rear Head Room (in.)	37.5	37.8	38.5	37.8	38.5	37.8	37.8	37.2	37.2	37.4
Front Shoulder Room (in.)	54.4	56.8	56.8	56.8	56.8	56.8	56.8	56.8	56.8	56.8
Rear Shoulder Room (in.)	54.2	55.9	55.9	55.9	55.9	55.9	55.9	55.9	55.9	55.9
Front Hip Room (in.)	53.5	NA	NA	NA	NA	NA	NA	NA	NA	NA
Rear Hip Room (in.)	53.3	NA	NA	NA	NA	NA	NA	NA	NA	NA
Front Leg Room (in.)	41.4	41.7	41.7	41.7	41.7	41.7	41.7	41.7	41.7	41.7
Rear Leg Room (in.)	34.6	34.2	34.2	34.2	34.2	34.2	34.2	34.2	34.2	34.2
Luggage Capacity (cu ft.)	10.7	11.1	32.7	11.1	32.7	11.1	11.1	11.1	11.1	32.1
Number of Cylinders	6	6	6	6	6	6	6	8	8	8
Displacement (liters)	3	2.5	2.5	2.5	2.5	3	3	4.4	4.4	4.4
Horsepower @ RPM	225@5900	184@6000	184@6000	184@6000	184@6000	225@5900	225@5900	282@5400	282@5400	282@5400
Torque @ RPM	214@3500	175@3500	175@3500	175@3500	175@3500	214@3500	214@3500	324@3600	324@3600	324@3600
Fuel Capacity	16.6	18.5	18.5	18.5	18.5	18.5	18.5	18.5	18.5	18.5
EPA City (mpg) - Manual	20	20	19	NA	NA	21	NA	15	NA	NA
EPA Hwy (mpg) - Manual	27	29	27	NA	NA	30	NA	23	NA	NA
EPA City (mpg) - Auto	17	NA	NA	19	19	NA	18	NA	18	15
EPA Hwy (mpg) - Auto	25	NA	NA	27	26	NA	28	NA	24	21

specifications

SPECIFICATIONS MILEAGE TABLES	Z3 2.5i Roadster	Z3 3.0i Coupe	Z3 3.0i Roadster	BUICK Century Custom/Limited	LeSabre Custom/Limited	Park Avenue Base	Park Avenue Ultra	Regal GS	Regal LS
Length (in.)	159.4	158.5	159.4	194.6	200	206.8	206.8	196.2	196.2
Width (in.)	68.5	68.5	68.5	72.7	73.5	74.7	74.7	72.7	72.7
Height (in.)	50.9	51.4	50.9	56.6	57	57.4	57.4	56.6	56.6
Curb Weight (lbs.)	2899	2943	2910	3368	3567	3778	3884	3543	3438
Wheelbase (in.)	96.3	96.3	96.3	109	112.2	113.8	113.8	109	109
Front Head Room (in.)	37.6	36.7	37.6	39.4	38.8	39.8	39.8	39.4	39.4
Rear Head Room (in.)	NA	NA	NA	37.4	37.8	38	38	37.4	37.4
Front Shoulder Room (in.)	51.7	51.7	51.7	58	59.1	59.2	59.2	58	58
Rear Shoulder Room (in.)	NA	NA	NA	57.1	58.7	58.7	58.7	57.1	57.1
Front Hip Room (in.)	54.1	54.1	54.1	54.4	56.1	56.4	56.4	54.4	54.4
Rear Hip Room (in.)	NA	NA	NA	53.3	56.6	55.7	55.7	53.3	53.3
Front Leg Room (in.)	41.8	41.8	41.8	42.4	42.4	42.4	42.4	42.4	42.4
Rear Leg Room (in.)	NA	NA	NA	36.9	39.9	41.4	41.4	36.9	36.9
Luggage Capacity (cu ft.)	5	9	5	16.7	18	19.1	19.1	16.7	16.7
Number of Cylinders	6	6	6	6	6	6	6	6	6
Displacement (liters)	2.5	3	3	3.1	3.8	3.8	3.8	3.8	3.8
Horsepower @ RPM	184@6000	225@5900	225@5900	175@5200	205@5200	205@5200	240@5200	240@5200	200@5200
Torque @ RPM	175@3500	214@3500	214@3500	195@4000	230@4000	230@4000	280@3200	280@3600	220@4000
Fuel Capacity	13.5	13.5	13.5	17.5	18.5	18.5	18.5	17.5	17.5
EPA City (mpg) - Manual	20	21	21	NA	NA	NA	NA	NA	NA
EPA Hwy (mpg) - Manual	27	28	28	NA	NA	NA	NA	NA	NA
EPA City (mpg) - Auto	19	19	19	20	19	19	18	18	20
EPA Hwy (mpg) - Auto	26	27	25	29	30	30	28	28	30

specifications

		CADILLAC								CHEVROLET	
		Catera	DeVille Base	DeVille DTS	Eldorado ESC	Eldorado ETC	Seville SLS	Seville STS		Camaro Base Convertible	
Length (in.)		192.2	207.2	207.2	200.6	200.6	201	201		193.5	
Width (in.)		70.3	74.5	74.5	75.5	75.5	75	75		74.1	
Height (in.)		56.4	56.7	56.7	53.6	53.6	55.7	55.4		51.8	
Curb Weight (lbs.)		3770	3978	4047	3814	3865	3986	4027		3500	
Wheelbase (in.)		107.4	115.3	115.3	108	108	112.2	112.2		101.1	
Front Head Room (in.)		38.7	38.2	38.2	37.8	37.8	38.2	38.2		38	
Rear Head Room (in.)		38.4	38.4	38.4	38.3	38.3	38	38		39	
Front Shoulder Room (in.)		54.6	60.4	60.4	58.2	58.2	59.1	59.1		57.4	
Rear Shoulder Room (in.)		55.9	60.1	60.1	57.6	57.6	58	58		43.5	
Front Hip Room (in.)		54.9	56.4	56.4	57.6	57.6	55.6	55.6		53.5	
Rear Hip Room (in.)		55.2	56.7	56.7	55.7	55.7	57.5	57.5		43.7	
Front Leg Room (in.)		42.2	42.4	42.4	42.6	42.6	42.5	42.5		43	
Rear Leg Room (in.)		37.5	43.2	43.2	35.5	35.5	38.2	38.2		26.8	
Luggage Capacity (cu ft.)		14.5	19.1	19.1	15.3	15.3	15.7	15.7		7.6	
Number of Cylinders		6	8	8	8	8	8	8		6	
Displacement (liters)		3	4.6	4.6	4.6	4.6	4.6	4.6		3.8	
Horsepower @ RPM		200@6000	275@5600	300@6000	275@5600	300@6000	275@5600	300@6000		200@5200	
Torque @ RPM		192@3600	300@4000	295@4400	300@4000	295@4400	300@4000	295@4400		225@4000	
Fuel Capacity		18	18.5	18.5	19	19	18.5	18.5		16.8	
EPA City (mpg) - Manual		NA	NA	NA	NA	NA	NA	NA		19	
EPA Hwy (mpg) - Manual		NA	NA	NA	NA	NA	NA	NA		31	
EPA City (mpg) - Auto		17	17	17	17	17	17	17		19	
EPA Hwy (mpg) - Auto		24	27	27	27	27	27	27		31	

specifications

	Camaro Base Coupe	Camaro Z28 Convertible	Camaro Z28 Coupe	Cavalier Base Coupe	Cavalier Base Sedan	Cavalier LS Sedan	Cavalier Z24 Coupe	Corvette Convertible	Corvette Coupe	Corvette Z06 Hardtop
Length (in.)	193.5	193.5	193.5	180.9	180.9	180.9	180.9	179.7	179.7	179.7
Width (in.)	74.1	74.1	74.1	68.7	67.9	67.9	68.7	73.6	73.6	73.6
Height (in.)	51.2	51.8	51.2	53	54.7	54.7	53	47.8	47.7	47.7
Curb Weight (lbs.)	3306	3574	3439	2617	2676	2676	2749	3210	3214	3116
Wheelbase (in.)	101.1	101.1	101.1	104.1	104.1	104.1	104.1	104.5	104.5	104.5
Front Head Room (in.)	37.2	38	37.2	37.6	38.9	38.9	37.6	37.6	37.9	37.8
Rear Head Room (in.)	35.2	39	35.2	36.6	37.2	37.2	36.6	NA	NA	NA
Front Shoulder Room (in.)	57.4	57.4	57.4	53.9	54.6	54.6	53.9	55.3	55.3	55.3
Rear Shoulder Room (in.)	55.8	43.5	55.8	54.9	53.9	53.9	54.9	NA	NA	NA
Front Hip Room (in.)	53.5	53.5	53.5	50	50.8	50.8	50	54.2	54.2	54.2
Rear Hip Room (in.)	45.9	43.7	45.9	49.5	50.6	50.6	49.5	NA	NA	NA
Front Leg Room (in.)	43	43	43	41.9	41.9	41.9	41.9	42.7	42.7	42.7
Rear Leg Room (in.)	26.8	26.8	26.8	32.7	34.4	34.4	32.7	NA	NA	NA
Luggage Capacity (cu ft.)	12.9	7.6	12.9	13.2	13.6	13.6	13.2	13.9	24.8	13.3
Number of Cylinders	6	8	8	4	4	4	4	8	8	8
Displacement (liters)	3.8	5.7	5.7	2.2	2.2	2.2	2.4	5.7	5.7	5.7
Horsepower @ RPM	200@5200	310@5200	310@5200	115@5000	115@5000	115@5000	150@5600	350@5600	350@5600	385@6000
Torque @ RPM	225@4000	340@4000	340@4000	135@3600	135@3600	135@3600	155@4400	360@4000	360@4000	385@4800
Fuel Capacity	16.8	16.8	16.8	14.3	14.3	14.3	14.3	18.5	18.5	18.5
EPA City (mpg) - Manual	19	19	19	23	23	NA	22	19	19	19
EPA Hwy (mpg) - Manual	31	28	28	33	33	NA	32	28	28	28
EPA City (mpg) - Auto	19	18	18	23	23	23	21	18	18	NA
EPA Hwy (mpg) - Auto	31	26	26	29	29	32	28	26	26	NA

SPECIFICATIONS MILEAGE TABLES

specifications

	Impala Base	Impala LS	Malibu Base/LS	Monte Carlo LS	Monte Carlo SS	Prizm Base/Lsi	CHRYSLER	300M	Concorde LX	Concorde LXi
Length (in.)	200	200	190.4	197.9	197.9	174.2		197.8	209.1	209.1
Width (in.)	73	73	69.4	72.3	72.3	66.7		74.4	74.4	74.4
Height (in.)	57.3	57.3	56.4	55.2	55.2	53.7		56	55.8	55.8
Curb Weight (lbs.)	3389	3466	3051	3340	3395	2403		3591	3495	3566
Wheelbase (in.)	110.5	110.5	107	110.5	110.5	97		113	113	113
Front Head Room (in.)	39.2	39.2	39.4	38.1	38.1	39.3		38.3	38.3	38.3
Rear Head Room (in.)	36.8	36.8	37.6	36.5	36.5	36.9		37.7	37.2	37.2
Front Shoulder Room (in.)	59	59	55.5	58.3	58.3	52.8		58.8	59.1	59.1
Rear Shoulder Room (in.)	58.9	58.9	55.3	57.8	57.8	52.2		58.7	58.4	58.4
Front Hip Room (in.)	56.5	56.5	52	55.2	55.2	50.5		57.4	56.3	56.3
Rear Hip Room (in.)	55.7	55.7	52	55.5	55.5	51.2		59.1	56.8	56.8
Front Leg Room (in.)	42.2	42.2	41.9	42.4	42.4	42.5		42.2	42.2	42.2
Rear Leg Room (in.)	38.4	38.4	38	35.8	35.8	33.2		39.1	41.6	41.6
Luggage Capacity (cu ft.)	18.6	18.6	17.1	15.8	15.8	12.1		16.8	18.7	18.7
Number of Cylinders	6	6	6	6	6	4		6	6	6
Displacement (liters)	3.4	3.8	3.1	3.4	3.8	1.8		3.5	2.7	3.2
Horsepower @ RPM	180@5200	200@5200	170@5200	180@5200	200@5200	125@5800		250@6400	200@5800	225@6300
Torque @ RPM	205@4000	225@4000	190@4000	205@4000	225@4000	125@4000		250@3900	190@4850	225@3800
Fuel Capacity	17	17	14.8	17	17	13.2		17.2	17	17
EPA City (mpg) - Manual	NA	NA	NA	NA	NA	32		NA	NA	NA
EPA Hwy (mpg) - Manual	NA	NA	NA	NA	NA	41		NA	NA	NA
EPA City (mpg) - Auto	21	20	20	21	20	30		18	20	19
EPA Hwy (mpg) - Auto	32	30	29	32	30	40		26	28	27

SPECIFICATIONS MILEAGE TABLES

specifications

	LHS	Sebring LX Convertible	Sebring LX Coupe	Sebring LX Sedan	Sebring LXi Convertible	Sebring LXi Coupe	Sebring LXi Sedan	Sebring Limited Convertible	Lanos Hatchback
Length (in.)	207.7	193.7	190.2	190.7	193.7	190.2	190.7	193.7	160.4
Width (in.)	74.4	69.4	70.3	70.6	69.4	70.3	70.6	69.4	66.1
Height (in.)	56	55	53.7	54.9	55	53.7	54.9	55	56.4
Curb Weight (lbs.)	3574	3332	3100	3574	3428	3183	3316	3428	2447
Wheelbase (in.)	113	106	103.7	108	106	103.7	108	106	99.2
Front Head Room (in.)	38.3	38.7	38.5	37.6	38.7	38.5	37.6	38.7	38.9
Rear Head Room (in.)	37.2	37	36	35.8	37	36	35.8	37	37.8
Front Shoulder Room (in.)	58.8	56.3	52.2	55.2	56.3	52.7	55.2	56.3	53.5
Rear Shoulder Room (in.)	58.4	48.9	52.4	54.7	48.9	52.4	54.7	48.9	53.5
Front Hip Room (in.)	57.4	52.4	52.7	52.5	52.4	52.2	52.5	52.4	NA
Rear Hip Room (in.)	59.3	44.7	49.5	53.1	44.7	49.5	53.1	44.7	NA
Front Leg Room (in.)	42.2	42.4	42.3	42.3	42.4	42.3	42.3	42.4	42.8
Rear Leg Room (in.)	41.6	35.2	34	38.1	35.2	34	38.1	35.2	34.6
Luggage Capacity (cu ft.)	18.7	11.3	16.3	16	11.3	16.3	16	11.3	8.8
Number of Cylinders	6	6	4	4	6	6	6	6	4
Displacement (liters)	3.5	2.7	2.4	2.4	2.7	3	2.7	2.7	1.6
Horsepower @ RPM	253@6400	200@5900	140@5500	150@5200	200@5900	200@5500	200@5900	200@5900	105@5800
Torque @ RPM	255@3950	192@4300	155@4000	167@4400	192@4300	205@4500	192@4300	192@4300	106@3400
Fuel Capacity	17	16	16.3	16	16	16.3	16	16	12.7
EPA City (mpg) - Manual	NA	NA	22	NA	NA	20	NA	NA	25
EPA Hwy (mpg) - Manual	NA	NA	30	NA	NA	28	NA	NA	35
EPA City (mpg) - Auto	18	20	20	20	20	19	20	20	22
EPA Hwy (mpg) - Auto	26	28	27	30	28	27	29	29	32

DAEWOO

specifications

	Lanos Sedan	Lanos Sport	Leganza SE/SX/CDX	Nubira Sedan	Nubira Wagon	Intrepid ES	Intrepid R/T	Intrepid SE	Neon Highline
Length (in.)	166.8	160.4	183.9	177	179	203.7	203.7	203.7	174.4
Width (in.)	66.1	66.1	70	66.9	67.7	74.7	74.7	74.7	67.4
Height (in.)	56.4	56.4	56.6	56.3	57.9	55.9	55.9	55.9	56
Curb Weight (lbs.)	2522	2447	3102	2800	2888	3489	3511	3471	2567
Wheelbase (in.)	99.2	99.2	105.1	101.2	101.2	113	113	113	105
Front Head Room (in.)	38.9	38.9	39.3	39	39	38.3	38.3	38.3	39.1
Rear Head Room (in.)	37.8	37.8	37.8	38.1	39.5	37.5	37.5	37.5	36.8
Front Shoulder Room (in.)	53.5	53.5	55.9	55	55	59	59	59	53.4
Rear Shoulder Room (in.)	53.5	53.5	55.9	54.3	54.3	58.1	58.1	58.1	52.8
Front Hip Room (in.)	NA	NA	NA	NA	NA	56.2	56.2	56.2	52.4
Rear Hip Room (in.)	NA	NA	NA	NA	NA	56.6	56.6	56.6	52.9
Front Leg Room (in.)	42.8	42.8	42.3	42	42	42.2	42.2	42.2	42.4
Rear Leg Room (in.)	34.6	34.6	38.2	34.7	34.7	39.1	39.1	39.1	34.8
Luggage Capacity (cu ft.)	8.8	8.8	14.1	13.1	19.4	18.4	18.4	18.4	11.8
Number of Cylinders	4	4	4	4	4	6	6	6	4
Displacement (liters)	1.6	1.6	2.2	2	2	2.7	3.5	2.7	2
Horsepower @ RPM	105@5800	105@5800	131@5200	129@5400	129@5400	202@5800	242@6400	200@5800	132@5600
Torque @ RPM	106@3400	106@3400	148@2800	136@4400	136@4400	195@4200	248@3950	190@4850	130@4600
Fuel Capacity	12.7	12.7	15.8	13.7	13.7	17	17	17	12.5
EPA City (mpg) - Manual	25	25	20	22	22	NA	NA	NA	27
EPA Hwy (mpg) - Manual	35	35	28	31	31	NA	NA	NA	33
EPA City (mpg) - Auto	22	22	20	22	22	20	18	20	24
EPA Hwy (mpg) - Auto	32	32	28	31	31	28	26	29	31

DODGE

SPECIFICATIONS MILEAGE TABLES

specifications

	Stratus ES/SE	Stratus R/T/SE		Crown Victoria Base/LX	Escort ZX2	Focus LX/SE Sedan	Focus SE Wagon	Focus ZTS	Focus ZX3	Mustang Base Convertible
Length (in.)	190.7	187.2		212	175.2	174.9	178.2	174.9	168.1	183.2
Width (in.)	70.6	70.3		78.2	67.4	66.9	66.9	66.9	66.9	73.1
Height (in.)	54.9	53.7		56.8	52.3	56.3	53.9	56.3	56.3	53.2
Curb Weight (lbs.)	NA	3012		3946	2478	2564	2717	2564	2551	3203
Wheelbase (in.)	108	103.7		114.7	98.4	103	103	103	103	101.3
Front Head Room (in.)	37.6	38.5		39.4	38	39.3	39.3	39.3	39.3	38.1
Rear Head Room (in.)	35.8	36		38	35.1	38.5	39.9	38.5	38.7	35.8
Front Shoulder Room (in.)	55.2	52.2		60.8	50.8	53.7	53.7	53.7	53.6	53.7
Rear Shoulder Room (in.)	54.7	52.4		60.3	48.7	53.7	53.7	53.7	53.5	41.4
Front Hip Room (in.)	50.5	51.9		57.1	51.1	49.4	49.4	49.4	49.4	52.3
Rear Hip Room (in.)	53.4	49.5		58.7	45.1	49.5	49.5	49.5	49.5	41
Front Leg Room (in.)	42.3	42.3		42.5	42.5	43.1	43.1	43.1	43.1	42.6
Rear Leg Room (in.)	38.1	34		39.6	33.4	37.6	37.6	37.6	37.6	29.9
Luggage Capacity (cu ft.)	16	16.3		20.6	11.8	12.9	37.5	12.9	18.6	7.7
Number of Cylinders	6	6		8	4	4	4	4	4	6
Displacement (liters)	2.7	3		4.6	2	2	2	2	2	3.8
Horsepower @ RPM	200@5800	200@5500		225@4750	130@5750	110@5000	130@5300	130@5300	130@5300	193@5500
Torque @ RPM	195@4200	205@4500		270@4000	127@4250	125@3750	135@4500	135@4500	135@4500	225@2800
Fuel Capacity	16	16.3		19	12.8	13.2	13.2	13.2	13.2	15.7
EPA City (mpg) - Manual	NA	20		NA	26	28	25	25	25	19
EPA Hwy (mpg) - Manual	NA	28		NA	33	36	33	33	33	29
EPA City (mpg) - Auto	20	19		18	25	25	25	25	25	19
EPA Hwy (mpg) - Auto	29	27		25	33	33	31	31	31	27

SPECIFICATIONS MILEAGE TABLES

FORD

specifications

	Mustang Base Coupe	Mustang Cobra Convertible	Mustang Cobra Coupe	Mustang GT Convertible	Mustang GT Coupe	Taurus LX/SE-ZV	Taurus SE Wagon	Taurus SEL/SES	Accord LX Sedan
Length (in.)	183.2	183.5	183.5	183.2	183.2	197.6	197.7	197.6	188.8
Width (in.)	73.1	73.1	73.1	73.1	73.1	73	73	73	70.3
Height (in.)	53.1	53.5	53.2	53.2	53.1	56.1	57.8	56.1	56.9
Curb Weight (lbs.)	3064	3560	3430	3429	3237	3355	3519	3408	2888
Wheelbase (in.)	101.3	101.3	101.3	101.3	101.3	108.5	108.5	108.5	106.9
Front Head Room (in.)	38.1	38.1	38.1	38.1	38.1	40	39.4	40	40
Rear Head Room (in.)	35.5	35.8	35.5	35.8	35.5	38.1	38.9	38.1	37.6
Front Shoulder Room (in.)	53.6	53.6	53.6	53.6	53.6	57.3	57.3	57.3	56.9
Rear Shoulder Room (in.)	52.1	41.4	52.1	41.4	52.1	56.6	56.6	56.6	56.1
Front Hip Room (in.)	52.3	52.3	52.3	52.3	52.3	54.5	54.5	54.5	54.9
Rear Hip Room (in.)	47.4	41	47.4	41	47.4	55.7	55.4	55.7	54.1
Front Leg Room (in.)	42.6	42.6	42.6	41.8	41.8	42.2	42.2	42.2	42.1
Rear Leg Room (in.)	29.9	29.9	29.9	29.9	29.9	38.9	38.5	38.9	37.9
Luggage Capacity (cu ft.)	10.9	7.7	10.9	7.7	10.9	17	38.8	17	14.1
Number of Cylinders	6	8	8	8	8	6	6	6	4
Displacement (liters)	3.8	4.6	4.6	4.6	4.6	3	3	3	2.3
Horsepower @ RPM	193@5500	320@6000	320@6000	260@5250	260@5250	153@4900	153@4900	200@5650	135@5400
Torque @ RPM	225@2800	317@4750	317@4750	302@4000	302@4000	185@3900	185@3900	200@4400	145@4700
Fuel Capacity	15.7	15.7	15.7	15.7	15.7	18	18	18	17.1
EPA City (mpg) - Manual	19	NA	NA	18	18	NA	NA	NA	25
EPA Hwy (mpg) - Manual	29	NA	NA	25	25	NA	NA	NA	32
EPA City (mpg) - Auto	19	18	18	18	18	20	18	20	23
EPA Hwy (mpg) - Auto	27	25	25	25	25	27	26	27	30

SPECIFICATIONS MILEAGE TABLES

HONDA

specifications

	Accord LX/EX - Coupe	Accord LX/EX - Sedan	Accord LX/EX - Coupe	Accord LX/EX - Sedan	Accord Value Package	Civic DX/LX - Coupe	Civic DX/LX - Sedan	Civic EX Coupe	Civic EX Sedan	Civic EX/LX - Sedan
Length (in.)	186.8	188.8	186.8	188.8	188.8	174.7	174.6	174.7	175.1	175.1
Width (in.)	70.3	70.3	70.3	70.3	70.3	67.7	67.5	67.7	67.1	67.1
Height (in.)	55	57.3	55.3	56.9	56.9	55.1	56.7	55.1	54.7	54.7
Curb Weight (lbs.)	2976	3285	3241	3020	2888	2405	2421	2553	2564	2465
Wheelbase (in.)	105.1	106.9	105.1	106.9	106.9	103.1	103.1	103.1	103.2	103.2
Front Head Room (in.)	38	38.5	38	38.5	40	39	39.8	36.9	38	39.8
Rear Head Room (in.)	36.5	36.5	36.5	36.5	37.6	35.4	37.2	35	36.3	37.2
Front Shoulder Room (in.)	56	56.9	56	56.9	56.9	52.8	52.6	52.8	52.6	52.6
Rear Shoulder Room (in.)	55.4	56.1	55.4	56.1	56.1	52.6	52	52.6	52	52
Front Hip Room (in.)	52.1	54.9	52.1	54.9	54.9	50.2	51.2	50.2	51.2	51.2
Rear Hip Room (in.)	46.1	54.1	46.1	54.1	54.1	46.7	49.8	46.7	49.8	49.8
Front Leg Room (in.)	42.6	42.1	42.6	42.1	42.1	42.5	42.2	42.7	42.2	42.2
Rear Leg Room (in.)	32.4	37.9	32.4	37.9	37.9	32.8	36	32.5	36	36
Luggage Capacity (cu ft.)	13.6	14.1	13.6	14.1	14.1	12.9	12.9	12.9	12.9	12.9
Number of Cylinders	4	6	6	4	4	4	4	4	4	4
Displacement (liters)	2.3	3	3	2.3	2.3	1.7	1.7	1.7	1.7	1.7
Horsepower @ RPM	150@5700	200@5500	200@5500	150@5700	135@5400	115@6100	115@6100	127@6300	127@6300	115@6100
Torque @ RPM	152@4900	195@4700	195@4700	152@4900	145@4700	110@4500	110@4500	114@4800	114@4800	110@4500
Fuel Capacity	17.1	17.1	17.1	17.1	17.1	13.2	13.2	13.2	13.2	13.2
EPA City (mpg) - Manual	25	NA	NA	25	NA	30	30	32	32	32
EPA Hwy (mpg) - Manual	32	NA	NA	32	NA	39	39	37	37	39
EPA City (mpg) - Auto	23	20	20	23	23	30	30	31	31	30
EPA Hwy (mpg) - Auto	30	28	28	30	30	38	38	38	38	38

specifications

	Civic HX Coupe	Civic LX Coupe	Insight Base	Prelude Base/SH	S2000	Accent Hatchback	Accent Sedan	Elantra GLS Sedan	Sonata Base
Length (in.)	174.7	174.7	155.1	178	162.2	166.7	166.7	177	185.4
Width (in.)	67.7	67.7	66.7	69	68.9	65.7	65.7	67.7	71.6
Height (in.)	55.1	55.1	53.3	51.8	50.6	54.9	54.9	56.1	55.5
Curb Weight (lbs.)	2434	2465	1847	2954	2809	2280	2240	2635	3072
Wheelbase (in.)	103.1	103.1	94.5	101.8	94.5	96.1	96.1	102.7	106.3
Front Head Room (in.)	39	39	38.8	37.9	34.6	38.9	38.9	39.6	39.3
Rear Head Room (in.)	35.4	35.4	NA	35.3	NA	38	38	38	37.6
Front Shoulder Room (in.)	52.8	52.8	50.5	53.8	50.2	52.8	52.8	54.7	56.9
Rear Shoulder Room (in.)	52.6	52.6	NA	50	NA	52.4	52.4	53.5	55.7
Front Hip Room (in.)	50.2	50.2	48.7	52.1	49.8	54.1	54.1	53	55.9
Rear Hip Room (in.)	46.7	46.7	NA	41	NA	53	53	55.6	54.3
Front Leg Room (in.)	42.7	42.7	42.9	43	44.3	42.6	42.6	43.2	43.3
Rear Leg Room (in.)	32.5	32.5	NA	28.1	NA	32.8	32.8	35	36.2
Luggage Capacity (cu ft.)	12.9	12.9	16.3	8.7	5	16.1	10.7	11	13.2
Number of Cylinders	4	4	3	4	4	4	4	4	4
Displacement (liters)	1.7	1.7	1	2.2	2	1.6	1.6	2	2.4
Horsepower @ RPM	117@6100	115@6100	73@5700	200@7000	240@8300	105@5500	105@5500	140@6000	149@5500
Torque @ RPM	111@4500	110@4500	91@2000	156@5250	153@7500	97@4000	97@4000	133@4800	156@3000
Fuel Capacity	13.2	13.2	10.6	15.9	13.2	11.9	11.9	14.5	17.2
EPA City (mpg) - Manual	36	32	61	22	20	27	27	25	22
EPA Hwy (mpg) - Manual	44	39	68	27	26	37	37	33	30
EPA City (mpg) - Auto	35	30	NA	21	NA	25	25	24	21
EPA Hwy (mpg) - Auto	40	38	NA	26	NA	35	35	33	28

SPECIFICATIONS MILEAGE TABLES

HYUNDAI

specifications

	Sonata GLS	Sonata GLS w/Leather	Tiburon	XG300 Base	INFINITI	G20 Luxury/Touring	I30 Luxury/Touring	Q45 Base/Touring	JAGUAR	S-Type V6
Length (in.)	185.4	185.4	170.9	191.5		177.5	193.7	199.6		191.3
Width (in.)	71.6	71.6	68.1	71.9		66.7	70.2	71.7		71.6
Height (in.)	55.5	55.5	51.7	55.9		55.1	56.5	56.9		55.7
Curb Weight (lbs.)	3069	3069	2633	3604		2950	3342	4007		3650
Wheelbase (in.)	106.3	106.3	97.4	108.3		102.4	108.3	111.4		114.5
Front Head Room (in.)	39.3	39.3	38	39.7		40	40.5	37.6		40.5
Rear Head Room (in.)	37.6	37.6	34.4	38		36.8	37.4	36.9		36.9
Front Shoulder Room (in.)	56.9	56.9	53.5	56.9		53.1	56.4	56.7		56.3
Rear Shoulder Room (in.)	55.7	55.7	49.2	56.2		53.2	56.2	56.7		56.2
Front Hip Room (in.)	55.9	55.9	52.4	NA		52.3	54.3	55.7		NA
Rear Hip Room (in.)	54.3	54.3	47.8	NA		51.9	53	55.7		NA
Front Leg Room (in.)	43.3	43.3	43.1	43.4		41.5	43.9	43.6		43.1
Rear Leg Room (in.)	36.2	36.2	29.9	37.2		34.6	36.2	35.9		37.7
Luggage Capacity (cu ft.)	13.2	13.2	12.8	14.5		13.5	14.9	12.6		11.7
Number of Cylinders	6	6	4	6		4	6	8		6
Displacement (liters)	2.5	2.5	2	3		2	3	4.1		3
Horsepower @ RPM	170@6000	170@6000	140@6000	192@6000		145@6000	227@6400	266@5600		240@6800
Torque @ RPM	166@4000	166@4000	133@4800	178@4000		136@4800	217@4000	278@4000		221@4500
Fuel Capacity	17.2	17.2	14.5	18.5		15.9	18.5	21.4		18.4
EPA City (mpg) - Manual	20	20	23	NA		24	NA	NA		NA
EPA Hwy (mpg) - Manual	28	28	31	NA		31	NA	NA		NA
EPA City (mpg) - Auto	20	20	21	19		23	19	18		18
EPA Hwy (mpg) - Auto	27	27	30	27		30	26	23		25

SPECIFICATIONS MILEAGE TABLES

specifications

	S-Type V8	KIA	Rio Base	Sephia Base	Sephia LS	Spectra GS	Spectra GSX	LEXUS	ES 300	GS 300
Length (in.)	191.3		165.9	174.4	174.4	176.2	176.2		190.2	189.2
Width (in.)	71.6		65.9	66.9	66.9	66.9	66.9		70.5	70.9
Height (in.)	55.7		56.7	55.5	55.5	55.5	55.5		54.9	55.9
Curb Weight (lbs.)	3770		2103	2478	2551	2560	2575		3373	3638
Wheelbase (in.)	114.5		94.9	100.8	100.8	100.8	100.8		105.1	110.2
Front Head Room (in.)	38.6		39.4	39.6	39.6	36.6	36.6		38	39
Rear Head Room (in.)	36.4		37.6	37.7	37.7	37.7	37.7		36.2	37.4
Front Shoulder Room (in.)	56.3		53	53.8	53.8	53.8	53.8		55.6	57.7
Rear Shoulder Room (in.)	56.7		53.2	54.2	54.2	54.2	54.2		54.1	56.6
Front Hip Room (in.)	NA		51.6	52.1	52.1	52.1	52.1		53.3	55
Rear Hip Room (in.)	NA		53.2	54	54	54	54		53.4	56.1
Front Leg Room (in.)	43.1		42.8	43.3	43.3	43.1	43.1		43.5	44.5
Rear Leg Room (in.)	37.7		32.7	34.4	34.4	34.4	34.4		34.4	34.3
Luggage Capacity (cu ft.)	11.7		10.2	10.4	10.4	11.6	11.6		13	14.8
Number of Cylinders	8		4	4	4	4	4		6	6
Displacement (liters)	4		1.5	1.8	1.8	1.8	1.8		3	3
Horsepower @ RPM	281@6100		96@5800	125@6000	125@6000	125@6000	125@6000		210@5800	220@5800
Torque @ RPM	287@4300		98@4500	108@4500	108@4500	108@4500	108@4500		220@4400	220@3800
Fuel Capacity	18.4		11.9	13.2	13.2	13.2	13.2		18.5	19.8
EPA City (mpg) - Manual	NA		22	24	24	24	24		NA	NA
EPA Hwy (mpg) - Manual	NA		30	29	29	29	29		NA	NA
EPA City (mpg) - Auto	17		25	21	21	21	21		19	18
EPA Hwy (mpg) - Auto	24		30	30	30	30	30		26	24

specifications

	GS / GS 430	LS 300	LS 430	**LINCOLN** Continental	LS V6 Auto	LS V6 Manual	LS V8	Town Car Cartier	Town Car Cartier L
Length (in.)	189.2	176.6	196.7	208.4	193.9	193.9	193.9	215.3	221.3
Width (in.)	70.9	67.7	72	73.6	73.2	73.2	73.2	78.2	78.2
Height (in.)	55.9	54.9	58.7	55.9	56.1	56.1	56.1	58	58
Curb Weight (lbs.)	3707	3270	3955	3848	3593	3598	3692	4047	4047
Wheelbase (in.)	110.2	105.1	115.2	109	114.5	114.5	114.5	117.7	123.7
Front Head Room (in.)	39	39.1	39.6	38.9	40.4	40.4	40.4	39.2	39.2
Rear Head Room (in.)	37.4	37.7	38	38	37.5	37.5	37.5	37.5	37.5
Front Shoulder Room (in.)	57.7	57.7	58.3	57.1	57.7	57.7	57.7	60.6	60.6
Rear Shoulder Room (in.)	56.6	56.6	58.2	56.6	57	57	57	60.3	60.3
Front Hip Room (in.)	55	55	56.7	55.7	53	53	53	57.3	57.3
Rear Hip Room (in.)	56.1	56.1	57.3	56.5	54.4	54.4	54.4	58	58
Front Leg Room (in.)	44.5	43.4	44	41.9	42.8	42.8	42.8	42.6	42.6
Rear Leg Room (in.)	34.3	32.2	37.6	38	37.4	37.4	37.4	41.1	41.1
Luggage Capacity (cu ft.)	14.8	10.1	20.2	18.4	13.5	13.5	13.5	20.6	20.6
Number of Cylinders	8	6	8	8	6	6	8	8	8
Displacement (liters)	4.3	3	4.3	4.6	3	3	3.9	4.6	4.6
Horsepower @ RPM	300@5600	215@5800	290@5600	275@5750	210@6500	210@6500	252@6100	235@4750	235@4750
Torque @ RPM	325@3400	218@3800	320@3400	275@4750	205@4750	205@4750	267@4300	276@4000	276@4000
Fuel Capacity	19.8	19.8	22.2	20	18	18	18	19	19
EPA City (mpg) - Manual	NA	NA	NA	NA	NA	NA	NA	NA	NA
EPA Hwy (mpg) - Manual	NA	NA	NA	NA	NA	25	NA	NA	NA
EPA City (mpg) - Auto	18	18	18	17	18	NA	17	18	18
EPA Hwy (mpg) - Auto	23	23	25	25	25	NA	24	25	25

specifications

	Town Car Executive	Town Car Executive L	Town Car Signature		626 4-Cyl	626 V6	MX-5 Miata Base/LS	Millenia Base	Millenia S	Protege DX/LX
Length (in.)	215.3	221.3	215.3		187.4	187.4	155.3	189.8	189.9	174
Width (in.)	78.2	78.2	78.2		69.3	69.3	66	69.7	69.7	67.1
Height (in.)	58	58	58		55.1	55.1	48.4	54.9	54.9	55.5
Curb Weight (lbs.)	4047	4047	4047		2864	3023	2332	3241	3355	2449
Wheelbase (in.)	117.7	123.7	117.7		105.1	105.1	89.2	108.3	108.3	102.8
Front Head Room (in.)	39.2	39.2	39.2		39.2	38.4	37.1	39.3	37.9	39.3
Rear Head Room (in.)	37.5	37.5	37.5		37	32	NA	37	36.5	37.4
Front Shoulder Room (in.)	60.6	60.6	60.6		56.3	56.3	49.7	55.1	55.1	53.9
Rear Shoulder Room (in.)	60.3	60.3	60.3		55.9	55.9	NA	54.2	54.2	53.4
Front Hip Room (in.)	57.3	57.3	57.3		53.8	53.8	49.2	53	53	NA
Rear Hip Room (in.)	58	58	58		54.5	54.5	NA	55.7	55.7	NA
Front Leg Room (in.)	42.6	42.6	42.6		43.6	43.6	42.8	43.3	43.3	42.2
Rear Leg Room (in.)	41.1	41.1	41.1		34.6	34.6	NA	34.1	34.1	35.4
Luggage Capacity (cu ft.)	20.6	20.6	20.6		14.2	14.2	5.1	13.3	13.3	12.9
Number of Cylinders	8	8	8		4	6	4	6	6	4
Displacement (liters)	4.6	4.6	4.6		2	2.5	1.8	2.5	2.3	1.6
Horsepower @ RPM	220@4750	235@4750	220@4750		125@5500	165@6000	155@6500	170@5800	210@5300	105@5500
Torque @ RPM	265@4000	275@4000	265@4000		127@3000	161@5000	125@5500	160@4800	210@3500	107@4000
Fuel Capacity	19	19	19		16.9	16.9	12.7	18	18	13.2
EPA City (mpg) - Manual	NA	NA	NA		26	21	23	NA	NA	29
EPA Hwy (mpg) - Manual	NA	NA	NA		32	27	28	NA	NA	34
EPA City (mpg) - Auto	18	18	18		22	20	22	20	20	26
EPA Hwy (mpg) - Auto	25	25	25		28	26	28	27	28	33

SPECIFICATIONS MILEAGE TABLES

MAZDA

specifications

	Protege ES	MERCEDES-BENZ C-Class C240	C-Class C320	CLK-Class CLK 320 Convertible	CLK-Class CLK 320 Coupe	CLK-Class CLK 430 Convertible	CLK-Class CLK430 Coupe	E-Class E320 AWD Sedan	E-Class E320 AWD Wagon
Length (in.)	174	178.3	178.3	180.3	180.3	180.3	180.3	189.4	190
Width (in.)	67.1	68	68	67.8	67.8	67.8	67.8	70.8	70.8
Height (in.)	55.5	55.2	55.2	54.3	54	54.3	54	56.7	59.3
Curb Weight (lbs.)	2537	3310	3395	3566	3213	3665	3323	3823	4043
Wheelbase (in.)	102.8	106.9	106.9	105.9	105.9	105.9	105.9	111.5	111.5
Front Head Room (in.)	39.3	38.8	38.8	37.5	36.9	37.5	36.9	37.6	37.6
Rear Head Room (in.)	37.4	41.7	41.7	36.5	35.8	36.5	35.8	37.2	37
Front Shoulder Room (in.)	53.9	53.1	53.1	52.9	52.9	52.9	52.9	56.3	56.3
Rear Shoulder Room (in.)	53.4	54.3	54.3	48	50.4	48	50.4	57.1	57.1
Front Hip Room (in.)	NA	55.1	55.1	53.7	53.7	53.7	53.7	54.9	54.9
Rear Hip Room (in.)	NA	56	56	44.2	45.9	44.2	45.9	55.9	55.9
Front Leg Room (in.)	42.2	41.4	41.4	41.9	41.9	41.9	41.9	41.3	41.3
Rear Leg Room (in.)	35.4	33	33	27.4	31.2	27.4	31.2	36.1	36.5
Luggage Capacity (cu ft.)	12.9	15.3	15.3	5.7	11	5.7	11	15.3	43.8
Number of Cylinders	4	6	6	6	6	8	8	6	6
Displacement (liters)	1.8	2.6	3.2	3.2	3.2	4.3	4.3	3.2	3.2
Horsepower @ RPM	122@6000	168@5500	215@5700	215@5700	215@5700	275@5750	275@5750	221@5600	221@5600
Torque @ RPM	120@4000	177@4500	221@3000	229@3000	229@3000	295@3000	295@3000	232@3000	232@3000
Fuel Capacity	13.2	16.2	16.2	16.4	16.4	16.4	16.4	21.1	18.5
EPA City (mpg) - Manual	26	NA	NA	NA	NA	NA	NA	NA	NA
EPA Hwy (mpg) - Manual	30	NA	NA	NA	NA	NA	NA	NA	NA
EPA City (mpg) - Auto	24	20	19	20	21	18	18	20	20
EPA Hwy (mpg) - Auto	29	26	26	28	29	24	25	27	27

specifications

	E-Class E320 RWD Sedan	E-Class E320 RWD Wagon	E-Class E430 AWD Sedan	E-Class E430 RWD Sedan	SLK SLK230 Kompressor	SLK SLK320 Roadster	Cougar I4	Cougar S	Cougar V6
Length (in.)	189.4	190	189.4	189.4	157.9	157.9	185	185	185
Width (in.)	70.8	70.8	70.8	70.8	67.5	67.5	69.6	69.6	69.6
Height (in.)	56.7	59.3	56.7	56.7	50.4	50.4	52.2	52.2	52.2
Curb Weight (lbs.)	3624	3856	3944	3757	3055	3099	2861	3103	3013
Wheelbase (in.)	111.5	111.5	111.5	111.5	94.5	94.5	106.4	106.4	106.4
Front Head Room (in.)	37.6	37.6	37.6	37.6	37.4	37.4	37.8	37.8	37.8
Rear Head Room (in.)	37.2	37	37.2	37.2	NA	NA	34.7	34.7	34.7
Front Shoulder Room (in.)	56.3	56.3	56.3	56.3	51.7	51.7	53.9	53.9	53.9
Rear Shoulder Room (in.)	57.1	57.1	57.1	57.1	NA	NA	51.3	51.3	51.3
Front Hip Room (in.)	54.9	54.9	54.9	54.9	54.7	54.7	51.2	51.2	51.2
Rear Hip Room (in.)	55.9	55.9	55.9	55.9	NA	NA	46.1	46.1	46.1
Front Leg Room (in.)	41.3	41.3	41.3	41.3	42.7	42.7	42.6	42.6	42.6
Rear Leg Room (in.)	36.1	36.5	36.1	36.1	NA	NA	33.2	33.2	33.2
Luggage Capacity (cu ft.)	15.3	43.8	15.3	15.3	3.6	3.6	14.5	14.5	14.5
Number of Cylinders	6	6	8	8	4	6	4	4	6
Displacement (liters)	3.2	3.2	4.3	4.3	2.3	3.2	2	2.5	2.5
Horsepower @ RPM	221@5600	221@5600	275@5750	275@5750	190@5500	215@5700	125@5500	196@6750	170@6250
Torque @ RPM	232@3000	232@3000	295@3000	295@3000	200@2500	229@3000	130@4000	165@4250	165@4250
Fuel Capacity	21.1	18.5	21.1	21.1	15.9	15.9	16	16	16
EPA City (mpg) - Manual	NA	NA	NA	NA	20	18	23	NA	20
EPA Hwy (mpg) - Manual	NA	NA	NA	NA	29	27	34	NA	29
EPA City (mpg) - Auto	20	20	17	18	23	21	NA	20	20
EPA Hwy (mpg) - Auto	28	28	23	25	30	27	NA	29	29

MERCURY

specifications

	Grand Marquis GS/LS	Sable GS Wagon	Sable GS/LS - Sedan	Sable LS Premium Sedan	Sable LS Premium Wagon	MITSUBISHI	Diamante ES/LS	Eclipse GS	Eclipse GT	Eclipse RS
Length (in.)	211.9	197.8	199.8	199.8	197.8		194.1	175.4	175.4	175.4
Width (in.)	78.2	73	73	73	73		70.3	68.9	68.9	68.9
Height (in.)	56.8	57.8	55.5	55.5	57.8		53.9	51.8	51.8	51.8
Curb Weight (lbs.)	3958	3546	3369	3364	3473		3549	2985	3120	2935
Wheelbase (in.)	114.7	108.5	108.5	108.5	108.5		107.1	100.8	100.8	100.8
Front Head Room (in.)	39.4	39.4	39.8	39.8	39.4		37.6	37.9	37.9	37.9
Rear Head Room (in.)	38.1	38.9	36.7	36.7	38.9		36.3	34.9	34.9	34.9
Front Shoulder Room (in.)	60.1	57.3	57.3	57.3	57.3		55.9	52.2	52.2	52.2
Rear Shoulder Room (in.)	60.3	56.7	56.6	56.6	56.7		56	52	52	52
Front Hip Room (in.)	58	54.4	54.4	54.4	54.4		54.3	51.9	51.9	51.9
Rear Hip Room (in.)	58.7	55.4	55.7	55.7	55.4		55.8	44.3	44.3	44.3
Front Leg Room (in.)	42.5	42.2	42.2	42.2	42.2		43.6	42.3	42.3	42.3
Rear Leg Room (in.)	38.4	38.5	38.9	38.9	38.5		36.6	30	30	30
Luggage Capacity (cu ft.)	20.6	38.4	16	16	38.4		14.2	16.9	16.9	16.9
Number of Cylinders	8	6	6	6	6		6	4	6	4
Displacement (liters)	4.6	3	3	3	3		3.5	2.4	3	2.4
Horsepower @ RPM	220@4750	155@4900	155@4900	200@5650	200@5650		210@5000	147@5500	200@5500	147@5500
Torque @ RPM	265@4000	185@3950	185@3950	200@4400	200@4400		231@4000	158@4000	205@4500	158@4000
Fuel Capacity	19	15	15	15	15		19	16.4	16.4	16.4
EPA City (mpg) - Manual	NA	NA	NA	NA	NA		NA	22	20	22
EPA Hwy (mpg) - Manual	NA	NA	NA	NA	NA		NA	30	28	30
EPA City (mpg) - Auto	18	18	20	20	19		18	20	20	20
EPA Hwy (mpg) - Auto	25	26	27	27	26		25	27	28	27

specifications

	Eclipse Spyder GS	Eclipse Spyder GT	Galant 4-Cyl	Galant V6	Mirage DE Coupe	Mirage ES Sedan	Mirage LS Coupe	Mirage LS Sedan	NISSAN Altima XE/GXE/SE/GLE
Length (in.)	175.4	175.4	187.8	187.8	168.1	173.6	168.1	173.6	185.8
Width (in.)	68.9	68.9	68.5	68.5	66.5	66.5	66.5	66.5	69.1
Height (in.)	52.8	52.8	55.7	55.7	53.5	53.5	53.5	53.5	55.9
Curb Weight (lbs.)	3042	3241	3031	3252	2183	2437	2293	2503	2851
Wheelbase (in.)	100.8	100.8	103.7	103.7	95.1	98.4	95.1	98.4	103.1
Front Head Room (in.)	39.4	39.4	39.9	39.9	38.6	39.8	38.6	39.8	39.4
Rear Head Room (in.)	34.5	34.5	37.7	37.7	35.8	37.4	35.8	37.4	37.7
Front Shoulder Room (in.)	52.2	52.2	54.5	54.5	53.6	53.6	53.6	53.6	55.7
Rear Shoulder Room (in.)	42.2	42.2	54.2	54.2	53.6	52.8	53.6	52.8	54.8
Front Hip Room (in.)	51.9	51.9	52.4	52.4	53.2	53.2	53.2	53.2	52.5
Rear Hip Room (in.)	41.3	41.3	53.9	53.9	47.6	52.2	47.6	52.2	52.6
Front Leg Room (in.)	42.3	42.3	43.5	43.5	43	43	43	43	42
Rear Leg Room (in.)	29.4	29.4	36.3	36.3	31.1	33.5	31.1	33.5	33.9
Luggage Capacity (cu ft.)	7.2	7.2	14.6	14.6	11.5	11.5	11.5	11.5	13.8
Number of Cylinders	4	6	4	6	4	4	4	4	4
Displacement (liters)	2.4	3	2.4	3	1.5	1.8	1.8	1.8	2.4
Horsepower @ RPM	147@5500	200@5500	145@5500	195@5500	92@5000	113@5500	113@5500	113@5500	155@5600
Torque @ RPM	158@4000	205@4500	155@3000	205@4500	93@3000	116@4500	116@4500	116@4500	156@4400
Fuel Capacity	16.4	16.4	16.3	16.3	12.4	12.4	12.4	12.4	15.9
EPA City (mpg) - Manual	22	20	NA	NA	32	28	28	28	23
EPA Hwy (mpg) - Manual	30	27	NA	NA	39	36	36	36	31
EPA City (mpg) - Auto	20	19	21	20	28	26	26	26	21
EPA Hwy (mpg) - Auto	27	26	28	27	35	32	32	32	28

SPECIFICATIONS MILEAGE TABLES

specifications

	Maxima GXE/SE/GLE	Sentra SE	Sentra XE/GXE		Alero Coupe - GL2/GLS	Alero Coupe - GX/GL/GL1	Alero Sedan - GL2/GLS	Alero Sedan - GX/GL/GL1	Aurora 3.5	Aurora 4.0
Length (in.)	190.5	177.5	177.5		186.7	186.7	186.7	186.7	199.3	199.3
Width (in.)	70.3	67.3	67.3		70.1	70.1	70.1	70.1	72.9	72.9
Height (in.)	56.5	55.5	55.5		54.5	54.5	54.5	54.5	56.7	56.7
Curb Weight (lbs.)	3199	2674	2548		2997	2997	3046	3046	3686	3803
Wheelbase (in.)	108.3	99.8	99.8		107	107	107	107	112.2	112.2
Front Head Room (in.)	40.5	39.9	39.9		38.4	38.4	38.4	38.4	38.6	38.6
Rear Head Room (in.)	37.4	37	37		36.5	36.5	37	37	37.7	37.7
Front Shoulder Room (in.)	56.9	52.5	52.5		53.6	53.6	53.6	53.6	58.9	58.9
Rear Shoulder Room (in.)	56.2	52.6	52.6		54.6	54.6	52.6	52.6	58.4	58.4
Front Hip Room (in.)	55.3	52.1	52.1		50.9	50.9	50.9	50.9	55.4	55.4
Rear Hip Room (in.)	53.7	52.3	52.3		51.2	51.2	51.5	51.5	56.1	56.1
Front Leg Room (in.)	44.8	41.6	41.6		42.2	42.2	42.2	42.2	42.5	42.5
Rear Leg Room (in.)	36.2	33.7	33.7		35.5	35.5	35.5	35.5	38	38
Luggage Capacity (cu ft.)	15.1	11.6	11.6		14.6	14.6	14.6	14.6	14.9	14.9
Number of Cylinders	6	4	4		4	4	4	4	6	8
Displacement (liters)	3	2	1.8		2.4	2.4	2.4	2.4	3.5	4
Horsepower @ RPM	222@6400	145@6400	126@6000		150@5600	150@5600	150@5600	150@5600	215@5550	250@5600
Torque @ RPM	217@4000	136@4800	129@2400		155@4400	155@4400	155@4400	155@4400	230@4400	260@4400
Fuel Capacity	18.5	13.2	13.2		14.3	14.3	14.3	14.3	18.5	17.5
EPA City (mpg) - Manual	22	24	27		22	NA	22	NA	NA	NA
EPA Hwy (mpg) - Manual	27	31	35		32	NA	32	NA	NA	NA
EPA City (mpg) - Auto	19	24	26		21	21	21	21	19	17
EPA Hwy (mpg) - Auto	26	30	33		29	29	29	29	28	25

SPECIFICATIONS MILEAGE TABLES

OLDSMOBILE

specifications

	Intrigue GX/GL/GLS	Neon Highline	Prowler	Bonneville SE/SLE	Bonneville SSEi	Firebird Base Convertible	Firebird Base Coupe	Firebird V8 Convertible
Length (in.)	195.9	174.4	165.3	202.6	202.6	193.4	193.4	193.8
Width (in.)	73.6	67.4	76.5	74.2	74.2	74.5	74.5	74.5
Height (in.)	56.6	56	50.9	56.6	56.6	52.7	52	52.4
Curb Weight (lbs.)	3434	2567	2850	3633	3716	3490	3323	3623
Wheelbase (in.)	109	105	113.3	112.2	112.2	101.1	101.1	101.1
Front Head Room (in.)	39.3	39.1	37.4	38.7	38.7	37.2	37.2	37.2
Rear Head Room (in.)	37.4	36.8	NA	37.3	37.3	35.3	35.3	35.3
Front Shoulder Room (in.)	58	53.4	51.6	59	59	57.4	57.4	57.4
Rear Shoulder Room (in.)	57	52.8	NA	58.4	58.4	55.8	55.8	55.8
Front Hip Room (in.)	55.6	52.4	52.1	55.7	55.7	52.8	52.8	52.8
Rear Hip Room (in.)	54.8	52.9	NA	56.4	56.4	44.4	44.4	44.4
Front Leg Room (in.)	42.4	42.4	42.9	42.6	42.6	42.9	42.9	42.9
Rear Leg Room (in.)	36.9	34.8	NA	38	38	28.9	28.9	28.9
Luggage Capacity (cu ft.)	16.4	11.8	3	18	18	7.6	12.9	7.6
Number of Cylinders	6	4	6	6	6	6	6	8
Displacement (liters)	3.5	2	3.5	3.8	3.8	3.8	3.8	5.7
Horsepower @ RPM	215@5500	132@5600	253@6400	205@5200	240@5200	200@5200	200@5200	310@5200
Torque @ RPM	230@4400	130@4600	255@3950	230@4000	280@3200	225@4000	225@4000	340@4000
Fuel Capacity	18	12.5	12.2	18.5	18.5	16.8	16.8	16.8
EPA City (mpg) - Manual	NA	27	NA	NA	NA	19	19	19
EPA Hwy (mpg) - Manual	NA	33	NA	NA	NA	31	31	28
EPA City (mpg) - Auto	19	24	17	19	18	19	19	18
EPA Hwy (mpg) - Auto	28	31	23	30	28	31	31	26

PLYMOUTH

PONTIAC

SPECIFICATIONS MILEAGE TABLES

specifications

	Firebird V8 Coupe	Grand Am GT Coupe	Grand Am GT Sedan	Grand Am SE Coupe/SE1 Coupe	Grand Am SE Sedan/SE1 Sedan	Grand Prix GT Coupe	Grand Prix GT Sedan	Grand Prix GTP Coupe	Grand Prix GTP Sedan	Grand Prix SE Sedan
Length (in.)	193.4	186.3	186.3	186.3	186.3	197.5	197.5	197.5	197.5	197.5
Width (in.)	74.5	70.4	70.4	70.4	70.4	72.7	72.7	72.7	72.7	72.7
Height (in.)	52	55.1	55.1	55.1	55.1	54.7	54.7	54.7	54.7	54.7
Curb Weight (lbs.)	3369	3168	3091	3066	3116	3429	3496	3494	3559	3384
Wheelbase (in.)	101.1	107	107	107	107	110.5	110.5	110.5	110.5	110.5
Front Head Room (in.)	37.2	38.3	38.3	38.3	38.3	38.3	38.3	38.3	38.3	38.3
Rear Head Room (in.)	35.3	37.6	37.2	37.2	37.6	36.5	36.7	36.5	36.7	36.7
Front Shoulder Room (in.)	57.4	53.6	53.7	53.7	53.6	58.5	58.5	58.5	58.5	58.5
Rear Shoulder Room (in.)	55.8	52.8	55	55	52.8	57.9	57.2	57.9	57.2	57.2
Front Hip Room (in.)	52.8	52.6	52.4	52.4	52.6	55.7	55.7	55.7	55.7	55.7
Rear Hip Room (in.)	44.4	52.4	49.3	49.3	52.4	57	54.3	57	54.3	54.3
Front Leg Room (in.)	42.9	42.1	42.1	42.1	42.1	42.4	42.4	42.4	42.4	42.4
Rear Leg Room (in.)	28.9	35.5	35.5	35.5	35.5	35.9	35.8	35.9	35.8	35.8
Luggage Capacity (cu ft.)	12.9	14.6	14.6	14.6	14.6	16	16	16	16	16
Number of Cylinders	8	6	6	4	4	6	6	6	6	6
Displacement (liters)	5.7	3.4	3.4	2.4	2.4	3.8	3.8	3.8	3.8	3.1
Horsepower @ RPM	310@5200	175@5200	175@5200	150@5600	150@5600	200@5200	200@5200	240@5200	240@5200	175@5200
Torque @ RPM	340@4000	205@4000	205@4000	155@4400	155@4400	225@3600	225@3600	280@3600	280@3600	195@4000
Fuel Capacity	16.8	15.2	15.2	15.2	15.2	17.5	18	17.5	18	18
EPA City (mpg) - Manual	19	NA	NA	22	22	NA	NA	NA	NA	NA
EPA Hwy (mpg) - Manual	28	NA	NA	32	32	NA	NA	NA	NA	NA
EPA City (mpg) - Auto	18	21	21	21	21	20	20	18	18	20
EPA Hwy (mpg) - Auto	26	32	32	29	29	30	30	28	28	29

specifications

	Sunfire GT Coupe	Sunfire SE Coupe	Sunfire SE Sedan	**PORSCHE** Boxster Base	Boxster S	**SAAB** 9-3 Base 2-Door	9-3 Base 4-Door	9-3 SE 4-Door
Length (in.)	182	182	181.8	171	171	182.2	182.2	182.2
Width (in.)	68.4	68.4	67.9	70.1	70.1	67.4	67.4	67.4
Height (in.)	53	53	54.7	50.8	50.8	56.2	56.2	56.2
Curb Weight (lbs.)	2771	2606	2644	2778	2855	2990	3160	3150
Wheelbase (in.)	104.1	104.1	104.1	95.2	95.2	102.6	102.6	102.6
Front Head Room (in.)	37.6	37.6	38.9	38.4	38.4	39.3	39.3	39.3
Rear Head Room (in.)	36.6	36.6	37.2	NA	NA	37.9	37.9	37.8
Front Shoulder Room (in.)	54.1	54.1	54.6	51.7	51.7	52.4	52.4	52.4
Rear Shoulder Room (in.)	54.8	54.8	53.9	NA	NA	52.6	52.6	52.6
Front Hip Room (in.)	48.7	48.7	50.9	53.4	53.4	NA	NA	NA
Rear Hip Room (in.)	49.5	49.5	51.1	NA	NA	NA	NA	NA
Front Leg Room (in.)	42.1	42.1	42.1	44	44	42.3	42.3	42.3
Rear Leg Room (in.)	32.6	32.6	34.3	NA	NA	34.1	34.1	34.1
Luggage Capacity (cu ft.)	12.4	12.4	13.1	9.1	9.1	21.7	21.7	21.7
Number of Cylinders	4	4	4	6	6	4	4	4
Displacement (liters)	2.4	2.2	2.2	2.7	3.2	2	2	2
Horsepower @ RPM	150@5600	115@5000	115@5000	217@6500	250@6250	185@5500	185@5500	205@5500
Torque @ RPM	155@4400	135@3600	135@3600	192@4500	225@4500	194@2100	194@2100	209@2200
Fuel Capacity	14.3	14.3	14.3	17	17	16.9	16.9	16.9
EPA City (mpg) - Manual	22	22	22	19	18	21	21	22
EPA Hwy (mpg) - Manual	32	32	32	27	26	29	29	30
EPA City (mpg) - Auto	21	23	23	17	17	21	21	21
EPA Hwy (mpg) - Auto	28	32	29	25	24	28	28	28

specifications

	9-3 SE Convertible	9-3 Viggen 2-Door	9-3 Viggen 4-Door	9-3 Viggen Convertible	9-5 2.3t Sedan	9-5 2.3t Wagon	9-5 Aero Sedan	9-5 Aero Wagon	9-5 SE V6t Wagon	9-5 SE V6t Sedan
Length (in.)	182.2	180.9	180.9	180.9	189.2	189.3	189.2	189.2	189.3	189.2
Width (in.)	67.4	67.4	67.4	67.4	70.6	70.6	70.6	70.6	70.6	70.6
Height (in.)	56	55.7	55.7	55.5	57	61.1	57	61.1	61.1	57
Curb Weight (lbs.)	3210	3130	3180	3220	3280	3640	3410	3640	3760	3410
Wheelbase (in.)	102.6	102.6	102.6	102.6	106.4	106.4	106.4	106.4	106.4	106.4
Front Head Room (in.)	38.9	39.3	39.3	38.9	37.1	38.7	37.1	38.7	38.7	37.1
Rear Head Room (in.)	37.8	37.9	37.8	37.8	37.6	37.6	37.6	37.6	37.6	37.6
Front Shoulder Room (in.)	52.5	52.4	52.4	52.5	56.9	56.9	56.9	56.9	56.9	56.9
Rear Shoulder Room (in.)	41.8	52.6	52.6	41.8	56.5	56.5	56.5	56.5	56.5	56.5
Front Hip Room (in.)	NA	NA	NA	NA	NA	NA	NA	NA	NA	NA
Rear Hip Room (in.)	NA	NA	NA	NA	NA	NA	NA	NA	NA	NA
Front Leg Room (in.)	42.3	42.3	42.3	42.3	42.4	42.4	42.4	42.4	42.4	42.4
Rear Leg Room (in.)	33.2	34.1	34.1	33.2	36.6	36.6	36.6	36.6	36.6	36.6
Luggage Capacity (cu ft.)	10	21.7	21.7	10	15.9	37	15.9	37	37	15.9
Number of Cylinders	4	4	4	4	4	4	4	4	6	6
Displacement (liters)	2	2.3	2.3	2.3	2.3	2.3	2.3	2.3	3	3
Horsepower @ RPM	205@5500	230@5500	230@5500	230@5500	185@5500	185@5500	230@5500	230@5500	200@5000	200@5000
Torque @ RPM	209@2200	258@2500	258@2500	258@2500	207@1800	207@1800	258@1900	258@1900	229@2500	229@2500
Fuel Capacity	16.9	16.9	16.9	16.9	18.5	18.5	18.5	19.8	18.5	18.5
EPA City (mpg) - Manual	22	20	20	20	21	21	21	21	NA	NA
EPA Hwy (mpg) - Manual	30	31	31	31	30	28	28	28	NA	NA
EPA City (mpg) - Auto	21	NA	NA	NA	20	19	19	19	18	19
EPA Hwy (mpg) - Auto	28	NA	NA	NA	29	26	26	26	26	26

SPECIFICATIONS MILEAGE TABLES

specifications

	L-Series L100/L200	L-Series L300	L-Series LW200	L-Series LW300	S-Series SC1	S-Series SC2	S-Series SL/SL1	S-Series SL2	S-Series SW2
Length (in.)	190.4	190.4	190.4	190.4	180.5	180.5	178.1	178.1	178.1
Width (in.)	69	69	69	69	68.2	66.82	66.4	66.4	66.4
Height (in.)	56.4	56.4	57.3	57.3	53	53	55	55	55.6
Curb Weight (lbs.)	2910	3153	3075	3230	2368	2436	2332	2399	2452
Wheelbase (in.)	106.5	106.5	106.5	106.5	102.4	102.4	102.4	102.4	102.4
Front Head Room (in.)	39.3	39.3	39.3	39.3	38.6	38.6	39.3	39.3	39.3
Rear Head Room (in.)	38	38	39.6	39.6	35.8	35.8	38	38	39.2
Front Shoulder Room (in.)	55.7	55.7	55.7	55.7	54.6	54.6	53.9	53.9	54
Rear Shoulder Room (in.)	56.1	56.1	56.1	56.1	50.4	50.4	53.1	53.1	53.1
Front Hip Room (in.)	51.7	51.7	51.7	51.7	50	50	49.2	49.2	49.2
Rear Hip Room (in.)	54	54	54	54	47.7	47.7	50.2	50.2	50.2
Front Leg Room (in.)	42.3	42.3	42.3	42.3	42.6	42.6	42.5	42.5	42.5
Rear Leg Room (in.)	34.4	34.4	34.7	34.7	31	31	32.8	32.8	30.7
Luggage Capacity (cu ft.)	17.5	17.5	29.4	29.4	11.4	11.4	12.1	12.1	24.9
Number of Cylinders	4	6	4	6	4	4	4	4	4
Displacement (liters)	2.2	3	2.2	3	1.9	1.9	1.9	1.9	1.9
Horsepower @ RPM	137@5800	182@5600	137@5800	182@5600	100@5000	124@5600	100@5000	124@5600	124@5600
Torque @ RPM	147@4400	190@3600	147@4400	190@3600	114@2400	122@4800	114@2400	122@4800	122@4800
Fuel Capacity	17.9	17.9	17.9	17.9	12.1	12.1	12.1	12.1	12.1
EPA City (mpg) - Manual	25	NA	NA	NA	28	27	29	27	27
EPA Hwy (mpg) - Manual	33	NA	NA	NA	40	38	40	38	38
EPA City (mpg) - Auto	24	20	24	20	26	25	27	25	25
EPA Hwy (mpg) - Auto	33	26	32	26	36	35	37	35	35

SATURN

specifications

	Impreza 2.5 RS Coupe	Impreza 2.5 RS Sedan	Impreza L Coupe	Impreza L Sedan	Impreza L Wagon	Impreza Outback Outback Sport	Legacy Sedan	Legacy Wagon	Outback L.L. Bean Wagon
Length (in.)	172.2	172.2	172.2	172.2	172.2	172.2	184.4	187.4	187.4
Width (in.)	67.1	67.1	67.1	67.1	67.1	67.1	68.7	68.7	68.7
Height (in.)	55.5	55.5	55.5	55.5	55.5	55.5	55.7	59.6	63.3
Curb Weight (lbs.)	2820	2825	2730	2735	2835	2835	3345	3450	3715
Wheelbase (in.)	99.2	99.2	99.2	99.2	99.2	99.2	104.3	104.3	104.3
Front Head Room (in.)	38	38	39.2	39.2	39.2	39.2	38.1	38.5	38.5
Rear Head Room (in.)	36.7	36.7	36.7	36.7	37.4	37.4	36.6	37.2	37.2
Front Shoulder Room (in.)	52.6	52.6	52.6	52.6	52.6	52.6	53.9	53.9	53.9
Rear Shoulder Room (in.)	52.2	51.8	52.2	51.8	51.8	51.8	53.6	53.6	53.6
Front Hip Room (in.)	51.8	51	51.8	51	51	51	51.3	51.3	51.3
Rear Hip Room (in.)	53.1	53	53.1	53	52.6	52.6	51.9	51.9	51.9
Front Leg Room (in.)	43.1	43.1	43.1	43.1	43.1	43.1	43.3	43.3	43.3
Rear Leg Room (in.)	32.5	32.5	32.5	32.5	32.4	32.4	34.2	34.3	34.3
Luggage Capacity (cu ft.)	11.1	11.1	11.1	11.1	25.5	25.5	12.4	34.3	34.3
Number of Cylinders	4	4	4	4	4	4	4	4	6
Displacement (liters)	2.5	2.5	2.2	2.2	2.2	2.2	2.5	2.5	3
Horsepower @ RPM	165@5600	165@5600	142@5600	142@5600	142@5600	142@5600	165@5600	165@5600	212@6000
Torque @ RPM	166@4000	166@4000	149@3600	149@3600	149@3600	149@3600	166@4000	166@4000	210@4400
Fuel Capacity	15.9	15.9	15.9	15.9	15.9	15.9	16.9	16.9	16.9
EPA City (mpg) - Manual	21	21	23	23	23	23	21	21	NA
EPA Hwy (mpg) - Manual	28	28	29	29	29	29	28	28	NA
EPA City (mpg) - Auto	23	23	23	23	23	23	22	22	20
EPA Hwy (mpg) - Auto	28	28	29	29	29	29	27	27	27

SUBARU

SPECIFICATIONS MILEAGE TABLES

specifications

	Outback Limited Sedan	Outback VDC Wagon	Outback Wagon		Esteem 1.8 Sedan	Esteem 1.8 Wagon	Swift GA/GL		Avalon XL/XLS	Camry 4-Cyl
Length (in.)	184.4	187.4	187.4		166.3	172.2	149.4		191.9	188.5
Width (in.)	68.7	68.7	68.7		66.1	66.5	62.6		71.7	70.1
Height (in.)	58.3	63.3	63.3		53.9	55.9	54.7		57.7	55.4
Curb Weight (lbs.)	3495	3735	3425		2227	2359	1895		3439	2998
Wheelbase (in.)	104.3	104.3	104.3		97.6	97.6	93.1		107.1	105.2
Front Head Room (in.)	38.1	38.5	40.2		39.1	38.8	39.1		38.7	38.6
Rear Head Room (in.)	36.6	37.2	39.1		37.2	38	36		37.9	37.6
Front Shoulder Room (in.)	53.9	53.9	53.9		51.8	51.8	48.9		58.4	56.2
Rear Shoulder Room (in.)	53.6	53.6	53.6		52.1	52.1	48.9		58.1	56.1
Front Hip Room (in.)	51.3	51.3	51.3		50.8	50.8	47.2		55.2	54
Rear Hip Room (in.)	51.9	51.9	51.9		48.2	48.2	43.9		55.1	54.1
Front Leg Room (in.)	43.3	43.3	43.3		42.3	42.3	42.5		41.7	43.5
Rear Leg Room (in.)	34.2	34.3	34.3		34.1	34.1	32.2		40.1	35.5
Luggage Capacity (cu ft.)	12.4	34.3	34.3		12	24	8.4		15.9	14.1
Number of Cylinders	4	6	4		4	4	4		6	4
Displacement (liters)	2.5	3	2.5		1.8	1.8	1.3		3	2.2
Horsepower @ RPM	165@5600	212@6000	165@5600		122@6300	122@6300	79@6000		210@5800	136@5200
Torque @ RPM	166@4000	210@4400	166@4000		117@3500	117@3500	75@3000		220@4400	150@4400
Fuel Capacity	16.9	16.9	16.9		12.7	12.7	10.3		18.5	18.5
EPA City (mpg) - Manual	21	NA	21		28	27	36		NA	24
EPA Hwy (mpg) - Manual	28	NA	28		35	34	42		NA	33
EPA City (mpg) - Auto	22	20	22		26	26	30		21	23
EPA Hwy (mpg) - Auto	27	27	27		33	33	34		29	32

SPECIFICATIONS MILEAGE TABLES

SUZUKI

TOYOTA

www.edmunds.com

EDMUNDS® NEW CARS

specifications

	Camry V6	Camry Solara SE	Camry Solara SE Convertible	Camry Solara SE V6	Camry Solara V6 Convertible	Celica GT	Celica GTS	Corolla CE/S/LE	Echo Coupe	Echo Sedan
Length (in.)	188.5	190	190	190	190	170.5	170.5	174	163.2	163.2
Width (in.)	70.1	71.1	71.1	71.1	71.1	68.3	68.3	66.7	65.4	65.4
Height (in.)	55.4	55.1	55.1	55.1	55.1	51.4	51.4	54.5	59.4	59.4
Curb Weight (lbs.)	3175	3120	3120	3230	3230	2425	2500	2405	2020	2030
Wheelbase (in.)	105.2	105.1	105.1	105.1	105.1	102.4	102.4	97	93.3	93.3
Front Head Room (in.)	38.6	38.3	38.3	38.3	38.3	38.4	38.4	39.3	39.8	39.8
Rear Head Room (in.)	37.6	36.3	36.3	36.3	36.3	35	35	36.9	37.8	37.8
Front Shoulder Room (in.)	56.2	55.3	55.3	55.3	55.3	52.6	52.6	52.8	52.3	51.8
Rear Shoulder Room (in.)	56.1	52.9	52.9	52.9	52.9	50.6	50.6	52.2	51	50.7
Front Hip Room (in.)	54	53.6	53.6	53.6	53.6	51.3	51.3	50.5	51.1	51.1
Rear Hip Room (in.)	54.1	49.3	49.3	49.3	49.3	46.8	46.8	51.2	51	51
Front Leg Room (in.)	43.5	43.3	43.3	43.3	43.3	44.1	44.1	42.5	41.1	41.1
Rear Leg Room (in.)	35.5	35.2	36.3	35.2	36.3	27	27	33.2	35.2	35.2
Luggage Capacity (cu ft.)	14.1	14.1	13.8	14.1	13.8	16.9	16.9	12.1	13.6	13.6
Number of Cylinders	6	4	4	6	4	4	4	4	4	4
Displacement (liters)	3	2.2	2.2	3	3	1.8	1.8	1.8	1.5	1.5
Horsepower @ RPM	194@5200	136@5200	136@5200	200@5200	200@5200	140@6400	180@7600	125@5800	108@6000	108@6000
Torque @ RPM	209@4400	150@4400	150@4400	214@4400	214@4400	125@4200	133@6800	125@4000	105@4000	105@4000
Fuel Capacity	18.5	18.5	18.5	18.5	18.5	14.5	14.5	13.2	11.9	11.9
EPA City (mpg) - Manual	20	24	NA	20	NA	28	23	32	34	34
EPA Hwy (mpg) - Manual	27	33	NA	27	NA	33	32	41	41	41
EPA City (mpg) - Auto	20	23	21	20	19	NA	NA	30	32	32
EPA Hwy (mpg) - Auto	27	32	29	27	26	NA	NA	39	38	38

SPECIFICATIONS MILEAGE TABLES

EDMUNDS® NEW CARS   www.edmunds.com

specifications

	MR2 Spyder Base	Prius Base		Cabrio GL/GLS/GLX	Golf GL	Golf GL TDI	Golf GLS	Golf GLS 1.8T	Golf GLS TDI	Golf GTI GLS
Length (in.)	153	169.6		160.4	164.9	164.9	164.9	164.9	164.9	164.9
Width (in.)	66.7	66.7		66.7	68.3	68.3	68.3	68.3	68.3	68.3
Height (in.)	48.8	57.6		56	56.9	56.9	56.9	56.9	56.9	56.9
Curb Weight (lbs.)	2195	2765		2825	2772	2782	2869	2915	2943	2860
Wheelbase (in.)	96.5	100.4		97.4	98.9	98.9	98.9	98.9	98.9	98.9
Front Head Room (in.)	37.3	38.8		38.7	38.6	38.6	38.6	38.6	38.6	37.4
Rear Head Room (in.)	NA	37.1		36.6	37.4	37.4	37.4	37.4	37.4	36.5
Front Shoulder Room (in.)	51	52.8		54.1	53.7	53.7	53.7	53.7	53.7	53.7
Rear Shoulder Room (in.)	NA	52.2		46.5	52.7	52.7	52.7	52.7	52.7	52.7
Front Hip Room (in.)	49.8	50.7		52.8	NA	NA	NA	NA	NA	NA
Rear Hip Room (in.)	NA	51.9		51.9	NA	NA	NA	NA	NA	NA
Front Leg Room (in.)	42.2	41.2		42.3	41.5	41.5	41.5	41.5	41.5	41.5
Rear Leg Room (in.)	NA	35.4		31.1	33.5	33.5	33.5	33.5	33.5	33.5
Luggage Capacity (cu ft.)	1.9	11.8		8	18	18	18	18	18	18
Number of Cylinders	4	4		4	4	4	4	4	4	4
Displacement (liters)	1.8	1.5		2	2	1.9	2	1.8	1.9	1.8
Horsepower @ RPM	138@6400	70@4500		115@5200	115@5200	90@3750	115@5200	150@5700	90@3750	150@5700
Torque @ RPM	125@4400	82@4200		122@2600	122@2600	155@1900	122@2600	155@1750	155@1900	155@1750
Fuel Capacity	12.7	11.9		13.7	14.5	14.5	14.5	14.5	14.5	14.5
EPA City (mpg) - Manual	25	NA		24	24	42	24	25	42	25
EPA Hwy (mpg) - Manual	30	NA		31	31	49	31	31	49	31
EPA City (mpg) - Auto	NA	52		22	22	34	22	23	34	23
EPA Hwy (mpg) - Auto	NA	45		28	28	44	28	29	44	29

VOLKSWAGEN

specifications

	Golf GTI GLX	Jetta GL	Jetta GL TDI	Jetta GLS	Jetta GLS 1.8T	Jetta GLS TDI	Jetta GLS VR6	Jetta GLX	New Beetle 1.8T	New Beetle 2.0L
Length (in.)	164.9	172.3	172.3	172.3	172.3	172.3	172.3	172.3	161.1	161.1
Width (in.)	68.3	68.3	68.3	68.3	68.3	68.3	68.3	68.3	67.9	67.9
Height (in.)	56.9	56.9	56.9	56.9	56.9	56.9	56.9	56.9	59.5	59.5
Curb Weight (lbs.)	2999	2893	2975	2908	2952	2983	3045	3144	2921	2769
Wheelbase (in.)	98.9	98.9	98.9	98.9	98.9	98.9	98.9	98.9	98.9	98.9
Front Head Room (in.)	37.4	38.6	38.6	38.6	38.6	38.6	38.6	37.4	41.3	41.3
Rear Head Room (in.)	36.5	36.9	36.9	36.9	36.9	36.9	36.9	36.5	36.7	36.7
Front Shoulder Room (in.)	53.7	53.7	53.7	53.7	53.7	53.7	53.7	53.7	52.8	52.8
Rear Shoulder Room (in.)	52.7	52.5	52.5	52.5	52.5	52.5	52.5	52.5	49.3	49.3
Front Hip Room (in.)	NA	NA	NA	NA	NA	NA	NA	NA	NA	NA
Rear Hip Room (in.)	NA	NA	NA	NA	NA	NA	NA	NA	NA	NA
Front Leg Room (in.)	41.5	41.5	41.5	41.5	41.5	41.5	41.5	41.5	39.4	39.4
Rear Leg Room (in.)	33.5	33.5	33.5	33.5	33.5	33.5	33.5	33.5	33.5	33.5
Luggage Capacity (cu ft.)	18	13	13	13	13	13	13	13	12	12
Number of Cylinders	6	4	4	4	4	4	6	6	4	4
Displacement (liters)	2.8	2	1.9	2	1.8	1.9	2.8	2.8	1.8	2
Horsepower @ RPM	174@5800	115@5200	90@3750	115@5200	150@5700	90@3750	174@5800	174@5800	150@5700	115@5200
Torque @ RPM	181@3200	122@2600	155@1900	122@2600	155@1750	155@1900	181@3200	181@3200	155@1750	122@2600
Fuel Capacity	14.5	14.5	14.5	14.5	14.5	14.5	14.5	14.5	14.5	14.5
EPA City (mpg) - Manual	20	24	42	25	25	42	19	19	25	24
EPA Hwy (mpg) - Manual	28	31	49	31	31	49	28	28	31	31
EPA City (mpg) - Auto	NA	22	34	20	23	34	19	19	23	22
EPA Hwy (mpg) - Auto	NA	28	45	28	29	45	26	26	29	28

SPECIFICATIONS MILEAGE TABLES

specifications

	New Beetle GLS	New Beetle GLX	New Beetle TDI	Passat GLS Sedan	Passat GLS V6 4MOTION Sedan	Passat GLS V6 4MOTION Wagon	Passat GLS V6 Sedan	Passat GLS V6 Wagon	Passat GLS Wagon	Passat GLX 4MOTION Sedan
Length (in.)	161.1	161.1	161.1	184.1	184.1	183.8	184.1	183.8	183.8	184.1
Width (in.)	67.9	67.9	67.9	68.5	68.5	68.5	68.5	68.5	68.5	68.5
Height (in.)	59.5	59.5	59.5	57.6	57.5	59	57.6	59	59	57.5
Curb Weight (lbs.)	2785	2959	2867	3043	3473	3574	3151	3244	3136	3502
Wheelbase (in.)	98.9	98.9	98.9	106.4	106.4	106.4	106.4	106.4	106.4	106.4
Front Head Room (in.)	41.3	41.3	41.3	39.7	39.7	39.7	39.7	39.7	39.7	37.8
Rear Head Room (in.)	36.7	36.7	36.7	37.8	37.8	37.9	37.8	37.9	37.9	37.3
Front Shoulder Room (in.)	52.8	52.8	52.8	55.8	55.8	55.8	55.8	55.8	55.8	55.8
Rear Shoulder Room (in.)	49.3	49.3	49.3	54.6	54.6	54.6	54.6	54.6	54.6	54.6
Front Hip Room (in.)	NA	NA	NA	NA	NA	NA	NA	NA	NA	NA
Rear Hip Room (in.)	NA	NA	NA	NA	NA	NA	NA	NA	NA	NA
Front Leg Room (in.)	39.4	39.4	39.4	41.5	41.5	41.5	41.5	41.5	41.5	41.5
Rear Leg Room (in.)	33.5	33.5	33.5	35.3	35.3	35.3	35.3	35.3	35.3	35.3
Luggage Capacity (cu ft.)	12	12	12	15	10	36	15	39	39	10
Number of Cylinders	4	4	4	4	6	6	6	6	4	6
Displacement (liters)	2	1.8	1.9	1.8	2.8	2.8	2.8	2.8	1.8	2.8
Horsepower @ RPM	115@5200	150@5700	90@3750	150@5700	190@3200	190@3200	190@6000	190@6000	150@5700	190@6000
Torque @ RPM	122@2600	155@1750	155@1900	156@1750	206@	206@	206@3200	206@3200	155@1750	206@3200
Fuel Capacity	14.5	14.5	14.5	16.4	16.4	16.4	16.4	16.4	16.4	16.4
EPA City (mpg) - Manual	24	25	42	22	20	20	20	20	22	NA
EPA Hwy (mpg) - Manual	31	31	49	31	29	29	29	29	31	NA
EPA City (mpg) - Auto	22	23	34	20	18	17	18	18	20	18
EPA Hwy (mpg) - Auto	28	29	44	28	26	24	26	26	28	26

specifications

	Passat GLX 4MOTION Wagon	Passat GLX Sedan	Passat GLX Wagon	VOLVO	C70 HT Convertible	C70 HT Coupe	C70 LT Convertible	S40 A Sedan	S60 2.4M Sedan	S60 2.4AT Sedan
Length (in.)	183.8	184.1	183.8		185.7	185.7	185.7	177.8	180.2	180.2
Width (in.)	68.5	68.5	68.5		71.5	71.5	71.5	67.6	71	71
Height (in.)	59	57.6	59		56.3	56.3	56.3	56	56.2	56.2
Curb Weight (lbs.)	3603	3180	3272		3601	3601	3601	2767	3230	3439
Wheelbase (in.)	106.4	106.4	106.4		104.9	104.9	104.9	100.9	106.9	106.9
Front Head Room (in.)	37.8	37.8	37.8		39.2	38.8	39.2	38.7	38.7	38.7
Rear Head Room (in.)	37.9	37.3	37.9		38.8	36.6	38.8	37.2	37.9	37.9
Front Shoulder Room (in.)	55.8	55.8	55.8		55.5	55.5	55.5	54	56.2	56.2
Rear Shoulder Room (in.)	54.6	54.6	54.6		44.9	52.2	44.9	54.1	55.5	55.5
Front Hip Room (in.)	NA	NA	NA		NA	55.2	NA	51.7	55	55
Rear Hip Room (in.)	NA	NA	NA		NA	55.2	NA	51.7	54.6	54.6
Front Leg Room (in.)	41.5	41.5	41.5		41.3	41.3	41.3	41.4	42.6	42.6
Rear Leg Room (in.)	35.3	35.3	35.3		34.6	34.6	34.6	32.7	33.3	33.3
Luggage Capacity (cu ft.)	36	15	39		7.9	13.1	7.9	13.2	13.9	13.9
Number of Cylinders	6	6	6		5	5	5	4	5	5
Displacement (liters)	2.8	2.8	2.8		2.3	2.3	2.4	1.9	2.4	2.4
Horsepower @ RPM	190@6000	190@6000	190@6000		236@5400	236@5400	190@5100	160@5100	168@5900	197@5000
Torque @ RPM	206@3200	206@3200	206@3200		244@2400	244@2400	199@1800	170@1800	170@4500	210@1800
Fuel Capacity	16.4	16.4	16.4		18.5	18.5	18.5	15.8	18.5	21.1
EPA City (mpg) - Manual	NA	20	20		21	21	NA	NA	21	NA
EPA Hwy (mpg) - Manual	NA	29	29		28	28	NA	NA	28	NA
EPA City (mpg) - Auto	18	18	18		20	20	20	22	21	21
EPA Hwy (mpg) - Auto	26	26	26		26	27	27	32	28	28
SPECIFICATIONS MILEAGE TABLES										

specifications

	S60 T5 Sedan	S80 2.9	S80 T6	S80 T6 Executive	V40 A Wagon	V70 2.4T Wagon	V70 T5 Wagon	V70 XC AWD
Length (in.)	180.2	189.8	189.8	189.8	177.8	185.4	185.4	186.3
Width (in.)	71	72.1	72.1	72.1	67.6	71	71	73.2
Height (in.)	56.2	57.2	57.2	57.2	56.1	58.7	58.7	61.5
Curb Weight (lbs.)	3439	3600	3600	3600	2822	3369	3369	3699
Wheelbase (in.)	106.9	109.9	109.9	109.9	100.9	108.5	108.5	108.8
Front Head Room (in.)	38.7	38.9	38.9	38.9	38.7	39.3	39.3	39.3
Rear Head Room (in.)	37.9	37.6	37.6	37.6	38.3	38.9	38.9	38.9
Front Shoulder Room (in.)	56.2	58	58	58	54	56.2	56.2	56.2
Rear Shoulder Room (in.)	55.5	56.9	56.9	56.9	54.1	55.9	55.9	55.9
Front Hip Room (in.)	55	NA	NA	NA	51.7	55	55	55
Rear Hip Room (in.)	54.6	NA	NA	NA	51.7	54.8	54.8	54.8
Front Leg Room (in.)	42.6	42.2	42.2	42.2	41.4	42.6	42.6	42.6
Rear Leg Room (in.)	33.3	35.9	35.9	37.9	32.7	35.2	35.2	35.2
Luggage Capacity (cu ft.)	13.9	14.2	14.2	14.2	30.2	37.5	37.5	37.5
Number of Cylinders	5	6	6	6	4	5	5	5
Displacement (liters)	2.3	2.9	2.8	2.8	1.9	2.4	2.3	2.4
Horsepower @ RPM	247@5200	197@6000	268@5400	268@5400	160@5100	197@6000	247@5200	197@6000
Torque @ RPM	243@2400	207@4200	280@2100	280@2100	170@1800	210@2000	243@2400	210@1800
Fuel Capacity	21.1	21.1	21.1	21.1	15.8	21.1	21.1	18.5
EPA City (mpg) - Manual	21	NA	NA	NA	NA	NA	NA	NA
EPA Hwy (mpg) - Manual	28	NA	NA	NA	NA	NA	NA	NA
EPA City (mpg) - Auto	20	19	19	19	22	21	21	18
EPA Hwy (mpg) - Auto	27	27	26	26	32	27	27	25

SPECIFICATIONS MILEAGE TABLES

In 1994, the National Highway Traffic Safety Administration (NHTSA—www.nhtsa.dot.gov) changed the way they rate frontal crash-test performances of the cars and trucks they run into a fixed barrier at 35 mph. Instead of the confusing numerical scale that had been in place for years, NHTSA decided to make the data more user-friendly for interested consumers by converting to a five-star rating system. This system is just like the one used by the movie reviewer in your local paper and the lucky folks AAA employs to travel around the world eating and sleeping in the best restaurants and hotels. Boy, they've got it rough, don't they?

For frontal-impact NHTSA crash tests, the scale is as follows:

1 Star	46 percent or better chance of life-threatening injury
2 Stars	a 36-45 percent chance of life-threatening injury
3 Stars	a 21-35 percent chance of life-threatening injury
4 Stars	a 11-20 percent chance of life-threatening injury
5 Stars	10 percent or less chance of life-threatening injury

We convert the NHTSA scale as follows:

1 Star	Very Poor
2 Stars	Poor
3 Stars	Average
4 Stars	Good
5 Stars	Excellent

In 1997, NHTSA began testing side-impact protection as well as frontal-impact protection. For side-impact testing, NHTSA runs a deformable barrier into the side of a car twice, once at the front passenger's level and once at the rear passenger's level. As with frontal-impact testing, the side-impact test is conducted at 5 mph above the federal standard, which means the deformable barrier hits the car at 38 mph.

For side-impact NHTSA crash tests, the scale is as follows:

1 Star	26 percent or better chance of life-threatening injury
2 Stars	a 21-25 percent chance of life-threatening injury
3 Stars	a 11-20 percent chance of life-threatening injury
4 Stars	a 6-10 percent chance of life-threatening injury
5 Stars	5 percent or less chance of life-threatening injury

We convert the NHTSA scale as follows:

1 Star	Very Poor
2 Stars	Poor
3 Stars	Average
4 Stars	Good
5 Stars	Excellent

The Insurance Institute for Highway Safety (IIHS — www.hwysafety.org) began conducting offset frontal crash tests in 1995. The offset test is conducted at 40 mph, and vehicles crash into a fixed barrier just like in the NHTSA testing, but only half of the front of the vehicle contacts the barrier. The IIHS claims this test, at this speed, more accurately reflects the most deadly real-world crash situations. Offset crash tests do not conform to the scale listed above. Instead, the IIHS rates a vehicle good, acceptable, marginal or poor. There are currently no federally mandated offset crash standards that automakers must meet by law.

The IIHS also conducts bumper-bashing tests. They run cars and trucks into barriers at 5 mph to see how much damage results, in terms of dollars. Front ends are smacked into flat and angled barriers, and they back vehicles into poles and angled barriers. Each vehicle is crashed four times; the lower the total cost for repair after all four tests, the better the vehicle scores. Federal law requires bumpers on passenger cars that can withstand an impact at 2.5 mph. Light trucks are not required to meet bumper-strength standards.

Following are the results of crash testing conducted on trucks since 1994, presented in alphabetical order by make and model. All test results are applicable to the 2000/2001 equivalent of the listed model, with one caveat. Most of the models tested after 1998 come equipped with depowered airbags, and some even have two-stage inflators that sense the speed of impact and vary airbag deployment force. Until the vehicle is re-tested by NHTSA, it is unknown how the presence of a depowered or two-stage airbag will affect occupant safety.

Crash Scores for 2000 and 2001 Cars

Acura Integra
    NHTSA Frontal Crash Driver — Good
    NHTSA Frontal Crash Passenger — Average
    NHTSA Side Crash Front Occupant — Not Tested
    NHTSA Side Crash Rear Occupant — Not Tested
    IIHS Offset — Not Tested
    IIHS Bumper Bash — Not Tested

Acura RL
    NHTSA Frontal Crash Driver — Good
    NHTSA Frontal Crash Passenger — Good
    NHTSA Side Crash Front Occupant — Not Tested
    NHTSA Side Crash Rear Occupant — Not Tested
    IIHS Offset — Not Tested
    IIHS Bumper Bash — Not Tested

Audi A4
    NHTSA Frontal Crash Driver — Good
    NHTSA Frontal Crash Passenger — Excellent
    NHTSA Side Crash Front Occupant — Not Tested
    NHTSA Side Crash Rear Occupant — Not Tested
    IIHS Offset — Not Tested
    IIHS Bumper Bash — Not Tested

Audi A6
    NHTSA Frontal Crash Driver — Not Tested
    NHTSA Frontal Crash Passenger — Not Tested

NHTSA Side Crash Front Occupant	Not Tested
NHTSA Side Crash Rear Occupant	Not Tested
IIHS Offset	Acceptable
IIHS Bumper Bash	Acceptable

Audi A8

NHTSA Frontal Crash Driver	Excellent
NHTSA Frontal Crash Passenger	Excellent
NHTSA Side Crash Front Occupant	Not Tested
NHTSA Side Crash Rear Occupant	Not Tested
IIHS Offset	Not Tested
IIHS Bumper Bash	Not Tested

Audi S4

NHTSA Frontal Crash Driver	Good
NHTSA Frontal Crash Passenger	Excellent
NHTSA Side Crash Front Occupant	Not Tested
NHTSA Side Crash Rear Occupant	Not Tested
IIHS Offset	Not Tested
IIHS Bumper Bash	Not Tested

BMW 3 Series

NHTSA Frontal Crash Driver	Not Tested
NHTSA Frontal Crash Passenger	Not Tested
NHTSA Side Crash Front Occupant	Not Tested
NHTSA Side Crash Rear Occupant	Not Tested
IIHS Offset	Good
IIHS Bumper Bash	Marginal

BMW 5 Series

NHTSA Frontal Crash Driver	Not Tested
NHTSA Frontal Crash Passenger	Not Tested
NHTSA Side Crash Front Occupant	Not Tested
NHTSA Side Crash Rear Occupant	Not Tested
IIHS Offset	Good
IIHS Bumper Bash	Poor

Buick Century

NHTSA Frontal Crash Driver	Good
NHTSA Frontal Crash Passenger	Average
NHTSA Side Crash Front Occupant	Average
NHTSA Side Crash Rear Occupant	Average
IIHS Offset	Acceptable
IIHS Bumper Bash	Acceptable

Buick LeSabre

NHTSA Frontal Crash Driver	Excellent
NHTSA Frontal Crash Passenger	Excellent
NHTSA Side Crash Front Occupant	Good
NHTSA Side Crash Rear Occupant	Good
IIHS Offset	Good
IIHS Bumper Bash	Marginal

Buick Park Avenue

NHTSA Frontal Crash Driver	Not Tested
NHTSA Frontal Crash Passenger	Not Tested
NHTSA Side Crash Front Occupant	Not Tested

NHTSA Side Crash Rear Occupant	Not Tested
IIHS Offset	Good
IIHS Bumper Bash	Acceptable
Buick Regal	
NHTSA Frontal Crash Driver	Good
NHTSA Frontal Crash Passenger	Average
NHTSA Side Crash Front Occupant	Average
NHTSA Side Crash Rear Occupant	Average
IIHS Offset	Acceptable
IIHS Bumper Bash	Acceptable
Cadillac Catera	
NHTSA Frontal Crash Driver	Not Tested
NHTSA Frontal Crash Passenger	Not Tested
NHTSA Side Crash Front Occupant	Not Tested
NHTSA Side Crash Rear Occupant	Not Tested
IIHS Offset	Good
IIHS Bumper Bash	Poor
Cadillac Deville	
NHTSA Frontal Crash Driver	Average
NHTSA Frontal Crash Passenger	Good
NHTSA Side Crash Front Occupant	Good
NHTSA Side Crash Rear Occupant	Good
IIHS Offset	Not Tested
IIHS Bumper Bash	Not Tested
Cadillac Eldorado	
NHTSA Frontal Crash Driver	Good
NHTSA Frontal Crash Passenger	Good
NHTSA Side Crash Front Occupant	Not Tested
NHTSA Side Crash Rear Occupant	Not Tested
IIHS Offset	Not Tested
IIHS Bumper Bash	Not Tested
Cadillac Seville	
NHTSA Frontal Crash Driver	Not Tested
NHTSA Frontal Crash Passenger	Not Tested
NHTSA Side Crash Front Occupant	Not Tested
NHTSA Side Crash Rear Occupant	Not Tested
IIHS Offset	Good
IIHS Bumper Bash	Marginal
Chevrolet Camaro	
NHTSA Frontal Crash Driver	Good
NHTSA Frontal Crash Passenger	Excellent
NHTSA Side Crash Front Occupant	Average
NHTSA Side Crash Rear Occupant	Good
IIHS Offset	Not Tested
IIHS Bumper Bash	Not Tested
Chevrolet Cavalier	
NHTSA Frontal Crash Driver	Average (Coupe); Good (Sedan)
NHTSA Frontal Crash Passenger	Good
NHTSA Side Crash Front Occupant	Very Poor
NHTSA Side Crash Rear Occupant	Poor (Coupe); Average (Sedan)

IIHS Offset	Poor
IIHS Bumper Bash	Acceptable
Chevrolet Impala	
NHTSA Frontal Crash Driver	Excellent
NHTSA Frontal Crash Passenger	Excellent
NHTSA Side Crash Front Occupant	Good
NHTSA Side Crash Rear Occupant	Good
IIHS Offset	Good
IIHS Bumper Bash	Marginal
Chevrolet Malibu	
NHTSA Frontal Crash Driver	Good
NHTSA Frontal Crash Passenger	Good
NHTSA Side Crash Front Occupant	Poor
NHTSA Side Crash Rear Occupant	Good
IIHS Offset	Acceptable
IIHS Bumper Bash	Marginal
Chevrolet Prizm	
NHTSA Frontal Crash Driver	Good
NHTSA Frontal Crash Passenger	Good
NHTSA Side Crash Front Occupant	Avg. (w/o side airbag); Good (w/side airbag)
NHTSA Side Crash Rear Occupant	Average
IIHS Offset	Acceptable
IIHS Bumper Bash	Good
Chrysler 300M	
NHTSA Frontal Crash Driver	Average
NHTSA Frontal Crash Passenger	Good
NHTSA Side Crash Front Occupant	Good
NHTSA Side Crash Rear Occupant	Average
IIHS Offset	Poor
IIHS Bumper Bash	Marginal
Chrysler Cirrus	
NHTSA Frontal Crash Driver	Average
NHTSA Frontal Crash Passenger	Good
NHTSA Side Crash Front Occupant	Average
NHTSA Side Crash Rear Occupant	Poor
IIHS Offset	Poor
IIHS Bumper Bash	Marginal
Chrysler Concorde	
NHTSA Frontal Crash Driver	Good
NHTSA Frontal Crash Passenger	Good
NHTSA Side Crash Front Occupant	Good
NHTSA Side Crash Rear Occupant	Average
IIHS Offset	Marginal
IIHS Bumper Bash	Marginal
Chrysler LHS	
NHTSA Frontal Crash Driver	Average
NHTSA Frontal Crash Passenger	Good
NHTSA Side Crash Front Occupant	Good
NHTSA Side Crash Rear Occupant	Average

IIHS Offset	Poor
IIHS Bumper Bash	Marginal
Chrysler PT Cruiser	
NHTSA Frontal Crash Driver	Poor
NHTSA Frontal Crash Passenger	Good
NHTSA Side Crash Front Occupant	Good
NHTSA Side Crash Rear Occupant	Excellent
IIHS Offset	Not Tested
IIHS Bumper Bash	Not Tested
Chrysler Sebring Convertible	
NHTSA Frontal Crash Driver	Good
NHTSA Frontal Crash Passenger	Good
NHTSA Side Crash Front Occupant	Not Tested
NHTSA Side Crash Rear Occupant	Not Tested
IIHS Offset	Not Tested
IIHS Bumper Bash	Not Tested
Chrysler Sebring Coupe	
NHTSA Frontal Crash Driver	Excellent
NHTSA Frontal Crash Passenger	Excellent
NHTSA Side Crash Front Occupant	Not Tested
NHTSA Side Crash Rear Occupant	Not Tested
IIHS Offset	Not Tested
IIHS Bumper Bash	Not Tested
Daewoo Leganza	
NHTSA Frontal Crash Driver	Not Tested
NHTSA Frontal Crash Passenger	Not Tested
NHTSA Side Crash Front Occupant	Not Tested
NHTSA Side Crash Rear Occupant	Not Tested
IIHS Offset	Poor
IIHS Bumper Bash	Marginal
Dodge Intrepid	
NHTSA Frontal Crash Driver	Good
NHTSA Frontal Crash Passenger	Good
NHTSA Side Crash Front Occupant	Good
NHTSA Side Crash Rear Occupant	Average
IIHS Offset	Marginal
IIHS Bumper Bash	Marginal
Dodge Neon	
NHTSA Frontal Crash Driver	Good
NHTSA Frontal Crash Passenger	Good
NHTSA Side Crash Front Occupant	Average
NHTSA Side Crash Rear Occupant	Average
IIHS Offset	Marginal
IIHS Bumper Bash	Acceptable
Dodge Stratus	
NHTSA Frontal Crash Driver	Average
NHTSA Frontal Crash Passenger	Good
NHTSA Side Crash Front Occupant	Average
NHTSA Side Crash Rear Occupant	Poor

IIHS Offset	Poor
IIHS Bumper Bash	Marginal

Ford Crown Victoria

NHTSA Frontal Crash Driver	Excellent
NHTSA Frontal Crash Passenger	Excellent
NHTSA Side Crash Front Occupant	Good
NHTSA Side Crash Rear Occupant	Good
IIHS Offset	Not Tested
IIHS Bumper Bash	Not Tested

Ford Escort ZX2

NHTSA Frontal Crash Driver	Not Tested
NHTSA Frontal Crash Passenger	Not Tested
NHTSA Side Crash Front Occupant	Very Poor
NHTSA Side Crash Rear Occupant	Good
IIHS Offset	Not Tested
IIHS Bumper Bash	Not Tested

Ford Focus

NHTSA Frontal Crash Driver	Excellent (Coupe); Good (Sedan)
NHTSA Frontal Crash Passenger	Excellent (Coupe); Good (Sedan)
NHTSA Side Crash Front Occupant	Average (Sedan)
NHTSA Side Crash Rear Occupant	Good (Sedan)
IIHS Offset	Not Tested
IIHS Bumper Bash	Not Tested

Ford Mustang

NHTSA Frontal Crash Driver	Good
NHTSA Frontal Crash Passenger	Good
NHTSA Side Crash Front Occupant	Average
NHTSA Side Crash Rear Occupant	Average
IIHS Offset	Not Tested
IIHS Bumper Bash	Not Tested

Ford Taurus

NHTSA Frontal Crash Driver	Excellent
NHTSA Frontal Crash Passenger	Excellent
NHTSA Side Crash Front Occupant	Average
NHTSA Side Crash Rear Occupant	Average
IIHS Offset	Good
IIHS Bumper Bash	Acceptable

Honda Accord

NHTSA Frontal Crash Driver	Good
NHTSA Frontal Crash Passenger	Good
NHTSA Side Crash Front Occupant	Good (Coupe); Good (Sdn) (both w/side airbag)
NHTSA Side Crash Rear Occupant	Good (Coupe); Excellent (Sdn) (both w/side airbag)
IIHS Offset	Acceptable
IIHS Bumper Bash	Acceptable

Honda Civic

NHTSA Frontal Crash Driver	Excellent
NHTSA Frontal Crash Passenger	Excellent
NHTSA Side Crash Front Occupant	Excellent (w/side airbag)

NHTSA Side Crash Rear Occupant	Excellent (Coupe); Good (Sdn) (both w/side airbag)
IIHS Offset	Acceptable
IIHS Bumper Bash	Acceptable

Honda Insight

NHTSA Frontal Crash Driver	Good (Coupe) (2001)
NHTSA Frontal Crash Passenger	Good (Coupe) (2001)
NHTSA Side Crash Front Occupant	Not Tested
NHTSA Side Crash Rear Occupant	Not Tested
IIHS Offset	Not Tested
IIHS Bumper Bash	Not Tested

Hyundai Elantra

NHTSA Frontal Crash Driver	Excellent
NHTSA Frontal Crash Passenger	Good
NHTSA Side Crash Front Occupant	Average
NHTSA Side Crash Rear Occupant	Very Poor
IIHS Offset	Acceptable
IIHS Bumper Bash	Acceptable

Hyundai Sonata

NHTSA Frontal Crash Driver	Not Tested
NHTSA Frontal Crash Passenger	Not Tested
NHTSA Side Crash Front Occupant	Not Tested
NHTSA Side Crash Rear Occupant	Not Tested
IIHS Offset	Acceptable
IIHS Bumper Bash	Marginal

Infiniti I30

NHTSA Frontal Crash Driver	Good
NHTSA Frontal Crash Passenger	Good
NHTSA Side Crash Front Occupant	Good
NHTSA Side Crash Rear Occupant	Good
IIHS Offset	Not Tested
IIHS Bumper Bash	Not Tested

Infiniti Q45

NHTSA Frontal Crash Driver	Not Tested
NHTSA Frontal Crash Passenger	Not Tested
NHTSA Side Crash Front Occupant	Not Tested
NHTSA Side Crash Rear Occupant	Not Tested
IIHS Offset	Marginal
IIHS Bumper Bash	Poor

Kia Sephia

NHTSA Frontal Crash Driver	Not Tested
NHTSA Frontal Crash Passenger	Not Tested
NHTSA Side Crash Front Occupant	Average
NHTSA Side Crash Rear Occupant	Good
IIHS Offset	Poor
IIHS Bumper Bash	Marginal

Lexus ES 300

NHTSA Frontal Crash Driver	Good
NHTSA Frontal Crash Passenger	Excellent
NHTSA Side Crash Front Occupant	Excellent

NHTSA Side Crash Rear Occupant	Good
IIHS Offset	Not Tested
IIHS Bumper Bash	Not Tested

Lexus GS 300

NHTSA Frontal Crash Driver	Not Tested
NHTSA Frontal Crash Passenger	Not Tested
NHTSA Side Crash Front Occupant	Not Tested
NHTSA Side Crash Rear Occupant	Not Tested
IIHS Offset	Good
IIHS Bumper Bash	Poor

Lexus GS 400

NHTSA Frontal Crash Driver	Not Tested
NHTSA Frontal Crash Passenger	Not Tested
NHTSA Side Crash Front Occupant	Not Tested
NHTSA Side Crash Rear Occupant	Not Tested
IIHS Offset	Good
IIHS Bumper Bash	Poor

Lincoln Continental

NHTSA Frontal Crash Driver	Not Tested
NHTSA Frontal Crash Passenger	Not Tested
NHTSA Side Crash Front Occupant	Not Tested
NHTSA Side Crash Rear Occupant	Not Tested
IIHS Offset	Acceptable
IIHS Bumper Bash	Good

Lincoln LS

NHTSA Frontal Crash Driver	Not Tested
NHTSA Frontal Crash Passenger	Not Tested
NHTSA Side Crash Front Occupant	Not Tested
NHTSA Side Crash Rear Occupant	Not Tested
IIHS Offset	Good
IIHS Bumper Bash	Marginal

Lincoln Town Car

NHTSA Frontal Crash Driver	Good
NHTSA Frontal Crash Passenger	Good
NHTSA Side Crash Front Occupant	Good
NHTSA Side Crash Rear Occupant	Good
IIHS Offset	Not Tested
IIHS Bumper Bash	Not Tested

Mazda 626

NHTSA Frontal Crash Driver	Good
NHTSA Frontal Crash Passenger	Excellent
NHTSA Side Crash Front Occupant	Average
NHTSA Side Crash Rear Occupant	Average
IIHS Offset	Acceptable
IIHS Bumper Bash	Acceptable

Mazda Millenia

NHTSA Frontal Crash Driver	Good
NHTSA Frontal Crash Passenger	Excellent
NHTSA Side Crash Front Occupant	Not Tested
NHTSA Side Crash Rear Occupant	Not Tested

IIHS Offset	Acceptable
IIHS Bumper Bash	Marginal

Mazda Protege

NHTSA Frontal Crash Driver	Good
NHTSA Frontal Crash Passenger	Good
NHTSA Side Crash Front Occupant	Average
NHTSA Side Crash Rear Occupant	Good
IIHS Offset	Acceptable
IIHS Bumper Bash	Marginal

Mercedes-Benz C-Class

NHTSA Frontal Crash Driver	Not Tested
NHTSA Frontal Crash Passenger	Not Tested
NHTSA Side Crash Front Occupant	Average
NHTSA Side Crash Rear Occupant	Good
IIHS Offset	Not Tested
IIHS Bumper Bash	Not Tested

Mercedes-Benz E-Class

NHTSA Frontal Crash Driver	Not Tested
NHTSA Frontal Crash Passenger	Not Tested
NHTSA Side Crash Front Occupant	Not Tested
NHTSA Side Crash Rear Occupant	Not Tested
IIHS Offset	Acceptable
IIHS Bumper Bash	Poor

Mercury Grand Marquis

NHTSA Frontal Crash Driver	Excellent
NHTSA Frontal Crash Passenger	Excellent
NHTSA Side Crash Front Occupant	Good
NHTSA Side Crash Rear Occupant	Good
IIHS Offset	Not Tested
IIHS Bumper Bash	Not Tested

Mercury Sable

NHTSA Frontal Crash Driver	Excellent
NHTSA Frontal Crash Passenger	Excellent
NHTSA Side Crash Front Occupant	Average
NHTSA Side Crash Rear Occupant	Average
IIHS Offset	Good
IIHS Bumper Bash	Acceptable

Mitsubishi Galant

NHTSA Frontal Crash Driver	Good
NHTSA Frontal Crash Passenger	Good
NHTSA Side Crash Front Occupant	Excellent
NHTSA Side Crash Rear Occupant	Good
IIHS Offset	Acceptable
IIHS Bumper Bash	Acceptable

Mitsubishi Mirage

NHTSA Frontal Crash Driver	Not Tested
NHTSA Frontal Crash Passenger	Not Tested
NHTSA Side Crash Front Occupant	Not Tested
NHTSA Side Crash Rear Occupant	Not Tested

IIHS Offset	Poor
IIHS Bumper Bash	Marginal

Nissan Altima
NHTSA Frontal Crash Driver	Good
NHTSA Frontal Crash Passenger	Excellent
NHTSA Side Crash Front Occupant	Average
NHTSA Side Crash Rear Occupant	Average
IIHS Offset	Marginal
IIHS Bumper Bash	Acceptable

Nissan Maxima
NHTSA Frontal Crash Driver	Good
NHTSA Frontal Crash Passenger	Good
NHTSA Side Crash Front Occupant	Good
NHTSA Side Crash Rear Occupant	Good
IIHS Offset	Acceptable
IIHS Bumper Bash	Marginal

Nissan Sentra
NHTSA Frontal Crash Driver	Not Tested
NHTSA Frontal Crash Passenger	Not Tested
NHTSA Side Crash Front Occupant	Not Tested
NHTSA Side Crash Rear Occupant	Not Tested
IIHS Offset	Acceptable
IIHS Bumper Bash	Acceptable

Oldsmobile Alero
NHTSA Frontal Crash Driver	Good
NHTSA Frontal Crash Passenger	Good
NHTSA Side Crash Front Occupant	Average (Sedan)
NHTSA Side Crash Rear Occupant	Average (Sedan)
IIHS Offset	Poor
IIHS Bumper Bash	Not Tested

Oldsmobile Aurora
NHTSA Frontal Crash Driver	Not Tested
NHTSA Frontal Crash Passenger	Not Tested
NHTSA Side Crash Front Occupant	Average
NHTSA Side Crash Rear Occupant	Good
IIHS Offset	Not Tested
IIHS Bumper Bash	Not Tested

Oldsmobile Intrigue
NHTSA Frontal Crash Driver	Good
NHTSA Frontal Crash Passenger	Poor
NHTSA Side Crash Front Occupant	Average
NHTSA Side Crash Rear Occupant	Very Poor
IIHS Offset	Acceptable

Plymouth Neon
NHTSA Frontal Crash Driver	Good
NHTSA Frontal Crash Passenger	Good
NHTSA Side Crash Front Occupant	Average
NHTSA Side Crash Rear Occupant	Average
IIHS Offset	Marginal
IIHS Bumper Bash	Acceptable

Pontiac Bonneville
- NHTSA Frontal Crash Driver — Not Tested
- NHTSA Frontal Crash Passenger — Not Tested
- NHTSA Side Crash Front Occupant — Not Tested
- NHTSA Side Crash Rear Occupant — Not Tested
- IIHS Offset — Good
- IIHS Bumper Bash — Marginal

Pontiac Firebird
- NHTSA Frontal Crash Driver — Good
- NHTSA Frontal Crash Passenger — Excellent
- NHTSA Side Crash Front Occupant — Average
- NHTSA Side Crash Rear Occupant — Good
- IIHS Offset — Not Tested
- IIHS Bumper Bash — Not Tested

Pontiac Grand Am
- NHTSA Frontal Crash Driver — Good
- NHTSA Frontal Crash Passenger — Good
- NHTSA Side Crash Front Occupant — Average (Sedan)
- NHTSA Side Crash Rear Occupant — Average (Sedan)
- IIHS Offset — Poor
- IIHS Bumper Bash — Marginal

Pontiac Grand Prix
- NHTSA Frontal Crash Driver — Good
- NHTSA Frontal Crash Passenger — Good
- NHTSA Side Crash Front Occupant — Not Tested
- NHTSA Side Crash Rear Occupant — Not Tested
- IIHS Offset — Acceptable
- IIHS Bumper Bash — Acceptable

Pontiac Sunfire
- NHTSA Frontal Crash Driver — Average (Coupe); Good (Sedan)
- NHTSA Frontal Crash Passenger — Good
- NHTSA Side Crash Front Occupant — Very Poor
- NHTSA Side Crash Rear Occupant — Poor (Coupe); Average (Sedan)
- IIHS Offset — Poor
- IIHS Bumper Bash — Acceptable

Saab 9-3
- NHTSA Frontal Crash Driver — Good
- NHTSA Frontal Crash Passenger — Good
- NHTSA Side Crash Front Occupant — Not Tested
- NHTSA Side Crash Rear Occupant — Not Tested
- IIHS Offset — Acceptable
- IIHS Bumper Bash — Acceptable

Saab 9-5
- NHTSA Frontal Crash Driver — Not Tested
- NHTSA Frontal Crash Passenger — Not Tested
- NHTSA Side Crash Front Occupant — Not Tested
- NHTSA Side Crash Rear Occupant — Not Tested
- IIHS Offset — Acceptable
- IIHS Bumper Bash — Marginal

Saturn LS
- NHTSA Frontal Crash Driver — Good
- NHTSA Frontal Crash Passenger — Excellent
- NHTSA Side Crash Front Occupant — Poor
- NHTSA Side Crash Rear Occupant — Good
- IIHS Offset — Acceptable
- IIHS Bumper Bash — Good

Saturn S-Series
- NHTSA Frontal Crash Driver — Excellent
- NHTSA Frontal Crash Passenger — Excellent
- NHTSA Side Crash Front Occupant — Average
- NHTSA Side Crash Rear Occupant — Average
- IIHS Offset — Acceptable
- IIHS Bumper Bash — Good

Subaru Impreza
- NHTSA Frontal Crash Driver — Good
- NHTSA Frontal Crash Passenger — Good
- NHTSA Side Crash Front Occupant — Not Tested
- NHTSA Side Crash Rear Occupant — Not Tested
- IIHS Offset — Not Tested
- IIHS Bumper Bash — Not Tested

Subaru Legacy
- NHTSA Frontal Crash Driver — Good
- NHTSA Frontal Crash Passenger — Good
- NHTSA Side Crash Front Occupant — Not Tested (Sedan); Good (Wagon)
- NHTSA Side Crash Rear Occupant — Not Tested (Sedan); Excellent (Wagon)
- IIHS Offset — Good
- IIHS Bumper Bash — Acceptable

Subaru Outback Sport
- NHTSA Frontal Crash Driver — Good
- NHTSA Frontal Crash Passenger — Good
- NHTSA Side Crash Front Occupant — Not Tested
- NHTSA Side Crash Rear Occupant — Not Tested
- IIHS Offset — Not Tested
- IIHS Bumper Bash — Not Tested

Suzuki Swift
- NHTSA Frontal Crash Driver — Good
- NHTSA Frontal Crash Passenger — Good
- NHTSA Side Crash Front Occupant — Not Tested
- NHTSA Side Crash Rear Occupant — Not Tested
- IIHS Offset — Not Tested
- IIHS Bumper Bash — Not Tested

Toyota Avalon
- NHTSA Frontal Crash Driver — Not Tested
- NHTSA Frontal Crash Passenger — Not Tested
- NHTSA Side Crash Front Occupant — Good
- NHTSA Side Crash Rear Occupant — Excellent
- IIHS Offset — Good
- IIHS Bumper Bash — Acceptable

Toyota Camry
- NHTSA Frontal Crash Driver — Good
- NHTSA Frontal Crash Passenger — Excellent
- NHTSA Side Crash Front Occupant — Avg. (w/o side airbag); Good (w/side airbag)
- NHTSA Side Crash Rear Occupant — Average
- IIHS Offset — Good
- IIHS Bumper Bash — Good

Toyota Camry Solara
- NHTSA Frontal Crash Driver — Not Tested
- NHTSA Frontal Crash Passenger — Not Tested
- NHTSA Side Crash Front Occupant — Average
- NHTSA Side Crash Rear Occupant — Excellent
- IIHS Offset — Not Tested
- IIHS Bumper Bash — Not Tested

Toyota Corolla
- NHTSA Frontal Crash Driver — Good
- NHTSA Frontal Crash Passenger — Good
- NHTSA Side Crash Front Occupant — Avg. (w/o side airbag); Good (w/side airbag)
- NHTSA Side Crash Rear Occupant — Average
- IIHS Offset — Acceptable
- IIHS Bumper Bash — Good

Volkswagen Golf
- NHTSA Frontal Crash Driver — Not Tested
- NHTSA Frontal Crash Passenger — Not Tested
- NHTSA Side Crash Front Occupant — Not Tested
- NHTSA Side Crash Rear Occupant — Not Tested
- IIHS Offset — Acceptable
- IIHS Bumper Bash — Good

Volkswagen Jetta
- NHTSA Frontal Crash Driver — Excellent
- NHTSA Frontal Crash Passenger — Excellent
- NHTSA Side Crash Front Occupant — Good
- NHTSA Side Crash Rear Occupant — Good
- IIHS Offset — Acceptable
- IIHS Bumper Bash — Good

Volkswagen New Beetle
- NHTSA Frontal Crash Driver — Good
- NHTSA Frontal Crash Passenger — Good
- NHTSA Side Crash Front Occupant — Excellent
- NHTSA Side Crash Rear Occupant — Average
- IIHS Offset — Good
- IIHS Bumper Bash — Good

Volkswagen Passat
- NHTSA Frontal Crash Driver — Excellent
- NHTSA Frontal Crash Passenger — Excellent
- NHTSA Side Crash Front Occupant — Good
- NHTSA Side Crash Rear Occupant — Good
- IIHS Offset — Good
- IIHS Bumper Bash — Good

Volvo S70
- NHTSA Frontal Crash Driver — Excellent
- NHTSA Frontal Crash Passenger — Excellent
- NHTSA Side Crash Front Occupant — Good
- NHTSA Side Crash Rear Occupant — No Data
- IIHS Offset — Good
- IIHS Bumper Bash — Marginal

Volvo S80
- NHTSA Frontal Crash Driver — Excellent
- NHTSA Frontal Crash Passenger — Excellent
- NHTSA Side Crash Front Occupant — Excellent
- NHTSA Side Crash Rear Occupant — Excellent
- IIHS Offset — Good
- IIHS Bumper Bash — Poor

Volvo V70
- NHTSA Frontal Crash Driver — Excellent
- NHTSA Frontal Crash Passenger — Excellent
- NHTSA Side Crash Front Occupant — Good
- NHTSA Side Crash Rear Occupant — No Data
- IIHS Offset — Good
- IIHS Bumper Bash — Marginal

TOWN HALL

Get answers from our editors, discover smart shopping strategies and share your perspectives in this interactive forum of both experts and consumers. Just enter the following address into your Web browser:

Where smart shoppers talk about cars, trucks, and related consumer topics.

REVIEW

2001 Chrysler Sebring

Slick, Even When Standing Still

BY NEIL DUNLOP

The launch of the 2001 Sebring Coupe and Sedan represents a belief by Daimler-Chrysler's brain trust that, beginning soon, baby boomers (age 35 to 55) will abandon pickups, minivans and sport-utility vehicles in favor of midsize, near-luxury sedans. The Sebring project is a critical effort for Chrysler, which lags behind Honda, Toyota, Ford and GM in market penetration—not surprising when you consider that trucks make up three-quarters of Chrysler's sales.

Chrysler didn't go into the new Sebring half-heartedly either. The company has spent $985 million on the sedan project so far (that figure also includes development of the new Dodge Stratus Sedan). Figures aren't available for the cost of developing the coupe as it was done in conjunction with Mitsubishi, but it likely cost many millions as well.

Consider it money well spent. In terms of drivability, performance, equipment and looks, the new Sebrings will make boomers happier than an inside tip on an Internet stock.

During a sunny day in June at DaimlerChrysler's Chelsea Proving Grounds in Ann Arbor, Mich., a group of journalists were given a preview of these impressive new vehicles.

Sebring Sedan

Testing began with the totally redesigned Sebring Sedan, which replaces the Chrysler Cirrus. Good looks first impress beholders of the new car. It's more stylized and modern looking than its predecessor and certainly more exciting than the Honda Accord and Toyota Camry with which it will compete. The Sebring retains Chrysler's trademark cab-forward design and it has borrowed the elliptical, eggcrate grille that is signature on the larger Chrysler Concorde and LHS. The forward slope of its roofline gives the impression of sleek, aerodynamic speed (in fact, the company claims to have designed the new Sebring to provide less air turbulence and resistance and better water flow in wet conditions). The sides are simple, unencumbered by detail (the sleek door handles and trim are body color and meld into the body). The rear is reminiscent of Chrysler's successful luxury 300M—high, squared and somehow haughty in departure. The overall effect is of slick movement, even when it's standing still.

Inside, the sedan is comfortable and noticeably roomy in front and back (thanks to the cab-forward design). The charcoal-leather interior of the testers was elegant, complemented by the chrome-ringed, black-on-white gauges (also borrowed from the 300M and LHS). Faux walnut burl accents lend a warm feel to the sculpted dash. The interior is more comfortable and attractive than the 2000 Toyota Camry and Honda Accord, which were on hand for comparison.

Out on the test track, the Sebring Sedan is a taut performer. The body was redesigned to provide 13 percent less twist and 33 percent less bend than last year's model. The added stiffness is obvious while cornering and also provides a better connection to the road, reminiscent of European sedans such as BMW, Volvo and Mercedes. The effect is a more fun to drive vehicle.

Chrysler also worked hard to reduce noise and vibration in this sedan: aerodynamics were improved; the front door glass was made thicker; parts of the frame were injected with insulating foam;

and full wheelhouse shields were added to deflect wheel noise. It worked. The Sebring is noticeably quieter than the Accord and about even with the Camry.

The Sebring's steering system was redesigned to include a front crossmember that increases stiffness for better handling and responsiveness. Rebound shocks were also added to keep the wheels more closely allied with the pavement and improve road feel without sacrificing comfort. Also, the 15-inch standard wheels (up 1 inch from last year) improve ride and handling (16-inch wheels are optional). The effect is a smooth ride that is much quieter than the Accord's, equal if not better than the Camry's, and a definite improvement over the Cirrus.

The Sebring's 2.4-liter four-cylinder powerplant (standard in the LX) is adequate, but hardly thrilling. At 147 horsepower it's no weakling, but it has to work harder to get up to cruising speeds. If you don't mind trading speed when accelerating and passing for improved gas consumption, the LX engine is a nice compromise between performance and economy.

The 2.7-liter V6 that is standard on the LXi and optional on the LX is a different story. Essentially the same twin-cam V6 used in Chrysler's larger sedans, it smoothly delivers 200 spirited horsepower (at 5900 rpm), a whopping 32 more ponies than the current 2.5-liter V6. The LXi is equipped with a four-speed automatic that includes Chrysler's "AutoStick" clutchless shifting mechanism for drivers who want more aggressive upshifts and downshifts. Most drivers will likely never use this quasi-manual shifting system, but for passing on hills or at highways speeds it works well. Adding driver input to transmission shifts can help make a mundane drive more fun, too.

While whipping around the test track at speeds inadvisable on public roads, the Sebring Sedan lent confidence to our exertions and never once betrayed an unwilling heart. Standard four-wheel disc brakes, enlarged from last year, and the optional ABS Plus system added assurance. Similar to ABS systems used in BMWs and Volkswagens, the Plus system reduces yaw (fishtailing) and prevents spinout by applying the rear brakes independent of each other, thereby making smoother, straighter emergency stops possible. Should a collision be beyond your control, dual front airbags are standard and side airbag curtains that protect front and rear passengers are optional.

Sebring Coupe

The new Sebring Coupe is an alltogether different animal. Borrowing heavily from the Mitsubishi

Eclipse and Galant (all three are made at the Mitsubishi Motor Assembly plant in Normal, Ill.), it looks much like a Japanese car. It shares a similar profile and styling cues with the Sebring Sedan, but is much more aggressive, starting with its lower, sharper nose. The below-bumper, elliptical egg-crate grille with built-in fog lamps is reminiscent of the Concorde's front end with more than a little influence from classic Ferrari grilles. The coupe's roofline is raked and streamlined like the sedan, but its side windows are much thinner, creating an even more aggressive need-for-speed look. And, while the Sebrings' rear ends mimic that of the 300M, the coupe's circular, inset reverse lights look sportier. If the sedan looks sleek, elegant and speedy, the coupe looks sexy, raw and fast.

The coupe's interior also reflects this difference. More sporty and less elegant, it is nearly identical to the Eclipse's interior with a few wooden accents and a more muscular than tailored look. Also, from inside the Sebring Coupe, the low profile side windows and high sills are quite noticeable, giving the impression of being in a sports car, yet the coupe offers similar comfort to the sedan—in the front seats only. As in many coupes, ingress and egress to the rear seats is awkward and would make even Fred Astaire seem clumsy.

On the track, the coupe is good fun, especially the five-speed manual. The Mitsubishi-derived, 200-horsepower 3.0-liter V6 provides similar acceleration to the sedan, but the coupe's aggressive profile and standard 16-inch tires lend attitude and superior road grip to its performance. Also, the coupe's single-piece body was redesigned to provide a 90 percent improvement in bending resistance and a 9 percent increase in twist resistance over the old model. This increased rigidity and an added front strut tower brace and sport-tuned suspension system give the coupe great feel and handling on all road conditions.

The coupe's AutoStick is also set up for more aggressive driving. It uses an intuitive up-down shift pattern, as opposed to the sedan's side-to-side movement. It can shift un-

photos courtesy of DaimlerChrysler AG

der full throttle, skip shift, and it does not share the sedan's auto upshift mechanism, which automatically upshifts before redline. The Sebring Coupe outperformed the Accord, Solara and Mustang V6 on the track, offering better performance, similar handling and superior road feel and ride comfort.

Both the LX Coupe and Sedan come with an impressive array of standard features, including air conditioning, cruise control, four-wheel disc brakes, six-speaker stereo, four-speed automatic tranny, tilt steering wheel, power trunk release and power windows, locks and mirrors. Upgrading to the LXi adds 16-inch aluminum wheels, leather seats, eight-way power driver's seat, fog lamps, remote keyless entry, compass and temperature display, and a seven-speaker Infinity sound system with cassette and CD.

Baby boomers might find that if the kids are grown and gone, rendering the days of lugging camping equipment or a soccer team around to a cherished memory, it makes sense to ditch the minivan or SUV and buy a Sebring of either stripe. But the car's appeal isn't limited to folks seriously pondering the use of Grecian Formula as part of the morning grooming ritual. Young singles will find Sebring Coupe's upscale style and peppy performance pleasing, while young families can enjoy style and grace with plenty of room to take the kids to grandma's house in the Sebring Sedan.

Whatever the case may be, the 2001 Sebring sure makes the Chrysler brain trust look like they know what they're doing.

WARRANTIES

All new vehicles sold in America come with at least three warranties, and many include roadside assistance. Described below are the major types of warranties and assistance provided to consumers.

Basic: Your basic warranty covers everything except items subject to wear and tear, such as oil filters, wiper blades, and the like. Tires and batteries often have their own warranty coverage, which will be outlined in your owner's manual. Emissions equipment is required by the federal government to be covered for eight years or 80,000 miles.

Drivetrain: Drivetrain coverage takes care of most of the parts that make the car move, like the engine, transmission, drive axles and driveshaft. Like the basic warranty, parts subject to wear and tear like hoses and belts are not covered. However, most of the internal parts of the engine, such as the pistons and bearings, which are subject to wear and tear, are covered by the drivetrain warranty. See your owner's manual or local dealer for specific coverage.

Rust or Corrosion: This warranty protects you from rust-through problems with the sheetmetal. Surface rust doesn't count. The rust must make a hole to be covered. Keep your car washed and waxed, and rust shouldn't be a problem.

Roadside Assistance: Most manufacturers provide a service that will rescue you if your car leaves you stranded, even if it's your fault. Lock yourself out of the car? Somebody will come and open it up. Run out of gas? Somebody will deliver some fuel. Flat tire? Somebody will change it for you. See your owner's manual for details, or ask the dealer about specifics.

Make	Basic (yrs/mi)	Drivetrain (yrs/mi)	Rust/Corrosion (yrs/mi)	Roadside Assistance (yrs/mi)
Acura	4/50,000	4/50,000	5/Unlimited	4/50,000
AM General	3/36,000	3/36,000	6/100,000	None Available
Audi	4/50,000	4/50,000	12/Unlimited	4/Unlimited
BMW	4/50,000	4/50,000	6/Unlimited	4/50,000
Buick	3/36,000	3/36,000	6/100,000	3/36,000
Cadillac	4/50,000	4/50,000	6/100,000	4/50,000
Chevrolet	3/36,000	3/36,000	6/100,000	3/36,000
Chrysler	3/36,000	3/36,000	5/100,000	3/36,000

WARRANTIES

Make	Basic (yrs/mi)	Drivetrain (yrs/mi)	Rust/Corrosion (yrs/mi)	Roadside Assistance (yrs/mi)
Daewoo	3/36,000	5/60,000	5/Unlimited	3/36,000
Dodge	3/36,000	3/36,000	5/100,000	3/36,000
Ford	3/36,000	3/36,000	5/Unlimited	3/36,000
GMC	3/36,000	3/36,000	6/100,000	3/36,000
Honda	3/36,000	3/36,000	5/Unlimited	None Available
Hyundai	5/60,000	10/100,000	5/100,000	5/Unlimited
Infiniti	4/60,000	6/70,000	7/Unlimited	4/Unlimited
Isuzu	3/50,000	10/120,000 (except Hombre)	6/100,000	5/60,000
Jaguar	4/50,000	4/50,000	6/Unlimited	4/50,000
Jeep	3/36,000	3/36,000	5/100,000	3/36,000
Kia	5/60,000	10/100,000	5/100,000	5/Unlimited
Land Rover	4/50,000	4/50,000	6/Unlimited	4/50,000
Lexus	4/50,000	6/70,000	6/Unlimited	4/Unlimited
Lincoln	4/50,000	4/50,000	5/Unlimited	4/50,000
Mazda	3/50,000	3/50,000	5/Unlimited	3/50,000
Mercedes	4/50,000	4/50,000	4/50,000	Unlimited
Mercury	3/36,000	3/36,000	5/Unlimited	3/36,000
Mitsubishi	3/36,000	5/60,000	7/100,000	3/36,000
Nissan	3/36,000	5/60,000	5/Unlimited	None Available
Oldsmobile	3/36,000	5/60,000	6/100,000	3/36,000
Plymouth	3/36,000	3/36,000	5/100,000	3/36,000
Pontiac	3/36,000	3/36,000	6/100,000	3/36,000
Porsche	4/50,000	4/50,000	10/Unlimited	4/50,000
Saab	4/50,000	4/50,000	6/Unlimited	4/50,000
Saturn	3/36,000	3/36,000	6/100,000	3/36,000
Subaru	3/36,000	5/60,000	5/Unlimited	3/36,000
Suzuki	3/36,000	3/36,000	3/Unlimited	None Available
Toyota	3/36,000	5/60,000	5/Unlimited	None Available
Volkswagen	2/24,000	10/100,000 (except EuroVan)	12/Unlimited (except Cabrio)	2/Unlimited
Volvo	4/50,000	4/50,000	8/Unlimited	4/Unlimited

* All data sourced directly from manufacturer customer assistance telephone operators.

There's plenty of talk these days about dealer holdback, and we suppose we're to blame for some of the hype over this manufacturer kickback to dealers. We've been reporting holdback data for years. But many consumers don't understand what the dealer holdback is, what it is used for, and what the holdback's role is in the deal-making process. Let's try to clear up some of the confusion.

What is Dealer Holdback?

Dealer holdback is a percentage of the MSRP or invoice of a new vehicle that is paid to the dealer by the manufacturer to assist with the dealership's financing of the vehicle. It is almost always non-negotiable, because it is designed to help the dealer cover some of the extraordinary costs of doing business. Think of it as a forced-savings plan for the dealer. However, by knowing about the holdback, you can use it to your advantage. First, a little more background.

The total invoice cost of the car is due to the manufacturer, payable by the dealership, when the vehicle is ordered, not when it is sold. Car dealerships must have an inventory on hand through which the consumer can browse and perhaps select a vehicle. Consequently, they must borrow money from the bank to pay for that inventory. The manufacturer pays for financing and maintenance for the first 90 days the vehicle is on the lot, in the form of a quarterly check called a holdback. After the first 90 days, the dealership dips into its own pocket, and into its own profit, to finance the car. Fortunately, most cars don't stay on the lot for three full months.

This amount is "invisible" to the consumer because, unlike the destination charge, it does not appear as an itemized fee on the window sticker and is included in the invoice cost of the car. If the car sells within 90 days of arrival on the dealer's lot, the dealer is guaranteed a profit even if the vehicle is sold to you at cost. Because of the holdback, the dealer can advertise a car at $1 over invoice and still make hundreds of dollars on the sale.

For example, let's say you're interested in a Ford with a Manufacturer's Suggested Retail Price (MSRP) of $20,500, including optional equipment and destination charge. Dealer invoice on this hypothetical Ford is $18,000, including optional equipment. The holdback for all Ford vehicles, amounts to 3 percent of the total MSRP or, in this case $615. (The destination charge should not be included when figuring the holdback.) So, on this particular Ford, the true dealer cost is actually $17,385, plus destination charges. Even if the dealer sells you the car for invoice, which is unlikely, he would still be making as much as $615 on the deal when his quarterly check arrived. That is profit to the dealer only; the sales staff doesn't see any of it.

Begin your calculation by finding the Edmunds.com® True Market Value[sm] (TMV[sm]) price that is listed our Web site at www.edmunds.com. TMV[sm] prices represent what the vehicle is actually selling for in the marketplace. If the TMV[sm] for this Ford is, say, $18,540 plus the destination charge, the dealer will make $540 above the invoice price and as much as $615 on the holdback. Also, you still get a good deal by paying $1,960 less than the MSRP. (Remember, this price doesn't include destination charges, additional fees, tax, or license plates.)

However, the true "profit" of holdback money depends on how long the car has been on the lot. If our hypothetical Ford had been sitting there for 45 days before you bought it, the dealer's holdback profit is only half of what it could have been, cutting the total profit on the deal by $300. At the 90-day mark, holdback profit has disappeared.

Dealer holdback allows dealers to advertise big sales. Often, ads promise that your new car will cost you just "$1 over/under invoice!" Additionally, the dealer stands to reap further benefits if there is some sort of dealer incentive or customer rebate on the car. Generally, sale prices stipulate that all rebates and incentives go to the dealer. Using the example above, let's see what happens when there is a rebate.

Suppose our hypothetical Ford has a $1,000 rebate in effect. You need to subtract that $1,000 rebate (remember, the dealer is keeping the rebate) from the dealer invoice of $18,000, which results in a new dealer invoice of just $17,000. In this example, TMV^{sm} is 3 percent over dealer invoice, which means your offer should be $510 over invoice, (plus destination, taxes*, and fees) or $17,510. The dealer is still making $1,110 in profit ($510 + $600 holdback) and you're paying $2,990 less than the MSRP. Remember, the longer the car has been in the dealer's inventory, the less money the dealer is making from holdbacks.

Almost all dealerships consider holdback money sacred, and are unwilling to share any portion of it with the consumer. Don't push the issue. Your best strategy is to avoid mentioning that you know the holdback amount and what it is during negotiations. Mention holdback only if the dealer gives you some song-and-dance about not making any money when you know that isn't true.

Using a hypothetical Ford in our example also brings us to a new issue regarding holdbacks. Ford Motor Company is trying to boost customer service ratings, and to do so, has decided to offer qualifying Blue Oval dealers a "rebate" on the invoice price of all 2001 Fords and Mercurys invoiced after September 1, 2000. The "rebate" amounts to 1.25 percent of the total invoice, and only Ford dealers who've earned Blue Oval status from the automaker will qualify. The company has estimated that only 70 percent of Ford retailers will gain Blue Oval certification, so when buying a Ford, be careful where you shop. A better deal might be available at a certified Blue Oval Store. A similar program will be instituted for Lincoln products and dealers, but those that obtain certification will receive 2.5% of the total invoice back in the form of a check.

So how can you truly benefit from holdback information? Well, if the dealership doesn't have that pretty green color you're interested in, and they can't find it at another dealership in the area, they have to order it directly from the manufacturer. If that's the case, make sure that they know that you know about the holdback. If a vehicle is special-ordered, holdback money is pure profit, and you will need to factor this into price negotiations.

Domestic manufacturers (Ford and GM) and the Chrysler half of DaimlerChrysler generally offer dealers a holdback equaling 3 percent of the total sticker price, or MSRP, of the car. Import manufacturers (Honda, Nissan, Toyota, etc.) provide varying holdback amounts that are equal to a percentage of total MSRP, base MSRP, total invoice or base invoice.

When calculating a holdback, use the following guidelines.
If a holdback is off the:
- Total MSRP, consumers must include the MSRP price of all options before figuring the holdback.
- Base MSRP, consumers must figure the holdback before adding desired options.
- Total Invoice, consumer must include the invoice price of all options before figuring the holdback.
- Base Invoice, consumers must figure the holdback before adding desired options.

Following is a current list of makes and the amount of the 2001 dealer holdback.

Make	Holdback
Acura	2% of the Base MSRP
Audi	No Holdback
BMW	No Holdback
Buick	3% of the Total MSRP
Cadillac	3% of the Total MSRP
Chevrolet	3% of the Total MSRP
Chrysler	3% of the Total MSRP
Daewoo	One-price sales. Customer pays MSRP.
Dodge	3% of the Total MSRP
Ford	3% of the Total MSRP + additional 1.25% rebate of Total Invoice to Blue Oval Dealers for 2001 models invoiced after September 1, 2000 (see note in above paragraph)
GMC	3% of the Total MSRP
Honda	2% of the Base MSRP (except Prelude, which has no holdback)
Hyundai	2% of the Total Invoice
Infiniti	1% of the Base MSRP (holdback) + 2% of the Base Invoice (floorplanning allowance)
Isuzu	3% of the Total MSRP
Jaguar	2.2% of the Base Invoice
Jeep	3% of the Total MSRP
Kia	3% of Base Invoice
Land Rover	No Holdback
Lexus	2% of the Base MSRP
Lincoln	2% of the Total MSRP + 2.5% rebate of Total Invoice to Certified Dealers for 2001 models
Mazda	2% of the Base MSRP
Mercedes-Benz	3% of the Total MSRP
Mercury	3% of the Total MSRP + additional 1.25% rebate of Total Invoice to Blue Oval Dealers for 2001 models invoiced after September 1, 2000 (see note in above paragraph)
Mitsubishi	2% of the Base MSRP
Nissan	2% + 1% of the Total Invoice (holdback + floorplanning allowance)
Oldsmobile	3% of the Total MSRP
Plymouth	3% of the Total MSRP
Pontiac	3% of the Total MSRP
Porsche	No Holdback
Saab	2.2% of the Base MSRP
Saturn	3% of Total MSRP. But with one-price sales, this is a moot point. The customer pays MSRP.
Subaru	3% of the Total MSRP (Amount may differ in Northeastern U.S.)
Suzuki	2% of the Base MSRP
Toyota	2% of the Base Invoice (Amount may differ in Southern U.S.)
Volkswagen	2% of the Base MSRP
Volvo	1% of the Base MSRP

* Incentives and rebates are actually deducted from the transaction price after Uncle Sam has collected taxes. We have taken editorial license with the process in this example for the sake of keeping it simple.

LEASING TIPS

You've seen the ads: VW Jetta for $189 a month. Jeep Grand Cherokee for $249 a month. Lincoln Navigator for $399 a month. Wow! You can't believe your eyes. Actually, you probably shouldn't believe your eyes when you read such ads—at least not until you've read the fine print.

Like most shoppers, you want to lease the car of your choice for the lowest possible price. Leasing is attractive because of low payments and the prospect of driving a new car every two or three years. Many people figure that a car payment is an unavoidable fact of life, and they might as well drive "new" rather than "old." True, leasing is an attractive alternative, but there are some things you need to understand about leasing before jumping in feet first.

What is Leasing?

Leasing is, well, renting. There are a few differences, however. When you rent a car you pay more for an expensive car than for a cheesy little compact. But when you lease, you can sometimes get *more* car for *less* money. Another advantage to leasing is that you only pay for the amount of the car's value that you use. This is like going to the grocery store and getting a pound of bananas, but not paying for the peels.

Here's how it works:

Say you want to lease a $20,000 car for three years. At the end of the lease the car will have depreciated (decreased in value) to $10,000. You've used up $10,000 of its value. Divide this $10,000 by 36 to get your monthly payments. Pretty simple, huh?

But wait a second. You need to pay interest on that $10,000. And tax and license fees. And all cars don't depreciate evenly. But still, that's the basic idea.

Leasing's Hot Buttons

In every financial deal there are the significant figures and then there are the related fees that don't affect the bottom line much. When you shop for a lease you need to understand the four important figures and watch them carefully:

Capitalized Cost: Lease payments are based on the capitalized cost, which is the selling price of the car. The price of the car is negotiable, so you should negotiate this price first, then have the dealer write you a lease based on this cost.

Residual Value: This is the predicted value of the vehicle at the end of the lease term, and is expressed as a percentage of the MSRP (the sticker price). Typically, a car is worth half its value after three years. Sometimes, dealers raise the residual value to lower monthly payments. This is OK, unless you plan to buy the car at the end of the lease.

Money Factor: This is lease-speak for "interest rate." It plays a big part in the calculation of a lease payment. If the money factor is expressed as a percentage, convert the percentage to the money factor by dividing by 24 (yes, it's 24 regardless of the term of the lease). For example, a 7 percent (.07) interest rate converts to a .0029 money factor.

Term of the Lease: This is the length, in months, you lease the car for. Popular leases are 24, 36, 48 and 60 months. Some lease companies write leases for 38 or 42 months. The 36-

month lease makes the most sense because most cars will be covered by the factory warranty for the entire term of the lease.

Later on we'll show you how to calculate an estimated lease payment. You'll see that these four figures will have the biggest effect on what you have to pay each month.

How to Lease

Never walk into a dealership and announce that you want to lease a car. Don't talk payment yet, either. Once a salesperson identifies you as a payment shopper, you're a dead duck. Any competent dealer can find a way to make a car fit your budget while maximizing profit. Concentrate on finding a car you like, and know **before** you go into the dealership what you can afford. This means you should figure out what you have to pay for the car (if you were buying it—which you aren't) and *approximately* what your lease payment will be.

Calculating a lease payment to the penny is nearly impossible, particularly when the lease is subsidized by the automaker, but you can arrive at a ballpark figure by using the following formula, which we will illustrate using a $23,000 car on a three-year lease.

Lease Payment Estimating

If you are the type of person who likes to work the numbers yourself, you can calculate a "bottom line lease." This is the very best deal you could get. If you get payments within $20 a month of this you will have done well.

To calculate a bottom line lease payment you will need several figures:

1. **MSRP of the vehicle.** Find this price in this book.
2. **The money factor.** This is the interest rate the lease is based on. To get this, call the dealer or get the information from your credit union. A common interest rate is 9% percent (as a money factor this would be .00375).
3. **Lease Term** — Again, we recommend 36-month lease, to ensure warranty coverage.
4. **Residual value of the car.** Call the bank or dealer to find the residual rate. Most cars have a residual value of about 50 – 55 percent for a 36-month lease.

A Sample Lease Calculation

In the following example, we have chosen a vehicle that has a sticker price of $23,000. You have negotiated the price down to $20,000. We'll also assume that the interest rate is 9 percent and the residual value is 57 percent. What are the monthly payments on a three-year lease?

The first step is to find out how much of the car's value you will use. In other words, down the road three years, what will it be worth? In this example, the MSRP of $23,000 is multiplied by the residual value of 57% percent.

$23,000 X .57 = $13,110

The car will be worth $13,110 at the end of the 36-month lease. Since the car *was* worth $20,000 (after you negotiated it down) and it will be worth $13,110, you will be using $6,890 of the car's value.

$20,000 - $13,110 = $6,890

The $6,890 is then broken into 36 monthly payments of $191.39.

Before you get excited about how low this payment is, remember that this figure doesn't include interest or tax. Finding the interest amount is the second half of the calculation. Interest on a lease in computed in a peculiar way. You add the negotiated price of the car to the residual value and multiply this by the money factor.

($20,000 + $13,110) X .0037 = $122.50

Finally, these two figures are added together to give you the approximate bottom line monthly lease payment.

$191.39 + $122.50 = $294.03

Remember, this figure does not include taxes or fees and doesn't take into consideration any down payment or upfront money such as rebates or incentives.
The formula looks like this:

1.	Sticker Price of the car + options	$23,000
2.	**Times** the residual value percentage	X .57%
3.	**Equals** the residual value	= $13,110
4.	Invoice price of car – incentives (net capitalized cost)	$20,000
5.	**Minus** the residual (From line 3)	- $13,110
6.	**Equals** the depreciation over 36 months	= $ 6,890
7.	Depreciation (Line 6) divided by term in months	÷ 36
8.	Equals the monthly depreciation payment	= $191.39
9.	Net capitalized cost (From line 4)	$20,000
10.	Plus the residual (From line 3)	+ $13,110
	Equals	= $33,110
11.	Times the money factor	X .0037
12.	**Equals** money factor payment portion	= $122.50
13.	Monthly depreciation payment (from line 8)	$191.39
14.	**Plus** money factor payment portion (from line 12)	+ $122.50
15.	**Equals** bottom monthly lease payment	= $313.89

Don't forget that you haven't paid tax yet, and this is significant. To find out how much tax you will pay, multiply the monthly lease payment by the sales tax. In this case:

$$\$313.89 \times .0825 = \$25.89$$

This has increased your monthly payment to $339.78.

In the above example, you could reduce your monthly payment by putting more money down. (Most leases require about $1,000 in "drive-off fees." Some of this money is loan initiation, some of it is security deposit and some goes toward the down payment.) The down payment would be subtracted from line 4, the invoice price of the car.

Residual Rates

Keep in mind that every vehicle will have a unique residual value, based on its popularity, its resale value and its reputation for reliability. The residual value is dependent on the term of the lease. Also remember that the above formula doesn't take the following into account: delivery and handling (D&H fees), documentation fees, the cost of license plates or trade-in values. The trade-in value and any cash down payment should be deducted from the capitalized cost before calculating the lease.

Since the residual rate has such an effect on the monthly payment, it would be nice to know which cars have high residual rates. There are lease calculators on the Internet that are extremely helpful. You can choose a sample vehicle, type in basic information and get a table of results. In this way, you can see how the residual rates vary from one lending institution to the next.

If you're *upside down* on your trade—your car is worth less than you owe on the loan—you'll need to add the difference between the balance due on the loan and the trade-in value to the capitalized cost.

The example we illustrated is a straightforward lease with no factory subsidy. In *subsidized leases*, the interest rates are very low and residual rates are very high. Subsidized leases allow dealers to lower payments by artificially raising residual values or lowering the capitalized cost through dealer incentives. You can easily recognize a subsidized lease. Any nationally or regionally advertised lease is generally subsidized by the manufacturer to keep lease payments low. The $189 per month VW Jetta is an example of a subsidized lease payment. It is based on a 1.9 percent APR. If you read the fine print you see that it is a 48-month lease, tax and license fees have not been added, and it requires a $2,500 payment at signing.

Once you find a car you can afford, negotiate the sticker price and then explore leasing based on the negotiated price. Ask what the residual value is and subtract any rebates or incentives from the capitalized cost, and remember that you'll need to pay tax to Uncle Sam for that discount. Use the formula above to calculate a ballpark figure, and if the dealer balks at your conclusion, ask to see the figures they base their payment on.

Your best bet when leasing is to choose a model with a subsidized lease. Payments are low, terms are simple to understand, and they are the only true bargain in the world of leasing.

Lower Payments?

Low payments aren't a fallacy with leasing, when taken in proper context. Yes, you can get into a car with less money down, and pay less for that car for three years. But if you buy the car (with a larger down payment, and higher monthly payments) you will eventually own it. Even though it might not be worth much on the market, it could still be dependable transportation for you, or a nice pass-along vehicle for a family member.

There are several other factors that should be kept in mind. When leasing, tax is calculated only on the payment; when buying, tax is calculated on the entire selling price. In other words, you are taxed only for the portion of the car's value that you use.

Other factors, like fluctuating interest rates, down payments, and contractual obligations can also affect the lease vs. buy scenario. Additionally, vehicle condition can have a tremendous affect on value. A few dents, dings or scratches could easily make a lease the more expensive proposition, with charges for worn tires, excessive mileage and cosmetic repair likely to top $1,000 at the end of the contract.

When trying to determine if leasing or buying is right for you, carefully weigh all the factors that can affect payments over the term of the lease or loan, including the way you drive and maintain a vehicle.

Restrictions

Leasing restricts your use of a vehicle. Mileage allowances are limited, modifications to the vehicle can result in hefty fines at the end of the lease, and if the vehicle is not in top condition when it is returned, wear-and-tear charges may be levied. Many dealers and financing institutions will be more lenient if you buy or lease another vehicle from them at the end of your term, but if you drop off the car and walk, prepare yourself for the possibility of some lease-end hassles.

Be sure to define these limitations at the beginning of the lease so that you know what you're getting yourself into. Find out what will be considered excessive in the wear-and-tear department and try to negotiate a higher mileage limit.

One strategy to avoid additional charges is to pay for extra miles up front (usually at about .10 a mile) rather than paying the over-mileage penalty on the back end (often at .15 a mile).

Pros & Cons

The lists below summarize the pros and cons of leasing vs. buying:

Advantages of Leasing
- Lower monthly payments
- Lower down payment
- You can drive a *better* car for *less* money each month
- Lower repair costs (with a three-year lease, the factory warranty will cover you)
- You can drive a new car every two or three years
- No trade-in hassles at the end of the lease
- You pay sales tax only on the portion of the car you finance

Disadvantages of Leasing
- You don't own the car at the end of the lease
- Your mileage is limited to a set amount, typically 10-15,000 a year
- Lease contracts are more confusing because the terminology is unfamiliar
- Leasing is more expensive in the long run
- Wear-and-tear charges can add up
- It's hard to terminate a lease early if your driving needs change

Advantages of Buying
- Pride of ownership – you can do with your car as you please
- Car buying is more economical in the long run
- No mileage penalty
- Increased flexibility – you can sell the car whenever you want

Disadvantages of Buying:
- Higher down payment
- Higher monthly payments
- You are responsible for maintenance costs (or have to buy an extended warranty)
- Trade-in or selling hassles
- Your money is tied up in a car, which depreciates, rather than an investment which appreciates

Certain lifestyles may work better with leasing. For instance, if you entertain business clients, leasing allows you to drive a luxury vehicle for less money (and there may be a tax write off for certain professions). Other people just like to drive a brand-new car every three years. So ultimately, leasing isn't only a dollars and cents question—it's about personal tastes and priorities.

Lease-end

Studies show that consumers generally like leases—until the lease ends. The reason for their apprehension is rooted in the dark days of open-end leasing, when Joe Lessee was dealt a sucker punch by the lessor on the day Joe returned the car to the leasing agent. Back then, residual values were established at the beginning of the lease, but the lessee was responsible for the difference between the residual value and the fair market value at the end of the lease. The resulting lease-end charges maxxed out credit cards and gave leasing a bad rep.

Leasing has changed. And with today's *closed-end* leases (the only type of lease you should consider), the lease-end fees are generally reasonable, unless the car has 100,000 miles on it, a busted-up grille and melted chocolate smeared into the upholstery. Dealers and financial institutions want you to buy or lease another car from them, and might be understanding about excess mileage and abnormal wear. After all, if they hit you with a bunch of trumped up charges you're not going to remain a loyal customer, are you?

Additionally, closed-end leasing establishes a set, non-negotiable residual value for the car in advance, at the beginning of the lease. Also, any fees or charges you may incur at the lease-end are spelled out in detail before you sign the lease. All the worry is removed by the existence of concrete figures. But keep in mind that if you take your business elsewhere, you're going to be facing a bill for items like worn tires, paint chips, door dings, and the like.

Another leasing benefit is the myriad of choices you have at the end of the term. Well, maybe not a myriad, but there are four, which is more than you have after two or three years of financing. They are:

1. **Return the car to the dealer and walk away from it** after paying any applicable charges like a termination fee, wear-and-tear repairs, or excessive mileage bills. Of course, if you don't plan to buy or lease another car from the dealer, you may get hit for every minor thing, but those are the risks.

2. **Buy the car** from the dealer for the residual value established at the beginning of the lease. If the car is in good shape, the residual value is probably lower than the true value of the car, making it a bargain, and many leasing companies will guarantee financing at the lowest interest rate available at the time your lease ends. If you've trashed the lease car, compare the lease-end wear-and-tear charges to the devaluation in worth the vehicle has suffered while in your care. You might be surprised to find that it's easier and less expensive to just give the car back and pay the fines.

3. **Use any equity in the car as leverage in a new deal** with the dealer. Since residual values are sometimes set artificially high, the car is not likely to be worth more than the residual value at lease-end under these circumstances. But a well-maintained, low-mileage lease car might allow the dealer to knock up to a couple of thousand bucks off your next deal.

4. **Sell the car yourself** and pay off the residual value, pocketing whatever profit you make.

Closing the Gap

If you decide to lease your next car, you may have to review your lease contract to make sure it includes "gap insurance." This protects you in case you get in an accident, or the vehicle is stolen, and the insurance company will not pay what you owe the bank. This means you might have to come up with $3,000 or $4,000 out of your own pocket.

In some cases involving an accident or a theft, the insurance company is willing to pay only the current market value of the vehicle. Since new cars depreciate steeply in the first year, there may be a gap between the current market value of the car and the amount you owe on it. Gap insurance pays this additional amount.

Most leasing contracts include gap coverage. But if they don't you can be in for a nasty surprise if your car is wrecked or stolen. Make sure to ask if gap insurance is included. If it isn't, call your insurance company to arrange for the additional coverage.

Conclusion

Closed-end leasing is a win-win situation for everybody except people who want to keep their cars for a good long time. The manufacturer sells more cars, the dealer sells more cars, and you get low payments and a new car every couple of years. However, it is important to stress that you never own the car and leasing can be quite restrictive. If you're a low-mileage driver who maintains cars in perfect condition, don't like tying up capital in down payments and don't mind never-ending car payments, leasing is probably just right for you. If you're on the road all day every day, beat the stuffing out of your wheels, enjoy a 'customized' look or drive your cars until the wheels fall off, buy whatever it is you're considering, because it will be less expensive in the long run.

2001 Honda Accord

 # SINGLE COPIES / ORDER FORM

Please send me:

☐ **USED CARS & TRUCKS: PRICES & RATINGS** (includes S&H) **$14.99**

☐ **NEW CARS**
— American & Import (includes S&H) **$14.99**

☐ **NEW TRUCKS [PICKUPS, VANS & SPORT UTILITIES]**
— American & Import (includes S&H) **$14.99**

Name _____
Email _____
Address _____
City, State, Zip _____
Phone _____

PAYMENT: __ MASTERCARD   __ VISA   __ CHECK or MONEY ORDER $_____

Make check or money order payable to:
Edmunds.com, Inc. P.O. Box 338, Shrub Oaks, NY 10588
For more information or to order by phone, call **(914) 962-6297**

Credit Card # _____ Exp. Date: _____
Cardholder Name: _____
Signature _____

Prices above include shipping within the U.S. and Canada only. Other countries, please add $7.00 to the price ($14.99+7.00) per book (via air mail) and $2.00 to the price ($14.99+2.00) per book (surface mail). Please pay through an American Bank or with American Currency. Rates subject to change without notice.

Edmunds.com In The News

YAHOO! "Fire up your Web browser and make a beeline for Edmunds Online. Edmunds has been publishing those handy pocket-sized automotive price guides since 1966. You'll find buying strategies, information on current rebates and incentives, and plenty of auto prices." —*Yahoo! For Newspapers, April 10, 2000*

"A good example of a metamediary in the automobile market is Edmunds, which has created a valuable data franchise by giving **BUSINESS 2.0** away information about new and used auto pricing, dealer cost and holdbacks, reliability, auto-buying advice, and auto reviews. Edmund's generates tremendous traffic on its site, which has been ranked as one of the most heavily trafficked as well as one of the most usable Web sites." —*Business 2.0, March 2000*

THE WALL STREET JOURNAL. "Edmunds.com Inc., an auto-information company, has a well-trafficked Web site and a brand name car buyers trust, a rarity in the automotive universe." —*The Wall Street Journal, July 11, 2000*

"In the process of going online, they've (Edmunds.com has) transformed their corporate identity from **www.THECARCONNECTION.com** print powerhouse into a dot-com destination for auto information and discussion, where even some top auto executives admit they lurk to see what people are talking about." —*The Car Connection, August 7, 2000*

Forbes.com "...when you start to haggle, Edmunds' information is invaluable... Ample info on both new and used cars." -*Forbes, February 28, 2000*

"Edmunds.com, the site of the automotive publisher, is packed with information, including photos and reviews **GANNETT** of various models." —*Gannett News Service, April 30, 2000*

Consumer Reports "At Edmunds.com you can get a free list of competing cars, specifications, safety features and prices for the vehicle and for every available option." —*Editors of Consumer Reports, April 17, 2000*

 **SUBSCRIPTIONS / ORDER FORM**

BUYER'S PRICE GUIDES

Please send me a one year subscription for:

☐ **USED CARS & TRUCKS: PRICES & RATINGS**
AMERICAN & IMPORT (package price includes $10.00 S&H) **$36.80**
Canada $42.80/Foreign Countries $50.80 (includes air mail S&H)
4 issues/yr

☐ **NEW CARS**
AMERICAN & IMPORT (package price includes $10.00 S&H) **$36.80**
Canada $42.80/Foreign Countries $50.80 (includes air mail S&H)
4 issues/yr

☐ **NEW TRUCKS [PICKUPS, VANS & SPORT UTILITIES]**
AMERICAN & IMPORT (package price includes $10.00 S&H) **$36.80**
Canada $42.80/Foreign Countries $50.80 (includes air mail S&H)
4 issues/yr

Name _____
Email _____
Address _____
City, State, Zip _____
Phone _____

PAYMENT: ___ MC ___ VISA ___ Check or Money Order-Amount $_____   Rates subject to change without notice

Make check or money order payable to:
Edmunds.com, Inc. P.O.Box 338, Shrub Oaks, NY 10588
For more information or to order by phone, call **(914) 962-6297**

Credit Card # _____ Exp. Date: _____
Cardholder Name: _____
Signature _____

☐ Yes, I would like to participate in surveys to assist Edmunds.com further meet my needs as a car-shopping consumer.

Notes